# THE COMPLETE BOOK OF
# THOROUGHBRED HORSE RACING

# THE COMPLETE BOOK OF
# THOROUGHBRED
# HORSE RACING

## Tom Biracree
## and Wendy Insinger

DOLPHIN BOOKS
DOUBLEDAY & COMPANY, INC., GARDEN CITY, NEW YORK
1982

Library of Congress Cataloging in Publication Data
Biracree, Tom, 1947–
    The complete book of thoroughbred horse racing.
    Includes index.
    1. Horse-racing.   2. Race horses.   3. Thorough-
bred horse.   4. Horse breeding.   5. Horse race
betting.   I. Insinger, Wendy.   II. Title.
SF334.B47       798.4'3'0973
AACR2
ISBN: 0-385-15676-6
Library of Congress Catalog Card Number 80–1650

To Banknote, the hopeful,
To Manny Dober, the fighter,
To Tanta Prisa, the source,
And to all the champions, near champions, potential champions, and just plain racehorses in whose blood the fire of the three foundation sires burns.
Long may they run.

# ACKNOWLEDGMENTS

With many thanks to:

Christine and Gary Heimerle of Scargo Farm, for their candid and firsthand lessons in the breeding business.

Frank Smith of Elloree Training Center, for his careful explanations of the training process.

Trainer Robert DeBonis, for his patience on hectic mornings.

Terrance Collier and the Fasig-Tipton Company, for their generous donation of time and resources.

Mrs. Thomas Waller of Tanrackin Farm, for her sage advice.

Dr. William O. Reed, D.V.M., for his permission to watch him perform equine surgery.

Dr. Howard Gill, D.V.M., for being one of the best broodmare men anywhere.

E. Barry Ryan of Normandy Farm for his much-needed supply of critical expertise and good Bourbon whiskey.

and to:

Roberto Lira of Tilly Foster Stock Farm, John Hettinger of Akindale Farm, Mr. and Mrs. Phillip Sagarin and the officials and employees of the NYRA for their invaluable assistance.

The public relations directors of the great majority of U.S. racetracks, for generously providing me with track programs, condition books, and other invaluable information.

The management of Finger Lakes Race Track, for the intimate exposure to racing and racing people that was critical in shaping this work.

Trainer Bill Strange, for his time and for a career that demonstrates what being a horseman is all about.

The *Daily Racing Form,* for its wonderful coverage of the sport of kings and for its kind permission to use copyrighted material.

Jim Menick, a dedicated racing fan who conceived and nurtured this book. For showing the patience and persistence of Tanta Prisa in dealing with the authors, two often unruly foals.

and finally, to:

an old, dead gelding named Cartersville, for providing the inspiration for the "Life of the Horse"* sections. In his heart he was a champ.

All of the credit for accuracy should be given to them; the errors are sadly our own.

* Although the characters are real, certain sections of the "Life of the Horse" (written entirely by Wendy Insinger) have been fictionalized to heighten dramatic effect or illustrate particular points and techniques.

# Contents

# Introduction

This book is a unique guide to Thoroughbred racing that will become an invaluable, well-thumbed addition to the library of every horse-racing fan.

Since over forty thousand books on the "sport of kings" have been published, this claim may seem more than a bit presumptuous. Eyebrows may raise even further when we offer as proof of our claim the apparently mundane reason that we believe the vast majority of people who attend the races end up losers.

What's original, however, is that we don't define "losing" strictly as "going home with less money." Rather, we mean that few racegoers derive the kind of full enjoyment from their trips to the track that they so richly deserve. The reason is that even the most regular racegoers tend to be far more poorly informed about their favorite sport than are baseball, football or basketball fans.

Because wagering on horses is legal, because odds are flashed minute by minute on tote boards, payoffs printed in daily newspapers and takeout percentages endlessly debated in legislatures, Thoroughbred racing has all too often been considered solely a gambling industry rather than a sport. The racegoer has thus been treated not as a fan, but as a gambler, like those who habituate casinos, buy lottery tickets or play the numbers. As a result, daily newspaper sports sections have traditionally devoted little space to racing, other than printing daily entries and results. Books directed to horseplayers contained, for the most part, simplified gambling systems of dubious value. These books were found not in the "Sports" section of bookstores, but in the "Games" section.

But beginning in 1973, when the charismatic Secretariat swept the first Triple Crown in over two decades, increasing attention has been paid to Thoroughbred racing as an exciting sport. Massive publicity has attended the subsequent Triple Crown victories of Seattle Slew and Affirmed, the thrilling victories and tragic death of the filly Ruffian, the climb to the all-time money-winning title of Spectacular Bid. In 1977, jockey Steve Cauthen became one of the most celebrated sports personalities in the last twenty years, and he was named Athlete of the Year by *Sports Illustrated*. In 1978, in one telling sign of the new popularity of racing, CBS Sports signed a five-year agreement to televise ten races a year from New York tracks.

This "discovery" of Thoroughbred racing brought to light the truth about racegoers—that the great majority of them were spectators as well as participants, sports fans as well as handicappers. These enthusiasts are engaged emotionally as well as intellectually in their sport, just like those who follow and bet on other professional sports.

Unlike those other fans, however, the horseplayer is still starved for the kind of information that will allow him or her to fully appreciate and enjoy the spectacle of his sport and allow him or her to make the most intelligent use of the average $116 wagered on each trip to the track. The football or baseball fan/bettor has the advantage of a lifetime familiarity with his sport. In addition, the newspaper daily provides voluminous statistics as well as articles evaluating the current condition and relative abilities of athletes; the philosophy, methods and skill of coaches; the conditions under which the games are to be played.

Few racing fans, on the other hand, are introduced to their sport until they reach adulthood. Daily newspaper coverage of racing is at best scanty. The only reliable information on racing, the *Daily Racing Form,* is unavailable in many areas and costs $456.25 a year.

This book fills the void by providing the first accessible, comprehensive explanation of the sport for neophyte and regular race-goers. This book covers the history and traditions of the sport. It includes descriptions and records of great horses, sires, breeders, trainers, jockeys and stables. The book provides an explanation of the mechanics of Thoroughbred racing: of breeding, ownership, training and riding; of the way in which individual races are organized, filled and conducted; of the operation of racetracks. Finally, while not specifically a handicapping guide, the book covers the mathematics of wagering and an overview of the most popular and successful theories of handicapping and betting.

Our goal in writing this book was to ensure that every one of our readers is a winner. We can't and won't do that by offering a dozen or two simplistic systems for you to follow rigidly. Rather, we're enriching you by providing a companion for your days at the races, a continually fascinating storehouse of information and lore about this wonderful sport. We hope you'll find using it a little like going to a baseball game with Casey Stengel, a football game with Ara Parsegian, a basketball game with Red Auerbach—or, best of all, going to the paddock with Eddie Arcaro.

"A bad day at the track is better than a good day anywhere else."
—John Nerud, Trainer

# Part One
# THE THOROUGHBRED

---

# The Champion

No single better image of the champion racehorse exists than the picture of Secretariat pounding down the stretch in the Belmont Stakes 31 lengths ahead of his closest pursuers. The majestic "Big Red," the first Triple Crown winner in twenty-five years, so enthralled the American public that a new interest in the sport of Thoroughbred racing was born. The awe and affection of horsemen, too, was captured by this chestnut colt. In both appearance and performance, no horse has ever come closer to the ideal than Secretariat.

An ideal held in the mind's eye is vital to true appreciation of any athlete in any sport. It is this ideal to which professional baseball, football and basketball scouts hold up the attributes of prospects, rating them on a scale of 1 to 10. Becoming a knowledgeable sports fan means first learning which attributes professionals deem important, then, through observation, developing a rating scale of one's own.

Professional horsemen—breeders, owners, trainers, jockeys' agents, jockeys—are also scouts whose income depends on their ability to evaluate relative abilities of their athletes, the Thoroughbreds. Becoming a knowledgeable racing fan and a successful horseplayer depends on developing the same kind of keen judgment. Unfortunately, the racegoer often starts with a more serious handicap than does the fan who follows sports that have human athletes—unfamiliarity with the horse's physical capabilities.

We all know what it feels like to run, to jump, to throw. At the very least, physical education classes in school provide experience in the basic rules of sports and in the rudiments of the skills practiced by the athletes we watch on television. We understand immediately how strength helps a football tackle; speed, a wide receiver; height, a basketball center.

Since the invention of the horseless carriage, however, our contact with horses is generally limited to watching them on the racetrack or on the movie screen. While we can instinctively sense the magnificence of a horse like Secretariat as compared with a $2,500 claimer, we lack the understanding to explain it, or, more to the point, to fully understand professional horsemen when they explain it.

That's why this book begins with the athlete, the Thoroughbred. To understand horse racing and the decisions made by owners, jockeys and trainers, we've first of all got to know the animal that makes the sport possible. The first step in becoming a winner at the track is understanding how horses are bred and raised, and their physical and mental characteristics.

## GREAT HORSES: SECRETARIAT

Only a handful of athletes in this century have, through the combination of performance and personality, captured the public imagination so thoroughly that their names are synonymous with their sport. The small list includes Babe Ruth in baseball, Arnold Palmer in golf, Jesse Owens in track—and Secretariat in Thoroughbred racing. Perhaps never in the million or more matings of Thoroughbred horses have genes combined more splendidly to produce the "super horse."

Every part of the history of this legendary equine performer is colorful and dramatic, even his breeding. Secretariat's dam, Something-royal, was owned by Christopher Chenery's Meadow Stable. In the 1960s, Chenery began sending two mares a year to be mated to the great stallion Bold Ruler, who was owned by Mrs. Gladys Phipps. Every two years, after one pair of foals had been born and the mares had been remated, Chenery and Mrs. Phipps would flip a coin, with the winner getting the first choice from the first crop and the loser the first choice from the second crop.

In August 1969, Chenery's daughter, Penny Tweedy, and Mrs. Phipps's son Ogden met for a coin toss both wanted to lose. The reason was that one of the mares had come up barren the second year. That meant the winner got the choice of one of the two live foals, but the loser got two foals—the second live foal and the foal carried by Somethingroyal, the mare that had conceived the second year. That foal, which Penny Tweedy won by "losing," was Secretariat.

By the time the chestnut colt was a yearling, his talent was obvious—but his first trip to the track almost proved to be his last. An instant after the gates opened for his first race, Secretariat was slammed by the horses on either side of him. It was the kind of accident that has ruined countless racing careers. Fortunately, Secretariat survived the collision and surged forward toward the leaders. Unfortunately, his inexperienced rider got him into heavy traffic several times in the short, 5½-furlong contest. Still, Secretariat finished with a blinding burst of speed to finish fourth. It was the only time he was to be off the board in his career.

The defeat was followed by a smashing maiden victory eleven days later, then a string of close-to-track-record victories, marred only by his disqualification (for bearing in on Stop the Music) from first to second in the Champagne Stakes. The performance was the talk of the Thoroughbred world—so impressive that Secretariat became the first two-year-old ever voted Horse of the Year. At the end of that first racing season, Secretariat was sold to a syndicate for a record $6 million.

After opening his three-year-old campaign with victories in the Bay Shore and Gotham Stakes, Secretariat shocked a big crowd at Aqueduct, which had made him a 1–3 favorite, by finishing a dull third in the Wood Memorial, his last prep for the Kentucky Derby.

No horse had won the Triple Crown since Citation in 1948, and the Thoroughbred world, which had considered Secretariat a shoe-in, now buzzed with rumors that he was a flash in the pan.

In the 1973 Derby, for the first time in nine races, Secretariat was not an odds-on favorite, but his smashing 2½-length triumph in the Kentucky Derby record time of 1:59.4 sent his reputation soaring. Two weeks later, in a Preakness made controversial by a malfunctioning timer that may have cost him another record, Secretariat won the second jewel of the Triple Crown by 2½ lengths.

On June 9, 1973, over 67,000 people crammed into Belmont Park to cheer Secretariat on to victory. The performance of "Big Red" surpassed their wildest dreams as he roared to an incredible 31-length victory in the Belmont in a world-record time of 2:24 for the mile-and-a-half. Many observers thought it the finest single performance in racing history.

Secretariat was to suffer two defeats later in the season, but he finished with two smashing victories over the best turf horses in the world in his first two races on the grass. For the second year in a row, he was voted Horse of the Year.

Retired to begin his career at stud, Secretariat provided drama for a final time when he failed his first fertility test. The kind of rumors that had buzzed after his defeat in the Wood Memorial now had Secretariat a $6 million dud in the breeding shed, but once again the chestnut colt rallied by getting more than 90 percent of his first crop of mares in foal. Although he has not yet proved the kind of absolute champion in the breeding shed that he has on the track, Secretariat has produced enough quality horses, including General Assembly and Terlingua, to rank well up in the top 1 percent of all standing sires.

*Racing Record:*

| STS. | 1ST | 2ND | 3RD | WON |
|------|-----|-----|-----|-----|
| 21 | 16 | 3 | 1 | $1,316,808 |

# Section 1

# Breeding

*"Breed the best to the best and hope for the best."*
*—The breeder's rule*

According to Webster's dictionary, the word "thorough" means "marked by completeness, as with full attention to detail." This adjective, wedded to the word "bred," is the perfect title for the modern racehorse, for the Thoroughbred was the product of the wisdom and dedication with which English horse owners selectively bred horses on the basis of racing ability. To this day, the foundation of the sport of Thoroughbred racing is that fascinating, exciting experiment of "thorough breeding."

We call breeding an "experiment," because each Thoroughbred results from the mysterious, infinitely complicated way in which the millions of genes from the sire and dam combine. After over three centuries of intense effort, horsemen still haven't found anything near an exact mating formula that guarantees a champion racehorse or even reliable winners. That's why many racing writers dismiss breeding as a "genetic lottery."

Thoroughbred breeding isn't a mere game of chance, though, any more than the development of the breed in the first place was a matter of luck. Rather, it is a business that rewards in-depth knowledge, shrewd judgment and hard work. Assuming risks in order to gain rewards, breeders invest time, energy and money in the three or more years from conception to the time the name of the horse is dropped into the entry box for the first time. The "thoroughness" with which this process is carried out plays a large part in each horse's performance at the track and thus, ultimately, in the breeder's success.

Because this process takes place far from the grandstand, and because it is almost totally ignored in the daily newspapers and handicapping guides, it is largely a mystery to the racing fan. In this section, we'll try to demystify the process. We'll explain how natural selection, aided by planned breeding efforts, produced the Thoroughbred racehorse. We'll look at the modern breeder and the breeding industry. We'll explain what makes a good sire and a good dam, and we'll unravel the mysteries of pedigrees and how breeding decisions are made. Finally, we'll go behind the scenes to a breeding farm to follow a single foal from conception to the auction ring.

# The Development of the Thoroughbred

## THE EVOLUTION OF THE HORSE

Long before man gave the horse the opportunity to become a professional athlete, the process of evolution had already made it the best amateur runner on earth. Natural selection over millions of years crafted the characteristics that man would later refine to produce the Thoroughbred.

Both man and the horse were evolutionary infants together 70 million years ago, when the great dinosaurs became extinct and mammals became the dominant players on the earth's stage. The "Adam" of the modern horse was *Eohippus,* a creature about the size of a spring lamb who roamed the forests that covered much of Europe, North America and Africa. This four-toed animal, which depended on nimbleness to escape predators, browsed the forest for leaves, shoots and twigs while, in the trees above, the small, shrew-like primates that would evolve into modern man swung.

The ancestors of both horse and man were woodland creatures until about 12 million years ago, when great environmental changes resulted in the replacement of most of the earth's forests by vast, grassy plains. The first hominoids (human-like primates) moved from the trees to the ground and adapted by walking upright on two legs. Similarly, with the change in environment, the progenitors of the horse could no longer depend on nimbleness and thick cover to escape predators. Instead, survival on the plains depended first of all on acute sensory perception. Because natural selection fa-

vored taller animals who could see over the grass and animals with a wider range of vision, after millions of years the surviving species were twice the height of *Eohippus* and had eyes on the side of the head that produced nearly 360-degree vision. The animals became extraordinarily sensitive to changes in their environment, to sudden sounds and smells. They banded in herds for further protection.

## WHATEVER BECAME OF THE HORSE'S TOES?

The horse's leg, from the knee down, has most of the same bones as the human hand from wrist to middle fingertip. If your third metacarpal, the bone that runs from your wrist to your middle knuckle, grew a foot long and eight inches in diameter, it would simulate a horse's cannon bone. Your knuckle is the fetlock joint, and the three segments of your middle finger, with their corresponding joints are the equivalent of the long pastern, the short pastern and the coffin bone. You have to imagine that the tip of your finger is a flat, heart-shaped surface wrapped in a gigantic fingernail that extends all the way up to the middle of your finger. *Eohippus* never had an opposable thumb, but it had three other fingers, which remain vestigially to remind the aristocrats of the horse world of their humble origins. The index and ring fingers retreated up the leg to become splint bones which lie like two slivers behind the cannon bone and serve no useful function. The pinkie moved up the inside of the leg to become a small, gray oval growth known as a "chestnut" or "night-eye." Fittingly, since all night-eyes are unique in shape, they are used to "fingerprint" horses for the purposes of identification.

Secondly, once a predator was spotted, speed and endurance were needed to escape it. Running on one toe rather than four allowed fuller extension of the limbs, and the tip of that toe hardened to provide protection from the hard ground. The backbone became rigid and horizontal to anchor the large muscle masses needed for acceleration. The long leg bones levering these muscle masses meant efficiency of energy once full speed was reached. The neck, lengthened both for grazing and for balance in running, supported a complex brain devoted to muscle coordination and acute sensory perception.

The development of these characteristics, which are essentially those of the modern horse, was enhanced by the animal's social hierarchy. For protection, the horse had become a herd animal, and these herds were led by one dominant stallion who fiercely reserved for himself the right to mate with his mares. Weak or inferior animals never got the chance to breed. Thus, only the males best suited for survival had the opportunity to pass along their genes to subsequent generations.

The great ice ages of the Pleistocene period (which began about one million years ago) applied one more test to the ancestors of both horse and man—that of hardiness. When the glaciers retreated for the last time, a single species, *Equus caballus,* remained. This stocky, sand-brown animal, about thirteen hands tall (one hand equals four inches), inhabited Central Asia. Gradually, *Equus caballus* migrated to China, India, Asia Minor and Europe. Varieties of the species, called breeds, were produced as the horse adapted to the new environments. One important element in those environments was man.

## MAN AND THE HORSE

According to Greek myth, the horse sprang from the waters at the command of Poseidon, god of the sea. The Arabs believed that Allah created the horse from strong gusts of the West Wind. These metaphors were occasioned not only by man's awe of the power and speed of the animal, but also by an unquenchable, capricious spirit that seemed as divinely inspired as that of wind and wave. The fierce will that enabled survival during millions of years of harsh conditions was indelibly stamped on the horse. Domestication of the horse to this day means individually breaking every animal by what Donald Braider has called "patient exercises of man's will and wit."

These "exercises" took tens of thousands of years to develop. Man was long one of the horse's predators, hunting the animal for its meat and hide. Such hunts are represented on the walls of Paleolithic caves in France and Spain. Because of the horse's

**MAIN EVOLUTIONARY LINE OF THE HORSE**

| Million Years Ago | Name | Height | | Fore feet | Hind feet |
|---|---|---|---|---|---|
| 55 | Eohippus | 3 hands | | Weight-bearing central pad and 4 hooved toes | Weight-bearing central pad and 3 hooved toes |
| 35 | Mesohippus | 6 hands | | Weight-bearing central pad and 3 hooved toes | |
| 25 | Merychippus | 10 hands | | Weight-bearing central hooved toe. Two reduced side toes. | |
| 10 | Pliohippus | 12 hands | | Weight-bearing central hooved toe. No recognizable side toes. | |
| 1 to present | Equus | | | Present-day horses | |

recognition of man as a predator and because of its strong inbred instincts to flee,
the animal proved far harder to tame than
to kill. It probably wasn't until 4500 B.C.,
long after the domestication of dogs and
cattle, that nomadic tribes of Central Asia
became the first horsemen.

By the beginning of recorded time, horses
were playing integral parts in the civilizations of Egypt, China, India and Asia
Minor. Hittite cuneiforms dating back to
1600 B.C. contained detailed instructions on
the raising and care of horses. Sophisticated
horsemanship, which is the skill in training
horses for specific tasks, was vital in the
formation of the Greek and Roman em-
pires.

With sophistication in training, however,
did not come sophistication in breeding.
Man's domestication of the horse had a
strong but decidedly mixed effect on the evolution of the different breeds. Man did
provide food and protection from predators, which led to substantial increases in
the size and power of the heavier horse
breeds. But the need for large numbers of
animals for use in war, commerce and agri-
culture led to the breeding of inferior animals that never would have obtained the
chance to breed in the selective social hierarchy of the herd. As a result, increasing
numbers of coarse, unsound animals of hap-
hazardly mixed blood were produced. When
the Greeks and Romans needed animals of
special quality for specific purposes like
racing, they imported them rather than bred
them.

It was not until after the fall of Rome
that a new civilization rising from the sands
of Arabia began to interfere systematically
in the 70-million-year-old evolutionary
process. The initiative of the Bedouin tribes
in breeding as well as training horses for a
specific purpose not only produced an animal crucial to the military conquests of
Islam; it was also the first vital step in the
process that would result in man's creation
of the Thoroughbred one thousand years
later.

## THE MAGIC OF THE HORSE

"When God created the horse, he said to the
magnificent creature: 'I have made thee unlike
any other. All the treasures of the earth shall
lie between thy eyes . . . Thou shalt fly
without wings and conquer without sword."
—THE KORAN

Since the dawn of civilization, man and the
horse have enjoyed a uniquely important sym-
biotic relationship. The horse bore man's many
burdens, carried man off to war and the hunt,
and provided pleasure in games and sport. In
return, man not only cared for his steeds, but
developed for the horse's strength and speed
and spirit a combination of awe and affection
that approached worship. Said the Greek
Xenophon:

Horses are god-like creatures, higher than
all others, formed of the sea, wind, and
earth, but mightier than all of these, because
with the strength of the sea, the swiftness of
the wind, and the stability of the earth, he
makes his rider an earth god.

Even today, when the horse plays no practical role in most of our lives, the sight of Thoroughbred racehorses parading in the paddock
or pounding down the stretch gives rise to a
shadow of that age-old feeling. To quote
D. H. Lawrence:

Far back, far back in our soul the horse
prances . . . The horse! The horse! The
symbol of surging potency and power of
movement, of action, in men.

## THE EASTERN HORSE

No weaklings, man or beast, long survive in
the desert. The horses of Egypt, Turkey
and Mesopotamia were well regarded for
their stamina and courage throughout ancient times. Of 14 winning racehorses celebrated in odes by the Greek poet Pindar, 12

were of Eastern blood. Similarly, 37 of 42 champions listed on a Roman wall inscription of 75 A.D. had been imported from North Africa.

The qualities of the desert horse were vastly refined and augmented by the Bedouins of Arabia, who began importing horses from Egypt sometime after the birth of Christ. The Arabs' fanaticism about bloodlines was codified in the Koran and was enhanced by the horse's importance in the holy wars of Islam. Horses personified the honor of their owners and of the whole tribe. Pedigrees were handed down orally from father to son, and no Bedouin ever lied about a pedigree.

The standards sought by the Arabs are best shown by a legend concerning the founding of the breed. Supposedly, the prophet Mohammed deprived one hundred mares of water for three days of harsh desert travel. Finally, the frantic horses were released within sight of a river. Just as they approached the water, the horn of battle was blown. Five mares responded. These became the "mares of the Prophet," from whom the *asil,* or "animals of pure blood," descended.

The Arabs fiercely protected the *asil* from contamination. Before battle, they sewed up the vaginas of their "war mares" to prevent misalliance. Once a mare mated with a stallion of impure blood, it was considered forever contaminated. Finally, every young horse was subjected to a harsh test of courage and stamina. When a colt or filly was mounted for the first time, its master rode the animal at full speed over fifty miles of burning sand and rock. He then plunged it into water deep enough for swimming. If, after this, the horse was able to eat normally, its purity of blood was considered confirmed.

The courage and stamina of the Arabian horse resulted from physical traits enhanced by centuries of selective breeding. Arab horses were often called "drinkers of the wind," reflecting their extraordinary respiratory capacity. Arabs had wide, flared nostrils, a very large windpipe, and a deep chest that provided room for the kind of lung expansion necessary for endurance. The weight-carrying ability of the small (fourteen to fifteen hands) Arab came from the power of the long, high hindquarters that sprung from a very short back. The Arab's sturdy bones and large joints resulted in unusual soundness.

Ultimately, however, the influence of Arabian horses depended not so much on their physical characteristics, but on their ability to pass on those characteristics to their progeny. Centuries of inbreeding and of strict attention to purity of blood made the Arab extraordinarily "prepotent." This means that when Arabs mated with horses of another breed, the Arabs' characteristics would tend to predominate in the foals. As a result, according to horse authority Margaret Cabell Self, "the Arabian horse is the 'foundation strain' of all light horses of the present day."

As the armies of Islam swept across North Africa into Spain, and eastward through Asia Minor, the influence of their horses likewise spread. Crosses with native breeds produced the Barb (horses of the Barbary Coast—Morocco, Algeria and Tunisia), the Spanish Barb (horses descended from North African stock mated with native heavy-horse stock), and the Turk. As a result of the Crusades, the influence of the Eastern horse became significant in Mediterranean Europe, primarily in Italy. There it stopped, waiting hundreds of years for a profound change in warfare in northern Europe.

## THE ENGLISH HORSE

Like the Arab chieftains, the nobles of northern Europe depended on the horse first and foremost to wage war—but the qualities they needed in their steeds were totally different from those of the armies of Islam. The heavily armored Norman knights who conquered England in 1066 sat astride huge horses that could bear up to 450 pounds. For the next four hundred years, the most prized animals were the largest of the "great" horse breeds that had developed in the colder climates.

In the 1400s, however, that rapidly changed. When the English archers decimated a larger army of helpless mounted warriors at the Battle of Agincourt in 1415, the age of the armored knight came to an end. Cavalry became a means of outflanking and surprising an enemy, and suddenly speed and endurance, rather than weight-carrying ability, became the main criteria for a war-horse.

Animals suitable for this purpose, however, were scarce in England. The light-horse breeds of England were primarily ponies, swift and nimble, but too small to stand up to the grueling uses of war. Some haphazard and mostly unsuccessful efforts to produce more suitable horses by mating ponies with heavier breeds ended with the destruction of much of the British horse population during the War of the Roses (1455–85). After the war, the English were forced to turn to large-scale importing to augment native breeding stock. Most of the imports were Spanish or Italian breeds that had a high percentage of the blood of the Eastern horses so admired by English noblemen who had participated in the Crusades.

The importation of these animals produced a marked general improvement in the English light-horse stock, but had little influence on the quality of racing stock. The Romans had introduced racing to Britain during their occupation of the area. Racing continued through the Middle Ages, primarily as one of a number of diversions at fairs and celebrations, but the sport held no special interest for the English horse breeders. With the constant internal and external threats to England's unity and sovereignty, the nobleman was almost a full-time warrior. His prime recreation was hunting, an activity that also put meat on his table. Until the seventeenth century, the purpose of horse importing and breeding was primarily the production of horses for war and hunting.

Then, with the defeat of the Spanish Armada in 1588, the last serious external threat to England was destroyed. After the civil wars and the short Protectorate (1653–58) of Oliver Cromwell, a remarkable degree of internal unity was achieved. With the restoration of Charles II, a long era of stability and leisure for the English nobleman began. All sorts of sporting activities blossomed. Because of the intense interest of the King, the sport of horse racing was prominent among these. Charles II was a fun-loving sort who once remarked, "God will never damn a man for allowing himself a little pleasure." Charles II both owned and rode horses, and his patronage of racing, especially at Newmarket, has caused him to be known as "the father of the British turf."

With the active support of the crown, many Englishmen, nobility and gentry alike, began to concentrate feverishly on the breeding of horses solely for performance on the racetrack. In a stunningly short time, a new breed of horse, specifically designed for racing, would be created.

## BREEDING FOR PERFORMANCE

In a scant two hundred years, the English created a brand new breed of racehorse, an indisputably separate and superior animal, able to cover a racecourse distance faster than any other breed in the world. To understand why this was accomplished in such short order, we need only to look back to the Arabs. The extraordinarily influential Arabian horse was a result of a rigorous selection process—only the fittest animals survived the harsh conditions of desert warfare—plus a rigorous system of inbreeding based on pedigree or purity of blood. Beginning in earnest in the mid-seventeenth century, English breeders began to select breeding stock according to a single, very narrow criterion—outstanding success on the racetrack. They also began to keep rec-

ords of matings, so that they could repeat successful couplings. Increasingly detailed record-keeping translated to increasingly narrow inbreeding. The result was a very rapid improvement in racing ability and in the vital prepotency of the best racers.

Although the "why" of the development of the Thoroughbred is clear, the "how" is somewhat clouded by the lack of totally accurate records of the first hundred years or so of this breeding effort. Most authorities agree, however, that the first results were produced by mating stallions of pure Eastern blood—primarily Arabian—with native mares of mixed breeding.

This pattern was produced by the nature of the native stock and the difficulties in importing quality horses. The English light horses of the early seventeenth century were predominantly of pony stock, variously mixed with heavy-horse breeds and the previously imported Spanish and Italian horses. They had speed, but, according to one authority of the time, "were small, poorly boned, and incapable of bearing weight or severe usage." The most common type of race at this time consisted of successive four-mile heats. Obviously, the endurance and courage of the pure Arab were vital to improving performance—but pure Arabian horses were expensive and hard to find. Arab mares were valued so highly by their owners that they were virtually unobtainable at any price. The logical result was the importation of stallions, which could service a large number of mares.

Approximately 160 Eastern stallions entered England in the century following the Restoration. These stallions were bred to the available mixed English stock, then bred back based on racing performance. So rigorous was the selection process that every single Thoroughbred in the world today traces back in tail-male (sire to grandsire to great-grandsire, etc.) to just three of these imported stallions—the Darley Arabian, the Byerly Turk, and the Godolphin Arabian. These male lines survived through a single descendant each: Eclipse (Darley Arabian), Matchem (Godolphin Arabian) and Herod (Byerly Turk).

## GREAT HORSES: THE FOUNDATION SIRES

Every Thoroughbred racing today traces back in the direct male line (tail-male) to one of three imported Eastern stallions—the Byerly Turk, the Darley Arabian, and the Godolphin Arabian. None of these horses ever raced. Genetically, the single descendants through which their lines survived—Herod, Eclipse, and Matchem—are far more important. But historically, the stories of these "foundation sires" are excellent examples of the circuitous ways the Eastern bloodstock that produced the Thoroughbred arrived in England.

### The Byerly Turk

In his *Sporting Calendar* of 1743, John Cheny wrote, "I have been assured by a person of rank and great honour that the horse called by sportsmen the Byerly Turk . . . was in fact an Arabian." This black horse, who was foaled about 1679, had probably been captured or bought from the Arabs by a Turkish officer who rode him off to the wars in Hungary. He was in turn captured by Captain Robert Byerly at the seige of Buda in 1687. Three years later, as Colonel of the Sixth Dragoon Guards, Byerly used the horse as a charger in the Irish wars. He then sent him to stud in 1691. The Byerly Turk stood until approximately 1698.

The blood of the Byerly Turk survives through his great-grandson Herod, foaled in 1758. Herod, a good but not great racehorse, sired the winners of more than one thousand races. Only about 5 percent of modern Thoroughbreds trace back to Herod in tail-male, including Waya, champion mare of 1979.

### The Darley Arabian

The Darley Arabian, one of the few stallions imported directly from the Middle East, was foaled in 1700. In 1704, Thomas Darley, a merchant in Aleppo, Syria, purchased and sent home to his father this horse, which came from, he wrote, "the most esteemed race among the Arabs." The horse stood at stud at

Aldby Stud in Yorkshire for twenty-six years, being intensively inbred to Darley's mares.

Except for the unbeaten Flying Childers, the Darley Arabian was not an especially successful sire of winners. However, through his great-great-grandson, Eclipse, he became the progenitor of 80 percent of the modern Thoroughbreds.

## The Godolphin Arabian

The story of the Godolphin Arabian is the most colorful of the tales of the three foundation sires. Foaled in Yemen in 1724, this horse was exported to Tunis, then was shipped as a present to the King of France by the Bey of Morocco. Because he arrived in France from the Barbary Coast, and because of a painting that gives him a "Barbish" look, this horse is sometimes erroneously referred to as the Godolphin Barb.

According to a romantic but unverifiable story, a Mr. Edward Coke found the Godolphin Arabian pulling a water cart in Paris in 1729. More likely, Coke purchased the horse privately and sold him to the 2nd Earl of Godolphin for his stud near Newmarket. Through his grandson Matchem, foaled in 1748, the Godolphin Arabian's direct male line accounts for about 15 percent of today's Thoroughbreds. His American line included the great Man o' War and Triple Crown winner War Admiral.

---

Similarly, Australian Bruce Lowe and German Hermann Goos, independently of each other, traced the tail-female (dam to granddam to great-granddam, etc.) back to forty-three "taproot" mares whose lines still survived at the end of the nineteenth century.

Of course, tracing tail-male and tail-female lines doesn't account for the influence other stallions had through their female offspring or mares through their male foals. It does, however, give an excellent picture of the extraordinary degree of selection and inbreeding applied to this new breed of racing horse.

This selection and inbreeding was made possible in large part by the formalization of complete record-keeping of racing records and pedigrees. The Arabs had kept every horse's complete pedigree in a pouch placed around each horse's neck (often also containing amulets). British breeders didn't begin keeping similar records until the early 1600s. In 1727, John Cheny began publication of a *Sporting Calendar,* which, for the first time, listed the results of all races run that year and some pedigrees of racing animals. After three changes of ownership, the responsibility for the calendar was given to James Weatherby, whose family had served as accountant to the wealthy members of the recently formed Jockey Club. Weatherby plunged himself into exhaustive research on pedigrees and, in 1791, published the monumental "Introduction to the General Stud Book," in which he traced every currently racing animal back as far as existing records would allow—some as far back as 1711. In 1773, Volume I of the General Stud Book was issued, listing foals of the previous two years. To this day, in succeeding volumes, the Weatherby family has meticulously recorded the pedigree of every Thoroughbred foal born in England and Ireland.

The introduction and strict maintenance of a Stud Book was the final, vital step in the establishment of the "thorough"-bred horse. This "completeness, as with full attention to detail," served the breeding and racing endeavors in four important ways:

1. Ensuring against false and inaccurate pedigrees.
2. Providing full and fraud-proof means of identification.
3. Giving breeders the data for making sensible mating decisions.
4. Preventing the introduction of undesirable genes by untested stock.

The last reason was of special concern by the nineteenth century. The racing ability of these animals reached such a level that the addition of "foreign" or "unproven" blood produced negative results that took several generations to breed out. Originally, the criteria for admission to the General Stud Book was simply being a racehorse, but the designation "thoroughbred" and admission to the General Stud Book came to depend on the tracing back of a horse, in all branches and for many generations, to horses already admitted to the General Stud Book. Thus, the production of race animals had become strictly a matter of inbreeding.

## GREAT HORSES: ECLIPSE

On May 3, 1769, a five-year-old chestnut descendant of the Darley Arabian made his first public appearance in a race at Epsom. This ungainly-looking horse, named for the solar eclipse during which he was born, had been purchased as a yearling for a mere seventy-five guineas. Eclipse proved a difficult colt to manage, but when he finally got into serious training, word of his ability rapidly spread to the numerous touts that congregated around the racetracks. At that time, winning a race required capturing two four-mile heats. In the first heat of his first race, Eclipse won easily, at 4–1 odds.

The odds dropped dramatically for the second heat. Looking for more than the paltry profit a win bet would provide, a brash Irish gambler named Dennis O'Kelly offered to name the exact placing of the four horses in the second heat. O'Kelly then uttered the most famous phrase in Thoroughbred racing: "Eclipse first, the rest nowhere." "Nowhere" meant "distanced," beaten by 240 yards, the theoretical limit to the placing judge's vision. All "distanced" horses were considered unplaced. Sure enough, after toying with the other horses for three miles, Eclipse pulled off to win by nearly a quarter of a mile.

In the seventeen months before his retirement, Eclipse was never beaten or even ex-

tended. He won at least eighteen recorded races, including eleven King's Plates, contested at four miles under a weight of 168 pounds. It is doubtful that any horse in racing history was as superior to the competition of his day.

The key to Eclipse's ability was his tremendous stride length. His hindquarters, peculiarly, were an inch higher than his withers, giving him great length from the point of the hip to the hock. Long, sloping shoulders gave him the reach to match the push provided by his long hind legs. Finally, his fiery temperament made him an unparalleled competitor.

Retired to stud, Eclipse proved as successful a sire as he was a racehorse, producing another windfall for gambler Dennis O'Kelly. After that famous first race, O'Kelly had purchased a half interest in Eclipse for 650 guineas. He later bought out the other owner for an additional 1,100 guineas. When Eclipse began producing offspring that demonstrated his speed and competitiveness, his stud fee jumped from 10 guineas to 50 guineas. O'Kelly's profit on his 1,750-guinea investment was 25,000 guineas.

O'Kelly earned his money, for much of Eclipse's success at stud came from the Irish gambler's recognition that the sturdy female descendants of Herod would make excellent mates for his lightly fleshed horse. The mating of the Eclipse and Herod lines was racing's first and perhaps most important "nick"—the breeder's term for a combination of two bloodlines that produces better than average racing results.

Although Eclipse sired three Derby winners, his most influential product of that nick was a colt tagged by his owner with an unglamorous name—Potato. Things got worse when a stableboy, instructed to paint the name over the horse's stall, misspelled it as Potoooooooo. In pedigrees, the name was soon rendered Pot-8-os, perhaps the strangest name in Thoroughbred history.

Pot-8-os, bred to another Herod mare, produced the Derby winner Waxy. Waxy, inbred to his own daughter by a mare out of Herod's son Highflyer, sired the influential Derby winner Whalebone. From this line came 139 of 170 1979 graded stakes winners.

Given Eclipse's ability as a racehorse and his influence as a sire, no more fitting name could have been chosen for American racing's top honors than the Eclipse Awards.

## THE TAIL-MALE LINE: ECLIPSE TO SECRETARIAT

Eclipse
  Pot-8-os
    Waxy
      Whalebone
        Sir Hercules
          Irish Birdcatcher
            The Baron
              Stockwell
                Doncaster
                  Bend Or
                    Bona Vista
                      Cyllene
                        Plymelus
                          Phalaris
                            Pharos
                              Nearco
                                Nasrullah
                                  Bold Ruler
                                    SECRETARIAT

---

## THE MODERN THOROUGHBRED

The modern Thoroughbred, produced by generations of selective breeding, stands eight inches taller than his ancestors of 240 years ago and can run a mile twelve seconds faster. Designed by nature to run from predators and destined by man to run toward a finish line, this modern racehorse is a distillation of all the finest qualities epitomized by his species. Wind, bone, blood, temperament, willingness and heart are commingled to just the right degree to produce the speed of a sprinter and the endurance of a stayer. Three inbred characteristics distinguish the Thoroughbred from all other breeds: speed over distance, competitive nerve, and that elusive quality known only as heart, the refusal to quit no matter what the challenge. Knowing neither the point of its destination, nor the reason it is asked to reach it so fast, the ideal Thoroughbred is born to run, bred to win, and will literally race to the death.

## BREED COMPARISON

The unique characteristics of the Thoroughbred can best be illustrated by comparing it to the modern descendants of its Arab ancestors and to the two other popular racing breeds, Quarter Horses and Standardbreds. While other breeds excel at specific types of tasks, the Thoroughbred is the most versatile equine athlete.

The *Arab* is the foundation strain for all modern light breeds and one modern draft breed, the Percheron. Thoroughbreds, Quarter Horses and Standardbreds all trace back directly to the three Arabian foundation sires.

Arabs are stayers. Although the average Arab stands only 14.3 to 15.1 hands tall, it has the wind capacity and strength of a much larger horse. It has one less vertebra than other breeds, making its back short, straight and easy to carry. Its long, flat muscles are reachers, rather than pushers, and they do not tire easily. The most versatile of all breeds, Arabs have been successful as runners, hunters, jumpers, cow ponies, dressage horses and park hacks. However, an Arab would be left in the dust of a Quarter Horse's early speed and would badly trail a Thoroughbred over a distance of a mile and a half. The best twelve-furlong time ever recorded by an Arab was 2:45.75—21.75 seconds slower than Secretariat's world-record time set in the 1973 Belmont Stakes.

The *Quarter Horse* is a sprinter. It stands about 15 to 16 hands high and weighs as much as 1,200 pounds; its skeleton is similar to the Arab's. The Quarter Horse's masses of short, bunchy muscles contribute to its short bursts of intense speed, but cause it to tire easily at fast paces. The Quarter Horse is mostly push, with limited reaching ability. Agile enough to spin 180 degrees on one hind foot or cut a cow from the herd, Quarter Horses have inherited both the quiet temperament and hardiness of their desert fathers. Like Arabs, they can live off the land and they have few soundness problems except in cases of extreme inbreeding. Compared to a Thoroughbred, the Quarter Horse is short-coupled, stands low to the ground, and has a thick neck, a heavy chest and an upright pastern. It is an "easy keeper," requiring only a few quarts of grain a day to stay "in good flesh." Although the Quarter Horse is descended from many types of mares, all Quarter Horses trace their genealogies back to the Godolphin Arabian, through the English Thoroughbred Janus, which stood in Virginia from 1756 to 1780. Recently, in an effort to improve the breed for racing purposes, many Quarter Horses have been bred to animals of mixed Thoroughbred-Quarter Horse stock. Matings such as this are producing a larger, less stockily built horse. Only time will tell how this influx of Thoroughbred blood will affect sprinting ability. The day may come when Quarter Horses are renamed three-eighths horses or half-milers.

The *Thoroughbred* combines the most powerful qualities of the sprinter and the stayer. It is known for its intense, sustained speed. Standing between 15.3 and 16.3 hands high and weighing from 900 to 1,200 pounds, it is the horse world's most sensational athlete. Its large skeleton is longer-boned and finer than that of the Arab or the Quarter Horse. It combines long, lean reaching muscles with short, bunchy pushing muscles to get the maximum length and power out of each stride. An enormous heart and huge lungs give it the stamina to sustain repeated thrusts of its driving legs long after other breeds have become fatigued. Unlike all other breeds, which were developed by man to perform some useful work, the Thoroughbred is designed solely for sport. Like any fine machine, it requires constant care to stay in good working order. The modern American Thoroughbred is often capable of producing more speed than its body can tolerate. It has disastrous leg problems from the knee downward and is prone to all sorts of minor ailments, such as coughs and colds, that make it totally unsuited to life without man. High-strung and often difficult to handle, Thoroughbreds have a naturally fast metabolism, which makes it hard to keep

weight on them even if they are not working hard. What it sacrifices in soundness, the Thoroughbred more than makes up for in courage and competitive spirit. Its blood has been used to improve many modern breeds and it is still the most popular horse for top equestrian pursuits, including show jumping, steeplechasing, three-day eventing and flat racing.

The *Standardbred* is a trotter or a pacer. Because of the nature of its gait, it is a stayer, rather than a speed horse. Measuring from 15.1 to 16.0 hands and weighing about 1,000 pounds, a very fast Standardbred can trot a mile in 1:56. A mediocre one, which can do it in 2:11, would still beat a Thoroughbred or a Quarter Horse, as long as they were trotting. A Standardbred is built to trot or pace, whichever gait comes naturally to it. It is a medium-sized, sturdy horse with a long barrel and long legs and a low head carriage. Its musculature is similar to the Thoroughbred's, for it relies on the powerful, piston-like ac-

## HORSE FACTS

World horse population: 75,000,000
Number of breeds: More than thirty
Age: Full maturity at age seven; average life-span, twenty years
Longest-lived horse: Sixty-two years, Old Billy, foaled in England, 1760
Longest-lived Thoroughbred: Forty-two years, Tango Duke, bay gelding, foaled 1935
Heaviest horse: 3,200 pounds, Brooklyn Supreme, purebred Belgian
Tallest horse: 21.1 hands (7'1"), Firpon, Percheron-Shire cross Big Jim, Clydesdale
Tallest Thoroughbred racer: 18.2 hands (6'2"), Fort D'Or, foaled 1963 in Ireland
Smallest horse: Smallest breed is Falabella, average adult standing 15" to 30"

tion of its haunches to drive it forward and the long reach of its front legs to cover the ground. Although it has the heart to fight to the finish, it is a calm, amiable animal which can survive happily turned out in a field and is not prone to serious soundness problems except after years of repeated stress. Like the Quarter Horse, the Standardbred is a truly American breed, but it, too, traces back to an Arabian forebearer, the Darley Arabian, through Hambletonian by the English Thoroughbred, Messenger.

# The Breeding Industry

If the foundation of racing is breeding, American racing rests on the sturdiest support of the Thoroughbred world. Since World War II, the American breeding industry has established itself as the strongest one in any racing country. Although a huge expansion in the number of racing days has caused big problems for the sport, the continued courage and commitment of the Thoroughbred breeder remains the best reason for optimism about an eventual solution to these problems.

## THE THOROUGHBRED IN AMERICA

Ancestors of the horse had roamed the American continent for 60 million years, but the species became extinct during the ice ages. The continent remained horseless until January 1519, when Cortez landed in Mexico with eleven stallions and five mares. These Spanish horses, which had a great deal of Eastern blood as a result of the Moorish conquest, adapted well to the New World. Within one hundred years, great herds of wild horses were roaming the continent.

The English settlers of America brought with them their strong interest in racing. As early as 1668, biannual races for the Governor's Cup were conducted on Long Island. By the eighteenth century, colonists were importing horses of the evolving breed of Thoroughbreds, many of whom were mated to half-breed American mares. The Revolutionary War disrupted the importa-tion, but by the nineteenth century the efforts of American breeders were as sophisticated and successful as that of their British counterparts.

In 1868, after twenty years of research, Col. Sanford D. Bruce published the first volume of the American Stud Book, which would serve the same purposes for American racing as the General Stud Book did for that of Great Britain.

For many years, there was complete reciprocity between the stud books of the two countries, allowing free interchange of blood. This changed abruptly in 1913, however, with the passage by the English Jockey Club of the Jersey Act, which declared that only horses that could be traced in all their lines to animals previously registered in the General Stud Book would be accepted for future registration. All American Thoroughbreds traced back in tail-male to the three English "foundation sires," but the female line included many half-breeds. The result was to exclude the majority of horses bred outside England and Ireland.

The reason for the Jersey Act was a crisis in the American breeding industry. Anti-gambling sentiment in the United States in the first decade of the twentieth century resulted in the reduction of the number of U.S. tracks from 313 in 1897 to 25 in 1908. In 1910, betting was prohibited in New York, and the tracks shut down for two years. With nowhere to sell and race their animals, American breeders threatened to flood the English market, and the English Jockey Club secured passage of the Jersey Act to block such a move.

This protectionism, however, greatly benefited the American breeding industry in the long run. When racing resumed in America, as it soon did, American breeders were free to import the best foreign blood-stock to improve their product, while British breeders, denied access to fresh blood, suffered from over-reliance on close in-breeding. In 1949, in the face of the obvious superiority of the American-bred horse, the English Jockey Club repealed the Jersey Act.

## BREEDING TODAY

Up until World War II, the breeding of Thoroughbreds was generally considered a pastime of the landed gentry and Social Register types. In truth, almost all the racing stock was produced by a relatively small number of farms in Virginia and Kentucky, with the heart of the business found in the bluegrass country around Lexington. In these halcyon days, the leading breeder of the year might have produced as many as 6 percent of the winners of all the races won in the United States.

Since the war, though, and particularly in the last twenty years, breeding Thoroughbreds has become big business—one of the fastest-growing industries in the country. In 1940, 6,003 new foals were registered with the Jockey Club. By 1960 that number had grown to 12,550, and by 1979 it was 32,114. The increase in the last nineteen years was an astounding 143 percent. The proceeds to breeders from the 20 percent of those foals sold at auction was more than $150 million; the income of the industry as a whole, more than a third of a billion.

The first major reason for this growth has been the great increase in the number of races run annually. By 1940, all of the nation's tracks had ousted bookmakers and instituted pari-mutuel wagering. Since World War II, state governments have increasingly found taxing pari-mutuel handles an attractive source of revenue. As a result,

## THOROUGHBRED FOAL REGISTRATIONS

| YEAR | NO. OF FOALS | YEAR | NO. OF FOALS |
|------|------|------|------|
| 1803–1892 | 3,950 | 1938 | 5,696 |
| 1893–1896 | 5,940 | 1939 | 6,316 |
| 1897 | 2,992 | 1940 | 6,003 |
| 1898 | 2,940 | 1941 | 6,805 |
| 1899 | 3,080 | 1942 | 6,427 |
| 1900 | 3,476 | 1943 | 5,923 |
| 1901 | 3,784 | 1944 | 5,650 |
| 1902 | 3,600 | 1945 | 5,819 |
| 1903 | 3,440 | 1946 | 6,579 |
| 1904 | 3,990 | 1947 | 7,705 |
| 1905 | 3,800 | 1948 | 8,434 |
| 1906 | 3,840 | 1949 | 8,770 |
| 1907 | 3,780 | 1950 | 9,095 |
| 1908 | 3,080 | 1951 | 8,944 |
| 1909 | 2,340 | 1952 | 8,759 |
| 1910 | 1,950 | 1953 | 9,062 |
| 1911 | 2,040 | 1954 | 9,031 |
| 1912 | 1,900 | 1955 | 9,195 |
| 1913 | 1,722 | 1956 | 9,791 |
| 1914 | 1,702 | 1957 | 10,793 |
| 1915 | 2,120 | 1958 | 11,159 |
| 1916 | 2,128 | 1959 | 11,935 |
| 1917 | 1,680 | 1960 | 12,550 |
| 1918 | 1,950 | 1961 | 14,475 |
| 1919 | 1,665 | 1962 | 14,870 |
| 1920 | 1,833 | 1963 | 15,911 |
| 1921 | 2,035 | 1964 | 17,347 |
| 1922 | 2,352 | 1965 | 18,768 |
| 1923 | 2,763 | 1966 | 20,131 |
| 1924 | 2,921 | 1967 | 21,754 |
| 1925 | 3,272 | 1968 | 22,977 |
| 1926 | 3,632 | 1969 | 24,033 |
| 1927 | 4,182 | 1970 | 24,954 |
| 1928 | 4,503 | 1971 | 25,487 |
| 1929 | 4,903 | 1972 | 26,312 |
| 1930 | 5,137 | 1973 | 27,292 |
| 1931 | 5,266 | 1974 | 27,794 |
| 1932 | 5,256 | 1975 | 28,896 |
| 1933 | 5,158 | 1976 | 29,500 |
| 1934 | 4,924 | 1977 | 30,724 |
| 1935 | 5,038 | 1978 | 32,114 |
| 1936 | 5,042 | 1979 | 33,360 |
| 1937 | 5,535 | 1980 | 33,170+ |

state racing commissions have authorized an increasing number of racing days. From 1960 to 1980, annual racing dates jumped from 4,304 to 7,443 (up 73 percent) and the number of races went from 37,661 to 68,236 (up 81 percent). Obviously, a lot more horses had to be bred to fill these races and compete for purses that rose 380 percent over the same period.

The 81 percent increase in the number of races wasn't the only factor in the 143 percent increase in foals. In recent years, the quality of American breeds and the advantages provided by a declining dollar have meant a large increase in foreign buyers at U.S. auctions. In 1979, the three yearling colts that sold for more than $1 million apiece were all purchased by foreign investors.

The domestic and international demand for racing stock has meant a huge increase in the price of young horses, particularly those with breeding as well as racing potential. The average price for yearlings sold at the prestigious summer auctions rose from $11,503 in 1960 to $160,427 in 1980—an astounding 1,295 percent increase. The average for all other yearlings sold rose 586 percent over the same period. With prices like that, Thoroughbreds have joined art, gold and collectibles as hedges against inflation.

Increasingly, these yearlings came from farms far from bluegrass country. The output of a breeding farm has a direct relationship to the amount of land available. When the demand rose, the traditional horse farms of Kentucky could not meet it. The industry moved into other states where land was available. In recent years, nineteen states have wooed new investment by establishing lucrative breeder award programs. In 1979, the *American Racing Manual* listed breeding farms in forty-eight of the fifty states.

Expansion of the industry has not been accomplished without problems. The increase in quantity has not been matched by an increase in quality, as stallions and mares who would not previously have been considered breeding stock were pressed into service. Also, the rise in the price of racing stock has not been matched by an equal rise in purse value, which straps those owners whose primary source of income is racing revenue. These problems present difficulties to the racing industry that will be discussed in more detail in subsequent chapters.

On the whole, though, the renaissance of the American breeding industry is an optimistic development. Knowledge of how the business operates will certainly aid the racing fan in his investments at the track, and those with a surprisingly small amount of capital may find an opportunity for lucrative participation as investors in their favorite sport.

## THE BREEDER

In racing, the *breeder* of a horse is defined as the *owner* of the mare at the time of foaling. Some are "backyard" breeders, who keep a mare or two on a farm used primarily for other purposes. Others, numerically the majority, board their mares and foals year round at professional breeding farms. Finally, the names that appear year after year at the top of the leading-breeder lists are those breeding farms that breed their own mares as well as stand stallions and board the mares of other breeders.

Breeders produce foals for one of two reasons: to sell or to race. Selling the offspring of one's mares is called *commercial* or *market* breeding. The largest of the commercial breeders—E. P. Taylor, Spendthrift Farms, Claiborne Farms, Bluegrass Farm, Gainesway Farm—send scores of yearlings to auction each year. Keeping foals to race is called *home* breeding. The names and racing silks of the leading home breeders are familiar to racing fans at all major tracks—Calumet Farm, Elmendorf

Farm, Greentree Stable, and Harbor View Farm.

The long-term success of a breeder, commercial or home, ultimately rests on the performance of his foals on the racetrack. Huge windfall profits can come from a sudden series of stakes wins that send the value of a mare and her subsequent foals soaring. Steady profits, though, in the face of the many risks of the business, result only from concentrating on making every foal a winner.

## ANNUAL LEADING AMERICAN BREEDER—MONEY WON

| YEAR | BREEDER | STARTS | 1ST | 2ND | 3RD | AMT. WON |
|------|---------|--------|-----|-----|-----|----------|
| 1923 | John E. Madden | | 419 | 366 | 323 | $ 623,630 |
| 1924 | Harry Payne Whitney | | 272 | 201 | 235 | 482,865 |
| 1925 | John E. Madden | | 383 | 374 | 376 | 535,790 |
| 1926 | Harry Payne Whitney | | 351 | 322 | 308 | 715,158 |
| 1927 | Harry Payne Whitney | | 271 | 306 | 234 | 718,144 |
| 1928 | Harry Payne Whitney | | 234 | 291 | 269 | 514,832 |
| 1929 | Harry Payne Whitney | | 278 | 284 | 234 | 825,374 |
| 1930 | Harry Payne Whitney | | 294 | 295 | 281 | 698,280 |
| 1931 | Harry Payne Whitney | | 264 | 241 | 244 | 582,970 |
| 1932 | Harry Payne Whitney Estate | | 244 | 236 | 217 | 560,803 |
| 1933 | Harry Payne and Cornelius V. Whitney | | 282 | 276 | 320 | 342,866 |
| 1934 | Harry Payne and Cornelius V. Whitney | | 310 | 295 | 287 | 320,955 |
| 1935 | Arthur B. Hancock | | 392 | 245 | 252 | 359,218 |
| 1936 | Arthur B. Hancock | | 310 | 271 | 265 | 362,762 |
| 1937 | Arthur B. Hancock | | 279 | 279 | 223 | 416,558 |
| 1938 | Cornelius V. and Harry Payne Whitney | | 154 | 170 | 169 | 374,049 |
| 1939 | Arthur B. Hancock | | 242 | 240 | 261 | 345,503 |
| 1940 | Joseph E. Widener | | 184 | 161 | 153 | 317,961 |
| 1941 | Calumet Farm (Warren Wright) | | 124 | 127 | 110 | 528,211 |
| 1942 | Mrs. Payne Whitney (Greentree Stable) | | 175 | 161 | 163 | 536,173 |
| 1943 | Arthur B. Hancock | | 346 | 330 | 315 | 619,049 |
| 1944 | Calumet Farm (Warren Wright) | | 253 | 227 | 231 | 990,612 |
| 1945 | E. E. Dale Shaffer (Coldstream Stud) | | 227 | 147 | 142 | 791,477 |
| 1946 | Mereworth Farm | | 341 | 352 | 344 | 962,677 |
| 1947 | Calumet Farm (Warren Wright) | | 266 | 207 | 168 | 1,807,432 |
| 1948 | Calumet Farm (Warren Wright) | | 227 | 189 | 160 | 1,559,850 |
| 1949 | Calumet Farm (Warren Wright) | | 270 | 206 | 209 | 1,515,181 |
| 1950 | Calumet Farm (Warren Wright) | | 243 | 219 | 231 | 1,090,286 |
| 1951 | Calumet Farm (Mrs. Gene Markey) | | 260 | 180 | 217 | 1,198,107 |
| 1952 | Calumet Farm (Mrs. Gene Markey) | | 256 | 217 | 209 | 2,060,590 |
| 1953 | Calumet Farm (Mrs. Gene Markey) | | 236 | 168 | 169 | 1,573,803 |
| 1954 | Calumet Farm (Mrs. Gene Markey) | | 201 | 145 | 176 | 1,139,609 |
| 1955 | Calumet Farm (Mrs. Gene Markey) | | 203 | 175 | 148 | 999,737 |
| 1956 | Calumet Farm (Mrs. Gene Markey) | | 208 | 156 | 163 | 1,528,727 |
| 1957 | Calumet Farm (Mrs. Gene Markey) | | 178 | 157 | 124 | 1,469,473 |
| 1958 | Claiborne Farm (A. B. Hancock, Sr. and A. B. Hancock, Jr.) | | 146 | 128 | 133 | 1,414,355 |
| 1959 | Claiborne Farm (A. B. Hancock, Jr.) | | 147 | 144 | 138 | 1,322,595 |
| 1960 | Cornelius V. Whitney | | 108 | 106 | 92 | 1,193,181 |
| 1961 | Calumet Farm (Mrs. Gene Markey) | | 156 | 120 | 144 | 1,078,894 |
| 1962 | Rex C. Ellsworth | | 185 | 181 | 155 | 1,678,769 |
| 1963 | Rex C. Ellsworth | 1,468 | 194 | 166 | 150 | 1,465,069 |

| YEAR | BREEDER | STARTS | 1ST | 2ND | 3RD | AMT. WON |
|---|---|---|---|---|---|---|
| 1964 | Bieber-Jacobs Stable (I. Bieber and H. Jacobs) | 2,282 | 271 | 271 | 256 | $1,301,677 |
| 1965 | Bieber-Jacobs Stable (I. Bieber and H. Jacobs) | 2,233 | 259 | 278 | 269 | 1,994,649 |
| 1966 | Bieber-Jacobs Stable (I. Bieber and H. Jacobs) | 1,785 | 216 | 238 | 217 | 1,575,027 |
| 1967 | Bieber-Jacobs Stable (I. Bieber and H. Jacobs) | 1,702 | 183 | 182 | 219 | 1,515,414 |
| 1968 | Claiborne Farm (A. B. Hancock, Jr.) | 797 | 147 | 116 | 95 | 1,493,189 |
| 1969 | Claiborne Farm (A. B. Hancock, Jr.) | 728 | 111 | 96 | 98 | 1,331,485 |
| 1970 | Harbor View Farm (L. Wolfson) | 2,856 | 366 | 342 | 323 | 1,515,861 |
| 1971 | Harbor View Farm (L. Wolfson) | 3,160 | 394 | 348 | 358 | 1,739,214 |
| 1972 | Leslie Combs II | 1,693 | 240 | 191 | 203 | 1,578,851 |
| 1973 | Elmendorf Farm (Max Gluck) | 1,604 | 220 | 173 | 175 | 2,128,080 |
| 1974 | Edward P. Taylor | 2,480 | 329 | 326 | 314 | 1,926,937 |
| 1975 | Edward P. Taylor | 2,604 | 344 | 366 | 310 | 2,369,145 |
| 1976 | Edward P. Taylor | 2,718 | 356 | 381 | 313 | 3,022,181 |
| 1977 | Edward P. Taylor | 2,968 | 409 | 417 | 401 | 3,414,169 |
| 1978 | Edward P. Taylor | 2,869 | 442 | 417 | 381 | 3,387,945 |
| 1979 | Edward P. Taylor | 2,671 | 353 | 356 | 360 | 3,001,108 |
| 1980 | Edward P. Taylor | 2,191 | 305 | 270 | 266 | 3,111,006 |

## 1980 LEADING BREEDERS OF STAKES WINNERS

| | |
|---|---|
| E. P. Taylor | 15 |
| Nelson Bunker Hunt | 11 |
| Westerly Stud Farms | 11 |
| Claiborne Farm | 8 |
| Elmendorf Farm | 8 |
| Golden Chance Farms | 7 |
| Lasater Farm | 7 |
| Nuckols Brothers | 7 |
| Farnsworth Farms | 6 |
| Mrs. Henry D. Paxson | 6 |
| Tartan Farms | 6 |
| Bwamazon Farm | 5 |
| Crimson King Farm | 5 |
| Thomas Gentry | 5 |
| Ogden Mills Phipps | 5 |
| Marvin L. Warner | 5 |

## THE BREEDING FARM

The *American Racing Manual* lists nearly four thousand Thoroughbred breeding farms. These farms range in size from giants like Spendthrift Farms, which stands dozens of stallions and boards hundreds of mares, to small farms with a handful of mares. The size of the farm isn't nearly as important as the quality of prenatal and postnatal care provided to a mare and its subsequent foal. One reason is that superior care can substantially reduce the likelihood of death caused by one of the staggering number of ailments and accidents to which mares and foals can fall prey. The second reason is that, just as the care of human infants is so crucial to their development, the treatment of the foal has an extraordinary influence on its eventual performance on the racetrack.

The life on the breeding farm follows a similar routine on large and small farms alike. It is a life demanding enormous dedication, hard work, knowledge and compassion. These characteristics are typified by Chris and Gary Heimerle of Scargo Farm, whom we've chosen to profile in this book.

# Life of the Horse: 1. Foaling

Come the beginning of March, the brood-mares are restless. Under the ice-edged starlight, in the quiet barns of Scargo Farm in New York State, thirty pregnant Thoroughbreds pace and shift their pendulous bulk from foot to foot in the dark. Eleven months ago, these mares consummated their carefully arranged marriages in efficient, if somewhat dispassionate, union with the proper equine strangers. Then, they lazed barefooted through the long summer, growing fatter on lush pasture and good alfalfa hay. In the hot weather, they crowded together in the shady corners of fields and stood in pairs, head to tail, and swished the flies from each other's flickering eyelids. As the days became shorter, the mares grew long, thick coats. For a while they were frisky in the sharp mornings, startling each other and snorting as they broke into a trot at the sound of Canadian geese or a hunter's gunshot. Then the ground froze and their feet began to slip under their growing burdens. In February, dreamy-eyed and wide as boats, they became withdrawn, preoccupied with the strangeness of their bodies, the way they had to stagger bow-legged and watch all the time so they didn't bump their bellies going in and out of the stall doors. Now it is March and, one by one, they become anxious. Inside and out, they are swollen, watchful, stretched to the point of aching. Nervously, they wait for their precious cargo to be delivered into the night.

"Tanta's gonna foal tonight," says Gary Heimerle, who with his wife, Chris, has owned and managed Scargo Farm for the last six years. "She's waxed over and she's started to drip."

Gary is a short, keen-eyed young man with "Popeye"-shaped biceps. He was a top horse-show horseshoer before settling among the twenty-two acres and four white barns of Scargo to breed Thoroughbreds for sale as yearlings.

Tanta Prisa is an eight-year-old Thoroughbred broodmare of Argentine descent. A temperamental chestnut, she belongs to the Heimerles and, eleven months ago, was bred to a stallion named Sir Wimborne, who stands at Akindale Farm in New York State.

Their union, like all marriages of Thoroughbred bloodlines, was carefully arranged. Both Tanta and Sir Wimborne are from respected equine families. Tanta's sire, *Pronto (an asterisk indicates that a horse was foreign-born), begat many classic winners when he stood at Haras El Turf in Argentina. In the late 1960s, while *Pronto's most famous son, *Practicante, was being named Argentine Horse of the Year, Sir Wimborne's father, Sir Ivor, was winning some of Europe's most prestigious races and being named 1968 Horse of the Year in England. He retired to become the world's leading sire of stakes winners for 1976. Sir Wimborne, who sold for $100,000 as a yearling, won two stakes races in Ireland as a two-year-old before a sinus infection forced him into early retirement. During his first year at stud, he proved his potency with a 94 percent conception rate. Although he was "unproven" as a sire of runners (his first foals were yearlings and so had never been tested as to their racing ability), the Heimerles found five other good reasons to breed Tanta to him: price, pedigree, conformation, temperament and performance.

A market breeder tries to find a stallion which will complement his mare's weaknesses and whose stud fee is equal to about one quarter of her worth. Sir Wimborne had a good pedigree and nearly perfect conformation. At $3,500, the stud fee was reasonable, in spite of the fact that it was the highest in New York State at the time. If Tanta had had a conformational defect, such as knock-knees, the Heimerles might have looked around for a stud known for "throwing" good knees to the foals he sired. As it was, it was hoped both that Sir Wimborne would pass on his exceptionally kind attitude to counteract Tanta's nervousness and that the fact that he had matured early into a good racehorse would complement the fact that she had not won any races until she was a three-year-old.

Three hundred and fifty-three days ago, Tanta Prisa, bred of Argentine bloodlines and raced in the United States, met Sir Wimborne, bred in Kentucky and raced in Ireland, on the immaculate bluestone floor of the breeding shed at Akindale Farm in upstate New York. If all went well, the mingling of their international bloodlines would produce a sound, straight-legged, well-balanced horse, kind enough to train, mean enough to run, and able to win at two, three and four years of age. The foal would be a breeder's dream: the perfect horse.

Tanta does not remember her brief moments with Sir Wimborne. She knows only the hot flashes now passing over her body, the headlong, splitting feeling of this thing inside her about to move.

Alternately, she waits in a corner, listening, or walks up and down the sixteen-foot length of the foaling stall, distraught. Her bag (udder) is so full that a yellow "wax" has formed over each of her two teats and milk has begun to drip from one teat onto her hind foot, where it dries on her hair in a clear crust. Tanta keeps picking that foot up and putting it down again, warily. She was a barren mare last year, unable to get "in foal." The year before that, she was a "maiden," giving birth to her first and only foal, Manny Dober.

"Has she started sweating?" asks Chris. A tough-minded but gentle woman in her early thirties, Chris broke yearlings and handled stallions both at Akindale and at Tanrackin Farm in Bedford, New York, before going into the breeding business. Red-headed, jovial but quick to spot the first signs of change in a horse's behavior or physiology, Chris walks down the darkened aisle. Going into stalls one by one, she performs the nightly ritual of patting brood-mares' chests to check for sweating, which may be a sign of impending parturition or of dangerous colic. If colic, the name applied to ailments of gas, indigestion or constipation in horses, is not avoided or treated promptly, it can be fatal to both mare and foal. Horses are unable to throw up, and colic is the cause of 50 percent of all equine deaths.

"She's not sweating yet," says Gary, entering the mare's stall with a horseman's stealth and lifting her tail to one side. "Easy, Tanta," he says, patting the mare's rump as she looks around angrily as if to kick. "Don't be stupid." When the mare is ready to foal, the muscles, tendons, ligaments and bone tissue of her pelvis are softened to a jelly-like consistency by the release of hormones. This softening eases the foal's journey from the uterus through the birth canal, to the outside world.

In Tanta's stall, all is in readiness. Six inches of fresh, yellow straw imported from

Canada cover the concrete floor with a bed deep enough so that a horse lying down will not scrape its feet against the concrete while trying to get up and absorbent enough to soak up the enormous amount of water released during foaling. A white plastic bucket containing clean towels, sterilized scissors, iodine solution, antibiotics, a thermometer, and a one-pint enema bottle with a rubber tube is near the stall door. The overhead light, recessed in the ceiling, is left on so that Tanta's progress may be watched from the house on closed-circuit television. A Panasonic camera mounted from a tall pole in the barn's center aisle monitors the activity in her stall and may be rotated by remote control to observe the mares in the three stalls nearest hers. This system allows the comfort of a warm house to attendants who must stay up all night, every night, during foaling season to keep an eye on the mares. It also permits the prospective mothers the kind of privacy they need in order to relax and settle in to the business of foaling. Horses are instinctively fearful in times of stress—a carryover from their methods of survival in the wild. Many mares refuse to foal when there is a person around, even one they know very well.

"Knowing Tanta," says Chris with resignation, "she'll probably wait until four in the morning to drop the damn foal." Most Thoroughbreds are born between midnight and 3 A.M., another inbred protective characteristic.

Scargo Farm is a relatively new breeding farm, started in response to the New York-bred Program. Although the farm is supported by the out-of-state mares which come there to foal each year and by the stallion it stands, Take Your Place, Tanta and the three other broodmares owned by the Heimerles are the cornerstones of Scargo's future. For market breeders, success comes from producing yearlings which have a good market value and do well at the track later on.

Tanta Prisa, Argentine broodmare, is a daughter of champions. In her own racing days, she won three races during her three-

and four-year-old years. A yearling out of a mare from a good South American running family is not guaranteed to bring a high price at a North American bloodstock sale, though. Few Americans are familiar with Argentine bloodlines, and most buyers want a horse which will mature early and win while it is still young.

"When you go to breed a horse for a sales prospect," says Chris Heimerle as she sits on her sofa in front of the closed-circuit television, watching the gray ghost of Tanta Prisa pace across the screen, "you look for a stallion that showed good form as a two-year-old. People who buy horses don't want to have to wait until the horse is four or five years old before it starts winning races. In Tanta's case, we knew she was a good horse because Roberto Lira [the astute Chilean farm manager of Tilly Foster Stock Farm, owned by the Edward Benedicts], who knows the South American bloodlines, told us she was from a good family and that the races she had won were good ones. Roberto said she was a nice mare and we should breed her to somebody nice, so we chose Sir Wimborne [by Sir Ivor—Cap and Bells by Tom Fool] because he was the nicest horse standing in New York at the time. He is classically bred, which means he is from good horses which have gone on to produce other good horses. He is a half-brother to Drone. He has good conformation, which is important when you are breeding sales horses. And, he was undefeated at two in Europe [winning two grade II stakes]. We had to borrow the money to breed to him because he stands for $3,500 and we couldn't afford to pay cash. When this foal arrives, we're calling it Banknote because we had to take out a banknote to pay John Hettinger at Akindale the stud fee. But like John Finney at Fasig-Tipton says, 'Breeding to a $1,500 horse is like trying to catch lightning in a bottle.'" She glances back at the television nervously.

Tanta lies down, then gets up again and snatches at some hay from the hayrack. For several hours, she alternately paces and rests fitfully while Chris and Gary sit in front of the TV. She is three weeks over-due, and with each day the possibility that the foal will be stillborn increases. If the foal is dead inside her, the mare's life is in grave danger, too. Infection, difficult to cure in the reproductive systems of mares, even with antibiotics, is bound to set in.

"She's a survivor," mutters Gary, almost to himself.

Tanta's ears twitch back and forth warily, as if she senses the threat of impending birth or death.

Then, finally, around midnight, with all the drama of a faucet beginning to run, Tanta's water breaks. The fetal fluid cascades down her legs and the white amniotic sack pops out and hangs like a big white water balloon under her tail. This is the first visible phase of foaling. The foal has moved into the birth canal and is positioned to be born. During the next phases, the body should emerge in six stages: both front feet, then the tip of the nose resting on the knees, the head, the brow and neck, the shoulders and, finally, the hips and hind legs. Chris and Gary pull on jackets and rush across the driveway through drizzling, cold March rain to the barn. If any phase takes longer than ten minutes, Tanta may need help.

"That stupid mare," mutters Chris under her breath. "It's just like her not to lie down."

They enter the stall quietly, but Tanta stiffens at the sight of them. Her bronze coat gleams purple with sweat and the veins pulsate across the topography of her shoulders and flanks. Gary moves quietly behind her and examines the contents of the white balloon.

"Only one foot and the nose showing," he reports.

"She's scared," says Chris. "She's only had one other foal. Horses won't lie down when they're frightened. Their instinct is to run away from what they fear and if they're thinking about running away, they're sure as hell not going to lie down." Tanta Prisa has no place to run to in the 16- by 12-foot stall. In a normal foaling, the mare lies down to give birth and the foal's two front

feet appear, followed by the nose. Tanta's foal has a leg twisted back on itself, so that it is too bulky to fit through the birth canal. Most mares who foal standing up need some human assistance. Mares which present their foals in an unorthodox posture— be it upside down, twisted in some way, or backwards—almost invariably require human help. Straightening the leg is a delicate procedure; if the amniotic sack and the umbilical cord break before the foal's shoulders are through the birth canal, it will not have room to expand its chest to draw breath and will asphyxiate.

Tanta gives three gigantic contractions in a row, but nothing happens. Most Thoroughbred births take between three and twenty minutes. Thirty-five minutes have passed, and this foal is definitely stuck. Gary phones Roberto Lira at Tilly Foster to come and help them pull it out.

Roberto arrives so quickly and so noiselessly that he seems to have been there all along. With his help, the foal is pushed partially back into the mare, so that there is less danger of breaking the umbilical cord and more room to coax the bent foot forward into the birth canal. Time is of the essence because, once foaling has begun, any delay can prove fatal. After two hours, there would be little hope of a live birth. Tanta senses that the moment has come for her big effort. She pushes down hard with all the muscles of her huge abdomen, with contractions strong enough to break a man's arm. As she pushes, Gary and Roberto stand right behind her, pulling the foal's legs down steadily toward her hocks in rhythm with the birth contractions. The first pull gets the feet and head to emerge. Tanta contracts again and moans as they pull the shoulders through her pelvis. The shoulders are the broadest part of the foal's body and, once they are out, the rest follows, in a gush of blood and birth fluid. The umbilical cord breaks. Chris quickly rips the tough amniotic sack open and wipes the mucus from the foal's nose so it can breathe its first breaths. Because this foal had to be pulled out, the cord broke early, and the foal was shortchanged of the extra blood in the placenta that should have passed into her veins. The foal's lips and closed eyelids look blue as it lies wet and motionless in the straw. Gary once had to give artificial respiration (mouth to nose, because horses can't breathe out of their mouths) to save a foal that didn't start breathing at birth. He holds his hand near the foal's nostrils to feel for breath. Banknote is not stillborn. Her little ribs begin to heave in and out like an accordion. She is simply one of the 10 percent of all foals which do not have a normal birth. As soon as the foal is out, white heat lamps are turned on to keep her from catching cold.

"A foal will lie down under white lamps, but it won't stay lying down under red lamps," explains Chris. "I leave the lamps on for three days to keep the foal warm. I don't care if people think I'm babying my foals. I think it's important for them to have a good foundation in life." The filly is wet, flecked with straw, shivering. Chris rubs it with a towel to promote circulation, the same way that a mare's tongue licking it all over would. Tanta, still confused about what exactly was causing all that agony a few moments ago, has still not "claimed" the foal. The ragged navel stump is left uncut and doused with iodine. It is better not to cut it and create a possible route for infection to enter. Eventually it will atrophy and fall off. Chris sticks her finger in the foal's mouth and it automatically sucks on the tip. Everyone breathes a sigh of relief.

Gary gathers up the strands of placenta and amniotic sack which still hang from under Tanta's tail and ties them in a big knot. The afterbirth weighs between ten and twenty pounds. If it remains inside the mare longer than three hours, infection or possibly laminitis is likely to set in. Tying it up helps to keep the mare from stepping on it, and applies a slight downward pull to help the afterbirth detach itself from the uterine wall in one piece. There is blood sticking to Tanta's hocks, and the big, shiny white-and-purple ball of membranes dangles like a pendulum between her hind legs.

Once Tanta is taken care of, everyone, including her, stands back to take a look at what sort of filly she has brought into the world. The attendants want to see that the newborn is eager to get up; that it gains stability on its soft, "feathered" feet, which have no hard horn yet to protect the sensitive structures; that it has a sucking reflex (which this foal has shown by sucking on Chris's finger) and will be able to suck its mother's first milk which contains the valuable colostrum (the mare's antibodies). Dummy foals, those which cannot suck, often die of disease soon after birth. To help orphan foals, the Heimerles collect colostrum from mares when they have the opportunity, and freeze it in plastic containers for future use. Although the antibodies in the first milk protect the foal for the first three months of life, at which point it begins to develop its own immunities, it is the first twenty-four hours that are most crucial. After twenty-four hours have elapsed, the young horse's body cannot benefit from the colostrum. A foal may not be examined by a veterinarian for insurance purposes until it has been alive twenty-four hours, because this is the period of most frequent fatality for young horses.

Slowly, the little, wet bundle of bone and fur sticks out its tiny nose, flares its downy nostrils, and squints to open its eyes and see what sort of world it has been brought into.

When Banknote opens her eyes in the bright stall light, she sees two entirely different images. Out of her left eye she sees her mother's legs turning in the straw and a large, chestnut nose swooping down at her. Out of her right eye, she sees three people standing about ten feet behind her and staring at her from the other side of the stall. From that moment, all the filly wants to do is stand up and run.

When horses lived in herds in the wild, foals which could not stand and run a few moments after being born were a delectable treat for predators. Attracted by the smell of the afterbirth, carnivores were more than happy to devour any foal which could not flee with the herd. All horses still carry with them the instinct to run from fear-inducing situations. The same impulse that kept

Tanta from lying down, and the same impulse that tells Banknote to try to stand up, is the impulse that caused the horse to evolve into a runner and that tells it to run from the starting gate or from the snap of the whip.

"She's a nice-looking filly," remarks Roberto as Banknote makes her first attempt to scramble to her feet. The bones of her legs are still soft and her hind legs curl up under her belly like a dog's. During the first few hours after birth, a foal's legs are so malleable that sometimes serious defects can be straightened out before they have time to solidify.

"Yeah, look at that," says Gary delightedly. "She has nice straight front legs." As he says it, Banknote quivers and falls onto her head.

"Good bone, too," says Chris. Even at this age, it is possible to see certain physical characteristics that will contribute to the foal's conformation in adult life.

The moment Banknote is on her feet, Tanta decides to "claim" her. Suddenly protective, she rushes between the attendants and the filly and flattens her ears. "Oh, Tanta," says Chris, "just don't step on her. Be careful." Some mares are so enthusiastic about protecting their foals that they step on them and kill them, or crush a precious leg, in their efforts to defend them. Others hate their foals on sight and purposely try to savage them, as well as any human attendants. Foals from such mares must be given to nurse mares at once.

Respecting Tanta's motherly, if somewhat witchy, instincts, Chris, Gary and Roberto clear out of the stall, but wait nearby, watching as Banknote finds her balance on all four feet and immediately begins searching for a first meal between her mother's forelegs. The foal's vision is not fully developed at birth. Even if it were, she wouldn't know where to find what she is looking for. Tanta, more interested in defending her property than in helping it find its first meal, alternately rubs her big nose against the foal's rump and then mills around it in frantic circles. Banknote sucks the air, blindly, with curled, red lips.

"Tanta," mutters Chris, "why don't you stand still and let that foal eat?"

Finally, the tiny muzzle plunges accidentally under Tanta's flank, grabs the teat and sucks heartily. Although vigilance will continue for the next twenty-four hours, the worst is over. The foal is delivered, and has stood up and nursed. It is not a "sleeper" (a foal with blood poisoning) which is indicated by an inability to stand and is often untreatable. Its eyelids are attached normally, neither inverted nor folded outward. It has nursed successfully, indicating that it is not a "dummy" and probably has no ruptured or defective organs. It has received the colostrum, which provides it with antibodies, and has not reacted by turning yellow in the gums and eye-whites, a sign that the blood type of mare and foal are incompatible and that her colostrum may be fatal to it. Some foals are born with contracted tendons, a condition in which the feet are curled up and cannot be straightened, so that the foal tries to walk on the front of its fetlock joints. This filly, on her feet within ten minutes of being foaled, is strong of constitution and sound of limb. The afterbirth has fallen loose from the mare in one piece and has been removed from the stall. Tanta has accepted the foal and it is chasing her around the stall between gulps of milk.

After one last peek at the newborn, Chris and Gary return to the house to observe its progress through the night on the closed-circuit TV, so the mother and foal can get to know each other in peace. Anything can still happen. In spite of all signs being good, foals can suddenly weaken and die a few hours after birth from a variety of congenital and infectious diseases. Nevertheless, the picture looks 100 percent brighter than it did three hours earlier, when the foal was twisted and Tanta refused to lie down. Chris fills in an "F" in the box for March 2, 1979, in Tanta's column of the broodmare chart. A black triangle in the box would mean "not in season," a red triangle would indicate "in season," a green triangle would indicate "bred," but an "F" means "foaled."

"Here, Max," says Chris joyfully to one of the Heimerles' four Vizslas, "want to help us celebrate the birth of the new foal?" The silky brown hound delightedly laps Bourbon and Coke from her outstretched glass.

On the TV screen, Banknote has lain down to nap on her soft bed of straw. Tanta stands over her, flicking her ears warily. From now on, Chris and Gary will take every precaution to prevent this foal from coming to harm, but much of the responsibility is Tanta's. Although there is danger that the mare may hurt her child inadvertently, the few foals raised on the bottle usually don't turn out the same as those raised by mares. They are "pets," but they are almost never the sort of tough, independent, horse-wise horses required to muscle their way to the front of the herd and fight to the finish.

# The Breeding Decision

*"If you plant beans, beans is what you're going to get."*
*—Old breeding axiom*

Successful breeding demands the ultimate combination of shrewdness and horsemanship. A breeder must first of all have the ability to properly evaluate stallions and mares. On the basis of these evaluations, it must be decided which is the right stallion to breed to the mare purchased. Then, a breeding farm that will provide the most skillful care, from conception to foaling to preparation for sale, must be chosen. Finally, the questions of if, when and how to sell the foal must be answered. Of course, all of the above must be based on sound economic judgment, taking into account the amount of money available for investment versus the likely return.

## HEREDITY

The basis of Thoroughbred breeding is heredity, the process through which characteristics are transmitted genetically from parents to offspring. While no one has been able to control or predict exactly how the millions of genes will combine, scientists have been able to come up with certain "laws" or probabilities that partially predict how the process will work in a given case. Whether they understand the workings of these genetic laws or not, successful Thoroughbred breeders use them when they play the percentages.

The most important principle for breeders is Galton's Law of Hereditary Influence. This genetic law states that "the parents of an individual together contribute, on an average, 50 percent of the total inherited characteristics, the grandparents together 25 percent, the third generation ancestors together 12½ percent, . . ." and so on. This means that, on the average, the sire's and the dam's contribution is one-fourth each, the grandparents' one-sixteenth each, the great-grandparents' one sixty-fourth each, and so on.

Two extremely important conclusions can be drawn from that. First of all, the far most influential members of the family tree are the first two generations. No matter how splendid the great-grandsire of a horse was, for example, its direct genetic contribution is only one sixty-fourth. Secondly, the phrase "on the average" indicates that certain individuals can and do pass on more than their share of their characteristics. Those that do so consistently are said to be "prepotent." Improving any breed depends on finding and utilizing individuals who are both outstanding and prepotent.

What this means for Thoroughbred breeders is, in a nutshell, that the first step in producing the best racehorses is seeking out the sire and the dam with the best racing performance. The second step is looking at the pedigree, or family tree, to evaluate the level of racing performance and the prepotency, or success with which that performance has been passed along. Finally, when stallions and mares begin to reproduce, their demonstrated prepotency has to be added to the above equation.

Success as a breeder means developing the ability to evaluate and to weigh the relative importance of racing performance, pedigree and breeding performance of both stallions and mares, then deciding what two individuals would make the best match.

## THE LANGUAGE OF PEDIGREE

```
                                | Third Sire
                   | Grandsire  |
            | Sire | Second Sire|
Horse       |                   |
            | Dam  | Broodmare Sire
                   | Grand Dam  |
                   | Second Dam |
                                | Third Dam
```

Horse, *by* Sire, *out of* Dam *by* Broodmare Sire
  e.g.: Secretariat, *by* Bold Ruler, *out of* Somethingroyal *by* Princequillo
*Relationships:*
*Full* brother or sister: by *same* sire out of *same* dam
  e.g.: Quadratic, by *Quadrangle* out of *Smartaire*
    Smart Angle, by *Quadrangle* out of *Smartaire*
*Half* brother or sister: by *different* sire out of *same* dam
  e.g.: Sir Gaylord, by Turn-to out of *Somethingroyal*
    Secretariat, by Bold Ruler out of *Somethingroyal*
By *same* sire out of *different* dam: just referred to as *by same sire:*

e.g.: Spectacular Bid by *Bold Bidder* out of Spectacular
    Cannonade, by *Bold Bidder* out of Queen Sucree

Male *Line*
Tail-Male        Sire to grandsire to great-
Top Line         grandsire, etc.

Female *family*
Tail-female      Dam to granddam to great-
Bottom line      granddam, etc.

*Sire's* offspring are its *progeny* or its *get.*
*Dam's* offspring are its *produce.*
A *horse* becomes a *stallion* when sent to stud, a *sire* when the first of its get wins a race.
A *mare* becomes a *broodmare* when sent to be bred, a *dam* when its first foal drops, a *producer* when its first foal races.
*Inbreeding:* The degree of inbreeding is referred to as *crosses,* and is notated by generation as follows:

If Nasrullah appears twice in the third generation of a horse, it would be *inbred to Nasrullah 3 × 3.*
If Nasrullah appears in the third generation and in the fourth generation, it would be *inbred to Nasrullah 3 × 4.*

### Special Marks

An *asterisk* indicates that the horse was foreign-born.
  e.g.: Bold Ruler, by *Nasrullah out of Miss Disco
*Black Type* means the horse was a stakes winner or was stakes-placed (finished second or third). Stakes winners' names appear in bold black type with all letters capitalized. Stakes-placed names appear in bold black type with only the first letter capitalized.

## NOTE: THE ORIGIN OF THE WORD "PEDIGREE":

The word denoting the horse's family tree comes from the old French *pie de grue*, meaning "crane's foot." The three-line mark denoting the succession in family trees looks like the mark of a bird's foot, hence the nickname that became "pedigree."

## THE STALLION

In the marketplace of the Thoroughbred world, stallion services are hawked with Madison Avenue slickness and used-car-lot vociferation. The reason is that the ownership of a successful stallion is the most lucrative prize in all of racing. The stud fees of an elite stallion can easily top a million dollars a year. Even a stallion standing for the relatively modest fee of $2,500 can become a millionaire during his stud career if his book is filled every breeding season.

The 63,728 horses that raced in North America in 1979 were sired by 7,910 stallions. Of these, only about 700 had ten or more offspring racing. These, together with the 300 to 400 stallions whose first crops haven't gotten to the track, or who are standing for their first season, make up the pool of the truly "commercial" stallions from which a serious breeder would select a mate for his mare. The new breeder leafing through the thousand pages of stallion profiles in the *Blood-Horse Stallion Register* can find the task bewildering. Amidst the din of the often extravagant hucksterism of the business, the successful breeder is the one who develops a method and sticks to it.

Many breeders select stallions first of all by geographic location. They may want to breed to a stallion standing in a certain location because of convenience; because they must to qualify for a state breeder's incentive program; or because they don't want to incur large transportation costs.

After location is dealt with, however, breeders evaluate potential sires in light of the three criteria pointed out in our discussion of heredity—racing performance, pedigree and performance as a sire. In this evaluation, breeders are guided by a dollar value that is supposed to reflect the quality of the stallion. This dollar value is the stallion's stud fee.

### Stud Fees

The stud fee is the charge for having a broodmare serviced by a stallion. This fee, which can range from $100 to over $100,000, reflects the stallion owner's appraisal of the market value of his animal at any time. The owner who sets the fee at the right level attracts a full book of the best possible quality mares. Setting the fee too high makes the book hard to fill; pegging it too low means losing money as well as attracting lower quality mares.

In most cases, stallion services are offered with a "live-foal guarantee." This means that the stud fee is not payable until the foal stands and nurses. For some of the highest-priced stallions, however, partial or full payment is demanded by September 1 of the year bred. If a live foal isn't obtained, the mare owner either gets a refund or a free service the next season.

For top stallions, the stud fee is often listed as "private." This means that the owner or, in the case of a syndicate, the shareholder, wants to negotiate privately, in light of his own objectives. A common arrangement is for a mare to be bred to a stallion for two successive seasons, with the stallion owner and the breeder each taking a foal. Losing a coin flip for the first foal under a similar agreement gave Penny Tweedy title to the great Secretariat.

The stud fees of most sires are advertised well in advance of the breeding season. Breeders use this stud fee to compile a list of stallions of roughly comparable quality to their mare. Such a determination is very important, for breeding to a stallion of higher quality is likely to produce a foal whose price wouldn't justify the investment. Breeding too low, on the other hand, can produce a foal that's not salable at all.

For a rough rule of thumb, the stud fee should be one quarter of the value of the mare. That is, a mare worth $30,000 should be bred to a horse standing for $7,500, with the acceptable range running from $5,000 to $10,000. After the breeder has made a list of stallions in his price range, he makes his own evaluation of whether they're worth the money. A stallion's services are sometimes offered at no charge to "approved mares" by syndicates that seek to build a young stud's reputation.

## STALLION SYNDICATION

Since standing a successful stallion is so lucrative, stallion prospects command high prices. In many cases, these horses are purchased by groups of investors who spread the cost and the risk. These groups are called syndicates.

The total value of a stallion prospect is determined by his racing performance and pedigree, and thus has a relationship to the projected stud fee. This relationship, however, is not constant for all levels of quality. The stud fee is an indication of the likelihood of a stallion becoming a successful sire. The lower the stud fee is, the higher the odds of failure are thought to be, and the greater are the difficulties of attracting investors. Thus, the value of a share in a horse standing for $1,000 may be set at a conservative 2½ times the stud fee, or $2,500. For a horse standing for $2,500, the multiplier may be 4, and the price of a share $10,000. For top-quality prospects, the multiplier may be 6 or more.

The total number of shares averages forty. This figure is a reflection of the consensus that a stallion is good for approximately one hundred covers a season, with an average of between two and three covers needed to impregnate each mare. In the case of the best horses, the owners who actually raced the animal commonly retain a number of shares. In the case of Secretariat's owner, Penny Tweedy, it was five shares; in the case of Hawksworth Farm, owner of Spectacular Bid, twenty shares. The trainer of the horse customarily receives a share, and the regular rider, if there was one, may receive one or more free seasons. The syndicator, usually one of the large breeding farms, may receive shares as compensation for its services.

The shareholders of stallions like Affirmed, Spectacular Bid and Secretariat are primarily interested in breeding their mares to these animals. As the value of the stallion decreases, however, shareholders are more likely to be pure investors. In these cases, the syndicate manager sets a stud fee, books mares, collects the fees and distributes the net proceeds to the shareholders. In addition to the substantial income that can result if the stallion is successful, participation in the syndication also carries tax advantages. Breeding stock is considered a capital investment. Shareowners may depreciate their investment over ten years, which is the length of time considered by the IRS to be the useful life of a stallion. If the share in the stallion is sold at a profit, this sum is taxed at the advantageous capital gains rate.

## LEADING HORSE SYNDICATIONS

| HORSE | YEAR | SYNDICATION PRICE |
|---|---|---|
| Spectacular Bid | 1980 | $22,000,000 |
| Troy | 1979 | 16,500,000 |
| Exceller | 1979 | 15,000,000 |
| Affirmed | 1978 | 14,400,000 |
| Alleged | 1978 | 13,000,000 |
| Seattle Slew | 1978 | 12,000,000 |
| Empery & Youth* | 1976 | 12,000,000 |
| The Minstrel | 1977 | 9,000,000 |
| What a Pleasure | 1976 | 8,000,000 |
| Wajima | 1975 | 7,200,000 |
| J. O. Tobin | 1978 | 7,200,000 |
| Secretariat | 1973 | 6,080,000 |
| Nijinsky II | 1970 | 5,440,000 |
| Coastal | 1979 | 5,400,000 |
| Majestic Light | 1979 | 5,400,000 |
| Riva Ridge | 1973 | 5,120,000 |
| Honest Pleasure | 1976 | 5,120,000 |
| Vaguely Noble | 1968 | 5,000,000 |
| Mill Reef | 1973 | 5,000,000 |
| Key to the Mint | 1973 | 4,800,000 |
| Buckpasser | 1967 | 4,800,000 |
| Caro | 1977 | 4,600,000 |
| Foolish Pleasure | 1975 | 4,500,000 |
| Bold Forbes | 1976 | 4,160,000 |
| Little Current | 1974 | 4,000,000 |

* Combined Syndicate

### Evaluating the Stallion

The process of weighing a horse's credentials—of setting and evaluating the stud fee—is a little like deciding which man or woman would make the best mate to produce a close-to-ideal human being. There are a few generalizations, but a lot of room is left for personal preference.

The most glittering credential, as far as racehorses are concerned, is superior racing performance. Triple Crown winners like Affirmed and Seattle Slew, million-dollar-plus earners like Spectacular Bid and Exceller, and foreign champions like Nijinsky II automatically command high prices. Multiple major stakes winners with earnings in the half-million-dollar range and up are stallion prospects regardless of pedigree.

For horses with a less spectacular record of racing performance, pedigree becomes more important. While the most impeccable pedigree will not enable an unraced or unsuccessful horse to earn anywhere near the kind of stud fee commanded by star performers (remember Galton's Law about the decreased influence of the second generation and beyond), it can give a stallion a chance to prove himself in the breeding shed.

The highest probability of breeding a champion is found with those stallions descended from proven prepotent sires who have in turn sired prepotent sires. For example, among the leading stallions currently standing in North America, Northern Dancer (No. 2) has sired Nijinsky II (No. 3) and Lyphard (No. 5). The great Italian champion Ribot is represented by Graustark (10) and Tom Rolfe (12), who in turn sired, respectively, Key to the Mint (6) and Hoist the Flag (4). Mr. Prospector (7) and Exclusive Native (9) are both by Raise a Native (19). Bold Ruler, whose direct male line includes seven of the last ten Kentucky Derby winners, is the sire of Secretariat (13). What a Pleasure (23) sired Foolish Pleasure and Honest Pleasure. Bold Bidder (26) sired Spectacular Bid.

To try to make some sense out of the rather unscientific way in which racing performance and pedigree are weighed, we're going to look at some stallions who stood their first season at stud in 1980. Since they hadn't yet sired any foals, their stud fees reflect an evaluation of their racing performances and their pedigrees.

*Stud Fee: $40,000—Alydar*

### ALYDAR, ch, 1975
**Raise a Native—Sweet Tooth, by On-and-On**

| Age(s) | Starts | 1st | 2nd | 3rd | Earnings |
|---|---|---|---|---|---|
| 2–4 | 26 | 14 | 9 | 1 | $957,195 |

**WON** Champagne-G1, Sapling-G1, Flamingo-G1, Blue Grass-G1, Travers-G1. Whitney-G2, Great American, Tremont S., Florida Derby-G1, Arlington Classic-G2, Nassau County H.-G3. 5½ furlongs to 1¼ miles.

**2ND** Kentucky Derby-G1, Laurel Futurity-G1, Preakness-G1, Belmont-G1, Futurity-G1, Hopeful-G1, Remsen S.-G2, Oaklawn-G2, Carter H.-G2.

**3RD** Suburban H.-G1.

Brother to winner Hopefully On (3 wins, $21,800), half-brother to 3 winners, including **OUR MIMS** (6 wins, 3 and 4, $368,034, champion 3-year-old filly, C.C.A. Oaks-G1, etc.). Out of **Sweet Tooth** (10 wins, 2 to 4, $86,004; 2nd Alcibiades S.; broodmare of the year in 1977), sister to Plum Plum (10 wins, $58,340; dam of **PRUNEPLUM;** granddam of **Rich Cream**), half-sister to 6 winners, including **SUGAR PLUM TIME** (9 wins, $198,856, Firenze H.-G2, etc.), **PLUM BOLD** (4 wins, $81,907, Juvenile S. at Belmont, etc.; sire in South Africa). Second dam **PLUM CAKE** (8 wins, $43,901, Jasmine S.; etc.).

**Calumet Farm, Lexington**

NOTE: Since 1972, a committee of racing experts has annually determined which of the approximately 2,000 U.S. stakes races attract the highest quality competition. Designated "graded stakes," these approximately 270 races are further subdivided, from most to least prestigious, into Grade 1 races (G1), Grade 2 races (G2) and Grade 3 races (G3).

In the 1978 Whitney Stakes at Saratoga, the three-year-old Alydar rolled to a smashing ten-length victory over an excellent field of older horses. This demonstrated superiority against the finest competition convinced horsemen that this handsome chestnut colt was one of the finest horses of the decade, just a notch below the Triple Crown winners. His value at stud was augmented further by the success of his sire, Raise a Native, whose progeny include Exclusive Native, the sire of Affirmed, whom Alydar dueled in those thrilling Triple Crown races. The combination of brilliant performance and pedigree set Alydar's stud fee at $40,000, $15,000 higher than such established stallions as Key to the Mint and Mr. Prospector, another son of Raise a Native.

### Stud Fee: $15,000—Smarten

**SMARTEN, dk b or br, 1976**
**Cyane—Smartaire, by \*Quibu**

| Age(s) | Starts | 1st | 2nd | 3rd | Earnings |
|--------|--------|-----|-----|-----|----------|
| 2–3 | 26 | 11 | 8 | 1 | $711,031 |

**WON** American Derby-G2, Ohio Derby-G2, Illinois Derby-G3, Woodlawn-G3, Senatorial S., City of Miami, Marylander H., Pennsylvania Derby. 7 furlongs to 1½ miles.
**2ND** Travers-G1, Secretariat-G2, Playpen S., Arkansas Derby-G2, Meadowlands Cup-G2, Discovery-G3, Rutgers H.-G3.
**3RD** Tropical Park Derby-G3.
Half-brother to 6 winners, including **SMART ANGLE** (6 wins at 2, 1979, $341,682, Selima-G1, Frizette-G1, Matron-G1, Spinaway-G1, Adirondack-G3, Luck Penny S.; etc.), **QUADRATIC** (6 wins, $233,941, Cowdin S.-G2, etc.). Out of winning sister to **TEACHER'S ART** (5 wins, $121,494, Alcibiades S.; dam of **BEAT INFLATION**), half-sister to **Teacher's Beau.**
**Windfields Farm Maryland, Chesapeake City, Maryland**

Smarten's seven stakes wins and earnings of $711,031 are certainly impressive. Unlike Alydar, though, this colt never beat older horses, and in the most important stakes he chased the very best colts of his class—General Assembly, Golden Act, and Spectacular Bid. On the pedigree side, his sire, Cyane, ranks thirtieth on the list of current stallions, but the average sale price of his yearlings is only one-third that of Raise a Native's progeny. His dam, however, is Smartaire, who has also produced multiple stakes winner Quadratic and 1979 two-year-old champion filly Smart Angle. This female line, plus the unusual durability he demonstrated in starting 26 times in two years, placed his stud fee at $15,000, $5,000 higher than his sire, Cyane.

### Stud Fee: $10,000—Cox's Ridge

**COX'S RIDGE, b, 1974**
**Best Turn—Our Martha, by \*Ballydonnell**

| Age(s) | Starts | 1st | 2nd | 3rd | Earnings |
|--------|--------|-----|-----|-----|----------|
| 2–5 | 28 | 16 | 4 | 4 | $667,172 |

**WON** Metropolitan-G1, Oaklawn-G2, Excelsior-G2, Discovery-G3, Queens County-G3, Stuyvesant-G3, Razorback-G3, Minuteman-G3, Governor's Cup H., Rosemont, Tom Fool S. 7 furlongs to 1¾6 miles.
**2ND** Amory L. Haskell H.-G1, Whitney S.-G2.
**3RD** Jockey Club Gold Cup-G1, Californian S.-G1, Nassau County H.-G3.
Half-brother to **FREEO** (2 wins at 2, 1979, $46,090, Pilgrim S.), **Lawrence W.** (16 wins, $52,850; 3rd Nebraska Derby).
**Claiborne Farm, Paris, Kentucky**

Cox's Ridge was a top New York handicap horse who won eleven stakes races, including the Grade I Metropolitan Handicap. Like Smarten, though, he failed to defeat the very best horses of his class. Cox's Ridge is by Best Turn, who, like Cyane, is a son of Turn-to. Best Turn also sired the 1979 Filly Triple Crown winner, Davona Dale, and his stud fee has reached $25,000. The female family of Cox's Ridge is quite undistinguished, though, in comparison to that of most major stakes winners. The female family is the main reason his stud fee is $10,000.

### Stud Fee: $7,500—Medaille D'Or

**MEDAILLE D'OR, ch, 1976**
**Secretariat—Fanfreluche, by Northern Dancer**

| Age(s) | Starts | 1st | 2nd | 3rd | Earnings |
|--------|--------|-----|-----|-----|----------|
| 2–3 | 17 | 3 | 5 | 4 | $148,750 |

**WON** Coronation Futurity. 1⅛ miles.
**2ND** Cup and Saucer, Clarendon S., Winnipeg Futurity.
**3RD** Colin, Summer S.
Champion two-year-old colt in Canada.
Half-brother to 4 winners, **L'ENJOLEUR** (15 wins, $546,079, horse of the year and champion colt at 2 and 3 in Canada, Laurel Futurity-G1, Queen's Plate, etc.; sire), **LA VOYAGEUSE** (12 wins to 4, 1979, $258,601, champion 3-year-old filly in Canada, Canadian Oaks, etc.), **GRAND LUXE** (10 wins, $114,349, La Merced, Fury S.; etc.), **L'Extravagante** (3 wins, $28,318; 3rd Canadian

Oaks). Out of **FANFRELUCHE** (11 wins, 2 and 3, $238,688, horse of the year and champion filly at 3 in Canada, champion 3-year-old filly in U.S., broodmare of the year in 1978 in Canada, Alabama S., etc.), sister to **BARACHOIS** (4 wins, $37,729, Plate Trial; etc.; sire), half-sister to 2 winners, including **COCO LA TERREUR** (13 wins, $64,662, Queenston S., etc.; sire). Second dam **CIBOULETTE** (14 wins, $54,131, Princess Elizabeth S., etc.).

**Windfields Farm Maryland, Chesapeake City, Maryland**

Medaille D'Or's lone stakes victory in the Coronation Futurity won him the title of champion Canadian two-year-old, but he failed to win in five tries at age three. His pedigree, however, is outstanding. His sire, Secretariat, has already won Juvenile Sire of the Year honors. His dam is the champion Canadian mare, Fanfreluche, out of the great Northern Dancer. Fanfreluche has produced four other stakes winners. This bold-type-studded pedigree is responsible for the $7,500 stud fee.

*Stud Fee: $5,000—Jose Binn*

**JOSE BINN, ch, 1976**
**Vertee—Miss Prompt, by Mr. Randy**

| Age(s) | Starts | 1st | 2nd | 3rd | Earnings |
|--------|--------|-----|-----|-----|----------|
| 2 | 6 | 3 | 1 | 1 | $161,317 |

**WON** Arlington-Washington Futurity-G1, Great American S. 5½ to 6½ furlongs.
**2ND** Tremont S.
**3RD** Youthful S.
Out of **Miss Prompt** (4 wins, $42,617; 2nd Brigantine S.), sister to Randy's Ready (9 wins to 6, 1979, $36,277), half-sister to 3 winners, including **RICKS JET** (7 wins, $78,723, Hibiscus S.; 3rd Tremont S.-G3). Second dam unraced sister to Steve's Vow (13 wins, $35,725). Third dam **Nantua** (4 wins, $21,957; 3rd Pollyanna, Alcibiades S.), sister to 3 winners, including Nirulla (9 wins, $32,440), half-sister to winners Stunning Upset (dam of **Maresi**), Propellant (dam of **Frosty Pop**).

**Pen-Mor Farm, Long Island, New York**

Yearling buyers looking for quick return on their investment often favor horses who showed great ability at age two. Before an injury halted his career, Jose Binn was considered one of the very best colts of his year, winning the rich Grade I Arlington-Washington Futurity. His pedigree, however, is relatively undistinguished. Jose Binn's stud fee is $5,000 because of his precociousness as a two-year-old and because he is standing in New York State, which has the richest of the breeders-award programs.

*Stud Fee: $2,500—Pumpkin Moonshine*

**PUMPKIN MOONSHINE, b, 1974**
**Cyane—Witching Hour, by Thinking Cap**

| Age(s) | Starts | 1st | 2nd | 3rd | Earnings |
|--------|--------|-----|-----|-----|----------|
| 2–5 | 34 | 6 | 8 | 6 | $199,909 |

**WON** Lamplighter-G3, Riggs H.-G3, Ventnor S., Japan Racing Association H. 1 mile to 1¹⁄₁₆ miles.
**2ND** Excelsior-G2, Toboggan H.
**3RD** Assault H.
Out of Witching Hour (3 wins, $10,385; sister to **SMART**, 19 wins, $365,244, Gallant Fox H., etc., sire; **TEMPTED**, 18 wins, $330,760, champion handicap mare, Beldame, etc.). Brother to 4 winners, including **SALEM** (7 wins, $203,488, Futurity S., etc.; sire), **TINGLE STONE** (9 wins, $168,535, Test S.-G3, etc.).

**J. T. Lundy Farm, Midway, Kentucky**

Pumpkin Moonshine, another son of Cyane, was an honest handicap horse who chased Cox's Ridge in some of the latter's victories. With four stakes wins in thirty-four races, winnings well into six figures, and a moderately good pedigree, Pumpkin Moonshine is an example of the type of horse who is given the opportunity to hook up at this lower rung of the ladder of true commercial success.

**Evaluating Stallion Performance**

Racing performance and pedigree translate into a stud fee that is a rough prediction of the kind of stallion a horse is likely to be. Once its progeny reach the racetrack, the stud fee moves up or down based on their performance. The breeder looking at stallions first of all relies on a number of statistical measures of sire performance:

1. *Average-Earnings Index:* In 1948, Joe Estes of *The Blood-Horse,* the magazine published by the Thoroughbred Owners and Breeders Association, devised this ingenious measure of the cumulative level of performance of all a stallion's progeny. The Average-Earnings Index (A-EI) is a cumulative measure of the average annual earnings of all racing progeny of one sire, related to the average annual earnings of all runners.

For example, in 1980, 64,499 starters earned an average total purse of $6,589. A sire whose get averaged exactly this figure would have an A-EI of 1.00. A sire whose progeny averaged twice that figure would have an A-EI of 2.00.

Because the A-EI is an index, it eliminates the factor of inflation and allows comparison of the relative success of two different sires' progeny in different years or decades. It also places the emphasis on quality, rather than quantity, as does a ranking by total career earnings.

Vaguely Noble leads current sires with an A-EI of 5.22, followed by Stop the Music at 5.13. As you can see from the table below, of 3,214 current sires who have been represented by 40 or more runners, only 39 have an A-EI over 3.00; only 5 percent have an index of 2.00 or more; only 33 percent are better than average.

## AVERAGE-EARNINGS INDEX OF 3,214 CURRENT SIRES

| A-EI RANGE | % SIRES AT OR ABOVE LEVEL | NO. OF SIRES |
|---|---|---|
| 4.00+ | .5% | 15 |
| 3.00 – 3.99 | 1.2% | 24 |
| 2.00 – 2.99 | 5.0% | 123 |
| 1.60 – 1.99 | 10.6% | 180 |
| 1.00 – 1.59 | 32.8% | 711 |
| .80 – .99 | 48.2% | 495 |
| .00 – .79 | 100.0% | 1,666 |

2. *Percentage of Winners:* For most sires, this is a measure of the relative overall soundness of their progeny. A figure over 60 percent is very good; the top among the seventy current leading stallions is Kentucky Derby winner Dust Commander's 80 percent.

This percentage tends to be lower for the very top sires, for two reasons. First, sires having a significant number of horses running in Europe have a lower percentage, because European horses are more lightly raced. Secondly, fillies with high value as broodmares are not allowed to drop down into claiming races to get a win, and this reduces the winning percentages for their sires.

3. *Percentage of two-year-old winners:* Yearling buyers looking for a quick return on their money look for a sire with a high percentage of progeny able to win at age two. The average for all stallions in 1980 was 14 percent two-year-old winners. Percentages over 30 percent are an indication of general precocity; the best of the top seventy current stallions is Vice Regent's 45 percent.

4. *Percentage of Stakes Winners:* This crucial figure is the key to the chances of a sire's producing the kind of outstanding success that means big profits in Thoroughbred racing. The average of all foals is about 2.5 percent. Successful stallions average 10 percent stakes winners. Of current sires, the leading percentage is the 20 percent of Northern Dancer and his son Nijinsky II.

After a breeder looks at a sire's statistics, he digs back into the records of that sire's best runners to uncover their general characteristics. First of all, the breeder looks for negative conformational problems and temperamental traits: foot problems, weak knees, intractability. Secondly, he looks for indications of special abilities: speed, staying power, durability, courage under pressure, performance on the turf, performance under poor track conditions. Finally, he looks at the kind of mare (both in racing performance and pedigree) that seems to make the best cross for a particular stallion.

Deciding exactly which stallion to breed to his mare is the culmination of the breeder's research. Before we discuss how the final decision is made, we have to take a look at the all-important broodmare.

## ANNUAL LEADING SIRES—
## MONEY WON

| YEAR | NAME | PER-FORMERS | RACES WON | AMOUNT |
|------|------|-------------|-----------|--------|
| 1860 | Revenue | 10 | 46 | $ 49,450 |
| 1861 | Lexington | 13 | 27 | 22,425 |
| 1862 | Lexington | 5 | 14 | 9,700 |
| 1863 | Lexington | 10 | 25 | 14,235 |
| 1864 | Lexington | 13 | 38 | 28,440 |
| 1865 | Lexington | 31 | 87 | 58,750 |
| 1866 | Lexington | 34 | 112 | 92,725 |
| 1867 | Lexington | 33 | 86 | 54,030 |
| 1868 | Lexington | 33 | 92 | 68,340 |
| 1869 | Lexington | 36 | 81 | 56,375 |
| 1870 | Lexington | 35 | 82 | 129,360 |
| 1871 | Lexington | 40 | 102 | 109,095 |
| 1872 | Lexington | 28 | 82 | 71,915 |
| 1873 | Lexington | 23 | 71 | 71,565 |
| 1874 | Lexington | 23 | 70 | 51,889 |
| 1875 | Leamington | 18 | 32 | 64,518 |
| 1876 | Lexington | 12 | 34 | 90,570 |
| 1877 | Leamington | 21 | 49 | 41,170 |
| 1878 | Lexington | 16 | 36 | 50,198 |
| 1879 | Leamington | 24 | 56 | 70,837 |
| 1880 | Bonnie Scotland | 35 | 137 | 135,700 |
| 1881 | Leamington | 23 | 67 | 139,219 |
| 1882 | Bonnie Scotland | 36 | 169 | 103,475 |
| 1883 | Billet | 17 | 48 | 89,998 |
| 1884 | Glenelg | 32 | 108 | 69,862 |
| 1885 | Virgil | 24 | 56 | 73,235 |
| 1886 | Glenelg | 34 | 136 | 113,638 |
| 1887 | Glenelg | 33 | 120 | 120,031 |
| 1888 | Glenelg | 33 | 134 | 130,746 |
| 1889 | Rayon d'Or | 27 | 101 | 175,877 |
| 1890 | St. Laise | 27 | 105 | 185,005 |
| 1891 | Longfellow | 52 | 143 | 189,334 |
| 1892 | Iroquois | 34 | 145 | 183,026 |
| 1893 | Himyar | 27 | 138 | 249,502 |
| 1894 | Sir Modred | 36 | 137 | 134,318 |
| 1895 | Hanover | 40 | 133 | 106,908 |
| 1896 | Hanover | 42 | 157 | 86,853 |
| 1897 | Hanover | 54 | 159 | 122,374 |
| 1898 | Hanover | 43 | 124 | 118,590 |
| 1899 | Albert | 19 | 64 | 95,975 |
| 1900 | Kingston | 33 | 110 | 116,368 |
| 1901 | Sir Dixon | 24 | 94 | 165,682 |
| 1902 | Hastings | 29 | 63 | 113,865 |
| 1903 | Ben Strome | 24 | 91 | 106,965 |
| 1904 | Meddler | 21 | 55 | 222,555 |
| 1905 | Hamburg | 30 | 60 | 153,160 |
| 1906 | Meddler | 21 | 54 | 151,243 |
| 1907 | Commando | 12 | 34 | 270,345 |
| 1908 | Hastings | 36 | 93 | 154,061 |
| 1909 | Ben Brush | 19 | 67 | 75,143 |
| 1910 | Kingston | 13 | 41 | 85,220 |

| YEAR | NAME | PER-FORMERS | RACES WON | AMOUNT |
|------|------|------------:|----------:|-------:|
| 1911 | Star Shoot | 36 | 103 | $ 53,895 |
| 1912 | Star Shoot | 44 | 126 | 79,973 |
| 1913 | Broomstick | 31 | 114 | 76,009 |
| 1914 | Broomstick | 31 | 90 | 99,043 |
| 1915 | Broomstick | 47 | 108 | 94,387 |
| 1916 | Star Shoot | 87 | 218 | 138,163 |
| 1917 | Star Shoot | 81 | 167 | 131,674 |
| 1918 | Sweep | 33 | 69 | 139,057 |
| 1919 | Star Shoot | 55 | 108 | 197,233 |
| 1920 | Fair Play | 27 | 72 | 269,102 |
| 1921 | Celt | 52 | 124 | 206,167 |
| 1922 | McGee | 57 | 125 | 222,491 |
| 1923 | The Finn | 16 | 31 | 285,759 |
| 1924 | Fair Play | 45 | 84 | 296,204 |
| 1925 | Sweep | 65 | 185 | 237,564 |
| 1926 | Man o' War | 26 | 49 | 408,137 |
| 1927 | Fair Play | 38 | 77 | 361,518 |
| 1928 | High Time | 55 | 109 | 307,631 |
| 1929 | Chicle | 41 | 88 | 289,123 |
| 1930 | Sir Gallahad III | 16 | 49 | 422,200 |
| 1931 | St. Germans | 15 | 47 | 315,585 |
| 1932 | Chatterton | 47 | 93 | 210,040 |
| 1933 | Sir Gallahad III | 49 | 78 | 136,428 |
| 1934 | Sir Gallahad III | 55 | 92 | 180,165 |
| 1935 | Chance Play | 38 | 88 | 191,465 |
| 1936 | Sickle | 48 | 128 | 209,800 |
| 1937 | The Porter | 45 | 104 | 292,262 |
| 1938 | Sickle | 43 | 107 | 327,822 |
| 1939 | Challenger II | 42 | 99 | 316,281 |
| 1940 | Sir Gallahad III | 63 | 102 | 305,610 |
| 1941 | Blenheim II | 30 | 64 | 378,981 |
| 1942 | Equipoise | 36 | 82 | 437,141 |
| 1943 | Bull Dog | 75 | 172 | 372,706 |
| 1944 | Chance Play | 71 | 150 | 431,100 |
| 1945 | War Admiral | 26 | 59 | 591,352 |
| 1946 | Mahmoud | 47 | 101 | 638,025 |
| 1947 | Bull Lea | 61 | 128 | 1,259,718 |
| 1948 | Bull Lea | 63 | 147 | 1,334,027 |
| 1949 | Bull Lea | 73 | 165 | 991,842 |
| 1950 | Heliopolis | 77 | 167 | 852,292 |
| 1951 | Count Fleet | 64 | 124 | 1,160,847 |
| 1952 | Bull Lea | 65 | 136 | 1,630,655 |
| 1953 | Bull Lea | 56 | 107 | 1,155,846 |
| 1954 | Heliopolis | 76 | 148 | 1,406,638 |
| 1955 | Nasrullah | 40 | 69 | 1,433,660 |
| 1956 | Nasrullah | 50 | 106 | 1,462,413 |
| 1957 | Princequillo | 75 | 147 | 1,698,427 |
| 1958 | Princequillo | 65 | 110 | 1,394,540 |
| 1959 | Nasrullah | 69 | 141 | 1,434,543 |
| 1960 | Nasrullah | 64 | 122 | 1,419,683 |
| 1961 | Ambiorix | 73 | 148 | 936,976 |
| 1962 | Nasrullah | 62 | 107 | 1,474,831 |
| 1963 | Bold Ruler | 26 | 56 | 917,531 |

| YEAR | NAME | PER-FORMERS | RACES WON | AMOUNT |
|---|---|---|---|---|
| 1964 | Bold Ruler | 44 | 88 | $1,457,156 |
| 1965 | Bold Ruler | 51 | 90 | 1,091,924 |
| 1966 | Bold Ruler | 51 | 107 | 2,306,523 |
| 1967 | Bold Ruler | 63 | 135 | 2,249,272 |
| 1968 | Bold Ruler | 57 | 99 | 1,988,427 |
| 1969 | Bold Ruler | 59 | 90 | 1,357,144 |
| 1970 | Hail to Reason | 53 | 82 | 1,400,839 |
| 1971 | Northern Dancer | 44 | 93 | 1,288,580 |
| 1972 | Round Table | 65 | 98 | 1,199,933 |
| 1973 | Bold Ruler | 41 | 74 | 1,488,622 |
| 1974 | T. V. Lark | 98 | 121 | 1,242,000 |
| 1975 | What a Pleasure | 90 | 101 | 2,011,878 |
| 1976 | What a Pleasure | 85 | 108 | 1,622,159 |
| 1977 | Dr. Fager | 79 | 124 | 1,593,079 |
| 1978 | Exclusive Native | 63 | 106 | 1,969,867 |
| 1979 | Exclusive Native | 75 | 110 | 2,903,995 |
| 1980 | Raja Baba | 111 | 152 | 2,632,382 |

## ANNUAL LEADING JUVENILE SIRES
### (Amount Won)

| YEAR | SIRE | WINNING PERFORMERS | RACES WON | AMOUNT |
|---|---|---|---|---|
| 1914 | *Ogden | 19 | 56 | $ 33,911 |
| 1915 | Broomstick | 11 | 38 | 178,546 |
| 1916 | Alambala | 5 | 16 | 56,280 |
| 1917 | Peter Quince | 6 | 18 | 48,537 |
| 1918 | Sweep | 12 | 39 | 97,947 |
| 1919 | Fair Play | 4 | 17 | 90,002 |
| 1920 | Peter Pan | 7 | 30 | 92,965 |
| 1921 | Runnymede | 7 | 23 | 128,195 |
| 1922 | *Allumeur | 1 | 5 | 94,847 |
| 1923 | Black Toney | 11 | 37 | 115,745 |
| 1924 | Ultimus | 10 | 31 | 104,349 |
| 1925 | *Sun Briar | 1 | 7 | 121,630 |
| 1926 | *Wrack | 12 | 22 | 112,504 |
| 1927 | Luke McLuke | 1 | 6 | 111,905 |
| 1928 | High Time | 18 | 44 | 229,100 |
| 1929 | Mad Hatter | 10 | 24 | 77,735 |
| 1930 | Pennant | 5 | 17 | 182,950 |
| 1931 | *Dis Donc | 13 | 34 | 247,916 |
| 1932 | Pompey | 11 | 28 | 141,025 |
| 1933 | *Royal Minstrel | 8 | 16 | 102,395 |
| 1934 | Chance Shot | 8 | 17 | 94,900 |
| 1935 | *Sir Gallahad III | 13 | 31 | 102,670 |
| 1936 | Pompey | 6 | 11 | 87,150 |
| 1937 | *Pharamond II | 22 | 41 | 105,875 |
| 1938 | John P. Grier | 7 | 20 | 95,535 |
| 1939 | Black Toney | 1 | 6 | 135,090 |
| 1940 | *Bull Dog | 14 | 28 | 100,676 |

| YEAR | SIRE | WINNING PERFORMERS | RACES WON | AMOUNT |
|------|------|--------------------|-----------|--------|
| 1941 | Good Goods | 6 | 24 | $ 118,425 |
| 1942 | *Bull Dog | 8 | 26 | 221,332 |
| 1943 | *Bull Dog | 14 | 33 | 178,344 |
| 1944 | Case Ace | 10 | 28 | 230,525 |
| 1945 | *Sickle | 7 | 13 | 188,150 |
| 1946 | *Mahmoud | 18 | 40 | 283,983 |
| 1947 | Bull Lea | 11 | 31 | 420,940 |
| 1948 | War Admiral | 6 | 23 | 346,260 |
| 1949 | Roman | 18 | 38 | 227,604 |
| 1950 | War Relic | 14 | 35 | 272,182 |
| 1951 | Menow | 6 | 13 | 247,700 |
| 1952 | Polynesian | 12 | 28 | 341,730 |
| 1953 | Roman | 15 | 33 | 550,966 |
| 1954 | *Nasrullah | 14 | 31 | 625,692 |
| 1955 | *Nirgal | 12 | 24 | 293,800 |
| 1956 | *Nasrullah | 10 | 30 | 422,573 |
| 1957 | Jet Jewel | 3 | 8 | 360,402 |
| 1958 | *Turn-to | 8 | 25 | 463,280 |
| 1959 | Determine | 6 | 14 | 411,765 |
| 1960 | *My Babu | 9 | 18 | 437,240 |
| 1961 | Bryan G. | 9 | 25 | 428,810 |
| 1962 | *Nasrullah | 9 | 17 | 574,231 |
| 1963 | Bold Ruler | 9 | 17 | 343,585 |
| 1964 | Bold Ruler | 11 | 36 | 967,814 |
| 1965 | Tom Fool | 5 | 15 | 592,871 |
| 1966 | Bold Ruler | 9 | 24 | 941,493 |
| 1967 | Bold Ruler | 12 | 34 | 1,126,844 |
| 1968 | Bold Ruler | 11 | 27 | 609,243 |
| 1969 | Prince John | 5 | 11 | 418,183 |
| 1970 | Hail to Reason | 9 | 16 | 473,244 |
| 1971 | First Landing | 9 | 17 | 551,120 |
| 1972 | Bold Ruler | 6 | 14 | 541,990 |
| 1973 | Raise a Native | 7 | 18 | 311,002 |
| 1974 | What a Pleasure | 13 | 21 | 387,748 |
| 1975 | What a Pleasure | 16 | 25 | 611,071 |
| 1976 | Raja Baba | 13 | 26 | 419,872 |
| 1977 | In Reality | 8 | 16 | 432,596 |
| 1978 | Secretariat | 5 | 12 | 600,617 |
| 1979 | Mr. Prospector | 16 | 30 | 671,707 |
| 1980 | Raja Baba | 10 | 20 | 846,672 |

* Foreign-bred. Note: Prior to 1962, amount won included earnings only from juvenile winning performers.

LEADING ACTIVE SIRES

| STALLION YEAR FOALED (WHERE STANDS) SIRE | CROPS | FOALS | RUNNERS | WINNERS | 2 YO WINNERS | STAKES WINNERS | CUM. A-EI |
|---|---|---|---|---|---|---|---|
| 1. Vaguely Noble (GB) 1965 (Ky.), Vienna | 9 | 319 | 213-67% | 138-43% | 41-13% | 32-10% | 5.22 |
| 2. Stop the Music, 1970 (Ky.), Hail to Reason | 2 | 56 | 42-75% | 24-43% | 16-29% | 4- 7% | 5.13 |
| 3. Northern Dancer, 1961 (Md.), Nearctic | 13 | 369 | 294-80% | 239-65% | 99-27% | 71-19% | 5.06 |
| 4. Nijinsky II, 1967 (Ky.), Northern Dancer | 7 | 225 | 175-78% | 140-62% | 52-23% | 46-20% | 4.82 |
| 5. Key to the Mint, 1969 (Ky.), Graustark | 4 | 99 | 63-64% | 38-38% | 14-14% | 12-12% | 4.60 |
| 6. Mr. Prospector, 1970 (Ky.), Raise a Native | 3 | 115 | 85-74% | 63-55% | 40-35% | 17-15% | 4.46 |
| 7. Sir Ivor, 1965 (Ky.), Sir Gaylord | 9 | 293 | 224-76% | 155-53% | 54-18% | 50-17% | 3.87 |
| 8. Lyphard, 1969 (Ky.), Northern Dancer | 5 | 190 | 157-83% | 109-57% | 43-23% | 27-14% | 3.86 |
| 9. Exclusive Native, 1965 (Ky.), Raise a Native | 9 | 270 | 204-76% | 168-62% | 79-29% | 30-11% | 3.84 |
| 10. In Reality, 1964 (Fla.), Intentionally | 9 | 229 | 182-79% | 162-71% | 71-31% | 30-13% | 3.69 |
| 11. Graustark, 1963 (Ky.), Ribot | 12 | 314 | 234-75% | 183-58% | 51-16% | 34-11% | 3.65 |
| 12. Forli (Arg) 1963 (Ky.), Aristophanes | 10 | 286 | 200-70% | 120-42% | 45-16% | 33-12% | 3.48 |
| 13. Halo, 1969 (Md.), Hail to Reason | 3 | 63 | 47-75% | 29-46% | 12-19% | 6-10% | 3.47 |
| 14. Roberto, 1969 (Ky.), Hail to Reason | 4 | 108 | 86-80% | 58-54% | 27-25% | 15-14% | 3.39 |
| Tom Rolfe, 1962 (Ky.), Ribot | 11 | 311 | 241-77% | 166-53% | 34-11% | 33-11% | 3.39 |
| 16. Tentam, 1969 (Md.), Intentionally | 4 | 101 | 81-80% | 61-60% | 29-29% | 11-11% | 3.31 |
| 17. Damascus, 1964 (Ky.), Sword Dancer | 9 | 304 | 223-73% | 171-56% | 65-21% | 30-10% | 3.30 |
| 18. Naskra, 1967 (Ky.), Nasram | 5 | 114 | 95-83% | 66-58% | 23-20% | 15-13% | 3.21 |
| 19. Raise a Native, 1961 (Ky.), Native Dancer | 14 | 424 | 295-70% | 225-53% | 81-19% | 56-13% | 3.18 |
| 20. King's Bishop, 1969 (Md.), Round Table | 4 | 101 | 78-77% | 57-56% | 31-31% | 14-14% | 3.13 |
| 21. Bold Bidder, 1962 (Ky.), Bold Ruler | 12 | 346 | 272-79% | 197-57% | 84-24% | 38-11% | 3.07 |
| Secretariat, 1970 (Ky.), Bold Ruler | 4 | 130 | 94-72% | 64-49% | 20-15% | 10- 8% | 3.07 |
| 23. Ack Ack, 1966 (Ky.), Battle Joined | 6 | 177 | 128-72% | 85-48% | 29-16% | 17-10% | 2.98 |

| STALLION YEAR FOALED (WHERE STANDS) SIRE | CROPS | FOALS | RUNNERS | WINNERS | 2 YO WINNERS | STAKES WINNERS | CUM. A-EI |
|---|---|---|---|---|---|---|---|
| 24. His Majesty, 1968 (Ky.), Ribot | 5 | 129 | 97-75% | 65-50% | 33-26% | 12- 9% | 2.97 |
| Stage Door Johnny, 1965 (Ky.), Prince John | 9 | 202 | 151-75% | 105-52% | 17- 8% | 25-12% | 2.97 |
| 26. Best Turn, 1966 (Ky.), Turn-to | 6 | 156 | 112-72% | 82-53% | 30-19% | 11- 7% | 2.95 |
| Hawaii (S. Afr.) 1964 (Ky.), Utrillo II | 8 | 193 | 142-74% | 102-53% | 41-21% | 17- 9% | 2.95 |
| 28. What a Pleasure, 1965 (Fla.), Bold Ruler | 9 | 288 | 238-83% | 172-60% | 76-26% | 31-11% | 2.91 |
| 29. *Dust Commander, 1967 (Ky.), Bold Commander | 5 | 66 | 62-94% | 53-85% | 10-15% | 7-11% | 2.90 |
| Explodent, 1969 (Ky.), Nearctic | 4 | 79 | 65-82% | 47-59% | 26-33% | 5- 6% | 2.90 |
| 31. Caro (Fr) 1967 (Ky.), Fortino II | 6 | 178 | 136-76% | 90-51% | 41-23% | 21-12% | 2.85 |
| 32. Icecapade, 1969 (Ky.), Nearctic | 4 | 122 | 106-87% | 73-60% | 41-34% | 17-14% | 2.84 |
| 33. Little Current, 1971 (Ky.), Sea-Bird | 3 | 73 | 52-71% | 34-47% | 13-18% | 6- 8% | 2.82 |
| 34. Cyane, 1959 (Va.), Turn-to | 14 | 275 | 220-80% | 173-63% | 65-24% | 35-13% | 2.75 |
| 35. Golden Eagle (Fr) 1965 (Calif.), Right Royal | 3 | 67 | 41-61% | 27-40% | 12-18% | 5- 7% | 2.71 |
| 36. Dewan, 1965 (Ky.), Bold Ruler | 7 | 217 | 170-78% | 118-54% | 38-18% | 22-10% | 2.70 |
| 37. Grey Dawn (Fr) 1962 (Ky.), Herbager | 11 | 305 | 266-87% | 206-68% | 80-26% | 32-10% | 2.69 |
| 38. Riverman (Fr) 1969 (Ky.), Never Bend | 5 | 166 | 131-79% | 86-52% | 43-26% | 25-15% | 2.68 |
| 39. Ramsinga, 1963 (Fla.), Prince Taj | 9 | 66 | 53-80% | 39-59% | 17-26% | 6- 9% | 2.66 |
| 40. Hold Your Peace, 1969 (Fla.), Speak John | 4 | 107 | 79-74% | 58-54% | 29-27% | 8- 7% | 2.65 |
| 41. Arts and Letters, 1966 (Ky.), Ribot | 7 | 176 | 132-75% | 87-49% | 27-15% | 15- 9% | 2.64 |
| Nodouble, 1965 (Fla.), Noholme II | 7 | 196 | 161-82% | 121-62% | 45-23% | 25-13% | 2.64 |
| Ole Bob Bowers, 1963 (Mich.), Prince Blessed | 7 | 76 | 56-74% | 42-55% | 21-28% | 4- 5% | 2.64 |
| 44. Majestic Prince, 1966 (Ky.), Raise a Native | 8 | 226 | 160-71% | 106-47% | 30-13% | 17- 8% | 2.63 |
| 45. Big Spruce, 1969 (Ky.), Herbager | 3 | 91 | 63-69% | 41-45% | 10-11% | 6- 7% | 2.62 |
| 46. First Landing, 1956 (Va.), Turn-to | 17 | 363 | 299-82% | 231-64% | 85-23% | 25- 7% | 2.60 |
| 47. Lothario, 1971 (N.Y.), Nashua | 3 | 46 | 23-50% | 8-17% | 6-13% | 2- 4% | 2.58 |

| STALLION | YEAR FOALED (WHERE STANDS) | SIRE | CROPS | FOALS | RUNNERS | WINNERS | 2 YO WINNERS | STAKES WINNERS | CUM. A-EI |
|---|---|---|---|---|---|---|---|---|---|
| 48. Pontoise, 1970 (N.Y.), Cornish Prince | | | 3 | 29 | 23-79% | 17-59% | 6-21% | 1- 3% | 2.56 |
| 49. Raja Baba, 1968 (Ky.), Bold Ruler — | | | 5 | 224 | 163-73% | 116-52% | 49-22% | 22-10% | 2.53 |
| 50. Rollicking, 1967 (Md.), Rambunctious | | | 5 | 77 | 65-84% | 52-68% | 34-44% | 10-13% | 2.52 |
| 51. Nashua, 1952 (Ky.), Nasrullah | | | 21 | 568 | 486-86% | 379-67% | 148-26% | 70-12% | 2.51 |
| 52. Sham, 1970 (Ky.), Pretense | | | 4 | 127 | 91-72% | 58-46% | 29-23% | 12- 9% | 2.50 |
| 53. Riva Ridge, 1969 (Ky.), First Landing | | | 4 | 112 | 81-72% | 55-49% | 24-21% | 10- 9% | 2.46 |
| Vice Regent, 1967 (Can.), Northern Dancer | | | 6 | 122 | 102-84% | 92-75% | 56-46% | 19-16% | 2.46 |
| 55. Mount Hagen, 1971 (Ky.), Bold Bidder | | | 3 | 102 | 89-87% | 52-51% | 16-16% | 6- 6% | 2.45 |
| Mr. Leader, 1966 (Ky.), Hail to Reason | | | 7 | 237 | 190-80% | 144-61% | 69-29% | 19- 8% | 2.45 |
| 57. Native Charger, 1962 (Ky.), Native Dancer | | | 12 | 299 | 237-79% | 167-56% | 68-23% | 28- 9% | 2.43 |
| 58. Le Fabuleux (Fr) 1961 (Ky.), Wild Risk | | | 12 | 313 | 215-69% | 141-45% | 26- 8% | 30-10% | 2.41 |
| Spring Double, 1963 (Md.), Double Jay | | | 8 | 157 | 131-83% | 109-69% | 41-26% | 15-10% | 2.41 |
| Verbatim, 1965 (Ky.), Speak John | | | 7 | 186 | 157-84% | 130-70% | 66-35% | 24-13% | 2.41 |
| 61. Sharpen Up (GB) 1969 (Ky.), Atan | | | 5 | 150 | 136-91% | 89-59% | 59-39% | 17-11% | 2.40 |
| 62. Wig Out, 1967 (Fla.), Bolero | | | 6 | 84 | 58-69% | 41-49% | 18-21% | 4- 5% | 2.39 |
| 63. Our Native, 1970 (Ky.), Exclusive Native | | | 3 | 86 | 61-71% | 40-47% | 21-24% | 7- 8% | 2.38 |
| 64. Gummo, 1962 (Calif.), Fleet Nasrullah | | | 11 | 264 | 222-84% | 161-61% | 53-20% | 18- 7% | 2.37 |
| Prove Out, 1969 (Ky.), Graustark | | | 3 | 82 | 52-63% | 31-38% | 9-11% | 5- 6% | 2.37 |
| 66. Drone, 1966 (Ky.), Sir Gaylord | | | 8 | 246 | 194-79% | 147-60% | 75-30% | 25-10% | 2.36 |
| Tri Jet, 1969 (Fla.), Jester | | | 2 | 37 | 30-81% | 18-49% | 12-32% | 3- 8% | 2.36 |
| 68. Friend's Choice, 1966 (Md.), Crimson Satan | | | 6 | 44 | 35-80% | 23-52% | 1- 2% | 2- 5% | 2.35 |
| 69. Bagdad, 1956 (Ky.), Double Jay | | | 18 | 390 | 331-85% | 258-66% | 91-23% | 28- 7% | 2.32 |
| Everetts Last, 1967 (Okla.), Everett Jr. | | | 6 | 26 | 22-85% | 11-42% | 2- 8% | 1- 4% | 2.32 |
| Olden Times, 1958 (Ky.), Relic | | | 13 | 428 | 362-85% | 289-68% | 113-26% | 43-10% | 2.32 |
| Pretense, 1963 (Calif.), Endeavour II | | | 9 | 224 | 169-75% | 112-50% | 36-16% | 13- 6% | 2.32 |
| T.V. Commercial, 1965 (Md.), T. V. Lark | | | 7 | 154 | 130-84% | 104-68% | 42-27% | 12- 8% | 2.32 |

## LEADING SIRES OF 1980
## OF TWO-YEAR-OLDS

Through 1979

| STALLION (WHERE STANDS) YEAR FOALED, SIRE | 2YOS/RNRS | WNRS/WINS | STAKES WNRS/WINS | (CHIEF EARNER, EARNINGS) | TOTAL EARNINGS | 2YOS | 2YO WNRS | PER CENT |
|---|---|---|---|---|---|---|---|---|
| 1. Raja Baba (Ky.) 1968, Bold Ruler | 52/21 | 9/19 | 4/8 | (Well Decorated, $306,097) | $839,895 | 175 | 39 | 22% |
| 2. ¶Foolish Pleasure (Ky.) 1972, What a Pleasure | 27/11 | 8/16 | 3/5 | (Prayers 'n Promises, $156,921) | $547,544 | — | 24 | 32% |
| 3. Mr. Prospector (Ky.) 1970, Raise a Native | 40/24 | 15/20 | 2/4 | (Miswaki-Fr., Eng., $112,959) | $470,409 | 75 | — | 25% |
| 4. Lord Gaylord (Md.) 1970, Sir Gaylord | 8/4 | 2/7 | 1/4 | (Lord Avie, $439,240) | $452,005 | 12 | 3 | 25% |
| 5. Riva Ridge (Ky.) 1969, First Landing | 24/13 | 5/9 | 1/3 | (Tap Shoes, $197,084) | $373,390 | 86 | 19 | 22% |
| 6. ¶Elocutionist (Ky.) 1973, Gallant Romeo | 42/16 | 8/12 | 1/2 | (Recitation-Eng., Fr., $209,188) | $372,893 | — | 38 | 45% |
| 7. Vice Regent (Can.) 1967, Northern Dancer | 36/23 | 18/29 | 4/5 | (Kushog, $68,190) | $367,809 | 85 | 79 | 33% |
| 8. Lt. Stevens (Ky.) 1961, Nantallah | 38/17 | 11/20 | 4/5 | (Mamzelle, $105,921) | $352,421 | 236 | 51 | 32% |
| 9. Al Hattab (Ky.) 1966, The Axe II | 37/24 | 10/20 | 2/5 | (Pass the Tab, $129,287) | $318,976 | 159 | 93 | 36% |
| 10. Northern Dancer (Md.) 1961, Nearctic | 31/12 | 6/13 | 2/5 | (Storm Bird-Eng., Ire., $169,181) | $317,859 | 338 | 77 | 28% |
| 11. Grey Dawn II (Ky.) 1962, Herbager | 26/12 | 3/6 | 1/3 | (Heavenly Cause, $269,819) | $298,421 | 279 | 14 | 23% |
| 12. Apalachee (Ky.) 1971, Round Table | 32/16 | 9/19 | 2/2 | (High Counsel, $115,980) | $285,014 | 61 | 5 | 33% |
| 13. Brent's Prince (Ohio) 1972, Proud Clarion | 23/16 | 10/24 | 3/10 | (Brent's Star, $88,095) | $270,016 | 15 | 112 | 31% |
| 14. Noholme II (Fla.) 1956, Star Kingdom | 27/14 | 6/11 | 2/4 | (Adirondack Holme, $99,697) | $262,916 | 357 | 7 | 18% |
| 15. Key to the Kingdom (Ky.) 1970, Bold Ruler | 52/25 | 10/18 | 1/2 | (Silver Express-Fr., $55,766) | $250,221 | 40 | 14 | 26% |
| 16. Our Native (Ky.) 1970, Exclusive Native | 34/14 | 7/12 | 2/3 | (Native Fancy, $113,675) | $248,702 | 53 | 80 | 31% |
| 17. Diplomat Way (Fla.) 1964, Nashua | 45/26 | 11/20 | 3/3 | (Fine Aroma, $34,964) | $245,043 | 258 | 31 | 20% |
| 18. Nodouble (Fla.) 1965, Noholme II | 43/25 | 14/24 | 3/3 | (Double Sonic, $45,216) | $241,386 | 153 | 68 | 26% |
| 19. What a Pleasure (Fla.) 1965, Bold Ruler | 29/12 | 5/7 | 1/1 | (Fairway Phantom, $157,767) | $240,492 | 262 | 21 | 41% |
| 20. Rollicking (Md.) 1967, Rambunctious | 25/17 | 10/20 | 2/5 | (John's Roll, $79,153) | $239,055 | 51 | 53 | 20% |
| 21. Buckpasser (1963–78) Tom Fool | 37/15 | 9/13 | 2/2 | (Akureyri, $86,686) | $237,911 | 269 | 23 | 28% |
| 22. Roberto (Ky.) 1969, Hail to Reason | 28/15 | 4/7 | 1/2 | (Robellino-Eng., $108,462) | $235,734 | 81 | 105 | 26% |
| 23. Olden Times (Ky.) 1958, Relic | 31/15 | 8/10 | 2/2 | (Ancient Regime-Fr., $90,731) | $230,419 | 401 | 7 | 25% |
| 24. Stop the Music (Ky.) 1970, Hail to Reason | 29/19 | 9/14 | 1/2 | (Cure the Blues, $131,102) | $230,177 | 28 | — | — |
| 25. ¶Master Derby (Ky.) 1972, Dust Commander | 37/17 | 7/12 | 2/4 | (Masters Dream, $80,550) | $228,921 | — | — | — |

*Through 1979*

| STALLION (WHERE STANDS) YEAR FOALED, SIRE | 2YOS/RNRS | WNRS/WINS | STAKES WNRS/WINS | (CHIEF EARNER, EARNINGS) | TOTAL EARNINGS | 2YOS | 2YO WNRS | PER CENT |
|---|---|---|---|---|---|---|---|---|
| 26. Accipiter (Ky.) 1971, Damascus | 36/18 | 9/12 | 1/2 | (Beldale Flutter-Eng., Belg., $131,640) | $226,535 | 34 | 5 | 15% |
| 27. Tri Jet (Fla.) 1969, Jester | 20/14 | 6/12 | 1/1 | (Triocala, $81,461) | $225,929 | 16 | 6 | 38% |
| 28. Ruritania (1969–78), Graustark | 23/13 | 7/13 | 3/4 | (Frost King, $164,318) | $225,881 | 82 | 18 | 22% |
| 29. ¶Valid Appeal (Fla.) 1972, In Reality | 26/14 | 7/11 | 1/2 | (Sezyou, $91,214) | $224,583 | — | — | — |
| 30. ¶Sir Wimborne (N.Y.) 1973, Sir Ivor | 31/16 | 7/10 | 1/1 | (Genuine Regret, $105,881) | $222,614 | — | — | — |
| 31. Iron Ruler (Fla.) 1965, Never Bend | 45/30 | 13/18 | 2/3 | (Incredible John, $33,292) | $219,514 | 207 | 67 | 32% |
| 32. Hold Your Peace (Fla.) 1969, Speak John | 33/17 | 11/24 | 1/3 | (Wander Kind $37,422) | $217,565 | 72 | 18 | 25% |
| 33. Bold Joey (Phil.) 1968, Bold Combatant | 18/6 | 5/9 | 1/3 | (Bold and Gold, $172,180) | $217,444 | 32 | 9 | 28% |
| 34. Riverman (Ky.) 1969, Never Bend | 34/12 | 7/9 | 2/2 | (Dunphy-Fr., $70,331) | $212,966 | 133 | 36 | 27% |
| 35. Bravest Roman (Japan) 1972, Never Bend | 31/23 | 17/26 | 3/3 | (Rodger Rinehart, $37,609) | $210,765 | 19 | 9 | 47% |
| 36. Raise a Bid (Fla.) 1968, Raise a Native | 30/22 | 13/19 | 2/3 | (Lockjaw, $77,962) | $210,497 | 75 | 34 | 45% |
| 37. Lyphard (Ky.) 1969, Northern Dancer | 39/16 | 9/12 | 2/3 | (Phydilla-Fr., $78,711) | $210,260 | 150 | 34 | 23% |
| 38. In Reality (Fla.) 1964, Intentionally | 33/13 | 9/12 | 1/2 | (Truly Bound, $95,532) | $208,697 | 197 | 60 | 30% |
| 39. Our Michael (Ky.) 1963, Bolero | 34/23 | 14/24 | 2/3 | (Legend Heiress, $36,100) | $208,675 | 140 | 56 | 40% |
| 40. Barachois (Fla.) 1969, Northern Dancer | 46/28 | 13/24 | 1/1 | (Bara Prince, $30,374) | $207,876 | 76 | 34 | 45% |
| 41. Halo (Md.) 1969, Hail to Reason | 24/10 | 2/7 | 1/4 | (Rainbow Connection, $181,600) | $203,273 | 41 | 10 | 25% |
| 42. Nijinsky II (Ky.) 1967, Northern Dancer | 41/13 | 7/11 | 2/2 | (De La Rose, $93,431) | $202,571 | 184 | 43 | 23% |
| 43. Caro (Ky.) 1967, Fortino | 30/10 | 8/10 | 2/2 | (Tropicaro-Fr., $71,673) | $199,835 | 147 | 33 | 22% |
| 44. Torsion (Ky.) 1970, Never Bend | 41/28 | 12/21 | 1/2 | (Contorsionist, $40,085) | $192,770 | 65 | 19 | 29% |
| 45. Native Royalty (Ky.) 1967, Raise a Native | 42/21 | 9/17 | 1/1 | (Stutz Finwhale, $55,845) | $190,792 | 122 | 39 | 32% |
| 46. Terresto (Calif.) 1964, Intentionally | 29/9 | 5/8 | 1/2 | (Loma Malad, $155,000) | $187,751 | 64 | 13 | 20% |
| 47. Bold Tactics (1963–79), Bold Ruler | 10/6 | 2/8 | 1/3 | (Bold Ego, $176,686) | $184,672 | 147 | 26 | 18% |
| 48. ¶Nostrum (Ky.) 1971, Dr. Fager | 17/9 | 6/10 | 1/1 | (Prosper, $87,808) | $184,519 | — | — | — |
| 49. Irish Castle (Ky.) 1967, Bold Ruler | 27/14 | 5/8 | 2/2 | (Irish Playboy-Fr., $61,247) | $173,837 | 167 | 40 | 24% |
| 50. Gunflint (Fla.) 1963, Rough 'n Tumble | 12/8 | 2/5 | 1/1 | (Carolina Command, $164,233) | $172,803 | 170 | 64 | 38% |

*FOOTNOTE: Bold Ruler led sires in juvenile progeny earnings six times in the 1960s and 1970s, and on four other occasions prior to 1980 sons of Bold Ruler have led the list—What a Pleasure (1974, 1975), Raja Baba (1976), and Secretariat (1978).*

# RANKING SIRES: NUMBER OF
## STAKES WINNERS

| | NAMED FOALS THROUGH 1980 | TOTAL SW | PER CENT |
|---|---|---|---|
| 1. Nasrullah, 1940–59, Nearco | 420 | 99 | 23.6% |
| 2. Court Martial, 1942–66, Fair Trial | 504 | 96 | 19.0% |
| 3. Bold Ruler, 1954–71, Nasrullah | 355 | 82 | 23.1% |
| 4. Round Table, 1954, Princequillo | 398 | 81 | 20.4% |
| 5. Northern Dancer, 1961, Nearctic | 369 | 71 | 20.1% |
| 6. Nashua, 1952, Nasrullah | 568 | 70 | 12.3% |
| 7. Broomstick, 1901–31, Ben Brush | 280 | 69 | 24.6% |
| 8. Mahmoud, 1933–62, Blenheim II | 408 | 68 | 16.7% |
| 9. Ribot, 1952–72, Tenerani | 418 | 66 | 15.8% |
| 10. Teddy, 1913–36, Ajax | 356 | 65 | 18.3% |
| 11. Man o' War, 1917–47, Fair Play | 379 | 64 | 16.9% |
| Princequillo, 1940–64, Prince Rose | 480 | 64 | 13.3% |
| 13. Star Shoot, 1898–1919, Isinglass | 478 | 61 | 12.8% |
| 14. Herbager, 1956–76, Vandale | 424 | 60 | 14.2% |
| Khaled, 1943–68, Hyperion | 524 | 60 | 11.5% |
| Blenheim II, 1927–58, Blandford | 530 | 60 | 11.3% |
| Sir Gallahad III, 1920–49, Teddy | 567 | 60 | 10.6% |
| 18. Never Bend, 1960–77, Nasrullah | 359 | 58 | 16.2% |
| Bull Lea, 1935–64, Bull Dog | 377 | 58 | 15.4% |
| 20. Royal Charger, 1942–61, Nearco | 363 | 57 | 15.7% |
| 21. Raise a Native, 1961, Native Dancer | 424 | 56 | 13.2% |
| 22. Alibhai, 1938–60, Hyperion | 395 | 54 | 13.7% |
| Roman, 1937–60, Sir Gallahad III | 410 | 54 | 13.2% |
| 24. Heliopolis, 1936–59, Hyperion | 346 | 53 | 15.3% |
| T. V. Lark, 1957–75, Indian Hemp | 367 | 53 | 14.4% |
| 26. Bull Dog, 1927–54, Teddy | 343 | 52 | 15.2% |
| 27. Ambiorix, 1946–75, Tourbillon | 423 | 51 | 12.1% |
| 28. Sir Ivor, 1965, Sir Gaylord | 293 | 50 | 17.1% |
| Sir Gaylord, 1959, Turn-to | 402 | 50 | 12.4% |
| Prince John, 1953–79, Princequillo | 543 | 50 | 9.2% |
| 31. Beau Pere, 1927–47, Son-in-Law | 286 | 49 | 17.1% |
| Nearctic, 1954–73, Nearco | 335 | 49 | 14.6% |
| 33. Peter Pan, 1904–33, Commando | 245 | 48 | 19.6% |
| 34. Fair Play, 1905–29, Hastings | 260 | 47 | 18.1% |
| Gallant Man, 1954, Migoli | 461 | 47 | 10.2% |
| 36. Nijinsky II, 1967, Northern Dancer | 225 | 46 | 20.4% |
| Sweep, 1907–31, Ben Brush | 395 | 46 | 11.6% |
| 38. Native Dancer, 1950–67, Polynesian | 304 | 45 | 14.8% |
| Johns Joy, 1946–72, Bull Dog | 425 | 45 | 10.6% |
| Double Jay, 1944–71, Balladier | 449 | 45 | 10.0% |
| 41. Blue Larkspur, 1926–47, Black Servant | 289 | 44 | 15.2% |
| Eight Thirty, 1936–65, Pilate | 299 | 44 | 14.7% |
| 43. Sickle, 1924–43, Phalaris | 297 | 43 | 14.5% |
| King of the Tudors, 1950–74, Tudor Minstrel | 371 | 43 | 11.6% |
| Olden Times, 1958, Relic | 431 | 43 | 10.0% |
| 46. Hail to Reason, 1958–76, Turn-to | 308 | 41 | 13.3% |
| Tudor Minstrel, 1944–71, Owen Tudor | 477 | 41 | 8.6% |
| Fleet Nasrullah, 1955–79, Nasrullah | 555 | 41 | 7.8% |
| 49. Black Toney, 1911–38, Peter Pan | 221 | 40 | 18.1% |
| Olympia, 1946–74, Heliopolis | 324 | 40 | 12.3% |
| War Admiral, 1934–59, Man o' War | 371 | 40 | 10.8% |
| Barbizon, 1954, Polynesian | 531 | 40 | 7.5% |

## GREAT HORSES: NASRULLAH

In 1939, the Aga Khan bred Mumtaz Begum, a mare from one of England's outstanding speed lines, to the great Italian-bred champion Nearco. The resulting foal was Nasrullah, a bay colt of impressive racing potential.

The potential was never fully actualized, however, because Nasrullah soon displayed temperamental traits that made him one of Thoroughbred history's most noted "bad actors." Nasrullah's behavior included mulish refusals to train, operatic displays of temperament in the paddock, and the tendency to suddenly quit in the middle of the course of a race. Although he was the top-weighted two-year-old colt of his year, he failed to win a classic race.

When he did condescend to get serious, Nasrullah displayed the stunning speed of his mother's line. He lacked the stamina of the true stayer, but he did win five races at distances up to 1¼ miles.

At stud, however, Nasrullah attained true greatness. In 1944, the colt was purchased by Joseph McGrath and sent to Ireland. In 1949, Nasrullah was sold to a syndicate headed by A. B. (Bull) Hancock for $372,000 and was sent to America to stand at Hancock's Claiborne Farm. This purchase marked the beginning of the modern trend of syndication of stallions for large sums of money.

Nasrullah's temperament didn't improve at all when he arrived at his new home. He still had no use for human beings, and he developed a reputation for carrying a grudge. Col. Floyd Sager, vet at Claiborne Farm, tells the story of trying to give Nasrullah a tetanus shot. When a groom tried to put a twitch on the mean-eyed bay, Nasrullah reared up to the ceiling with rage and flung himself violently across the stall. Attempts to calm him only resulted in more vicious attacks. Sager wrote, "Nasrullah's dead and buried, but he never did get that tetanus shot." After that, whenever Nasrullah heard Sager's voice, he would bare his teeth and charge. He bore a similar hatred for Bull Hancock, and wouldn't mount a mare with the owner of Claiborne Farm anywhere in sight.

Nasrullah's success at stud more than made up for his outrageous behavior, though. In 1951, the success of his progeny in England made him the leading sire. He went on to win the same honors in America in 1955, 1956, 1959, 1960 and 1962, becoming the only stallion ever to head the list in both countries. Out of 420 foals, Nasrullah sired 99 stakes winners (highest of any stallion in North America in this century). Of his foals, 90 percent were runners, 70 percent were winners, 38 percent were two-year-old winners and 23.6 percent were stakes winners.

Nasrullah was also a great sire of sires. Four of his offspring are also on the list of the century's top sires of stakes winners: Bold Ruler (2); Nashua (5); Never Bend (24); and Fleet Nasrullah (43). He was also a great broodmare sire.

| | Nearco | Pharos |
| Nasrullah | | Nogara |
| | Mumtaz Begum | Blenheim II |
| | | Mumtaz Mahal |

## THE BROODMARE

Because of the numbers of their progeny, stallions draw most of the attention from racing fans and writers, but the dam's genetic contribution is equal to that of the sire. In today's expanding market, the quality mares that are the key to success as a breeder are fetching premium prices. In the last six years, the average price for broodmares sold at the Keeneland Fall Sale of Breeding Stock has jumped 258 percent, from $16,540 to $59,349.

Because so many more mares than stallions become breeding stock, the word "quality" is more broadly defined and thus more difficult to predict. The factors used in evaluating the mare are the same ones used in judging a stallion—racing performance, pedigree and the record of the broodmare's foals. The initial value of the mare, like the stud fee of the stallion, is based on the first two characteristics. However, because this appraisal is often based on more subjective data than that of the stallion, and because a broodmare is judged on a handful of offspring rather than the scores of a stallion's progeny, the value is intensely volatile. We'll give examples of that volatility when we discuss pedigree and broodmare production.

## Racing Performance

As with a stallion, a mare's performance on the track is the surest indication of the quality of her produce as a broodmare. The price of the relatively few champions can reach high into six figures. The price for mares with a single stakes win is also very high, for this group has produce records (i.e., records for getting in foal) that compare with the very top stallions—those with several major stakes victories. A survey of the progeny of two hundred stakes-winning mares by *The Blood-Horse* showed 61.9 percent winners and 10.7 percent stakes winners, figures slightly above the averages for the top seventy current stallions.

The same survey showed that the two hundred winning mares produced 59.1 percent winners and 4.8 percent stakes winners, well above average. Mares that placed in a race did slightly less well, with a sharper drop-off for unplaced animals. Unraced mares produced only 46.4 percent winners and 1.5 percent stakes winners.

## Pedigree

Pedigree plays a far greater part in determining the value of a mare than of a stallion. In particular, the produce records of the broodmare prospect's dam is especially important. At minimum, a buyer likes to see a female line of steady producers (as opposed to chronically barren mares) of winning performers. A stakes-winning full or half brother or sister greatly increases the value of a broodmare; outstanding success of the relative can send it soaring.

## GREAT HORSES: PRINCEQUILLO

Imported from England to America in 1941 as a yearling, Princequillo proved to be such a slow developer that he entered in claiming races as a two-year-old. At three, however, he won at a distance of 1½ miles, and with another win in the two-mile Jockey Gold Cup, began to attract some attention as a true "stayer."

This quality, however, did not exactly lead to breeders clamoring for his services. Most American races are run at short and middle distances, where speed is of the essence. Princequillo was purchased by Bull Hancock's father and sent to Virginia, where he would be close to the breeders who had expressed interest in him—breeders of horses for the grueling long-distance steeplechases.

When Bull Hancock came home from World War II and took over management of Claiborne Farm, he started to drum up business for Princequillo. Gradually, interest built as his performers hit the track. Soon, steeplechase breeders couldn't find room in his book.

In 1956 and 1957, Princequillo headed the list of American sires. He has gotten a total of 64 stakes winners, including the outstanding racehorses Round Table (sire of 79 stakes winners) and Prince John (sire of 49 stakes winners). His male progeny have shared their father's staying power and have generally proved to be superior grass racers.

Princequillo's major contribution to the American turf, however, may have been his influence as a broodmare sire. His female offspring have proven superior mates to speed sires, providing the staying power for horses competing at the classic distances. Princequillo has led the list of broodmare sires eight times, and his offspring, particularly Prince John, have also demonstrated this ability.

|  |  | Rose Prince |
|  | Prince Rose |  |
|  |  | Indolence |
| Princequillo |  |  |
|  |  | Papyrus |
|  | Cosquilla |  |
|  |  | Quick Thought |

Recent auction prices reflect the influence of the performance of a mare's relatives. Syrian Sea, full sister to Secretariat, sold at auction in 1979 for $1.6 million. Come to Market, a $24,000 earner at the track, sold at auction for a quarter of a million dollars when her half-brother, Bold Forbes, won the Kentucky Derby and Belmont Stakes.

Just as certain sires produce good sires, other stallions are excellent sires of broodmares. The most notable broodmare sire of the last few decades was Princequillo, sire of Secretariat's dam, Somethingroyal. A stallion who appears high on the annual list of leading broodmare sires will enhance the value of the prospective producer.

## ANNUAL LEADING BROODMARE SIRES
### (Money Won)

| YEAR | BROODMARE SIRE | PERF. | 1ST | AMOUNT |
|------|----------------|-------|-----|--------|
| 1937 | Sweep | 140 | 271 | $ 382,744 |
| 1938 | Fair Play | 129 | 254 | 408,369 |
| 1939 | *Sir Gallahad III | 95 | 168 | 480,018 |
| 1940 | High Time | 134 | 247 | 335,807 |
| 1941 | Sweep | 115 | 217 | 462,587 |
| 1942 | *Chicle | 113 | 205 | 533,572 |
| 1943 | *Sir Gallahad III | 195 | 365 | 703,301 |
| 1944 | *Sir Gallahad III | 236 | 447 | 1,024,290 |
| 1945 | *Sir Gallahad III | 236 | 362 | 1,020,235 |
| 1946 | *Sir Gallahad III | 276 | 475 | 1,529,393 |
| 1947 | *Sir Gallahad III | 273 | 465 | 1,458,309 |
| 1948 | *Sir Gallahad III | 302 | 433 | 1,468,648 |
| 1949 | *Sir Gallahad III | 317 | 537 | 1,393,104 |
| 1950 | *Sir Gallahad III | 345 | 542 | 1,376,629 |
| 1951 | *Sir Gallahad III | 341 | 587 | 1,707,823 |
| 1952 | *Sir Gallahad III | 344 | 567 | 1,656,221 |
| 1953 | *Bull Dog | 234 | 490 | 1,941,345 |
| 1954 | *Bull Dog | 243 | 459 | 1,780,267 |
| 1955 | *Sir Gallahad III | 336 | 591 | 1,499,162 |
| 1956 | *Bull Dog | 228 | 420 | 1,683,908 |
| 1957 | *Mahmoud | 171 | 283 | 2,593,782 |
| 1958 | Bull Lea | 172 | 252 | 1,645,812 |
| 1959 | Bull Lea | 189 | 335 | 1,479,375 |
| 1960 | Bull Lea | 196 | 352 | 1,915,881 |
| 1961 | Bull Lea | 196 | 364 | 1,632,559 |
| 1962 | War Admiral | 120 | 348 | 1,654,396 |
| 1963 | Count Fleet | 205 | 332 | 1,866,809 |
| 1964 | War Admiral | 212 | 351 | 2,028,459 |
| 1965 | Roman | 217 | 368 | 2,394,944 |
| 1966 | *Princequillo | 191 | 287 | 2,007,184 |
| 1967 | *Princequillo | 215 | 323 | 2,311,709 |
| 1968 | *Princequillo | 219 | 299 | 2,116,648 |
| 1969 | *Princequillo | 215 | 275 | 2,196,327 |
| 1970 | *Princequillo | 209 | 261 | 2,454,097 |
| 1971 | Double Jay | 202 | 290 | 2,051,296 |
| 1972 | *Princequillo | 238 | 297 | 2,722,783 |
| 1973 | *Princequillo | 241 | 322 | 3,071,322 |
| 1974 | Olympia | 174 | 297 | 2,300,121 |

* Foreign-bred.

| YEAR | BROODMARE SIRE | PERF. | 1ST | AMOUNT |
|------|----------------|-------|-----|--------|
| 1975 | Double Jay | 238 | 329 | $2,233,642 |
| 1976 | *Princequillo | 202 | 266 | 2,778,695 |
| 1977 | Double Jay | 233 | 300 | 2,696,490 |
| 1978 | Crafty Admiral | 172 | 260 | 2,295,375 |
| 1979 | Prince John | 204 | 135 | 2,856,904 |
| 1980 | Prince John | 210 | 282 | 3,434,042 |

## 50 LEADING BROODMARE
### SIRES, 1970–1980

| BROODMARE SIRE | YEAR-STARTERS | TOTAL MONEY EARNED | CUM. AVERAGE-EARNINGS INDEX |
|----------------|---------------|--------------------|------------------------------|
| 1. Buckpasser, 63 | 138 | $ 3,706,145 | 4.20 |
| 2. Graustark, 63 | 188 | 3,692,884 | 2.98 |
| 3. Northern Dancer, 61 | 420 | 7,256,242 | 2.96 |
| 4. Tom Fool, 49 | 1,146 | 15,352,312 | 2.79 |
| 5. Quibu, 42 | 516 | 6,836,305 | 2.72 |
| 6. Nasrullah, 40 | 2,035 | 21,011,879 | 2.71 |
| Preciptic, 42 | 190 | 2,113,363 | 2.71 |
| 8. Never Bend, 60 | 368 | 5,890,551 | 2.62 |
| 9. Hail to Reason, 58 | 770 | 10,776,996 | 2.59 |
| 10. Sir Gaylord, 59 | 613 | 8,968,506 | 2.55 |
| 11. Native Dancer, 50 | 1,806 | 21,765,760 | 2.52 |
| 12. Bold Ruler, 54 | 1,275 | 16,595,403 | 2.51 |
| 13. Princequillo, 40 | 3,392 | 34,313,917 | 2.45 |
| 14. Round Table, 54 | 842 | 11,349,994 | 2.43 |
| Summer Tan, 52 | 1,008 | 11,481,502 | 2.43 |
| 16. Prince John, 53 | 1,824 | 22,351,874 | 2.39 |
| 17. T. V. Lark, 57 | 505 | 6,726,157 | 2.38 |
| 18. Bold Bidder, 62 | 186 | 2,684,401 | 2.33 |
| Swaps, 52 | 1,325 | 14,374,022 | 2.33 |
| 20. Boldnesian, 63 | 208 | 3,049,340 | 2.30 |
| 21. Nantallah, 53 | 695 | 8,217,597 | 2.28 |
| 22. Amerigo, 55 | 635 | 7,843,329 | 2.27 |
| 23. War Admiral, 34 | 2,343 | 18,262,376 | 2.26 |
| 24. First Landing, 56 | 818 | 9,680,471 | 2.24 |
| Greek Game, 54 | 240 | 2,893,919 | 2.24 |
| 26. Intentionally, 56 | 696 | 8,522,959 | 2.19 |
| 27. Traffic Judge, 52 | 1,230 | 13,906,866 | 2.18 |
| 28. Double Jay, 44 | 3,076 | 30,854,424 | 2.17 |
| Hasty Road, 51 | 1,456 | 15,256,777 | 2.17 |
| 30. Counterpoint, 48 | 474 | 4,082,721 | 2.13 |
| Speak John, 58 | 197 | 2,656,060 | 2.13 |
| 32. Jet Action, 51 | 549 | 5,393,764 | 2.10 |
| 33. Tim Tam, 55 | 969 | 10,699,810 | 2.09 |
| 34. Cornish Prince, 62 | 227 | 2,987,351 | 2.06 |
| 35. Nearctic, 54 | 1,262 | 13,708,411 | 2.05 |
| 36. Better Self, 45 | 1,468 | 12,154,991 | 2.02 |
| My Babu, 45 | 1,605 | 13,984,926 | 2.02 |
| 38. Chieftain, 61 | 359 | 4,322,290 | 2.01 |
| Clandestine, 55 | 290 | 3,451,120 | 2.01 |

| BROODMARE SIRE | YEAR-STARTERS | TOTAL MONEY EARNED | CUM. AVERAGE-EARNINGS INDEX |
|---|---|---|---|
| 40. Gallant Man, 54 | 997 | $11,001,157 | 2.00 |
| Ribot, 52 | 875 | 9,098,459 | 2.00 |
| 42. Bupers, 61 | 233 | 2,842,416 | 1.99 |
| 43. Olympia, 46 | 2,309 | 20,270,912 | 1.98 |
| 44. Ridan, 59 | 434 | 5,042,211 | 1.96 |
| Thinking Cap, 52 | 559 | 5,477,065 | 1.96 |
| 46. Count Fleet, 40 | 3,208 | 24,010,743 | 1.93 |
| 47. Roman, 37 | 2,524 | 18,088,921 | 1.91 |
| 48. Dedicate, 52 | 838 | 6,560,575 | 1.88 |
| 49. Crimson Satan, 59 | 290 | 3,306,020 | 1.87 |
| Warfare, 57 | 673 | 7,066,491 | 1.87 |

## Produce Records

The first thing breeders look at when evaluating a producing broodmare is her record of getting in foal, for a barren mare produces no income. On the average, mares get in foal about 60 percent of the time. Breeders shy away from mares that have turned up barren two or more years in a row or who have a record of losing foals.

Obviously, though, the most important evidence of a mare's quality is the racing performance of her offspring. One outstanding runner can bring about an amazing jump in the value of the mare. For example, Flying Tammie was purchased at an auction in 1973 for $17,500. After her first foals had indicated that she would be no more than a producer of allowance class horses, she was resold in 1977 for $7,700. The next year, her son Mac Diarmida won 12 of 14 races and was named champion grass horse. In 1979, Flying Tammie was resold at auction for $1 million.

Such a dramatic change in fortune is unusual. As a general rule, the first three foals indicate the quality of horse a mare will produce. The best foals are more likely to be in the first seven or eight a mare produces. Perhaps because of the loss of some vitality, quality generally drops off above age fourteen.

## THE ECONOMICS OF BREEDING

The extraordinary demand for bloodstock has brought a flood of interest in Thoroughbred breeding. To give you an idea of the costs of playing this new investment game, we'll use as an example a mare costing $30,000.

Since bloodstock is a capital investment, the cost of the mare can be depreciated. The maximum useful age of a broodmare is considered by the IRS as sixteen. The minimum depreciation period is twenty-four months, for mares fourteen and over. The maximum, for broodmares six or under, is ten years. We'll assume our $30,000 mare is eight years old, and use a straight-line depreciation over the eight-year life.

The average broodmare gets in foal two of every three years, so we'll charge 1½ years of her expenses to the production of each foal. We'll also assume a $7,500 stud fee, assume that the foal and the mare will both be insured, and assume the foal will be sold at auction as a yearling. The numbers come up like this:

*Investment in one foal:*

| | |
|---|---:|
| Depreciation (1½ yrs. at $3,750 per year) | $ 5,625 |
| Board for mare (1½ yrs. at $5,000 per year) | 7,500 |
| Vet care and shoeing for mare (1¼ years) | 600 |
| Stud fee | 7,500 |
| Insurance for mare (4½ percent of value per year) | 2,025 |
| Board of foal from weaning to sale (11 months) | 3,400 |
| Insurance on foal (assume 5 percent of value, say $30,000) | 2,250 |
| Vet care and shoeing for foal | 150 |
| Transportation | 500 |
| Auction nomination fee | 150 |
| TOTAL INVESTMENT | $29,700 |

What are the chances of making a profit on this investment? In today's market, pretty good, especially if the foal qualifies for one of the more lucrative breeder-incentive programs. First of all, in 1980, 32 percent of the horses offered sold for $20,000+, a range in which a foal from this quality coupling should fall. Secondly, the average value of quality breeding stock has been increasing twice as fast as inflation, making the mare more valuable each year. Finally, using New York as an example, the breeder of a New York-bred horse gets 25 percent of that animal's purse earnings. Career earnings of $30,000 would return $7,500 to the breeder.

On the downside, of course, are considerable risks: the foal could have conformational defects that would reduce its value to little or nothing; the mare could come up barren more often than average. In today's market, though, breeders dealing in quality stock are more often than not coming up winners.

---

## The "Good" Female Line

In summing up the combination of racing performance, pedigree and production record that makes a "good" broodmare, we don't have the assistance of a published dollar figure like the stud fee to help us determine relative worth. All we can do is provide three examples of how a broodmare is evaluated.

*Fanfreluche, dam of Medaille D'Or*

Fanfreluche, b. 1967, 21s, SW, $238,688, 5 f, 4 SW, 23.61 AEI

Northern Dancer, b. 1961, 18s, SW, $580,647, 307 f, 58 SW, 5.40 AEI

Ciboulette, dk. b. 1961, 33s, SW, $54,131, 6 f, 3 SW, 11.07 AEI

Nearctic, 1954, 47s, SW, $152,384, 335 f, 49 SW, 2.75 AEI

Natalma, 1957, 7s, wnr, $16,015, 11 f, 3 SW, 8.87 AEI

Chop Chop, 1940, 11s, SW, $36,600, 205 f, 29 SW, 1.37 AEI

Windy Answer, 1955, 21s, SW, $41,945, 6 f, 3 SW, 7.28 AEI

FANFRELUCHE. 11 wins at 2 and 3, $238,688, Alabama S., Manitoba Centennial Derby, Benson and Hedges Invitational H. (ntr), Quebec Derby, Selene S., Bison City S., Natalma S., Princess Elizabeth S., Fleur de Lys S., 2nd Spinster S., Queen's Plate S., Canadian Oaks, Wonder Where S., etc., champion 3-year-old filly. Dam of 4 other foals—

L'ENJOLEUR (Buckpasser). 15 wins at 2 and 3, $546,079, Laurel Futurity S. (gr. I), Carling O'Keefe Invitational H., Queen's Plate S., Ontario Foaled S., Prince of Wales S., Coronation Futurity S., Manitoba Derby, Cup and Saucer S., Quebec Derby, etc. Sire.

LA VOYAGEUSE (Tentam). 11 wins, 2 to 4, 1979, $232,081, champion 3-year-old filly in Canada, Canadian Oaks S., Bison City S., Ontario Matron H., Hendrie H., 2nd Duchess S., City of Miami H., Whimsical S., Seaway S., Canadian S., Belle Mahone S.

GRAND LUXE (Sir Ivor). 10 wins at 3 and 4, $114,349, Convenience S., La Merced S., Fury S., 2nd Bonnie Miss S., Hibiscus S., 3rd Hawthorne H.

L'EXTRAVAGANTE (Le Fabuleux). 3

wins at 3, $28,318, 3rd Canadian Oaks S.

CIBOULETTE. 14 wins, 2 thru 4, $54,131, Shady Well S., Duchess S., Princess Elizabeth S., Maple Leaf S., 2nd Quebec Derby, 3rd Fury S., etc. Dam of 6 other foals, including—

COCO LA TERREUR. 13 wins, 2 thru 4, $64,662, Midsummer H. (ntr), Woodstock S., Queenston S., City of St. James-Assiniboia H., 2nd Fleur de Lys S., 3rd Friar Rock S. Sire, 1.10 Average-Earnings Index.

BARACHOIS. 4 wins at 2 and 3, $37,729, Plate Trial S., 2nd Queen's Plate S., 3rd Woodstock S., Marine S., etc. Sire, 1.80 Average-Earnings Index.

ERIMO CIBOULETTO. 3 wins at 2 and 3 in Japan.

WINDY ANSWER. 10 wins at 2 and 3, $41,945, Star Shoot S., Selene S., Nassau S., Hersey S., Fairbanks H., etc. Dam of 5 other foals—

COOL RECEPTION. 10 wins, $153,477, Coronation Futurity, Cup and Saucer S., Carleton S., Summer S., Marine S., 2nd Belmont S., etc.

BREEZY ANSWER. 2 wins at 2, $18,040, Princess Elizabeth S., 2nd Canadian Oaks S., etc. Dam of stakes winner Arctic Blizzard (sire).

ICY REPLY. 5 wins at 2 and 3, $15,370, 2nd Star Shoot S., 3rd Selene S. Producer.

PRIZE ANSWER. Unraced. Dam of stakes winner Noble Answer.

NORTHERN ANSWER. Sire, 1.46 Average-Earnings Index.

Fanfreluche qualifies as a superior broodmare on racing performance, pedigree and production. She was a multiple stakes winner, Canadian Horse of the Year in 1970, out of outstanding racer and broodmare sire Northern Dancer. Her dam and granddam were both stakes winners and stakes producers. Of Fanfreluche's five foals to date, four have been stakes winners and the other stakes placed. Of the foals, L'Enjoleur is a winner of over a half million dollars and stands at stud for a fee of $25,000; La Voyageuse was a champion three-year-old filly in Canada. This female line added considerably to Medaille D'Or's rating as a stallion prospect.

*Witching Hour, dam of Pumpkin Moonshine*

Witching Hour, b. 1960, 15s, wnr, $10,385, 8 f, 3 SW, 7.31 AEI

Thinking Cap, b. 1952, 59s, SW, $208,415, 163 f, 5 SW, 1.41 AEI

Enchanted Eve, ch. 1949, 29s, wnr, $32,230, 13 f, 2 SW, 7.41 AEI

Rosemont, 1932, 23s, SW, $168,750, 110 f, 13 SW, 2.07 AEI

Camargo, 1944, 59s, SW, $82,755, 4 f, 1 SW, 14.15 AEI

Lovely Night, 1936, 41s, SW, $55,660, 147 f, 7 SW, 1.17 AEI

Poupee, 1941, 9s, wnr, $2,700, 9 f, 9 wnrs, 1.81 AEI

The Porter

Garden Rose

Heliopolis

Misleading

Pilate

Snooze

Quatre Bras II

Marcella Miss

WITCHING HOUR. 3 wins at 3, $10,385. Dam of 8 other foals, including—

SALEM (Cyane). 7 wins at 2 and 3, $203,488, Futurity S., Saranac S., 3rd Withers S. Sire, 1.44 Average-Earnings Index.

TINGLE STONE (Cyane). 10 wins at 3 and 4, 1979, $196,571, Test S. (gr. III), Busher H., Dark Mirage S., Hydrangea H., 2nd Shuvee H. (gr. II).

CHEATIN TIME (Quarter Deck) Winner at 2 and 3, $14,950.

FREEDOM SUIT (Cyane). 6 wins, 2 thru 5.

SEVEN GABLES (Cyane). 7 wins at 3 and 5.

ENCHANTED EVE. 4 wins at 2 and 3, $32,230, 2nd Comely H., Alabama S., 3rd Ladies H. Dam of 12 other foals, including—

SMART. 19 wins, 2 thru 6, $365,244, Manhattan H. (ntr), Massachusetts H. twice, Gallant Fox H., Valley Forge

H., etc. Sire, 1.20 Average-Earnings Index.

TEMPTED. 18 wins, 2 thru 5, $330,760, champion handicap mare of 1959, Diana H. twice, Beldame H., Ladies H. (nAr), Maskette H. twice, Alabama S., Jersey Belle S., New Castle S., Jeanne d'Arc S., etc. Dam of stakes winner Lead Me On. Granddam of stakes winners Tell Me All, Brokerette (to 4, 1979), Bishop's Choice (at 3, 1979).

SETH WHO. 7 wins, 3 thru 5, $34,950. Sire, .54 Average-Earnings Index.

SET A CAP. 5 wins at 3, $16,950. Dam of stakes winner Pinch Pie.

KYRENIA. Winner at 3 and 4, $5,040. Dam of stakes winner Enchanted Native.

ONE RIB. 2 wins at 3, $10,600. Producer.

POPPERDOPPER. 4 wins, 3 thru 5, $23,010.

CLOUD NINE. Winner at 2 and 3, $6,375.

INSTANT SIN. Winner at 3, $3,024. Dam of stakes winner Misgivings, stakes-placed Menage a Trois.

Witching Hour was a winning mare of modest racing abilities, out of the moderate sire Thinking Cap. Her dam, however, the stakes-placed Enchanted Eve, was an excellent broodmare. Enchanted Eve's two stakes winners both earned in excess of $300,000—one, Tempted, was a champion handicap mare of such note that a grade III stakes for two-year-old fillies was named after her. Enchanted Eve's daughters also proved excellent broodmares, with four stakes producers. Thus, Witching Hour was a good broodmare prospect who has proved to be a good broodmare. Pumpkin Moonshine's female line is appropriate to his stud fee.

*Our Martha, dam of Cox's Ridge*

Our Martha, ch. 1961, 25s, wnr, $6,045, 6 f, 1 SW, 6.92 AEI

Ballydonnell, ch. 1952, 41s, SW, $48,323, 156 f, 6 SW, .95 AEI

Corday, ch. 1946, 1s, unpl., 6 f, 6 wnrs, .76 AEI

Ballogan, 1939, 15s, SW, $3,365, 1.18 AEI

O'Donnell, 1941, 11s, wnr, $1,056, 4 f, 1 SW, 2.07 AEI

Carrier Pigeon, 1937, 11s, wnr, $5,400, 215 f, 6 SW, 1.03 AEI

Galleon Gold, 1928, unraced, 6 f, 2 wnrs, .64 AEI

OUR MARTHA. 3 wins at 3 and 4, $6,045. Dam of 6 other foals, including—

LAWRENCE W. (Golden Ruler). 15 wins, 2 thru 6, $50,750, 3rd Nebraska Derby.

KINOVILLE KORNER (Beauguerre), 6 wins at 2 and 4, $16,965.

FREEO (Tom Tulle). Winner at 2, 1979, $16,640.

COLONEL E. SMITH (Ky. Colonel). Winner at 3 and 4, $3,626.

SIMPLY FURIOUS (Delta Judge). Winner at 3, $3,390.

CORDAY. Dam of 5 other foals—

BOB'S DAY. 7 wins, 3 thru 5, $12,559.

MISS AGOO. 16 wins, 2 thru 8.

MISS DOGETTE. 5 wins at 2 and 3. Dam of stakes winner Rail Rider (6 wins to 3, 1979, CKRM Futurity, etc.).

ENGAGE ME. 13 wins, 2 thru 7.

SUITS ME. Winner at 2.

Our Martha won three races, but won only $6,045. Her sire, Ballydonnell, had a very mediocre average earnings index of .95. Neither her dam nor her granddam won a race or produced a stakes-winning or -placed horse. In addition to Cox's Ridge, Our Martha has produced another stakes winner and a stakes-placed animal. Her produce record is surprising in light of her racing performance and pedigree. Cox's Ridge is considered to have a weak female line, which only his superior performance on the racetrack overcame.

# BREEDING SYSTEMS

Driven by the human need to find a "sure thing," horsemen over the centuries have labored long and hard to find within the process of heredity a foolproof system to follow in making breeding decisions. In particular, with the pedigrees of every single animal having been traced back over two thousand years, breeders have found it hard to resist playing with this data to come up with a mathematical formula for evaluating breeding potential. Unfortunately, nature has so far refused to cooperate in turning its probabilities into certainties.

Three systems, however, have generated sufficient staying power so that they're often mentioned in breeding articles: Colonel Vuillier's Dosage System; Dr. Varola's Dosage Diagram; and the Bruce Lowe System. Today, many breeders check with one or more of these systems in much the same way many people check their horoscopes—out of habit, out of curiosity, out of a vague feeling that there's a kernel of truth in the process.

## Colonel Vuillier's Dosage System

In the early twentieth century, after an exhaustive study of every available Thoroughbred pedigree, Colonel Vuillier concluded that fifteen stallions and one mare appeared with remarkably similar frequency in the pedigrees of outstanding racehorses. Using the percentages of influence of each generation from Galton's Law, he computed exact mathematic "dosages" of the blood of each of these fifteen stallions and the one mare that should be present in the "ideal" horse. Thus, low dosages of one or more lines in a stallion meant looking for a mare with surpluses in those same areas.

Colonel Vuillier was hired by the Aga Khan, a famous horse breeder, to run his operation, a task at which Vuillier and his wife were quite successful. The consensus of opinion is, however, that their success came not from the mathematics of their system, but from their reliance on obtaining the best breeding stock, then mating it to balance such important characteristics as speed and stamina.

## Dr. Varola's Dosage Diagram

Dr. Franco Varola, an Italian lawyer, updated Vuillier on the basis of twentieth-century sires. After exhaustive study, Varola selected sires which he felt were the most important influences on the breed. These sires, which he named *chefs de race or* "heads of breed," now number 120. Varola then divided the *chefs de race* into five groups according to the aptitude, or "way of being a Thoroughbred," demonstrated by their progeny. These five groups are Brilliant, Intermediate, Classic, Stout and Professional. These five are really points on a continuum that ranges from the speed and inconsistency of the "brilliant" horse to the extreme consistency and stamina of the "professional" horse. In the middle is the "classic" horse, the ideal balance of speed and stamina.

To appraise an individual animal, one adds up the sires from each of the five groups in the horse's pedigree. The sum is expressed as a dosage diagram, like that, for example, of Spectacular Bid: 6–9–21–24–6. While the ideal diagram would have the highest number in the middle or "classic" group, the higher number of *chefs de race* on the right side, the stamina side, is common for quality handicap animals.

Varola further supplied an index of consistency, arrived at by dividing the first number, the "brilliant" total, into the sum of the other four. A consistency rating between six and ten is considered ideal.

## The Bruce Lowe System

While Vuillier and Varola placed most of their importance on sire lines, others concentrated on the female families. The most exhaustive investigation of these was conducted by an Australian, Bruce Lowe. Lowe traced back every winner of three English classic races—the English Derby, the English Oaks, and the St. Leger—to 43 dams that he tabbed "taproot mares." These mares were ranked by the number of descendants who won these three races. Thus, descendants in tail-female of Tregonwell's Natural Barb were No. 1, those of Burton's Barb Mare were No. 2, all the way to No. 43. The family number of any individual horse is determined by which of these mares it descended from on the female side.

Lowe then designated the first five families

as "running" families, and their numbers were printed in italics. Another grouping he dubbed "sire" families, in which the stallion element was supposed to be especially important.

All this effort is of some historical interest, but today breeding experts find little practical value in Lowe's classifications.

---

## THE BREEDING DECISION

In their "Introduction to the Thoroughbred Horse," prepared under the auspices of the Thoroughbred Owners and Breeders Association, J. A. Estes and Joe Palmer close their discussion of breeding with the following statement: "In the matter of breeding Thoroughbreds, opinions are rampant and accepted principles are few." In the last three hundred years, horsemen and scientists alike have invested enormous time in experiments to find a specific recipe for Thoroughbred breeding that would guarantee a champion, but anything close to a scientific formula has steadfastly eluded all of them. Horsemen today do have the benefit of easily accessible computer-generated statistics, which makes quantitative analysis of performance and pedigree less tedious. In making the final breeding decision, however, breeders today, like those a hundred years ago, must rely on a few proven generalizations tempered by their own experience and instincts.

### Quality

The most oft-repeated generalization about mating Thoroughbreds is "breed the best to the best and hope for the best." In our discussions of the stallion and the mare, we've presented ample statistics that prove, beyond a doubt, that animals demonstrating superior racing ability tend, on the average, to demonstrate superior ability as breeding stock. To a lesser extent, the abilities of the close families of stallions and mares have a similar correlation. Finally, the progeny records of sires and broodmares have proved fairly reliable in predicting the racing ability of future offspring.

For breeders with large capital resources, their goal is literally breeding the best to the best. These breeders are the ones who pay up to $950,000 for a stallion share, or $2,000,000 for a mare. They are the riverboat gamblers of the Thoroughbred world, having the ability to wager large amounts on the prospects of hitting the jackpot with a Secretariat, an Affirmed, a Dahlia.

The vast majority of breeders, though, are concerned with breeding the best to the best within a specific quality range that's largely determined by price. Since the breeder is by definition the owner of the mare, he first of all evaluates the quality and characteristics of his animal. Then he looks for a stallion of similar quality whose characteristics complement the characteristics of the broodmare.

By quality, we mean, again, the potential or demonstrated probability of the racing quality of the offspring. For example, a stakes-winning mare, who statistically can be expected to produce 10 percent stakes winners, should be bred to a stallion whose average approximates that. The value of such a mare is likely to be $100,000 or more; the stud fee of such a top stallion, $25,000 and up. The same rough approximation between mare value and stud fee holds true as the quality diminishes.

To complement the mare, breeders look for some characteristics that *compensate* for the mare's liabilities and some that *enhance* the mare's positive points.

The primary compensating factor is conformation. We didn't specifically discuss conformation in discussing the stallion and broodmare, because serious conformational problems are almost always automatic disqualifiers when considering an animal as breeding stock. However, since no horses have perfect conformation, it is a major consideration in breeding two horses. For example, an animal from a family that tends toward foot problems should be bred to an animal from a family with sound feet. While such compensation doesn't always work, breeding animals with similar problems almost guarantees that the problem will occur in the foal.

*Temperament* is another compensating characteristic. Many horsemen prefer calm mares, for their disposition is likely to be imitated by the foal. Mares from families noted for their intractability, like the Nasrullah family, should be bred to stallions from more well-balanced lines.

*Precocity,* the likelihood of progeny winning at age two, is a third factor. Except for the relatively few home breeders whose goal is the elusive breeding of high-class stamina horses, most breeders prefer precocious foals. A mare whose foals are likely to develop early would be bred to a stallion of similar bent. The same kind of stallion would be sought as a compensating factor for a mare with opposite traits.

Precocity has a direct relationship to *speed,* because most two-year-old races are sprints. In addition, more than 65 percent of all races for older horses in 1980 were also at a distance of less than one mile. Lack of speed is the main reason why more than 29,000 horses were unable to win even one race in 1980. It is unwise to breed two animals who don't both have the ability to get rolling before the distance tops one mile. The most successful formula for achieving the elusive goal of breeding champions seems to be to breed a horse with championship speed at one mile to a stakes winner who has demonstrated ability to stay at longer distances.

*Special racing characteristics* should be enhanced. With the increased popularity of turf racing, mares from families successful on the grass should be mated with stallions from similar lines. The increase in year-round racing has increased the value of animals from families who've shown success on less-than-perfect racing surfaces.

The last point brings us to the final conclusion that matings should be based on successful experiences. At the most basic level, a mating between two animals that has produced a good racehorse is more likely to do so again. Certain crosses between families have an increased likelihood of working well. This is what is meant by "nicks." Finally, every breeder develops over the years an instinctual judgment based on close examination of the appearance and performance of the results of thousands of matings. In the long run, those who work hardest developing this kind of judgment get the best luck in the genetic game of chance called Thoroughbred breeding.

## STATE BREEDING PROGRAMS

Within the past ten years, nineteen states have instituted incentive programs to attract breeders of Thoroughbred horses. By offering cash payoffs in the form of breeder awards, stallion awards and greatly increased purses in special, restricted races, the states hope to create a home-bred industry. The theory is that the indigenous Thoroughbred industry will create jobs, boost horse-related businesses, and increase pari-mutuel revenues at the tracks. The funding for most breeder-incentive programs is derived from a set percentage of the pari-mutuel take. Although all breeder programs have attracted a lot of attention, the most generous and perhaps the most successful is the New York State Thoroughbred Breeding and Development Fund Corporation.

The New York Fund has been set by law at 0.5 percent of the state's handle of the on- and off-track pari-mutuel pool. As of 1981, the estimated financing of the New York Fund had reached $8,000,000. Offering roughly five restricted overnight races (which are open only to registered New York-breds) per condition book (issued every two weeks), New York pegs its purses about 40 percent higher than the purses offered in comparable races open to non-state-bred horses. The purse incentive is not the major attraction, however. Any time a qualified New York-bred horse wins, places or shows in *any* race run in New York, the owner of the dam receives 25 percent of the money earned by her foal and the owner of the sire gets a bonus equal to 15 percent of the money earned by his get. Although incentive programs in other states work much the same way, the New York Fund is the richest and the most attractive in the country.

Needless to say, because of the great benefits they offer, state breeding programs enforce strict residency and breeding regulations on mares and stallions whose foals are to be registered as state-bred Thoroughbreds. States currently offering breeder-incentive programs are:

| | |
|---|---|
| ARIZONA | NEBRASKA |
| ARKANSAS | NEW MEXICO |
| CALIFORNIA | NEW JERSEY |
| COLORADO | NEW YORK |
| FLORIDA | OHIO |
| ILLINOIS | OREGON |
| KENTUCKY | PENNSYLVANIA |
| LOUISIANA | WASHINGTON |
| MARYLAND | WEST VIRGINIA |
| MICHIGAN | |

Specific information regarding the requirements and incentives for each program may be obtained by writing to the American Horse Council, 1700 K Street N.W., Washington, D.C. 20006.

## GREAT HORSES: BOLD RULER

On April 6, 1954, Bull Hancock watched the birth of two foals in adjoining stalls at his Claiborne Farm. The first one to drop was the great Round Table, champion horse of 1958, champion grass horse for three successive years, winner of $1,749,869 and sire of 79 stakes winners. Those achievements make Round Table one of the couple of dozen most notable horses of the century. Yet, for all that, the foal that was born one half hour later that night had an even greater influence on racing in America. That foal was Bold Ruler.

Bold Ruler was by Nasrullah, out of Miss Disco, a tough, honest mare who won four stakes in 54 career starts. As a foal, Bold Ruler was thin and ungainly, and he began to demonstrate the susceptibility to illness and accidents that was to plague him throughout his life. As a two-year-old, he first demonstrated the brilliant speed that was later to carry him to victory in 23 of 33 starts, including the Preakness. His most famous victory was his smashing defeat of arch-rivals Gallant Man and Round Table in the 1½-mile Trenton Handicap, a triumph that won him Horse of the Year honors in 1957.

After recurring leg injuries ended his career, Bold Ruler was sent to stud. He got off to a slow start when his first crop was slow to develop as two-year-olds, but in 1963 his Lamb Chop became a champion three-year-old filly. In 1964, Bold Lad was named champion two-year-old colt and Queen Empress champion two-year-old filly—an unprecedented double for a sire. Out of the same crop came Bold Bidder, winner of nearly half a million dollars in 1965 and 1966.

Before he died of cancer in 1971, Bold Ruler sired 82 stakes winners out of 355 foals, a magnificent 23.1 percent. His average earnings index of 7.73 is the highest in history. Bold Ruler was sire of the year eight times, including every year from 1963 to 1968. Seven of the ten Kentucky Derby winners of the 1970s came from his line.

Bold Ruler has also been proved an incredible sire of sires. No less than thirteen of his offspring sired graded stakes winners in 1979. The most noted sires in the Bold Ruler line are Bold Bidder, sire of Cannonade and Spectacular Bid; What a Pleasure, sire of Honest Pleasure and Foolish Pleasure; Irish Castle, sire of Bold Forbes; Bold Commander, sire of Dust Commander; and, of course, Secretariat.

| | | |
|---|---|---|
| | | Nearco |
| | Nasrullah | |
| | | Mumtaz Begum |
| Bold Ruler | | |
| | | Discovery |
| | Miss Disco | |
| | | Outdone |

# Life of the Horse: 2. Early Life

---

## Breeding Season

From her mother, Banknote inherited her strong bone and her chestnut color. From her father, she inherited a sweet, trusting temperament and the kind eye and intelligent head with which Sir Wimborne stamps most of his get. Stallions which "stamp their get" (or transmit particular characteristics to their offspring) are said to be prepotent. Although many breeders believe that anywhere from 50 percent to 90 percent of a horse's makeup is directly traceable to the mare (through a combination of genetic and environmental influence), certain stallion families are renowned for passing on specific physical or mental qualities.

"We believe that it's 70 percent the mare," says Chris on her way down to the barn at 6:30 the next morning to check on the new foal. "If more than 30 percent of it is the stallion, I'll eat my hat. But a lot of people believe it's all the stallion, so if you are raising a sales product, you have to consider what is fashionable and what people want to buy."

The wooden barn door slides open and the four closest mares, particularly Tanta, look up from their feed tubs and move around so that they are standing between the noise and their young foals.

"Personally," says Chris, twisting the faucet above Tanta's bucket to fill it to the brim, "I think the most important thing in any horse is attitude. You can have the best-looking horse, but if he doesn't have the attitude, he won't walk out of the starting gate. Look at Carry Back and Forego. They weren't such fancy-bred horses, but they sure could run."

"He must have had some pain threshold, that Forego," interjects Gary, appearing from the depths of the aisle with an enema bottle. "He must have been sore as hell most of the time," he continues, referring to the three-time Horse of the Year's infamously bad left ankle. "That pounding on the track really tests a horse's ability to bear pain. They finally had to retire the sucker because if he'd have broken down on the track and they had had to put him down, there would have been a riot. The crowd would probably have killed the owner." Forego, before he was castrated, was reportedly so vicious that he nearly killed several handlers, biting them as hard as he could and then refusing to let go. Until he was cured of his "studdishness," he also had difficulty with his performance on the track.

# COLOR

A horse's coat color, like human hair color, is genetically determined. Because the gene pool of registered Thoroughbreds has been restricted for more than three hundred years, certain colors are characteristic to the breed.

The Jockey Club recognizes only six coat colors for Thoroughbreds:

*Black:* The entire coat, including the muzzle, flanks and legs, must be black, with the exception of white markings.

*Bay:* The entire coat varies from a yellow-tan to a bright auburn. The mane, the tail and the lower portions of the leg are black, unless white markings are present.

*Dark Bay or Brown:* The entire coat color varies, from brown with large areas of tan on the head, shoulders, flanks, insides of the thighs and the upper portions of the legs, to brown with tan hairs on the muzzle and/or flanks, but too marginal to be specified in color.

*Chestnut:* The entire coat varies from a yellow-red to a red-yellow to a golden yellow. The mane, tail and legs are also red (the same color as the coat of the horse). Rarely, a chestnut horse is found to be so light in color as to give the appearance of a palomino or so dark in color that it shows numerous black hairs throughout its coat.

*Gray:* Most of the coat is a mixture of black and white hairs. In the young horse, the black hair predominates, but as the horse ages, the white hair increases and the markings tend to fade. A gray horse may have distinct white markings, or it may have faded markings. It always has a gray or black mane, tail and legs.

*Roan:* Most of the coat is a mixture of red and white hairs. In the young horse, red hair predominates, but as it ages, the white hair increases. If the red hair comes from the bay pattern, the mane, tail and legs will be black. If the red hair comes from the chestnut pattern, the mane, tail and legs will be red. Roan horses may have distinct or indistinct white markings.

## Skin Color

All Thoroughbreds have black skin, which they inherited from their Arab forefathers. The dark pigmentation, which protected the horse from the intense desert sun, has prevailed, except in the case of white markings (which grow from pink skin patches) and the extremely rare instances of pure-white Thoroughbreds.

## White Thoroughbreds

All white horses are considered to be gray unless they have pink skin and blue eyes. From 1896 to 1963, not a single white Thoroughbred was registered, and the odds against one being born were considered to be three million to one, but in 1963, Kentucky Colonel, a chestnut horse by a black sire and a brown grandsire, sired two white foals. One of the two, a filly named White Beauty, produced two more white fillies, in 1975 and 1977. In the same year that White Beauty was foaled, another white Thoroughbred was dropped in France, and in 1977, Brimstar, a bay mare, foaled a pure-white colt in New York State. As a result of these births, the odds of getting a white foal have dropped to about 25,000 to one. Although all gray Thoroughbreds can be traced back to one sire, the great horse Drone (foaled 1823), the origin of all white Thoroughbreds remains a mystery.

## Frequency of Coloring

Because the genes for bay coloring are dominant, the majority of Thoroughbreds are bay. The second most common color, chestnut, though genetically recessive, has been the hue of a lot of good horses. Blacks and grays, which are much rarer, are often great crowd pleasers.

The colors of the 105 winners of the Kentucky Derby roughly reflect the proportion of coloring of the top-quality horses: 42 bays; 35 chestnuts; 21 dark bay or brown; 4 blacks; 3 grays.

## The Mythology of Color

From the beginning of man's association with the horse, legends and myths have inevitably attached to the various colors of the steeds on which they depended. While in our modern, rational age no one has found any conclusive evidence linking color to temperament or speed, horsemen continue to have their prejudices. Black horses have a reputation for meanness; bays for willingness; chestnuts for flightiness; and roans for sluggishness.

The most persistent prejudice seems to be against roans. Perhaps because of the "muddy" color of their coat, perhaps because the splotchiness hides muscle definition, many horsemen shy away from roans. This prejudice is shared by the betting public. Track surveys show that when betting odds are more or less equal, a roan will be far the least wagered-on horse.

Curiously, horses, too, seem to have their prejudices about color. If a gray horse is turned out in a field of bays, or a black horse put into a pasture of chestnuts, the group may ostracize or even savage it, though they will be tolerant of a new horse of their own shade. It is believed that this "racist" behavior is less related to the actual color (since horses are fairly color-blind) than to the lightness or darkness of the strange horse's coat.

---

"Certain families," comments Chris, "are known for their meanness. Nasrullah was so mean, they say he used to hold a grudge and would go after people he hadn't seen for two years if they had once done something to him he didn't like. All the Nasrullahs have that sort of temperament. Sometimes aggressive horses make the best runners, but they sure are a pain to live with."

Banknote seems to have a delightful attitude. Friendly and curious, when the stall door opens she peers around behind Tanta's tail and tiptoes shyly forward. The little coffin bone inside her still-soft hoof completed its ossification in utero and has already reached its mature growth. She weighs about one hundred pounds and is a little over a yard tall; her spindly legs are only about one-half as wide as they will be. Even though she is only 60 percent of her adult height and 47 percent of her adult length, Banknote is big for a filly. She is

bigger than many colts. Tanta's age may have something to do with this. Studies have shown that Thoroughbred mares between the ages of eight and twelve tend to produce the tallest foals with the largest cannon bones.

After Banknote is used to their presence and Tanta has settled herself angrily in one corner of the stall, Gary lets the filly sniff his fingers and then puts his right arm over her back and his left arm around the front of her chest to hold her while Chris gives her a quick enema. Banknote, surprised, squeals to the scowling Tanta, hop-kicks with her long hind legs, and flaps her short, furry rag of a tail in disgust. The moment she is released, she bounces back behind Tanta, who leers disapprovingly. The filly needs the enema to prevent constipation caused by meconium—the accumulation of waste material left over from intrauterine life.

Banknote spends the rest of her first day on earth in the foaling stall with Tanta, demanding meals every hour (a good sign, since a foal that stops nursing is usually sick), napping frequently and entertaining the veterinarian, who takes her temperature with a rectal thermometer (it is normal at 101 degrees) and says he will be back the next day to vet her out for insurance purposes.

"We don't take any foals outside until the insurance forms have been sent in," says Chris the next morning after the vet has proclaimed everything alright. It is a warm March day, hay-dusted sunshine streaming through the wide barn door, which is kept open to provide good ventilation. The body heat and fluid created by 25 broodmares in a dark barn produces an almost tropical environment in which bacteria flourish if the supply of fresh air and dry bedding is insufficient. Horses, even foals, can deal with cold air as long as they are not damp or in a draft. "It's important to get the mare out as soon as possible, though," says Chris, "even if it's raining or the footing is bad on the second day, we might turn the mare out by herself for five minutes. It helps her to shake loose and clean out anything left in her uterus. If it's sunny and the foal goes out, it gets its first dose of vitamin D."

As Gary walks into the stall and puts his arm around Banknote's neck so he can slip a tiny halter over her nose, she remembers the sensation of the enema and hops and struggles to get away from him. A horse's strongest mental faculty is its memory, and man's greatest training aid is his ability to get horses to remember the right things. Gary makes no effort to punish Banknote, but holds her persistently until she stops struggling and relaxes into submission. Then he gently slips the halter over her head. Banknote has just had her first lesson about people.

"The first rule of raising horses," exclaims Gary, petting the foal for a long moment and, at last, letting her bounce back to her mother: "Never, ever let a horse get away from you from day one. We put the halters on and take them off every day until they are weaned, just so they get used to being handled. It's a hell of a lot easier to start teaching them you're the master when you are still stronger than they are."

Later on in the day, Banknote is taken outside for the first time. Tanta is led out to a small paddock. Banknote follows, with Chris wrapped lightly around her, one hand on the halter and the other arm firmly around the foal's rump. Any attempt to lead Banknote at this tender age might cause irreparable bone damage to her neck if she pulled back against the lead shank. "We don't start leading them," says Chris, "until they learn to follow their heads."

Chris holds Banknote firmly while the mare is let go in the dirt paddock, kicking and bucking. When Tanta trots back, remembering that she has a foal, the danger that she might accidentally damage it is over. Banknote is let go to sniff the dirt, the air and the fence rails. She tests her legs in a few circles around her mother. Then, startled by the flutter of a sparrow's wing, she charges back to huddle sideways under the protective arch of the mare's great head and neck. After a brisk trot around the fence line with Banknote's nose pressed to Tanta's belly, the two are taken in. Ten

minutes is enough for the first day. And in the week that follows, the two are turned out for longer and longer periods, but always with attendants watching to make sure that the foal, which is highly susceptible to pneumonia, does not become overheated or lie down on the cold ground.

Eight days after being born, Banknote, along with Tanta, is moved to a smaller, unmonitored stall, so that another expectant mare can be observed in the foaling stall. Although she is still on milk, Banknote has begun to play with mouthfuls of hay from the tolerant Tanta's manger. She spends more time in darkness (only the foaling stalls are lighted around the clock), but she is beginning to learn the routine of the breeding farm.

At 5:30 A.M. the stereo comes on, piping music and news of world events through all of the farm buildings, less to keep the horses informed than to prepare them for the constant loudspeakers they will hear when they get to the track. (The Heimerles believe in getting the horses accustomed to noise from the very start, and do not hesitate to drive trucks, farm machines, or even motorcycles through the barns to teach the foals they raise not to be skittish.) There are hoofbeats on the concrete floor of the stallion barn as Gary lets Take Your Place out for his morning run. The big bay is so dark that he looks black in the dawn. He has to be turned out when there are no mares around because if he sees them, he frets, trying to herd them from the confines of his paddock. It's hard enough to keep weight on studs during the breeding season without having them burn it off through nervous upset. At age seven, "Tippy," as he is called familiarly, is still a young stallion. Another successful product of the Princequillo-Nasrullah nick, undefeated as a two-year-old, he was syndicated for $10,000 a share and stands for $3,500. He races alongside the five-foot-high fence of the stallion paddock on the graceful legs which once carried his jockey to victory in England's Observer Gold Cup, a Grade I stakes. Trumpeting to invisible mares across the New York hilltops, he is all fire and taut magnificence, but it still remains to be seen whether or not he will pass the class he carries in his veins on to future generations.

By six, Banknote hears the creaking of the wheelbarrow and the pleasant sound of grain being scooped into the feed tubs. Tanta circles the stall impatiently and bites deep into her ration when it appears. Lactating mares, which produce as much as five hundred quarts of milk monthly, have ravenous appetites and a special need for protein, calcium and phosphorus. They receive a 90 percent protein mixture of oats, corn, soybean meal and vitamin supplements. Extra trace minerals come from the red block-mineral "lick" in the tub. Banknote nibbles at a few of the grains that dribble from Tanta's mouth, but decides she wants to stick mainly to milk for a while longer. Some mornings, out of boredom, she teethes on the stall door or wisps of hay. This alfalfa, so dry and green that it smells of August, is rich in calcium, phosphorus and the bulky fiber essential to equine digestion. After breakfast, Tanta drinks a few gallons of the fresh water that has been drawn for her. She will consume eight to fifteen gallons during the day. Banknote lies down and naps in the middle of the stall.

At ten of seven, Chris comes quietly to the stall door and rouses the filly, so she is awake and standing up. Once all the foals are on their feet, Toga Nut, the teaser, is led down the aisle to pay a visit to all the mares who are not in foal. He is a stallion, but not of the quality used for breeding. His job is to try to arouse each mare so the handler can determine if she is "in season" and willing to be bred. While Toga is nuzzling mares in one part of the barn, Tanta and Banknote are taken outside to a pasture by themselves. After Tanta's first heat period they will be turned out with another mare and foal, but until that time, Tanta will be overly jealous of her foal and possibly dangerous to other mares.

By eight, all of the mares and foals, except for the newborn, are out in their different fields. Mares with young foals are paired, after they have passed their first heat period. The barren mares (those which did not get "in foal" last year) are kept separate from the mares still due to foal. The yearlings are separated by sex. The lusty "Tippy" sulks back in his stall, while Romantic Lead (the other stallion Scargo stands) takes his place in the stallion paddock. Unlike "Tippy," the relatively inexperienced Romantic Lead is content to leave the mares in peace. He is still recovering from being at the racetrack, where colts are beaten for even looking sideways at a filly or a mare.

From eight to eleven, while the horses exercise or graze or sleep, the stalls are mucked out and covered with fresh bedding, both to discourage the growth of bacteria and to keep the horses' feet from rotting from standing in wet, soiled shavings. The water buckets are scrubbed and refilled. Fresh alfalfa is loaded into the hay ricks. The barn floor is swept immaculate for their return.

In the early afternoon, various farm tasks are done. Stalls are rebuilt; veterinarians arrive to examine the barren mares or to treat the condition of a foal which has been born blind, or with a crooked leg or a cleft palate. As far as Banknote is concerned, though, nothing happens until two or three o'clock, when she and Tanta are led back to their stall for the evening meal. The feed tub lies in the aisle, but a strange man is waiting next to it.

"Here she is," says Chris to the vet. An older man who looks very strong and healthy in his bright blue overalls, Dr. Gill is known as one of the best broodmare men in New York. As Chris shoves Banknote into the stall and slips the twitch, a loop of rope attached to a thick, wooden baton, over Tanta's upper lip, Gill pulls a shoulder-length, disposable plastic glove over his arm in preparation for examining the mare's recovery from parturition. Tomorrow will be the ninth day since Banknote's delivery, the normal time for the onset of Tanta's "foal heat." If her internal organs have healed sufficiently and a new follicle has in fact developed, she will be bred back immediately to Take Your Place. The Heimerles, who own a share of his syndicate and also stand him at Scargo, believe that his winning two-year-old form and indomitable temperament will combine with Tanta's excellent bone and conformation to produce an exceptional horse.

"This is her eighth day," says Chris, backing the mare around so that her rear end faces Gill in the stall door and twisting the wooden baton to tighten the loop of the twitch around Tanta's lip. As long as the mare is concentrating on the twitch and afraid to move for fear of ripping her lip off, she will not try to kick the vet. "We haven't teased yet."

As his assistant holds Tanta's tail curled back and Chris tightens the twitch to control the mare's upflung head, Gill disinfects his glove and does a speculum examination of Tanta's uterus. He checks for any inflammation, swelling or abrasions that might make it unsafe to breed her.

"Okay, it looks like she's healed up pretty good. She's cleaned out well, but there's some sign of a hematoma just easing up. That might open up if you try to breed her back too soon," he informs Chris. He works his hand into Tanta's rectum to examine her ovaries, removing large wads of manure and throwing them onto the floor as he goes.

"Here we are," he says once his arm is fully inside her. "Okay, I'm at your left ovary. Not much to get excited about here." Tanta shivers as he palpates her.

"Ho, Tanta," growls Chris. "Watch out, she can be a people kicker." With his arm still inside the mare, Gill steps deftly to the side.

"Now here, on the right, she's got a halfway decent follicle, a medium-large follicle, soft, good tone, active. This mare you could breed in about two to three days," he says as he finishes, sliding his arm out and peeling off the glove. If the follicle is small, hard and blended to the ovary, it is an indication that the egg is not well developed and will be a long time in breaking away

and passing into the Fallopian tube, where it can be fertilized.

"How big was the entrance to the cervix?" asks Chris. Tanta is shut in the stall now and Chris is making notes about the mare's condition on her monthly ovary charts. These charts, kept for every broodmare at Scargo, record the vet's findings and give a pictorial representation of the condition of each ovary at each checkup during the month. Careful chart-keeping helps the breeder determine the mare's fertility pattern and the optimum days on which she should be bred.

"Cervix was about two fingers." For breeding purposes, the cervix should be open from two to three fingers' width to permit sperm to pass through. "Personally, I wouldn't breed this mare right away. I'd let her get over the soreness a little more, then try to catch her later on in the season. But there's nothing really wrong with her. You could go ahead if you don't think you'll have another chance."

Mares come into season every fourteen to twenty-four days for periods lasting as long as thirty days (in the case of a false heat) or as few as three. Ovulation occurs 20 to 40 hours before the heat period ends. Due to the unpredictability of this crucial period, mares are usually covered close to the expected end of their heat periods and, if they are still in heat two days later, covered again. Covering the mare when she is not fertile is a waste of the stud's energy, because most stallions are bred to forty-five mares a year and are only good for about two and a half covers per mare in a breeding season. Besides, repeated attempts at impregnation can be injurious to the mare. With Gill's expert help, Scargo managed to get in foal 96 percent of the mares sent there in 1979. The national average is about 70 percent. Their success is attributable to thrice-weekly vet visits, high stallion fertility, a very reliable teaser and, perhaps most of all, close observation of each mare's individual behavior patterns during her cycle.

"If she shows to the teaser tomorrow, we might breed her back right away. She was barren last year and she goes in and out of season so fast she's hard to catch."

Ever since 1833, when the Jockey Club changed the communal Thoroughbred birthday from May 1 to January 1 of the year foaled, broodmare fertility has been a primary concern. For racing purposes, all horses born during the course of a year are considered to be one year old on the subsequent New Year's Day, regardless of whether they were foaled on January 2 or at 11:59 P.M. on December 31. Foals like Banknote, which were conceived in March or April and dropped in February or March of the following year, have a physiological head start when they get to the racetrack.

One of the greatest liabilities a Thoroughbred breeder can have is a barren broodmare. Not only does he have to carry the $3,600 and upward cost of keeping the mare for an entire year until he can try breeding her again, but he forfeits any money he might have gained from the sale of the foal as a yearling.

Small commercial breeders like the Heimerles cannot afford to have a mare go barren. With their entire life savings and two years of hard work spent renovating Scargo, mostly by hand, they are counting on the sale of foals like Banknote to help pay back loans and help them to invest in more mares. Tanta was a wedding present, given to them in part because she had been barren in 1977. Through careful management they got her in foal in 1978 and the result was Banknote. As Gary explains, "It takes two and a half years to realize any profit in this business. The first year, you breed the mare and then, eleven months later, if she doesn't colic or get struck by lightning or run through a fence or something, you get a foal. If you're lucky, it's born with all its legs on right and it doesn't have any congenital defects. Then, for the next six months, you have to hope it doesn't die of pneumonia or the mare doesn't step on it during the night. After that you wean it and for the whole next year you pray that it doesn't get kicked in the leg by one of the other yearlings or get twisted up in something or come down with some terrible in-

fection. By the time you rub it up and teach it some manners and load it in the van for auction in August, you've devoted a year and a half to raising the horse, not to mention the cost of the stud fee and the year of mare care while you were waiting for her to foal. That's two and a half years and even when you lead it off the truck at the sales, there's no guarantee somebody's going to buy it. What if it doesn't sell, or dies before you get to the sales, and your mare comes out of the season barren? It's three more years before you've got something to take to the sales again."

It is a blustery March morning, exactly two weeks after Banknote was brought into the world, and it proves to be a frightening day for the filly because it is also the third day of Tanta's foal heat. At 7 A.M., Toga, the teaser, makes his way down the steamy aisle, snorting softly, his journey punctuated by the sound of sharp kicks against the stable walls by mares who are not in season. This morning, the bay stallion, led by Gary, pauses in front of Tanta's stall. Chris enters to hold Banknote still and observe the mare's reaction to Toga. Although many farms tease the mare out of the stall behind a teasing board which separates the mare and the teaser, the Heimerles prefer to tease in the stall.

Based on the opinion of Dr. Gill and Toga, the Heimerles decide when to breed each mare. The vet can tell if the mare has a viable follicle, but only the teaser can determine whether the mare is willing to accept a stallion. Most mares will only accept a stallion when they are ovulating, though there are exceptions. The teaser serves two functions. He helps discover the mare's fertility and protects "Tippy" from being kicked in a way that might ruin both his breeding future and his owners' investment.

"Come on, Toga," says Gary, leading the stallion toward the inhospitable Tanta. "You want to talk to her?" Toga sticks his neck into the stall toward Tanta and dutifully nuzzles her face. Tanta looks quickly at Banknote, who is cowering in Chris's grasp, then back to Toga.

"Come on, Tiger," says Gary, "talk to

this one." Toga takes a wary step into the stall and nibbles Tanta's neck. For a moment she looks like she might try to savage him, wrinkling her upper lip back to reveal strong gums and teeth. A mare will try to kill a teaser if she thinks her foal is in danger, though some mares are more violent than others. Generally, once the mares have become accustomed to the practice, the Heimerles find that most of them can be teased in their stalls with no one holding the foal. In this manner, an entire barnful of twenty mares can be teased by two people in about a half hour. Knowing Tanta, however, they are not taking any chances of Banknote getting hurt accidentally. Toga rubs his huge head hard against Tanta's shoulder. Suddenly, she wheels around, arches her tail, squats and urinates on his front feet. Toga sniffs her tail with interest. Hormonally, mares are most apt to accept a stallion when they are in the "foal heat."

"She's winking," says Gary, meaning that she is opening and closing her vulva to attract the teaser. "Come on, Toga," he urges. Toga, inhaling deep gusts of her scent through one nostril, moves closer, pushing his head against her flank in preparation to mount. Tanta squats a little deeper and makes no attempt to kick.

"She's not super hot, but she's showing," says Gary, backing Toga away with the lead shank and slamming the stall door. "I say we breed her today before it's too late." Chris releases Banknote and they proceed to the next stall.

"Okay, Toga, how do you like this one?" The mare takes one look at him, pins her ears, and strikes the wall right next to his leg with a quick report of her hind foot. Toga steps politely back into the aisle.

"That's not too bad," says Chris.

"No, it wasn't a bad kick. She might come in later on in the week."

Some mares will never "show" to a teaser, but may display small attitude changes when they come into season, refraining from kicking out or swishing their tails violently when he tries to interest them. Good teasers are hard to find. Toga is a successful one because he is quiet. At

first Toga had to be given testosterone to get him interested, but this made him too aggressive, so treatment was stopped. By that time he had accepted his role.

"Mares don't like a noisy teaser," says Gary. "They want to fight the teaser to protect the foals, and they won't show. You've got to have a gentleman for a teaser. But you've got to train the mare to be a lady, too. Everything has to be socially acceptable."

In the late afternoon, after all the chores are done and the horses have been "put up" for the night, Tanta is taken down to the breeding shed. It is Banknote's first separation from her mother and the filly is frantic, rearing up and clawing with her tiny feet against the sides of the stall, squealing through her small, wrinkled nose and rolling her eyes desperately.

"The breeding shed is no place for a foal," says Chris, leading Tanta into the cool, high-ceilinged, cinder-block structure. Light filters through a row of high clerestory windows. The hard dirt floor is neatly raked and the only sound is water running in a small washroom at one end of the large, open space.

Tanta, ears flicking to listen for Banknote, is stood next to the wall of the washroom. A pale-blue, hinged board is swung up next to her to pin her in place.

"I've seen people take foals into the breeding shed," says Chris, fitting a twitch over Tanta's lip so the attendant can wash her before breeding, "and I've seen the stallion try to kill the foal."

Tanta's tail is wrapped in gauze. She winks slightly, displaying the pink lining of her vulva to the attendant as swabs of cotton soaked in water, Ivory liquid and disinfectant wash her external genitalia. A leather lead shank with a twelve-inch chain on one end is snapped to her halter and the chain is passed over her tongue like a bit to give the handler extra control. For the final teasing, though, the twitch is removed.

"Our whole purpose," explains Gary, leading Toga into the softly lit shed, "is not to get the stallion hurt. We always tease without the twitch so we can tell if the mare will stand or kick when we go to breed her. If they don't want to be bred so badly that they kick the teaser, they probably aren't ovulating anyway."

There is a whinny from one of the stallion stalls as Toga's hooves resound on the concrete walkway. Tanta, still trapped in the angle of the board and the wall, chews the chain in her mouth apprehensively. Both in teasing and in breeding, every attempt is made to keep procedures as natural as possible, simulating the rituals mating horses go through in the wild. If the mare is ready to breed, no hobbles are strapped on to keep her from kicking, because an angry mare can break hobbles and clumsy stallions can get tangled up in them. If restraint is required, it is usually provided in the form of tying up one of the mare's front legs so she cannot kick out behind. Some farms use tranquilizers, but this can be dangerous. Occasionally, a tranquilized mare will "wake up" and, not remembering her foal, kick it to death when it tries to nurse.

"Okay," says Gary. "Set her up."

Chris takes Tanta to the center of the shed to meet Toga. Many farms would separate them with a teasing board, but Toga is a docile, mannerly teaser, so Scargo is able to tease all but the most violent mares "head to head."

"Okay," says Gary after Tanta has lowered her head and hind end in submission to Toga's nips at her neck, "let's jump her." Tanta, tail arching and vulva winking, is deftly turned around.

"Okay, fella," says Gary, clucking and slapping Toga's neck as a signal that he should mount her. The horse rears up, pinches Tanta's belly between his forelegs, and bites down on her withers to hold her in place. For a few seconds, he hovers above her, bug-eyed, trying to enter, but each time he thrusts toward her, a teasing shield blocks his entry.

"Alright, down, down," commands Gary when Tanta has dropped her head and relaxed her hips in total submission. Feeling the chain against his gums, Toga reluctantly slides off the mare. Still gazing sidelong at her figure, shimmering in a last ray of afternoon sunlight, he nips furiously at a few blades of grass as Gary leads him out the side door.

The teaser is an essential element of any successful stud farm operation. Without the services, or mock services, of such stallions, many fewer horses would be sent to the starting gate each year. Although his life seems one of endless frustration, like the mythic Sisyphus, Toga was saved from going to the killer's to become Scargo's teaser. Out of a sense of fairness and to keep Toga from souring on his work the Heimerles try to breed Toga to several cross-bred mares at the end of the season.

Now it is twilight in the breeding shed. Tanta stands in the center like the dark statue of a horse, waiting just as Toga left her because her instincts and the person standing next to her tell her not to budge. The only sound is the stereo playing, "Teen-aged girl on a Saturday night. I've never seen such a beautiful sight," blasting down from the high roof beams. All memories of Banknote seem forgotten in the cool, dim room smelling of antiseptic and horse sweat.

Then, Take Your Place comes in, led by Gary. Lean, but fit, he has not begun to lose the one hundred to two hundred pounds stallions often drop during the busy breeding season. Although they loaf for eight months of the year, stallions cover anywhere from twenty-five to fifty mares several times between February 15 and mid-June, often having to "double," or cover two mares a day, in the hectic final weeks. Overweight stallions are predisposed to dying of coronary attacks in the breeding shed, so it is the Heimerles' practice to keep the stallions they stand "in good flesh" throughout the season, but not flabby or overfed. At the sight of Tanta, Take Your Place tosses his head against the chain. Scenting Toga in the air, he surveys the room jealously.

"You can turn her around," says Chris to the attendant holding Tanta. The top muscle of the mare's neck quivers nervously under her mane at the sight of Tippy. A

## THE STALLION STATION

Most Thoroughbred breeding farms that stand a stallion also keep mares or board many of the mares booked to their stud. A more modern concept in breeding is the stallion station, where mares come to be serviced. This superdeluxe stud barn may stand as many as fifteen stallions, but provides no mare-care facilities.

The stallions living at the station each have a huge stall, a private paddock and a personal groom. The mares visit them by appointment only. During the hectic end of the breeding season, a well-organized stallion station can breed a mare every three to five minutes.

When the mare arrives, she is unloaded and travels through a circuit that is a sort of breeding assembly line. First, she is led down a corridor and washed. She continues along that corridor to the teaser, who stands in his permanent stall and teases her. She then continues around the corner to the holding area (from which she is also exposed to the teaser), and finally arrives in the breeding shed. As she is being bred, another mare is in the holding area, another in the teasing area, and another entering the wash stall. When the cover is over, the mare is taken directly outside and loaded into her van while a fresh stud is led in to cover the next mare.

hoofprint of dirt flies out from under her left hind foot.

"You better tighten up that twitch," says Chris.

Never taking an eye from Tanta, Tippy prances, arching his neck and tail in the characteristic posture of an excited horse. He is backed up into one corner of the room to be washed.

"Now, bring her one step forward," instructs Gary. With Tanta's approach, Tippy paws the floor and drops his penis out of its sheath. The minute Chris leans under him to wash it, he rears twelve feet straight up-

ward and strikes out wildly, lunging toward Tanta. Chris leaps back, but Gary stands beneath the horse in the confusion of slashing hooves.

"You son of a bitch. Get back there now. Get back," he growls, reefing the chain links back so hard that they rattle against the stallion's teeth. Tippy totters backward and nearly loses his balance.

"Now stand," says Gary, giving the chain an extra yank for good measure as Tippy lands again on his two front feet. This time he stays still while Chris washes him, both to prevent infection and to guard against the dreaded equine venereal disease, CEM.

"Alright," says Gary, slapping Tippy's neck to excite him as if they are in a stallion fight, "you can turn her around now. This horse is ready." Tippy, smelling the mare's scent on Gary's arm, snaps at him as they approach Tanta slowly. Gary slaps the stallion on the neck again. "You want a stud to be a little aggressive. We try to keep everything as natural as possible and let the horses go through the same kind of breeding ritual they go through in the wild."

Tanta stands stock-still, winking rhythmically. Her ears flit and strain to hear the stallion approaching slowly and invisibly from behind. His head pops into her view as he nips her left flank. Then Gary clucks, pushes Tippy's jaw onto Tanta's rump and holds it there until he rears and mounts her. Tanta's bones sink under the weight of the huge stomach crashing down and she freezes while Tippy dances on two hind feet in a semicircle around her hind hooves. Chris runs over to insert him. The wooden end of the twitch is braced against Tanta's shoulder to keep the stallion's thrusts from shoving her forward. Her eyes glaze over in a look of catatonic boredom and her teeth stick out, her upper lip twisted back by the rope loop.

"Did he do it?" asks Gary, as Tippy "flags" his tail up and down a few times, a common signal that the stallion has ejaculated.

"I think so. Sometimes he'll fool you, though," says Chris. Tippy collapses over Tanta as if to fall asleep.

"Okay, come on down. Down," Gary insists.

Tippy slides off, his penis "flared" at the end like a funnel. Chris rushes to catch some semen on a glass slide and takes it to the washroom to observe under the microscope. If the sperm are visible, it means the stud ejaculated. Horses with low fertility rates; slow breeders, which take half an hour to mount the mare; and shy breeders, which are prone to premature ejaculation, present great difficulties for the stud farm manager. Because artificial insemination of Thoroughbreds is not permitted by the Jockey Club (the resulting foal cannot be registered and therefore will be unable to race), sperm count and stallion-handling techniques are of great concern. Young studs, just off the track, are used to being roundly beaten for even looking at or whinnying to a filly. Suddenly they are asked to do something which for their entire life they have been punished for even thinking about. A very timid horse will sometimes be left alone with a mare in a special honeymoon suite, like that at Fountainhead Farm's Stallion Station in Lexington, to overcome his fears in private. Enthusiastic studs like Tippy, who tend to be "rushers," need severe disciplinary measures just to keep them from picking the handler up in their teeth and tossing him across the room in an effort to get to the mare.

"Was it a cover?" asks Gary, still holding Tippy in case they have to try again.

"Yeah," says Chris. "Boy, he's fertile. They were swimming around all over the place."

As soon as the cover is confirmed, Tanta is taken out the door and led up the drive to rejoin the frantic Banknote. Tippy scans the shed for his lost mare. Once he is put away, muffled whinnies from behind his stall door beckon his herd of one, but she is already out of hearing and there is no response. Some stallions become so oversexed during the breeding season that they must wear hard, rubber stallion rings around the ends of their penises to prevent them from masturbating.

The next day, the Heimerles try to breed Tanta to Tippy again, but she kicks out at the sight of him, and refuses to let him near her without a fuss. Although she knowingly tolerated Toga, she refused to have anything to do with the real stud. Assuming that her violent reaction was due to the sudden hormonal change mares experience after ovulation, they decided not to risk wasting Tippy's virility. He has thirty-nine other mares in his "book" for this season, and his failure to cover them successfully would necessitate the return of all stud fees. Even if he gets the mares in foal, his fee is not officially due until the foals stand and nurse.

Unresponsive to the teaser every day thereafter, Tanta is examined by Dr. Gill on her eighteenth post-cover day and her cervix is sealed tightly, indicating that she is in foal. It is not until the thirtieth post-cover day, however, that her pregnancy is conclusive. She is still nursing Banknote. Meanwhile the new embryo inside her has already survived the most threatening period of its development.

# *Weaning*

Tanta, "the survivor," Tanta of the flashing hooves and the eyes that squint like black jewels at the slightest noise, turns out to be a good mother. More protective than affectionate, she bosses Banknote with her nose and teeth, teaching her both alertness and obedience. The filly has to learn two things: to run from fear and to trust and obey a master. Tanta, at times almost feral in her paranoia, instinctively lays the emotional foundation for a successful racehorse.

"When we breed a racehorse, we are breeding for nerves, kind of, for speed," says Chris, sauntering into Tanta's stall to hold the filly while the vet gets ready to give her her first vaccinations. "If the mare is independent, like Tanta, the foal will be, too. If the mare is dominant in the herd, the foal will be dominant. If the mare is clean in her stall, the foal will take after that and if the mare is a pig, you'll have a pig of a foal."

Banknote's nostrils puff with suspicion as the vet approaches, offering one of his large, antiseptic hands for her to sniff. She twists her neck and glints her gaze down sideways at him, as if she senses the other hand, hidden behind him, cupping the hypodermic. Chris fondles the filly's nose to keep her relaxed.

At the first sting of the needle in the left side of her neck, Banknote flinches.

"Okay, it's okay," whispers Chris softly, steadying the filly with strokes of her hand, but leaving the lead rope slack. More than anything else, a horse fears restraint. The fear of not being able to run away from danger is genetically embedded in its nerves. Banknote stands still, quivering, but bound only by the delicate tie of Chris's enveloping reassurance. A tightening of the lead rope right now would cause the filly to panic and fight. The horse that learns to associate the vet with claustrophobic restraint and painful struggles will probably fear him for life and be unwilling to stand quietly for future treatment.

"It has always been Chris's and my intention to produce a salable commodity," explains Gary, standing by Tanta in a corner of the stall to keep her from interfering. "We want to raise something that is socially acceptable, horses that are not afraid and will not hurt themselves through stupidity."

At age three months, Banknote submits warily to her first battery of vaccinations. She has passed the danger point as far as early childhood diseases are concerned and is old enough to be inoculated against the four most feared equine ailments: tetanus, the bacteria of which reside in horse manure (and to which Banknote was initially immune because Tanta received a booster two months before foaling); Eastern or Western encephalomyelitis, a fatal sleeping sickness; rhinopneumonitus, a respiratory disease which is usually not fatal to the animal, but which causes abortion in mares; and influenza, which, though not usually fatal itself, often induces pneumonia, a widespread killer of foals. For the rest of her life, Banknote will receive annual boosters against them.

"Alright there, girlie, that's it," mutters the vet, plucking out the last needle and giving the impatient Banknote a gentle pat on the chest.

The veterinarian is a constant figure in the life of every racehorse. The horse that is treated with sympathy during the early visits will learn to tolerate the discomfort or pain of veterinary treatments, because it understands that the vet is not going to harm it. With improper handling, horses have been known to become vicious and dangerous around vets and horseshoers. Thoroughbred horses are quick to remember an unkindness and can be stubborn as mules when it comes to resisting against doing something they fear or dislike. These qualities, so admirable if they can be channeled into the will to win, become destructive character flaws if the horse is not properly socialized.

Gary leads Tanta out to the aisle.

"Come on, dummy, come with your mother," says Chris, gently indicating which way Banknote should move with a slight forward pull of the lead rope. Once the foals have learned to "follow their heads," they are no longer "two-handed" by attendants. While the foals are still young, they are body-shadowed. Attendants place one arm around the tiny chest and another over the still-low back to control what direction the foal moves in. This method of "two-handing" keeps the foal from hurting itself either by running away or by straining its soft bones in an effort to resist being led.

Banknote is usually willing to follow her mother, but seeing the still-frightening vet in the aisle, she rears and pulls back against the lead rope. Prepared for this, an attendant standing behind the filly clucks to her and taps her smartly on the rump. Encouraged both by the sight of Tanta disappearing at the end of the barn in a fit of nickering and by the fear of the unaccustomed tapping coming from behind, Banknote lunges forward, yanking Chris with her. Chris manages to keep her in a steady trot until they reach Tanta's flank, but makes no serious effort to slow her down or punish her as long as she is in control.

"We don't mind running them in and out of the barn at first," says Gary, as Chris lets Banknote loose to tear across the misted paddock. "After all, they are supposed to be racehorses and racehorses are supposed to want to run forward. All of their early training is forward, forward, forward. The worst thing you can teach a horse is that if it doesn't want to go someplace, it can back up."

From the first moment she drew breath, every contact the filly has had with people has been directed to shaping her body and mind toward two ultimate goals: the sales ring in Kentucky and the as-yet-unspecified racetrack where, one summer afternoon, she will look into the eyes of others like her and show the world the stuff of which she is made.

Destiny is a long way off, though. Throughout the spring and summer and early fall, Banknote romps, teases, makes discoveries. Her slender legs, agile as a pianist's fingers, play in whimsical rhythms across the long fields, trotting, turning, cantering, racing, rearing, bouncing against her

## MEASUREMENTS OF FOALS

| | WEIGHT (LBS.) | | HEIGHT (IN.) | | CANNON BONE (IN.) | |
|---|---|---|---|---|---|---|
| DAYS | COLTS | FILLIES | COLTS | FILLIES | COLTS | FILLIES |
| 2 | 115 | 113 | 39½ | 39¼ | 4$\frac{15}{16}$ | 4⅞ |
| 30 | 216 | 213 | 43⅝ | 43½ | 5½ | 5¼ |
| 60 | 301 | 297 | 46¾ | 46½ | 5⅞ | 5¾ |
| 120 | 430 | 420 | 50½ | 50 | 6¼ | 6⅛ |
| 180 | 540 | 520 | 53 | 52⅜ | 6⅝ | 6½ |
| 365 | 795 | 750 | 57½ | 56¾ | 7¾ | 7½ |
| 540 | 960 | 885 | 60¾ | 60 | 8⅜ | 8⅛ |

Address all communications to: REGISTRY OFFICE, THE JOCKEY CLUB, 380 MADISON AVENUE, NEW YORK, NY 10017
TO REGISTER AT THE $60.00 RATE, APPLICATIONS MUST BE POSTMARKED ON OR BEFORE AUGUST 31 OF THE FOAL'S BIRTH
YEAR. FROM SEPTEMBER 1 TO DECEMBER 31, THE FEE IS $85.00. Full fee must accompany application. Make checks payable to The Jockey Club.
Submission of application gives consent to The Jockey Club to blood-type foal and either or both parents if they are owned by you. Blood-typing may be required
because this foal is chosen by random selection or if specific need for verification of parentage arises.

# APPLICATION FOR FOAL REGISTRATION
## (PLEASE PRINT OR TYPE. DO NOT USE PENCIL.)

Date: August 27, 197_

**1. ADDRESS INQUIRIES ON THIS APPLICATION TO:**
Name: Geraghty-Heimerle, Christine
Scargo Farm
Address: Carmel, N.Y. 10512
Telephone: ( 914 ) 279-5021

**2. BREEDER OF FOAL:** (Owner of mare at time foal was dropped)
Name: Geraghty-Heimerle, C.
Address: Scargo Farm
P.O. Box O
Carmel, N.Y. 10521

**3. OWNER OF FOAL:** SAME AS BREEDER [X]
Name:
Address:

**4. PRESENT OWNER OF MARE:** SAME AS BREEDER [X]
Name:
Address:

**5. FARM, STATE, COUNTRY WHERE FOAL WAS DROPPED:**
Farm: Scargo Farm
State: New York
Country: U.S.A. [X]    Other:

**6. MARE BRED BACK TO:**
Stallion Name: Take Your Place    4/1/79 (first cover date) (last cover)
Stallion Name: (first cover date) (last cover)

**7. NAME CLAIMED FOR FOAL** (LIVE FOAL ONLY):
(1)
(2)
(3)
(4)
(5)
(6)

**8. IF NO LIVE FOAL, INDICATE REASON:**

**9. IS THIS FOAL A TWIN?** YES [ ] NO [X]
What happened to other twin?

**10. PRIMARY FOAL DATA:**
Sex:    Color (check only one box):
☐ Colt    ☐ Black    ☐ Bay
☐ Gelding    ☐ Dk Bay or Br    ☐ Gray
[X] Filly    [X] Chestnut    ☐ Roan
Date of foaling: March 2 1979
(month) (day) (year)

**11. DAM:**
Name: TANTA PRISA    Color: CH
Year of birth: 71
Pedigree
By: *PRONTO
Out of: *CAMEROLA

**12. SIRE:**
Name: SIR WIMBORNE    Color: B
Year of birth: 73
Pedigree
By: SIR IVOR
Out of: CAP AND BELLS
(OTHER COVERING STALLION)
Name:

**13. DAM IDENTIFICATION:**
A mare must be identified when her first foal is registered and each time she changes ownership thereafter. If identification is called for, outline all white markings of dam on diagrams. If there are no white markings, check box. ☐

FOREHEAD
EYE LEVEL
CENTER OF FACE
BRIDGE OF NOSE
BETWEEN NOSTRILS
UPPER LIP
LOWER LIP

L.F. R.F. L.F. R.F. R.H. L.H.    R.H. L.H.    L.F. R.F. L.H. R.H.

**14. DAM'S TATTOO NUMBER:**
A7658

**15. MAIL CERTIFICATE TO:**
Name: Geraghty-Heimerle, Christine
Address: Scargo Farm
P.O. Box O, Carmel, N.Y. 10512

**16. SIGNATURE:**

Owner of foal or authorized agent

## FOAL DESCRIPTION:

Give complete written description of all markings and characteristics in the following order: (1) head; (2) left fore leg; (3) left hind leg; (4) right hind leg; right fore leg; (6) body, including cowlicks; (7) brands, scars, physical abnormalities. Indicate accurately if markings are to left or right of center. If there is no white markings on the foal, please state NO WHITE MARKS. Whether or not the foal has white markings, all cowlicks should be accurately reported.

(1) Head: Star to right side of median extending from middle of forehead to eye level.
Median cowlick just above eye level.  Median cowlick at top of forehead under forelock.
(3) Left hind leg: pastern and part of ankle marking higher on outside and back
than inside and front.  (5) Right foreleg:  intermittent coronet marking on front
inside and outside of leg, higher in back toward center.  (6) Body cowlick on upper
third of neck midway between crest of neck and jugular groove on left side.  Cowlick
midway to withers on crest of neck on left side.  Cowlick on crest of neck on upper one
third of right side of neck.  Cowlick on crest of neck proximal to withers on right side.
Cowlick on jugular groove of upper one-third of right side of neck.

## DIAGRAMS:

Outline all white markings of foal on diagrams below. Mark locations of cowlicks with an X.

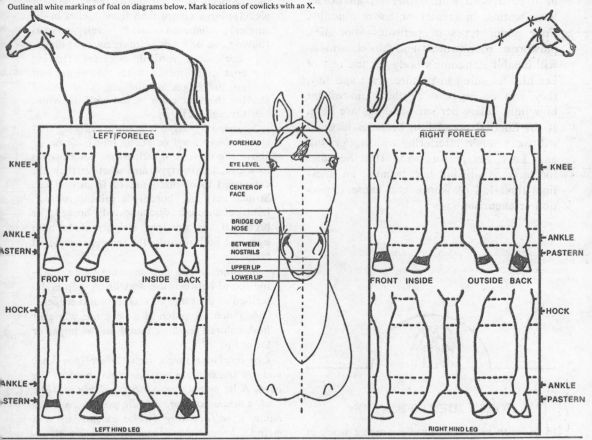

## ENCLOSE SIGNED SERVICE CERTIFICATE:

A service certificate which reports the covering dates that resulted in this foal must accompany this application for registration. If the mare was covered by more than one stallion and blood analysis of the foal eliminates all but one potential sire, only that stallion's service certification is needed to complete the registration process. The service certificate must be signed by the stallion owner or by an authorized agent.

## ENCLOSE A SET OF FOUR (4) PHOTOGRAPHS OF THE FOAL:

(1) front view of foal, including head, body, and legs. Face markings must be clearly visible.
(2) left side of head and body, including legs
(3) right side of head and body, including legs
(4) rear view of lower legs, including heels

friend, a colt out of Mark's Pet, racing again, stopping short to sniff the changing breeze.

Every four weeks, Banknote's feet are trimmed and she receives a dose of what will be a lifelong unpleasantness, worming medicine. Because she has always had nice straight legs and a straight "way of going" (or moving), she does not require the corrective trimming that is done on some of the other foals to encourage them to grow out of any conformational flaws they may have been born with. However, all horses have worms, in greater or lesser quantity. Four major types of parasites—bot flies, pinworms, roundworms and bloodworms—will inhabit Banknote's body for the rest of her life. Breeding in pasture grass and hay, they will be ingested regularly no matter how immaculate her surroundings are kept. If the internal population becomes large, it will weaken her, interfering with her growth and, later, her performance. If it becomes too large, it will kill her, because an intestinal tract full of worms can cause impaction or aneurism.

## HORSE IDENTIFICATION

In order to race or to produce racing stock in the United States, a horse must be registered by the Jockey Club. As of 1980, any foal has to be identified by three separate methods: written physical descriptions of body markings and characteristics; photographs of the front, rear and both sides of the foal, as well as life-size pictures of all four leg "chestnuts"; and blood typing. The purpose of this identification is to protect the buying and betting public from misrepresentation of bloodstock.

## Markings

All markings are both drawn onto blank horse diagrams and described in words. The markings are of three types: head markings, leg markings and body markings. The head and leg markings are white hair that grows out of pink (or unpigmented) skin.

*Head markings,* which almost invariably occur between the top of the forehead and the base of the upper lip, are of four types:

1. *Star:* A star is a solid collection of white hair found on the forehead. Its description includes size, shape and position on the forehead, such as: small (the shape of a nickel); large (more than three inches in diameter); diamond-shaped; oval; pointed (having one or more points); narrow; diagonal; horizontal; vertical; bordered (having the coat color mixed with the white hair around the edges of the star); or mixed (having the coat color mixed with the white hair throughout).

2. *Stripe:* A stripe is a white marking that starts at eye level or below and ends on or above the upper lip. Stripes are described as to width, length, type and whether they are connected to or disconnected from the star. Stripes may be: bordered; mixed; narrow; faint; connected; disconnected; broken; or broad. If the star and stripe include both eyes and both nostrils, the face is considered "bald."

3. *Snip:* A snip is a separate white marking found between the nostrils. A snip is described in the same way as stars and stripes.

4. *Patch:* A patch is a separate white or flesh-colored marking found on the upper or lower lip.

*Leg markings* rarely occur above the knee and are much more variable than those of the head. A horse may have, progressively, a *white heel,* a *white coronet,* a *white pastern,* a *white ankle,* a *half-stocking* (white extends up and includes lower half of cannon bone), a *three-quarters stocking* (white extends three-quarters of the way up the cannon bone), a *full stocking* (white extends all the way up the cannon bone), and many variations within the above. Irregular smatterings of white from hoof to shoulder or stifle are also common, and must be noted on horse identification forms.

The *body markings* consist of:

1. *Odd markings:* Most commonly, black

spots on chestnut horses, or large white patches on a Thoroughbred of any color.

2. *Dimples:* Dimples in muscles under the skin are considered characteristics if they are permanent and easily seen. Usually, they occur at the point of one or both shoulders and in the neck muscles.

3. *Cowlicks:* Cowlicks are the centers of hair whorls. They are permanent, and cannot be brushed or clipped away. Most horses have a cowlick on the forehead above eye level. Some have two forehead cowlicks or a cowlick on the side of the neck. Cowlicks are described in terms of their location and their relationship to each other (i.e., double horizontal cowlicks, double diagonal cowlicks, etc.).

## Distinctive Characteristics

Any distinguishing conformational characteristics are noted on identification certificates, such as: lop ears (ears which do not point straight ahead); roman nose (a convex area between the eyes and the muzzle); parrot-mouth (upper teeth protrude beyond the lower teeth); or leg flaws, such as cow hocks, sickle hocks, etc. Also noted are scars and firing marks.

## Chestnuts

Chestnuts are horny growths that are found on each of the horse's legs, just above the knees of the front legs, and just below the hocks of the hind legs. The chestnuts are considered to be vestigial toes; since no two have exactly the same outline, they serve as the horse's fingerprints. The average chestnut (or *night eye*, as they are sometimes called) is about the length of a finger and is between one half inch and two inches wide. They do not change in size or shape during the horse's lifetime. On rare occasions, a horse will be born without one or both hind chestnuts.

## Blood Type

Blood typing of all American Thoroughbreds was begun by the Jockey Club in 1977. Because each horse's blood has a combination of characteristics related to immune response and protein makeup that has less than a one-in-ten-thousand chance of being identical to that of another horse, blood typing is the most sophisticated form of equine classification. Since general blood types are inherited, blood typing is also useful in validating pedigree.

Once the information on the foal registration form is verified, a *certificate* is issued that validates the horse's identity for racing and breeding purposes. This laminated document looks like a college I.D., only larger and fancier. On one side is a copy of the foal registration document, on the other the photographs of the horse, pedigree information and the names of the breeder, owner and trainer.

For all Thoroughbreds intended to be raced, an identification number is issued by the Jockey Club. This number is *tattooed* on the inside of the horse's upper lip. Tattoo numbers are checked against the Jockey Club's records prior to each race.

## The Mythology of Markings

There are as many superstitions about a horse's markings as about its color. The most common is an oft-repeated rhyme about leg markings:

> "One white foot, run it for your life.
> Two white feet, give it to your wife.
> Three white feet, give it to your man.
> Four white feet, sell it if you can."

Some horses, like the Triple Crown winner Count Fleet, or Equipoise, the great "Chocolate Soldier" and world-record holder at a mile for many years, displayed the one white foot to prove the rhyme. But Swaps, one of fourteen twentieth-century horses in the Daily Racing Form Hall of Fame, would have been quite a prize for a wife, with his two white feet.

The "man" who received three-white-footed Secretariat and the similarly handicapped Triple Crown winner Whirlaway would have earned a fortune from his gift horse. A disgruntled seller of Lexington or Gallant Fox, both of which had the dreaded four white feet, would not only have endured the misery of seeing them blaze to many victories on the track, but would have felt twice the fool when they went to stud. Lexington was America's leading sire for fourteen years, and Gallant Fox has the distinction of being the only Triple Crown winner to sire another Triple Crown winner (Omaha).

On August 27, just about six months after Banknote was foaled, Chris sends in her application for registration with the Jockey Club. A form detailing her blood-lines and markings is submitted for approval and future identification purposes, but the "name claimed for foal" blank is left empty. Although "Banknote" is her "stable name," her racing name will have to be approved by the Jockey Club, under its strict regulations. Because Banknote is part of a sales crop, she will remain officially, "Chestnut Filly, Property of Scargo Farm" until she is sold.

"Part of the fun of being a new owner is getting to name your yearling," says Gary.

Thoroughbreds' names are usually related to their family names to indicate lineage. Count Fleet, for instance, was by Reigh Count and out of Quickly. Calumet Farm's great sire Bull Lea was by Bull Dog and out of Rose Leaves. Occasionally, horses are named after people. Dr. Fager, holder of the world record for the mile, was named after the doctor who pulled his owner through a rough illness. Good horses tend to have good names, but some owners seem to intentionally make fun of their animals with bad ones. Probably the worst name ever given to a horse was Bed Pan, who did manage to win over $36,000. The breeder can only hope that the owner will do his carefully nurtured progeny justice.

Symbolically, registration is Banknote's first step toward becoming an independent horse. A few days after the form is sent in, she begins the first concrete step toward adulthood, the weaning from Tanta, her dam.

At Scargo, weaning takes place in two phases. First, all of the fillies and their dams are weaned from all of the colts and their dams. The Mark's Pet colt takes the separation from his best friend hard, galloping the fence line, screeching out and trying to climb the rails in search of her. The parting is necessary. Although Banknote is still immature, if she and the colt were still romping in the same field in January, there would be a good chance of her getting "in foal" before she was physically one year old. From now on, Banknote will socialize only with members of her own sex. Her next close contact with a male horse will be exposure to the teaser and brief moments in the breeding shed, after she has retired from racing.

The second phase of weaning occurs more gradually. One brilliant September day, all of the fillies and their mothers are taken into an unfamiliar field. The fillies are enchanted. Banknote wanders off, nosing each tuft of grass, testing the fence lines, eyeing the odd shapes of the sunlight shifting through strange treetops. At last, Banknote looks up to check on Tanta's whereabouts, but the mare is gone. Forever. She cannot hear Tanta's maternal screams dying behind the closed barn doors high on the hill.

After about three hours, Tanta gives up. She has time now to become preoccupied with the new foal growing inside her. Banknote, surrounded by a field of calm mares and foals, settles down until nightfall. It only takes one night to wean a horse, but that night is the loneliest one of the horse's life.

"The mare's temperament often determines who will get weaned first," explains Gary, putting the suddenly frightened Banknote into a stall by herself for the first time. "We took Tanta and Amber Dancer first because Amber was very old and her foal was big and was taxing her system demanding milk, and Banknote was one of the oldest foals. The kid only really gets nervous the first night alone. They squeal all night long, but it's done by morning. It just seems like it takes a month to wean them because you wean a new one every night."

"The mare is like a security blanket for the foal," Chris adds. "In the wild, the mother would kick the foal away at around nine months of age, so we take them at six months to prevent any injury."

Banknote survives her night, squealing and crashing fitfully against the oak stall door. As the days progress, more and more mares are removed from the field, one at a time, until they are all gone. The mares, including Tanta, are turned out in a separate field to "dry out" their milk bags. Exercise helps them to absorb the milk so they do not develop mastitis, a painful congestion of the udder. Because horses, being herd animals, are extremely suggestible, the method of taking only one or two mares away at a time ensures that the relaxed attitude of the herd will prevail over the excited weanlings. A field of weanlings, all separated from their dams for the first time, can work themselves into such a frenzy that some are badly hurt or even killed by crashing against fences while trying to find their mothers.

"Lee Eaton, who handles a lot of yearlings, says that you have to remember that horses are predisposed to self-destruction," explains Chris. "We try to do everything we can to minimize the danger of having them hurt themselves, but if you breed horses you've got to have a fatalistic attitude. You know, through statistics, that a certain percent are going to kill themselves. All you can do is make everything as safe as you possibly can and then pray that the bunch you've got are survivors. Every time you turn them out in a new field, you just shut your eyes and hope for the best."

## ASTROLOGY

In 1961, *The Blood-Horse* magazine caused a furor in the Thoroughbred world by announc-ing plans to stop publishing astrological signs. For centuries, many horsemen have relied upon the moon signs of the zodiac to indicate to them the most auspicious time for performing various activities. Just as the moon influences the tide, its signs are believed to influence certain parts of the body. Moon

| 1980 | JANUARY | 1980 |
| --- | --- | --- |

| Sun. | Mon. | Tue. | Wed. | Thu. | Fri. | Sat. |
| --- | --- | --- | --- | --- | --- | --- |
| | | 1 | 2 | 3 | 4 | 5 |
| 6 | 7 | 8 | 9 | 10 | 11 | 12 |
| 13 | 14 | 15 | ♑ | 17 | 18 | 19 |
| 20 | 21 | ♈ | 23 | 24 | 25 | 26 |
| 27 | 28 | 29 | 30 | 31 | | |

### THE "SIGN" IN JANUARY

| 1 | ♊ | Arms | 18 | ♒ | Legs |
| --- | --- | --- | --- | --- | --- |
| 2 | ♋ | Breast | 20 | ♓ | Feet |
| 4 | ♌ | Heart | 22 | ♈ | Head |
| 6 | ♍ | Bowels | 24 | ♉ | Neck |
| 9 | ♎ | Kidneys | 27 | ♊ | Arms |
| 11 | ♏ | Loins | 29 | ♋ | Breast |
| 14 | ♐ | Thighs | 31 | ♌ | Heart |
| 16 | ♑ | Knees | | | |

signs, which change every two to three days, are: Aries (head), Taurus (neck), Gemini (arms), Cancer (breast), Leo (heart), Virgo (bowels), Libra (kidneys), Scorpio (loins), Sagittarius (thighs), Capricorn (knees), Aquarius (legs) and Pisces (feet). When the moon sign corresponds to a certain body part, stress in the areas of the body above that part is supposed to be lessened. For instance, foals are weaned when the sign is in the legs (to aid in the rapid drying up of the mare's udder) and colts are castrated when the sign is in the knees. In spite of modern methods of breeding-farm management, tradition prevailed. *The Blood-Horse* still prints the monthly positions of the signs.

# The Thoroughbred Auction

Until the late eighteenth century, Thoroughbred racing was the province of a small group of noblemen and landed gentry who bred and traded horses primarily among themselves. In 1766, when a shrewd Yorkshireman named Richard Tattersall rented a piece of property behind London's Hyde Park Corner, the scope of racing considerably widened. Tattersall, who managed the extensive stables of the Second Duke of Kingston, as a sideline assisted many owners in the private buying and selling of horses. Soon he had a reputation for excellent judgment and absolute honesty. To capitalize on this reputation, he began to hold twice-weekly public sales of horses on the Hyde Park Corner property. The Thoroughbred auction soon opened the sport to many new owners and spurred the development of the true commercial breeding industry.

Today, the Thoroughbred auction remains the focal point of commercial breeding. While only 21 percent of the registered Thoroughbred yearlings were sold at auction in 1980, these represent a much larger percentage of the quality animals. The auction results determine the price levels at which horses are sold privately, and play a decisive role in setting the prices of racing and breeding stock.

Auctions can be a thrilling process for participants and spectators alike. Investors and the shrewd bloodstock agents that serve as their advisers scour the sales for bargains like the $17,500 for which Seattle Slew was purchased, or the $15,200 a Puerto Rican businessman paid for Bold Forbes. The auctioning process itself has the tension of a high-stakes poker game. Breeders and

buyers never know when an unexpected bidding war will send prices soaring toward the million-dollar mark.

For those interested in investing in Thoroughbreds at some point, following the auctions is the best way to develop good judgment about how the combination of pedigree and conformation translates into auction price and, later, racing performance.

## BIG PLAYERS IN THE AUCTION GAME

### Robert Sangster

Gambling is both the vocation and avocation of this forty-six-year-old resident of the Isle of Man. Sangster operates the Vernons football pool out of Liverpool, England, taking bets by mail from 114 countries. Vernons, which also runs lotteries in the United States and Australia, grosses $500 million annually.

Sangster pours a substantial portion of the profits into Thoroughbred horses. For several years, Sangster has been extraordinarily active at the prestigious summer yearling sales. In 1979, Sangster and his associate purchased twenty-three yearlings for $10,840,000—an astounding 16 percent of the gross of the Keeneland and Saratoga select sales. Together with those of his bids that drive up the prices on top yearlings he doesn't get (his agent dropped out of the bidding on the record $1.7 million colt at $1.6 million), this activity makes Sangster the single most influential individual in the North American yearling market, and a major reason for the huge increases in top yearling prices.

Most of Sangster's purchases are sent to trainer Vincent O'Brian's huge farm in Ireland, for future racing in Ireland, Britain and France. Many are ridden by the young American jockey sensation Steve Cauthen, who Sangster signed in 1979 for a reputed $400,000 a year.

## Nelson Bunker Hunt

Domination is a family trait inherited along with his father's oil billions by Nelson Bunker Hunt. Hunt suffered severe losses in 1980 in an attempt to corner the world silver market, but since his entry into the Thoroughbred market in 1953, his stature in the industry has steadily risen.

Hunt currently owns more than one thousand Thoroughbreds, housed at his racing stables in the United States, Europe and Australia, and at his breeding farms in Kentucky and New Zealand. Among the great horses he has raced and/or bred are Dahlia, Youth, Nobiliary, Empery, Exceller and Mississippian. Annually, his name appears on the lists of both leading U.S. breeders and owners.

His breeding operation, which specializes in the highest-quality yearlings, has become so significant that, beginning in 1979, Hunt has organized his own summer sale rather than consign to Keeneland and Saratoga as he had done in the past. In 1980, the fifty-three yearlings that he offered brought in $10,313,000, an average of $194,585—nearly the same average as the select Keeneland sale and $83,000 higher than that of Saratoga. In the 1979 Hunt sale, a filly by Bold Forbes out of Goofed, dam of the great racehorse and sire Lyphard, sold for a then-record $1.45 million.

In addition to selling, Hunt is also a major buyer, particularly of breeding stock. In 1979, he was the leading buyer at the Keeneland Fall Sale of Breeding Stock, purchasing twenty-three mares for $3,518,000. Hunt also assures himself of future breeding rights to champion stallions by accepting one-quarter interest in any colt he sells at auction, provided the buyer is interested in partnership.

## YEARLING SALES

In 1980, 7,079 yearlings were sold at auction, an all-time record. The average price was $29,683, another all-time record. Since 1975, the average has leaped an astounding 171 percent.

Traditionally, the most prestigious yearling sales have been the July Select Keeneland Sale and the August Select Saratoga sale. To qualify as one of the five hundred or so animals to enter the ring in these events, a yearling must have a glittering pedigree and must pass a rigorous conformation inspection. In 1980, the 534 animals sold at these two auctions averaged $156,468, an increase of 202 percent since 1975. Also in 1980, billionaire horse owner and breeder Nelson Bunker Hunt conducted a separate sale at which fifty-three yearlings bred by his Bluegrass Farm sold for an average of $194,585.

These sale prices have been pushed up in recent years by the influx of foreign investors taking advantage of the decline of the American dollar. The all-time record yearling, a Northern Dancer colt, was purchased in 1981 by the British Bloodstock Agency. In 1979, foreign buyers spent $20,856,000 at Keeneland, 44 percent of the total purchases.

Although the American tracks offer the largest purses in the world, the top four colts and top three fillies sold in 1979 were sent to race in Europe. Because of the high value of these animals as breeding stock, their owners prefer to cut down the risk of injury by having them brought along in the more leisurely European style, and by having them race exclusively on grass.

While the relative value of animals sold at auction can be predicted on the basis of pedigree and conformation, the making of a million-dollar yearling is still a mysterious process. The Hoist the Flag colt that sold for $1.6 million is an example. In 1974, breeder Tom Gentry paid $60,000 for fifteen-year-old Royal Dowry, the dam of 1969 two-year-old filly champion Tudor Queen. Royal Dowry was in foal to Jacinto, and the resultant filly sold at auction for

$20,000. Royal Dowry produced a colt by Hoist the Flag that sold at auction in 1977 for $150,000. The next foal she produced was by Protagonist—like Hoist the Flag, a two-year-old champion—but this yearling brought only $15,000.

In 1979, the full brother to the $150,000 colt stepped into the ring at Keeneland. This time the bidding soared quickly to $1,025,000. Minutes later, the hammer came down at $1,600,000, over ten times the price of the 1977 colt.

## LEADING SIRES OF SALE YEARLINGS

### (With Three or More Sale Yearlings)
### 1980

| | SALE YRLGS. | HIGHEST PRICE | LOWEST PRICE | AVERAGE PRICE | TIMES NAT'L. AVG. |
|---|---|---|---|---|---|
| Northern Dancer | 13 | $1,400,000 | $180,000 | $537,308 | 18.1 |
| Lyphard | 10 | 1,700,000 | 85,000 | 453,000 | 15.3 |
| Hoist the Flag | 12 | 1,050,000 | 37,000 | 349,333 | 11.8 |
| Exclusive Native | 18 | 1,600,000 | 27,000 | 318,444 | 10.7 |
| Nijinsky II | 16 | 775,000 | 105,000 | 261,563 | 8.8 |
| The Minstrel | 15 | 900,000 | 110,000 | 261,133 | 8.8 |
| Secretariat | 15 | 530,000 | 42,000 | 221,933 | 7.5 |
| In Reality | 8 | 410,000 | 75,000 | 198,000 | 6.7 |
| Roberto | 16 | 500,000 | 45,000 | 177,688 | 6.0 |
| What a Pleasure | 8 | 895,000 | 43,000 | 174,875 | 5.9 |
| Bold Forbes | 26 | 800,000 | 35,000 | 170,654 | 5.8 |
| Graustark | 11 | 625,000 | 52,000 | 167,455 | 5.6 |
| Vaguely Noble | 19 | 375,000 | 67,000 | 160,474 | 5.4 |
| L'Enjoleur | 12 | 850,000 | 20,000 | 158,333 | 5.3 |
| Blushing Groom | 16 | 650,000 | 25,000 | 153,563 | 5.2 |
| Sir Ivor | 21 | 475,000 | 65,000 | 152,476 | 5.1 |
| Caro | 19 | 565,000 | 24,000 | 142,579 | 4.8 |
| Raise a Native | 23 | 400,000 | 32,000 | 139,304 | 4.7 |
| Key to the Mint | 16 | 360,000 | 17,000 | 134,375 | 4.5 |
| Youth | 12 | 235,000 | 28,000 | 131,750 | 4.4 |
| Raja Baba | 23 | 330,000 | 23,000 | 129,478 | 4.4 |
| Dance Spell | 21 | 275,000 | 22,000 | 129,333 | 4.4 |
| Forli | 13 | 320,000 | 36,000 | 127,462 | 4.3 |
| Honest Pleasure | 13 | 250,000 | 20,000 | 117,923 | 4.0 |
| Bold Bidder | 17 | 250,000 | 35,000 | 116,118 | 3.9 |
| Mr. Prospector | 8 | 250,000 | 52,000 | 113,625 | 3.8 |
| Damascus | 7 | 225,000 | 37,000 | 113,143 | 3.8 |
| Foolish Pleasure | 10 | 240,000 | 32,000 | 110,700 | 3.7 |
| Tom Rolfe | 12 | 300,000 | 37,000 | 107,083 | 3.6 |
| Snow Knight | 14 | 550,000 | 2,500 | 104,000 | 3.5 |
| Stage Door Johnny | 7 | 320,000 | 22,000 | 102,714 | 3.5 |
| Master Derby | 14 | 310,000 | 22,500 | 102,607 | 3.5 |
| Prince John | 4 | 195,000 | 35,000 | 100,500 | 3.4 |
| Wajima | 21 | 250,000 | 21,000 | 95,143 | 3.2 |
| Olden Times | 23 | 320,000 | 25,000 | 90,739 | 3.1 |
| Stop the Music | 14 | 260,000 | 12,500 | 87,536 | 3.0 |

| | SALE YRLGS. | HIGHEST PRICE | LOWEST PRICE | AVERAGE PRICE | TIMES NAT'L. AVG. |
|---|---|---|---|---|---|
| Vice Regent | 12 | $215,000 | $19,000 | $ 87,167 | 2.9 |
| Majestic Light | 11 | 250,000 | 17,000 | 87,000 | 2.9 |
| Gummo | 6 | 335,000 | 15,000 | 80,167 | 2.7 |
| Best Turn | 9 | 155,000 | 28,000 | 78,000 | 2.6 |
| Gallant Romeo | 15 | 350,000 | 11,500 | 76,700 | 2.6 |
| Elocutionist | 19 | 175,000 | 25,000 | 76,316 | 2.6 |
| Cornish Prince | 20 | 175,000 | 30,000 | 74,850 | 2.5 |
| Run Dusty Run | 5 | 200,000 | 16,000 | 74,800 | 2.5 |
| Ack Ack | 12 | 285,000 | 11,000 | 73,667 | 2.5 |
| Icecapade | 14 | 160,000 | 35,000 | 72,643 | 2.5 |
| Little Current | 17 | 140,000 | 13,000 | 72,588 | 2.5 |
| Riva Ridge | 14 | 160,000 | 15,500 | 72,205 | 2.4 |
| King Pellinore | 17 | 165,000 | 18,000 | 71,647 | 2.4 |
| Gallant Man | 5 | 185,000 | 25,000 | 71,600 | 2.4 |

## TOP TEN YEARLING COLTS SOLD AT AUCTION

| YEAR | SIRE–DAM | PRICE |
|---|---|---|
| 1981 | Northern Dancer—South Ocean | $3,500,000 |
| 1981 | Northern Dancer–Sweet Alliance | 3,300,000 |
| 1981 | Northern Dancer–Bernie Bird | 2,950,000 |
| 1980 | Lyphard–Stylish Genie | 1,700,000 |
| 1981 | Hoist the Flag–Native Street | 1,600,000 |
| 1979 | Hoist the Flag-Royal Dowry | 1,600,000 |
| 1980 | Exclusive Native–La Jalouse | 1,600,000 |
| 1976 | Secretariat–Charming Alibi | 1,500,000 |
| 1979 | Nijinsky II–Syrian Sea | 1,400,000 |
| 1980 | Northern Dancer–Gold Digger | 1,400,000 |

## TOP TEN YEARLING FILLIES SOLD AT AUCTION

| YEAR | SIRE–DAM | PRICE |
|---|---|---|
| 1979 | Bold Forbes–Goofed | $1,450,000 |
| 1979 | Empery–Charming Alibi | 1,100,000 |
| 1981 | Alleged–Runaway Bride | 1,000,000 |
| 1980 | The Minstrel–Mrs. Peterkin | 900,000 |
| 1980 | Bold Forbes–Goofed | 800,000 |
| 1980 | Exclusive Native–Won't Tell You | 800,000 |
| 1979 | Secretariat–My Charmer | 750,000 |
| 1980 | Bold Forbes–Gazala II | 750,000 |
| 1981 | Northern Dancer–Barely Even | 725,000 |
| 1981 | Lyphard–Miss Carmie | 700,000 |

The enormous sums paid at these auctions represent the latest fashions in Thoroughbred breeding, but they don't guarantee success on the racetrack. The world-record sales yearling as of 1978 was a colt named Canadian Bound, by Secretariat out of Charming Alibi, dam of the all-time leading money-winning mare, Dahlia. Despite the $1.5 million he commanded, Canadian Bound was a failure on the racetrack. In 1980, he was sent to stud for a paltry $1,000 stud fee.

To date, the biggest winner in this high-stakes game were the purchasers of the Bold Bidder colt, Spectacular Bid. Obtained in 1973 for the sum of $37,000, Spectacular Bid earned $2,781,607 on the track. When he was retired, he was syndicated for $22,000,000, nearly six hundred times his initial price. This kind of return is the reason investors pour money into the yearling auctions.

## LEADING ANNUAL YEARLING AUCTIONS

*July*
Fasig-Tipton Kentucky Summer Sale (Lexington, KY)
Keeneland Summer Select Sale (Lexington, KY)
Bluegrass Farm Sale (Lexington, KY)
*August*
California Thoroughbred Breeders Association (Del Mar, CA)
Saratoga Select Sale (Saratoga Springs, NY)
New York State Breeders Association Select Sale (Saratoga Springs, NY)
*September*
Canadian Horse Society Sale (Ontario, Canada)
Fasig-Tipton Kentucky Fall Preferred Sale (Lexington, KY)
Keeneland Fall Sale (Lexington, KY)

## PINHOOKING

Pinhooking is the practice of buying horses as weanlings or yearlings and conditioning them over the winter to resell as yearlings or two-year-olds-in-training. Because pinhooking is highly speculative, successful pinhookers must be expert horsemen with a good sense of market value. Pinhookers look for a horse by a sire and out of a dam whose runners seem to be on the way up; they hope that by the time they are ready to sell a prospect, there will be more black type in its pedigree. On the other hand, they avoid families of horses that are mainly producing cheap claimers. The idea is to buy a horse with reasonably good conformation and a respectable, if not fashionable, pedigree at the lower end of the middle-price range. To make a profit, pinhookers have to be able to at least double their money in about six months, selling an unproven Thoroughbred.

Pinhookers often avoid such things as South American bloodlines (which are unfamiliar to most American buyers), foals from older mares, and full brothers or sisters to top horses (which many buyers believe won't measure up). Pinhookers also look for a horse with a pretty head, an elegant topline, and a straight hind leg, none of which technically affects running ability, but all of which have eye appeal.

In the fall, pinhookers break their yearlings and prepare them for the two-year-old sales beginning in January. They like to show a horse that is sound, in good health, mannerly, dead fit and ready to go. This entails feeding supplements and sometimes hormones to promote muscular growth. Showmanship is very important. The advantage to the buyer is that although he is paying a higher price, he is getting more of a sure thing. The horse is trained, ready to race, and has proven its soundness and suitability, at least in light breezing. Although pinhooking can be done anywhere along the line of a horse's career, yearlings are the most popular pinhook prospects.

## OTHER AUCTIONS

Thoroughbreds are auctioned at every stage of their career. After yearling sales, the most common types of auctions are:

1. *Weanlings auctions:* Buying a six- to eight-month-old foal in the hope of reselling it for a profit as a yearling is the riskiest proposition in all of racing. The people who play this game, requiring the highest degree of nerve and market savvy, are called "pinhookers." In 1980, 1,480 weanlings sold for an average $14,277.

2. *Two-year-old sales:* Most untried two-year-olds are sold in January, February and March. In 1980, 2,373 were sold for an average of $17,546.

3. *Horses of racing age:* Many horses offered at racing age are from dispersals of racing stables caused by an owner's death or by the dissolution of a partnership. Quality and price vary widely in relationship to the quality of the stable being dispersed, but top horses are seldom sold this way.

4. *Broodmare auctions:* Broodmares head the list of fall sales of breeding stock. Most broodmares are sold in foal, with the estimated value at auction of the foal a prime consideration in the total purchase price. In the 1980 Fall Keeneland Sale, four broodmares in foal sold for more than $900,000 each. Top price of $2 million went for Street Dancer, a thirteen-year-old daughter of Native Dancer out of Beaver Street. The $2 million represents the highest price ever paid for a broodmare at public auction.

Barren and maiden mares are also offered at auction, but seldom bring the prices commanded by mares in foal. The average price for the 1,263 broodmares sold at Keeneland in 1980 was $59,349, a jump of 34 percent from 1979.

5. *Stallion shares and seasons:* Buyers of high-quality mares often seek shares in top stallions or one-season rights to a top stallion at the auction ring. Top price for a stallion share at auction, to date, is $950,000 for one share in Lyphard.

# Life of the Horse: 3. The Yearling

## Sales Preparation

On January 1, Banknote, along with every other Thoroughbred weanling, celebrates her first birthday. On March 5, three days after the anniversary of Banknote's real birth date, Tanta drops another big-boned foal, "stamped" with Tippy's bay markings and unruly temperament. Like many mares, she repeats her former foaling pattern. She refuses to lie down and the foal has to be pulled out. On March 6, Manny Dober, a three-year-old filly and Tanta's first foal, places second in the sixth race at Aqueduct. The race is restricted to New York-bred horses. Like Tanta, Manny Dober has waited until age three to show her form. In April, she breaks her maiden at Aqueduct, running the mile and seventy yards and winning by five lengths.

The Heimerles, hearing this broadcast, celebrate with a glass of white wine.

"I just upped Banknote's insurance at Fasig-Tipton to $15,000 last week," grins Chris. "Boy, if that Manny Dober would just win a few more races before the September sales, we'd be all set."

In order to break even on a yearling, the breeder has to make at least three times the stud fee. Sir Wimborne's stud fee was $3,500, so the Heimerles have to sell Banknote for $10,500 just to cover their costs. Although they believe that she is worth more than $15,000 and have nominated her for the preferred sale of yearlings at Fasig-Tipton in Kentucky, she is insured for that amount simply because that is what they can afford.

"A yearling's insurance premium is five percent of the figure it is insured for," says Gary. "You have to insure them for the amount you absolutely can't afford to lose. After all, what if you spend thousands of dollars on insurance and then the damn fool lives?"

Nomination for the preferred sale costs $100. This fee, which pays for a representative of Fasig-Tipton to inspect the yearling for certain standards of conformation and pedigree, is credited against the $150 entry fee, if the yearling is accepted. Because preselected yearlings are supposedly of a higher quality than those at the open sales, they are expected to bring a higher price, and usually do.

"We are nominating Banknote because we think she has a nice enough pedigree and she has good conformation. She's got her knees facing in the same direction as her feet and her ankles. The examiner from Fasig-Tipton, when he comes around, will look for yearlings with straight legs and no blemishes. Even if the pedigree is good, the horse won't be accepted if he has one foot pointing east and the other foot pointing west. The whole thing," sighs Chris, "is just to try to avoid any sort of accident that will raise a bump."

Out in the paddocks, the yearlings gallop wildly. They ram into each other at top speed, or they rear up onto each other's backs, while galloping, to hitch a ride. They dive and charge at each other's flying legs. By summer, the colts are so rambunctious that they must be turned out in separate paddocks to keep them from playing too hard. The fillies, more docile in their play, hang around the edge of the fence nearest the stallion paddock like bored teenagers slouching on a street corner. They chomp on the wooden fence rails and on each other, pushing and shoving to test their dominance and strength.

Banknote, now the tallest and most athletic, is the leader of her group. There is a dash of Tanta's fire in her eye, an independent toss to her head and an ease with which she shoves the other fillies out of the way. She is alert when Tanta and her new foal are turned out alone for a few hours in the stallion paddock, but there is no whinny of recognition, no sign of knowledge that one year ago she and Tanta had shared a glimmer of impending birth or death. Banknote watches the new foal, fascinated by its enthusiastic speed and sudden clumsiness. She doesn't seem certain that the bundle of legs and energy is really a horse.

"Tanta dropped another nice one, didn't she?" says Gary. "Sort of a nasty little sucker, but I don't mind seeing them nasty. Those are the ones that survive at the track."

The fillies, led by Banknote, thunder in a high-speed chase to the farthest end of the paddock, as if to prove they're just as good as that little whippersnapper. It is a peaceful afternoon on the farm; morning chores are done and there is another good hour

before it's time to put the horses up for the night.

"You know what," exclaims Chris, surveying the house, the neat barns, the fields —only two years earlier choked with weeds, now full of lazing horses—"last week somebody offered me twice as much money for Tanta as she's insured for." She leans for a rare, restful moment on the white fence post, strands of sunlight glittering through her red hair.

"You know what I told him, though," says Gary. "You can buy all the golden eggs you want, but not the goose that lays them." He laughs.

"What's that?" asks Chris, her eyes still shut to the sunlight.

"What?" says Gary.

"That noise," says Chris, sighing and opening her eyes to look around. "Oh my God, what are those fillies up to?"

The fillies are stampeding wildly and skidding into the far corner of the field. One of them, unable to stop in time, has jumped the fence. It trots jauntily but skittishly along the roadside near the white rails. In the dappled sunlight it is impossible to see which one it is. The only certainty is that the slightest movement— a passing car or a child on a bicycle—could startle it and set it running onto the nearby intersection with the highway. The Heimerles cannot even run or drive down to the fence line.

"Quick," says Chris. "I'll get Billy and Teresa." While Chris gets organized, Gary takes a lead rope and begins the long, slow creep down through the paddock to try to rescue the other fillies before they injure themselves trying to join the one on the road. The plan is to send Teresa, the farm manager, in one direction and Billy, her assistant, in the other direction. They will creep down to the road and trap the filly between them so that the only direction she can run is back up the farm's driveway, where Chris will be waiting. If Gary can catch the other fillies and bring them up to the barn, the one on the road will be encouraged to rejoin the herd.

"Oh, Jesus," mutters Chris as the filly

trots gaily into view at the bottom of the hill and skitters across the road. It is Banknote. "Where the hell is Billy? Where's Teresa? Can't they get down there any faster than that?"

Banknote, pleased by her new freedom but a bit timid, dawdles by a drainage ditch, nibbling the tops of the unchewed grass. An airplane roars overhead and she hops to attention. Gary sidles cautiously down to the three excited fillies and manages to grasp two of their halters. The third filly follows as he leads her playmates toward the barn, but Banknote, bred for her independent spirit, doesn't budge.

Horses are predisposed to self-destruction. They do not consider the consequences of their actions. Although they have excellent memories, they fear the unfamiliar. When afraid, they will run from that fear, even if it means running into something else.

As Banknote stands on the road, squinting at her playmates, a pickup truck on its way to the highway rolls toward her. Billy and Teresa have reached the road now. Teresa gets the driver to stop the truck. Billy steps, in slow motion, toward the filly. Her shadow wavers, black and startled, on the pavement. A sudden noise from behind right now, and she will run right through Billy and out to the highway. The noise comes. It is not the sound of cars, but the sound of her friends' hoofbeats from the top of the driveway. She snorts once at the truck's fender, glances at Billy, then jogs up the hill to Chris.

"Easy. Easy," mumbles Chris, almost as much to herself as to Banknote, when she gets hold of the halter. "Let's put them all in for the night now, anyway," she says to Gary.

"Yeah. Then at least we won't have to worry about them until tomorrow."

Banknote, breathing heavily with excitement, follows her friends into the yearling stalls.

Perhaps, if the truck hadn't come, she would have gone back to the barn anyway. Perhaps, if Gary hadn't shifted the other fillies onto the driveway at just that mo-ment, beckoning her with their herd noises, she would have ended her life on the hood of someone's car in the middle of the highway intersection. Perhaps, if she hadn't been the strongest and most courageous of her group, she wouldn't have been the one that got out. The same qualities that predispose a horse to self-destruction predispose it to race, to win.

As the days get longer and hotter, Banknote and the other yearlings spend their days in the cool of the yearling barn. Some yearlings, at other farms, are "shed raised" —left in a large field with a shed for shelter and communal feeding. Banknote, though, stays neat, blemish- and fly-free, in her private stall in the coed equine dormitory. Fortunately for the Heimerles, she did not raise a bump or a blemish during her excursion on the road. Now it is midsummer and her only exercise time is a few hours each dark, lake-scented evening.

"We are raising a salable commodity," says Gary, leading Banknote out into the aisle. "If we leave the yearlings outside, they won't be as big and fat by sale time. Some people say shed-raising is better because it makes them tougher, but if you bring them in every day, you raise each horse as an individual. We can see if they are hurt. We know how much each one is eating and what its manure looks like."

Banknote leads quietly now, following her handler wherever he asks her to go. She has had lessons in the Chiffney bit, a special leading bit designed to attach to her halter. She has learned to respect the tug of metal against her gums, to stop and stand on cue, to trust and obey the signals of the person next to her the way she once trusted and obeyed Tanta's brusque commands.

Gary places her in the center of the aisle and snaps ropes to either side of her halter. She stands calmly in the "cross-ties" to be groomed.

"In the beginning, we start playing with them and rubbing them in the stall," says Gary, watching Billy brush Banknote's coat to a glossy sheen. "While they're eating is a good time. Later, we put them on a lead shank and introduce them to the different brushes, one at a time. They are groomed for about fifteen minutes once or twice a day. It's hard work, too, isn't it?" he says to Billy, who groans. "The guy who is rubbing on the horse has to exert some pressure to bring up the oils in the skin. If he's doing it right, by the end, he's going to be sweating." Banknote, slightly bored, nibbles at the cross-tie ropes.

"The worst thing that can happen to you when you get to the sale is to get a horse that won't go back into its stall," says Chris, stooping down to paint Banknote's hooves with her own homemade hoof dressing. This application of a concoction of pine tar and peanut oil, a thrice-weekly ritual, helps keep the filly's hooves moist and accustoms her to having them painted as they will be for the sale. "You can't have it out with the horse right there in front of the buyers," Chris continues. "You have to train the horse so that when you cluck, he knows he'll get crucified if he doesn't go back into the stall."

"We try to trick them into socially acceptable behavior," explains Gary, "not force them to do something for twenty or twenty-five minutes and get into an argument. We try to take the terror out of things for the young horses and socialize them so that they don't flip out and gash their heads open or try to kill you out of fear or disobedience."

"By the end, it gets to the point where even if they do misbehave, you don't dare hit them because they might freak out and raise a bump or a blemish on themselves,"

Chris adds with the sigh of someone who's been there before. "This is the sales crop. This is what it's all about. This is what you stayed up all night for and worried about the runny nose, the scrape on the leg, the somersault when he ran to the gate and you hoped he didn't break his back. Every horse here is worth at least ten to thirty thousand dollars. As September approaches, everything is low-key, but very intense."

Before actually going to the sale, Banknote will learn to "load" (walk into the horse van) and will be driven for short rides away from the farm with the other yearlings. Six weeks before the sale, she will get her first light shoes. By the time she gets her sale set, she will be used to having metal tacked to her feet. The repeated lessons, walking briskly and standing at attention on the Chiffney bit, will help her to show off her almost perfect conformation to best advantage under the auctioneer's spotlights.

Now, on this late June day, she stands stamping her foot impatiently in the aisle to shake off a fly and flares her huge nostrils to the sweet smell of clover wafting in from the hills. Her youth is practically over, but in this moment she is innocent, unaware of the life of bone-splitting stress and driving competition that lies before her. Coat burnished, young muscles flexing with untested speed, she still has time before she is called upon to show the world whether she will live up to the promise of her conformation and regal bloodlines, or simply be another also-ran.

# At the Sale

On the morning of September 1, Banknote is loaded into the horse van. For sixty days she has been groomed and polished. The crest of her neck and her prominent, sloping shoulder blades reflect the early light. Although her pedigree has only been rated a "4" on the inspection scale, due mainly to Tanta's South American lineage and the fact that Sir Wimborne is an unproven sire, her well-balanced and nearly perfectly proportioned conformation was given the scale's highest mark, a "10." Unfortunately, neither pedigree nor conformation of the highest standard can guarantee success on the racetrack. It is the purpose of "selected" and the slightly less prestigious "preferred" sales, such as the one Banknote is headed for, to even the odds for buyers who are the true gamblers of the racing world. Statistically, well-bred, well-built horses perform more commendably than ill-bred, poorly formed horses. However, there is no scale by which to predict the will to win. Even the practiced Fasig-Tipton inspectors cannot look into a horse's heart.

Banknote is boisterous, as always. Her new shoes clank on the driveway, thud on the rubber ramp. With Gary at her side, she lunges anxiously into the dark trailer. What matters to her now is being first, and she doesn't bother to take a last look at the fields and barns she will never see again. Once inside, she passes manure, as all horses do upon entering a trailer, then spreads her feet and braces herself for the long ride to Kentucky. For a while, she nibbles at hay or drowses to the rhythm of the tires vibrating up through her legs. Tied safely in her narrow compartment, she knows that this ride is longer, something is different. For the next full year of her life, every day will be a surprise.

Up in the cab, Chris and Gary are restless.

"Your horse must appear perfect in Kentucky," says Chris. "You can have the most perfect horse in the world, but if it's too small, some people won't buy it. Some people look for bone. Some people like to see white on a horse's legs and some people don't. All day there will be people coming around to inspect the yearlings they've marked down in the Fasig-Tipton sales catalog. We'll be sitting in our Scargo Farm director's chairs, smiling. By the end of the day, you're so sore from smiling, your whole face aches."

Late in the night, Banknote arrives in Lexington and enthusiastically scents her first whiffs of the famous bluegrass. The van wends down Paris Pike, past the Normandy Farm of E. Barry Ryan, past Spendthrift Farms, where generations of Combses have raised generations of Nashuas and Raise a Natives, past Greentree and Elmendorf and Gainesway, where Lyphard, Riverman, Vaguely Noble and other stallions of international repute live in a style known only to Arab sheiks and reigning Thoroughbred studs. Here the climate is temperate, the soil soft and springy under the hoof, the sweet grass and water enriched by the deep limestone and mineral base. Here humanity and geology are united in their celebration of equine supremacy. Lexington is one town in which there are more monuments to horses than there are to people. Kentucky is as close to heaven as most Thoroughbreds ever get.

The van turns into Fasig-Tipton's Newtown Paddocks, where Banknote and 385 other yearlings are bedded for the night in assigned stalls, equipped with pedigree cards and hip number notations. Banknote's card tells that she is by Sir Wimborne and out of Tanta Prisa by *Pronto. (The asterisk indicates that Pronto was a foreign horse.) The hip number, which will be pasted to Banknote's haunch before she goes into the sales ring, is the catalog number given her by Fasig-Tipton, the largest auctioneer, by volume, of Thoroughbreds in the United States. Hip numbers, which designate the order of sale, are given out randomly so that all of the most desirable animals will not come to the block in a clump.

Banknote does not know that she is stabled with some of the potential champions of her generation. Her fuzzy black nostrils wrinkle and squeal petulantly at six the next morning when she spies Chris and Gary hustling down the barn aisle to muck out her stall. All manure must be dumped into burlap sacks for removal from this pristine yearling motel. Fasig-Tipton provides the bedding, but the Heimerles have brought along their own buckets, feed, and stall screens painted in Scargo's colors: beige, white and dark brown.

Dressed in their farm colors throughout the sale, Chris and Gary spend hour after hour smiling, leading Banknote out of the stall, "setting her up" at attention for people's inspection, talking to buyers, smiling and smiling more. Although she is not the best-bred yearling in the sale, Banknote attracts attention because of her size, her bright chestnut color and her straight, unblemished legs.

Strange people mill all around her: fat men with large hats, rumpling papers and smelling of cigars; laughing women in larger straw hats; and other men who just walk up to her stall door and squint. She eyes them nervously, but her good manners prevail and she manages to handle herself well in public, standing tall and neither kicking out nor struggling against the lead rope. Some people mark her page in the catalog. Others just stand in front of her and look at her legs, then walk behind her and look at her legs, make a mental note and walk on down to the next yearling waiting to be inspected.

"Nice-looking filly," says one man to Chris. "A Sir Wimborne, eh?"

"Yes," smiles Chris. "She's got her daddy's eye and head."

"Nice-looking filly," he says again. "Thanks."

"Thank you," she smiles after him. "Why doesn't he just buy her?" she whispers to Gary after the man has left. They stay by the stalls until 9 P.M.

The next day is the most trying. This is sales day. Chris and Gary spend the morning getting Banknote ready because, as Chris puts it, "You've got to show off your horse to the best advantage. It's got to be shiny, healthy and in good flesh."

Banknote's mane, which was pulled (thinned out) to a length of six inches, is touched up. Her feet are painted with Chris's special hoof dressing and then wiped with a rag so her feet look natural, "like a horse that's been out in the grass playing." Chris insists that all of her crop look like "normal horses." Some of the other yearlings have braided manes or hooves painted an artificial-looking black.

When the fifth horse ahead of Banknote is called into the sales arena, Chris and Gary take Banknote up to join the four other horses in the walking ring. Fasig-Tipton employees in white coats communicate by walkie-talkie, preparing to lead the next yearling down the chute and into the enclosed amphitheater where the buyers sit and the auctioneer chants furiously from a tall wooden podium, reiterating the horse's good points and minimizing the bad ones to sell his wares. Fasig-Tipton receives 5 percent of the purchase price of each horse sold. The owners may "put a reserve" on the horse, which means that they may set a figure below which they will not sell it. Owners are encouraged to keep their reserves within reason, however, because Fasig-Tipton charges a fee for its services if the horse goes home unsold.

Banknote has settled easily into the walking ring. Her number is called and a man in a white coat comes over to lead her into the spotlights of the small sales ring. At the end of the chute the auctioneer's gavel is pounding out the sale of the previous yearling.

"Come on, kid," says Gary, giving her one last rub on the nostrils. "I know you can do it."

Without a backward glance, she perks up her ears and follows the strange man in white down the chute and onto a circle of green carpet in the center of a large amphitheater. Hot white spotlights pour down on her through the atmosphere heavy with cigarette smoke and human want. High above, in the podium behind her, sit auctioneer Ralph Retler and announcer John M. S. Finney, who is also the president of Fasig-Tipton. Just as good Thoroughbreds usually come from good running families, top humans in the racing business are often bred to their work. John Finney is the son of Humphrey Finney, the man who brought showmanship to horse peddling and who put Fasig-Tipton on the map. Great auctioneers generally come from auctioneering families. Retler is one of the exceptions; he trained for the job after having worked in other areas of the horse business.

"Hip number three forty-five," shouts Retler, pounding his gavel on the podium and startling Banknote, who lunges toward the front-row seats.

"This chestnut filly, property of Scargo Farm," intones John Finney in his booming, ecclesiastical voice, "is half-sister to winner Manny Dober, out of a winning daughter of *Pronto, he a stakes winner in Argentina and three times leading sire in Argentina. On her top line, she is by the good young son of Sir Ivor, Sir Wimborne, a stakes winner of three races in England and Ireland. His first crop are two-year-olds of 1980 and he is the sire of the stakes-winning filly, Genuine Regret, who came in first in yesterday's Mohawk Stakes at Belmont Park in New York. Let me remind you, ladies and gentlemen, that this filly is a registered New York bred and eligible for the generous awards of the New York State program."

The gavel in Ralph Retler's hand beats quick rhythms on the podium as he picks up the auctioneer's chant.

"An whadoihear, whadoihear, whadoihear, bevita, bevita, bevita, bevita. Doihear a five, five, five, five, doihear a ten, ten. Five ten five ten FIVE. Whoillgotahseven. Seven, ten, seven, ten, bevita, bevita, bevita."

Banknote, excited by the hammered-out rhythms, kicks out at the wooden podium nervously, but the striking of her hoof is barely audible above the hypnotic mumbo-jumbo of the sales pitch.

Chanting as a method of auctioneering is a particularly American custom and was originated around the turn of the century

---

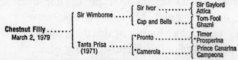

**Hip No.** Property of Scargo Farm     **Barn 10G**
**345**     **Chestnut Filly**

Half-sister to winner Manny Dober (at 3, 1980, $19,552). Out of winning half-sister to Bite The Bullet (12 wins, $59,796), Cameronia (dam of CALVADOS). Second dam *CAMEROLA, sister to Canela Fina (dam of FLEUR SEVEN), half-sister to *CORVETTE II, etc.

| | | | |
|---|---|---|---|
| | | Sir Ivor .......... | Sir Gaylord / Attica |
| | Sir Wimborne ..... | | |
| Chestnut Filly....... | | Cap and Bells ..... | Tom-Fool / Ghazni |
| March 2, 1979 | | *Pronto ............ | Timor / *Prosperina |
| | Tanta Prisa ...... | | |
| | (1971) | *Camerola ......... | Prince Canarina / Campeona |

By SIR WIMBORNE (1973), stakes winner of 3 races in 3 starts in England and Ireland, Royal Lodge S.-G II, National S.-G II. Brother to stakes winner Lady Capulet. His first foals are 2-year-olds of 1980. Sire of Sir Ivor, horse of the year.

**1st dam**
TANTA PRISA, by *Pronto. 3 wins at 3 and 4, $13,875. This is her second foal. Dam of—
  Manny Dober (f. by Native Heritage). Winner at 3, 1980, $19,552.

**2nd dam**
*CAMEROLA, by *Prince Canarina. 5 wins at 4 and 5 in Argentina, Premio Gran Bretana at San Isidro, 3rd Premio Antonio Cane at La Plata; 2 wins at 6, $13,850 in U. S. Dam of—
  Bite the Bullet. 12 wins, 3 to 6, $59,796.
  Cameronia. Unraced. Dam of—
    CALVADOS. 7 wins, 2 to 5, 1979 in South Africa, Smirnoff Plate, Administrators Champion Juvenile S., Durban Merchants H., 2nd Somerset Plate, Summerveld S., Cape of Good Hope Nursery S., 3rd Breeders' Challenge S., Newbury Chairman's S.

**3rd dam**
CAMPEONA, by Filon. Winner at 3 in Argentina. Half-sister to Coquimbo, Catalan, Clamoreo. Dam of 7 foals to race, all winners, including—
  *CORVETTE II. 13 wins, 2 to 5 in Argentina, Premio General Francisco B. Bosch, 2nd Polla de Potrancas, 3rd Premio Republica de Venezuela, Premio Miguel Angel y Thomas Juarez Celman, all at San Isidro, La Plata and Mendoza. Producer. Granddam of COULISSE (5 wins, $29,380, Tattling H.).
  CAIO DUILIO. 5 wins at 3 and 4 in Argentina, Premio Pretexto, Premio Dart, 2nd Premio Provincia de Buenos Aires, 3rd Premio General Jose de San Martin, Premio Asociacion Bonaerense de Propietarios de Caballos de Cerrera, etc. all at La Plata.
  *CAMEROLA. Stakes winner, see above.
  Fay Crocker. Winner at 3, 2nd Premio Seleccion at La Plata. Producer.
  Canela Fina. Winner at 2, 3 and 4 in England. Dam of FLEUR SEVEN (Dansks Oaks, Mowerinalob in Denmark).

7/80

by the Bain brothers of Bourbon, Kentucky. Their father preached as a temperance lecturer, so they combined his style with the country wit and singsong chants of bluegrass tobacco and livestock auctioneers and introduced it to the slightly more refined circle of the Thoroughbred sales ring. The famed team of auctioneer George Swineboard and announcer Humphrey Finney perfected this technique to such a degree that, during the Forties, they were known for being able to empty every wallet in the sales pavilion faster than a band of pickpockets. Swineboard not only chanted, he bullied and joked with potential buyers, playing their egos against their insecurities.

"If you've got a hundred thousand dollars to spend, stay right where you are," he might boom down arrogantly as a particularly choice animal was led into the arena. "Otherwise, get the hell out of the way." If the bidding lagged and it appeared that the horse would sell for less than it was worth, he might prod with, "Now, look aheah boys, you can't take it with you. Are you gonna let this little lady steal a Nashua colt right out from under your noses?"

Using this aggressive and personalized mode of auctioneering, Fasig-Tipton managed to convert what was once a buyer's into a seller's market and to accelerate the pace at which horses were sold from three or four to eighteen per hour. In the Eighties, yearlings sell at an average rate of twenty-five per hour and for an average price of $19,318, except in the select summer sales at Keeneland and Saratoga, where the average leaps as high as $160,427. With the expansion of today's market, auctioneers do not have Swineboard and Finney's advantage of knowing each of the bidders personally. They must tailor their style to the pulse of a changing market filled with new faces.

"Doihear a twelve, twelve, twelve, twelve, twelve, twelve, twelve . . ." Retler pipes on, as Banknote flinches nervously under the startling lights. Chris and Gary watch from far away, afraid to breathe, afraid to move for fear of jinxing anything. "FIFTEEN. Willyahgive a seventeen, eighteen, seventeen. SEVENTEEN. EIGHTEEN. NINETEEN. TWENTY. Twenty, twenty, twenty, twenty, twenty, twen-tee. SOLD. For twenty thousand dollars."

"Hip ⚹346," shouts Retler as Banknote is led out of the ring and replaced by another young Thoroughbred. "This bay colt," pontificates John Finney, "half-brother to winner Willie's Aatlas, out of winner Tax Credit, second dam the winner Easy Credit, she a full sister to the stakes-winning Donut King . . ." Chris and Gary, standing at the end of one of the long rows of seats, barely hear him.

"She did it, she did it," mutters Gary through his grin, for Banknote has brought exactly the price they had hoped for.

"Banknote. Banknote's gone. My baby's gone," sobs Chris, relieved that the filly has sold, but still unable to hold back a few motherly tears. "We'll never see her again."

"Oh, Jesus," says Gary, guiding her out into the daylight. "It's just a horse."

After a brief celebration, they are driving on the long road back toward Scargo Farm, where the people toil, the horses laze, and the dogs drink Coke with Bourbon. Somewhere, in the musty twilight of a horse van, Banknote braces her legs against the vibrations of an unfamiliar highway and hurtles closer to her destiny—a training farm and then the racetrack.

# Section 2

# Conformation

*"In the matter of judging the conformation of a prospective racehorse, it must be remembered that it is the judge, rather than the horse, who is on trial. The speed of a horse is not likely to be affected in the least by the opinion of a man who walked around him once or twice."*

—The Blood-Horse

# The Ideal Running Machine

**Areas of A Horse**

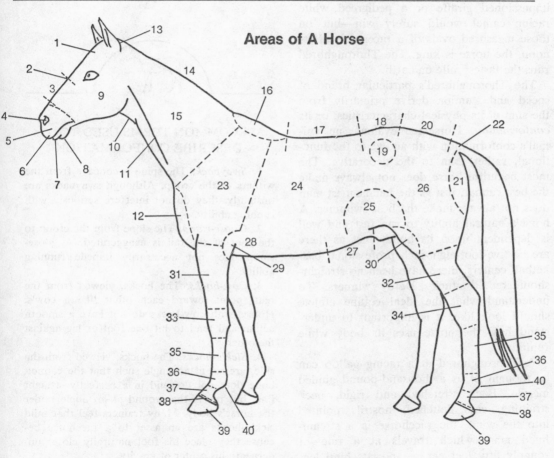

| | | | |
|---|---|---|---|
| 1 Forehead | 11 Jugular Groove | 21 Buttock | 31 Forearm |
| 2 Center of Face | 12 Point of Shoulder | 22 Root of Tail | 32 Gaskin |
| 3 Bridge of Nose | 13 Poll | 23 Shoulder | 33 Knee |
| 4 Nostril | 14 Crest | 24 Barrel | 34 Hock |
| 5 Muzzle | 15 Neck | 25 Flank | 35 Cannon |
| 6 Upper Lip | 16 Withers | 26 Thigh | 36 Ankle |
| 7 Lower Lip | 17 Back | 27 Abdomen | 37 Pastern |
| 8 Under Lip | 18 Loin | 28 Girth | 38 Coronet |
| 9 Cheek | 19 Point of Hip | 29 Elbow | 39 Hoof |
| 10 Throat Latch | 20 Rump | 30 Stifle | 40 Fetlock |

The Thoroughbred is the consummate professional runner of the animal kingdom. As fleet as the lightweight jackrabbit, a good Thoroughbred at the top of its form can outsprint a greyhound at the quarter-mile, becomes an unsporting match for the cheetah at three-eighths of a mile, and will leave even the most determined ostrich stretching its neck out in vain at the three-quarter marker. It can accomplish all this despite the 125-pound handicap of rider and tack. At distances of ten miles or more, an impassioned giraffe or a pedigreed white racing camel would surely win—but on those measured ovals of a racegoer's afternoon, the horse is king. The Thoroughbred runs the fastest mile on earth.

The Thoroughbred's particular brand of speed and stamina derive primarily from the sum of its physical characteristics, or its *conformation*. Horsemen evaluate an animal's conformation with an eye to the functional, rather than to the decorative. The most beautiful horse does not always make the best runner, just as the handsomest man does not always make the best swimmer. A horse's natural ability to run fast and well is dependent upon its build. Just as there are no five-foot-eight-inch professional basketball centers, there have been no straight-shouldered Kentucky Derby winners. To understand what the ideal equine athlete should look like, it is important to understand how the horse uses its body while running.

A Thoroughbred at a racing gallop can be thought of as a thousand-pound guided missile. Back stretched and rigid, neck straining, ears flattened, nostrils pointed into the wind, the racehorse is a streamlined mass which travels at a rate of roughly fifty feet per second. Its hind legs push against the ground to propel the missile forward. Its front legs follow through, reaching out to carry the momentum onward and pitch it into the air. The head and neck provide the balance, swinging forward, then back to prevent momentum from sending the horse head over heels. The heart and lungs provide the fuel needed to resist fatigue and fight to the finish line.

Mechanically, then, the fastest horse is the one which can run straightest, push hardest, reach out farthest, balance with the least effort, and last the longest. Judging conformation is simply a question of recognizing which physical characteristics work best together to make the ideal equine running machine.

## COMMON TERMS USED TO DESCRIBE CONFORMATION

1. *Swayback:* The spine is concave from the withers to the croup. Although swaybacks are unsightly, they do not interfere seriously with running ability.

2. *Goose-rump:* The slope from the croup to the root of the tail is exaggerated. A goose-rump does not necessarily impede running ability.

3. *Cow-hocks:* The hocks, viewed from the rear, point toward each other like a cow's. Horses with cow-hocks do not have a smooth action and tend to hit one foot or leg against the other.

4. *Sickle-hocks:* The hocks, viewed from the side, are set at an angle such that the cannon bone does not descend in a perfectly straight line, but meets the ground at an angle under the horse's body. Many trainers feel that mild sickle-hocks are an asset to a racehorse because they place his foot naturally closer underneath his center of gravity.

On the other hand, hocks which place the line of the cannon bone out behind the point of buttock are considered undesirable because they prevent the horse from getting his hind legs under his center of gravity sufficiently.

5. *Back at the knee (calf-kneed):* There is a concave line from the forearm to the fetlock joint. Undue strain is thrown onto the tendons and the horse is unable to extend the leg properly.

6. *Over at the knee:* The knee is, or seems, permanently bent forward. Although not ideal, this sort of conformation tends to relieve strain from the tendons and does not necessarily interfere with the horse's usefulness.

7. *Tied in below the knee:* The leg looks pinched in behind the knee joint, indicating weak tendons and poor bone.

8. *Toe-in conformation:* The horse is pigeon-toed and may have a tendency to stumble.

9. *Toe-out conformation:* The horse is duck-footed and probably lacks speed due to an unbalanced gait.

10. *Ewe-neck:* The top line of the neck is concave. A ewe-neck does not interfere with running ability.

11. *Close-coupled:* The horse has a short back and his ribs extend close to his loins. Sprinters, like Quarter Horses, are usually close-coupled.

12. *Slab-sided:* The ribs are flat, as opposed to well sprung and rounded. Flat ribs indicate restricted room for the heart and lungs, and thus diminished endurance.

13. *Roman nose:* The head, viewed from the side, is convex, indicating draft ancestry.

14. *Dish-faced:* The head, viewed from the side, is concave, emphasizing Arab ancestry.

15. *Pig-eyed:* The eye is small and round. Pig-eyed horses have a reputation for stubbornness.

## THE BACK

The construction of an ideal racehorse begins with a good, strong back. The back is the roof beam for the rib cage, which houses the vital organs. It is also the driveshaft which unites the front and hind ends, and through which the energy is transferred from rear to front.

To gallop, the horse stiffens its spine and propels itself forward with its long hind

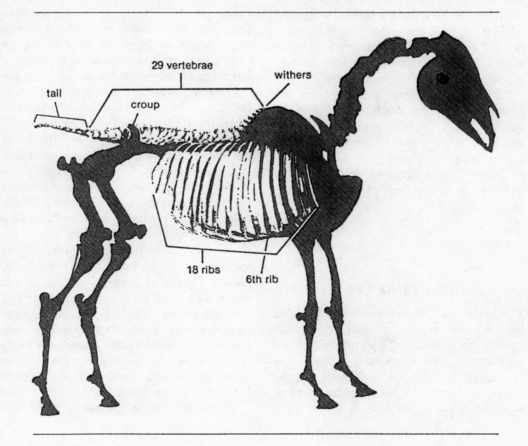

legs and strong rear muscles. To run fast, a horse should have a relatively short back. A short back is easier to keep straight and rigid than a long one. A horse can't attain very efficient forward propulsion if it is thrown off balance at every step by a spine that wobbles up and down or back and forth like a wet noodle. A horse that wastes motion wobbling tires more easily than the horse which can propel its energy along the shortest distance from rear to front, a straight line.

A relatively short back is important for a second reason. The horse's center of gravity is right behind its heart, exactly between its two sixth ribs. To run its fastest, the horse has to be able to swing its hind legs far enough forward to hit the ground well underneath the center of gravity. The horse that has trouble "getting its hind legs underneath him" has a hard time transferring its energy properly from rear to front. For this reason, the horse's length (which is measured from the point of the shoulder to the point of the buttock) should be shorter than its height at the withers and the croup. A back (and therefore, a length) which is short in proportion to the length of the legs means longer, more efficient strides.

Finally, a horseman wouldn't want an animal that has "too much room behind the saddle." More distance than the width of one hand between the last rib and the flank means "weak loins" and a "strung out" way of going. The purpose of the back is to unite the front and hind ends, not to push them apart.

## THE HIND LEG

The horse has "rear-wheel drive." Its hind legs are its engine, pushing downward against the ground and upward against the backbone to drive the animal forward. The two major parts of the hind limb are the *upper leg,* formed by the hipbone (running from the point of the buttock to the stifle joint) and the gaskin (running from the stifle joint to the hock), and the *lower leg,* formed by the cannon bone, the fetlock joint, the pastern bone, and the hoof.

Although a prima ballerina lacing the ribbons of her toe shoes around her dainty ankles might scorn the thought, a racehorse is basically a thousand-pound ballet dancer. It runs on its toes, just as she does, and although she might insist on a slight difference in their derrieres, both move their legs in nearly the same way. If you want to know how a horse moves its hind legs, imagine that you're that ballerina. Swing your leg forward, straighten it, and let your toes fall to the floor in front of you as far as they can reach. Then bend your knee, thrust your weight forward, push down on the balls of your foot, spring up off your toes, and straighten your leg out behind you. The horse swings its hind legs and springs off its toes in much the same way.

Just as few good ballerinas are short and stocky, so, too, few good racehorses have short leg bones between hock and hip. Stride length is dependent, first of all, on long, strong gaskins. Secondly, to ensure a full range of movement for the hind leg, the "angles of power" should be wide. That is, the wider the angle at which the hipbone meets the thighbone and at which the gaskin meets the hock, the farther the horse can swing its hind feet forward underneath its center of gravity.

The horse has one huge advantage over the human runner and the ballerina, which helps account for its superior swiftness. Instead of sneakers or silk toe shoes, the horse has elongated feet which act as springs. From the hock to the hoof, the horse's leg contains the bones found between the human ankle and the first joint of the middle toe. The leg has no muscles from the hock down. Rather, several long tendons, like giant rubber bands, run along the back of the hock joint, the cannon bone, the fetlock joint and the pastern bone, then attach to the foot.

When the horse pushes against the

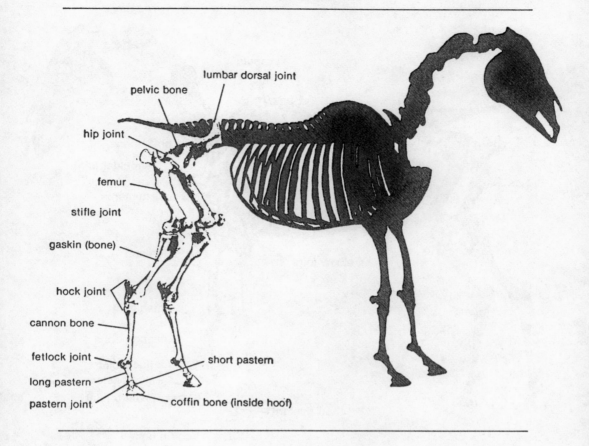

lumbar dorsal joint
pelvic bone
hip joint
femur
stifle joint
gaskin (bone)
hock joint
cannon bone
fetlock joint
long pastern
pastern joint
short pastern
coffin bone (inside hoof)

ground, he drives his gaskin down into his hock joint and his cannon bone down into his fetlock joint. As these joints bend, the leg bones cock the tendons in the same way that the tip of a pencil, in the hands of a schoolboy, might be used to cock a rubber band. As the horse's weight is pushed over the top of the leg, the bones align and the joints straighten, releasing their tension on the tendons in the same way that fingers let go of a rubber band. The tendons act as a slingshot against the horse's leg bones. The pencil shoots forward, and so does the horse.

To create the maximum cocking action, the lower leg should be straight (so straight that a plumb line could be dropped from the point of the buttock through the point of the hock to the fetlock joint). The hocks should be "low to the ground" and the cannon bones short in relation to the rest of the leg. The function of the cannon bone is to help cock the slingshot, but it is the thigh and the gaskin that reach forward to extend the leg and push down on it.

## THE FORELEG

The forelegs are the reachers. They stretch out to catch the momentum provided by the hind legs and swing the horse into the air. The major parts of the foreleg are the shoulder (running from the withers to the point of the shoulder); the upper arm (running from the point of the shoulder to the elbow); the forearm (running from the elbow to the knee joint); and the lower leg (which corresponds to the lower hind leg).

A horse can have the best pushing ability

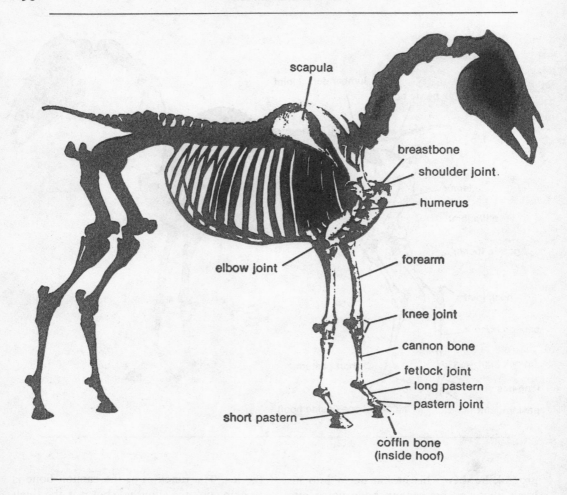

scapula

breastbone

shoulder joint

humerus

forearm

elbow joint

knee joint

cannon bone

fetlock joint

long pastern

pastern joint

short pastern

coffin bone
(inside hoof)

in the world, but if its forearms are short or its shoulders straight, it won't be able to move very fast. With a sloping shoulder and long, strong upper arms and forearms, the horse can reach out far in front of it and push down hard against the ground. Ideally, the slope of the shoulder from the withers to the point of the shoulder should be forty-five degrees.

As a horse tires, it tires in its forelimbs first. One reason is that, due to the added bulk of its head and neck, it carries about 60 percent of its weight on its front legs. In addition, its front legs have only one "slingshot" instead of two—the knee is straight, not providing the powerful bending and cocking action of the angle of the hock. Thus the forearms need to be strong

and muscular to keep pushing the horse into the air.

From the knee down, the front leg is similar to the hind leg, but it has to bear more concussion and thus is more prone to injury. To withstand the 22,800 inch-pounds applied to the front leg in each stride, the horse must have straight knees, strong tendons and "good bone." A knee that is not straight, either back to front or side to side, will cause undue stress on tendons and ligaments, producing much the same kind of knee injury human athletes suffer. The tendons have to be strong enough to absorb 85 percent of the force applied to the leg and return 80 percent of it in the "slingshot" effect. "Good bone" refers to the circumference and density of the cannon bone, which, if too thin or soft, tends to crack or develop calcium deposits (splints) under stress. Light-boned horses are also prone to develop "bowed" tendons, a tendon which bulges out behind the line of the leg and thus can't be fully stretched to produce the proper slingshot effect.

## BALANCE BETWEEN REAR AND FRONT

More than any individual quality, a horse must be well balanced from rear to front. Too much of one quality cannot compensate for a deficiency in the other. If the push is too powerful for the reach, the horse will have to slow down to keep from falling on its nose. If its push is less powerful than its reach, it will not have the power to keep moving at high speed. Thus, a horse has to have a shoulder angle that complements the angle of its hips, and a height at the withers that is about the same as the height of the croup. The horse is thus well balanced, with the front legs reaching out at the same angle and distance as the hind legs can push.

## MUSCLES

The Thoroughbred is the horse kingdom's middle-distance runner. To excel at distances from three-quarters of a mile to two miles, it must have the proper combination of two kinds of muscles. Short, bunchy muscles provide power at the expense of endurance, because they use blood more quickly. A Quarter Horse has blinding speed for a quarter-mile because it primarily has these strong, quickly contracting muscles.

An Arabian horse, on the other hand, has long, flat muscles designed to sustain a swinging rhythm over long distances. The Arab takes a long time to get up to top speed, but it relies on reach and inertia to maintain its stride for up to one-hundred-mile rides.

The Thoroughbred has a combination of these two kinds of muscles. The power is in the rear. The hindquarters should be so heavily muscled that the horse's hind legs touch underneath its tail. Bulging muscles in the shoulder, on the other hand, mean only extra "lumber" to carry, and muscle-bound joints that obstruct the ability to reach. Just as a missile is streamlined in front, so should a horse be.

## THE FOOT

Horsemen often remark, "no foot, no horse." This is because when a horse pounds down on its foot at a racing gallop, it's applying 3,420 inch-pounds of energy to a weight-bearing surface about the size of a human hand.

The foot is really the horse's toe. It is specially designed to absorb shock and provide traction. The two toe bones—the short pastern and the coffin bone—are wrapped in a covering of skin, blood vessels and nerves (the sensitive foot). This entire package is coated with the purple-black horn of the hoof, which protects it like a wrap-around toenail, and it is cushioned by the callus-like fibers of the heel and frog.

If you look at the print left by a horse's foot, you will see an imprint that looks as if someone tried to push a heart into the open end of a horseshoe. The rounded parts of the heart are the bulbs of the horse's heels, the wedge is the frog, and the horseshoe shape is the wall of the hoof.

When a horse's foot contacts the ground, the heart-shaped frog acts as a cushion, expanding and pushing outward, causing the walls of the hoof to widen about one-twentieth of an inch. Inside the foot, six hundred primary tissues and seventy-two hundred secondary layers are compacted. Due to the delicate interlocking of this tissue, the relatively tiny, sensitive foot distributes the impact of the horse's weight over an area equivalent to eight square feet.

As the horse's weight passes over the top of its leg, the weight-bearing surface moves forward from heel to toe. The sole, which is domed, digs into the dirt to help the horse push off. As the leg rises, the whole foot

contracts to its original size. Because the horse has no valves in the veins of its feet, the expansion and contraction of the foot not only help absorb the shock, they also pump the blood back up the leg.

The angle at which the pastern bone meets the hoof is vital in the shock-absorbing process. An angle of forty-five degrees —the same angle at which the withers meets the shoulder—is desirable. If the pas-

DRAWINGS BY PATRICIA GREENE

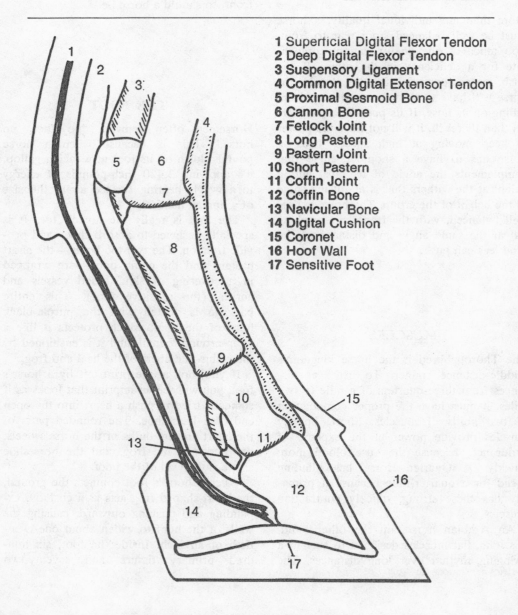

1 Superficial Digital Flexor Tendon
2 Deep Digital Flexor Tendon
3 Suspensory Ligament
4 Common Digital Extensor Tendon
5 Proximal Sesmoid Bone
6 Cannon Bone
7 Fetlock Joint
8 Long Pastern
9 Pastern Joint
10 Short Pastern
11 Coffin Joint
12 Coffin Bone
13 Navicular Bone
14 Digital Cushion
15 Coronet
16 Hoof Wall
17 Sensitive Foot

# Underside of Hoof

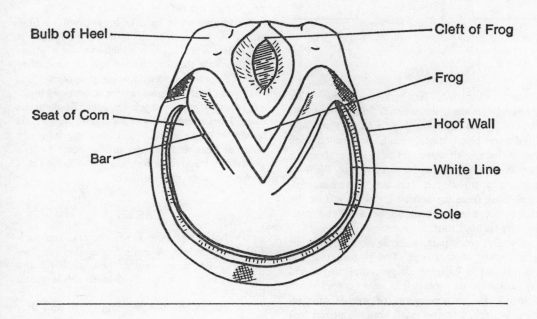

Bulb of Heel — Cleft of Frog — Frog — Seat of Corn — Hoof Wall — Bar — White Line — Sole

tern angle is too upright, the horse's toe bone is driven into the ground and the shock of landing is directed to the cannon bone and the knee, rather than to the tendons and the tissue layers of the hoof. If the pastern angle is too sloping, the cannon bone may drive the fetlock joint all the way into the ground, straining the tendons or causing a compound fracture of the sesmoid bones (the bones of the fetlock joint). Such sesmoid fractures are twice as common as any other racing fracture; it was this injury that caused the destruction of the great racing filly Ruffian.

## HEAD AND NECK

Ever since 1937, when the New York Racing Association declared that horses officially win by touching their noses to the finish line (to end arguments about outstretched feet), a long, slender neck has been an asset to a horse. But the most important function of the horse's head and neck is to balance its forward movement and keep it from somersaulting down the track.

Together, the head and neck weigh between fifty and seventy pounds. As the horse pushes off with its hind legs, the head and neck dive forward, streamlining the body and encouraging forward momentum. The head continues to descend until the front legs strike the ground, thus carrying the weight of the horse forward to its farthest point of balance and lightening the load borne by the forelegs at the moment of impact. As the front legs pitch the horse on into the air, the head and neck swing up and back, tilting the horse's weight back toward its haunches in preparation for the next push of the hind legs.

The head and neck rise and fall from four to ten inches each stride, about 240 times in a mile. A long neck encourages longer strides; a short neck means shorter strides and a tendency to tire over a distance. A heavy head is not only "common" to look at, but it drags a horse down in front like a lead weight.

## VISION

A horse, like a bird, has eyes on the side of its head. It can see a wide visual field (about 340 degrees) with some overlap in front, but has a 20-degree blind spot behind. Its eyeballs are twice the size of ours and it can see about as far as we do: several hundred yards. Without moving a muscle, it can see something approaching from far behind it on the left or the right, but it must turn its head sideways to look at its hind foot.

For the most part, a horse sees a different picture out of each eye. The picture plane it sees is flat collage of shapes, undistinguished by solidity or color (it sees colors only faintly). Depth perception, or stereoscopic vision, is limited to the small area about ten feet in front of the horse's face, where its two separate visual fields converge and begin to overlap.

With its head in the grazing position, the horse has the widest visual range and the least depth perception. Because its most acute visual quality is the perception of movement in the flat picture plane, this stance was ideal for the perception of predators slinking across the landscape. To this day, a horse will instinctively shy or run from the sudden movement of an unfamiliar object, even something as harmless as fluttering paper.

As a horse raises its head, it increases its stereoscopic vision, but also widens the blind spot behind it. The Thoroughbred, with its relatively more frontally placed eyes, has better depth perception and ability to focus forward than other horses. It may see objects at a distance ahead more clearly, but it doesn't have as good a view of the horses coming up behind it. No horse which is facing forward can see its jockey, though it may get glimpses of the rider's arms and legs.

Because horses hate to go into unfamiliar, dark places, or any place they can't see, full, one-eyed blinkers are sometimes used to totally cover the eye of a horse which tends to veer in a certain direction. The use of a one-cup blinker on the right eye successfully cured Triple Crown winner Whirlaway of bearing out away from the rail.

Horses' eyes are usually brown, with a blue pupil. A horse with a blue or pink iris is known as a wall-eye, a watch-eye, or a glass-eye. Because these variations are unusual, they must be noted for identification purposes.

If you want to know where a horse is looking, though, don't watch its eyes. Look at its ears. Horses generally coordinate sight- and sound-seeking, because their hearing is nearly twice as keen as their vision. If a horse's ear is pointed in your direction, chances are that it is giving you a good once-over.

## TEETH

Every horse has twelve molars and ten incisors in each jaw. A male horse also has two "tushes," or canine teeth; thus, stallions and geldings have a total of 46 teeth while mares have 44.

The molars are the grinding teeth, and they need frequent attention. Because the horse's upper jaw is wider than the lower jaw, the outer edges of the upper teeth get no wear and tend to become sharply pointed. These points irritate the horse and make chewing difficult. At regular intervals they must be filed off. This procedure, known as "floating" the teeth, is not painful to the horse.

The incisors provide the best method for telling a horse's age. At about age two and a half, the two central permanent incisors push out the baby teeth. At age four, the permanent lateral incisors come in; by age five, all the baby teeth are gone.

If one examines the teeth of a five-year-old, it will be noted that each tooth has a depression in its center, the outside enamel being raised. By age six, the central incisors are worn smooth, and by age seven, the lateral incisors. By age eight, all of the incisors have "aged." From this point on, it is much more difficult to determine the horse's age. A rough approximation can be obtained by a brown groove that appears on the upper corner teeth near the gum line. This line extends down the tooth with age, reaching the bottom at age twenty, and from then on receding back up toward the gum.

## COMPARATIVE MEASUREMENTS OF TWO GREAT HORSES

|  | LARGE HORSE MAN O' WAR | SMALL HORSE AFFIRMED |
|---|---|---|
| Sex | Colt | Colt |
| Age | 3 | 3 |
| Weight | 1,200 | 1,000 |
| Height (withers) | 16.2¼ hands | 15.3 hands |
| Girth | 76½" | 73½" |
| Point of shoulder to point of shoulder | 16½" | 15" |
| Point of shoulder to point of hip | 49" | 48" |
| Buttock to ground | 58½" | 55" |

## HEART AND LUNGS

Resisting fatigue means providing sufficient oxygen to the muscles. To remain fleet over a distance, a horse first of all has to be able to "drink the wind." Since it can't breathe through its mouth, the horse should have large, well-developed nostrils. It also needs plenty of space for the windpipe. Some horsemen judge this by making sure they can easily insert a fist between the jawbones where they join the throat latch.

To allow for adequate lung capacity, the horse should be "deep through the heart." The higher the withers and the farther the underline of the horse extends below the point of the elbow, the more room there is for expansion of the lungs during muscular effort. The rib cage should be broad and "well sprung" and the chest, when viewed from the front, should appear elliptical (so there is room for expansion), rather than round.

The heart of a fit horse weighs about ten pounds, and at rest its pulse rate is thirty to forty beats per minute, as slow as or slower than that of top-level human marathon runners. A slow pulse rate means a muscular heart that provides more force per contraction. Thus, the faster the animal runs, the faster the heart can pump blood to deliver oxygen and remove fatigue-causing waste products from the muscles. (The short, bunchy muscles of the sprinter contract more quickly and more frequently than the elongated muscles of the stayer. They tire more easily because they require more oxygen and have less time to refuel between contractions.)

Two features of a horse's circulatory system greatly increase endurance. One is prominent veins. When a horse is moving at top speed, its heart tends to pump blood so quickly that its lungs and brain could be flooded. The veins bulge out during a race to keep the blood from flowing too quickly. Secondly, a horse's skin contains a network of blood vessels that act as reservoirs of glucose-rich blood that is released into the system during extended periods of exertion, providing a vital energy boost.

## A SPECIAL KIND OF "HEART"

When horsemen talk of "heart," they usually mean not the blood-pumping organ, but the horse's will to win. Racing hurts, and the horse suffers like a human runner. The quality that distinguishes one racehorse from another, and the Thoroughbred from other breeds, is the extent to which it will withstand the pain and keep on running as hard as it can until the race is finished. The greatest compliment a horseman can pay a horse is to say that it is "all heart." The most degrading thing that can be said of a racehorse is that it "has a heart like a pea."

While the final test of a horse's heart comes only in the stress of competition, horsemen believe that physical traits indicate the will to win, or at least to try all the way. Alert ears, large, domineering eyes and a proud head carriage are thought to connote a winning attitude. The proverbial "look of eagles," a gaze through which the horse conveys its sense of its own power and superiority, is rare and most sought after. Courage and willfulness, the qualities that make up heart, can be demonstrated both by a calm, regal bearing or a bold and fierce dominance. It takes a practiced observer to discern the challenging eye of a winner from the startled eye of a nervous horse, the white-edged eye of a frightened one, or the dull eye of a sick or lazy beast. The eyes and ears are the surest signs of a horse's thoughts and feelings, and for that reason their messages are well worth learning to decode.

## GREAT HORSES: AFFIRMED

Sam Riddle, the owner of Man o' War, once made the now-famous remark, "Thoroughbreds don't cry." By this he meant that they had the heart, or courage, to keep on trying no matter how badly the odds were stacked against them. Many are the legends of great Thoroughbred fanatics, like Black Gold and Dark Secret, both of whom broke a leg during a race, but refused to stop running until they crossed the finish line, still fighting.

Perhaps one of the greatest tests of heart in recent years was the two-year duel between two superior colts, Alydar and Affirmed. Both chestnuts, both schooled by top trainers, and both members of the same outstanding Raise a Native family, they typified all that is great in the Thoroughbred breed. Affirmed, standing only 15.3 hands, was a good little horse. Alydar, at 16.1½ hands was a good big horse. Although their girths were nearly the same, the common racing sentiment prevailed: a good big horse will always beat a good little one. What those who repeated that well-worn phrase forgot to take into account, however, was the fact that Affirmed was a fanatic. Once in the lead, he simply refused to let another horse pass him. What Affirmed always had to take into account was that Alydar was also a fanatic and refused to stop trying to pass no matter how consistently Affirmed beat him. Their duel, which covered nine miles and dominated two years of turf history, provided one of the most exciting Triple Crowns in American racing.

In spite of the fact that Affirmed had edged out Alydar in four of their six meetings, the big Calumet colt was the Derby favorite. An interesting aspect of the Alydar/Affirmed battles was the difference in their running styles. Alydar tended to break slowly from the gate and then come on strong from behind to challenge the leaders. Affirmed generally broke briskly and, once in the lead, flatly refused to relinquish his advantage. This pattern prevailed in the 1978 Kentucky Derby. Although Alydar chased Affirmed valiantly, the little Harbor View Farm colt won the race. This set the score at Affirmed: 5, Alydar: 2.

History repeated at Pimlico, but this time the big horse made an even more determined run for the lead and was beaten by only a neck. "Even if they went around again," said Affirmed's trainer, Laz Barrera, "he [Alydar] still wouldn't catch him." Few others, including Alydar himself, believed Barrera's vote of absolute confidence. The Calumet colt was favored in the one-and-a-half-mile Belmont, though there was another faction of knowing horsemen who believed that Alydar had lost out to Affirmed so many times that he was bound to give up (in essence, that Affirmed had "broken his heart") and that the race would be little more than a walkover.

The 111th running of the Belmont Stakes will be remembered by Ogden Phipps, president of the New York Racing Association, and everyone else who saw it as "The greatest horse race I have ever seen." Affirmed broke quickly from the gate, as expected, and hovered easily in second place. Alydar, having made his usual leisurely break from the gate, came up on the outside to challenge. Showing that he had the indomitable spirit of a great horse, he began his most ambitious assault on Affirmed, in spite of recent, hard-fought defeats that would have made a lesser horse quit trying.

Speeding rapidly to the head of the field, the good big horse and the good little horse passed the three-eighths pole eye-to-eye. Matching each other stride for stride, they completed the first mile in 1:37⅖. Muscles strained to the bursting point and neither horse giving quarter, they ran until Alydar, in the moment everyone had been waiting for, stuck his nose out just a fraction of an inch farther than Affirmed's. It seemed, in that instant, that the battle was finally won. The prolonged intensity of the pace, the assertive move by Alydar, would have caused most horses to back off and settle for a respectable second place.

For a moment, it looked as if Affirmed would tire and slow, but he now reached down to the depths of his "bottom," searching for that little extra something, that tiny ounce of greatness that makes a horse a Thoroughbred and a Thoroughbred a champion. Then, in one bold move of excruciating courage, the little horse with the enormous heart gathered every ounce of power that was in him and thrust his nose out a good three inches past Alydar's. That's where it stayed until the end of the race.

To this day, the question is still hotly debated. Which of the two colts had more heart: the one that just wouldn't be beaten, or the one that kept getting beaten, but came back in each race, trying harder and harder to win?

Alydar didn't know how to cry, and in that sense he exemplified the ideal Thoroughbred— but the fact remains that it was Affirmed who had that little something extra. As Laz Barrera put it when, the following summer, the good little Triple Crown winner thundered home under 132 pounds to win the Hollywood Gold Cup and become the first Thoroughbred to earn $2 million: "Affirmed is like my father. When you asked him for a quarter to go to the movies, he would have to look in all his pockets, but you knew he'd find one somewhere."

| | | Raise a Native |
| | Exclusive Native | |
| | | Exclusive |
| Affirmed | | |
| | | Crafty Admiral |
| | Won't Tell You | |
| | | Scarlet Ribbon |

*Racing Record:*

| STS. | 1ST | 2ND | 3RD | WON |
|------|-----|-----|-----|-----|
| 29 | 22 | 5 | 1 | $2,393,818 |

# The Stride: Conformation Put to the Test

In horse racing, greatness is measured in hundredths of a second and fractions of an inch. Imagine two horses running neck and neck as they approach the final furlong. If one horse can manage to stretch each of his feet just one-sixteenth of an inch farther forward than the feet of the other horse, it will win by a neck. Or, if their strides are of exactly equal length, the one that can complete each stride 0.01 of a second faster than the other will win by nearly two lengths. Running is a sequence of individual strides, and the horse that puts together the best sequence is the fastest.

A stride is one full launch cycle of the horse's body. The average racehorse covers about two and a half times its length every stride, or twenty-one to twenty-four feet. Stride length is the distance covered from the time one foot leaves the ground until that same foot touches down again. One stride at a racing gallop consists of four footsteps followed by an airborne period. If the horse is going to the left, the sequence is: right hind foot, left hind foot, right front foot, left front foot, airborne period. In other words: push, push, reach, reach, fly.

Stride time is broken down into two parts: stance time (when at least one foot is touching earth) and airborne time (when no feet are on the ground). Stance time is spent pushing forward; airborne time is spent moving forward, but with a loss of momentum. The ideal horse gets maximum push out of each leg while keeping airborne time to a minimum.

The greater the distance the horse travels over each leg individually, the longer its stride. Suppose a horse can cover a distance of six feet with each leg. If there is no overlap time (time when two feet are on the ground simultaneously) the horse will swing its weight forward perfectly from foot to foot and will travel twenty-four feet before becoming airborne. However, if two of the footsteps overlap totally—that is, if two of his feet strike and leave the ground at the same time—the horse will have traveled only eighteen feet before becoming airborne. Getting maximum push means reducing overlap time—those periods when more than one foot is on the ground—to a minimum.

All horses have some overlap time, usually during the period when they are transferring the thrust of their weight from the last-pushing hind foot to the first-reaching forefoot. Increased overlap time is the result of lack of balance or fatigue.

One cause of lack of balance in the stride is imbalance from front to rear (too much reach or too much push). A second cause is failure to "track straight" and "travel straight." If a horse "tracks straight," its hind feet follow the hoofprints of its front feet, just as the wheels on one side of a train follow the same track. If a horse "travels straight," its legs move directly forward without swinging outward (paddling) or swinging inward (winging) before being set down. Horses that are knock-kneed or pigeon-toed or have offset joints rarely track or travel straight. Overlap time is needed to provide the balance to compensate for crooked steps.

A horse with good balance and good conformation fatigues less easily, because each stride is more efficient. Fatigue in turn affects coordination: the stride shortens, and the horse drops back.

## GAITS OF THE HORSE

Gaits are the sequence in which a horse's feet strike the ground to produce movement. Just as a dance step is a pattern of footprints, a gait is a pattern of hoofprints. Inherent characteristics of certain gaits give them more speed potential than others. In general, the fewer feet required to support the horse at any given step, the greater its potential for speed.

The natural gaits of the horse are the walk, the trot or pace, and the gallop. The walk is a four-beat gait. Each foot leaves the ground separately and returns to the ground separately, but when that foot leaves the ground, the other three are planted. That is why the walk is the slowest gait.

The trot and the pace are two-beat gaits. In the trot, the diagonal pairs of legs leave the ground and strike the ground in unison (i.e., the right hind leg and the left front leg). In the pace, the lateral pairs of legs leave the ground and strike the ground in unison (i.e., both right legs). Two feet are always on the ground at the same time.

The racing gallop is a four-beat gait, with each foot leaving and striking the ground separately. Since overlap time is at a minimum, a Thoroughbred is able to gallop a mile faster than the fastest trotter can trot it. The galloping horse takes two forward strides for every one forward stride taken by the trotter.

## SECRETARIAT AND RIVA RIDGE— WHAT MAKES ONE HORSE FASTER?

There is an amazing photograph of Secretariat and Riva Ridge, nose to nose in the Marlboro Cup. The jockeys are crouched head to head. Both horses have their left front legs outstretched at exactly the same height and to exactly the same distance. In fact, there is only one thing that differentiates the two horses. Riva Ridge has his left hind foot and his right hind foot on the ground and is in the process of transferring his weight forward from one to the other. Secretariat has all of his weight on his right front leg and both of his hind legs are flung out high and far behind him. This is the crucial moment of the race, the instant at which Secretariat passed Riva Ridge to win by 3½ lengths. What this photograph illustrates is overlap time, the stride time wasted when more than one foot is in support of the horse's weight.

George W. Pratt, a professor of electrical engineering at M.I.T., analyzed the strides that Secretariat took to beat Riva Ridge in the Marlboro Cup. He found that Secretariat's average stride was 24'3" while Riva Ridge's average stride was 21'10". Secretariat's overlap time was 0.018 second per stride, Riva Ridge's overlap time was 0.115 second per stride. Secretariat, with his long stride and reduced overlap, only spent 0.006 of a second per stride longer in the air than Riva Ridge. This means he spent only a little bit more time in airborne deceleration than Riva Ridge did, but he spent much more time traveling forward over each leg individually. Because of his superior reaching ability and balance, he had low overlap. To catch up, Riva Ridge had to rely on the more fatiguing pushing ability. Eventually, he tired and had to drop back.

The lesson learned from the contest between Secretariat and Riva Ridge in the Marlboro Cup may someday benefit future buyers of Thoroughbred racehorses. Pratt has designed a special horseshoe made of aluminum. Each shoe is fitted with a "force transducer." The force transducer conveys an electrical broadcast to a magnetic tape which records the force of each hoofbeat and feeds it into a computer. The computer analyzes the horse's stride in 35,000 measurements per second and shows the relationship of each foot to each other foot, airborne time, stance time, and the timing of each stride. Pratt hopes this tool may someday be useful to buyers who want to compare the running styles of two yearling prospects or to trainers who want to identify the fine points of weakness in a horse's stride phrases and train accordingly.

# Section 3

# Ownership

Owning a Thoroughbred racehorse can provide some of the greatest thrills in sports. While ownership of professional sports teams requires millions of dollars, tens of thousands of people of far more modest means find themselves stepping proudly into the winner's circle at a racetrack while the public address system proclaims, "The winner of the fourth race is Mr. and Mrs. John Doe's Lifelong Dream." Participating in racing provides other pleasures; choosing racing colors to be displayed on the jockey's back; naming horses and choosing a stable name; visiting the backstretch to watch one's horse train and develop; bringing friends to the track to sit in an owner's box.

Of course, with the fun also come the bills. From a pure profit-and-loss standpoint, buying racehorses is an extremely risky investment. Depending on the caliber of the track, the cost of keeping a racehorse in training for a year averages $10,000 to $25,000. This includes the trainer's daily charge ($20 a day at small tracks, up to $50 at New York tracks), shoeing, veterinarian charges, jockey's fees, insurance, and transportation.

Offsetting these expenses is a horse's earnings. However, in 1980, the average horse earned $6,971. The median income

was $2,524, which means 32,250 horses earned under that figure. Only 18.7 percent of all horses earned more than $10,000 and only 5.6 percent earned more than $25,000. It's estimated that only one in ten horses earns a profit for its owner on the racetrack.

Why, then, in light of these rather dreary figures, do owners continue to purchase and run racehorses? The reasons are both financial and emotional, and they vary according to the classification into which the owner falls.

The first classification, which includes many of the names that perennially appear at the top of the Leading Money-winning Owners list, are the owner-breeders. The most famous of these is Calumet Farm, owner and breeder of eight Kentucky Derby winners, two Triple Crown winners and five winners of the "Horse of the Year" award. While these owner-breeders do their best to make a profit on the track, their most important reason for racing is to improve breeding potential. Losses sustained in their racing operation are exceeded by profits from standing stallions and from selling yearlings at auction.

The second classification is the entrepreneur—people with extensive business acumen and large capital acquired in other areas, who apply these resources in skill-fully managed, large-scale racing opera-tions. On the list of leading owners of 1980 are Thoroughbred capitalists Viola Sommer (widow of Sigmund Sommer), Dennis Heard, Murray Garren, Dan Lasater and Barry Schwartz.

Next are the owner-trainers, who are par-ticularly prominent at the smaller tracks across the country. The best-known of these entrepreneurs is Dale Baird, the "King of Waterford Park," whose skill with cheap claimers brings him annually near or at the very top of the lists of owners and trainers who have won the most races. These owner-trainers tend to be the most dedi-cated and hard-working people at the track. To cut costs, many act as their own grooms, hot-walkers and even exercise boys. The shrewdest among them earn a de-cent living year after year; the majority, buffeted constantly by the many ill fortunes of racing, are sustained only by occasional jobs with bigger stables and their continu-ing love of racing.

Finally, there is the small owner, a per-son successful in another business who pur-chases one or two or three horses to run at a local track. For many, ownership pro-vides useful tax advantages. Others find ownership a way to participate more closely in their favorite sport. Some, a minority, mistakenly view racing as a quick way to get rich. Very few small owners end up making money in the sport, but many get satisfaction, especially sharing the dream that someday they'll find the one horse like Stymie, a $1,500 claimer who went on to win over $900,000.

## RACING SILKS

The Romans were the first to require drivers to wear the colors of the interests they repre-sented. All horses competing in the Circus Maximus represented one of four factions—the blue, the red, the green and the white.

In England, identifying the contestants wasn't much of a problem in the days of two-horse matches. But when sweepstakes became popular, spectators had a difficult time distin-guishing the horses they'd wagered on. In Oc-tober 1762, the members of the Jockey Club met at Newmarket to discuss the problem. They decided:

> For the greater convenience of distinguishing the horses in running, and also for the prevention of disputes arising from not knowing the colours of each rider, the under-mentioned gentlemen have come to the resolution and agreement of having the colours annexed to the following names worn by their respective riders: The Stewards therefore hope, in the name of The Jockey Club, that the named gentlemen will take care that the riders be provided with dresses accordingly.

Nineteen owners were listed at the bottom—seven dukes, one marquis, four earls, one vis-count, one lord, two baronets and three com-moners. Among the colors chosen was "straw" by the Duke of Devonshire; the color is still used by the family and is considered the oldest racing color in existence.

Originally, all riders wore black hunting caps, but gradually, as the number and combi-nation of colors increased, black gave way to varied colors that served as part of the identification.

Today, in the United States, new owners must register their choice and pattern of colors with the Jockey Club. For a fee of $5 per year or $15 for three years, they receive exclusive use of their chosen colors and patterns. These silks must be worn whenever their horses race; substitute colors may be used only with the permission of the stewards, and a fine usually results even if permission is granted.

The cost of silks depends on the quality and complexity of the design. The price range is anywhere from $75 to upwards of $250 for one jacket-and-cap combination. Large stables need dozens of sets.

At each track, racing silks are stored in a room adjacent to the jockeys' quarters. The jockeys' valets are responsible for cleaning and maintaining the silks.

## LEADING OWNERS, MONEY WON—1980

| OWNER | STARTS | WINS | EARNINGS |
|---|---|---|---|
| Harbor View Farm | 572 | 103 | $2,207,576 |
| Viola Sommer | 515 | 101 | 1,888,791 |
| Tartan Stable | 335 | 52 | 1,803,113 |
| Hawksworth Farm | 318 | 69 | 1,630,500 |
| Loblolly Stable | 169 | 32 | 1,570,568 |
| Elmendorf | 528 | 67 | 1,482,417 |
| W. S. Farish 3rd | 295 | 70 | 1,076,233 |
| Rokeby Stable | 142 | 32 | 1,060,276 |
| N. B. Hunt | 294 | 34 | 901,852 |
| G. Ring | 249 | 41 | 875,214 |
| Mrs. H. D. Paxson | 222 | 50 | 857,754 |
| Saron Stable | 104 | 21 | 841,231 |
| R. L. Reineman Stable | 299 | 53 | 840,874 |
| F. W. Hooper | 509 | 59 | 839,247 |
| M. M. Garren | 447 | 58 | 815,949 |
| Dotsam Stable | 11 | 7 | 805,217 |
| Flying Zee Stable | 330 | 51 | 780,941 |
| J. M. Schiff | 108 | 28 | 773,563 |
| O. Phipps | 75 | 19 | 753,722 |
| Darby Dan Farm | 184 | 39 | 738,784 |
| Bwamazon Farm | 221 | 46 | 735,022 |
| B. K. Schwartz | 306 | 44 | 730,338 |
| Hickory Tree Stable | 149 | 36 | 719,985 |
| Windfields Farm | 213 | 55 | 719,505 |
| Buckland Farm | 304 | 25 | 690,941 |

## ANNUAL LEADING OWNERS— MONEY WON

| YEAR | OWNER | AMOUNT WON |
|---|---|---|
| 1902 | Green B. Morris | $ 98,350 |
| 1903 | William C. Whitney | 102,569 |
| 1904 | H. B. Duryea | 200,107 |
| 1905 | James R. Keene | 228,724 |
| 1906 | James R. Keene | 155,519 |
| 1907 | James R. Keene | 397,342 |
| 1908 | James R. Keene | 282,342 |
| 1909 | Samuel C. Hildreth | 159,112 |
| 1910 | Samuel C. Hildreth | 152,645 |
| 1911 | Samuel C. Hildreth | 47,473 |
| 1912 | John W. Schorr | 58,225 |
| 1913 | Harry Payne Whitney | 55,056 |
| 1914 | John W. Schorr | 85,326 |
| 1915 | L. S. Thompson | 104,106 |
| 1916 | H. Guy Bedwell | 71,100 |
| 1917 | A. King Macomber | 68,578 |
| 1918 | J. K. L. Ross | 99,179 |
| 1919 | J. K. L. Ross | $ 209,303 |
| 1920 | Harry Payne Whitney | 270,675 |
| 1921 | Rancocas Stable (Harry F. Sinclair) | 263,500 |
| 1922 | Rancocas Stable (Harry F. Sinclair) | 239,503 |
| 1923 | Rancocas Stable (Harry F. Sinclair) | 438,849 |
| 1924 | Harry Payne Whitney | 240,193 |
| 1925 | Glen Riddle Farm Stable (Samuel D. Riddle) | 199,143 |
| 1926 | Harry Payne Whitney | 407,139 |
| 1927 | Harry Payne Whitney | 328,769 |
| 1928 | Edward B. McLean | 234,640 |
| 1929 | Harry Payne Whitney | 362,305 |
| 1930 | C. V. Whitney | 385,972 |
| 1931 | C. V. Whitney | 422,923 |
| 1932 | C. V. Whitney | 403,681 |
| 1933 | C. V. Whitney | 241,292 |
| 1934 | Brookmeade Stable (Mrs. Dodge Sloane) | 251,138 |
| 1935 | A. G. Vanderbilt | 303,605 |
| 1936 | Milky Way Farm (Mrs. Ethel V. Mars) | 206,450 |
| 1937 | Mrs. Charles S. Howard | 214,559 |
| 1938 | H. Maxwell Howard | 226,495 |
| 1939 | Belair Stud (William Woodward) | 284,250 |
| 1940 | Charles S. Howard | 334,120 |
| 1941 | Calumet Farm (Warren Wright) | 475,091 |
| 1942 | Greentree Stable (Mrs. Payne Whitney) | 414,432 |
| 1943 | Calumet Farm (Warren Wright) | 267,915 |
| 1944 | Calumet Farm (Warren Wright) | 601,660 |
| 1945 | Maine Chance Farm (Mrs. Elizabeth N. Graham) | 589,170 |
| 1946 | Calumet Farm (Warren Wright) | 564,095 |
| 1947 | Calumet Farm (Warren Wright) | 1,402,436 |
| 1948 | Calumet Farm (Warren Wright) | 1,269,710 |
| 1949 | Calumet Farm (Warren Wright) | 1,128,942 |
| 1950 | Brookmeade Stable (Mrs. Dodge Sloane) | 651,399 |
| 1951 | Greentree Stable (Mrs. C. S. Payne & J. H. Whitney) | 637,242 |

| YEAR | OWNER | AMOUNT WON |
|------|-------|------------|
| 1952 | Calumet Farm (Mrs. Gene Markey) | $1,283,197 |
| 1953 | A. G. Vanderbilt | 987,306 |
| 1954 | King Ranch (Robert J. Kleberg, Jr.) | 837,615 |
| 1955 | Hasty House Farm (Mr. & Mrs. A. E. Reuben) | 832,879 |
| 1956 | Calumet Farm (Mrs. Gene Markey) | 1,057,383 |
| 1957 | Calumet Farm (Mrs. Gene Markey) | 1,150,910 |
| 1958 | Calumet Farm (Mrs. Gene Markey) | 946,262 |
| 1959 | Cain Hoy Stable (H. F. Guggenheim) | 742,081 |
| 1960 | C. V. Whitney | 1,039,091 |
| 1961 | Calumet Farm (Mrs. Gene Markey) | 759,856 |
| 1962 | Ellsworth Stable (Rex C. Ellsworth) | 1,154,454 |
| 1963 | Ellsworth Stable (Rex C. Ellsworth) | 1,096,863 |
| 1964 | Wheatley Stable (Mrs. Henry C. Phipps) | 1,073,572 |
| 1965 | Marion H. Van Berg | 895,246 |
| 1966 | Wheatley Stable (Mrs. Henry C. Phipps) | 1,225,861 |
| 1967 | Hobeau Farm (J. J. Dreyfus, Jr.) | 1,120,143 |
| 1968 | Marion H. Van Berg | 1,105,388 |
| 1969 | Marion H. Van Berg | 1,453,679 |
| 1970 | Marion H. Van Berg | 1,347,289 |
| 1971 | S. Sommer | 1,523,508 |
| 1972 | S. Sommer | 1,605,896 |
| 1973 | Dan R. Lasater | 1,498,785 |
| 1974 | Dan R. Lasater | 3,022,960 |
| 1975 | Dan R. Lasater | 2,894,726 |
| 1976 | Dan R. Lasater | 2,894,074 |
| 1977 | Elmendorf (Max Gluck) | 2,309,200 |
| 1978 | Harbor View Farm | 2,097,443 |
| 1979 | Harbor View Farm | 2,701,741 |
| 1980 | Harbor View Farm | 2,207,576 |

## BECOMING AN OWNER

There are four ways to become an owner: breeding a racehorse; purchasing a yearling at auction; buying a horse of racing age privately or at auction; and claiming horses at the track.

*Breeding* a horse to race requires by far the greatest amount of capital and carries the highest amount of risk, but also involves the best chance of producing the huge profit owners dream of. As we've seen in the "Economics of Breeding" section, the cost of breeding and raising a yearling from a "good" (i.e., $30,000) broodmare is about $29,000. The additional costs involved in getting that yearling to its first race, a time period that could be anywhere between eight and eighteen months, ranges from $6,000 to $15,000. That makes a total investment of $35,000 to $45,000 over a three- to four-year period before the horse has a chance to earn a cent. During this time, numerous accidents and illnesses can cost the horse its career or its life.

On the other hand, a horse whose breeding is good enough to carry these kinds of costs has the potential to become a stakes winner or even a champion. With the level of purses today, a single graded stakes win can return the breeding and raising costs, and continued success can bring, as we've seen, huge profits in the breeding shed.

*Buying a yearling at auction* is slightly more expensive than breeding a horse, but it reduces the risks. Before any money is expended, the horse has survived all the hazards of foaling and weaning, and its conformation can be carefully evaluated. Since breeders expect, and usually make, a profit on a well-turned-out colt or filly, the price paid exceeds the cost of raising the animal, but the length of time the auction buyer has to wait until his horse can race is far shorter than that of the breeder. The buyer does still, however, have to bear the costs of breaking, boarding and training the yearling.

Since auction yearlings, as a whole, are those with better-than-average racing potential, the auction buyer has a better-than-average chance that the horse will make a profit and, perhaps, become an animal of breeding value. The chance increases with the price paid. In 1980, the price range of auction yearlings was:

| PRICE RANGE | NO. | % |
|---|---|---|
| $100,000 or more | 468 | 6.6% |
| 50,000 to 99,999 | 490 | 6.9% |
| 10,000 to 49,999 | 2,523 | 35.6% |
| 5,000 to 9,999 | 1,295 | 18.3% |
| 4,999 or less | 2,303 | 32.9% |

Those that sold for $50,000 or more have a four-in-ten chance of returning a profit to their purchaser, and a one-in-ten chance of becoming a stakes winner.

Most owners get into the sport by *purchasing privately a horse of racing age*. This is the only method of purchasing horses of allowance and stakes quality (since they are not entered in claiming races). Besides, since in most states the only people eligible to claim are owners who've had a horse start in the current race meeting, private purchase of a racehorse is the only way to establish eligibility to claim.

The advantages of purchasing a horse privately are: the horse has established a racing record, which can be evaluated; there is the potential to earn a profit on the investment immediately; and the horse can be evaluated carefully by a trainer or a veterinarian before the sale is consummated. One disadvantage is that the horse has limited upside potential (because its price is based on demonstrated ability rather than potential). The second disadvantage is that the buyer usually pays a premium price in exchange for the opportunity to carefully inspect the merchandise.

In the United States, the majority of horses change hands through *claiming*. Thoroughbreds may only be claimed by registered owners or trainers authorized by them. The advantages of claiming are that the horse has demonstrated ability and can race immediately. The major disadvantage is the inability to ascertain the horse's physical condition ahead of time. In addition, once a claim is filed, the claimant owns the horse, as most state racing rules state, "whether it be alive or dead, sound or unsound, or injured during a race or after it."

While many horses racing for higher claiming prices move up into allowance company, the chances of making a profit on claiming horses are not bright. Although claiming races make up 71 percent of all races, they command only 46 percent of the purses allocated. Contents for cheap claimers, those with tags of under $5,000, make up 31 percent of all races, but get only 12 percent of all purses. That's why it takes unusual shrewdness and luck in the claiming game.

## THE ECONOMICS OF OWNERSHIP

Once an owner acquires a horse, he is faced with the expenses of maintaining it. Costs vary in different parts of the country and from track to track, but generally the cost increases with the quality of the horse and the purse structure of the track at which it is stabled.

Because of the wide variance in expenses and income, it is impossible to prepare an "average" profit-and-loss statement. However, to give you an idea of the kinds of costs involved in owning a racehorse, we'll use the example of a horse claimed at Aqueduct for $20,000 and raced in New York for one year. We'll assume that the horse raced sixteen times (the average for horses starting more than ten times), and chalked up two wins, two seconds, two thirds, and two fourths. We'll also assume that the horse spent two months of the year being "freshened" at a boarding farm.

*Expenses*

| | |
|---|---|
| Trainer's per diem (covers food, grooms, hot-walkers, exercise boys, trainer's expenses) 300 days @ $40 per day | $12,000 |
| Trainer's bonus (10% of all purse money) | 2,400 |
| Jockey's fees (10% of 1st money, $55 for 2nd, $45 for 3rd, $35 for others) | 1,955 |
| Jockey's insurance | 100 |
| Stable bonuses (1% of earnings) | 240 |
| Sales tax on original claiming price (8%) | 1,600 |
| Shoeing | 400 |

| | |
|---|---:|
| Veterinarian | $ 400 |
| Shipping (to track and to boarding farm) | 1,000 |
| Boarding per diem (65 days @ $10 per day) | 650 |
| Lead ponies for races ($10 per race) | 150 |
| Mortality insurance (8½% of horse's value) | 1,750 |
| Misc. (license, registration, etc.) | 100 |
| | $22,745 |

*Income*  (NOTE: Average purse value $12,000)

| | |
|---|---:|
| 2 wins (60% of $12,000 per win) | $14,400 |
| 2 seconds (22%) | 5,280 |
| 2 thirds (12%) | 2,880 |
| 2 fourths (6%) | 1,440 |
| | $24,000 |

As you can see, the owner's income just covered his expenses. While the numbers would change considerably, a horse with the same record should come close to breaking even at most tracks. Statistically, the average horse with three wins would make a profit for its owner.

## REQUIREMENTS FOR OWNERSHIP

Having the money to buy a horse doesn't necessarily guarantee that a person can become a horse owner. To ensure that the sport is conducted honestly state racing commissioners require every owner to apply for a license. As part of the license approval procedure, the owner's credit is checked, and his background may be investigated.

The owner must then decide if the horse is going to race under the individual's name or a stable name (officially known as an "assumed name"). All stable names must be approved by the Jockey Club, as are the chosen racing colors.

Many people seek to spread the costs and risks of ownership by forming partnerships. The Jockey Club limits such partnerships to no more than ten. Each individual must be registered with the Jockey Club, and each must meet the state licensing requirements.

Finally, the Jockey Club requires registration of the appointment of a trainer as the owner's "assigned agent," which gives the trainer the power to claim horses in the owner's name.

## CALUMET FARM

No stable in the modern age has ever dominated the sport like Calumet Farm. Between 1941 and 1963, Calumet led the list of winning owners twelve times and the list of leading breeders fourteen times. Eight Kentucky Derby winners carried the devil's red-and-blue silks, including Triple Crown winners Whirlaway and Citation.

Behind this racing dynasty was a fiercely competitive man named Warren Wright. Born in Springfield, Ohio, in 1875, Wright took over the family business, the Calumet Baking Powder Company, at age twenty-four. He made the company so successful he was able to sell it just before the Depression for $40 million.

In 1931, Wright inherited Calumet Farm, which, under his father's management, had bred trotting horses. Benefiting from the buying power of his fortune during the Depression, Wright plunged into Thoroughbred racing, purchasing the best racing stock available and obtaining the best possible advice. One of his expenditures involved joining with A. B. Hancock of Claiborne Farms in the importation of the stallion Blenheim II, at the then unheard-of price of $225,000.

From his first crop, Blenheim II produced Whirlaway, the colt that was to begin Calumet's long domination of American racing. This somewhat unruly chestnut colt followed a promising two-year-old campaign with a series of disappointing early performances at age three, including defeats in the Blue Grass Stakes and the Derby Prep. For the 1941 Kentucky Derby, the shrewd veteran Calumet trainer, Ben Jones, made two key moves. One was a modification of Whirlaway's blinkers. The second was obtaining the services of jockey Eddie Arcaro. Whirlaway cleaned up his act and blazed through the final quarter-mile of the Derby in an incredible 23⅗ seconds to win by eight lengths. The colt followed with easy triumphs in the Preakness and Belmont to capture the first of Calumet's two Triple Crowns.

Whirlaway's Derby victory was matched by that of another Calumet colt, Pensive, in 1944. In 1945, Wright's filly, Twilight Tear, became the first of her sex to be voted Horse of the Year. Then, in 1948, came the Triple Crown victories of the great Citation, who was sired by Bull Lea, a horse Warren Wright had purchased in the 1930s for $14,000. Citation's smashing victories led Calumet to the first million-dollar year ever chalked up by a stable.

That year was to be the acme of Wright's stewardship of Calumet Farm. Wright died in 1950, and ownership of the farm went to his wife, Lucille (who later married Admiral Gene Markey). Under her very able leadership, Calumet won Derbies in the 1950s with Hill Gail (1952), Iron Liege (1957) and Tim Tam (1958). In the same period, Calumet was leading owner for four years.

In 1963, however, Calumet slipped from the list of the top twenty owners for the first time since 1941. For the next decade the stable suffered a decline broken only when Forward Pass was named 1968 Kentucky Derby champion after the disqualification of Dancer's Image. Mrs. Markey continued to persevere, though, and in the late 1970s, racing fans rejoiced to see the devil's red-and-blue silks race to prominence again. In 1977, the Calumet filly, Our Mims, was named champion three-year-old filly. In that same year, Calumet's colt Alydar began his great series of duels with Affirmed. In 1979, Davona Dale became the first filly ever to capture both versions of the filly Triple Crown by winning the Kentucky Oaks, the Black-eyed Susan, the Acorn Stakes, the Mother Goose and the Coaching Club American Oaks. The dedication of Mrs. Markey and the skill of young trainer John Veitch had returned Calumet to racing's upper echelon.

# Life of the Horse: 4. Schooling

## Going South

Banknote, her inch-long lashes pulled back wide from the white edges of her blue-and-amber eyes, hurls through the long night in the large and unfamiliar van. The van is full of yearlings purchased at Lexington and Banknote, now surrounded by the strange herd, braces her legs to the unevenness of the highway, leaning into the curves, staring into a blackness smelling of oil, sweet hay, horse urine and hot rubber. Some of the other yearlings are sleeping, knees and stifle joints locked so that the bones and not the muscles support their weight. All the small, shadowy heads bob up and down to the truck's hypnotic rhythm.

The jolt of the van stopping in a gas station startles them, and they scramble on uncertain hooves. As the truck waits, filling up, they all begin to whinny in the dark. They whinny for mares who cannot hear them, for the people who have sold them, for the friends they have left behind, for any response outside the big, rectangular darkness inside the van. A bold and boisterous colt rears in his cross ties. Another

kicks impatiently at the sides of the truck. The timid quiver, hyperventilating through distended nostrils. Banknote, well-mannered but alert, stands poised to run, watching and listening, chewing nervously on her cross-tie rope.

The herd instinct is strong within her. When the yearling beside her strikes out and paws the floor, Banknote's hoof rises automatically and begins to strike out in the same cadence. Soon, every yearling in the van is pawing the rubber mats. There are no broodmares here now, no old horses who will stay quiet and set a calm tone for the group to emulate. These yearlings—corresponding in age to human ten-year-olds—are on their own.

When the van door opens, the pawing halts suddenly. Twenty ears perk up to the voice.

"Hush up, now. Hush up. We'll be there soon enough."

In with the voice comes a slice of blue light, soft and richly scented with the moisture evaporating from the skin of wild grapes and pine boughs. The air here is different from the harsh, dry air of New York State. It enters the van like a dream full of smells never smelled before, invigorating their nostrils, and the yearlings cease their pawing to sniff as the truck gradually revs up and returns them to the road's trance.

Traditionally, Thoroughbreds go south in the fall for training. For generations they have been shipped to Aiken, Camden and Columbia, South Carolina, or to Florida, to learn how to race. Thoroughbreds have no sense of cultural history, however, and Thoroughbred families are as disunited as they are incestuous.

Banknote, licking the wood panel of her stall to soothe herself, has never met her half-sister, Manny Dober. She does not know that two years earlier, Tanta's diminutive first filly (by Native Heritage) took a similar trip to Elloree Training Center in South Carolina one lonesome night. The horse has no sense of what the future holds in store. It knows only remembered sensations and the instinct for self-preservation at the moment in which it is living. Even if Banknote could hear the story of her sister, Manny Dober, it would no more change her future or her attitude than a twig would alter the course of a rushing waterfall. She is bred to run and to want to win, and her fate, like the fate of Manny Dober, was determined long before the night she was pulled from Tanta's womb and struggled to get up as fast as she could.

# School—Manny Dober

In South Carolina, the air is cool in the early morning, and heavy with the resin of pine needles. The sandhills covered with coniferous forest roll like waves for mile after silent mile. Pastures, undulating and rockless, spin intricate grids around the four white barns and three-quarter-mile track of Elloree Training Center, where one hundred Thoroughbreds have been sent to learn their trade.

It is mid-September of 1978 when Manny Dober arrives for training. Owned by her breeder, Philip Sagarin, Manny, unlike her younger half-sister Banknote, was not offered at a yearling sale, but kept to race.

Like all Thoroughbreds sent for a half year or more of teaching at $20 per day, this still gangly filly symbolizes the high hopes and true gambling spirit of the racehorse owner. In 1977, when Manny Dober was foaled, there were 27,649 two-year-olds registered with the Jockey Club. Of these, only 10,433, a little more than one-third, ever started in a race at two, and of those that started, less than half (4,062) were winners. The average purse distribution per two-year-old starter was $3,614, barely enough to pay back Manny's sire's stud fee of $1,000 and support Tanta for the year. Statistics like these don't seem to bother the true sportsman, for whom each new foal offers the potential to be the next champion. Superstition, hope and instinct are interwoven into the mentality of anyone who will risk thousands of dollars a year to find out if his spindly yearling will develop into one of the one in ten horses that earns its keep. Some try to squeeze their appeals to fortune or their incantations to the

spirits of great ancestors into the eighteen characters the Jockey Club permits them for the names of their horses. Sometimes, these efforts seem to work. Begoodtome was good to owner D. W. Lukas, winning $20,915. Sir Ivor Again, owned by Mrs. Tillylou Christopher, did not match Sir Ivor's earnings of $561,323, but did manage to win $146,515 by the end of his three-year-old year. Manny Dober, whose name seems oddly masculine for such a feminine-looking filly, is named after a friend of the Sagarins. Hoping to get all the edges possible, the Sagarins named the filly Manny Dober for luck, because "every time there is a raffle in a hat, the name Manny Dober gets pulled out."

## NAMING HORSES

Before the Jockey Club assumed control of the American Stud Book and jurisdiction over the naming of Thoroughbreds, duplication of names caused headaches for the entire industry. Today, with more than thirty thousand Thoroughbreds foaled each year, finding a suitable name can be a problem for owners, and registering names is a big job for the Jockey Club.

Until the early 1960s, names were restricted to fourteen characters, including spaces between words. As the Thoroughbred population grew, the limit was increased, first to sixteen, then to the present eighteen. The name of a gelding may be reused three years after its death, and the names of other horses fifteen years after their deaths. The names of famous racehorses such as Man o' War and Secretariat may never be reused. Names of celebrities or individuals may not be used without the written permission of the person involved.

Horse owners are urged to submit three to six possible names. Nearly 60 percent of the first choices are rejected because of duplication, overt commercialism or poor taste. Some owners submit ten to twenty choices before the Jockey Club computer check allows one name to be approved.

Traditionally, many owners have adapted names from that of the sire or the dam, or a combination of the two. The success at stud of Bold Ruler and his descendants has lead to a torrent of names beginning with "Bold"—more than four hundred such names of active horses are listed in the 1979 American Racing Manual. The Broodmare of the Year in 1979, Smartaire, produced a fine colt that was named Smarten and a fine filly named Smart Angle. The gray colt by Bold Bidder out of Spectacular was logically named Spectacular Bid.

Some breeders work hard to come up with more imaginative names suggested by those of the sire and the dam. Spectacular Bid's great-granddam, Danger Ahead, produced twin fillies appropriately called Stop On Red and Go On Green. When Prince John mated with Peroxide Blonde, the resulting colt became Stage Door Johnny. Even more cleverly, the filly by Nijinsky II (named after the famed ballet star) out of the bouncily named Glad Rags II was named Terpsichorist, which means "lively dancer."

Other owners range far and wide for inspiration. Some honor friends or associates—Dr. Fager was named after a neurosurgeon who operated on trainer John Nerud. The five-year-old son of owner Barry Schwartz liked reading the racing form better than children's books; in honor of his son's habit, Schwartz named a colt Degenerate Jon. Place names are commonly used—Temperence Hill and Cox's Ridge are both located near owner John Ed Anthony's Arkansas home.

Foreign languages are a frequent source of monikers: Toujours Pret ("always ready"); L'Enjoleur ("the flatterer"); and Taisez Vous

("shut up"). Other sports get their play: Fourth and Inches; Suicide Squeeze; Goal Keeper. Current dance trends are popular: Disco Dance and Do the Bump. Even imbibers have their offspring: Glass of Draft and Heresmudinyoureye. Finally, some owners can't help letting negative emotions creep into the naming process: caution (Dontpressyourluck); disappointment (Just Nosed Out); resignation (It's Only Money); and confusion (Who Am I).

---

Although neither her breeding nor her stature is as regal as Banknote's, Tanta's first filly embodies certain characteristics that were transmitted to Banknote as well. She is burnished chestnut with no white markings. She has a fine, alert head; she has no conformational defects; her legs and her way of going are straight. On the negative side, she stands under fifteen hands, small even for a filly. Her head, her feet and her rib cage seem too large for her underdeveloped body. Since neither Tanta nor Native Heritage was scrawny, her immaturity is attributed to shed-raising. Shed-raised weanlings, turned out into the fields twenty-four hours a day and fed communally, are thought by some breeders to make better racehorses because they have to fight for their food. Other breeders object to shed-raising because it is impossible to determine how much nutrition each young horse is receiving. Manny Dober's stablemate, Wandaful Candy J, has accompanied her to Elloree Training Center. Named for Sagarin's wife, Wanda was also shed-raised and is very small for her age.

Banknote, still in the embryonic stage when Manny began training, was about the size of a cat when Manny Dober, at seventeen months, reached 95 percent of her mature height. Her head and her body length are almost as developed as they will become; her elbow is as far from the ground as it will ever be, but the all-important bones of her legs, which will have to withstand the stresses of racing speeds, will continue to thicken and grow for at least six more months.

She and Wanda both look tough and wiry as they are led out of the van's night into the cool morning. Manny, sprightly and flashing Tanta's dark eyes, flares open her big, square nostrils, deeply inhales the pine air and turns it into a shrill blast of young horse breath whinnying across the track busy with horses. Wanda follows suit and the two strut down the van ramp, heads poking, ears flitting to the sound of every strange new hoofbeat falling through the mist. Not covered with baby fat like the sales yearlings, both Manny and Wanda are callow and unmuscled. It is the job of Frank Smith, manager of Elloree Training Center, to take these "babies" and transform them over the next six months into hard, competitive athletes.

"It's our job to help them grow up and develop into racehorses," says Frank, in that low, slow Southern drawl that frantic Thoroughbreds seem to love so well. "All that means developing the physical capability and the mental attitude to go to the track." He has trained more than nine hundred young racehorses during the past twenty years. Frank's calm, patient approach seems to work well with Manny Dober as she skitters and dances at the end of the lead rope. He just ignores her and keeps on walking a straight line and talking in his slow, soothing voice.

"Now this filly, well, she seems a little small and unruly. She was shed-raised, which means she wasn't handled that much. She seems to have a nice disposition, but she just isn't that used to being confident and obedient with people. What we'll do is get her used to being here and to being handled for a while."

Manny has not spent time in a stall since she was a foal with Tanta. She cleans up her ration of sweet feed—oats from Wisconsin, special vitamin and mineral supplements, and high-quality Canadian hay—but paces fretfully by herself. The whole first day at Elloree, she and Wanda whinny to each other. All yearlings develop special buddies, even during training, and Manny and Wanda, who have been together since birth, find the ten-foot separation of the aisle an imposition to their herd instinct.

The next morning, Manny meets Sigi for the first time. Sigi, one of Elloree's thirty employees, weighs only one hundred pounds and is known for her ability with tense or flighty yearlings.

"This one's a little green," Frank tells her in front of Manny's stall. "She hasn't been handled much and she might get a little confused at first, so we'll have to be kind of careful with her. Just sneak up on her slowly and I think she'll be alright."

Unlike many farm managers, Smith likes to use the same people as grooms that he uses as riders. Over the past four years, yearlings he has broken have earned over $1,000,000 at the track. Nine of them have been stakes winners. He attributes their success to slow, patient training and gentle handling. His method allows the young horse to spend most of its time with one person, whose voice and movements it learns to trust, both in the exercise ring and on foot.

While Frank saunters into the stall and offers his open hand for Manny to sniff, Sigi finds a soft dandy brush. Manny approaches Frank with suspicion and curiosity. While she is sniffing him, he snaps a lead rope to her halter ring so softly that she doesn't realize the rope now connects her to his hand.

"I don't like to tie a horse to a tie chain too early," he says, as Sigi, speaking shyly, enters the stall, offering the brush for Manny to inspect. The filly snorts down onto the bristles, then chomps them.

"Okay, okay," says Sigi gently. Placing one hand on Manny's chest, she begins to brush in downward strokes, following the direction in which the hair grows. At first, Manny tries to move away from the brush, but Frank places his hand on the other side of her neck to steady her. Each time she moves away, Frank and Sigi back off, just using their voices and light touches of their hands to keep her still and get her to accept the brush. Once, when the soft bristles sweeping across her underbelly tickle her,

Manny kicks out, but neither Sigi nor Frank make a move to punish her.

"Maybe if she keeps that up, we'll have to do something about it," Frank mutters, "but there's no sense in getting into a fight the first day. She doesn't seem mean like a real kicker. Probably she was just a little surprised or irritated. To the young horse, everything is new. If you move too fast or try to do too much too soon, you can get a horse hurt. The thing you have to remember is that we are dealing with a valuable animal which belongs to someone else. We like to keep them just as free of restraint as we can without having them hard to control. We handle them a lot in the stall, teach them to lead if they don't know that and to stand still and be brushed. Some take longer than others, but usually for the first week they're here we just try to get them to be satisfied with living with us."

After about fifteen minutes, Manny stamps her foot with impatience, telling them that she is sick of standing still for such a long time.

"Okay, just one more minute," whispers Sigi. She slides her hand down Manny's foreleg and presses the tendon firmly to get Manny to pick up her foot. At first, the filly doesn't understand and Sigi nudges her shoulder off-balance to indicate what she wants.

"Come on now, give it up."

Manny lifts her hoof, but fights, pawing the air to shake loose the small hands that hold it off the ground.

"Oh, don't be stupid," says Sigi, waiting for Manny to be still before finally setting the hoof down gently and moving on to the next one. It is frightening for the young horse to stand on only three legs, unbalanced and unable to run from danger, but horses must learn to lift up their feet for the farrier, who will change their shoes every four weeks. Sigi methodically repeats the lesson with each of the other feet.

Then, she scratches the side of Manny's withers and continues scratching all the way up the crest of her long neck. The filly's whole spine stretches out under the pleasant sensation. Her eyelids squeeze shut and she twists her neck sideways, enjoying the fingers' scratch.

"I guess that's plenty for today," says Frank, unsnapping the lead shank. "I'd say from her attitude, this one should settle pretty well. With any luck we can start breaking her by the beginning of next week. We like to give all the new ones a little time, just to see whether they're nasty or nippy or roguish before we even start to introduce them to a bridle or saddle. A lot of horses we get are almost broken before we get them. Others, like her, have hardly had more than a halter put on them. You have to spend time to gain their confidence without hurting their character or getting them so that they fear humans. Once they are leading and listening to us and standing quietly in the stall to be brushed, then we can think about backing them."

"Backing" is the process of teaching a horse to accept a rider's weight on its back. Before a horse is backed at Elloree, however, it is "bitted," or taught to accept and respond to the signals of a bit in its mouth. Both backing and bitting are essential steps in "breaking" a horse to ride. The term breaking, though it implies violent shattering of a horse's will, is really quite the opposite. At least in the case of reputable farms such as Smith's, it is a process of gentle persuasion through which the young animal learns to trust humans so thoroughly that it is more responsive to their commands than to its own fears or wishes. Both character, or honorable behavior, and high spirit are qualities highly valued in a racehorse. The trick of breaking is to make the animal docile and tractable enough to train without taking the will to fight out of it.

On October 1, just two weeks after her arrival, Manny Dober is introduced to the bridle and bit. By now, she has learned to stand still and be brushed from head to tail without fussing or kicking. In the process of developing Thoroughbred athletes, the complete daily brushing is not purely cosmetic. It stimulates circulation, massages muscles, and helps to keep the horse amused and relaxed. Early training and conditioning of the racehorse means not just developing specific running muscles, but also shaping the nervous system and mind of the animal so it will be able to function at top capacity. The neurotic horse, which frets or paces, wastes energy. This detracts from performance and predisposes the horse to serious digestive upsets and to injuring itself in the stall. Mental fitness is a key to any athlete's performance. Grooming not only tones the skin, but helps to fill up the twenty-two hours a day most racehorses at the peak of fitness spend standing in a twelve-foot-by-twelve-foot stall.

When Sigi enters, Manny lets out a muffled nicker and comes over to her at once. Sigi snaps the shank easily onto her halter and begins the routine of brushing to get Manny relaxed. Horses love a routine. The sameness of each day seems to pacify their often suspicious temperaments and to reassure them that nothing unanticipated, and therefore potentially harmful, is going to happen. When Sigi brings out the bridle and bit, Manny eyes it with interest and some trepidation. Her fear comes from the knowledge that any new object that is brought into her stall usually ends up touching her. She does not yet know the purpose of this device. She doesn't panic, however, because she has learned to trust Sigi more than she fears the unknown.

While Frank stands on one side holding the lead shank, Sigi's small, sensitive hands move slowly, tickling the bars of Manny's pink gums lightly so she will open her mouth, then slipping the metal bit between her teeth, over her tongue. While Manny is licking and chewing at the strange object in her mouth, Sigi slips the crown-piece of the bridle over her delicate ears and fastens the throat-latch.

"Easy, easy," she says, patting Manny's shoulder as the filly dives her neck forward, chewing furiously, tossing her head, trying to spit out or shake out the bit.

"Here, be a good girl, have some apple." Sigi offers Manny a quarter of an apple and the filly snatches it. Chewing the juicy pulp helps take her mind off the strange taste of

stainless steel and the slight pressure it exerts against the corners of her lips.

The purpose of the bit is to control the speed and direction of the horse's movement. The kind of bit used at Elloree Training Center is a full-cheek, jointed snaffle. It is shaped like the letter "H". The mild, light, five-inch-long horizontal bar fits over her tongue. It is "jointed" or hinged in the center. The bit lies on the flat space of gums (bars) between her incisors and her molars and the idea is to get her used to carrying the metal close to the sensitive parts of her mouth without fearing it. The vertical "cheeks," about the size and shape of fountain pens, lie alongside her muzzle and help to keep the bit from sliding through her mouth.

The bit is adjusted high and snug against the corners of Manny's lips, so she cannot get her tongue over it. Horses that learn to get their tongues over the bit to avoid its signals have to have their tongues strapped down with gauze ties during exercise and races. For the first lesson, no reins are attached to the bit. With her halter still on under the bridle, Manny is led around the stall to the left and then to the right. Later, with a rider, she will learn that the slight nutcracker action of the hinge on her tongue means to slow or stop, pressure on the right corner of her mouth means to turn right and pressure on the left corner means to turn left. Then, after she has become muscled up enough to gallop, she will learn to be "rated." A firmer bit pressure, applied to the sensitive bars of her mouth, will contain her energy in short, bursting strides, or dictate her pace while galloping or during a race.

Adjusting to the bit and bridle is usually not too frightening for the young horse. She is used to having a halter over her head and, as long as the bit causes her no pain, it is almost comforting to have a pacifier to roll her tongue against and gnaw on.

The saddle is much more frightening. Manny, like most youngsters, has never had weight on her back. Foals that are handled often and "two-handed," the way Banknote was, become used to an arm surrounding various parts of their bodies or putting slight amounts of pressure on their tender spines. The horse's instinct is to move away from strange or unpleasant sensations, especially from anything unknown going on behind it. Because the back is one of the most sensitive parts of the horse's body, Sigi pats Manny's spine and barrel for a while before slowly sliding the light exercise saddle over her withers. She eases the saddle backward, careful not to rub Manny's hair the wrong way, and gently fits it into place. Gradually, as the filly becomes accustomed to the feel of the leather next to her skin, Sigi allows the full weight of it to rest on her back. Manny arches her spine downward to escape the saddle, but it follows her. She puffs out air through red nostrils and cranes her head around to see what this thing is on her back.

"Steady now," says Sigi. As Manny straightens up again, realizing that the saddle will not harm her, Sigi reaches under her belly and fastens the girth very loosely to the saddle buckles. Horses naturally fight any constriction or restraint. Tightening the girth too much too soon often causes yearlings—especially fillies, which are more sensitive than colts—to become "cinch-bound", so frightened of the girth that they buck wildly to try to get away from it. A bad experience at this age can make a horse difficult to saddle for the rest of its life.

Once she accepts the saddle and girth, Manny is led around the stall in both directions. Day by day, the girth is tightened, one notch at a time, until the saddle is fastened securely. Only then is Manny led out of her stall and around the barn's shed row in both directions, wearing the saddle and bridle, her "tack," the equipment of her trade.

As soon as she seems comfortable carrying the weight of the saddle, Sigi is ready to "belly" her in the stall. At first, when Sigi lies across Manny's back, the filly buckles and sinks low, more from surprise than from strain. Frank, at her head, fiddles with her nostrils to placate her while Sigi stays steady to let her learn to adjust to the pressure and the new sensation.

Horses are always mounted from the left, a tradition left over from the time of the Romans. Because most soldiers were right-handed and carried their spears in that hand, it became a convention to hold the reins in the left hand while mounting and swing the spear up over the horse's back.

Each day, Sigi puts a little more weight on Manny and inches her body farther and farther toward the filly's right side, until Manny's back has learned to support her full one-hundred-pound weight. Then, lying on her belly over the saddle and stroking the filly's right shoulder to give her confidence, Sigi deftly lifts her right leg up over Manny's hindquarters and "straddles" her for the first time.

Sigi's weight slides around Manny Dober's ribs. Her legs envelop the filly. Manny sinks and bulges from side to side, testing the limits of the invisible thing wrapped around her. As Manny sucks deep breaths and wiggles and twists away from the rider, Sigi perches toward the front of the saddle, over the filly's strong withers, where Manny will feel the heaviness least, and glides her hands in long strokes down the filly's twitching neck.

Sigi's balance is good. Even when Manny crouches back on her hocks as if to sit down, the girl stays still, petting the horse and encouraging her to go forward with little clucks. Frank, still at the filly's head, fondles her nostrils and indicates to her with the rope that she should walk with him. It is very important that the filly learn that she cannot go backward to avoid the rider's weight and even more important that no matter what she does, the rider is able to stay on her back. Most evasions in horses are initiated from the hindquarters. The horse whose hind legs are moving forward cannot rear or buck or flip itself over backward. Sigi stays as still as possible to help Manny get used to and adjust for her weight. "It's important, especially with a horse with a bad attitude, not to get the rider thrown," Frank explains. "If the horse learns that it can toss off the weight, rather than carrying it, it may turn into a dangerous rogue who will try to throw its rider every time it is asked to do something it doesn't feel like doing."

Manny, with her nervous but tractable disposition, adjusts to the rider quickly. After two days of walking with Sigi on her back, reins are attached to the bit. As Frank leads her around the stall, Sigi begins to teach Manny the reins' turn signals. Eight days from the time she was backed, Manny is ready to go outside the stall and walk around the shed row with Sigi in the saddle. In two weeks she is jogging around the shed row with a "set" of other yearlings, first to the left and then to the right so that the muscles on each side of her body develop equally. Manny takes turns leading the set.

"Young horses learn from each other," explains Frank, watching the once terrified group of yearlings parade neatly down the long side of the barn. "You want a racehorse to learn from the start that he has to have his turn to be in front."

Six days later, Manny is ready to go to the paddock. In this fenced exercise ring, 125 feet wide and 250 feet long, she and the two other yearlings in her set begin work, jogging and cantering big, slow figure eights.

"We ride long here," says Frank, watching Manny begin to jog her first big, awkward circles to the right and to the left. "At the track the stirrups are short, but for training we like to keep our legs around the horse. You know there's an old saying, 'The longer you ride, the longer you ride.' Well, that's doubly true when you are breaking yearlings." Frank, who over his twenty years of training young horses has had a broken foot, a broken wrist, and a concussion, still rides and doesn't seem to blame the young horses for the injuries they have inflicted. "That's just part of the game. Certain ones are roughnecks. It's like raising a family of kids. It's a lot of fun, but it requires a whole lot of patience."

Manny Dober's feet step hesitantly across the strange dirt in the paddock. Her glistening chestnut haunches skitter and fishtail as she learns to balance Sigi's weight. Until the muscles of her back and gaskins are more developed, Manny will have difficulty stiffening her spine and carrying her rider directly forward. Sigi manages to keep her weight steady over Manny's shifting withers and guides the wobbly filly in a large circle with the right rein. The circle, because it forces Manny to bend her body and transport most of her load with her inside hind leg, is an ideal exercise both in balancing and in developing flexion and strength in the muscles and joints which will propel her in giant piston-like strokes down the hard-fought inches of sand at Suffolk Downs and Belmont Park. On those demanding afternoons not so far in her future, she will have to be able to balance all of her driving weight on the left edges of her hooves at each precarious stride, spinning a mile of distilled horsepower in a precise and direct oval of speed and will.

This morning, though, in the cool of the pine breeze, Manny's circles are more sideways than forward, as she veers from the slightest crinkle of a pinecone falling to earth. With her belly bulging out to one side and her head and neck swooping in the other direction, she tries to balance by squatting on spread hind feet. The pattern her hoofprints leave in the soft dirt looks like the magnified crayon scrawl of a preschooler's first attempt to draw a cloud. Sigi does not demand a perfect circle. She cares only that Manny keep moving forward, no matter what, and continue turning as best she can to the right. Gradually, she begins to squeeze her legs more strongly against Manny's sides, urging her to move on faster. The more definitively a horse is stepping forward with its hind legs, the better it is able to balance itself in motion and the straighter its body will be.

Manny starts to jog brightly for a few strides, looking balanced, confident and almost cocky as she shifts her weight from one diagonal pair of legs to the other in small, rhythmic bounces. Sigi smiles, enjoying the feel of the filly's newfound coordination. When they reach the corner of the paddock and Sigi opens the rein to turn her, though, Manny forgets that she has to bring her right hind leg farther underneath her center of gravity to pivot through the turn. Frightened by her own uncertainty, she stumbles, hops, rears, wheels backward in unsteady spins to the center of the paddock.

Horses are thousand-pound copy cats. Seeing Manny, the two other yearlings in her set twist wildly in sympathy, and soon all three riders are perching forward in the swirls of dust and terrified horseflesh.

The scene is intense, silent. If the riders scream, it will scare the yearlings and get them so upset that they may be impossible to calm down. If they pull on the reins, there is a good chance that the pain caused by the bit will frighten the yearlings even more and they will flip over backward trying to get away from it. If the young horses learn to associate turning with punishment or pain, they will be reluctant to approach that corner of the paddock again.

Sigi, hardly unseated by Manny's commotion, leans forward with loose reins and kicks the filly's sides to urge her forward. At last the message seems to get from Manny's ribs to her brain and she jogs unsteadily along the fence line, but when they return to the same corner where she lost her balance, Manny snorts and cringes with white-rimmed eyes. Once a horse has avoided something from fear, it is important to make it face the same fear and work through it as soon as possible.

The horse is the classic paranoid personality. Fear is its strongest emotion and memory is its most highly developed mental faculty. People who break yearlings have to be part athlete, part parent and part child psychiatrist. A fear created and left unresolved will haunt a horse's career like a recurring nightmare for trainers, exercise riders, jockeys and owners.

"Come on now," coos Sigi, as if the filly can understand her. Looking as if the farthest thing from her mind is whether or not Manny goes through the corner, she presses Manny's ribs hard with her right leg to help her bend her body into the turn and to get her to move her right leg farther forward. Rather than taking a strong hold on the reins and trying to force Manny to negoti-ate a perfect corner with the weapon of the bit, Sigi tries to teach Manny to engage her hind legs more actively and find her own way. In general, horses that are allowed to figure things out for themselves stay calmer than horses that are forced with strength or pain. Although gentle persuasion is more time-consuming at the beginning than brute force, it helps to develop the willing, trusting attitude that allows a horse to perform to its maximum potential.

"You'd be surprised," comments Frank, letting out a small sigh of relief as Manny trots through the turn quickly. She is nervous and unsteady, but her ears are cocked as she listens to Sigi, and her feet step boldly under the girl's weight. "They pick it up really fast if you just let them. Horses are a lot smarter than people give them credit for being. The thing is, you want them to be willing in their work."

Part of the mystique of training horses is that in spite of the fact that they are enormous, powerful animals, quite capable of breaking any of the equipment used to control them and of killing their handlers with a single kick, they seem generally benevolent in their attitude toward humans. Like children, they seek reassurance and, for a few kind words and gentle, consistent handling, they will work their hearts out trying to please.

Occasionally, however, trainers run across a roguish yearling—a colt or filly which, because it was badly brought up or because it was just born with a mean streak, has a serious character flaw. One famous trainer, Preston Burch, described a big French colt which gave him a lot of headaches. The colt would behave like a perfect gentleman, responding to the rider's commands, until, suddenly and with no apparent provocation, he would slump to the ground, roll over and try to crush the exercise rider. Most horsemen are accustomed to taking daily physical risks in order to develop horses properly, but the colt's actions made him both dangerous to his rider and totally useless as a race animal. Burch's only solution was to resort to the drastic tactic of "throwing" the yearling.

Throwing is the ultimate method of psychologically intimidating a horse without causing him physical injury. The next time the colt slumped to the ground with a boy up, Burch had the stable foreman pin the yearling to the ground. While the large man sat on the yearling's head so he couldn't move, Burch whipped him thoroughly. Being held down and unable to get up is the scariest situation a horse can be in. Being forced to suffer discomfort and fear while held on the ground by a man is so terrifying to the horse that he develops a healthy respect for the ability of humans to overpower him. Burch's yearling, like most yearlings that are thrown young enough, was cured of his bad character. Once the yearling is so strong that it cannot be held down, reforming a true rogue becomes nearly impossible. The horse that learns that it is stronger than humans and capable of intimidating them virtually reverts to a wild state.

After a few days of jogging big circles in both directions around the paddock, Manny has learned how to stretch her muscles and bend her hocks to carry Sigi's weight. Her feet dig more surely into the soft footing and, though it will be a few months until her back muscles and tendons are fully conditioned to withstand the stress of racing, she is ready to begin cantering in both directions around the paddock. The canter, which is a slow and contained gallop, demands better balance than the trot. Manny's balletic legs, which seem gangly for her underdeveloped body, adapt easily to the three-beat rhythm. Soon she is cantering big figure eights with Wanda behind her, changing leads in the air each time she changes direction.

For racing purposes, yearlings must learn to do a "flying change of leg" automatically each time they turn. In the canter, as in the racing gallop, one hind leg strikes the ground first, providing the strong, driving impetus for each stride. This force thrusts the horse's weight diagonally forward toward the opposite foreleg, called the "leading leg" because, though it is the last leg to strike the ground, it is the farthest forward

extension of the horse's body. If the right front leg is the leading leg, the horse is said to be "on the right lead." If the left front leg is the leading leg, the horse is said to be "on the left lead." The horse that only learns to gallop on one lead is rather like a pianist who only learns to play with one hand. Although such a player may be brilliant, the overdevelopment of one set of muscles at the expense of the other limits both endurance and range of performance.

A good sprinter, which may not have to make a single turn during a race, can get away with running on one lead, but it is as hard for the one-leaded horse to win at the classic distances as it is for the concert pianist to play one-handed Beethoven. Not only will the horse tire prematurely—by continually thrusting all of its motive force onto the same front limb, it will overstress the bones and break down more easily. One great virtuoso of the track, Alydar, was rumored not to change leads during a race. Although this did not keep him from giving championship performances, it may have contributed to the fracture that forced him into early retirement in the middle of his three-year-old season.

In the "flying change of leg" the horse learns to shift its thrusting energy from one set of legs to the other by retracting one hind leg and advancing the other in the air between strides. Executing a flying change is as natural to the horse as skipping is to a person. Manny, like most yearlings, picks this up quite easily, shifting legs on the turns as Sigi shifts her weight.

Just as people are right- or left-handed, horses are innately one-sided. Manny, who tends to favor her left side, has to spend more time cantering to the right. The object of the Elloree training program is to equalize tone, coordination and muscular strength throughout the horse's body, to build a "foundation" for the animal. Later, when she is trained specifically for racing, Manny Dober will be encouraged to become slightly left-sided, because all American races are run in a counter-clockwise direction. Meanwhile, it is Elloree's job to get this still-growing adolescent to the physical point at which there is no danger of her injuring herself during rigorous race training.

"The Thoroughbred is the only complete athlete there is," remarks Frank Smith, leaning against the rail of the three-quarter-mile training track and squinting through the mist at the top of the rise to watch for Manny Dober and her set to emerge from the barns and go through their morning gallop. It is late November, just ten weeks since Manny and Wanda, stunted, scruffy and suspicious, arrived to learn their purpose in life.

"There they are," says Frank, pointing to a shadowy line of horses picking their way gingerly through the sandhills. Manny Dober, at the front of the line, is the first to be revealed by a weak beam of sunshine, her alert and noble head etched against the gauzy dawn. Her whole body and way of carrying herself are different now. Nourished by ten quarts of oats a day and made fit by long, slow gallops of 1½ to 1¾ miles every morning, she is supple and hard. Gone is the soft baby fat, the wobbly pattern of her footsteps. Her back has developed enough to stand the strain of the person in the saddle and, because she has been brought along slowly, she has not suffered the most common injury to young horses in training, bucked shins. This condition, an inflammation of the cannon bone, causes the horse's legs to become sore and swollen. The horse is lame and the legs hurt so much that even a finger pointed at the shins can cause the horse to cringe. Most cases of bucked shins are curable with rest and poulticing. The ailment is the result of too much fast work too soon. It is a fact of American racing that many yearlings in training buck their shins unnecessarily due to efforts to get them out on the track competing before they are physically ready to run.

Although she has spent the last twenty-nine days being "legged up," or galloped slowly to build up her wind and muscle and to "put a bottom on her," Frank still doesn't feel Manny is up to being breezed. Most horses at Elloree are "breezed" lightly or allowed to "run off a little" once before

Christmas, usually about forty-five days after they first began galloping on the training track. Others, like Manny, who was immature for her age, need a longer "buildup program" during which their appetite and their growth are stimulated to bring them to a higher level of physical and mental maturity. It is the trainer's job to condition the horse's nervous system as well as its respiration, circulation, bone quality and muscular strength. To push Manny along right now might not only cause her physical injury, it might also get her into a frame of mind in which she wanted to fight the rider. Running is intoxicating to the young horse.

"That's what they're bred for and that's one of the quickest things they're going to respond to," explains Frank. "When we first ask them to run, we'll just cluck to them and move them on a little with our feet and our hands. You just keep nudging and keep asking and you hardly ever need to use a stick. If they try to get in a hurry about running, we just slow them down and make them remember that they've got to do it our way. But we don't even like to start breezing until we make sure that the horse wants to listen to us.

"Personally, I like a lazy horse. He's not going to hurt himself by overdoing. When you ask him, he's going to do it a lot easier than the one who is fractious. The nervous ones take so much out of themselves, but the lazy horse has a more relaxed nervous system."

Manny Dober, prancing onto the sand track and sidestepping daintily to avoid some vision she has seen rising out of the three-quarter-mile pole, is anything but lazy. She sucks the wind into the huge nostrils that look like they should belong to a horse twice her size and whinnies wildly back toward the distant barns.

"Easy there. Come on, Manny," says Sigi as the filly bounces around underneath her. "Let's go take a look at the starting gate. You'll see Wanda again soon enough."

Thoroughbred yearlings, like schoolchildren, are divided up by ability and achievement into slow and fast groups. Precocious horses are trained together so that they will be challenged by each other. The less talented and the immature are placed in a separate group so that they do not become discouraged or disheartened by having to compare themselves to more capable performers. As a rule, sprinters mature earlier than distance horses. The fast group consists for the most part of those older and physically more able yearlings which have shown that they will have some early speed and will not break down under the stress of heavier training. Because Frank has decided that Wanda is skeletally and emotionally more mature than Manny and will probably develop early enough to be entered in the first short sprints at the beginning of her two-year-old season, the buddies work in separate sets.

"They all start out on the same pattern and the same program," explains Frank. "Then they begin to be individuals. Now, this Manny, she looks like, with time, she could be a useful filly, but she's kind of slow developing. She has a good way of going, she travels alright, and she has the temperament, but she is small and immature for her age. Listen to that," he says as Manny bellows out another shrill cry for Wanda. "They love to talk, you know. They get all confused leaving the barn or they don't want to be without their buddies. They're like kids. You can just understand what they're feeling."

It is obvious what Manny is feeling as she approaches the sixteen-foot-tall and forty-foot-long starting gate for the first time. The six-stall contraption, with its high metal scaffolding, jail-cell doors and floating padded dividers, sends her balking backward, wheeling and diving into the bit. Although she has learned to gallop slowly forward, both on the rail and on the outside, abreast with the other yearlings, and to lead, be in the middle or bring up the rear as they simulate possible racetrack formations, she has yet to learn one of a racehorse's most important lessons: how to get off to a good start.

A race, particularly a short one, can be lost in the starting gate. Just as swimmers use the wall of the pool to compress their energy and push off, establishing momentum, racehorses must learn to compact their bodies to spring forward from the gate. As the horse crouches down, bending his hocks for action, his head and body drop a full twelve inches. A long metal "stumbling bar" on the ground behind the gate keeps his hooves from sliding backward and gives him something to push off from until he has established a toehold on the racing surface. When the gate opens, he lunges forward from both hind feet simultaneously and takes off.

There is no real way to teach a horse to break well, other than giving it the time to figure things out for itself. Horses that fear the gate so much that they have to be stuffed into it before each race, or those so nervous that they rear and fuss when the doors are shut, not only are dangerous to deal with, but also tend to stumble, shy, waver or even fall when they break. Although there are instances of famous runners like Bold Ruler falling to their knees when the gate opened and recovering to sprint past the field to victory, the average horse needs every fifth-of-a-second and quarter-inch edge it can get.

"The horse should be contented with what he is doing so that when he goes to the races he will conduct himself in a way that he's not a problem to deal with," explains Frank in his long, slow drawl as he ambles toward Manny, who is hyperventilating furiously through red, distended nostrils, as she canters in place like a malfunctioning hobbyhorse.

"Now what's your problem?" he asks, stopping a few feet in front of her. "Is that some sort of monster?"

Perhaps it is the engaging, gentlemanly tone of voice. Perhaps it is his solid, motionless, and totally relaxed air, radiant with paternal interest. Manny stands still, ears and eyes attentive only to him, looking like a child who is a little bit frightened but knows it is overreacting.

"Come on now," he says, snapping on a lead shank and leading her gently toward the gate. "It can't be as bad as all that."

Manny walks in short, tense steps, angling her haunches away from the gate. When they reach the big metal contraption looming out of the mist, she snorts down on its fender and freezes stiff waiting for it to snort back. When it doesn't do anything, she sticks out her tongue and licks the glossy paint.

Somewhere deep in her consciousness is the message that the world is divided into two sorts of things: those that want to eat her and those that she can eat. This starting gate, which is neither food nor predator, loses her interest quickly. She hesitates only a little when Frank leads her through one of the stalls for the first time, because it is only forty inches wide and the patterns of the shadows are moving underfoot.

The horse hates to enter into any narrow space in which its range of movement and vision are limited. Even when fully domesticated, it is always looking for the lurking danger and the way out. It hates to step onto any unfamiliar surface where the footing is unknown. The combination of poor depth perception and a naturally suspicious nature can transform a blanket on the ground into a bottomless pit and a shifting shadow into a predator rising up out of the earth.

Once through the gate, Manny walks into it willingly again and again. She learns to stand quietly while the back door is closed behind her. It is important to teach horses right from the beginning that, no matter what happens, they cannot back out. Horses which do not learn this often injure their jockeys, bucking and rearing over backward inside the gate.

At last, when her eyes are squinting closed with boredom, Frank unsnaps the lead shank, but Manny doesn't seem to notice. As he starts to amble off to study the rest of the set, she steps along beside him. When he stops by the fence rail, she nudges his elbow with her soft and bewhiskered muzzle.

"Sorry," he says. "That's it for today. If you're real good, though, you can come back and do it again tomorrow."

Back at the barn, Manny is sponged thoroughly with lukewarm water containing a body brace. A thin metal belt known as a sweat scraper is used to sluice excess water, sweat and dirt from her coat. This bath, the equivalent of a human shower, keeps her pores from getting clogged, relaxes her muscles and prepares her for the grooming routine that will be a part of her daily life at the track. Sigi runs a hand down each of Manny's still-tender legs, checking for any sign of swelling or inflammation.

Until she has reached the age of four, Manny's skeleton will not have completely ossified, or hardened. The bones of her lower legs, which must take the most punishment during training and racing, are still soft and prone to crack. Her tendons, which will someday be so powerful that they could keep her trotting even if all the muscles connecting to her knee were severed, are still weak. Osselets (ossifications of synovial fluid in the fetlock joint), splints (calcium deposits along the cannon bone) and tendon strains are all common injuries to yearlings in training. If they are discovered and treated in the early stages with massage, liniments, cold packs, bandages, poulticing and, primarily, rest, they will often disappear or resolve themselves into harmless blemishes through the body's natural healing processes. If ignored or undetected, they may become so severe that they limit the motion of the joint (osselets), fray the tendons which pass over them (splints), or cripple the horse for life (bowed tendons). It is an irony of American racing that most racehorses break down from training or racing long before their bodies reach full maturity.

On this brisk December day in South Carolina, though, Manny Dober, at age nineteen months, is radiant with adolescent health and soundness. Her eyes are clear, her bronze coat glimmers over compacted muscle, her legs, free of swelling or blemishes, are "tight" and "clean." She steps jauntily, four clear and even hoofbeats carrying her weight equally, marching down the drive beside the "hot-walker" who will walk her for forty-five minutes before putting her back in the stall.

The practice of hot-walking is absolutely

essential to the maintenance of a Thoroughbred in training. Full relaxation is as essential to muscle development as strenuous exercise. A good trainer would no more send a horse directly to its stall after a workout than a track coach would tell his runners to flop into bed immediately after a brisk thirty laps. Manny is walked to reoxidize her muscles, to prevent stiffness and cramping, and to make sure that excess blood does not get stuck in her feet. When her respirations per minute and body temperature have returned to normal levels, and her veins are "down," she is returned to her stall.

The horse has very poor circulation below the knee. It relies primarily upon the foot, expanding as it impacts the ground and contracting as it is lifted from the ground, to pump blood up the leg. If a horse is galloped and then left to stand, blood courses down into the foot faster than it is pumped back up. Eventually, the feet become hot, painful and so swollen with blood that the hoof cracks and separates from the inner foot. Once this "founder" occurs, the horse is usually irreversibly lame for life. When the veins that bulge out all over the horse's body during intense exercise are no longer evident, it is a good indication that circulation has returned to normal and the danger is over.

In the long afternoons, Manny is turned out in the sweet pasture grass to romp with the other fillies. On Sundays, she gets the whole day off. Around the end of December, she and the other yearlings, like any normal schoolchildren, have a few weeks of Christmas vacation. According to Frank, "They've got to have recess. Besides, the colts are less likely to get manly in their ways if they are turned out to play with the others, though there is the occasional bullish one who has to be turned out alone. The Christmas break lets them freshen up and unwind from all the work they've been doing. And it gives us a chance to worm them, trim their feet, have their teeth floated (rasping of the sharp edges that hinder chewing) and get them set up for the

first of the year when the serious work begins."

On January 1, 1979, Manny Dober becomes officially two years old, although her actual age is one year and eight months. While the more precocious Wanda begins a program of breezing, starting with short breezes of one-sixteenth to one-eighth of a mile, Manny is given another month off to develop more before being pushed to perform. In February, while Wanda is learning to breeze longer and longer distances approaching half a mile, Manny is put back into work, at first just galloping slowly and then gradually "being allowed to run off a little," just so she can get the feel of it. Then, around the end of February, Manny is put to her first real test. She is asked to break from the gate and breeze three-eighths of a mile.

Intelligent and quick to please, as are most fillies, Manny remembers well her careful instruction in the starting gate. First she learned to walk through, then to stand quietly, then to jog and canter from the stall with the front door open, and finally to break from the gate at a gallop with the front door shut. She strides almost eagerly into the small enclosure and stands patiently while the back and front doors are snapped shut.

"When I watch the horses breeze," says Frank, waiting for Manny to break, "I look to see what's in the horse. Just what's there. I don't clock them that much. I'm not really worried about how fast they go. I can tell if they can run or not and the clocking itself doesn't mean a whole lot. A good horse may work in the same time as a bad one. It's class and ability that count. I can watch a set work and I can pretty well tell the claimers from the allowance horses. Like one good trainer said, 'It doesn't matter how fast they run as long as it's fast enough.' "

Manny, poised on her hocks, one ear pricked back listening to Sigi, the other pricked forward down the track, seems anxious to live up to the challenges of racing life. When a gate opens, she springs. The bell goes off behind her, but she is already far down the track, streamlining her small body into the wind and digging her toes into the deep sand base in breathless, four-beat choreography. The strides pound out, past the eighth pole, past the three-sixteenths. She shows no burst of early speed, no sudden lightning dash. Her strides are not brilliant, but they are effortless and each one is exactly the same. Her legs, her breaths, her clockwork heart are generally mechanized to produce a perfectly even pace.

"Yep," says Frank. "I figured, though it's still a little early to tell, but I think if this one does anything she's going to have to go a distance. Wandaful Candy J was bred to be fast and early and she is fast and early. This one's female side is distance and she's bred to go long. You can see it in her stride. It's easy and it's even, but it has more endurance than pure speed."

When Sigi stands up in the stirrups and leans back to ease the filly at the three-eighths pole, the dull, brown sheen of sweat has just begun to dampen Manny's chest and flanks. Her breaths come as easily as if she were made of wind. When she has finally been rocked and cajoled down into a full halt, she lifts up her black muzzle to the silver-dollar sun, squints her eyes shut, and just whinnies and whinnies until the whole little valley edged in barn roofs and pine tips resounds with her pleasure squeals.

"A lot of them do that after they gallop," says Frank, chuckling. "It's fun for them and I guess it beats the doldrums of every day, though some people would say I'm nuts for thinking that."

A few weeks after her first breeze from the gate, Manny is asked to break and breeze with another horse.

"Some horses can't stand to work every day. They really feel the pressure and get emotional about it. Others thrive on work. Others are totally disinterested. They feel like, oh man, golly, I don't want to go out and do that again today. I just did that yesterday. It's a real challenge trying to figure out what each one needs. It's a pleasure, though. There's nothing like them." Frank Smith, anxious to see how Manny will respond in company, loads her and another, more seasoned yearling into the gate. The other yearling, also a distance prospect, but more mature than Manny, has shown a certain amount of class and the idea is to breeze them together so that they can help each other. The riders will keep them head to head so that the older yearling does not breeze too fast and so that Manny learns to improve her speed without getting discouraged by being beaten. Horses are influenced by the company they keep and it is hoped that any natural class Manny may possess will be brought out by non-threatening association with good horses.

Manny eyes the other yearling wickedly through the thin metal bars that separate them. Somewhere, in the taut linkage of her vertebrae, in the burning beneath her breastbone, in the deepening bend of her hocks, she knows what she is here for. Horses are more intelligent than people give them credit for being. The gate opens and they fly out of the chutes side by side. Whenever two horses run, it is a race.

Everything in Manny Dober's spirit tells her that she wants to be a racehorse. Although she is only fifteen hands tall (five feet to the top of her withers), her girth is as big as that of a sixteen-hand horse. Her enormous lungs and heart, her wide, well-developed feet, and her fine, proud head all look like they are waiting for her body to fill out and grow into them. She has still only reached 88 percent of her full growth and there is hope that her bones and musculature will catch up.

The fighting stare of Tanta is in her eyes. What she lacks in maturity, she makes up in sheer feistiness and will as she bolts along beside the other yearling. A bay filly with a long, sweeping stride, her opponent is capable of covering more ground and completing her stride phases faster than Manny, but it is Manny who keeps pressing her nose to the front, striving in the deepest fibers of her muscles to be first. Ears lying flat on her neckline in classic equine threat, blue-and-amber eyes fixed in challenge, Manny lugs forward on the bit, trying to pull the reins from Sigi's hands, while the big bay, more experienced and perhaps less ambitious, is easily rated. The three furlongs are not run with blistering speed, nor were they supposed to be, but Manny's attitude is evident. Her veins map the routes of blood under her soaking coat and she champs against the foaming bit, furious, when she is pulled up, that the race has ended before she had a chance to hit her longest strides and leave the bay in her dust. To the bay filly, a talented but indifferent runner, it was no contest. Given the signal, she could have opened up her stride and leaped past Manny at any designated moment. While Manny fusses and strikes out at the sand track with her front foot in anger and frustration, the big bay, hardly winded, stares off vacantly into the distance, where a mockingbird is plucking bits of cotton bandages up in its beak to weave into a nest.

Life's ironies are nowhere more apparent than on the racetrack. Manny has the heart and guts to become a great horse, but she is limited by her slight physique. The strapping bay filly, with her long stride and power to burn, has all the equipment Manny so desperately misses, but her lackadaisical attitude may prevent her from ever winning a race. Speed, without the desire to win, is useless. Boldness and determination are almost impossible to train for. "You can't change a horse's attitude, you just have to learn to live with it." This is why comparing horses only by comparing the times they clocked over the same distance is meaningless. As Joe Thomas at Windfields Farm once put it, "All great horses are fast but not all fast horses are great."

Attitude can compensate for a multitude of disabilities. It was sheer will to win that carried Assault to the 1946 Triple Crown victory on a malformed foot and earned him the title of the horse that "ran on three legs and a heart." It was indomitable fighting spirit verging on madness that drove Dark Secret down the homestretch of the 1934 Jockey Club Gold Cup. When he ruptured a tendon one-sixteenth of a mile from the finish, he forced all of his weight onto his good foot, shattering it, too, one step before the finish, but he crossed the line to win. Horses are predisposed to self-destruction, and horses with a winning attitude, be they cheap claimers or classics victors, are more predisposed to self-destruction than those that don't care.

The morning after Manny's first light breeze from the gate with another horse, she walks out of her stall limping. Sigi is the one who discovers it. The filly is dragging her toe and "going short" with her left hind leg. The diagnosis is that her stifle, the equivalent of the human knee joint, has become dislocated. Loose stifles are common to young horses that have not reached their full muscular development and over-exert themselves prematurely. Stifles can be "blistered"—burned with strong medicine to create tightening scar tissue—or "injected" with steroids to provide quick muscular relief, but Frank decides that rest, with very light work over a longer period of time, will be the most humane and sensible treatment.

"Rest is the best medicine for a young horse. She never has worked as well as I feel she could, and all that is saying is that she doesn't need to be rushing."

At the end of March, when the other two-year-olds, including Wanda, leave for racetracks around the country, Manny and a few others stay on to grow up more, physically or emotionally, before they are asked to push themselves to the limit in the stinging sand and crazed momentum of six furlongs of battling horseflesh. By late June of 1979, just two years and two months after she staggered to her feet beside the fierce-eyed Tanta and sucked her first gulp of mare's milk with red, curling lips, Manny is pronounced sound and fit enough to race.

There is a pine-scented drizzle in the gray air as Manny wends her way down the path to the waiting van. Clouds of steam spew from her nostrils and she moves elegantly now, like a thing of liquid fire burning its way through the atmosphere. Although she is still leggy and small for her age, there is a self-containment in the way her hind legs swing forward like metronomes, striking the earth directly beneath her heartbeat. She conveys a sense of grace more appropriate to a deer or a panther than to a domestic animal. She is an athlete, for better or worse. Her prehistoric instincts have been conditioned to harness her energy into the quintessential running machine.

In human terms, she is a little over fourteen years old—just pubescent. She is a "young" two-year-old, and in Frank's opinion, "She's been slow developing and stayers do develop slower than sprinters. She needs some racing to get herself together and show how she wants to run. She will have to run with relatively cheaper horses to win in shorter races, but I feel that if she does amount to anything, she will have to go a distance."

School days—the tranquil life of morning lessons on the quiet training track and afternoons spent frolicking in the peaceful, pine-scented pastures with other fillies— are over. Sigi, who patiently braved her first panicky conniptions and taught her to trust the hands and voice of a human rider better than she trusted her own instinct, has, along with Tanta, who taught her how to fight like a horse, faded from consciousness. She is in the van again, this time without Wanda to keep her company, headed for Suffolk Downs in Massachusetts. She was bred to be an athlete and an investment, to give pleasure to man, not to laze in an expensive field and pursue an active social life.

Horses are naturally gregarious animals, but like most modern horses, Manny leads a lonely existence, isolated from the herd. Some horses become so lonesome and fretful that they have to be given a pet goat or pony, which lives in their stall to keep them company. The closest Manny Dober will get to others of her own kind will be during those fifteen or twenty minutes a year that she spends stampeding through the flanks and shoulders of some driven herd hurtling around an oval track. In those brief, intimate meetings, the only instinct pulsing from her brain will be to get in front and prove that she is the best.

# Part Two

# THOROUGHBRED RACING

---

*"All great horses are fast but not all fast horses are great."*
—*Joe Thomas, Windfields Farm*

# Racing

When ancient civilizations developed the ability to write, their chronicles included detailed descriptions of the even-then long-established practice of racing horses. There is something so fundamentally compelling about the horse that racing became universal among civilizations that had the opportunity and the leisure to pursue it.

The culmination of mankind's age-old fascination with racing was the development of the supreme equine athlete, the Thoroughbred racehorse. Concurrent with this development was the growth of racing into a professional sport with wide public appeal. As we've seen, the purpose of the breeding industry today is still the production of the best possible racehorse.

If the purpose of horse racing today were simply to determine which horses were best, the sport would be easy to understand. Unfortunately, particularly in the United States, racing is a much more complicated proposition. The reasons lie in the difference between racing and other professional sports.

All sports are entertainment industries, deriving their income from fans who pass through the turnstiles or watch the sport on television. Unlike those other sports, however, racing receives the bulk of its income not from admission fees and television rights, but from the money that spectators wager on the outcome of races. Betting is a more overt and a more important part of the entertainment appeal of horse racing than it is of any other sport.

This legalized gambling is the feature that has contributed most to racing's ranking as the number-one American spectator sport. Along with the magnificent spectacle of Thoroughbred athletes competing, the horseplayer has the added challenge of matching his knowledge of the sport against the knowledge of his fellow racegoers, nine or ten times a day. No other sport combines thrilling action with intellectual challenge in quite the same way.

At the same time, however, the presence of gambling necessitates diligent management to maintain the integrity of the sport. Such management requires balancing the varied and often conflicting needs of horsemen, owners, track managements, state governments and racing fans.

Unfortunately, in the last twenty years, the scramble for racing revenue on the part of track managements and state governments has caused problems for horsemen and horseplayers. A huge expansion in racing dates has led to a precipitous decline in the quality of racing. Exotic wagering, with its higher takeout percentages, has squeezed more dollars out of racegoers while occasioning fix attempts that have called into question the integrity of the sport. The reluctance of state governments to adjust takeout percentages has caused purse increases to lag behind inflation, driving owners out of racing and horsemen out of business.

Fortunately, the combined efforts of the dedicated members of the Thoroughbred racing community have led to increasing recognition of the problems of racing. At the same time, the magnificent crop of horses of the 1970s—Secretariat, Seattle Slew, Forego, Affirmed, Spectacular Bid, and many more—have rekindled public interest in racing as a spectator sport. The combination of these two factors has arrested the sport's decline and holds out great hope for the future.

To be an expert spectator and participant, the racing fan needs in-depth knowledge about how the sport of racing is conducted. In this section, we'll cover the history of the sport of racing, the adminis-tration of the sport, the kinds of races and the conditions under which they're run and the racetrack facilities. We'll look at the life of the racehorse—how it's schooled, trained, cared for and ridden. We'll also look at how the horse race is supervised and how it's run.

# Section 4

# History of Horse Racing

*Heroin H.C.L. 12 grains*
*Aromatic spirits of ammonia 6 fluid ounces*
*Caffeine alkaloid 6 ounces*
*Spirits of nitroglycerin 2 ounces*
*Strychnine 6 grains*
*Brandy or alcohol quantity sufficient to make one quart*
*Formula used to "hop" a horse fifty years ago. The horse was supposed to be dosed with two ounces of this concoction, with a chaser of water, one half hour before post time.*

—*from* Fair Exchange

## RACING IN ANCIENT TIMES

The origins of horse racing lie hidden in that dark period before the beginning of recorded history when man first domesticated the horse. While historians continue to argue whether organized mounted racing preceded chariot racing, they know man did ride horses long before he harnessed them. Given man's competitive instinct and urge to gamble, no doubt prehistoric nomadic tribesmen wagered their day's hunting haul on which of their two mounts was the faster. Since mounted racing, unlike chariot racing, doesn't require a fixed course, though, archaeological evidence of such sporting activity is difficult to uncover.

By the time man began to keep written records, racing was well established as the sport of kings and emperors. Baked clay tablets unearthed in Turkish Asia Minor contain detailed descriptions of the training of racehorses by one Kikkulis, head trainer for the King of Mitanni about 1350 B.C. Hittite drawings show racing flourishing in the same millennium. The Greek poet Homer, who lived in the ninth century B.C., describes in great detail in *The Iliad* a chariot race around the walls of Troy that was held as part of a funeral ceremony. The solemn nature of the occasion, however, didn't preclude attempts to fix the race—and hotly argued claims of foul by the drivers.

The Greeks, in 776 B.C., founded the Olympic Games to honor the god Zeus. In 680 B.C., four-horse-chariot events became Olympic events, and thirty-two years later mounted races were added. The Greeks rode bareback in the mounted races, although they used saddle clothes and girths for hunting and war. A "mares only" race was added in 496 B.C., and soon afterward a race for boy riders, who were like our modern racing apprentices.

While racing was popular in Greece, in Rome the sport became a public obsession. From a schedule of twelve races a day under the Emperor Augustus (27 B.C.–A.D. 14), programs expanded to 100 races a day under Domitian A.D. 81–96). The racing brought daily life almost to a halt, as the historian Suetonius described: "There flocked such crowds of spectators from all parts, that most of the strangers were obliged to lodge in tents erected in the streets, or along roads near the city. Several in the throng were squeezed to death, including two senators." Citizens wagered huge sums to back one of four racing factions, which were identified by the colors the drivers and riders wore—the Blue, Green, White and Red. The Emperor Caligula was such an enthusiastic supporter of the Green that he designated his favorite horse a senator.

Since the sport of racing had always been closely allied with the use of horses in war, most Roman racing was chariot racing rather than mounted races. The significance of Roman racing, as it relates to modern Thoroughbred racing, was that for the first time in recorded history the sport had developed into an organized professional sport with wide popular participation, as opposed to a private contest between horse owners or a part of a religious ceremony. In later Roman times, drivers were full-time professionals; race records and pedigrees were publicly kept; the races were conducted by professional racing officials. Even the abuses were those of modern-day racing —drugging and injuring of horses, sabotaging chariots, bribing and intimidating drivers.

As the Dark Ages settled over Europe, organized racing in the Roman style was snuffed out. Such racing requires leisure, and men were far too preoccupied with war and with the hunting necessary to put meat on the table. Furthermore, access to the swift Eastern breeds was cut off, and neither the huge steeds that carried the armored knights nor the light ponies used for hunting were suitable as racehorses. It was not until a millennium after the fall of Rome that horse racing was once again to assume its age-old prominence.

## RACING IN GREAT BRITAIN

The Romans brought chariot racing with them when they conquered Britain in A.D. 43, but the sport didn't long survive their retreat. While, no doubt, individuals tested the relative abilities of the various light-horse breeds they used for hunting, no clear pattern of organized racing has been found until the twelfth century, when the Crusaders returned home full of admiration for the Eastern horses ridden by their foes. These horses began to be imported for use in hunting. To display the speed of the horses to prospective buyers, regular competitions were organized; a description of London around A.D. 1174 mentions that such racing was held at Smithfield every Friday. During the reign of Richard II (1189–99), the first known racing purse was offered—forty pounds of gold. The race was run over a three-mile course, with knights as riders. Richard's successor, King John, reportedly maintained a stable of racing animals.

In the next four hundred years, as mounted warfare changed from knights on huge steeds to swift cavalry, the influence of the light horse grew. However, racing remained a diversion to the nobility, whose preoccupations were war and hunting. As we pointed out in our description of the development of the Thoroughbred, only after the defeat of the Spanish Armada in 1588 and the Restoration of Charles II in 1660 did the nobility have the leisure to devote themselves full time to racing, which then reevolved into a professional sport.

The reevolution of racing took place in three stages. During the time of Charles II, racing was strictly an amateur sport. The most common type of race was the two-horse match race. These matches were, typically, agreements between two owners to run their horses against each other. The purse was a private wager, with a provision for a forfeit should one owner decide to pull his horse out. No standard rules existed, and no governing body supervised the races. The two owners arrived at the rules by mutual agreement, then got a neutral third party to make a record of the race conditions, hold the wager and supervise the contest in case of disputes. In the larger racing centers, some people became specialists in this recording function. One, John Cheny, "keeper of the match" at Newmarket, published in 1727 the first *Cheny's Horse Matches,* which was intended as a compilation of matches all over Britain. This book later evolved into the modern *Racing Calendar.*

By the time of Queen Anne (1702–14), racing was moving to stage two, that of a semi-professional sport. As more interest in racing was generated and more racehorses were bred, match racing gave way to races in which several horses competed. These races were conducted and supervised by racecourses that sprang up all over England. Each racecourse was autonomous; each race meeting set its own rules for the contests held under its auspices.

The most common type of race was that conducted in heats, with the winner being the first horse to capture two heats. To attract better-quality horses, racecourses began to offer bigger and bigger prizes. The most prestigious races of all were the *King Plates,* which were contested in four-mile heats by horses at least six years old, who carried 168 pounds.

While racing became an organized affair at this time, the sport was still largely the pastime of the large landowners or their friends. Betting was still a matter of individual wagers between participants and spectators.

One of the factors that moved racing to stage three, that of a truly professional sport, was the advent of the Industrial Revolution and the end of the agrarian economy. The costs of maintaining a horse for six years before it could bring any return grew considerably, bringing pressure to allow races for younger horses. By the 1760s, three-year-old racing was firmly established; in 1776, the first stakes race for two-year-olds was held. Since younger horses lacked the stamina to run a number of heats, heat racing was replaced by *dashes,* a dash being any race decided by a single heat.

Because investors could get a quicker return on their profit, breeding racehorses became a separate industry. Breeders directed their efforts to the development of speedy, precocious animals, rather than the sturdier, slower types required for heat racing. The goal for breeders became the kind of horse that remains the ideal Thoroughbred today—the three-year-old that can sustain high speed under moderate weights over distances ranging from one mile to a mile and a half.

The trend to dashes meant more races and more betting opportunities. Private wagering between individuals gave way to the bookmaker. Areas for betting rings were established at every racecourse, and income from these bookmaking activities contributed to rising purses for horse races.

Finally, with the rapid expansion of the sport came the need for a central governing authority. Around 1750, racing's elite formed the Jockey Club, which met at Newmarket to write complete rules of racing. These rules, which were published in the *Racing Calendar,* were adopted throughout England. When the Jockey Club acquired the *Racing Calendar* and the General Stud Book, its authority became supreme. The Jockey Club to this day continues to exercise virtually complete control over racing and breeding in England.

By the late 1800s, racing in England, under the supervision of the horse breeders who created the Thoroughbred, had achieved a rather orderly transition from an amateur activity to a widely popular professional sport. The people involved—the jockeys, trainers, grooms and racing officials—were professionals. Wagering had become institutionalized through the bookmaker.

# THE HISTORY OF RACING IN AMERICA

English settlers brought to the New World both the sport of racing and the developing racehorse, but the size and diversity of the new continent spawned diverse kinds of racing. The development of Thoroughbred racing was far less orderly than in the mother country.

In the first English colony in Virginia, every member of the King's Council had bred or raced horses in England, but the dense woodlands of their new land prohibited the kind of racing they had conducted at home. Instead, a new kind of racing developed—short dashes in a straight line down the main streets of the village. Although land was later cleared, many Americans, particularly on the frontier, continued to favor these races of a quarter mile or less. They developed a new breed—a combination of the Thoroughbred and the Indian ponies—that became known as the Quarter Horse.

Restriction of racing to the streets in towns and roads between towns also brought about races for horses pulling carriages. Horses were trained and raced in both the trotting and pacing gaits. Breeding for these gaits produced the Standardbred, an animal of great endurance. To this day, the classic American harness races are conducted in heats, a practice long abandoned by Thoroughbred racing.

In the New York colony, however, where open plains were available, the more traditional English match racing and heat racing were practiced. The first English governor of New York, Richard Nicholls, laid out the first full-sized American racecourse on Long Island in 1665. When large areas of land in the South were cleared for tobacco and other crops, traditional racing also began to flourish in Maryland, Virginia (which, until 1792, included what is now Kentucky), and South Carolina. In the 1700s, Thoroughbreds were regularly imported from England for breeding purposes.

The Revolutionary War brought racing in America to an abrupt halt. After the war, embargoes against trading with England slowed importation of Thoroughbreds to a trickle until about 1830. At the same time, lingering bad feelings about all things British led Americans to disdain the new British trend to dash racing. Match racing and the traditional three- and four-mile-heat races predominated until about the time of the Civil War.

By the end of the Civil War, though, American racing had undergone a profound change. The same kind of change from a purely agrarian to an industrial society that had occurred in England made the raising of racehorses too expensive a hobby for American breeders. Horsemen could no longer afford to wait until a horse was five or six years old before it could race, and they needed public patronage to provide more and bigger purses to defray expenses. This meant organization of racecourses to conduct daily programs consisting of several races.

The formation of the Saratoga Association in 1863 to conduct racing at the famed New York spa and gambling resort signaled the arrival of the new trend. The meetings at Saratoga were so popular that Wall Street financier and horseman Leonard W. Jerome decided that New York City, the nation's largest city, needed a racetrack too. Together with his friend, August Belmont, Jerome purchased an estate in Fordham, Long Island, and built a glittering racecourse called Jerome Park. To administer racing at the track, Jerome formed a jockey club that consisted of thirteen hundred of the nation's most socially, politically and financially prominent people.

The society figures who flocked to the opening of Jerome Park in September 1866 found a clubhouse that looked like a luxury hotel. Included in the facilities were spacious dining rooms, a huge ballroom, a skating rink, a trap-shooting range and overnight accommodations. The glittering display attracted many wealthy businessmen and horse owners from other states, who then went home to form their own jockey clubs and build their own new racing plants.

While the wealthy members of the newly formed jockey clubs provided the impetus for the new growth of racing, it was gambling that provided the fuel. The first bookmaker to take bets on races opened for business in Philadelphia in 1866. Soon, racetracks admitted bookmakers to their grounds. The opportunity to gamble at the track brought spectators in droves, and the daily fees that tracks charged the bookmakers augmented purses and produced profits for track operators.

These profits led to a huge expansion of racing. By 1894, an astounding total of 314 tracks were operating across the country. As might have been expected, many problems attended this rapid growth. Every track operated under its own rules and decided its own racing dates. No formal reciprocity among tracks concerning rule violators existed, and a person suspended by one track just moved to another. Some tracks were dominated by criminal elements who bribed politicians and policemen as well as jockeys and trainers.

At the same time, the sport lacked strict supervision of the breed. In the matter of names alone, enormous confusion existed. One historian counted, in the first two volumes of the American Stud Book, 102 females named "Fanny" and 139 horses named "John."

Recognizing the need for a central authority, an influential horse owner, Pierre Lorillard, invited track and stable owners to discuss the problem. The result was the formation in 1890 of a seven-member Board of Control. This organization made some progress, but many horsemen felt it was dominated by track managements more interested in profits than purses. In 1894, James Keene proposed the formation of a new organization modeled on the English Jockey Club. The Board of Control was absorbed by the Jockey Club, which consisted of fifty members and was managed by seven stewards.

Led by chairman August Belmont II, the Jockey Club began to rule racing with an iron hand. When it took over the American Stud Book in 1896, it exercised complete executive, judicial and legislative control over racing. The Jockey Club licensed all jockeys, owners, trainers and horses; appointed racing officials; allotted racing dates; enforced suspensions and fines; and supervised breeding. Any tracks that didn't heed the Jockey Club's dictates were branded outlaws, and horses that ran at outlaw tracks were barred from other tracks.

By the turn of the century, however, an emerging trend that the Jockey Club couldn't control began to have a profound effect on racing. This was the wave of anti-gambling sentiment that accompanied the burgeoning temperance movement. Beginning with Missouri and Illinois, state after state banned bookmaking and other gambling activities. Without the fees from bookmakers and the admission fees of the spectators they attracted, tracks folded in droves. By 1908, when New York State banned betting, the number of tracks had plummeted from 314 to just 25. Faced with dwindling attendance, even Belmont Park, the glamorous showcase of racing when it opened in 1905, closed its gates for 1911 and 1912.

Obviously, the closing of so many tracks desperately hurt the American breeding industry. With no income from gambling, the tracks that did stay open were forced to reduce purse levels drastically. As a result, Thoroughbreds were exported by the thousands, and many leading jockeys and trainers followed them overseas.

With the reduction in tracks, however, came the purge of much of the criminal element of the sport. The tracks that remained operated under the patronage and sanction of the politically and economically powerful membership of the Jockey Club. As the crest of the anti-gambling wave passed, respectability was slowly returned to racing.

The most important factor in the rebirth of racing in this century, however, was the introduction of pari-mutuel wagering. Pari-mutuel machines had been imported from France in the nineteenth century, but their introduction didn't survive the bitter opposition of bookmakers. However, in 1908, when the Louisville City Council decided to enforce a ban on bookmaking for Kentucky Derby Day, Churchill Downs' general manager, Col. Matt Winn, remembered eleven pari-mutuel machines that had been gathering dust since the 1870s. Winn hauled the machines out of storage. The mutuel machines attracted an astounding $67,570 in bets—five times the amount wagered with bookmakers for the previous year's Derby. The payoff on the winner, Stone Street, was $123.60, which pleased the public immensely. The experiment was a complete success.

Pari-mutuel wagering succeeded because it provided the tracks with a reliable source of profit; provided a higher level of purses to horsemen; provided bigger payoffs to bettors; reduced the chicanery connected with bookmaking; and, most important, provided a source of tax revenue that gave state governments a reason to legalize wagering on horse races. The latter became increasingly attractive during the Depression, when ten states authorized pari-mutuel wagering and the number of tracks increased by 70 percent. After World War II, many more states jumped on the bandwagon, and the number of races run tripled in the next two decades.

As state governments authorized expansion of the sport, they often came into conflict with the conservative Jockey Club. With a substantial source of revenue involved, the states were reluctant to leave the responsibility for regulating the sport in the hands of what many people called an "elitist" organization. Gradually, state legislatures approved the formation of state racing commissions that had the ultimate responsibility for making racing rules, for licensing racing personnel and for allocating racing dates. However, because of the expertise and the political influence of the members of the Jockey Club, states were reluctant to wrest complete control away from the organization. The result was a sharing of responsibility, and the partnership continues to this day.

# Section 5

# The Organization of American Racing

On the Bluegrass: "Its reputation for fast horses, beautiful women, virile men, and potent whisky is deserved, even if the adjectives do occasionally get mixed."

—Bradley Smith

Unlike in England, where the authority over racing rests primarily with the Jockey Club, racing in America is under the jurisdiction of three partners: the state racing commissions, the Jockey Club and the local racing associations.

## THE STATE RACING COMMISSION

State legislatures have invested in state racing commissions the licensing and rule-making authority for horse racing. The members of every commission are appointed by the governor of the state. Half serve without salary, and the rest receive only token remuneration. A significant number of commissioners have some background in racing, but the majority come from other fields, such as business, law and banking.

Under the licensing powers of the commissions comes the granting of racing days to local associations. The competition for "prime" dates between Thoroughbred tracks, and in many states between Thoroughbred tracks and harness tracks, sometimes results in intense lobbying. Such lobbying, in connection with the state's interest in increasing tax revenue, has led to an over-expansion that has hurt racing.

The state racing commissions also license everyone connected with racing—trainers, owners, jockeys, jockeys' agents, grooms, veterinarians, etc. The commissions make the rules of racing in each state, and they enforce these rules through suspensions, fines or bans.

Since racing is an interstate sport, adequate supervision requires full reciprocity between states. The individual commissions in 1934 formed the National Association of State Racing Commissioners, the constitution of which reads:

Every board and commission identified with or belonging to this association shall uphold the rulings of every other board and commission likewise identified with or belonging to this association. The denial of a license, or a suspension or revocation of a license by any member board or commission shall be deemed to be such a ruling.

The above means that if a jockey is suspended for seven days at a New York track, he can't ride during that period anywhere in the country. The reciprocity above, however, doesn't extend to granting licenses.

Every trainer, owner, etc. must be separately licensed by each state in which he or she operates.

Finally, the state racing commission appoints a steward for each track, who, with two others appointed by the Jockey Club and the local association, shares the responsibility for the day-to-day governing of that race meeting.

## THE JOCKEY CLUB

The membership of the Jockey Club is made up of the most powerful and influential owners and breeders in Thoroughbred racing. The members, who currently number ninety, are elected for life. While the Jockey Club no longer has the dictatorial power it once exercised, it remains an extraordinarily powerful force in the sport.

The Jockey Club has sole responsibility for the supervision of the Thoroughbred breed in this country. That large task includes the registration and identification of all Thoroughbreds; the registering of partnerships, stable names, horse names, and authorized agents; the maintenance of racing and breeding records. The Jockey Club also formulates rules of racing, which serve as the model for most of the rules adopted by state racing commissions. The Club appoints one of the three stewards who supervise every authorized race meeting. Finally, the Jockey Club conducts equine research and advises racing commissions and state governments on matters pertaining to racing and breeding.

### OFFICERS

Nicholas F. Brady, *Chairman*
Paul Mellon, *Vice-Chairman*
G. W. Douglas Carver, *Secretary-Treasurer*
Calvin S. Rainey, *Executive Director*
Robert L. Melican, *Deputy Executive Director*
Gilbert B. Razzetti, *Assistant Treasurer*
Board of Handicappers: Leonard C. Hale,
Frank E. (Jimmy) Kilroe, Thomas E. Trotter

### STEWARDS

Nicholas F. Brady            Paul Mellon
G. W. Douglas Carver   James B. Moseley
John W. Galbreath          Donald P. Ross, Jr.
Louis Lee Haggin 2d       John Hay Whitney
Stuart S. Janney, Jr.

### Members and Years of Election

Eslie Asbury (1953)
Lt. Col. Charles Baker (1975)
Thomas M. Bancroft, Jr. (1973)
William W. Bancroft (1976)
August Belmont 4th (1977)
James H. Binger (1976)
Albert C. Bostwick (1930)
George H. Bostwick (1942)
James Cox Brady, Jr. (1973)
Nicholas F. Brady (1966)
Baird C. Brittingham (1968)
G. W. Douglas Carver (1975)
Charles J. Cella (1974)
George M. Cheston (1965)
Stephen C. Clark, Jr. (1971)
Leslie Combs 2d (1959)
F. Eugene Dixon, Jr. (1958)
Jack J. Dreyfus, Jr. (1969)
William DuPont III (1981)
Thomas M. Evans (1978)
William S. Farish 3d (1970)
Anderson Fowler (1957)
Daniel M. Galbreath (1968)
John W. Galbreath (1955)
Richard L. Gelb (1978)
Edward H. Gerry (1956)
Henry A. Gerry (1956)
M. Tyson Gilpin (1955)
John K. Goodman (1978)
Gordon Grayson (1971)
Raymond R. Guest (1954)
Winston F. C. Guest (1962)
Louis Lee Haggin 2d (1951)
Seth W. Hancock (1978)
John W. Hanes (1952)
Leonard D. Henry (1976)
Fred W. Hooper (1975)
E. Edward Houghton (1976)
G. W. Humphrey, Jr. (1976)
Stuart S. Janney, Jr. (1954)
Walter M. Jeffords, Jr. (1968)
Richard I. G. Jones (1975)
Warner L. Jones, Jr. (1971)
Howard B. Keck (1963)
Francis Kernan (1960)

James R. Kerr (1978)
Peter F. F. Kissel (1968)
John S. Knight (1961)
Arthur F. Long (1981)
Gene Markey (1962)
Townsend B. Martin (1955)
Charles E. Mather 2d (1957)
Peter McBean (1965)
Donald M. McKellar (1977)
Paul Mellon (1947)
James P. Mills (1965)
John A. Morris (1928)
Thruston B. Morton (1974)
James B. Moseley (1970)
Walter F. O'Connell (1981)
John M. Olin (1969)
Perry R. Pease (1960)
W. Haggin Perry (1956)
James W. Phillips (1981)
Ogden Phipps (1939)
Ogden Mills Phipps (1965)
George A. Pope, Jr. (1962)
William Purdey (1979)
David P. Reynolds (1976)
Richard S. Reynolds, Jr. (1976)
Reuben F. Richards (1976)
Bernard J. Ridder (1979)
Joseph M. Roebling (1956)
William P. Rogers (1975)
Donald P. Ross, Jr. (1941)
Louis R. Rowan (1967)
E. Barry Ryan (1957)
John M. Schiff (1953)
Kenneth Schiffer (1978)
Reeve Schley, Jr. (1960)
Bayard Sharp (1952)
George Strawbridge, Jr. (1976)
E. P. Taylor (1953)
Charles H. Thieriot (1978)
Oakleigh B. Thorne (1981)
Daniel G. Van Clief (1955)
Alfred G. Vanderbilt (1937)
Joseph Walker, Jr. (1956)
Reginald N. Webster (1966)
Cortright Wetherill (1955)
C. V. Whitney (1930)
John Hay Whitney (1928)
Wheelock Whitney (1974)
P. A. B. Widener 3d (1955)

### HONORARY MEMBERS
Lord Howard de Walden (England)
Major Victor McCalmont (Ireland)

M. Marcel Boussac (France)
Hubert de Chaudenay (France)

---

## NATIONAL RACING ORGANIZATIONS

*The Jockey Club*
380 Madison Avenue
New York, NY 10017

*Thoroughbred Racing Associations of North America*
300 Marcus Ave., Suite 2W4
Lake Success, NY 11042

*Thoroughbred Owners and Breeders Association*
P. O. Box 358
Elmont, NY 11003

*National Association of State Racing Commissioners*
P. O. Box 4216
Lexington, KY 40504

*The American Horse Council*
1700 K St., NW, Suite 300
Washington, DC 20006

---

## THE LOCAL RACING ASSOCIATION

In racing parlance, racing associations are the racetrack operators. In the United States, associations may be private, profit-making corporations, nonprofit corporations like the New York Racing Association or public agencies like the New Jersey Sports and Exposition Authority. The associations conduct racing under licenses granted by and dates assigned by the state racing commission.

The local racing association is the organization that actually produces the entertainment for racing fans. It "hires" the best horsemen and horses; provides the facilities in which they race, train and live; under the rules of racing, cards programs that provide the best competition for fans and horsemen alike; attracts fans through advertising and promotion; and provides parking, seating, concessions and printed programs for the racegoers. In addition, the local association sells tickets to bettors; pays off winners; collects state, local and federal taxes; and collects and disburses jockeys' fees, fines, purses, payments for claimed horses, and stakes nomination and entry fees.

While the actions and rulings of state racing commissions and the Jockey Club have a profound effect on the overall well-being of the sport (just as the NCAA does on college sports, for example), the local association largely determines the quality of racing and the quality of entertainment provided for the fan.

# Section 6

# The Racing Program

The key to a racing association's success is the skill with which it puts together a racing program that attracts both racegoers and horsemen. Without fans who pay admission and place bets, there wouldn't be any income to operate the track and pay purses. Without the stables of enough horse owners, there wouldn't be anything to bet on. Keeping both horseplayer and horseman happy is a difficult task that requires diligent exercise of intelligence and diplomacy.

The job would be easy if tracks were able to offer nothing but programs of championship races. Everyone agrees that the Kentucky Derby, the Preakness and the Belmont Stakes, contests rich in pageantry and purse, which attract the highest-quality three-year-olds in training, are the ideal horse races. Not far behind are the Handicap Triple Crown (the Metropolitan, the Suburban and the Brooklyn handicaps), Belmont's Fall Championship Series (the Marlboro Cup, the Woodward Stakes and the Jockey Club Gold Cup), the Ruffian and Beldame stakes and the filly triple crown, the Acorn, Mother Goose and Coaching Club American Oaks, for fillies and mares, and the prestigious competitions that help determine the annual Eclipse Award winners.

Unfortunately, the above contests and their like make up only a couple of hundred of the nearly seventy thousand races run annually. Even if the money were available for more rich races, nowhere near enough championship-caliber horses exist to fill them. As we've seen, the breeding industry has been unable to produce more than 3 percent stakes winners, racing's "major league" athletes.

These couple of thousand major leaguers aren't anywhere near enough to run America's huge racing program. A major-league baseball team gets through a season with twenty-five players; a racetrack needs between one thousand and two thousand horses. In the peak summer months of July and August, an average of nearly three hundred races a day are carded at over forty U.S. tracks. Obviously, only a fraction of these can be important or "great" races. The task of the management of these racetracks is to make sure that as many as possible of these are "good" races.

The next question is, "What's a good race?" That depends on one's point of view. The racegoer, who's a spectator and participant, would probably cite a race in which the 6–1 shot chosen by his shrewd handicapping roared down the stretch to win by a nose. The key here, as track managements found out long ago, is *good prices* and *thrilling races*.

Three basic elements are needed to produce racing programs that maximize the number of "good" races that keep horseplayers happy. The first element is attracting the highest-quality horses possible, with "quality" meaning, at the minimum, animals sound enough and willing enough to perform reasonably reliably. Trying to decide which horse in a race will be least affected by various serious physical and mental afflictions is not handicapping, but guessing. Secondly, good races mean a large field, for small fields mean lopsided races and short prices. Finally, the field should be as evenly matched as possible. Just as few football fans enjoy a 40–0 game, racegoers quickly grow tired of a program of 3–5 shots galloping home ten lengths in front. As the saying goes, "It's differences of opinion that make a horse race." The challenge of ferreting out a winner from a well-matched field creates action at the betting windows; a three- or four-horse stretch duel brings an entire crowd roaring to its feet.

To a horseman, on the other hand, a "good" race is one with a large purse, but a small field, in which his or her horse has a big speed, class and weight advantage. A racing fan visits a track for excitement and the chance to win a few bucks. A horseman *has* to win purses to stay in business. Because the track depends on the racegoer for its income, it can't card races to make horses easy winners. Horsemen do expect a racing program that gives every horse in their barn a chance to compete in its own class every couple of weeks—and they need a purse structure that allows the average horse to earn its keep.

To be successful, a racetrack has to satisfy both its constituencies. The person charged with this important job is the track's *racing secretary* (at some tracks the job is split between a Director of Racing and a Racing Secretary). The single most important key to understanding how races are run and won is to understand how the racing secretary develops a racing program and creates the races that are run each day.

# Purse Money: The Barometer of Quality

The first step in developing a racing program is to assemble a pool of horses. Although Thoroughbreds are shipped all over the country for the rich stakes races, most races are filled by animals who live in the stables provided free of charge by track managements. The quality of the horses that fill these one thousand to two thousand stalls determines to a great extent the quality of racing at that track.

The major factor in the quality of horses brought to a track is that track's purse structure. Horses and horsemen are "free agents"—that is, they go where they can make the most money. In making the decision where to stable and race their stock, horsemen look at both the amount of purse money the track offers and the way that purse money is distributed.

## WHERE DOES PURSE MONEY COME FROM?

In its early days, when racing was an amateur sport, purses consisted solely of the wagers put up by the owners of the horses that were competing. If a horse was scratched after the wager was agreed on, a half-forfeit was paid to the other owner or owners. The winner of the contest took home the whole pot.

When racing became a professional sport, the owners' expenses soared. The purchase price of quality Thoroughbreds rose substantially; horses were boarded at training centers instead of on the home farm; professional trainers and riders had to be paid. Obviously, racing solely for purses made up of their own money meant that only a small percentage of lucky owners could meet these considerable costs.

To attract enough quality horses to fill fields, racetracks found that they had to supplement the entry fees or stakes put up by the owners. This additional purse money came from admission fees charged to the public and, somewhat later, license fees paid by bookmakers who did business at the track.

Today, in Great Britain, money paid by horse owners makes up about 24 percent of the purses in stakes races and 57 percent of the money in other contests. To keep this contribution from being ruinous, purse levels tend to be very low compared to purse levels in the United States.

Until the twentieth century, purses at American tracks came from the same three sources as purses in England—owners' entry fees and stakes, admission fees, and bookmaker license fees. However, the introduction of pari-mutuel wagering opened up a new and much larger source of revenue—the pari-mutuel pool. State governments took a percentage of the total money wagered on each race as tax revenue; track management took a percentage to defray the costs of operating the facility; and a percentage went to the purses for the horses' owners. Except for nomination fees to stakes races, all entry fees paid by owners were eliminated. Today, in the United States, over 97 percent of all purses paid come from pari-mutuel wagering. It was only when purses stopped coming out of the owners' pockets that the huge expansion of racing in this country was made possible.

## THE PURSE POOL

The exact percentage of the pari-mutuel pool that goes to purses varies from state to state, and from track to track. At some tracks the percentage is fixed by state law; at others it is set through negotiation between the track and the Horsemen's Benevolent and Protective Association (HBPA). This figure generally ranges from 3 percent to 7 percent on win, place and show betting, and generally rises on exotic wagering (exactas, trifectas, etc.).

Despite the differences in the formulas for determining purse money, the amount of money available can be correlated to the total pari-mutuel handle. The tracks with the highest daily average handle ($3 million to $4 million), such as Hollywood Park, Santa Anita and Belmont Park, distribute an average of over $150,000 a day in purse money. Tracks with handles of around $1 million a day (such as Bowie, Keystone and Keeneland) give away an average of $60,000 to $80,000 per program. For facilities like the Finger Lakes, which handle $300,000 to $400,000 a day, the average daily purse ranges from $20,000 to $30,000.

## PURSE STRUCTURE

Obviously, the total amount of money given away is a good indication of the quality of horses racing at any track. Within general ranges of daily purse levels, horsemen carefully look at exactly how the purse money is distributed when choosing a track at which to compete. This purse structure is arrived at by negotiation between the track and the HBPA, and conflict generally arises in two different areas.

The first is the matter of how the money is distributed within each race. In the early days of racing, only the winning owner received any purse money. By the late nineteenth century, prizes were awarded for second and third place also. However, since betting provided the support for racing, track managements continued to press for reserving most of the purse for the winner, to ensure that each horse entered in the race would try as hard as possible to win. These managements felt that significant purses for lower finishes encouraged horsemen to run horses too often in races where they had no intention of mounting an all-out effort to win, but rather hoped to snare enough money to pay expenses. Horsemen, on the other hand, have lobbied vigorously for broader distribution for purses, citing the large rise in training expenses and jockeys' fees.

The result is that purse distribution within a race varies considerably from track to track. The percent of purse that goes to the winner ranges from 55 percent at Del Mar to 65 percent at Churchill Downs. The number of places receiving money ranges from four at Aqueduct and Bowie to six at Suffolk Downs and the Finger Lakes. Below is a table showing the average purse distribution for all races run in 1980 and the percentages for representative tracks:

| FINISH | NAT'L AVERAGE | BELMONT | SANTA ANITA | CHUR. DOWNS | SUFFOLK |
|---|---|---|---|---|---|
| 1 | 59.7% | 60% | 55% | 65% | 60% |
| 2 | 20.1% | 22% | 20% | 20% | 20% |
| 3 | 11.5% | 12% | 15% | 10% | 10% |
| 4 | 5.9% | 6% | 7.5% | 5% | 5% |
| 5 | 2.1% | — | 2.5% | — | 3% |
| 6 | .8% | — | — | — | 2% |

The second area of contention between horsemen and track management is how the purse money is distributed among the different kinds of races. At every Thoroughbred racetrack, purse values for each race always rise with the quality of the race.

That is, a race for $3,500 claimers always has a larger purse than a similar race for $2,500 claimers. Claiming races have, on the average, lower purses than for allowance races, which in turn have a lower average purse than stakes races. The reason for this is that both horsemen and track management want to reward horses for moving up in class and penalize horses that are moving down in class.

The amount of purse money devoted to races for each class of horse and the amount of the increase in purse value from class to class is an area of intense negotiation. Since rich stakes races bring the track increased publicity and increased attendance, track managements often seek to devote a significant percentage of purse money to these contests. Horsemen, on the other hand, while recognizing the need for a representative stakes program, prefer an emphasis on increases in the minimum purse and increases in the average purse. In the last five years, owners have been losing ground as tracks compete for top-quality horses by raising purses in the richest races. From 1975 to 1980, total purse distribution rose 54 percent, but stakes purses rose 81 percent.

Nationally in 1980, stakes races made up 3.1 percent of the races run, but received 18.4 percent of the purse money. The percentage of purse money devoted to stakes reaches 25 percent at those tracks that seek to attract the highest-quality animals. At other tracks, which emphasize claiming races, the stakes percentage may be as low as 10 percent. A trainer without stakes-class horses obviously prefers the latter distribution.

| Aqueduct | $3,174,719 |
| Belmont Park | 2,973,367 |
| Aqueduct | 2,918,853 |
| Del Mar | 2,907,458 |
| Aqueduct | 2,619,923 |
| Oaklawn Park | 2,547,526 |
| Saratoga | 2,543,724 |
| Los Alamitos | 2,220,241 |
| Meadowlands | 1,964,033 |
| Hialeah Park | 1,905,047 |
| Pomona | 1,894,591 |
| Golden Gate Fields (Tanforan) | 1,805,561 |
| Bay Meadows | 1,800,356 |
| Ak-Sar-Ben | 1,649,365 |
| Bay Meadows (Tanforan) | 1,647,243 |
| Arlington Park | 1,627,241 |
| Golden Gate Fields | 1,606,007 |
| Sportsman's Park | 1,598,427 |
| Del Mar Fair | 1,569,380 |
| Monmouth Park | 1,567,770 |
| Bay Meadows Fair | 1,554,333 |

## HIGHEST AVERAGE NET DISTRIBUTION—1980

| MEETING | AVERAGE NET DISTRIBUTION |
| --- | --- |
| Belmont Park | $236,976 |
| Saratoga | 225,812 |
| Hollywood Park | 211,545 |
| Belmont Park | 206,033 |
| Santa Anita (Oak Tree) | 193,880 |
| Aqueduct | 192,865 |
| †Santa Anita | 183,071 |
| Aqueduct | 172,018 |
| Aqueduct | 152,261 |
| Del Mar | 132,290 |
| Oaklawn Park | 123,381 |
| Meadowlands | 123,034 |
| Arlington Park | 111,999 |
| Los Alamitos | 109,416 |
| Hialeah Park | 108,097 |
| Keeneland | 107,560 |
| Keeneland | 107,350 |
| Monmouth Park | 106,686 |
| Pomona | 105,872 |
| Sportsman's Park | 104,174 |
| Del Mar Fair | 101,250 |
| Churchill Downs | 99,703 |
| Hawthorne | 97,325 |
| Louisiana Downs | 95,710 |
| Gulfstream Park | 95,025 |

†1979–1980 Meeting.

## HIGHEST DAILY AVERAGE HANDLE—1980

| MEETING | DAILY AVERAGE MUTUEL HANDLE |
| --- | --- |
| Hollywood Park | $5,185,978 |
| Santa Anita | 4,629,947 |
| Santa Anita (Oak Tree) | 4,240,453 |
| Belmont Park | 3,425,659 |

# The Problem of Stall Space

While the purse structure and distribution is the prime factor in the overall quality of the horses racing at a track, the number of healthy horses available to race is also a major factor in the quality of racing. The more healthy horses, the larger the fields and the better the competition.

Unfortunately, the huge expansion in racing dates and number of races in the last two decades hasn't been matched by a comparable increase in stall space. Many tracks have found themselves unable to afford to purchase additional land on which to construct and maintain additional stalls. This shortage of stall space has two effects on racing. First of all, as a racing meeting progresses, the inevitable high proportion of injuries and ailments suffered by horses reduces the number of animals capable of racing. This means smaller fields and a wider range of abilities within each race, factors that tend to produce short-priced winners and dull contests. Secondly, horsemen who are unable to get enough stalls often try to compensate for the lost income by running the horses they do have too frequently. This, in turn, inevitably increases the number of horses breaking down.

Certain racing circuits alleviate part of the problem by stabling horses at idle tracks (for example, horses are stabled at Belmont when Aqueduct is racing, and at Santa Anita when Hollywood Park is racing), but even this doesn't meet the need. As a result, California has led a trend toward the opening of formal off-track training centers which provide supervised workouts as well as stall space. Unlike harness racing, where horses that have been idle for an extended period prove they're fit to race by competing in non-betting qualifying races, idle Thoroughbreds in most states must have an officially timed published workout before they're allowed to compete.

## FILLING THE STALLS

Until the problem of increasing stable areas is solved, however, each track's racing secretary is faced with the big job of filling his one thousand to two thousand stalls with the right mix of qualified, racing-fit Thoroughbreds. In handling stall allotments, racing secretaries face three major problems: more requests than available space; requests for stall space for horses that are not ready to run or may never run; and requests for space by trainers without a proper balance of horses in their barns.

They begin to whittle the applications down by eliminating horses that don't meet the track's minimum eligibility requirements. Below is an example of such requirements for the Maryland circuit:

**PIMLICO, BOWIE AND LAUREL will not accept entries for any horse which has started for a claiming price of less than $2,500, unless said horse has won for a claiming price of $2,500 or more, since starting for less than $2,500. Entries will not be accepted for any horse which has not been First, Second or Third in its last ten starts since starting for a claiming price of $3,000 or less. (Starter and optional claiming races will be considered claiming races in determing eligibility under any of the above rules.)**

**Entries will not be accepted for Maidens Five Years Old and Older.**

Next, the racing secretary sets an upper limit on the number of stalls a trainer or stable may have. The limit at Aqueduct and Belmont, for example, is forty-four stalls. At smaller tracks, the limit is usually lower.

Perhaps the most important consideration in evaluating how ready or able a horse is to race is the record of the trainer. Racing secretaries keep detailed records of how often a trainer's horses start and how well they race. They also carefully weigh a trainer's attitude. A trainer who has a record of cooperating by entering a horse when a race comes up short of a full field has a big edge over a trainer who refuses to enter a horse except under "perfect" conditions. Thus, a trainer whose horses race often and successfully, and who has a history of helping out the racing secretary, will receive the same number of stalls, or more, for the next meeting. An unsuccessful and uncooperative trainer may be cut off completely.

Finally, racing secretaries try to assign stalls in such a manner as to provide a good mix of horses of different levels of ability. A particular problem is dealing with the large number of untried two-year-olds, who may take a while to get to the track, and the large number of maidens, who may never show enough talent to win a race. To avoid having to card five or six maiden races a day, most racing secretaries use a ratio for each stable. At Longacres, for example, racing secretary Glen Williams allows eight two-year-old and eight three-year-old maidens for a stable with fourteen older winners. Twelve older horses means seven two-year-old and seven three-year-old maidens, etc. A rule of thumb used by other tracks is one two-year-old for every four older horses.

The stall problem doesn't end with the granting of allotments at the beginning of a race meeting. The average track loses twenty-five to fifty horses a week to injury, sales, ailments, etc. Since most contracts between horsemen and the track entitle a trainer to keep a stall until the end of a meeting, the racing secretary must be vigilant to see that those stalls are refilled with the right kind of horse. If horses aren't replaced promptly, short fields inevitably result.

## OFFICIAL REQUIREMENTS FOR STALL SPACE

To protect the racing public and the industry, horsemen must fulfill the following requirements established by the state racing commissions before being granted stall space:

1. Foal Certificates for every horse must be submitted to the Horse Identification Office.
2. Evidence must be presented proving that during the past year every horse has tested negatively for swamp fever (equine infectious anemia) using the Coggins Test.
3. All racing personnel, including owners, trainers and stable help, must be licensed by the State Racing Commission.
4. Partnerships' stable names, authorized agents and racing colors must be registered with the Jockey Club.
5. The full name of every person having an owner's interest in every horse must be disclosed to the racing secretary.
6. Trainers must submit a certificate to prove that they carry workman's compensation insurance on all their employees.

# Creating Races

Once the stalls are filled, the racing secretary is faced with the task of creating a program of interesting races in which, ideally, ten to twelve horses have a legitimate chance to win. These competitive contests are the races that attract the most interest from horseplayers and horsemen alike. The difficulties in arranging such matches, however, are substantial. The main problem is that no one has ever been able to come up with a reliable ranking that predicts how successfully horses will compete against each other.

In many individual sports, like tennis, such rankings are accomplished through a series of elimination matches that create a "ladder." Once that ladder is set up, a player can move up by beating the person above him, or drop by losing to the player below. Such challenges automatically compensate for the changes in physical condition and ability that inevitably affect every athlete, human or equine.

In Thoroughbred racing, two-horse matches began to lose popularity a century and a half ago. Because an average of fifteen hundred horses is needed for any racing meet, pre-meet elimination matches are obviously impossible. Equally impossible is any way for a racing secretary to monitor the considerable changes in each horse's condition and ability that take place from race to race, and even from day to day.

The best that the racing secretary can do is build his own ladder based on the recent performances of the horses from which he has to draw. The rung on the ladder to which a horse is assigned is referred to in racing as its "class."

## DEFINING "CLASS"

The word "class" is derived from the Greek word "klesis," which means "a calling or a summons." Since different kinds of summons produce different responses, "class" eventually came to mean "a number of things grouped together because of certain likenesses or common traits."

The job of a racing secretary relates to both the origin and the modern meaning of class. To produce the best possible races, he has to identify and specify certain "common traits" that "summon" ten or twelve evenly matched Thoroughbreds. Since the fundamental purpose of the sport is to win races and win money, those common traits that define "class" are the number and kind of races won and the amount of purse money won.

"What about breeding as a sign of class?" you may ask. Certainly we talked a good bit about pedigree in the breeding section of this book. As you'll remember, the importance of a horse's immediate ancestors had to do with an appraisal of the animal's breeding *potential*. Once the horse began producing offspring, the most important statistics became measures of performance, such as number and percentage of winners, number and percentage of stakes winners, and the average earnings index. In racing, a young horse coming to the track may start higher on the class ladder because his pedigree may indicate significant *potential,* but subsequent appraisals of class will be based on *performance*.

That brings up the second point, that class is *relative* and is *constantly changing.* Like the player on the tennis ladder, the racehorse challenges other animals in every race. Its performance determines whether it moves up or down. Given the fragility of the racehorse, the slide downward can be dramatic. A gelding's victories in stakes races at age four do it little good in races for $2,500 claimers at age nine, if it's been trounced several times recently by similar animals. As with people, a horse is known by the company it's been keeping.

The emphasis on recent performance in appraising class doesn't mean, however, that *class* is the same thing as *form. Class* is the ranking a horse has demonstrated through its past performances; *form* is its current condition, which determines whether it will equal, surpass, or fall short of the sum of its past performances, known as class. In making races and in assigning weights for handicaps, the racing secretary concentrates solely on objective analysis of past performances—that is, on demonstrated class. The racing secretary leaves it to the horseman to appraise the current *form* of his Thoroughbred. The horseman decides whether, for its next race, it has improved enough to challenge horses of a higher class, or whether it has deteriorated to the extent that it has to be entered against lower-class animals in order to win a purse. For the horseplayer, handicapping means evaluating both class and form—a very difficult task which we'll discuss later in the book.

For now, we'll explore the definition of class. Since the purpose of racing is winning races, the *first class distinction is between horses that win a race and those that don't.* Approximately 40 percent of all Thoroughbreds either never get to the racetrack or never "break their maidens." Of those

horses racing in 1980, 46 percent failed to win a race; only 28 percent won more than one race. The table below shows the hierarchy of horses as determined by races won in 1980:

| RACES WON | NO. OF RUNNERS | % OF RUNNERS | AVE. EARNINGS PER RUNNER | CUMU-LATIVE % LESS THAN |
|---|---|---|---|---|
| 0 | 29,944 | 46.5% | $ 1,092 | 46.5% |
| 1 | 16,643 | 25.8% | 6,068 | 72.3% |
| 2 | 9,180 | 14.2% | 11,454 | 86.5% |
| 3 | 4,658 | 7.2% | 17,648 | 93.7% |
| 4 | 2,267 | 3.5% | 25,561 | 97.2% |
| 5 | 1,018 | 1.6% | 32,122 | 98.8% |
| 6 | 449 | 0.7% | 39,830 | 99.5% |
| 7 | 215 | 0.3% | 47,298 | 99.8% |
| 8 | 75 | 0.1% | 75,836 | 99.9% |
| 9 | 37 | 0.1% | 92,418 | * |
| 10 | 8 | * | 50,019 | * |
| 11 | 4 | * | 88,290 | * |
| 12 | 0 | * | * | * |
| 13 | 1 | * | 17,000 | 100.0% |

Another indication of the importance of consistency as related to class is that horses that won at least one race earned, in addition to 100 percent of all first-place money, *84 percent* of all second-place money, *82 percent* of all third-place money, and a total of *93 percent* of all purse money awarded.

Along with number of races won, *an appraisal of class has to include an analysis of the kind of races won.* Since the late 1700s, when the epitome of the Thoroughbred became a three-year-old who could win at distances from a mile to a mile and a half, the classiest horse has been the rare three-year-old who proved its superiority by sweeping the "classic races"—the Triple Crown. Only eleven horses have accomplished this feat in the United States.

After the Triple Crown winners, the classiest horses are the nine annual Eclipse Award champions, which are chosen from among the winners of *graded stakes,* races that have been selected as the nation's most prestigious by a panel of distinguished experts. In 1980, 175 horses won these 277 events. Next come the winners of all *stakes* races, which represent less than 3 percent of each foal crop. In 1980, 1,404 horses

(2.2 percent of all starters) won the 2,092 stakes races (3.1 percent of races run).

Below stakes races are the other kinds of races, which, in descending order of class, are *handicaps, allowance races, claiming races,* and *maiden races.* Although overlapping of ability exists between kinds of races, a horse that consistently competes successfully in stakes races is considered higher class than a consistent allowance performer, who in turn has an edge over the claiming horse.

This "ladder" based on kinds of races is extremely useful when considering the horses racing at one track. However, as we've seen, the quality of racing varies considerably from track to track, based roughly on the amount of purse money available. Similarly, *the most reliable indication of the relative class of horses racing at different tracks is the purse value of the races in which they've been winning or placing.* For example, many stakes races at Fairmount Park have a total purse value of $8,500. These horses would, in all likelihood, be soundly trounced by $20,000 claimers at Aqueduct, who've been competing for $12,000 purses. At Suffolk Downs, an allowance race for "three-year-olds, non-winners of a race other than maiden or claiming" has a purse of $8,500; at Bowie, the purse for the same race is $10,000; at Santa Anita, $17,000. As a general rule, the winner of the Bowie race is of a higher "class" than the winner of the race at Suffolk, and in turn, the Bowie winner would be bested by the California horse.

Many horseplayers, recognizing the significance of purse in relationship to class, divide the number of races into the total earnings to get an "average earnings per race." Racing secretaries and sophisticated handicappers, on the other hand, are concerned primarily with the contests in which the horse provided an indication of class by winning. For example, a horse that has won 3 of 6 races with first prizes of $6,000 has an average earnings per race of $18,000 divided by 6, or $3,000. A horse that finished out of the money in 5 races with higher-class animals may drop down in

class and win a $12,000 first prize in the sixth race. The second horse's average earnings per race would be only $2,000, but its average earnings in races in which it won would be *$12,000,* twice the $6,000 of the first horse, which it in fact *out-classes.*

While total earnings are an unreliable way to handicap an individual horse race, the table below shows how ranges of individual earnings (in 1980) reflect an animal's overall class, just as the number of races won reflects class:

| RANGE OF INDIV. EARNINGS | NO. OF RUNNERS | % OF RUNNERS | CUMULATIVE % LESS THAN |
|---|---|---|---|
| None | 8,615 | 13.4% | 13.4% |
| $      999 or less | 14,020 | 21.7% | 35.1% |
| $   1,000 to $  4,999 | 19,626 | 30.4% | 65.5% |
| $   5,000 to $  9,999 | 10,141 | 15.8% | 81.3% |
| $ 10,000 to $14,999 | 4,549 | 7.0% | 88.3% |
| $ 15,000 to $24,999 | 3,929 | 6.1% | 94.4% |
| $ 25,000 to $49,999 | 2,547 | 3.9% | 98.3% |
| $ 50,000 to $99,999 | 794 | 1.3% | 99.6% |
| $100,000 or more | 277 | .4% | 100.0% |

The above table vividly points out perhaps the most serious problem in Thoroughbred racing. The estimated annual cost to keep a racehorse in training is $10,000 to $25,000 per year, but 81 percent of the horses that ran in 1980 earned less than $10,000. The cutoff point for the top 5 percent was a modest $25,000.

## WRITING THE CONDITION BOOK

The racing secretary has at his disposal the complete past-performances record of every horse stabled at his track. He reviews these past performances to separate them by class. His purpose is to card races that bring together horses as close in class as possible, while giving every horse at the track a chance to race.

He does this in three stages. First of all, he plans different *kinds of races*—stakes, handicaps, allowance races, claiming, and maiden races—each of which have different *conditions of entry.* The top races, stakes and handicaps, may be open to any horse that wishes to enter, but for the other kinds of races, the racing secretary writes conditions of entry which either *prevent a horse from being entered below its demonstrated class*, or which *severely penalize a horseman who drops his horse down into a lower class*.

Secondly, within each kind of race, the racing secretary writes *conditions of age, sex, distance,* and *racing surface* which are designed to further ensure competitive contests.

Finally, to each race are attached *conditions that modify* the weights carried by each horse. The purpose of these conditions is to produce more even contests between the horses that meet the race's entry conditions.

The results of the racing secretary's difficult work are published every two weeks in what is known, for obvious reasons, as the *Condition Book*. This book contains the conditions for nine or ten races

on each racing day for two weeks, plus alternate races for each program in case one or more scheduled races fails to attract enough entrants. Each volume of the condition book also contains reminders about upcoming stakes races, important racing rules that apply to that meeting, charts of division of purses, and often, lists of jockeys with the minimum weights at which they can ride.

This condition book is the horseman's bible, a publication eagerly awaited and pored over until it is dog-eared. No matter how skilled the racing secretary is, the conditions for every race give some horses advantages over others. A successful trainer is one who can shrewdly interpret conditions, then decide which races favor the current form of his horse. Reading the condition book is equally important to the jockey's agent, who must decide which horses he'd like his client to ride. Finally, deciphering

---

ENTRIES CLOSE THURSDAY

## Fifty-Ninth Day    Saturday, March 8

**FIRST RACE**                                                    CLAIMING
Purse $4,000. For Four-Year-Olds and Upward..........122 lbs.
Non-winners of two races since January 25, allowed...... 3 lbs.
A race ................................................. 6 lbs.
A race since January 18 .............................. 9 lbs.
Claiming price $3,000.                            **Six Furlongs**

**SECOND RACE**                                              MAIDEN
Purse $8,000. For Maidens, Three-Years-Old............120 lbs.
(Preference to non-starters for $7,500 or less).   **Six Furlongs**

**THIRD RACE**                                   STARTER/HANDICAP
"THE MISTER BREA HANDICAP"
Closing Wednesday, March 5
Purse $8,500. A Handicap for Three-Year-Olds and Upward, which have started for a Claiming Price of $6,500 or less since June 30, 1979. Weights and Declarations by 9:30 A.M., Thursday, March 6.
                                        **One Mile and One-Sixteenth**

**FOURTH RACE**                                           CLAIMING
Purse $16,000. For Four-Year-Olds and Upward..........122 lbs.
Non-winners of two races since January 25, allowed...... 3 lbs.
A race ................................................. 5 lbs.
A race since January 18 .............................. 8 lbs.
Claiming price $65,000; for each $2,500 to $60,000 ....... 1 lb.
(Races where entered for $55,000 or less not considered).
                                              **Seven Furlongs**

**FIFTH RACE**                                          ALLOWANCE
Purse $10,500. For Three-Year-Olds, which have never won a race other than Maiden or Claiming........................120 lbs.
Non-winners of a race other than Claiming at one mile or over since January 25, allowed .............. 3 lbs.
Such a race since December 15......................... 5 lbs.
Such a race since November 15......................... 8 lbs.
                                        **One Mile and One-Sixteenth**

**SIXTH RACE**                                          ALLOWANCE
Purse $19,000. For Four-Year-Olds and Upward, which have not won $6,625 twice other than Maiden. Claiming, Starter or Bonus Payment since August 30............................122 lbs.
Non-winners of $6,600 twice in 1980, allowed .......... 3 lbs.
Once ................................................. 5 lbs.
$5,700 twice since November 15......................... 7 lbs.
Once ................................................. 10 lbs.
(Maiden, Claiming, and Starter races not considered in estimating allowances).                         **Six Furlongs**

**SEVENTH RACE**                                        ALLOWANCE
Purse $23,000. For Four-Year-Olds and Upward, which have not won two races over one mile other than Maiden. Claiming. Starter or Hunt Meeting since September 15....................122 lbs.
Non-winners of $6,600 at one mile or over in 1980, allowed  3 lbs.
A race at one mile or over since December 15 .......... 5 lbs.
Such a race since November 15......................... 7 lbs.
A race at any distance since September 15 .............. 10 lbs.
(Maiden, Claiming, and Starter races not considered in estimating allowances).              **One Mile and One-Sixteenth**

**EIGHTH RACE**                                          HANDICAP
"THE DONETTA HANDICAP"
Closing Wednesday, March 5
Purse $20,000. A Handicap for Fillies and Mares, Three-Years-Old and Upward. Weights and Declarations by 9:30 A.M., Thursday, March 6.                                    **Six Furlongs**

**NINTH RACE**                                           HANDICAP
"THE JOHN B. CAMPBELL HANDICAP"
$100,000 Added
A Handicap for Three-Year-Olds and Upward. By subscription of $100 each, which should accompany the nomination, starters to pay $1,000 additional, with $100,000 added, of which 65% of all monies to the winner, 20% to second, 10% to third and 5% to fourth. Weights five days before the race. Starters to be named through the entry box by the usual time of closing.
Closed Friday, February 15, 1980 with — nominations.
                                        **One Mile and One-Quarter**

**TENTH RACE**                                           CLAIMING
Purse $8,500. For Four-Year-Olds and Upward..........122 lbs.
Non-winners of two races at one mile or over since January 25, allowed ............................. 3 lbs.
One such race......................................... 5 lbs.
Such a race since January 18 ......................... 8 lbs.
Claiming price $11,500; for each $1,000 to $9,500 ...... 1 lb.
(Races where entered for $8,500 or less not considered).
                                        **One Mile and One-Sixteenth**

the conditions of each race is critical to the success of the horseplayer, who's betting his or her money on the outcome of a race.

On page 159 are the two pages from a condition book that describe a day's planned racing program at Bowie. At first glance, the race conditions seem bewildering and complicated. However, in the following pages, we're going to explain in detail the kinds and conditions of races. By the end of the description, you'll be able to read and explain the race conditions like a professional horseman.

## GREATNESS IN THE THOROUGHBRED

As in any sport, arguments about the ultimate greatness or "class" rage on, unabated and unresolved, in Thoroughbred racing. Yet, certain measures that help define quality are available. One is time; the second, earnings; the third, the judgment of racing experts. Below are the listings of some "great" Thoroughbreds as defined by these measures:

### WORLD RECORDS

| DISTANCE | HORSE AGE WEIGHT TRACK AND DATE | TIME |
|---|---|---|
| 1–4 | Big Racket, 4, 114, Hipodromo de las Americas, Mexico City, Mexico; February 5, 1945 | :20⅘ |
| 2 1–2f | Tie Score, 5, 115, Hipodromo de las Americas, Mexico City, Mexico; February 5, 1946 | :26⅘ |
| 3–8 | Atoka, 6, 105, Butte, Mont.; September 7, 1906 | :33½ |
| 3 1–2f | Tango King, 6, 116, Northlands Park, Edmonton, Alta; Canada; April 22, 1978 | :38⅘ |
| 1–2 | Norgor, 9, 118, Ruidoso Downs, Ruidoso, New Mexico; August 14, 1976 | :44⅗ |
| 4 1–2f | Kathryn's Doll, 2, 111, Turf Paradise, Phoenix, Ariz.; April 9, 1967 | :50⅖ |
| | Dear Ethel, 2, 114, Miles Park, Louisville, Ky.; July 4, 1967 | :50⅖ |
| | Bold Liz, 2, 118, Sunland Park, Sunland, N. M.; March 19, 1972 | :50⅖ |
| | Scott's Poppy, 2, 118, Turf Paradise, Phoenix, Ariz.; February 22, 1975 | :50⅖ |
| | Foxen Canyon, 2, 119, Turf Paradise, Phoenix, Ariz.; April 13, 1977 | :50⅖ |
| 5–8 | Zip Pocket, 3, 122, Turf Paradise, Phoenix, Ariz.; April 22, 1967 | :55⅖ |
| | Big Volume, 4, 120, Fresno District Fair, Fresno, Calif.; October 15, 1977 | :55⅖ |
| 5 1–2f | Zip Pocket, 3, 129, Turf Paradise, Phoenix, Ariz.; November 19, 1967 | 1:01⅗ |
| 5 3–4f | Last Freeby, 4, 116, Timonium, Timonium, Md.; July 20, 1974 | 1:07⅕ |
| 3–4 Ⓣ | *Gelding, 2, by Blink—Broken Tendril, 3, 123, Brighton, England; August 6, 1929 | 1:06⅕ |
| | Grey Papa, 6, 112, Longacres, Seattle, Wash.; September 4, 1972 | 1:07⅕ |
| 6 1–2f | Best Hitter, 4, 114, Longacres, Seattle, Wash.; August 14, 1973 | 1:13⅘ |
| 7–8 | Triple Bend, 4, 123, Hollywood Park, Inglewood, Calif.; May 6, 1972 | 1:19⅘ |
| 1 | Dr. Fager, 4, 134, Arlington Park, Arlington Heights, Ill.; August 24, 1968 | 1:32⅕ |
| 1m40y | Impecunious, 3, 126, Rockingham Park, Salem Depot, N. H.; September 3, 1973 | 1:38⅖ |
| 1m70y | Drill Site, 5, Garden State Park, Cherry Hill, N.J.; October 12, 1964 | 1:38⅘ |
| Ⓣ | Aborigine, 6, 119, Penn National, Grantville, Pa.; August 20, 1978 | 1:37⅕ |
| 1 1–16 | Swaps, 4, 130, Hollywood Park, Inglewood, Calif.; June 23, 1958 | 1:39 |
| 1 1–8 Ⓣ | Tentam, 4, 118, Saratoga, Saratoga Springs, N.Y.; August 10, 1973 | 1:45⅖ |
| | Secretariat, 3, 124, Belmont Park, Elmont, N.Y.; September 15, 1973 | 1:45⅖ |
| Ⓣ | Crystal Water, 4, 116, Santa Anita Park, Arcadia, Calif.; February 20, 1977 | 1:45⅖ |

| DISTANCE | HORSE   AGE   WEIGHT   TRACK AND DATE | TIME |
|---|---|---|
| Ⓣ | Waya, 4, 115, Saratoga, Saratoga Springs, N.Y.; August 21, 1978 | 1:45⅖ |
| 1 3–16Ⓣ | Toonerville, 5, 120, Hialeah Park, Hialeah, Fla.; February 7, 1976 | 1:51⅖ |
| 1 1–4 Ⓣ | Double Discount, 4, 116, Santa Anita Park, Arcadia, Calif.; October 6, 1977 | 1:57⅖ |
| 1 5–16Ⓣ | Roberto, 3, 122, York, England; August 15, 1972 | 2:07 |
| 1 3–8 Ⓣ | Cougar II, 6, 126, Hollywood Park, Inglewood, Calif.; April 29, 1972 | 2:11 |
| 1 1–2 Ⓣ | Fiddle Isle, 5, 124, Santa Anita Park, Arcadia, Calif.; March 21, 1970 | 2:23 |
| 1 9–16 | Lone Wolf, 5, 115, Keeneland, Lexington, Ky.; October 31, 1961 | 2:37⅗ |
| 1 5–8 Ⓣ | Red Reality, 6, 113, Saratoga, Saratoga Springs, N.Y.; August 23, 1972 | 2:37⅘ |
| Ⓣ | Malwak, 5, 110, Saratoga, Saratoga Springs, N.Y.; August 22, 1973 | 2:37⅘ |
| 1m5½f | Distribute, 9, 109, River Downs, Cincinnati, Ohio; September 7, 1940 | 2:51⅗ |
| 1 3–4 | Noor, 5, 117, Santa Anita Park, Arcadia, Calif.; March 4, 1950 | 2:52⅘ |
| 1 7–8 Ⓣ | El Moro, 8, 116, Delaware Park, Wilmington, Del.; July 22, 1963 | 3:11⅘ |
| 2 Ⓣ | Polazel, 3, Salisbury, England; July 8, 1924 | 3:15 |
| 2m40y | Winning Mark, 4, 107, Thistledown, Cleveland, Ohio; July 20, 1940 | 3:29⅖ |
| 2m7–y | Sun n Shine, 4, 113, Hawthorne, Cicero, Ill.; October 19, 1974 | 3:30⅖ |
| 2 1–16 | Midafternoon, 4, 126, Jamaica, Jamaica, L. I.; November 15, 1956 | 3:29⅗ |
| 2 1–8 Ⓣ | Ceinturion, 5, 119, Newbury, England; September 19, 1923 | 3:35 |
| 2 3–16 | Santiago, 5, 112, Narragansett Park, Pawtucket, R. I.; September 27, 1941 | 3.51⅕ |
| 2 1–4 Ⓣ | Dakota, 4, 116, Lingfield, England; May 27, 1927 | 3:37⅗ |
| 2 3–8 Ⓣ | Pamroy, 4, 120, Goodwood Park, Sussex, England; August 1, 1973 | 4:10⅗ |
| 2 1–2 | Miss Grillo, 6, 118, Pimlico, Baltimore, Md.; November 12, 1948 | 4:14⅗ |
| 2 5–8 Ⓣ | Girandole, 4, 126, Goodwood Park, Sussex, England; July 31, 1975 | 4:38⅘ |
| 2 3–4 | Shot Put, 4, 126, Washington Park, Homewood, Ill.; August 14, 1940 | 4:48⅘ |
| 2 7–8 | ††Bosh, 5, 100, Tijuana, Mexico; March 8, 1925 | 5:23 |
| 3 | Farragut, 5, 113, Agua Caliente, Mexico; March 9, 1941 | 5:15 |
| 3 3–8 | Winning Mark, 4, 104, Washington Park, Homewood, Ill.; August 21, 1940 | 6:13 |
| 4 | Sotemia, 5, 119, Churchill Downs, Louisville, Ky.; October 7, 1912 | 7:10⅘ |

## ALL-TIME LEADING EARNERS

| | STARTS | 1ST | 2ND | 3RD | AMOUNT |
|---|---|---|---|---|---|
| John Henry, g '75 | 61 | 28 | 12 | 6 | $2,805,310 |
| Spectacular Bid, c '76 | 30 | 26 | 2 | 1 | 2,781,608 |
| • Affirmed, c '75 | 29 | 22 | 5 | 1 | 2,393,818 |
| •Kelso, g '57 | 63 | 39 | 12 | 2 | 1,977,896 |
| Forego, g '70 | 57 | 34 | 9 | 7 | 1,938,957 |
| •Round Table, c '54 | 66 | 43 | 8 | 5 | 1,749,869 |
| Exceller, c '73 | 33 | 15 | 5 | 6 | 1,654,003 |
| Dahlia, f '70 | 48 | 15 | 4 | 6 | 1,535,443 |
| Buckpasser, c '63 | 31 | 25 | 4 | 1 | 1,462,014 |
| Allez France, f '70 | 21 | 13 | 3 | 1 | 1,380,565 |
| Secretariat, c '70 | 21 | 16 | 3 | 1 | 1,316,808 |
| •Nashua, c '52 | 30 | 22 | 4 | 1 | 1,288,565 |
| Ancient Title, g '70 | 57 | 24 | 11 | 9 | 1,252,791 |
| Susan's Girl, f '69 | 63 | 29 | 14 | 11 | 1,251,668 |
| Carry Back, c '58 | 61 | 21 | 11 | 11 | 1,241,165 |
| Foolish Pleasure, c '72 | 26 | 16 | 4 | 3 | 1,216,705 |

| | STARTS | 1ST | 2ND | 3RD | AMOUNT |
|---|---|---|---|---|---|
| Seattle Slew, c '74 | 17 | 14 | 2 | 0 | $1,208,726 |
| Damascus, c '64 | 32 | 21 | 7 | 3 | 1,176,781 |
| Cougar II, c '66 | 50 | 20 | 7 | 17 | 1,162,725 |
| Riva Ridge, c '69 | 30 | 17 | 3 | 1 | 1,111,497 |
| Fort Marcy, g '64 | 75 | 21 | 18 | 14 | 1,109,791 |
| •Citation, c '45 | 45 | 32 | 10 | 2 | 1,085,760 |
| Native Diver, g '59 | 81 | 37 | 7 | 12 | 1,026,500 |
| Royal Glint, g '70 | 52 | 21 | 9 | 4 | 1,004,816 |
| Dr. Fager, c '64 | 22 | 18 | 2 | 1 | 1,002,642 |
| Troy, c '76 | 12 | 8 | 2 | 2 | 973,978 |
| Swoon's Son, c' 53 | 51 | 30 | 10 | 3 | 970,605 |
| Alydar, c '75 | 26 | 14 | 9 | 1 | 957,195 |
| Trillion, f '74 | 32 | 9 | 14 | 3 | 954,825 |
| John Henry, g '75 | 50 | 20 | 11 | 5 | 948,000 |
| Noble Dancer (GB), c '72 | 43 | 22 | 1 | 5 | 945,893 |
| Roman Brother, g '61 | 42 | 16 | 10 | 5 | 943,473 |
| •Stymie, c '41 | 131 | 35 | 33 | 28 | 918,485 |
| Flying Paster, c '76 | 23 | 10 | 7 | 2 | 907,060 |
| T. V. Lark, c '57 | 72 | 19 | 13 | 6 | 902,194 |
| Rheingold, c '69 | 17 | 9 | 4 | 1 | 901,099 |
| Bowl Game, g '74 | 22 | 11 | 5 | 5 | 899,383 |
| Shuvee, f '66 | 44 | 16 | 10 | 6 | 890,445 |
| Tiller, g '74 | 40 | 16 | 7 | 6 | 867,988 |
| Swaps, c '52 | 25 | 19 | 2 | 2 | 848,900 |
| Nodouble, c '65 | 42 | 13 | 11 | 5 | 846,749 |
| Crystal Water, c '73 | 25 | 9 | 3 | 3 | 845,072 |
| Honest Pleasure, c '73 | 25 | 12 | 6 | 2 | 839,997 |
| Sword Dancer, c '56 | 39 | 15 | 7 | 4 | 829,610 |
| Candy Spots, c '60 | 22 | 12 | 5 | 1 | 824,718 |
| Waya, f '74 | 29 | 14 | 6 | 4 | 823,066 |
| Golden Act, c '76 | 25 | 8 | 6 | 7 | 821,408 |
| Mongo, c '59 | 46 | 22 | 10 | 4 | 820,766 |
| •Armed, g '41 | 81 | 41 | 20 | 10 | 817,475 |
| Find, g '50 | 110 | 22 | 27 | 27 | 803,615 |
| Three Troikas, f '76 | 11 | 7 | 3 | 1 | 800,312 |

## NORTH AMERICA'S RECORD MONEY EARNERS

| DATE BECAME | RACE | RUNNER, FOALING DATE, SIRE | STS | 1ST | 2ND | 3RD | RECORD EARNINGS |
|---|---|---|---|---|---|---|---|
| May 13, 1845 | Won match with Fashion | BOSTON, 1833, ch. c, by Timoleon | 45 | 40 | 2 | 1 | $ 51,700 |
| Sept. 25, 1860 | Won a post stake | PEYTONA, 1839, ch. f, by Glencoe | 7 | 6 | 1 | - | 62,400 |
| Oct. 4, 1881 | Won overnight race | PLANET, 1855, ch. c, by Revenue | 31 | 27 | 4 | - | 69,700 |
| June 17, 1882 | Won Coney Island Cup | PAROLE, 1873, b. g, by Leamington | | | | | 69,891† |
| July 3, 1882 | Won overnight race | HINDOO, 1878, b. c, by Virgil | 35 | 30 | 3 | 2 | 71,875 |
| July 4, 1885 | Won Ocean Stakes | PAROLE, 1873, b. g, by Leamington | 138 | 59 | 28 | 17 | 82,816 |
| Aug. 29, 1889 | Won Express Stakes | MISS WOODFORD, 1880, br. f, by Billet | 48 | 37 | 7 | 2 | 118,270 |
| Aug. 4, 1892 | Won Eatontown Stakes | HANOVER, 1884, ch. c, by Hindoo | 50 | 32 | 14 | 2 | 118,887 |
| Aug. 29, 1893 | Won Futurity Stakes | KINGSTON, 1884, br. c, by Spendthrift | 138 | 89 | 33 | 12 | 140,195 |
| Oct. 12, 1920 | Won Kenilworth Gold Cup | DOMINO, 1891, br. c, by Himyar | 25 | 19 | 2 | 1 | 193,550 |
| Oct. 20, 1923 | Won International Special | MAN O' WAR, 1917, ch. c, by Fair Play | 21 | 20 | 1 | - | 249,465 |
| Sept. 6, 1930 | Won Lawrence Realization | ZEV, 1920, br. c, by The Finn | 43 | 23 | 8 | 5 | 313,639 |
| Aug. 1, 1931 | Won Arlington Handicap | GALLANT FOX, 1927, b. c, by Sir Gallahad III | 17 | 11 | 3 | 2 | 328,165 |
| March 2, 1940 | Won Santa Anita Handicap | SUN BEAU, 1925, b. c, by Sun Briar | 74 | 33 | 12 | 10 | 376,744 |
| July 15, 1942 | Won Massachusetts Handicap | SEABISCUIT, 1933, b. c, by Hard Tack | 89 | 33 | 15 | 13 | 437,730 |
| June 21, 1947 | Won Brooklyn Handicap | WHIRLAWAY, 1938, ch. c, by Blenheim II | 60 | 32 | 15 | 9 | 561,161 |
| July 5, 1947 | Won Sussex Handicap | ASSAULT, 1943, ch. c, by Bold Venture | | | | | 576,670† |
| July 12, 1947 | Won Butler Handicap | STYMIE, 1941, ch. c, by Equestrian | | | | | 595,500† |
| July 19, 1947 | Won Empire City Gold Cup | ASSAULT, 1943, ch. c, by Bold Venture | 42 | 18 | 6 | 7 | 675,470 |
| | | STYMIE, 1941, ch. c, by Equestrian | | | | | 678,500† |
| Oct. 9, 1947 | Won Sysonby Handicap | ARMED, 1941, br. g, by Bull Lea | 81 | 41 | 20 | 10 | 817,475 |
| Oct. 25, 1947 | Won Gallant Fox Handicap | STYMIE, 1941, ch. c, by Equestrian | 131 | 35 | 33 | 28 | 918,485 |
| June 3, 1950 | Won Golden Gate Mile | CITATION, 1945, b. c, by Bull Lea | 45 | 32 | 10 | 2 | 1,085,760 |
| May 19, 1956 | Won Camden Handicap | NASHUA, 1952, b. c, by Nasrullah | 30 | 22 | 4 | 1 | 1,288,565 |
| Oct. 11, 1958 | Won Hawthorne Gold Cup | ROUND TABLE, 1954, b. c, by Princequillo | 66 | 43 | 8 | 5 | 1,749,869 |
| Oct. 31, 1964 | Won Jockey Club Gold Cup | KELSO, 1957, dk.b/br. g, by Your Host | 63 | 39 | 12 | 2 | 1,977,896 |
| June 24, 1979 | Won Hollywood Gold Cup | AFFIRMED, 1975, ch. c, by Exclusive Native | 26 | 19 | 5 | 1 | 2,393,818 |
| June 8, 1980 | Won California Stakes | SPECTACULAR BID, 1976, gr. c, by Bold Bidder | 27 | 23 | 2 | 1 | 2,394,268† |
| Oct. 10, 1981 | Won Jockey Club Gold Cup | JOHN HENRY, 1975, g, by Ole Bob Bowers | 61 | 28 | 12 | 6 | 2,805,310† |

† Indicates earnings on day record established, all other figures represent total record upon retirement.

## ANNUAL LEADING HORSES—
## MONEY WON

| YEAR | HORSE | ACE | STS | 1STS | EARNINGS |
|------|-------|-----|-----|------|----------|
| 1902 | Major Daingerfield | 3 | 7 | 4 | $ 57,685 |
| 1903 | Africander | 3 | 15 | 8 | 70,810 |
| 1904 | Delhi | 3 | 10 | 6 | 75,225 |
| 1905 | Sysonby | 3 | 9 | 9 | 144,380 |
| 1906 | Accountant | 3 | 13 | 9 | 83,570 |
| 1907 | Colin | 2 | 12 | 12 | 131,705 |
| 1908 | Sir Martin | 2 | 13 | 8 | 78,590 |
| 1909 | Joe Madden | 3 | 15 | 5 | 44,905 |
| 1910 | Novelty | 2 | 16 | 11 | 72,630 |
| 1911 | Worth | 2 | 13 | 10 | 16,645 |
| 1912 | Star Charter | 4 | 17 | 6 | 14,655 |
| 1913 | Old Rosebud | 2 | 14 | 12 | 19,057 |
| 1914 | Roamer | 3 | 16 | 12 | 29,105 |
| 1915 | Borrow | 7 | 9 | 4 | 20,195 |
| 1916 | Campfire | 2 | 9 | 6 | 49,735 |
| 1917 | Sun Briar | 2 | 9 | 5 | 59,505 |
| 1918 | Eternal | 2 | 8 | 6 | 56,173 |
| 1919 | Sir Barton | 3 | 13 | 8 | 88,250 |
| 1920 | Man o' War | 3 | 11 | 11 | 166,140 |
| 1921 | Morvich | 2 | 11 | 11 | 115,234 |
| 1922 | Pillory | 3 | 7 | 4 | 95,654 |
| 1923 | Zev | 3 | 14 | 12 | 272,008 |
| 1924 | Sarazen | 3 | 12 | 8 | 95,640 |
| 1925 | Pompey | 2 | 10 | 7 | 121,630 |
| 1926 | Crusader | 3 | 15 | 9 | 166,033 |
| 1927 | Anita Peabody | 2 | 7 | 6 | 111,905 |
| 1928 | High Strung | 2 | 6 | 5 | 153,590 |
| 1929 | Blue Larkspur | 3 | 6 | 4 | 153,450 |
| 1930 | Gallant Fox | 3 | 10 | 9 | 308,275 |
| 1931 | Gallant Flight | 2 | 7 | 7 | 219,000 |
| 1932 | Gusto | 3 | 16 | 4 | 145,940 |
| 1933 | Singing Wood | 2 | 9 | 3 | 88,050 |
| 1934 | Cavalcade | 3 | 7 | 6 | 111,235 |
| 1935 | Omaha | 3 | 9 | 6 | 142,255 |
| 1936 | Granville | 3 | 11 | 7 | 110,295 |
| 1937 | Seabiscuit | 4 | 15 | 11 | 168,580 |
| 1938 | Stagehand | 3 | 15 | 8 | 189,710 |
| 1939 | Challedon | 3 | 15 | 9 | 184,535 |
| 1940 | Bimelech | 3 | 7 | 4 | 110,005 |
| 1941 | Whirlaway | 3 | 20 | 13 | 272,386 |
| 1942 | Shut Out | 3 | 12 | 8 | 238,872 |
| 1943 | Count Fleet | 3 | 6 | 6 | 174,055 |
| 1944 | Pavot | 2 | 8 | 8 | 179,040 |
| 1945 | Busher | 3 | 13 | 10 | 273,735 |
| 1946 | Assault | 3 | 15 | 8 | 424,195 |
| 1947 | Armed | 6 | 17 | 11 | 376,325 |
| 1948 | Citation | 3 | 20 | 19 | 709,470 |
| 1949 | Ponder | 3 | 21 | 9 | 321,825 |
| 1950 | Noor | 5 | 12 | 7 | 346,940 |
| 1951 | Counterpoint | 3 | 15 | 7 | 250,525 |

| YEAR | HORSE | AGE | STS | 1STS | EARNINGS |
|---|---|---|---|---|---|
| 1952 | Crafty Admiral | 4 | 16 | 9 | $ 277,225 |
| 1953 | Native Dancer | 3 | 10 | 9 | 513,425 |
| 1954 | Determine | 3 | 15 | 10 | 328,700 |
| 1955 | Nashua | 3 | 12 | 10 | 752,550 |
| 1956 | Needles | 3 | 8 | 4 | 440,850 |
| 1957 | Round Table | 3 | 22 | 15 | 600,383 |
| 1958 | Round Table | 4 | 20 | 14 | 662,780 |
| 1959 | Sword Dancer | 3 | 13 | 8 | 537,004 |
| 1960 | Bally Ache | 3 | 15 | 10 | 445,045 |
| 1961 | Carry Back | 3 | 16 | 9 | 565,349 |
| 1962 | Never Bend | 2 | 10 | 7 | 402,969 |
| 1963 | Candy Spots | 3 | 12 | 7 | 604,481 |
| 1964 | Gun Bow | 4 | 16 | 8 | 580,100 |
| 1965 | Buckpasser | 2 | 11 | 9 | 568,096 |
| 1966 | Buckpasser | 3 | 14 | 13 | 669,078 |
| 1967 | Damascus | 3 | 16 | 12 | 817,941 |
| 1968 | Forward Pass | 3 | 13 | 7 | 546,674 |
| 1969 | Arts and Letters | 3 | 14 | 8 | 555,604 |
| 1970 | Personality | 3 | 18 | 8 | 444,049 |
| 1971 | Riva Ridge | 2 | 9 | 7 | 503,263 |
| 1972 | Droll Role | 4 | 19 | 7 | 471,633 |
| 1973 | Secretariat | 3 | 12 | 9 | 860,404 |
| 1974 | Chris Evert | 3 | 8 | 5 | 551,063 |
| 1975 | Foolish Pleasure | 3 | 11 | 5 | 716,278 |
| 1976 | Forego | 6 | 8 | 6 | 401,701 |
| 1977 | Seattle Slew | 3 | 7 | 6 | 641,370 |
| 1978 | Affirmed | 3 | 11 | 8 | 901,541 |
| 1979 | Spectacular Bid | 3 | 12 | 10 | 1,279,334 |
| 1980 | Temperence Hill | 3 | 17 | 8 | 1,130,452 |

## RACING'S HALL OF FAME
## SARATOGA, NEW YORK

HORSES (YEAR ELECTED, YEAR FOALED)
Affirmed (1980, 1975)
Alsab (1976, 1939)
American Eclipse (1970, 1814)
Armed (1963, 1941)
Artful (1956, 1902)
Assault (1964, 1943)
Battleship (1969, 1927)
Bed o' Roses (1976, 1947)
Beldame (1956, 1901)
Ben Brush (1955, 1893)
Bewitch (1977, 1945)
Blue Larkspur (1957, 1926)
Bold Ruler (1973, 1954)
Bon Nouvel (1976, 1960)
Boston (1955, 1833)
Broomstick (1956, 1901)
Buckpasser (1970, 1963)
Busher (1964, 1942)
Bushranger (1967, 1930)

Carry Back (1975, 1958)
Challedon (1977, 1945)
Cicada (1967, 1959)
Citation (1959, 1945)
Colin (1956, 1905)
Commando (1956, 1898)
Count Fleet (1961, 1940)
Dahlia (1981, 1970)
Damascus (1974, 1964)
Dark Mirage (1974, 1965)
Desert Vixen (1979, 1970)
Devil Diver (1980, 1939)
Discovery (1969, 1931)
Domino (1955, 1891)
Dr. Fager (1971, 1964)
Elkridge (1966, 1938)
Equipoise (1957, 1928)
Exterminator (1957, 1915)
Fair Play (1956, 1905)
Fashion (1980, 1837)
Firenze (1981, 1884)
Forego (1979, 1971)

Gallant Bloom (1977, 1966)
Gallant Fox (1957, 1927)
Gallorette (1963, 1942)
Gamely (1980, 1964)
Good and Plenty (1956, 1900)
Grey Lag (1957, 1918)
Hanover (1955, 1884)
Hindoo (1955, 1878)
Imp (1965, 1894)
Jay Trump (1971, 1957)
Jolly Roger (1965, 1922)
Kingston (1955, 1884)
Kelso (1967, 1957)
L'Escargot (1977, 1963)
Lexington (1955, 1850)
Longfellow (1971, 1867)
Luke Blackburn (1955, 1877)
Man o' War (1957, 1917)
Miss Woodford (1967, 1880)
Myrtlewood (1979, 1933)
Nashua (1965, 1952)
Native Dancer (1963, 1950)
Native Diver (1978, 1959)
Northern Dancer (1976, 1961)
Neji (1966, 1950)
Oedipus (1978, 1941)
Old Rosebud (1968, 1911)
Omaha (1965, 1932)
Pan Zareta (1972, 1910)
Peter Pan (1956, 1904)
Regret (1957, 1912)
Reigh Count (1978, 1925)
Roamer (1981, 1911)
Roseben (1956, 1901)
Round Table (1972, 1954)
Ruffian (1976, 1972)
Ruthless (1975, 1864)
Salvator (1955, 1886)
Sarazen (1957, 1921)
Seabiscuit (1958, 1933)
Searching (1978, 1952)
Seattle Slew (1981, 1974)
Secretariat (1974, 1970)
Shuvee (1975, 1966)
Silver Spoon (1978, 1956)
Sir Archy (1955, 1805)
Sir Barton (1957, 1916)
Stymie (1975, 1941)
Susan's Girl (1976, 1969)
Swaps (1966, 1952)
Sword Dancer (1977, 1956)
Sysonby (1956, 1902)
Tom Fool (1960, 1949)
Top Flight (1966, 1929)
Twenty Grand (1957, 1928)
Twilight Tear (1963, 1941)

War Admiral (1958, 1934)
Whirlaway (1959, 1938)
Whisk Broom II (1979, 1907)

TRAINERS (YEAR ELECTED)

Lazaro Barrera (1979)
H. Guy Bedwell (1971)
Elliott Burch (1980)
Preston M. Burch (1963)
William Preston Burch (1955)
Fred Burlew (1973)
J. D. (Dolly) Byers (1967)
Frank E. Childs (1968)
William Duke (1956)
Louis Feustel (1964)
James Fitzsimmons (1958)
John M. Gaver (1966)
Thomas Healey (1955)
Samuel Hildreth (1955)
Max Hirsch (1959)
Thomas Hitchcock, Sr. (1973)
Hollie Hughes (1973)
John Hyland (1956)
Hirsch Jacobs (1958)
H. Allen Jerkens (1975)
Ben A. Jones (1958)
H. A. (Jimmy) Jones (1959)
Andrew Joyner (1955)
Lucien Laurin (1977)
J. Howard Lewis (1969)
Horatio Luro (1980)
Frank Martin (1981)
Henry McDaniel (1956)
William Molter, Jr. (1960)
Winbert Mulholland (1967)
John Nerud (1972)
John Rogers (1955)
James Rowe, Sr. (1955)
Robert A. Smith (1976)
D. M. (Mike) Smithwick (1971)
W. C. (Woody) Stephens (1976)
H. J. Thompson (1969)
Marion H. Van Berg (1970)
Sylvester Veitch (1977)
Robert W. Walden (1970)
Sherrill Ward (1978)
Frank Whiteley, Jr. (1978)
Charles Whittingham (1974)
Carey Winfrey (1975)
W. C. (Bill) Winfrey (1971)

JOCKEY (YEAR ELECTED)

Frank (Dooley) Adams (1970)
John Adams (1965)

Joe Aitcheson, Jr. (1978)
Edward Arcaro (1958)
Ted Atkinson (1957)
Braulio Baeza (1976)
Carroll Bassett (1972)
George H. Bostwick (1968)
Sam Boulmetis (1973)
Steve Brooks (1963)
Frank Coltiletti (1970)
Robert (Specs) Crawford (1973)
Lavelle (Buddy) Ensor (1962)
Laverne Fator (1955)
Andrew (Mack) Garner (1969)
Snapper Garrison (1955)
Henry Griffin (1956)
Eric Guerin (1972)
William Hartack (1959)
Albert Johnson (1971)
Willie Knapp (1969)
Clarence Kummer (1972)
Charles Kurtsinger (1967)
John Loftus (1959)
John Longden (1958)
Danny Maher (1955)
Linus McAtee (1956)
Conn McCreary (1974)
Rigan McKinney (1968)
James McLaughlin (1955)

Walter Miller (1955)
Isaac Murphy (1955)
Ralph Neves (1960)
Joe Notter (1963)
George Odom (1955)
Winnie O'Connor (1956)
Frank O'Neill (1956)
Ivan Parke (1978)
Gil Patrick (1970)
Laffit Pincay, Jr. (1975)
Sam Purdy (1970)
John Reiff (1956)
Earl Sande (1955)
Carroll Schilling (1970)
William Shoemaker (1958)
Willie Simms (1977)
Todhunter Sloan (1955)
A. Patrick Smithwick (1973)
James Stout (1968)
Fred Taral (1955)
Bayard Tuckerman, Jr. (1973)
Ron Turcotte (1979)
Nash Turner (1955)
Robert Ussery (1980)
George Woolf (1955)
Raymond Workman (1956)
Manuel Ycaza (1977)

# The Stakes Race

In sports, the word "stakes" means the wagers taken home by the winner of the contest. The best guess is that the word is derived from an old custom of placing the game or gold or whatever constituted the wager on a stake at the finish line of a race, to be snatched up by the winner on his way past.

In the earliest days of racing, races were matches between two owners who put up equal "stakes." Such two-horse contests meant, however, that the winner puts up 50 percent of his prize. Owners of good horses soon realized that they could get better returns on their money in contests between a larger number of horses. If five horses competed, for example, the owner of the winning animal would only be putting up 20 percent of his purse. Such races were called "sweepstakes," because the winning owner "swept" up the "stakes" of every entrant.

When racecourses sprang up all over England, they eagerly competed for the best-quality horses, which attracted the most spectators. As an incentive to the owners of these Thoroughbreds, tracks began the practice of adding money to the pooled stakes put up by the owners. Today in England, owners put up money to enter their horses in every race. In many races, this money is considered an "entry fee" and is absorbed into the track's general revenue pool, with the horses racing for a pre-announced purse that doesn't depend on the exact number of entries. Other races are true "sweepstakes," in that the money put up by the owners' contributions in stakes races is about half that of the other kind of race. Owners prefer stakes, and stakes tend to attract the higher-quality animals, but so many stakes are run that the designation "stakes race" in itself does not carry the connotation of quality that it does in the United States. Rather, in Britain, the important races are known as "principal" races.

The sweepstakes came to America with the English settlers, and sweepstakes made up a large proportion of the races run through the nineteenth century. The introduction of pari-mutuel wagering meant that owners no longer had to be called upon to pay entry fees in order to create significant purses. With many opportunities to race for free, owners were willing to continue to put up stakes in the most important races. To continue to attract the best-quality horses, racetracks made these "stakes" races the richest on their cards. For both reasons, "stakes" came to mean "highest quality competition."

## MATCH RACES

Match races between two horses, which in the early nineteenth century had been the most common and significant type of Thoroughbred contest, declined sharply in popularity after the Civil War. The important races became sweepstakes such as the Kentucky Derby, the Belmont Stakes, and the Handicap Triple Crown.

In this century, arguments about the relative merits of two great horses inevitably give rise to conversation about lettting the two go head-to-head in a special match race. Most of these matches—such as the much-talked-about Affirmed-Spectacular Bid match in 1979—drown in a sea of discussion about the track to be used, the distance, weight, and other details, but a small number of famous matches have taken place in the last sixty years.

The first rich match of the century pitted the great Man o' War against Sir Barton, the 1919 Triple Crown winner, for the then phenomenal purse of $80,000. "Big Red" trounced Sir Barton, drawing away to a seven-length victory at Kenilworth Park. Triple Crown winners fared poorly in two other matches: War Admiral lost to Seabiscuit by 4 lengths at Pimlico in 1938 and Whirlaway fell a nose short of Alsab in a thrilling duel at Narragansett Park in 1942.

The only time a special race was arranged to settle the relative merits of the Kentucky Derby winner versus the English Derby winner was an $85,000 match between the American horse Zev and the English horse Papyrus in 1923. Zev covered the mile-and-a-half distance at Belmont Park five lengths ahead of Papyrus.

In the first $100,000 match, then all-time earnings leader Armed trounced Assault at Belmont Park in 1947. In another $100,000 race in 1955, Nashua walloped Swaps at Washington Park. In a much more thrilling contest, the dollar record for a match race rose to $250,000 as the four-year-old filly Convenience beat the six-year-old mare Typecast by a head at Hollywood Park in 1972.

The richest race ever held also produced the most lopsided victory. In 1974, Chris Evert humiliated Miss Musket by 50 lengths at Hollywood Park to win $350,000.

The most recent significant two-horse contest produced a tragedy that may have cast a permanent pall over match racing. At Belmont Park, on July 6, 1975, undefeated Ruffian, who had sprinted to an early lead, broke down after 3½ furlongs of a 1¼-mile race against Foolish Pleasure. After desperate attempts to repair her leg failed, the gallant filly had to be destroyed.

Ever since racing underwent its tremendous expansion after World War II, racetracks have increasingly tried to attract attention to their feature races by labeling them as "stakes" races. The majority of these races are not designed to attract the best horses in the country, but rather are handicaps or allowance races which showcase the best animals in each age and sex group at that particular track. Instead of making up a large portion of the purse, nomination fees are generally set at 1 percent of the "added money" that the track puts up. That means, for example, that to enter a race with "$25,000 added" an owner would pay a total of $250. If ten horses enter, the purse would be increased by $2,500, or 10 percent. These nomination fees discourage frivolous entries of uncompetitive horses, and they do make up a nice "pot sweetener," but both these purposes are subservient to the fact that cachet is attached to a race when it is designated a "stakes."

## AMERICA'S OLDEST STAKES

| DATE | STAKE NAME (CURRENT SITE) |
|------|---------------------------|
| 1831 | Phoenix Handicap (Keeneland) |
| 1860 | Queen's Plate Stakes (Woodbine) |
| 1864 | Travers Stakes (Saratoga) |
| 1866 | Jerome Handicap (Belmont) |
| 1867 | Belmont Stakes (Belmont) |
|      | Champagne Stakes (Belmont) |
| 1868 | Ladies Handicap (Aqueduct) |
| 1870 | Dixie Handicap (Pimlico) |
| 1871 | Monmouth Oaks (Monmouth Park) |
| 1872 | Alabama Stakes (Saratoga) |
| 1872 | California Derby (Golden Gate Fields) |
|      | Preakness Stakes (Pimlico) |
| 1874 | Juvenile Stakes (Aqueduct) |
|      | Withers Stakes (Aqueduct) |
| 1875 | Clark Handicap (Churchill Downs) |
|      | Kentucky Derby (Churchill Downs) |
|      | Kentucky Oaks (Churchill Downs) |
| 1881 | Spinaway Stakes (Saratoga) |

## THE KINDS OF STAKES RACES

Despite the proliferation of stakes races, they still constitute a treat for the racing fan. Stakes only represent approximately 3 percent of the races run each year. Of the nearly 470,000 Thoroughbreds foaled between 1955 and 1980, only 12,390 (2.64 percent) have been stakes winners.

Understanding racing, though, means being able to decipher the levels of ability within the pool of stakes winners. That means following the statement "Stakes races attract the best horses" with the question "Best of what?" For the Kentucky Derby, the answer is easy: "The best three-year-olds in training in the United States." For the $8,500 added Sardonyx Stakes at Fairmount Park, the answer is "the best five-furlong-sprinting three-year-old fillies at the track." As with every race, understanding the *class* of a stakes begins with interpreting the *conditions* of the race.

## GREAT HORSES: MAN O' WAR

Fifty-three years before Secretariat, another "Big Red" was foaled—a horse that captured the public's imagination in exactly the same way as did the 1973 Triple Crown winner. Huge crowds, a large part of which had never seen a race before, flocked to racetracks to watch the immortal Man o' War rack up victory after smashing victory. Many racing experts agree with the evaluation of his stud groom, Will Harburt, who always referred to Man o' War as "de mostest hoss dat ever was."

The record of the big chestnut colt speaks for itself. Man o' War won twenty of twenty-one races. He never won by less than a length.

Despite not being pushed, he set three track records, two American records (for the mile and for the mile and a half) and three world records (1⅛ mi., 1⅜ mi., 1⅝ mi.). In the 1⅝-mi. Lawrence Realization, which he won by 100 lengths, Man o' War broke the world record by 6⅘ seconds; in his twenty-length victory in the 1⅜-mi. Belmont Stakes, he shattered the existing world mark by 3⅕ seconds. All of the above feats were accomplished competing against what horsemen believed was a fine crop of colts in his age group.

Man o' War was bred by Jockey Club Chairman August Belmont II at his Nursery Stud. When Belmont entered the Army during World War I, he offered his entire crop of yearlings for sale at Saratoga in 1918. Man o' War was purchased by Sam Riddle for $5,000, which was double the sale average, but his price was $9,000 below that of the top colt. This purchase turned out to be one of the great bargains in racing history.

Man o' War inherited his sire Fair Play's surly disposition, but, when he entered training, his ability soon shone through. Few horses have ever looked as much like champions. It was this Big Red's eyes that first called forth the expressions "the look of eagles" and "living flame." Racing writer Joe Palmer said "his very stillness was that of the coiled spring, of the crouched tiger."

His promise was such that in his very first race he was sent to the post as an odds-on three-to-five favorite, and he responded with what was to become a typical six-length victory. Five stakes victories in a row followed, but in the Sanford Stakes at Saratoga, Man o' War suffered his only defeat—at the hands of a horse appropriately named Upset. In the race, Man o' War was hampered by a poor start. When he got into gear in the short six-furlong contest, he got trapped in a pocket at the rail. Jockey John Loftus had to check the colt and move him far to the outside. Still, "Big Red" finished with a rush that left him a scant half-length from an undefeated record.

Man o' War recovered to finish his two-year-old campaign with victories in the rich Hopeful Stakes and the Belmont Futurity. He opened his three-year-old campaign at Pimlico with a length-and-a-half victory in the Preakness, then added the Withers and Belmont Stakes in the next four weeks. By the end of the year, his superiority was so well established that he was forced to carry a staggering 138 pounds in the Potomac Handicap. Still, Man o' War charged to victory in track-record time. He ended the year with an easy seven-length win in a match race against 1919 Triple Crown winner Sir Barton.

After the colt's three-year-old campaign, owner Sam Riddle decided to retire him to stud, despite huge offers to keep him in training. The main reason was the prospect of handicappers assigning damaging weight to a champion who had already been made to carry 138 pounds as a three-year-old. At stud, Man o' War was the first to command a $5,000 stud fee, and his success occasioned million-dollar purchase offers. Out of 379 foals, Man o' War got 64 stakes winners, an impressive 17 percent. In 1942, Man o' War replaced his own sire, Fair Play, as the all-time leading sire in money won by his offspring. His most famous foal was the 1937 Triple Crown winner, War Admiral.

*Racing Record:*

| STS. | 1ST | 2ND | 3RD | EARNINGS |
|------|-----|-----|-----|----------|
| 21 | 20 | 1 | 0 | $249,465 |

MAN O' WAR, by Fair Play out of Mahubah by *Rock Sand

## Age and Sex

Like all races, every stakes race carries restrictions. Two-year-olds, racing's neophytes, never compete against older horses. The modern emphasis on the three-year-old has resulted in nearly a third of all races run being restricted to that age group. The rest of the stakes run are open to older horses as well as, in most cases, three-year-olds.

Although, as Genuine Risk proved, top fillies can compete with colts, male horses are generally believed to have a physical advantage over females, especially at ages two and three and especially over a distance of ground. While fillies are free to enter almost every stakes race, tracks in recent years have carded an increasing number of stakes that give distaff campaigners a

chance to prove their ability against their own sex.

Below is a table of stakes races by age and sex in 1980:

| AGE | FILLIES ONLY | OTHER STAKES | TOTAL |
|-----|------|------|------|
| 2 | 147 | 307 | 454 |
| 3 | 258 | 387 | 645 |
| Older | 367 | 626 | 993 |
| Total | 772 | 1,320 | 2,092 |

## Open vs. Restricted Stakes

Since the purpose of stakes races is to attract the best horses, the most significant are those *open* to any horse that meets the age and sex conditions. An example is the Balboa Stakes at Del Mar, the conditions of which appear below. Any two-year-old whose owner pays the required fees can compete for the purse offered.

8th RACE             STAKE

**EIGHTH RUNNING OF THE
BALBOA STAKES
$30,000 ADDED**

FOR TWO-YEAR-OLDS. By subscription of $50 each, which shall accompany the nomination and $300 additional to start, with $30,000 Added, of which $6,000 to second, $4,500 to third, $2,250 to fourth and $750 to fifth. Weight 120 lbs. Non-winners of $12,500 at one mile or over, 3 lbs.; of such a race of $15,000 any distance, 5 lbs.; a race at one mile or over other than maiden or claiming, 7 lbs. Starters to be named through the entry box Sunday, August 26, by the closing time of entries. A Trophy will be presented to the owner of the winner.

                             ONE MILE

A little over a quarter of all stakes races, however, carry *restrictions* that generally mean the field is of lower quality than *open* races. The largest number of restricted stakes are for horses bred in the state in which the track is located. An example is the Conniver Handicap at Bowie:

EIGHTH RACE           HANDICAP

**"THE CONNIVER HANDICAP"
$25,000 Added**

A Handicap for Fillies and Mares. Three-Years-Old and Upward. Registered Maryland-Breds. By subscription of $50 each, which should accompany the nomination, starters to pay $200 additional, with $25,000 added, of which 65% of all monies to the winner, 20% to second, 10% to third and 5% to fourth. Weights five days before the race. Starters to be named through the entry box by the usual time of closing.

Closed Friday, February 15, 1980 with — nominations.

                        One Mile and One-Sixteenth

Others are restricted to horses racing at a track, such as the Silky Sullivan Handicap, the conditions of which read: "for three-year-olds and upward *stabled at Golden Gate Fields*." Finally, a number of stakes have restrictions involving *races won* (such as Rockingham's Bold Lad Stakes for *"non-winners of a sweepstakes"*), or involving *money won* (such as Golden Gate Fields Portola Stakes for *"non-winners of $15,000"*).

**Purse Value**

Although most stakes are open, most don't have purses large enough to tempt owners to ship horses in to compete. Generally, it takes purses of over $25,000 to persuade owners to *van* horses from nearby racing circuits, and purses of over $50,000 for them to *fly* horses in from farther distances. Below is a table of 1980 stakes races by ranges of "added money" offered by the tracks:

| ADDED MONEY | NO. OF STAKES | % OF STAKES |
|---|---|---|
| $0 to $9,999 | 394 | 19% |
| $10,000 to $24,999 | 571 | 27% |
| $25,000 to $49,999 | 629 | 30% |
| $50,000 to $99,999 | 339 | 16% |
| $100,000 and up | 159 | 8% |

## RICHEST AMERICAN STAKES EVENTS—1980

| STAKES | TRACK | WINNER'S PURSE | TOTAL PURSE |
|---|---|---|---|
| Jockey Club Gold Cup | Belmont Park | $329,400 | $549,000 |
| Super Derby | Louisiana Downs | 300,000 | 500,000 |
| Arling.-Wash. Fut. | Arlington Park | 240,885 | 428,975 |
| Hollywood Gold Cup | Hollywood Park | 220,000 | 400,000 |
| Santa Anita Hdcp. | Santa Anita | 190,000 | 350,000 |
| Kentucky Derby | Churchill Downs | 250,500 | 346,800 |
| Louisiana Downs Hdcp. | Louisiana Downs | 207,600 | 346,000 |
| Hollywood Derby | Hollywood Park | 195,250 | 330,250 |
| Meadowlands Cup | Meadowlands | 196,500 | 327,500 |
| Californian Stakes | Hollywood Park | 184,450 | 319,450 |
| Marlboro Cup | Belmont Park | 180,000 | 300,000 |
| Turf Classic | Aqueduct | 180,000 | 300,000 |
| Belmont Stakes | Belmont Park | 176,220 | 293,700 |
| Golden Harvest Hdcp. | Louisiana Downs | 174,660 | 291,100 |
| Swaps Stakes | Hollywood Park | 162,200 | 274,700 |
| Amory Haskell Hdcp. | Monmouth Park | 158,160 | 263,600 |
| Washington Pk. Stks. | Arlington Park | 155,880 | 259,800 |
| Preakness | Pimlico | 180,600 | 250,600 |
| Hollywood Invit. | Hollywood Park | 137,500 | 250,000 |
| Young America Stks. | Meadowlands | 150,000 | 250,000 |
| Washington D.C. Int. | Laurel | 150,000 | 250,000 |

Arlington Million instituted in 1981 at Arlington Park became the world's riches horse race: $1,000,000 (total purse), $600,000 (winner's purse).

## Nomination Procedure

The procedure for entering horses in stakes races requires filing of a nomination form and payment of a nomination fee, which usually ranges from $25 to $250. Below is the nomination form for the Coaching Club American Oaks, the third jewel in the filly Triple Crown:

| Triple Crown For Fillies - 3rd Leg |
|---|

## THE COACHING CLUB AMERICAN OAKS
### [GRADE I]
### $125,000 ADDED
### TO BE RUN SATURDAY, JUNE 28, 1980

**20**

**FOR FILLIES THREE YEAR OLD.** By subscription of $250 each, which should accompany the nomination: $1,000 to pass entry box, with $125,000 added. The added money and all fees to be divided 60% to the winner, 22% to second, 12% to third and 6% to fourth. Weight 121 lbs. Starters to be named at the closing time of entries. Trophies will be presented to the winning owner, trainer and jockey, and mementoes to the grooms of the first four finishers. A special permanent trophy will be presented to the owner of the winner of the Coaching Club American Oaks if the filly has also won the Acorn and the Mother Goose.

**Nominations Close Wednesday, June 11, 1980**

**ONE MILE AND A HALF**

| NAME OF HORSE | Color | Sex | Age | SIRE | DAM |
|---|---|---|---|---|---|
| | | F | 3 | | |
| | | F | 3 | | |
| | | F | 3 | | |
| | | F | 3 | | |
| | | F | 3 | | |

**In the above stake closing Wednesday, June 11, 1980, I enter the horses above specified under the conditions printed on the reverse side of this blank.**

☐ Check box if limousine service is desired. State time and day of arrival.

**To: The New York Racing Association Inc. P.O. Box 90, Jamaica, N.Y. 11417**

If this nomination is signed by other than the owner, the person signing represents that he is authorized to enter the above agreement on behalf of the owner.

OWNER _____

Permanent Address _____

_____
(City)    (State)    (Code)

Nomination made by _____

For the majority of stakes races, nominations close one to three weeks beforehand. The nearer the close of nominations is to post time, the surer the horseman is of the competition his horse will face and of the animal's fitness to run. This is important, because the nomination fee is forfeited if the horse doesn't compete.

The more prestigious stakes races are able to set the deadlines for nominations months in advance of the race. The Triple Crown races, for example, close on February 15. Horsemen tend to nominate every potentially talented three-year-old in their barns. The 1978 Derby, as a result, closed with 319 nominations; the Preakness with 247; the Belmont Stakes with 268.

By the entry date, however, the potential fields for these races have been reduced to a relative handful. In the Derby, owners pay $4,000 more to pass the entry box, then an additional $3,500 to start. The fee is split to allow an owner whose horse draws an unfavorable post position or who suffers a last-minute ailment or injury to withdraw without forfeiting the total $7,500 due.

Many stakes races with early nomination dates have provisions for entries by late-developing horses. In return for the privilege, however, the owners are forced to pay a heavy *supplementary nomination fee*. In the Belmont Stakes, for example, fees for horses nominated in February are $1,000 to pass the entry box and $2,000 more to start. The supplementary nomination fee is $5,000 to enter and $15,000 more to start. Coastal, the 1979 Belmont winner, and Temperence Hill, the 1980 Belmont Champion, were both supplementary nominees.

The most speculative of investments in stakes nominations are those for two-year-old races known as *futurities*. To keep a horse eligible for these races, owners have to make a series of escalating payments for periods up to a year. Some futurities re-

quire the first nomination to be paid while
the mare is still in foal. More common is
the sequence for the Arlington-Washington
Futurity of 1980, the richest in the United
States:

| AMOUNT | DATE TO BE PAID |
|---|---|
| $ 25 | August 15, 1979 |
| $ 75 | November 15, 1979 |
| $ 200 | March 1, 1980 |
| $ 300 | May 15, 1980 |
| $ 400 | July 1, 1980 |
| $ 500 | August 15, 1980 |
| $1,000 | September 4, 1980, to pass entry box |
| $1,000 | September 6, 1980, to start |
| $3,500 Total | |

A total of 668 horses were nominated on
the lower rung of the ladder. The total
nomination and eligibility payments totaled
in the neighborhood of $300,000. Com-
bined with the $100,000 added by the
track, this made a total purse of around
$400,000.

Finally, some important and rich races,
such as the Marlboro Cup and the Washington, D.C., International, are invita-
tionals. That is, the race is open only to
those top horses invited by the race organ-
izers. Although no nomination fees are paid
by the owners of the entrants, in terms of
class these contests are included in the category "stakes races."

## Conditions of Running

Calling together the best horses for a stakes
race doesn't necessarily mean that the winner has proven to be absolutely the best
horse in the field. The reason is that in only
a relatively small number of races do horses
of the same age and sex compete on equal
terms.

If no compensating factors were introduced into race competition, certain superior
Thoroughbreds would so dominate stakes
that entries by other horses would be discouraged. Since tracks card stakes races to
attract spectator interest, the racing secretary attempts to make the competition more

even by handicapping the entrants according to his evaluation of their ability or
through written conditions based on their
past performance.

The truly championship competitions
within age and sex groups and between age
and sex groups are conducted in races with
conditions known in racing as *scale
weights.* This means that all horses of the
same age and sex carry the same weight,
based on a scale we'll explain when we discuss handicap races in detail.

The prestigious Triple Crown races, obviously, are conducted for three-year-olds
carrying level weights. Of the races leading
up to the Triple Crown contests, racing experts place more importance on the results
of such contests as the Wood Memorial and
the Blue Grass Stakes than on the equally
rich Arkansas and Louisiana derbies.

One big reason is apparent when the conditions of the Wood and of the Arkansas
Derby, below, are compared:

### WOOD MEMORIAL
1⅛ MILES. (1.47) 54th Running WOOD
MEMORIAL $100,000 Added. 3-year-olds.
Weight, 126 lbs. By subscription of $200 each
which shall accompany the nomination; $500
to start, with $100,000 added. The added
money and all fees to be divided 60% to the
winner, 22% to second, 12% to third and
6% to fourth. Starters to be named at the
closing time of entries. Trophies will be presented to the winning owner, trainer and
jockey.

### ARKANSAS DERBY
Ninth Race OAKLAWN April 1, 1978
1⅛ MILES. (1.48⅗) THE ARKANSAS
DERBY $100,000 ADDED. 42nd Running. 3-
year-olds. By subscription of $100 each, which
shall accompany the nomination, $750 to pass
the entry box, $1,500 additional to start.
$100,000 added of which with the subscription,
entry box and starting fees to be divided 60%
to the winner, 20% to second, 10% to third,
6% to fourth and 4% to fifth. Weight, 126 lbs.
Non-winners of $25,000, allowed 3 lbs.
$15,000, 6 lbs. Two races other than maiden
or claiming, 9 lbs. Starters to be named
through the entry box Thursday, March 30 at
time of closing. The owner of the winner to
receive a trophy.

Obviously, owners of the very best horses prefer them to race on an equal footing with their rivals.

The same reasoning holds true in determining the very top races in other age groups. For two-year-olds, the $125,000 scale-weight Champagne Stakes is more prestigious than the $200,000 allowance-condition Young America Stakes. Horse of the Year and Older Horse or Gelding awards most often go to winners of the scale-weight Jockey Club Gold Cup and Woodward Stakes, with even prestigious handicaps like the Marlboro Cup rated a touch less important. For similar reasons, Grass Horse of the Year honors is decided by such scale-weight races as the Man o' War Stakes and the Washington, D.C., International. The seven-furlong Vosburgh Stakes at Aqueduct became the most important sprint of the year when it was changed from a handicap to a scale-weight race.

Unfortunately, only a handful of horses in each division can race competitively on a scale-weight basis. Differences in maturation rates for young two- and three-year-olds make their owners more willing to test them on the basis of scale weights, but by the time a horse reaches age four, its top ability has normally been determined. That's why, in order to get big fields, 746 of the 993 stakes open to older horses in 1980 were *handicaps*. An example is Gulfstream's Orchid Handicap.

**NINTH RACE**
**THE ORCHID HANDICAP (Grade III)**
**$100,000 Added**
**9 A HANDICAP FOR FILLIES AND MARES, THREE-YEAR-OLDS AND UPWARD.** By subscription of $150 each which shall accompany the nomination, $1,000 to pass the entry box and $1,000 additional to start, with $100,000 added. The added money and all fees to be divided 65% to first; 20% to second; 10% to third; 5% to fourth . . . Supplementary nominations may be made on or before Saturday, March 29 on payment of $5,000 each. Weights: Monday, March 31. This event will be di-

vided. Preference to highweights up to 16 horses. Starters to be named through the entry box on Thursday, April 3 by 10:30 A.M. Trophy to winning owner. **Closed Saturday, March 22 with nominations.**
**ONE MILE AND ONE-SIXTEENTH (On the Turf)**

The weights in a handicap are assigned by the racing secretary based on his appraisal of past performances. We'll explain how this is done in the section on handicap races.

Most stakes races for two- and three-year-olds not run under scale weights are conducted under *allowance* conditions. This means that the horses that haven't won a certain amount of money or a certain amount of races get *weight allowances*. The example below is Aqueduct's Bold Ruler Stakes:

**NINTH RACE—THE BOLD RULER**
**$75,000 Added**
**For Three-Year-Olds and Upward.** By subscription of $150 each, which shall accompany the nomination; $600 to pass the entry box, with $75,000 added. The added money and all fees to be divided 60% to the winner, 22% to second, 12% to third and 6% to fourth.

| | |
|---|---|
| Three-year-olds | 113 lbs. |
| Older | 126 lbs. |
| Winners of a race of $35,000 in 1980 an additional | 2 lbs. |
| Non-winners of a race of $75,000 in 1979–80 allowed | 3 lbs. |
| Of two races of $25,000 in 1980 | 5 lbs. |
| Of a race of $25,000 in 1980 | 7 lbs. |

Starters to be named at the closing time of entries. Trophies will be presented to the winning owner, trainer and jockey and mementoes to the grooms of the first four finishers.

**SIX FURLONGS**

We'll explain how these allowances are determined in our section on allowance races.

## Distance

A final consideration in looking at a stakes race is the distance over which it is run. As we saw in the breeding section, speed is easier to breed into a Thoroughbred than stamina. The classic horse is one that can carry speed over a distance longer than a mile. The classier races are those conducted at the longer distances.

Because they're still relative babies, most two-year-olds race in stakes held at sprint distances—five furlongs to a mile. For three-year-olds and older horses, the most prestigious and richest races are conducted at the longer distances, as demonstrated by the following table:

| DISTANCE | NO. OF STAKES | AVG. ADDED MONEY |
|---|---|---|
| Less than 6 f. | 85 | $ 9,619 |
| 6 f. | 348 | 21,862 |
| Between 6 and 8 f. | 212 | 23,944 |
| 8 to 8½ f. | 653 | 29,038 |
| 9 f. | 199 | 63,044 |
| 9½ f. | 14 | 65,000 |
| 10 f. | 57 | 110,175 |
| Over 10 f. | 70 | 84,679 |

## DISTINGUISHING THE QUALITY RACE

As we've seen, tracks attempt to heighten the interest in certain of their races by designating them stakes races. The relative importance of these stakes races is determined by a variety of different conditions: purse level; whether the race is open or restricted; how weights are determined; how nomination procedures are established; the distance at which they're run.

All the above factors are helpful in evaluating the conditions of races run at your track—but with more than two thousand stakes run annually, trying to pick out the most important is a very difficult and bewildering job.

Three races are easily recognized even by people who don't know in which direction horses race. These are the Kentucky Derby, the Preakness, and the Belmont Stakes, America's "classic" races, which make up the Triple Crown. Since 1973, a committee formed by the Thoroughbred Owners and Breeders Association (TOBA) has performed the valuable service of selecting and rating the most important of the other races. In that year, foreign racing authorities, seeking help in interpreting the past performances of potential breeding stock, suggested to the TOBA that it conduct an annual grading of stakes races similar to a grading program done for European racing in 1971.

Struck by the logic of this system, a committee made up of three each of racing officials, trustees of the TOBA, and editors of *The Blood-Horse* annually select the most important stakes races and classify these Grade I, Grade II, and Grade III. These graded stakes are the contests that determine the annual champions and distinguish the animals worthy of consideration as breeding stock. Below, we'll first discuss the *classic races,* then explore the *graded stakes races.*

# The Classic Races

The word classic means "most representative of the excellence of its kind." In Thoroughbred racing, the epitome of excellence is the three-year-old who demonstrates superiority at distances from a mile to a mile and a half. Races that have attained prestige as the ultimate test of the three-year-old have been given the special title "classic races." Winning a classic race is the most sought-after prize in all of racing.

## THE ORIGIN OF THE CLASSIC RACE

When racing first blossomed in Great Britain, heat races predominated. The ideal horse was the six-year-old who had the stamina to contest as many as four heats in one day. The classic tests of this ability were the King's Plates, the first of which was run in the time of Charles II. By the 1730s, fourteen King's Plates were contested all over Britain. No horse, however, competed in more than two or three Plates. The problem was distance: at this time, horses had to be walked to racing meets, which obviously limited a horse to competitions in the area in which it was trained.

In the middle 1700s, as we've seen previously, heat racing was replaced by dashes contested by younger horses. The ideal horse changed from the sturdy six-year-old to the speedy three-year-old. With the change in concept of the classic horse came new classic races to test its ability.

In 1776, a group of sportsmen, led by the Marquis of Rockingham and Lt. Gen. Anthony St. Leger of Park Hill, assembled at Doncaster, which had been a center of racing since before 1600. They decided to subscribe to a new sweepstakes for three-year-olds, to be run at a distance of two miles. In 1778, at the urging of Lord Rockingham, the race was named the St. Leger Stakes.

About the same time, the young 12th Earl of Derby took over from his uncle General Burgoyne (of Battle of Saratoga fame) a converted inn near the racing center of Epsom. The name of the inn was The Oaks. In 1778, perhaps inspired by the new sweepstakes for three-year-olds run at Doncaster, Lord Derby and his friends planned a sweepstakes for three-year-old fillies to be run the next summer and to be named after the inn. In 1779, Lord Derby won the first running of the Oaks with his filly, Bridget.

The next year, a second three-year-old sweepstakes was planned, this one for colts and fillies. Lord Derby tossed a coin with Sir Bunbury to determine after whom the race would be named. The coin determined that the new race would be, not the "Bunbury," but the Derby.

By the early nineteenth century, a need was felt for additional races to prove horses' all-around ability by trying them first at shorter distances. The obvious site for these new races was Newmarket, which had been the headquarters of British racing since the time of Charles II. The Jockey Club had been formed there in the mid-eighteenth century. In 1809, a mile race for three-year-old colts and fillies was established, the 2,000 Guineas. In 1814, a mile race for fillies only was added, the 1,000 Guineas.

To this day, these five races retain the title "classics." The English Triple Crown, which consists of the 2,000 Guineas, the Derby, and the St. Leger Stakes, is so hotly contested that only one horse in the last forty-five years, Nijinsky II, has captured all three.

### The English Classic Races

| RACE | DISTANCE | TRACK | WHEN RUN | 1ST RUNNING |
|------|----------|-------|----------|---------|
| 2,000 Guineas | 1 mile | Newmarket | April | 1809 |
| 1,000 Guineas (fillies) | 1 mile | Newmarket | April | 1814 |
| Derby | 1½ miles | Epsom | June | 1780 |
| Oaks (fillies) | 1½ miles | Epsom | June | 1779 |
| St. Leger Stakes | 1 mile, 6 fur., 127 yds. | Doncaster | Sept. | 1776 |

## ENGLISH TRIPLE CROWN WINNERS

| | |
|---|---|
| 1853 | West Australian |
| 1865 | Gladiateur |
| 1866 | Ormonde |
| 1891 | Common |
| 1893 | Isinglass |
| 1897 | Galtee More |
| 1899 | Flying Fox |
| 1900 | Diamond Jubilee |
| 1903 | Rock Sand |
| 1915 | Pommern |
| 1917 | Gay Crusader |
| 1918 | Gainsborough |
| 1935 | Bahram |
| 1970 | Nijinsky II |

## THE AMERICAN CLASSICS— THE TRIPLE CROWN

In the United States, the classic races are the famous Triple Crown contests: the Kentucky Derby, the Preakness, and the Belmont Stakes. Conducted in a short five-week time span, these races represent a stern test of speed, stamina, and durability. Winning a Triple Crown race brings a horse millions in the breeding shed.

Although the prestige of these races is well established today, it's only in the last forty or fifty years that they've been linked together as the Triple Crown. The history of the races is far more varied than that of the English classics. While the Belmont Stakes, like the British races, was begun and supported by racing's elite, the Preakness was contested at six different distances and three different tracks before it became the $1\frac{3}{16}$-mile middle jewel in the Triple Crown in 1932. The Kentucky Derby was an insignificant race for mediocre local horses before a promotional genius built it into America's most famous race.

Even today, the Triple Crown has its detractors. The races force young three-year-olds to run too far, too often, with too much weight, some say. More good horses have been ruined than helped by the Derby, others say—but even the most vociferous critics of the Derby can't deny the greatness of the horses who've performed magnificently in the Triple Crown races: Count Fleet, Citation, Native Dancer, Northern Dancer, Nashua, Majestic Prince, Riva Ridge, Secretariat, Seattle Slew, Affirmed, and Spectacular Bid. Those same horsemen would find themselves humming "My Old Kentucky Home" if fortune placed a speedy, precocious three-year-old in their barns.

## GREAT HORSES: CITATION

When racing experts talk about the greatest American horses of all time, three names invariably rise to the top: Man o' War, Secretariat, and Citation. While the relative merits of these three champions are ultimately undeterminable, Citation's three-year-old campaign was perhaps the greatest single year ever enjoyed by a racehorse.

Citation's two-year-old record showed eight victories in nine races, with his only defeat coming at the hands of his Calumet Farm stablemate, the filly, Bewitch, in the Washington Park Futurity. Citation was named champion two-year-old colt and ranked along with Bewitch at the top of the Experimental Free Handicap.

At the end of the three-year-old campaign, however, Citation's handicap weight was fifteen pounds greater than that of his nearest rival. While most three-year-olds campaign exclusively against their own age group until the second half of the year, Citation opened the season with two successive victories against older horses. He followed with two additional triumphs against his peers before suffering a one-length defeat in a six-furlong prep race at Havre de Grace. (The horse that beat him was Saggy, sire of the 1968 Derby and Preakness winner, Carry Back.) The setback was only temporary, as Citation went on to reel off fifteen consecutive victories.

Included in this streak was a sweep of the Triple Crown races that was accomplished so easily it seemed almost anti-climactic. Citation was such a favorite in the Kentucky Derby that Col. Matt Winn eliminated place and show wagering for the event. Citation won the Derby by three and a half lengths, the Preakness by five and a half, and the Belmont by eight. After demolishing all the three-year-olds, Citation began his campaign against older horses, capturing the Stars and Stripes Handicap by two lengths in track-record time. Later in the fall, he wiped out all suspicions about his stamina with a seven-length triumph in the two-mile Jockey Club Gold Cup. By the end of October, not a single horse was willing to challenge Citation in the winner-take-all Pimlico Invitational. Citation won in a walk-over.

By the end of 1948, Citation had won nineteen of twenty races at nine different tracks, at distances from six furlongs to two miles. He had been ridden by three different jockeys and had triumphed over fast, good, sloppy, muddy, and heavy surfaces. Citation was not only named Horse of the Year and best three-year-old, but won honors as best handicap horse as well. His earnings for the year, $708,470, set a new record.

Unfortunately, the rest of Citation's story is one of injury and frustration. Various ailments caused him to sit out an entire year. Not until January of his fifth year did he return, winning an allowance race at Santa Anita. In his subsequent eight starts he wound up with a lone victory and seven second-place finishes. Incredibly, in six straight races he was beaten in track-record time; more incredibly, five of those were new world records.

As a result, Citation was still nearly $100,000 short of becoming racing's first millionaire, so Calumet brought him back at age six after a ten-month layoff. The gallant horse started slowly, but finally snared a victory in his fifth start, the Argonaut Handicap. A second tough win followed in the American Handicap. Finally, on July 14, 1951, Citation, in his last race, grabbed the $100,000 first prize in the Hollywood Gold Cup. He retired with the coveted million-dollar career earnings total that his owners had pursued for three long years.

That moment of glory was to be Citation's last. The son of Bull Lea proved to be a keen disappointment at stud. Of 269 named foals (those registered with the Jockey Club), Citation produced only 12 stakes winners. His average earnings index was a mediocre 1.57.

*Race Record:*

| STS. | 1ST | 2ND | 3RD | EARNINGS |
|------|-----|-----|-----|----------|
| 45 | 32 | 10 | 2 | $1,085,760 |

CITATION, by Bull Lea out of Hydroplane II by Hyperion

---

*American Triple Crown Winners*

| | |
|---|---|
| Sir Barton | 1919 |
| Gallant Fox | 1930 |
| Omaha | 1935 |
| War Admiral | 1937 |
| Whirlaway | 1941 |
| Count Fleet | 1943 |
| Assault | 1946 |
| Citation | 1948 |
| Secretariat | 1973 |
| Seattle Slew | 1977 |
| Affirmed | 1978 |

*Derby-Preakness Winners*

| | |
|---|---|
| Burgoo King | 1932 |
| Pensive | 1944 |
| Tim Tam | 1958 |
| Carry Back | 1961 |
| Northern Dancer | 1964 |
| Kauai King | 1966 |
| Forward Pass | 1968 |
| Majestic Prince | 1969 |
| Canonero II | 1971 |
| Spectacular Bid | 1979 |
| Pleasant Colony | 1981 |

*Derby-Belmont Winners*

| | |
|---|---|
| Zev | 1923 |
| Twenty Grand | 1931 |
| Johnstown | 1939 |
| Shut Out | 1942 |
| Middleground | 1950 |
| Needles | 1956 |
| Chateaugay | 1963 |
| Riva Ridge | 1972 |
| Bold Forbes | 1976 |

*Preakness-Belmont Winners*

| | |
|---|---|
| Man o' War | 1920 |
| Pillory | 1922 |
| Bimelech | 1940 |
| Capot | 1949 |
| Native Dancer | 1953 |
| Nashua | 1955 |
| Damascus | 1967 |
| Little Current | 1974 |

# THE KENTUCKY DERBY

The Kentucky Derby, the fabled "Run for the Roses," is the most famous Thoroughbred horse race in the world. On the first Saturday in May, the attention of the entire sports world turns to Louisville and the spires of Churchill Downs. There, the three-year-olds who are talented and lucky enough to survive the rugged pre-Derby training will duel for the most prestigious racing title—Kentucky Derby winner.

It was this kind of prestige that the founder of the Derby, Col. M. Lewis Clark, Jr., had in mind when he conceived of a race that would serve as a showcase for the Kentucky breeding industry. After the Civil War, the heartland of American racing was New York's two tracks, Saratoga and Jerome Park. Although Kentucky-bred horses had proved their worth up north, the market for racehorses was rather small, causing serious problems for the industry. Col. Clark, a socially prominent man in his mid-twenties, began to talk of forming a jockey club, building a racecourse, and conducting a race meeting featuring rich stakes races that would attract the interest of wealthy Northern horsemen. In 1872, Clark journeyed to England to observe closely the classic Epsom Derby. He returned full of plans for a race modeled on that great English classic.

The persuasive Clark was finally able to assemble 320 patrons willing to put up $100 each to join the Louisville Jockey Club. Clark then leased eighty acres of land from his uncles, John and Henry Churchill, and on that property he built the Louisville Jockey Club course (later to be known as Churchill Downs). For the opening of the new track in 1875, he carded the first running of the race he prophesied would rival its English namesake in prestige—the Kentucky Derby.

With his characteristic energy, Clark then set out to promote the race, which was to be run at the Epsom Derby distance of 1½ miles. Forty-two owners paid $50 each to nominate their horses by the March 1, 1875, entry deadline. With $1,000 added, the total purse came to $3,100, with the winner getting $2,900. The race was scheduled for Monday, May 17, the first day of the inaugural race meeting.

By Derby eve, the field had been narrowed to thirteen colts and two fillies. The race had attracted considerable interest beyond the borders of Kentucky, and great excitement in Louisville. A holiday atmosphere filled the air as a huge crowd of 10,000 flocked into the brand-new racing grounds.

Finally, it was Derby time. Favored at 2 to 1 was the entry of gambler H. P. McGrath. McGrath's plan was to have one horse, Aristides, force the pace and tire out the speed horses, so that the more highly regarded Chesapeake could surge on to win. When the flag fell, however, Chesapeake got off dead last. Aristides moved to the front as planned. As the race progressed, Aristides' jockey, Oscar Lewis, kept looking around for his stablemate, but Chesapeake was nowhere in sight. As the crowd roared, Lewis set the chestnut colt down and, despite the pace, Aristides responded. The margin of victory for the "rabbit" part of McGrath's entry was one length. The time, 2:37¾ was the fastest ever clocked for a mile-and-a-half run by a three-year-old in the United States. The Derby had proved to be the smashing success Clark had planned.

The Derby continued to attract quality horses for the next decade, despite relatively low purses, but in 1886 came a quarrel which precipitated a long decline for the race. In that year, multi-millionaire horse owner James Ben Ali Haggin arrived in Louisville with a big string of horses, including his prize Derby nominee and namesake, Ben Ali. Haggin, a big gambler, was angered by a bookmakers' strike on Derby day. A Churchill Downs official responded by insulting Haggin, who immediately pulled his horses out of Louisville. Haggin was a powerful figure in New York racing, and the incident triggered a virtual boycott of the Derby by Eastern owners.

Another problem the Derby faced was the mile-and-a-half distance, which many horse owners felt was too far to risk sending good three-year-olds so early in the year. In 1894, only five horses showed up to compete in the Derby. The *Daily Louisville Commercial* called the field "a contest of dogs."

The decline in the prestige of the Derby was matched by the serious financial problems of Churchill Downs. The track looked like it was headed for oblivion when, in 1902, a successful merchant tailor named Matt Winn took over its management. Winn, a brilliant businessman and promoter, single-handedly transformed the

Kentucky Derby into the kind of event Colonel Clark had dreamed of.

Winn began his campaign by resuscitating the financial fortunes of Churchill Downs. A key element in this was his response to the Louisville City Council's decision to enforce a ban on bookmaking for the 1908 Derby. Winn was the man who remembered that the track had in storage four pari-mutuel machines that had been imported years before, then put aside to gather dust. The pari-mutuel machines proved to be popular with the public, and they provided an excellent source of income for the track. It was Winn's introduction of the pari-mutuel machines that was so influential in the return to health of the entire American racing industry.

Once Churchill Downs was healthy, Winn turned to courting the New York racing notables and the national racing press. He persuaded a number of wealthy owners, including August Belmont, to enter the 1914 Derby. The next year, Harry Payne Whitney entered his great filly, Regret. After Regret became the first filly ever to win the Derby, Whitney remarked, "I do not care if she never wins another race or if she never starts another race. She has won the greatest race in America."

After Whitney's imprimatur elevated the race in horsemen's eyes, Winn intensified his unprecedented wooing of the sporting press. No newsman ever paid for anything in Louisville during Derby week. Famous newspapermen like Grantland Rice and Damon Runyon wrote column after column that helped form the romance of the race. Movie newsreels didn't seem complete unless they included a clip of a Derby.

Also intensifying the public's interest in the race was the creation of the Winter (or Future) Book. The Winter Book was an opportunity to place wagers with bookmakers months before the Kentucky Derby. Such wagering was extremely popular with the public, which clamored for news of Derby contenders. Such major spring races as the Flamingo Stakes, the Santa Anita Derby, the Wood Memorial, and the Blue Grass Stakes became important not for

# HISTORY OF THE KENTUCKY DERBY

| YEAR | WINNER | MARGIN | SIRE | JOCKEY | TRAINER | SECOND | THIRD | PAYOFF | TIME | TRACK | DISTANCE | MONEY | STARTERS |
|---|---|---|---|---|---|---|---|---|---|---|---|---|---|
| 1875 | Aristides, ch. c | 1 | Leamington | O. Lewis | Ansel Williams | Volcano | Verdigris | 2-1 | 2:37 3/4 | Fast | 1 1/2 | $2,850 | 15 |
| 1876 | Vagrant, br. g. | 2 | Virgil | R. Swim | James Williams | Creedmoor | Harry Hill | 9-5 | 2:38 1/4 | Fast | 1 1/2 | 2,950 | 11 |
| 1877 | Baden Baden, ch. c | 2 | Australian | W. Walker | Ed Brown | Leonard | King William | 8-1 | 2:38 | Fast | 1 1/2 | 3,300 | 11 |
| 1878 | Day Star, ch. c. | 2 | Star Davis | J. Carter | Lee Paul | Himyar | Leveler | 3-1 | 2:37 1/4 | Good | 1 1/2 | 4,050 | 9 |
| 1879 | Lord Murphy, b. c. | 1 | Pat Malloy | C. Shauer | George Rice | Falsetto | Strathmore | 11-10 | 2:37 | Fast | 1 1/2 | 3,550 | 9 |
| 1880 | Fonso, ch. c. | 1 | King Alfonso | G. Lewis | Tice Hutsell | Kimball | Bancroft | 7-1 | 2:37 1/2 | Fast | 1 1/2 | 3,800 | 5 |
| 1881 | Hindoo, b. c. | 4 | Virgil | J. McLaughlin | James Rowe, Sr. | Lelex | Alhambra | 1-3 | 2:40 | Fast | 1 1/2 | 4,410 | 6 |
| 1882 | Apollo, ch. g. | 1/2 | Lever | B. Hurd | Green B. Morris | Runnymede | Bengal | 10-1 | 2:40 1/2 | Good | 1 1/2 | 4,560 | 14 |
| 1883 | Leonatus, b.c. | 3 | Longfellow | W. Donohue | Raleigh Colston | Drake Carter | Lord Raglan | 9-5 | 2:43 | Heavy | 1 1/2 | 3,760 | 7 |
| 1884 | Buchanan, ch. c. | | Buckden | I. Murphy | William Bird | Loftin | Audrain | 3-1 | 2:40 1/4 | Good | 1 1/2 | 3,990 | 9 |
| 1885 | Joe Cotton, ch. c. | nk | King Alfonso | E. Henderson | Alex Perry | Bersan | Ten Booker | 1-1 | 2:37 1/4 | Good | 1 1/2 | 4,630 | 10 |
| 1886 | Ben Ali, br. c. | 1/2 | Virgil | P. Duffy | Jim Murphy | Blue Wing | Free Knight | 1.72-1 | 2:36 1/2 | Fast | 1 1/2 | 4,890 | 10 |
| 1887 | Montrose, b. c. | 2 | Duke of Montrose | I. Lewis | John McGinty | Jim Gore | Jacobin | 10-1 | 2:39 1/4 | Fast | 1 1/2 | 4,200 | 7 |
| 1888 | Macbeth II, b. g. | 1 | Macduff | G. Covington | John Campbell | Gallifet | White | 8-1 | 2:38 1/4 | Fast | 1 1/2 | 4,740 | 7 |
| 1889 | Spokane, ch. c. | ns | Hyder All | T. Kiley | John Rodegap | Proctor Knott | Once Again | 10-1 | 2:34 1/2 | Fast | 1 1/2 | 4,880 | 8 |
| 1890 | Riley, b. c. | 2 | Longfellow | I. Murphy | Edward Corrigan | Bill Letcher | Robespierre | 4-1 | 2:45 | Heavy | 1 1/2 | 5,460 | 6 |
| 1891 | Kingman, b. c. | 1 | Glengarry | I. Murphy | Dud Allen | Balgowan | High Tariff | 1-2 | 2:52 1/4 | Good | 1 1/2 | 4,550 | 4 |
| 1892 | Azra, b. c. | ns | Reform | A. Clayton | John H. Morris | Huron | Phil Dwyer | 3-2 | 2:41 1/2 | Heavy | 1 1/2 | 4,230 | 3 |
| 1893 | Lookout, ch. c. | 5 | Troubadour | E. Kunze | Will McDaniel | Plutus | Boundless | 7-10 | 2:39 1/4 | Fast | 1 1/2 | 3,840 | 6 |
| 1894 | Chant, b. c. | 2 | Falsetto | F. Goodale | Eugene Leigh | Pearl Song | Sigurd | 1-2 | 2:41 | Fast | 1 1/2 | 4,020 | 5 |
| 1895 | Halma, blk. c. | 3 | Hanover | J. Perkins | Byron McClelland | Basso | Laureate | 1-3 | 2:37 1/2 | Fast | 1 1/2 | 2,970 | 4 |
| 1896 | Ben Brush, b. c. | ns | Bramble | W. Simms | Hardy Campbell | Ben Eder | Semper Ego | 1-2 | 2:07 3/4 | Good | 1 1/4 | 4,850 | 8 |
| 1897 | Typhoon II, ch. c. | hd | Top Gallant | F. Garner | J. C. Cahn | Ornament | Dr. Catlett | 3-1 | 2:12 1/2 | Heavy | 1 1/4 | 4,850 | 6 |
| 1898 | Plaudit, br. c. | nk | Himyar | W. Simms | J. E. Madden | Lieber Karl | Isabey | 3-1 | 2:09 | Good | 1 1/4 | 4,850 | 4 |
| 1899 | Manuel, b. c. | 2 | Bob Miles | F. Taral | Robert J. Walder | Corsini | Mazo | 11-20 | 2:12 | Fast | 1 1/4 | 4,850 | 5 |
| 1900 | Lieut. Gibson, b. c. | 4 | G. W. Johnson | J. Boland | Charles H. Hughes | Florizar | Thrive | 7-10 | 2:06 1/4 | Fast | 1 1/4 | 4,850 | 7 |
| 1901 | His Eminence, b. c. | 2 | Falsetto | J. Winkfield | F. B. VanMeter | Sannazarro | Driscoll | 3-1 | 2:07 3/4 | Fast | 1 1/4 | 4,850 | 5 |
| 1902 | Alan-a-Dale, ch. c. | ns | Halma | J. Winkfield | T. C. McDowell | Inventor | The Rival | 3-2 | 2:08 3/4 | Fast | 1 1/4 | 4,850 | 4 |
| 1903 | Judge Himes, b. c. | 3/4 | Esher | H. Booker | J. P. Mayberry | Early | Bourbon | 10-1 | 2:09 | Fast | 1 1/4 | 4,850 | 6 |
| 1904 | Elwood, b. c. | 1/2 | Free Knight | F. Pryor | C. E. Durnell | Ed Tierney | Brancas | 15-1 | 2:08 1/2 | Fast | 1 1/4 | 4,850 | 5 |
| 1905 | Agile, b. c. | 3 | Sir Dixon | J. Martin | Robert Tucker | Ram's Horn | Layson | 1-3 | 2:10 3/4 | Heavy | 1 1/4 | 4,850 | 3 |
| 1906 | Sir Huon, b. c. | 2 | Falsetto | R. Troxler | Peter Coyne | Lady Navarre | James Reddick | 11-10 | 2:08 45 | Fast | 1 1/4 | 4,850 | 6 |
| 1907 | Pink Star, b. c. | 2 | Pink Coat | A. Minder | W. H. Fizer | Zal | Ovelando | 15-1 | 2:12 3/5 | Heavy | 1 1/4 | 4,850 | 6 |
| 1908 | Stone Street, b. c. | 1 | Longstreet | A. Pickens | J. W. Hall | Sir Cleges | Dunvegan | $49.40 | 2:15 1/5 | Heavy | 1 1/4 | 4,850 | 8 |
| 1909 | Wintergreen, b. c. | 4 | Dick Welles | W. Powers | C. Mack | Miami | Dr. Barkley | 5.90 | 2:08 1/5 | Slow | 1 1/4 | 4,850 | 10 |
| 1910 | Donau, b. c. | 1/2 | Woolsthorpe | F. Herbert | George Ham | Joe Morris | Fighting Bob | 5.30 | 2:06 2/5 | Fast | 1 1/4 | 4,850 | 7 |
| 1911 | Meridian, b. c. | 3/4 | Broomstick | G. Archibald | A. Ewing | Governor Gray | Colston | 7.80 | 2:05 | Fast | 1 1/4 | 4,850 | 7 |
| 1912 | Worth, br. c. | nk | Knight of the Thistle | C. H. Shilling | Frank M. Taylor | Duval | Flamma | 3.60 | 2:09 2/5 | Muddy | 1 1/4 | 4,850 | 8 |
| 1913 | Donerail, b. c. | 1/2 | McGee | R. Goose | T. P. Hayes | Ten Point | Gowell | 184.90 | 2:04 45 | Fast | 1 1/4 | 5,475 | 8 |
| 1914 | Old Rosebud, b. g. | 8 | Uncle | J. McCabe | F. D. Weir | Hodge | Bronzewing | 3.70 | 2:03 2/5 | Fast | 1 1/4 | 9,125 | 7 |
| 1915 | Regret, ch. f. | 2 | Broomstick | J. Notter | James Rowe, Sr. | Pebbles | Sharpshooter | 7.30 | 2:05 2/5 | Fast | 1 1/4 | 11,450 | 16 |
| 1916 | George Smith, blk. c. | nk | Out of Reach | J. Loftus | Hollie Hughes | Star Hawk | Franklin | 10.30 | 2:04 | Fast | 1 1/4 | 9,750 | 9 |
| 1917 | Omar Khayyam, ch. c. | 2 | Marco | C. Borel | C. T. Patterson | Ticket | Midway | 27.60 | 2:04 3/5 | Fast | 1 1/4 | 16,600 | 15 |
| 1918 | Exterminator, ch. g. | 1 | McGee | W. Knapp | Henry McDaniel | Escoba | Viva America | 61.20 | 2:10 4/5 | Muddy | 1 1/4 | 14,700 | 8 |
| 1919 | Sir Barton, ch. c. | 5 | Star Shoot | J. Loftus | H. G. Bedwell | Billy Kelly | Under Fire | 7.20 | 2:09 4/5 | Heavy | 1 1/4 | 20,825 | 12 |
| 1920 | Paul Jones, br. g. | hd | Sea King | T. Rice | Wm. Garth | Upset | On Watch | 34.40 | 2:09 | Slow | 1 1/4 | 30,375 | 17 |
| 1921 | Behave Yourself, b. c. | hd | Marathon | C. Thompson | H. J. Thompson | Black Servant | Prudery | 19.30 | 2:04 1/5 | Fast | 1 1/4 | 38,450 | 12 |
| 1922 | Morvich, br. c. | 1 1/2 | Runnymede | A. Johnson | Fred Burlew | Bet Mosie | John Finn | 4.40 | 2:04 3/5 | Fast | 1 1/4 | 46,775 | 10 |
| 1923 | Zev, br. c. | 1 1/2 | The Finn | E. Sande | D. J. Leary | Martingale | Vigil | 40.40 | 2:05 2/5 | Fast | 1 1/4 | 53,000 | 21 |

| Year | Winner | Margin | Sire | Trainer | Jockey | Second | Third | Odds | Time | Dist. | Track | Value | Starters |
|------|--------|--------|------|---------|--------|--------|-------|------|------|-------|-------|-------|----------|
| 1928 | Reigh Count, ch. c. | 3 | Sunreigh | B.S. Michell | C. Lang | Misstep | Toro | 6.10 | 2:10 2/5 | 1 1/4 | Heavy | 55,375 | 15 |
| 1929 | Clyde Van Dusen, ch. g. | 2 | Man o' War | Clyde Van Dusen | L. McAtee | Nalshapur | Panchio | 8.00 | 2:10 4/5 | 1 1/4 | Muddy | 53,950 | 22 |
| 1930 | Gallant Fox, b. c. | 2 | Sir Gallahad III | James Fitzsimmons | E. Sande | Gallant Knight | Ned O. | 4.30 | 2:07 3/5 | 1 1/4 | Good | 50,725 | 21 |
| 1931 | Twenty Grand, b. c. | 4 | St. Germans | James Rowe, Jr. | C. Kurtsinger | Sweep All | Mate | 3.70 | 2:01 4/5 | 1 1/4 | Fast | 48,725 | 15 |
| 1932 | Burgoo King, ch. c. | 5 | Bubbling Over | H.J. Thompson | E. James | Economic | Stepenfetchit | 13.20 | 2:05 1/5 | 1 1/4 | Fast | 52,350 | 12 |
| 1933 | Brokers Tip, br. c. | ns | Black Toney | H.J. Thompson | D. Meade | Head Play | Charley O. | 19.80 | 2:06 4/5 | 1 1/4 | Good | 48,925 | 20 |
| 1934 | Cavalcade, br. c. | 2 1/2 | Lancegaye | R.A. Smith | M. Garner | Discovery | Agrarian | 5.00 | 2:04 | 1 1/4 | Fast | 28,175 | 13 |
| 1935 | Omaha, ch. c. | 1 1/2 | Gallant Fox | James Fitzsimmons | W. Saunders | Roman Soldier | Whiskolo | 10.00 | 2:05 | 1 1/4 | Good | 39,525 | 13 |
| 1936 | Bold Venture, ch. c. | hd | St. Germans | Max Hirsch | I. Hanford | Brevity | Indian Broom | 43.00 | 2:03 3/5 | 1 1/4 | Good | 37,725 | 18 |
| 1937 | War Admiral, br. c. | 1 3/4 | Man o' War | George Conway | C. Kurtsinger | Pompoon | Reaping Reward | 5.20 | 2:03 1/5 | 1 1/4 | Fast | 52,050 | 14 |
| 1938 | Lawrin, br. c. | 1 | Insco | Benjamin A. Jones | E. Arcaro | Dauber | Can't Wait | 19.20 | 2:04 4/5 | 1 1/4 | Fast | 47,050 | 20 |
| 1939 | Johnstown, b. c. | 8 | Jamestown | James Fitzsimmons | J. Stout | Challedon | Heather Broom | 3.20 | 2:03 2/5 | 1 1/4 | Fast | 46,350 | 10 |
| 1940 | Gallahadion, b. c. | 1 1/2 | Sir Gallahad III | Roy Waldron | C. Bierman | Bimelech | Dit | 72.40 | 2:05 | 1 1/4 | Fast | 60,150 | 8 |
| 1941 | Whirlaway, ch. c. | 8 | Blenheim II | Benjamin A. Jones | E. Arcaro | Staretor | Market Wise | 7.80 | 2:01 2/5 | 1 1/4 | Fast | 61,275 | 11 |
| 1942 | Shut Out, ch. c. | 2 1/2 | Equipoise | John M. Gaver | W.D. Wright | Alsab | Valdina Orphan | 5.80 | 2:04 2/5 | 1 1/4 | Fast | 64,225 | 15 |
| 1943 | Count Fleet, br. c. | 3 | Reigh Count | G.D. Cameron | J. Longden | Blue Swords | Slide Rule | 2.80 | 2:04 | 1 1/4 | Fast | 60,725 | 10 |
| 1944 | Pensive, ch. c. | 4 1/2 | Hyperion | Benjamin A. Jones | C. McCreary | Broadcloth | Stir Up | 16.20 | 2:04 1/5 | 1 1/4 | Fast | 64,675 | 16 |
| 1945 | Hoop Jr., ch. c. | 6 | Sir Gallahad III | Ivan H. Parke | E. Arcaro | Pot o' Luck | Darby Dieppe | 9.40 | 2:07 | 1 1/4 | Muddy | 64,850 | 16 |
| 1946 | Assault, ch. c. | 8 | Bold Venture | Max Hirsch | W. Mehrtens | Spy Song | Hampden | 18.40 | 2:06 3/5 | 1 1/4 | Slow | 96,400 | 17 |
| 1947 | Jet Pilot, ch. c. | hd | Blenheim II | Tom Smith | E. Guerin | Phalanx | Faultless | 12.80 | 2:06 4/5 | 1 1/4 | Slow | 92,160 | 13 |
| 1948 | Citation, b. c. | 3 1/2 | Bull Lea | Benjamin A. Jones | E. Arcaro | Coaltown | My Request | 2.80 | 2:05 2/5 | 1 1/4 | Fast | 83,400 | 6 |
| 1949 | Ponder, dk. c. b. | 3 | Pensive | Benjamin A. Jones | S. Brooks | Capot | Palestinian | 34.00 | 2:04 1/5 | 1 1/4 | Sloppy | 91,600 | 14 |
| 1950 | Middleground, ch. c. | 1 1/4 | Bold Venture | Max Hirsch | W. Boland | Hill Prince | Mr. Trouble | 17.80 | 2:01 3/5 | 1 1/4 | Fast | 92,650 | 14 |
| 1951 | Count Turf, b. c. | 4 | Count Fleet | Sol Rutchick | C. McCreary | Royal Mustang | Ruhe | 31.20 | 2:02 3/5 | 1 1/4 | Fast | 98,050 | 20 |
| 1952 | Hill Gail, dk. b. c. | 2 | Bull Lea | Benjamin A. Jones | E. Arcaro | Sub Fleet | Blue Man | 4.20 | 2:01 3/5 | 1 1/4 | Fast | 96,300 | 16 |
| 1953 | Dark Star, br. c. | hd | Royal Gem II | Edward Hayward | H. Moreno | Native Dancer | Invigorator | 51.80 | 2:02 | 1 1/4 | Fast | 90,050 | 11 |
| 1954 | Determine, gr. c. | 1 1/2 | Alibhai | Willie Molter | R. York | Hasty Road | Hasseyampa | 10.60 | 2:03 | 1 1/4 | Fast | 102,050 | 17 |
| 1955 | Swaps, ch. c. | 1 1/2 | Khaled | M.A. Tenney | W. Shoemaker | Nashua | Summer Tan | 7.60 | 2:01 4/5 | 1 1/4 | Fast | 108,400 | 10 |
| 1956 | Needles, b. c. | 3/4 | Ponder | H.L. Fontaine | D. Erb | Fabius | Come On Red | 5.20 | 2:03 2/5 | 1 1/4 | Fast | 123,450 | 17 |
| 1957 | Iron Liege, b. c. | ns | Bull Lea | H.A. Jones | W. Hartack | Gallant Man | Round Table | 18.80 | 2:02 1/5 | 1 1/4 | Fast | 107,950 | 15 |
| 1958 | Tim Tam, dk. b. c. | 1/2 | Tom Fool | H.A. Jones | I. Valenzuela | Lincoln Road | Noureddin | 6.20 | 2:05 | 1 1/4 | Fast | 116,400 | 9 |
| 1959 | Tommy Lee, b. c. | ns | Tudor Minstrel | Frank Childs | W. Shoemaker | Sword Dancer | First Landing | 9.40 | 2:02 1/5 | 1 1/4 | Fast | 119,650 | 14 |
| 1960 | Venetian Way, ch. c. | 3 1/2 | Royal Coinage | Vic Sovinski | W. Hartack | Bally Ache | Victoria Park | 14.60 | 2:02 2/5 | 1 1/4 | Good | 114,850 | 17 |
| 1961 | Carry Back, br. c. | 3/4 | Saggy | J.A. Price | J. Sellers | Crozier | Bass Clef | 7.00 | 2:04 | 1 1/4 | Good | 120,500 | 13 |
| 1962 | Decidedly, gr. c. | 2 1/4 | Determine | Horatio Luro | W. Hartack | Roman Line | Ridan | 19.40 | 2:00 2/5 | 1 1/4 | Fast | 119,650 | 15 |
| 1963 | Chateaugay, ch. c. | 1 1/4 | Swaps | James Conway | B. Baeza | Never Bend | Candy Spots | 20.80 | 2:01 4/5 | 1 1/4 | Fast | 108,900 | 9 |
| 1964 | Northern Dancer, b. c. | nk | Nearctic | Horatio Luro | W. Hartack | Hill Rise | The Scoundrel. | 8.80 | 2:00 | 1 1/4 | Fast | 114,300 | 12 |
| 1965 | Lucky Debonair, b. c. | nk | Vertex | Frank Catrone | W. Shoemaker | Dapper Dan | Tom Rolfe | 10.60 | 2:01 1/5 | 1 1/4 | Fast | 112,000 | 11 |
| 1966 | Kaual King, dk. b. or br. c. | 1/2 | Native Dancer | Henry Forrest | D. Brumfield | Advocator | Blue Skyer | 6.80 | 2:02 | 1 1/4 | Fast | 120,500 | 15 |
| 1967 | Proud Clarion, b. c. | 1 | Hail to Reason | Loyd Gentry | R. Ussery | Barbs Delight | Damascus | 62.20 | 2:00 3/5 | 1 1/4 | Fast | 119,700 | 14 |
| 1968 | *Forward Pass, b. c. | nk | On-and-On | Henry Forrest | I. Valenzuela | Francie's Hat | T. V. Commercial | 4.40 | 2:02 2/5 | 1 1/4 | Fast | 122,600 | 16 |
| 1969 | Majestic Prince, ch. c. | nk | Raise a Native | John Longden | W. Hartack | Arts and Letters | Dike | 4.80 | 2:01 4/5 | 1 1/4 | Fast | 113,200 | 8 |
| 1970 | Dust Commander, ch. c. | 5 | Bold Commander | Don Combs | M. Manganello | My Dad George | High Echelon | 32.60 | 2:03 2/5 | 1 1/4 | Good | 127,800 | 17 |
| 1971 | Canonero II, b. c. | 3 1/4 | Pretendre | Juan Arias | G. Avila | Jim French | Bold Reason | 19.40 | 2:03 1/5 | 1 1/4 | Fast | 145,500 | 20 |
| 1972 | Riva Ridge, b. c. | 3 1/4 | First Landing | Lucien Laurin | R. Turcotte | No Le Hace | Hold Your Peace | 5.00 | 2:01 4/5 | 1 1/4 | Fast | 140,300 | 14 |
| 1973 | Secretariat, ch. c. | 2 1/2 | Bold Ruler | Lucien Laurin | R. Turcotte | Sham | Our Native | 5.00 | 1:59 2/5 | 1 1/4 | Fast | 155,050 | 13 |
| 1974 | Cannonade, b. c. | 2 1/4 | Bold Bidder | W.C. Stephens | A. Cordero, Jr. | Hudson County | Agitate | 5.00 | 2:04 | 1 1/4 | Fast | 274,000 | 23 |
| 1975 | Foolish Pleasure, b. c. | 1 3/4 | What a Pleasure | LeRoy Jolley | J. Vasquez | Avatar | Diabolo | 5.80 | 2:02 | 1 1/4 | Fast | 209,600 | 15 |
| 1976 | Bold Forbes, dk. b. or br. c. | 1 | Irish Castle | Lazaro Barrera | A. Cordero, Jr. | Honest Pleasure | Elocutionist | 8.00 | 2:01 3/5 | 1 1/4 | Fast | 165,200 | 9 |
| 1977 | Seattle Slew, dk. b. or br. c. | 1 3/4 | Bold Reasoning | W.H. Turner, Jr. | J. Cruguet | Run Dusty Run | Sanhedrin | 3.00 | 2:02 1/5 | 1 1/4 | Fast | 214,700 | 15 |
| 1978 | Affirmed, ch. c. | 1 1/2 | Exclusive Native | Lazaro Barrera | S. Cauthen | Alydar | Believe It | 5.60 | 2:01 1/5 | 1 1/4 | Fast | 186,900 | 11 |
| 1979 | Spectacular Bid, gr. c. | 2 3/4 | Bold Bidder | Grover G. Delp | R. Franklin | General Assembly | Golden Act | 3.20 | 2:02 2/5 | 1 1/4 | Fast | 228,650 | 10 |
| 1980 | Genuine Risk, ch. f. | 1 | Exclusive Native | L. Jolley | J. Vasquez | Rumbo | Jaklin Klugman | 13.30 | 2:02 | 1 1/4 | Fast | 250,550 | 13 |
| 1981 | Pleas. Colony, dk. b. or br. c. | 3/4 | His Majesty | J. Campo | J. Velasquez | Woodchopper | Partez | 9.00 | 2:02 | 1 1/4 | Fast | 317,200 | 21 |

# HISTORY OF THE PREAKNESS STAKES

| YEAR | WINNER | MARGIN | SIRE | JOCKEY | TRAINER | SECOND | THIRD | PAYOFF | TIME | TRACK | DISTANCE | MONEY | STARTERS |
|---|---|---|---|---|---|---|---|---|---|---|---|---|---|
| 1873 | Survivor, b. c. | 10 | Vandal | G. Barbee | A. D. Pryor | John Boulger | Artist | 11-1 | 2:43 | Slow | 1 1/2 | $1,850 | 7 |
| 1874 | Culpepper, b. c. | 3/4 | Revolver | M. Donohue | Hugh Gaffney | King Amadeus | Scratch | 8-1 | 2:56 1/2 | Muddy | 1 1/2 | 1,900 | 5 |
| 1875 | Tom Ochiltree, b. c. | 2 | Lexington | L. Hughes | R. W. Walden | Viator | Bay Final | | 2:43 1/2 | Slow | 1 1/2 | 1,950 | 9 |
| 1876 | Shirley, b. g. | 4 | Lexington | G. Barbee | Wm. Brown | Rappahannock | Algerine | 2-1 | 2:44 3/4 | Good | 1 1/2 | 1,950 | 8 |
| 1877 | Cloverbrook, ch. c. | 2 | Vauxhall | C. Holloway | Jeter Walden | Bombast | Lucifer | | 2:45 1/2 | Good | 1 1/2 | 1,650 | 4 |
| 1878 | Duke of Magenta, b. c. | 2 | Lexington | C. Holloway | R. W. Walden | Bayard | Albert | 2-5 | 2:41 3/4 | Good | 1 1/2 | 2,100 | 3 |
| 1879 | Harold, ch. c. | 1 | Leamington | L. Hughes | R. W. Walden | Jericho | Rochester | 1-6 | 2:40 1/2 | Fast | 1 1/2 | 2,550 | 6 |
| 1880 | Grenada, b. c. | 3/4 | King Alfonso | L. Hughes | R. W. Walden | Oden | Emily F. | 7-10 | 2:40 1/2 | Good | 1 1/2 | 2,000 | 5 |
| 1881 | Saunterer, ch. c. | 1/2 | Leamington | T. Costello | R. W. Walden | Compensation | Baltic | 3-2 | 2:40 1/2 | Good | 1 1/2 | 1,950 | 6 |
| 1882 | Vanguard, b. c. | nk | Virgil | T. Costello | R. W. Walden | Heck | Col. Watson | 6.05-5 | 2:44 1/2 | Good | 1 1/2 | 1,250 | 3 |
| 1883 | Jacobus, b. c. | 4 | The Ill-Used | G. Barbee | R. Dwyer | Parnell | | 6.00-5 | 2:42 1/2 | Good | 1 1/2 | 1,635 | 2 |
| 1884 | Knight of Ellerslie, ch. c. | 2 | Eolus | S. Fisher | T. B. Doswell | Welcher | | 8.45-5 | 2:39 1/2 | Fast | 1 1/2 | 1,905 | 2 |
| 1885 | Tecumseh, b. c. | 2 | Attila | J. McLaughlin | Charles Littlefield | Wickham | John C. | 7.75-5 | 2:49 | Heavy | 1 1/2 | 2,160 | 4 |
| 1886 | The Bard, b. c. | 3 | Longfellow | S. Fisher | John Huggins | Eurus | Elkwood | 26.40-5 | 2:45 | Good | 1 1/2 | 1,525 | 5 |
| 1887 | Dunboyne, b. c. | 1 | Uncas | W. Donohue | W. Jennings | Mahoney | Raymond | 4-1 | 2:39 1/2 | Fast | 1 1/2 | 1,675 | 4 |
| 1888 | Refund, ch. c. | 3 | Sensation | F. Littlefield | R. W. Walden | Judge Murray | Glendale | 22.75-5 | 2:49 | Heavy | 1 1/2 | 1,185 | 4 |
| 1889 | Buddhist, b. c. | 8 | Hindoo | W. Anderson | J. Rogers | Japhet | | 5.75-5 | 2:17 1/2 | Fast | 1 1/4 | 1,130 | 2 |
| 1890 | Montague, ch. h., 5 | 3 | Mortemer | W. Martin | E. Feakes | Philosophy | Barrister | 5-4 | 2:38 3/4 | Fast | 1 1/2 | 1,185 | 4 |
| 1894 | Assignee, ch. c. | 3 | Spendthrift | F. Taral | Wm. Lakeland | Potentate | Ed Kearney | 4-1 | 1:47 1/4 | Fast | 1 1/16 | 1,830 | 14 |
| 1895 | Belmar, gr. c. | 1 | Belvidere | F. Taral | E. Feakes | April Fool | Sue Kittie | 3-1 | 1:50 1/2 | Fast | 1 1/16 | 1,350 | 7 |
| 1896 | Margrave, ch. c. | 1 | St. Blaise | H. Griffin | Byron McClelland | Hamilton II | Intermission | 5-4 | 1:51 | Fast | 1 1/16 | 1,350 | 4 |
| 1897 | Paul Kauvar, b. c. | 1 1/2 | Pirate of Penzance | Thorpe | T. P. Hayes | Elkins | On Deck | 6-1 | 1:51 1/4 | Sloppy | 1 1/16 | 1,420 | 7 |
| 1898 | Sly Fox, b. c. | 2 | Silver Fox | W. Simms | H. Campbell | The Huguenot | Nuto | 12-5 | 1:49 3/4 | Fast | 1 1/16 | 1,500 | 4 |
| 1899 | Half Time, ch. c. | 1 | Hanover | R. Clawson | F. C. Frisbee | Filigrane | Lackland | 1-1 | 1:47 | Fast | 1 1/16 | 1,580 | 3 |
| 1900 | Hindus, b. c. | hd | Volante | H. Spencer | J. H. Morris | Sarmatian | Ten Candles | 15-1 | 1:48 2/5 | Fast | 1 1/16 | 1,900 | 10 |
| 1901 | The Parader, b. c. | 2 | Longstreet | Landry | T. J. Healey | Sadie S. | Dr. Barlow | 20-9 | 1:47 1/5 | Heavy | 1-70 yds. | 1,605 | 7 |
| 1902 | Old England, b. c. | ns | Goldfinch | L. Jackson | G. B. Morris | Maj. Daingerfield | Namtor | 9-5 | 1:45 4/5 | Heavy | 1-70 yds. | 2,240 | 7 |
| 1903 | Flocarline, ch. f. | 1/2 | St. Florian | W. Gannon | H. C. Riddle | Mackey Dwyer | Rightful | 8-1 | 1:44 4/5 | Fast | 1-70 yds. | 1,875 | 6 |
| 1904 | Bryn Mawr, br. c. | 1 | Atheling | E. Hildebrand | W. F. Presgrave | Wotan | Dolly Spanker | 7-5 | 1:44 1/5 | Fast | 1-70 yds. | 2,355 | 10 |
| 1905 | Cairngorm, b. c. | hd | Star Ruby | W. Davis | A. J. Joyner | Klamesha | Coy Maid | 9-5 | 1:45 4/5 | Fast | 1-70 yds. | 2,200 | 10 |
| 1906 | Whimsical, ch. f. | 4 | Orlando | W. Miller | T. J. Gaynor | Content | Larable | 8-5 | 1:45 | Fast | 1-70 yds. | 2,355 | 10 |
| 1907 | Don Enrique, b. g. | 1 | Hastings | G. Mountain | John Whalen | Ethon | Zambesi | 15-1 | 1:45 2/5 | Slow | 1-70 yds. | 2,260 | 7 |
| 1908 | Royal Tourist, b. c. | 4 | Sandringham | E. Dugan | A. J. Joyner | Live Wire | Robert Cooper | 1-2 | 1:46 2/5 | Fast | 1 1/16 | 2,465 | 4 |
| 1909 | Effendi, br. c. | 1 | Previous | W. Doyle | F. C. Frisbee | Fashion Plate | Hilltop | 20-1 | 1:39 4/5 | Fast | 1 | 2,725 | 10 |
| 1910 | Layminster, ch. g. | 1/2 | Matchless | R. Estep | J. S. Healy | Dalhousie | Sager | 8-1 | 1:40 3/5 | Fast | 1 | 2,800 | 12 |
| 1911 | Watervale, b. c. | 1 | Watercress | E. Dugan | John Whalen | Zeus | The Nigger | 6-5 | 1:51 | Fast | 1 1/8 | 2,700 | 7 |
| 1912 | Colonel Holloway, br. c. | 5 | Ethelbert | C. Turner | D. Woodford | Bwana Tumbo | Tipsand | 2-1 | 1:56 3/5 | Slow | 1 1/8 | 1,450 | 7 |
| 1913 | Buskin, b. g. | nk | Hamburg | J. Butwell | John Whalen | Kleburne | Barnegat | $ 4.80 | 1:53 2/5 | Fast | 1 1/8 | 1,670 | 8 |
| 1914 | Holiday, b. g. | 3/4 | Broomstick | A. Schuttinger | J. S. Healy | Brave Cunarder | Defendum | 10.50 | 1:53 4/5 | Fast | 1 1/8 | 1,355 | 6 |
| 1915 | Rhine Maiden, b. f. | 1 1/2 | Watercress | D. Hoffman | Frank Devers | Half Rock | Runes | 13.90 | 1:58 | Muddy | 1 1/8 | 1,275 | 6 |
| 1916 | Damrosch, br. c. | 1 1/2 | Rock Sand | L. McAtee | A. G. Weston | Greenwood | Achievement | 14.90 | 1:54 4/5 | Fast | 1 1/8 | 1,360 | 9 |
| 1917 | Kalitan, b. c. | 2 | Rey Hindoo | Ev. Haynes | W. J. Hurley | Al M. Dick. | Kentucky Boy | 21.20 | 1:54 2/5 | Slow | 1 1/8 | 4,800 | 14 |
| 1918 | War Cloud, b. c. | 3/4 | Polymelus | J. Loftus | W. B. Jennings | Sunny Slope | Lanius | 5.40 | 1:53 3/5 | Slow | 1 1/8 | 12,250 | 10 |
| 1918 | Jack Hare, Jr., br. c. | 2 | Marathon | C. Peak | F. D. Weir | The Porter | Kate Bright | 3.80 | 1:53 2/5 | Good | 1 1/8 | 11,250 | 6 |
| 1919 | Sir Barton, ch. c. | 4 | Star Shoot | J. Loftus | H. G. Bedwell | Eternal | Sweep On | 4.80 | 1:53 | Fast | 1 1/8 | 24,500 | 12 |
| 1920 | Man o' War, ch. c. | 1 1/2 | Fair Play | C. Kummer | Louis Feustel | Upset | Wildair | 3.60 | 1:51 3/5 | Fast | 1 1/8 | 23,000 | 9 |
| 1921 | Broomspun, b. c. | 3/4 | Broomstick | F. Coltiletti | James Rowe, Sr. | Polly Ann | Jeg | 4.00 | 1:54 1/5 | Slow | 1 1/8 | 43,000 | 14 |
| 1922 | Pillory, ch. c. | hd | Olambala | L. Morris | T. J. Healey | Hea | June Grass. | 24.30 | 1:51 3/5 | Fast | 1 1/8 | 51,000 | 12 |

| Year | Winner | Margin | Sire | Second | Third | Jockey | Trainer | Track | Distance | Time | Odds | Value ($) | Starters |
|---|---|---|---|---|---|---|---|---|---|---|---|---|---|
| 1927 | Bostonian, blk. c. | 1/2 | Broomstick | Sir Harry | Whiskery | A. Abel | Fred Hopkins | Good | 1 3/16 | 2:01 3/5 | 8.00 | 53,100 | 12 |
| 1928 | Victorian, b. c. | ns | Whisk Broom II | Toro | Solace | R. Workman | James Rowe, Jr. | Fast | 1 3/16 | 2:00 1/5 | 20.70 | 60,000 | 18 |
| 1929 | Dr. Freeland, ch. c. | 1 | Light Brigade | Minotaur | African | L. Schaefer | T. J. Healey | Fast | 1 3/16 | 2:01 3/5 | 9.70 | 52,325 | 11 |
| 1930 | Gallant Fox, b. c. | 3/4 | Sir Gallahad III | Crack Brigade | Snowflake | E. Sande | James Fitzsimmons | Fast | 1 3/16 | 2:00 3/5 | 4.00 | 51,925 | 11 |
| 1931 | Mate, ch. c. | 1 1/2 | Prince Pal | Twenty Grand | Ladder | G. Ellis | J. W. Healey | Fast | 1 3/16 | 1:59 | 10.20 | 48,225 | 7 |
| 1932 | Burgoo King, b. c. | hd | Bubbling Over | Tick On | Boatswain | E. James | H. J. Thompson | Fast | 1 3/16 | 1:59 4/5 | 8.50 | 50,375 | 9 |
| 1933 | Head Play, ch. c. | 4 | My Play | Ladysman | Utopian | C. Kurtsinger | T. P. Hayes | Slow | 1 3/16 | 2:02 | 5.60 | 26,850 | 10 |
| 1934 | High Quest, b. c. | ns | Sir Gallahad III | Cavalcade | Discovery | R. Jones | R. A. Smith | Fast | 1 3/16 | 1:58 1/5 | 2.90 | 25,175 | 7 |
| 1935 | Omaha, ch. c. | 6 | Gallant Fox | Firethorn | Psychic Bid | W. Saunders | James Fitzsimmons | Fast | 1 3/16 | 1:58 2/5 | 3.90 | 25,325 | 8 |
| 1936 | Bold Venture, ch. c. | ns | St. Germans | Granville | Jean Bart | G. Woolf | Max Hirsch | Good | 1 3/16 | 1:59 | 5.70 | 27,325 | 11 |
| 1937 | War Admiral, br. c. | hd | Man o' War | Pompoon | Flying Scot | C. Kurtsinger | George Conway | Sloppy | 1 3/16 | 1:58 2/5 | 2.70 | 45,600 | 8 |
| 1938 | Dauber, ch. c. | 7 | Pennant | Cravat | Menow | M. Peters | R. E. Handlen | Muddy | 1 3/16 | 1:59 4/5 | 5.00 | 51,875 | 9 |
| 1939 | Challedon, b. c. | 1 1/4 | Challenger II | Gilded Knight | Volitant | G. Seabo | L. J. Schaefer | Fast | 1 3/16 | 1:59 4/5 | 14.40 | 53,710 | 6 |
| 1940 | Bimelech, b. c. | 3 | Black Toney | Mioland | Gallahadion | F. A. Smith | W. J. Hurley | Good | 1 3/16 | 1:58 3/5 | 3.80 | 53,230 | 9 |
| 1941 | Whirlaway, ch. c. | 5 1/2 | Blenheim II | King Cole | Our Boots | E. Arcaro | B. A. Jones | Fast | 1 3/16 | 1:58 4/5 | 4.30 | 49,365 | 8 |
| 1942 | Alsab, b. c. | 1 | Good Goods | Dead heat—Requested and Sun Again | | B. James | August Swenke | Good | 1 3/16 | 1:57 | 6.10 | 58,175 | 10 |
| 1943 | Count Fleet, br. c. | 8 | Reigh Count | Blue Swords | Vincentive | J. Longden | G. D. Cameron | Fast | 1 3/16 | 1:57 2/5 | 2.30 | 43,190 | 4 |
| 1944 | Pensive, ch. c. | 3/4 | Hyperion | Platter | Stir Up | C. McCreary | B. A. Jones | Fast | 1 3/16 | 1:59 1/5 | 5.30 | 60,075 | 7 |
| 1945 | Polynesian, br. c. | 2 1/2 | Unbreakable | Hoop, Jr. | Darby Dieppe | W. D. Wright | Morris Dixon | Fast | 1 3/16 | 1:58 4/5 | 26.00 | 66,170 | 9 |
| 1946 | Assault, ch. c. | nk | Bold Venture | Lord Boswell | Hampden | W. Mehrtens | Max Hirsch | Fast | 1 3/16 | 2:01 2/5 | 4.80 | 96,620 | 10 |
| 1947 | Faultless, br. c. | 1 1/4 | Bull Lea | On Trust | Phalanx | D. Dodson | H. A. Jones | Fast | 1 3/16 | 1:59 | 10.40 | 98,005 | 11 |
| 1948 | Citation, b. c. | 5 1/2 | Bull Lea | Vulcan's Forge | Bovard | E. Arcaro | H. A. Jones | Heavy | 1 3/16 | 2:02 2/5 | 2.20 | 91,870 | 4 |
| 1949 | Capot, br. c. | hd | Menow | Palestinian | Noble Impulse | T. Atkinson | J. M. Gaver | Fast | 1 3/16 | 1:56 | 7.00 | 79,985 | 9 |
| 1950 | Hill Prince, b. c. | 5 | Princequillo | Middleground | Dooly | E. Arcaro | J. H. Hayes | Slow | 1 3/16 | 1:59 1/5 | 3.40 | 76,115 | 6 |
| 1951 | Bold, b. c. | 7 | By Jimminy | Counterpoint | Alerted | E. Arcaro | P. M. Burch | Fast | 1 3/16 | 1:56 2/5 | 10.20 | 83,110 | 8 |
| 1952 | Blue Man, b. c. | 3 1/2 | Blue Swords | Jampol | One Count | C. McCreary | W. C. Stephens | Fast | 1 3/16 | 1:57 2/5 | 5.20 | 86,135 | 10 |
| 1953 | Native Dancer, gr. c. | nk | Polynesian | Jamie K. | Royal Bay Gem | E. Guerin | W. C. Winfrey | Fast | 1 3/16 | 1:57 4/5 | 2.40 | 65,200 | 7 |
| 1954 | Hasty Road, dk. b. c. | nk | Roman | Correlation | Hasseyampa | J. Adams | Harry Trotsek | Fast | 1 3/16 | 1:57 2/5 | 12.00 | 91,600 | 11 |
| 1955 | Nashua, b. c. | 1 | Nasrullah | Saratoga | Traffic Judge | E. Arcaro | James Fitzsimmons | Fast | 1 3/16 | 1:53 3/5 | 2.60 | 67,550 | 8 |
| 1956 | Fabius, b. c. | 3/4 | Citation | Needles | No Regrets | W. Hartack | H. A. Jones | Fast | 1 3/16 | 1:58 2/5 | 7.00 | 84,250 | 9 |
| 1957 | Bold Ruler, dk. b. c. | 2 | Nasrullah | Iron Liege | Inside Tract | E. Arcaro | James Fitzsimmons | Fast | 1 3/16 | 1:56 1/5 | 4.80 | 65,250 | 7 |
| 1958 | Tim Tam, dk. b. c. | 1 1/2 | Tom Fool | Lincoln Road | Gone Fishin' | I. Valenzuela | H. A. Jones | Fast | 1 3/16 | 1:57 1/5 | 4.20 | 97,900 | 12 |
| 1959 | Royal Orbit, ch. c. | 4 | Royal Charger | Sword Dancer | Dunce | W. Harmatz | Reggie Cornell | Fast | 1 3/16 | 1:57 | 15.20 | | 11 |
| 1960 | Bally Ache, b. c. | 4 | Ballydam | Victoria Park | Celtic Ash | R. Ussery | H. J. Pitt | Fast | 1 3/16 | 1:57 3/5 | 5.40 | | 6 |
| 1961 | Carry Back, b. c. | 3/4 | Saggy | Globemaster | Crozier | J. Sellers | J. A. Price | Fast | 1 3/16 | 1:57 3/5 | 4.00 | 121,000 | 9 |
| 1962 | Greek Money, ch. c. | ns | Greek Song | Ridan | Roman Line | J. Rotz | V. W. Raines | Fast | 1 3/16 | 1:56 1/5 | 23.80 | 126,200 | 11 |
| 1963 | Candy Spots, ch. c. | 3 1/2 | Nigromante | Chateaugay | Never Bend | W. Shoemaker | M. A. Tenney | Fast | 1 3/16 | 1:56 1/5 | 5.00 | 135,800 | 8 |
| 1964 | Northern Dancer, b. c. | 2 1/4 | Nearctic | The Scoundrel | Hill Rise | W. Hartack | Horatio Luro | Fast | 1 3/16 | 1:56 4/5 | 6.20 | 124,200 | 6 |
| 1965 | Tom Rolfe, b. c. | nk | Ribot | Dapper Dan | Hail to All | R. Turcotte | F. Y. Whiteley, Jr. | Fast | 1 3/16 | 1:56 1/5 | 9.20 | 128,100 | 9 |
| 1966 | Kauai King, dk. b. or br. c. | 1 3/4 | Native Dancer | Stupendous | Amberoid | D. Brumfield | Henry Forrest | Fast | 1 3/16 | 1:55 2/5 | 4.00 | 129,000 | 9 |
| 1967 | Damascus, b. c. | 2 1/4 | Sword Dancer | In Reality | Proud Clarion | W. Shoemaker | F. Y. Whiteley, Jr. | Fast | 1 3/16 | 1:55 1/5 | 5.60 | 141,500 | 10 |
| 1968 | Forward Pass, b. c. | 6 | On-and-On | Out of the Way | Nodouble | I. Valenzuela | Henry Forrest | Fast | 1 3/16 | 1:56 4/5 | 4.20 | 142,700 | 10 |
| 1969 | Majestic Prince, ch. c. | hd | Raise a Native | Arts and Letters | Jay Ray | W. Hartack | John Longden | Fast | 1 3/16 | 1:55 3/5 | 3.20 | 129,500 | 8 |
| 1970 | Personality, b. c. | nk | Hail to Reason | My Dad George | Silent Screen | E. Belmonte | John W. Jacobs | Sloppy | 1 3/16 | 1:56 1/5 | 11.00 | 151,300 | 14 |
| 1971 | Canonero II, b. c. | 1 1/2 | Pretendre | Eastern Fleet | Jim French | G. Avila | Juan Arias | Fast | 1 3/16 | 1:54 | 8.80 | 137,400 | 11 |
| 1972 | Bee Bee Bee, dk. b. or br. c. | 1 1/4 | Better Bee | No Le Hace | Key to the Mint | E. Nelson | D. W. Carroll | Good | 1 3/16 | 1:55 3/5 | 39.40 | 135,300 | 7 |
| 1973 | Secretariat, ch. c. | 2 1/2 | Bold Ruler | Sham | Our Native | R. Turcotte | Lucien Laurin | Fast | 1 3/16 | 1:54 2/5 | 2.60 | 129,900 | 6 |
| 1974 | Little Current, ch. c. | 7 | Sea-Bird | Neapolitan Way | Cannonade | M. Rivera | Lou Rondinello | Good | 1 3/16 | 1:54 3/5 | 28.20 | 156,500 | 13 |
| 1975 | Master Derby, ch. c. | 1 | Dust Commander | Foolish Pleasure | Diabolo | D. McHargue | W. E. Adams | Fast | 1 3/16 | 1:56 2/5 | 48.80 | 158,100 | 10 |
| 1976 | Elocutionist, b. c. | 3 1/2 | Gallant Romeo | Play the Red | Bold Forbes | J. Lively | Paul T. Adwell | Fast | 1 3/16 | 1:55 | 22.20 | 159,700 | 6 |
| 1977 | Seattle Slew, dk. b. or br. c. | 1 1/2 | Bold Reasoning | Iron Constitution | Run Dusty Run | J. Cruguet | W. H. Turner, Jr. | Fast | 1 3/16 | 1:54 2/5 | 2.80 | 138,600 | 9 |
| 1978 | Affirmed, ch. c. | nk | Exclusive Native | Alydar | Believe It | S. Cauthen | Lazaro Barrera | Fast | 1 3/16 | 1:54 1/5 | 3.00 | 136,200 | 7 |
| 1979 | Spectacular Bid, gr. c. | 5 1/2 | Bold Bidder | Golden Act | Screen King | R. Franklin | Grover G. Delp | Good | 1 3/16 | 1:54 1/5 | 2.20 | 165,300 | 5 |
| 1980 | Codex, ch. c. | 4 3/4 | Arts and Letters | Genuine Risk | Colonel Moran | A. Cordero | D. W. Lukas | Fast | 1 3/16 | 1:54 1/5 | 2.70 | 180,600 | 8 |
| 1981 | Pleas. Colony, dk. b. or br. c. | 1 | His Majesty | Bold Ego | Paristo | J. Velasquez | J. Campo | Fast | 1 3/16 | 1:54 3/5 | 5.00 | 200,800 | 13 |

# HISTORY OF THE BELMONT STAKES

| YEAR | WINNER | MARGIN | SIRE | JOCKEY | TRAINER | SECOND | THIRD | PAYOFF | TIME | TRACK | DISTANCE | MONEY | STARTERS |
|---|---|---|---|---|---|---|---|---|---|---|---|---|---|
| 1867 | Ruthless, b. f. | 1/2 | Eclipse | J. Gilpatrick | A. J. Minor | De Courcy | Rivoli | 1-4 | 3:05 | Slow | 1 5/8 | $ 1,850 | 4 |
| 1868 | General Duke, ch. c. | 2 | Lexington | R. Swim | A. Thompson | Northumberland | Fanny Ludlow | 1-2 | 3:02 | Heavy | 1 5/8 | 2,800 | 6 |
| 1869 | Fenian, ch. c. | 6 | Mickey Free | C. Miller | Jacob Pincus | Glenelg | Invercauld | 4-5 | 3:04 1/4 | Muddy | 1 5/8 | 3,350 | 8 |
| 1870 | Kingfisher, b. c. | nk | Lexington | E. Brown | Rollie Colston | Foster | Midday | 5-4 | 2:59 1/2 | Slow | 1 5/8 | 3,750 | 7 |
| 1871 | Harry Bassett, ch. c. | 3 | Lexington | W. Miller | David McDaniel | Stockwood | By-the-Sea | 1-1 | 2:56 | Fast | 1 5/8 | 5,450 | 8 |
| 1872 | Joe Daniels, ch. c. | 3/4 | Australian | J. Rowe | David McDaniel | Meteor | Shylock | 1-1 | 2:58 1/4 | Good | 1 5/8 | 4,500 | 9 |
| 1873 | Springbok, ch. c. | 3/4 | Australian | J. Rowe | David McDaniel | Count D'Orsay | Strachino | 18-1 | 3:01 3/4 | Heavy | 1 5/8 | 5,200 | 10 |
| 1874 | Saxon, br. c. | nk | Beadsman | G. Barbee | W. Prior | Grinstead | Aaron Pennington | 12-1 | 2:39 1/2 | Fast | 1 1/2 | 4,200 | 9 |
| 1875 | Calvin, br. c. | 2 | Tipperary | R. Swim | Ansel Williams | Aristides | Milner | 6-5 | 2:42 1/4 | Fast | 1 1/2 | 4,450 | 14 |
| 1876 | Algerine, b. c. | 1/2 | Abd-el-Kader | W. Donohue | T. W. Doswell | Fiddlesticks | Barricade | 6-1 | 2:40 1/2 | Fast | 1 1/2 | 3,700 | 5 |
| 1877 | Cloverbrook, ch. c. | 1 | Vauxhall | C. Holloway | Jeter Walden | Loiterer | Baden Baden | 5-1 | 2:46 | Heavy | 1 1/2 | 5,200 | 13 |
| 1878 | Duke of Magenta, b. c. | 2 | Lexington | G. Hughes | R. W. Walden | Bramble | Spartan | 7-10 | 2:43 1/2 | Muddy | 1 1/2 | 3,850 | 6 |
| 1879 | Spendthrift, ch. c. | 6 | Australian | G. Evans | Thomas Puryear | Monitor | Jericho | 1-1 | 2:42 3/4 | Slow | 1 1/2 | 4,250 | 6 |
| 1880 | Grenada, br. c. | nk | King Alfonso | W. Hughes | R. W. Walden | Ferncliffe | Turenne | 2-5 | 2:47 | Good | 1 1/2 | 2,800 | 6 |
| 1881 | Saunterer, ch. c. | nk | Leamington | T. Costello | R. W. Walden | Eole | Baltic | 5-2 | 2:47 | Heavy | 1 1/2 | 3,000 | 6 |
| 1882 | Forester, ch. c. | 5 | The Ill-Used | Lewis Stuart | Lewis Stuart | Babcock | Wyoming | 1-5 | 2:43 | Fast | 1 1/2 | 2,600 | 3 |
| 1883 | George Kinney, b. c. | 1 | Bonnie Scotland | J. McLaughlin | James Rowe, Sr. | Trombone | Renegade | 1-12 | 2:42 1/2 | Fast | 1 1/2 | 3,070 | 4 |
| 1884 | Panique, ch. c. | nk | Alarm | J. McLaughlin | James Rowe, Sr. | Knight of Ellerslie | Himalaya | 11-10 | 2:42 | Good | 1 1/2 | 3,150 | 4 |
| 1885 | Tyrant, ch. c. | 3 | Great Tom | P. Duffy | C. Claypool | St. Augustine | Tecumseh | 9-10 | 2:43 | Good | 1 1/2 | 2,710 | 6 |
| 1886 | Inspector B, b. c. | 1 | Enquirer | J. McLaughlin | Frank McCabe | The Bard | Linden | 6-5 | 2:41 | Fast. | 1 1/2 | 2,720 | 5 |
| 1887 | Hanover, ch. c. | 15 | Hindoo | J. McLaughlin | Frank McCabe | Oneko | Wyoming | 1-20 | 2:43 1/2 | Heavy | 1 1/2 | 2,900 | 2 |
| 1888 | Sir Dixon, br. c. | 15 | Billet | W. Hayward | Frank McCabe | Prince Royal | Renegade | 30-13 | 2:40 1/4 | Fast | 1 1/2 | 3,440 | 2 |
| 1889 | Eric, b. c. | 1/2 | Duke of Magenta | W. Hayward | John Huggins | Diablo | Zephyrus | 7-5 | 2:47 | Good | 1 1/2 | 4,960 | 3 |
| 1890 | Burlington, blk. c. | 2 | Powhattan | S. Barnes | Albert Cooper | Devotee | Padishah | 6-1 | 2:07 3/4 | Fast | 1 1/4 | 8,560 | 3 |
| 1891 | Foxford, b. c. | nk | Stratford | E. Garrison | M. Donovan | Montana | Laurestan | 8-1 | 2:08 3/4 | Fast | 1 1/4 | 5,070 | 6 |
| 1892 | Patron, b. c. | 6 | Falsetto | W. Hayward | Lewis Stuart | Shellbark | Rainbow | 1-6 | 2:17 | Muddy | 1 1/4 | 6,610 | 2 |
| 1893 | Comanche, ch. c. | hd | Sir Modred | W. Simms | Gus Hannon | Dr. Rice | Assignee | 20-1 | 1:53 1/4 | Fast | 1 1/8 | 5,310 | 5 |
| 1894 | Henry of Navarre, ch. c. | 1 1/2 | Knight of Ellerslie | W. Simms | Byron McClelland | Prig | Nankl Pooh | 1-10 | 1:56 1/2 | Muddy | 1 1/8 | 6,680 | 3 |
| 1895 | Belmar, gr. c. | hd | Belvidere | F. Taral | E. Feakes | Counter Tenor | Hamilton II | 6-1 | 2:11 1/2 | Heavy | 1 1/4 | 2,700 | 5 |
| 1896 | Hastings, br. c. | hd | Spendthrift | F. Griffin | J. J. Hyland | Handspring | | 8-5 | 2:24 1/2 | Fast | 1 3/8 | 3,025 | 4 |
| 1897 | Scottish Chieftain, br. c. | 1 | Inverness | J. Scherrer | Matt Byrnes | On Deck | Octagon | 9-5 | 2:23 1/4 | Fast | 1 3/8 | 3,550 | 6 |
| 1898 | Bowling Brook, b. c. | 6 | Ayrshire | F. Littlefield | R. W. Walden | Previous | Hamburg | 7-2 | 2:32 | Heavy | 1 3/8 | 7,810 | 4 |
| 1899 | Jean Bereaud, b. c. | hd | His Highness | R. Clawson | Sam Hildreth | Half Time | Glengar | 2-5 | 2:23 | Fast | 1 3/8 | 9,445 | 4 |
| 1900 | Ildrim, br. c. | ns | Kingston | N. Turner | H. Eugene Leigh | Petruchio | Missionary | 3-1 | 2:21 1/2 | Fast | 1 3/8 | 14,790 | 7 |
| 1901 | Commando, b. c. | 2 | Domino | H. Spencer | James Rowe, Sr. | The Parader | All Green | 7-10 | 2:21 | Fast | 1 3/8 | 11,595 | 3 |
| 1902 | Masterman, ch. c. | 2 | Hastings | J. Bullman | J. J. Hyland | Ranald | King Hanover | 3-1 | 2:22 1/2 | Fast | 1 3/8 | 13,220 | 6 |
| 1903 | Africander, b. c. | 2 | Star Ruby | J. Bullman | R. O. Miller | Whorler | Red Knight | 3-5 | 2:23 1/5 | Fast | 1 3/8 | 12,285 | 5 |
| 1904 | Delhi, br. c. | 4 | Ben Brush | G. Odom | James Rowe, Sr. | Grazlallo | Rapid Water | 8-5 | 2:06 3/5 | Fast | 1 1/4 | 11,575 | 8 |
| 1905 | Tanya, ch. f. | 1/2 | Meddler | E. Hildebrand | J. W. Rogers | Blandy | Hot Shot | 11-5 | 2:08 | Fast | 1 1/4 | 17,240 | 7 |
| 1906 | Burgomaster, br. c. | 4 | Hamburg | L. Lyne | J. W. Rogers | The Quail | Accountant | 2-5 | 2:20 | Fast | 1 3/8 | 22,700 | 6 |
| 1907 | Peter Pan, b. c. | 1 | Commando | G. Mountain | James Rowe, Sr. | Superman | Frank Gill | 7-10 | | Fast | 1 3/8 | 22,765 | 5 |
| 1908 | Colin, b. c. | hd | Commando | J. Notter | James Rowe, Sr. | Fair Play | King James | 1-2 | 2:21 3/5 | Sloppy | 1 3/8 | 22,765 | 4 |
| 1909 | Joe Madden, ch. c. | 8 | Yankee | E. Dugan | Sam Hildreth | Wise Mason | Donald Macdonald | 11-5 | 2:22 | Fast | 1 3/8 | 24,550 | 5 |
| 1910 | Sweep, br. c. | 6 | Ben Brush | J. Butwell | Sam Hildreth | Duke of Ormonde | | 1-10 | 2:22 | Fast | 1 3/8 | 9,700 | 2 |
| 1913 | Prince Eugene, b. c. | 1/2 | Hamburg | R. Troxler | James Rowe, Sr. | Rock View | Flying Fairy | 3-1 | 2:18 | Fast | 1 3/8 | 2,825 | 4 |
| 1914 | Luke McLuke, b. c. | 8 | Ultimus | M. Buxton | J. F. Schorr | Gainer | Charlestonian | 9-5 | 2:20 | Fast | 1 3/8 | 3,025 | 3 |
| 1915 | The Finn, blk. c. | 4 | Ogden | G. Byrne | E. W. Heffner | Half Rock | Pebbles | 7-5 | 2:18 2/5 | Fast | 1 3/8 | 1,825 | 3 |
| 1916 | Friar Rock, ch. c. | 3 | Rock Sand | E. Haynes | Sam Hildreth | Spur | Churchill | 5-2 | 2:22 | Muddy | 1 3/8 | 4,100 | 3 |
| 1917 | Hourless, br. c. | 10 | Negofol | J. Butwell | Sam Hildreth | Skeptic | Wonderful | 1-4 | 2:17 4/5 | Good | 1 3/8 | 5,800 | 3 |
| 1918 | Johren, b. c. | 2 | Spearmint | F. Robinson | Albert Simons | War Cloud | Cum Sah | 11-5 | 2:20 2/5 | Fast | 1 3/8 | 8,950 | 4 |
| 1919 | Sir Barton, ch. c. | 5 | Star Shoot | J. Loftus | H. Guy Bedwell | Sweep On | Natural Bridge | 7-20 | 2:17 2/5 | Fast | 1 3/8 | 11,950 | 3 |
| 1920 | Man o' War, ch. c. | 20 | Fair Play | C. Kummer | Louis Feustel | Donnacona | | 1-25 | 2:14 1/5 | Fast | 1 3/8 | 7,950 | 2 |
| 1921 | Grey Lag, ch. c. | 3 | Star Shoot | E. Sande | Sam Hildreth | Sporting Blood | Leonardo II | 2-1 | 2:16 4/5 | Fast | 1 3/8 | 8,650 | 4 |

| Year | Winner | Margin | Sire | Jockey | Trainer | Second | Third | Odds | Time | Track | Dist. | Value | St. |
|---|---|---|---|---|---|---|---|---|---|---|---|---|---|
| 1925 | American Flag, ch. c. | 8 | Man o' War | A. Johnson | G. R. Tompkins | Swope | Dangerous | 9-20 | 2:16 4/5 | Fast | 1 3/8 | 38,500 | 7 |
| 1926 | Crusader, ch. c. | 1 | Man o' War | A. Johnson | George Conway | Haste | Espino | 7-10 | 2:32 1/5 | Sloppy | 1 1/2 | 48,550 | 9 |
| 1927 | Chance Shot, b. c. | 1 1/2 | Fair Play | E. Sande | Peter Coyne | Flambino | Bois de Rose | 2-7 | 2:32 2/5 | Fast | 1 1/2 | 60,910 | 6 |
| 1928 | Vito, b. c. | 3 | Negofol | C. Kummer | Max Hirsch | Genie | Diavolo | 10-1 | 2:33 1/5 | Fast | 1 1/2 | 63,430 | 6 |
| 1929 | Blue Larkspur, b. c. | 3/4 | Black Servant | M. Garner | T. G. Hastings | African | Jack High | 13-10 | 2:32 4/5 | Sloppy | 1 1/2 | 59,650 | 8 |
| 1930 | Gallant Fox, b. c. | 3 | Sir Gallahad III | E. Sande | James Fitzsimmons | Whichone | Questionnaire | 8-5 | 2:31 3/5 | Good | 1 1/2 | 66,040 | 4 |
| 1931 | Twenty Grand, b. c. | 10 | St. Germans | C. Kurtsinger | James Rowe, Jr. | Sun Meadow | Jamestown | 4-5 | 2:29 3/5 | Fast | 1 1/2 | 58,770 | 3 |
| 1932 | Faireno, b. c. | 1 1/2 | Chatterton | T. Malley | James Fitzsimmons | Osculator | Flag Pole | 5-1 | 2:32 4/5 | Fast | 1 1/2 | 55,120 | 11 |
| 1933 | Hurryoff, b. c. | 1 1/2 | Haste | M. Garner | Henry McDaniel | Nimbus | Union | 15-1 | 2:32 3/5 | Fast | 1 1/2 | 49,490 | 9 |
| 1934 | Peace Chance, b. c. | 6 | Chance Shot | W. D. Wright | Peter Coyne | High Quest | Good Goods | 3-1 | 2:29 1/5 | Fast | 1 1/2 | 43,410 | 8 |
| 1935 | Omaha, b. c. | 1 1/2 | Gallant Fox | W. Saunders | James Fitzsimmons | Firethorn | Rosemont | 7-10 | 2:30 3/5 | Sloppy | 1 1/2 | 35,480 | 5 |
| 1936 | Granville, b. c. | ns | Gallant Fox | J. Stout | James Fitzsimmons | Mr. Bones | Hollyrood | 16-5 | 2:30 | Fast | 1 1/2 | 29,800 | 10 |
| 1937 | War Admiral, br. c. | 3 | Man o' War | C. Kurtsinger | George Conway | Sceneshifter | Vamoose | 9-10 | 2:28 3/5 | Fast | 1 1/2 | 28,020 | 7 |
| 1938 | Pasteurized, ch. c. | nk | Milkman | J. Stout | G. M. Odom | Dauber | Cravat | 8-1 | 2:29 2/5 | Fast | 1 1/2 | 34,530 | 6 |
| 1939 | Johnstown, b. c. | 5 | Jamestown | J. Stout | James Fitzsimmons | Belay | Gilded Knight | 1-8 | 2:29 3/5 | Fast | 1 1/2 | 37,020 | 6 |
| 1940 | Bimelech, b. c. | 3/4 | Black Toney | F. A. Smith | Wm. J. Hurley | Your Chance | Andy K. | $4.70 | 2:29 3/5 | Fast | 1 1/2 | 35,030 | 6 |
| 1941 | Whirlaway, ch. c. | 2 1/2 | Blenheim II | E. Arcaro | B. A. Jones | Robert Morris | Yankee Chance | 2.50 | 2:31 | Fast | 1 1/2 | 39,770 | 4 |
| 1942 | Shut Out, ch. c. | 2 | Equipoise | E. Arcaro | J. M. Gaver | Alsab | Lochinvar | 9.00 | 2:29 1/5 | Fast | 1 1/2 | 44,520 | 7 |
| 1943 | Count Fleet, br. c. | 25 | Reigh Count | J. Longden | G. D. Cameron | Fairy Manhurst | Deseronto | 2.10 | 2:28 1/5 | Fast | 1 1/2 | 35,340 | 3 |
| 1944 | Bounding Home, br. c. | 1/2 | Bull Dog | G. L. Smith | Matt Brady | Pensive | Bull Dandy | 34.70 | 2:32 1/5 | Fast | 1 1/2 | 55,000 | 7 |
| 1945 | Pavot, br. c. | 5 | Case Ace | E. Arcaro | Oscar White | Wildlife | Jeep | 6.20 | 2:30 1/5 | Fast | 1 1/2 | 52,675 | 8 |
| 1946 | Assault, ch. c. | 3 | Bold Venture | W. Mehrtens | Max Hirsch | Natchez | Cable | 4.80 | 2:30 4/5 | Fast | 1 1/2 | 75,400 | 7 |
| 1947 | Phalanx, b. c. | 8 | Pilate | R. Donoso | Syl Veitch | Tide Rips | Tailspin | 6.60 | 2:29 2/5 | Fast | 1 1/2 | 78,900 | 9 |
| 1948 | Citation, b. c. | 8 | Bull Lea | E. Arcaro | H. A. Jones | Better Self | Escadru | 2.40 | 2:28 1/5 | Fast | 1 1/2 | 77,700 | 8 |
| 1949 | Capot, br. c. | 1/2 | Menow | T. Atkinson | J. M. Gaver | Ponder | Palestinian | 13.20 | 2:30 1/5 | Fast | 1 1/2 | 60,900 | 8 |
| 1950 | Middleground, ch. c. | 1 | Bold Venture | W. Boland | Max Hirsch | Lights Up | Mr. Trouble | 7.40 | 2:28 3/5 | Fast | 1 1/2 | 61,350 | 9 |
| 1951 | Counterpoint, ch. c. | 4 | Count Fleet | D. Gorman | Syl Veitch | Battlefield | Battle Morn | 12.30 | 2:29 | Fast | 1 1/2 | 82,000 | 9 |
| 1952 | One Count, dk. br. c. | 2 1/2 | Count Fleet | E. Arcaro | Oscar White | Blue Man | Armageddon | 27.60 | 2:30 1/5 | Fast | 1 1/2 | 82,400 | 8 |
| 1953 | Native Dancer, gr. c. | nk | Polynesian | E. Guerin | W. C. Winfrey | Jamie K. | Royal Bay Gem | 2.90 | 2:28 3/5 | Fast | 1 1/2 | 82,500 | 6 |
| 1954 | High Gun, br. c. | nk | Heliopolis | E. Arcaro | Max Hirsch | Fisherman | Limelight | 8.90 | 2:30 4/5 | Fast | 1 1/2 | 89,000 | 13 |
| 1955 | Nashua, b. c. | 9 | Nasrullah | E. Arcaro | James Fitzsimmons | Blazing Count | Portersville | 2.30 | 2:29 | Fast | 1 1/2 | 83,700 | 8 |
| 1956 | Needles, b. c. | nk | Ponder | D. Erb | Hugh Fontaine | Career Boy | Fabius | 3.30 | 2:29 4/5 | Fast | 1 1/2 | 83,600 | 8 |
| 1957 | Gallant Man, b. c. | 8 | Migoli | W. Shoemaker | John Nerud | Inside Tract | Bold Ruler | 3.90 | 2:26 3/5 | Fast | 1 1/2 | 77,300 | 6 |
| 1958 | Cavan, ch. c | 6 | Mossborough | P. Anderson | Tom J. Barry | Tim Tam | Flamingo | 11.80 | 2:30 1/5 | Fast | 1 1/2 | 73,440 | 8 |
| 1959 | Sword Dancer, ch. c. | 3/4 | Sunglow | W. Shoemaker | J. Elliott Burch | Bagdad | Royal Orbit | 5.30 | 2:28 2/5 | Sloppy | 1 1/2 | 93,525 | 9 |
| 1960 | Celtic Ash, ch. c. | 5 1/2 | Sicambre | W. Hartack | Tom J. Barry | Venetian Way | Disperse | 18.80 | 2:29 3/5 | Fast | 1 1/2 | 96,785 | 7 |
| 1961 | Sherluck, dk. c. | 2 1/4 | Correspondent | B. Baeza | Harold Young | Globemaster | Guadalcanal | 132.10 | 2:29 1/5 | Fast | 1 1/2 | 104,900 | 9 |
| 1962 | Jaipur, dk. b. c. | ns | Nasrullah | W. Shoemaker | W. F. Mulholland | Admiral's Voyage | Crimson Satan | 7.70 | 2:28 4/5 | Fast | 1 1/2 | 109,550 | 8 |
| 1963 | Chateaugay, ch. c. | 2 1/2 | Swaps | B. Baeza | James P. Conway | Candy Spots | Choker | 11.00 | 2:30 1/5 | Good | 1 1/2 | 101,700 | 7 |
| 1964 | Quadrangle, b. c. | 2 | Cohoes | M. Ycaza | J. Elliott Burch | Roman Brother | Northern Dancer | 15.10 | 2:28 2/5 | Fast | 1 1/2 | 110,850 | 8 |
| 1965 | Hail to All, b. c. | 2 1/2 | Hail to Reason | J. Sellers | Eddie Yowell | Tom Rolfe | First Family | 7.30 | 2:28 2/5 | Fast | 1 1/2 | 104,150 | 8 |
| 1966 | Amberoid, dk. b. or br. c. | 2 1/2 | Count Amber | W. Boland | Lucien Laurin | Buffle | Advocator | 13.00 | 2:29 3/5 | Fast | 1 1/2 | 117,700 | 11 |
| 1967 | Damascus, b. c. | 2 1/2 | Sword Dancer | W. Shoemaker | F. Y. Whiteley, Jr. | Cool Reception | Gentleman James | 3.60 | 2:28 4/5 | Fast | 1 1/2 | 104,950 | 9 |
| 1968 | Stage Door Johnny, ch. c. | 1 1/4 | Prince John | H. Gustines | J. M. Gaver | Forward Pass | Call Me Prince | 10.80 | 2:27 1/5 | Fast | 1 1/2 | 117,700 | 9 |
| 1969 | Arts and Letters, ro. c. | 5 1/2 | Ribot | B. Baeza | J. Elliott Burch | Majestic Prince | Dike | 5.40 | 2:28 4/5 | Fast | 1 1/2 | 104,050 | 6 |
| 1970 | High Echelon, ro. c. | 3/4 | Native Charger | J. Rotz | John W. Jacobs | Needles N Pins | Naskra | 11.00 | 2:34 | Sloppy | 1 1/2 | 115,000 | 10 |
| 1971 | Pass Catcher, b. c. | 3/4 | All Hands | W. Blum | Eddie Yowell | Jim French | Bold Reason | 71.00 | 2:30 2/5 | Fast | 1 1/2 | 97,710 | 13 |
| 1972 | Riva Ridge, b. c. | 7 | First Landing | R. Turcotte | Lucien Laurin | Ruritania | Cloudy Dawn | 5.20 | 2:28 | Fast | 1 1/2 | 93,540 | 10 |
| 1973 | Secretariat, ch. c. | 31 | Bold Ruler | R. Turcotte | Lucien Laurin | Twice a Prince | My Gallant | 2.20 | 2:24 | Fast | 1 1/2 | 90,120 | 5 |
| 1974 | Little Current, ch. c. | 7 | Sea-Bird | M. Rivera | Lou Rondinello | Jolly Johu | Cannonade | 5.00 | 2:29 1/5 | Fast | 1 1/2 | 101,970 | 9 |
| 1975 | Avatar, ch. c. | nk | Graustark | W. Shoemaker | A. T. Doyle | Foolish Pleasure | Master Derby | 28.40 | 2:28 1/5 | Fast | 1 1/2 | 116,160 | 9 |
| 1976 | Bold Forbes, dk. b. or br. c. | nk | Irish Castle | A. Cordero, Jr. | Lazaro Barrera | McKenzie Bridge | Great Contractor | 3.80 | 2:29 | Fast | 1 1/2 | 117,000 | 10 |
| 1977 | Seattle Slew, dk. b. or br. c. | 4 | Bold Reasoning | J. Cruguet | W. H. Turner, Jr. | Run Dusty Run | Sanhedin | 2.80 | 2:29 3/5 | Muddy | 1 1/2 | 109,080 | 8 |
| 1978 | Affirmed, ch. c. | hd | Exclusive Native | S. Cauthen | Lazaro Barrera | Alydar | Darby Creek Road | 3.20 | 2:26 4/5 | Fast | 1 1/2 | 110,580 | 5 |
| 1979 | Coastal, ch. c. | 3 1/4 | Majestic Prince | R. Hernandez | David A. Whiteley | Golden Act | Spectacular Bid | 10.80 | 2:28 3/5 | Fast | 1 1/2 | 161,400 | 8 |
| 1980 | Temperence Hill, b. c. | 2 | Stop the Music | E. Maple | J. B. Cantey | Genuine Risk | Rockhill Native | 108.80 | 2:29 4/5 | Muddy | 1 1/2 | 176,220 | 10 |
| 1981 | Summing, b. c. | nk | Verbatim | G. Martens | Luis Barrera | Highland Blade | Pleasant Colony | 17.80 | 2:29 | Fast | 1 1/2 | 170,580 | 11 |

themselves, but for their significance vis-à-vis the upcoming Kentucky Derby.

Today, the Derby has joined the World Series, the Super Bowl and the Indianapolis 500 as one of the leading American sporting events. The Derby is as much a "happening" as it is a race. As such, it is racing's showcase.

## Kentucky Derby Facts

*The Winners:* 98 colts, 7 geldings (last Clyde Van Dusen in 1929), and 2 fillies (Regret in 1915 and Genuine Risk in 1980)
*Leading Owner:* Calumet Farm, 8 winners
*Leading Trainer:* Ben A. Jones, 6 winners
*Leading Jockeys:* Eddie Arcaro and Bill Hartack, 5 winners each
*Leading Breeder:* Calumet Farm, 8 winners
*Largest Field:* 23 in 1974
*Smallest Fields:* 3 in 1892 and 1905
*Favorites:* 47 of 107 favorites have won (44 percent). 17 of 28 odds-on favorites finished first
*Largest Payoff:* $184.90, Donerail (1913)
*Smallest Payoffs:* $2.80, Citation (1948) and Count Fleet (1943)
*Fastest Times:*

| | | |
|---|---|---|
| 1. | Secretariat (1973) | 1:59$\frac{2}{5}$ |
| 2. | Northern Dancer (1964) | 2:00 |
| 3. | Decidedly (1962) | 2:00$\frac{2}{5}$ |
| 4. | Proud Clarion (1967) | 2:00$\frac{3}{5}$ |
| 5. | Lucky Debonair (1965) | 2:01$\frac{1}{5}$ |
| 6. | Affirmed (1978) | 2:01$\frac{1}{5}$ |
| 7. | Whirlaway (1941) | 2:01$\frac{2}{5}$ |
| 8. | Middleground (1950) | 2:01$\frac{3}{5}$ |
| | Hill Gail (1952) | 2:01$\frac{3}{5}$ |
| | Bold Forbes (1976) | 2:01$\frac{3}{5}$ |

## THE PREAKNESS

In 1868, a group of Maryland gentlemen gathered at a dinner party at Saratoga. Impressed by the racing program conducted by the Saratoga Association, they decided that their home state needed a revival of the racing that had been halted by the Civil War, and they vowed to build a racecourse. The horsemen decided to inaugurate the racetrack with a feature called the Dinner Party Stakes. Excitement was so high, two years before the race, that thirty horses were nominated on the spot and a wagering pool was begun.

When these gentlemen returned home, they promptly re-formed the Maryland Jockey Club (begun originally in 1743 as the first jockey club in America). Under the chairmanship of Maryland's governor, Odin Bowie, the Jockey Club opened its new racetrack in October 1870. The track was named Pimlico, after an aquatic bird that skimmed Chesapeake Bay looking for food. On the card that first day was the long-awaited Dinner Party Stakes, which was won by a horse named Preakness.

Three years later, Pimlico carded a new stakes race for three-year-olds, to be run over the "classic" (i.e., Epsom Derby) distance of one and a half miles. The race was named after the famous Dinner Party Stakes winner, Preakness.

Racing in Maryland soon suffered a decline, however, and the Preakness stakes was plagued by small fields. From 1882 to 1889, a total of only twenty-three horses competed—an average of three per race. In 1890, the Maryland Jockey Club abandoned Pimlico, and the Preakness moved to Morris Park, New York, where it was run as a handicap. The race was then discontinued for three years before being resumed at Gravesend Course in Brooklyn from 1894 to 1908.

With racing on the decline in New York, the race came back to a reopened Pimlico in 1909. In 1912, the Maryland state government legalized pari-mutuel wagering, and Pimlico purses grew to the point where they became the highest in the nation. In 1918, the Maryland Jockey Club decided to emphasize the Preakness; they raised the purse from $4,800 to $24,500. This attracted fifteen entrants, and the race had to be split into two divisions (the only Triple Crown race ever split). In 1919, Sir Barton bested eleven other entrants on the way to the first sweep of the Preakness, the Kentucky Derby, and the Belmont Stakes. Although these three events weren't labeled yet as the Triple Crown, the prestige of the

Preakness had grown to equal that of the other two events.

From the time of its inception, the Preakness had sometimes been run before the Kentucky Derby, sometimes after. From 1932 on, it has remained between the Derby and the Belmont, as the middle jewel of the Triple Crown.

## Preakness Facts

*The Winners:* 98 colts, 4 fillies (last was Nellie Morse, 1924) 5 geldings (last was Holiday, 1914)

*Leading Owner:* Calumet Farm, 7 winners

*Leading Trainer:* R. W. Walden, 7 winners

*Leading Jockey:* Eddie Arcaro, 6 winners

*Largest Field:* 18 in 1928

*Smallest Fields:* 2 in 1883, 1884, 1889

*Favorites:* 55 of 108 (51 percent)

*Largest Payoff:* $48.80, Master Derby in 1975

*Smallest Payoffs:* $2.20, Citation (1948) and Spectacular Bid (1979)

*Fastest Times:*

|  |  |  |
|---|---|---|
| 1. | Canonero II (1971) | 1:54 |
| 2. | Spectacular Bid (1979) | 1:54⅕ |
| 3. | Codex (1980) | 1:54⅕ |
| 4. | Secretariat (1973) | 1:54⅖ |
| 5. | Seattle Slew (1977) | 1:54⅖ |
| 6. | Affirmed (1978) | 1:54⅖ |
| 7. | Nashua (1955) | 1:54⅗ |
| 8. | Little Current (1974) | 1:54⅗ |
| 9. | Pleasant Colony (1981) | 1:54⅗ |
| 10. | Elocutionist (1976) | 1:55 |

## THE BELMONT STAKES

In 1870, one year after the opening of Jerome Park, the American Jockey Club carded a stakes race for three-year-olds and named it after one of the most influential men in racing, August Belmont. The son of the biggest farmer in Germany's Rhine region, Belmont had come to the United States in 1837 as agent for the fabulously wealthy European banking family, the Rothschilds. He was an important horse owner and breeder before the Civil War. Along with Leonard Jerome, he played a crucial role in the founding of Jerome Park.

The Belmont Stakes did not suffer the ups and downs of the other two Triple Crown races. New York was the center of the best American racing, and most of the wealthy, influential owners and breeders considered winning the Belmont on their home track the acme of success.

The only decline the race suffered resulted from the anti-gambling fervor that swept through the country. The Belmont, which had been moved to Morris Park in 1900 and on to the new Belmont Park in 1905, was not held in 1911 and 1912. By the time the racing program at Belmont got back on its feet, the promotional wizardry of Col. Matt Winn had already made the Kentucky Derby the number-one race in the country in the public's eye.

To many horsemen, however, the one-and-a-half-mile Belmont remains the sternest test for three-year-olds.

## Belmont Stakes Facts

*Winners:* 111 colts, 2 fillies Ruthless (1867) and Tanya (1905)

*Leading Owner:* Belair Stud, 6 winners

*Leading Trainers:* James Rowe, Sr., and James (Sunny Jim) Fitzsimmons, 6 winners each

*Leading Jockeys:* J. McLaughlin and Eddie Arcaro, 6 winners each

*Largest Field:* 14 in 1875

*Smallest Fields:* 2 in 1887, 1888, 1892, 1910, 1920

*Favorites:* 57 of 114 (50 percent)

*Largest Pari-Mutuel Payoff:* $132.10, Sherluck (1961)

*Smallest Pari-Mutuel Payoff:* $2.20, Secretariat (1973)

*Fastest Times:*

|  |  |  |
|---|---|---|
| 1. | Secretariat (1973) | 2:24 |
| 2. | Gallant Man (1957) | 2:26⅗ |
| 3. | Affirmed (1978) | 2:26⅘ |
| 4. | Stage Door Johnny (1968) | 2:27⅕ |
| 5. | Riva Ridge (1972) | 2:28 |
| 6. | Count Fleet (1943) | 2:28⅕ |
| 7. | Citation (1948) | 2:28⅕ |
| 8. | Avatar (1975) | 2:28⅕ |
| 9. | Sword Dancer (1959) | 2:28⅖ |
| 10. | Quadrangle (1964) | 2:28⅖ |
| 11. | Hail to Ali (1965) | 2:28⅖ |

# Graded Stakes: The Championship Races

In any team sport, the contests that attract the most spectator and media interest are those that lead to the winning of championships. Early in the season, these may be games that test the relative strengths of the strong pre-season favorites. Later, key battles sort out the top contenders, who then move on to the final championship events, like the World Series and the Super Bowl.

Racing, too, has its leagues—the nine divisions for which Eclipse Award winners are chosen. However, since no "league standings" appear in daily newspapers or in racing programs, racing fans have a great deal of difficulty picking out the most important races in the season-long quest for championships.

In 1971, European authorities, faced with similar problems, designated the best of their stakes races "Pattern Races" and classified these by relative importance into Groups I, II, and III. Unable to determine which among the two thousand U.S. stakes races were indicative of superior racing ability and breeding potential, the Europeans recommended that the Thoroughbred Owners and Breeders Association adopt the same system. The TOBA agreed.

Each year the TOBA convenes a panel to undertake the grading of North American stakes. For the 1980 stakes, the panel consisted of racing officials Jimmy Kilroe of California, Tommy Trotter of Chicago, and Lenny Hale of New York; TOBA trustees Mr. Lenart Ringquist, Jacques Wimpfheimer, and L. P. Doherty; and the editor and executive editor of *The Blood-Horse*. In a pamphlet published by *The Blood-Horse,* the TOBA explains the procedure this panel follows in grading the stakes:

Primary criterion for grading stakes is the quality of horses attracted to the race in recent years. This necessarily is an imprecise standard, yet it embraces several factors—purse value, distance, prestige, competition—whose combined value is assessed and acted upon as to payment of stakes fees by owners and trainers of good horses.

Thus, the number of good horses in a field, or the lack thereof, reflects an appraisal by racing men of the importance of a stakes. This is a balanced appraisal, often weighing purse value against the value of the tradition attached to fixtures.

In addition to the primary consideration of the quality of fields attracted to the stakes in recent years, subjectively the panel members favor distance racing to sprint racing for three-year-olds and older horses; level weight or scale weight—for age rather than handicaps; and traditional fixtures whose names have become a signal of class in family pedigree notes, with a wait-and-see attitude toward rich new stakes.

As to objective criteria, the panel considers for grading no stakes with a purse value less than $40,000 added. . . . In addition, no stakes is considered for grading whose conditions contain restrictions other than for age or sex, that is, not considered are stakes restricted as to entries by place of foaling (state-bred races) or by previous racing performance.

The result of this rigorous process is the designation of those races in America that sharply and clearly define *class* in the Thoroughbred. In 1980, of the 64,497 horses that raced, only 175 (0.27 percent) were Graded Stakes winners. In 1980, 272 races at 33 tracks were designated Graded Stakes. Of these, 72 were Grade I, 93 Grade II, and 107 were Grade III. The table below shows where these races were run:

| TRACK | GR. I | GR. II | GR. III | TOTAL |
|---|---|---|---|---|
| Belmont Park | 17 | 16 | 7 | 40 |
| Aqueduct | 5 | 9 | 22 | 36 |
| Santa Anita | 14 | 10 | 11 | 35 |
| Hollywood Park | 9 | 10 | 9 | 28 |
| Saratoga | 4 | 5 | 5 | 14 |
| Monmouth Park | 4 | 2 | 6 | 12 |
| Arlington Park | 1 | 8 | 3 | 12 |
| Del Mar | – | 5 | 3 | 8 |
| Keeneland | 2 | 3 | 2 | 7 |
| Hialeah | 2 | 3 | 2 | 7 |
| Gulfstream Park | 2 | 2 | 3 | 7 |
| Meadowlands | 1 | 2 | 4 | 7 |
| Churchill Downs | 2 | – | 4 | 6 |
| Pimlico | 1 | 2 | 3 | 6 |
| Oaklawn Park | 1 | 3 | 1 | 5 |
| Laurel | 3 | – | 1 | 4 |
| Ak-Sar-Ben | – | 2 | 2 | 4 |
| Delaware Park | 2 | 1 | – | 3 |
| Atlantic City | 1 | 1 | 1 | 3 |
| Woodbine | 1 | – | 2 | 3 |
| Bowie | – | 1 | 2 | 3 |
| Golden Gate Fields | – | 1 | 2 | 3 |
| Hawthorne | – | 1 | 2 | 3 |
| Bay Meadows | – | 1 | 2 | 3 |
| Calder | – | – | 3 | 3 |
| Keystone | – | 2 | – | 2 |
| Fair Grounds | – | 1 | 1 | 2 |
| Detroit | – | 1 | – | 1 |
| Thistledown | – | 1 | – | 1 |
| Longacres | – | – | 1 | 1 |
| Fort Erie | – | – | 1 | 1 |
| Suffolk Downs | – | – | 1 | 1 |
| Sportsman's Park | – | – | 1 | 1 |
| | 72 | 93 | 107 | 272 |

For the racing fan and horseman alike, these events are the highlights of the racing season. Most important, it is the winners of these events, especially the Grade I races, that contend for the annual Eclipse Awards. We're going to look at these Graded Stakes by age and sex groups, then point out the races that play the most significant role in determining champions.

## ECLIPSE AWARDS

Beginning in 1936, two publications conducted separate pollings for Horse of the Year and divisional honors. The *Daily Racing Form* took a vote among its staff members, *Turf & Sport Digest* among selected sportswriters and sportscasters. In 1950, the Thoroughbred Racing Association began to poll the racing secretaries of its member tracks. This separate voting often resulted in more than one horse being named "champion." Six times, more than one Horse of the Year was named.

Finally, in 1971, the *Daily Racing Form* and the TRA polls were consolidated, and the members of the National Turf Writers Association were added as voters. All three organizations conducted separate polls, the results of each organization's voting counting as one vote for the top horse. In 1979, modifications were made in the vote-counting procedure to ensure that no more dual championships would result. Racing now has a single major program for honoring the finest horses in each division—the Eclipse Awards.

The horses listed in this book as champions from 1971 on are the Eclipse Award winners. Prior to 1971, the horses listed are those named in the poll conducted by the *Daily Racing Form*.

## THREE-YEAR-OLDS

| STAKES | TRACK | ADDED MONEY | FUR-LONGS |
|--------|-------|-------------|-----------|
| **Grade I** | | | |
| Belmont S. | Bel | $200,000 | 12 |
| Blue Grass S. | Kee | 100,000 | 9 |
| Flamingo S. | Hia | 125,000 | 9 |
| Florida Derby | GP | 200,000 | 9 |
| Hollywood Derby | Hol | 250,000 | 9 |
| Kentucky Derby | CD | 200,000 | 10 |
| Monmouth Inv. H. | Mth | 100,000 | 9 |
| Preakness S. | Pim | 200,000 | 9.5 |
| Santa Anita Derby | SA | 150,000 | 9 |
| Swaps S. | Hol | 200,000 | 10 |
| Travers S. | Sar | 125,000 | 10 |
| Wood Memorial S. | Aqu | 125,000 | 9 |
| | | | |
| **Grade II** | | | |
| Ak-Sar-Ben Gold Cup | Aka | $100,000 | 8.5 |
| American Derby | AP | 100,000 | 10 |
| Arkansas Derby | OP | 150,000 | 9 |
| Arlington Classic | AP | 100,000 | 10 |
| California Derby | GG | 150,000 | 8.5 |
| Cinema H. | Hol | 100,000 | 9T |
| Dwyer S. | Bel | 100,000 | 9 |
| Gotham S. | Aqu | 75,000 | 8 |
| Jerome H. | Bel | 100,000 | 8 |
| Lawrence Realization | Bel | 75,000 | 12T |
| Lexington H. | Bel | 75,000 | 10T |
| Louisiana Derby | FG | 125,000 | 9 |
| Ohio Derby | Tdn | 150,000 | 9 |
| Roamer H. | Aqu | 50,000 | 9.5 |
| San Felipe H. | SA | 100,000 | 8.5 |
| Saranac S. | Bel | 50,000 | 8T |
| Secretariat S. | AP | 125,000 | 12T |
| Silver Screen H. | Hol | 60,000 | 9 |
| Will Rogers H. | Hol | 50,000 | 8.5T |
| Withers S. | Aqu | 50,000 | 8 |
| | | | |
| **Grade III** | | | |
| Ak-Sar-Ben Pres. Cup | Aks | $ 75,000 | 9 |
| Bay Shore H. | Aqu | 50,000 | 7 |
| Del Mar Derby | Dmr | 75,000 | 9T |
| Discovery H. | Aqu | 50,000 | 9 |
| El Dorado H. | Hol | 50,000 | 8 |
| Fountain of Youth | GP | 40,000 | 8.5 |
| Hawthorne Derby | Haw | 75,000 | 8.5 |
| Illinois Derby | Spt | 150,000 | 9 |
| Jamaica H. | Aqu | 50,000 | 8 |
| Jim Dandy S. | Sar | 50,000 | 9 |
| La Jolla Mile | Dmr | 40,000 | 8T |
| Lamplighter H. | Mth | 50,000 | 8.5T |
| Long Branch S. | Mth | 40,000 | 8T |
| Marylander H. | Bow | 50,000 | 9 |
| Peter Pan S. | Bel | $ 50,000 | 9 |
| Round Table H. | AP | 50,000 | 9T |
| Rutgers H. | Med | 100,000 | 10 |
| San Vicente S. | SA | 60,000 | 7 |
| Swift S. | Aqu | 50,000 | 6 |
| Tropical Park Derby | Crc | 100,000 | 8.5 |
| Volante H. | SA | 50,000 | 9T |
| Woodlawn S. | Pim | 50,000 | 8T |

By far the most significant of the above are the three *Triple Crown* races—the Kentucky Derby, the Preakness, and the Belmont Stakes. These are America's classic races, the most prized championships in North American racing.

The importance of the Triple Crown makes the pre-Kentucky Derby races of interest to racing fans. In past years, Triple Crown contenders have generally followed three patterns in prepping for the "main event."

The first is the *Florida route,* the pattern followed by Spectacular Bid. The key races are, in order, the eight-and-a-half-furlong *Fountain of Youth* (Gr. III), the nine-furlong *Florida Derby* (Gr. I) and the nine-furlong *Flamingo Stakes* (Gr. I).

The second route is the *California* races, the prep used by Affirmed. Key races are the seven-furlong *San Vicenta Stakes* (Gr. III), the eight-and-a-half-furlong *San Felipe Handicap* (Gr. II), the nine-furlong *Santa Anita Derby* (Gr. I) and the nine-furlong *Hollywood Derby* (Gr. I).

The third common path is the *New York* races, where Secretariat prepped. Key races are the six-furlong *Swift Stakes* (Gr. III), the seven-furlong *Bay Shore Handicap* (Gr. III), and the eight-furlong *Gotham Stakes* (Gr. II).

Two races held in the two weeks preceding the Derby have been recognized for many years as the most significant predictors of success in the Run for the Roses. These are the nine-furlong *Wood Memorial* (Gr. I) at Aqueduct and the nine-furlong *Blue Grass Stakes* (Gr. I) at Keeneland.

Winning two of the three Triple Crown races usually wins a colt the Eclipse Award for three-year-olds. A late-maturing animal can come to prominence in the historic

Travers Stakes (Gr. I) at Saratoga in August, and can win the award with a good showing against older horses in Belmont's Fall Championship Series (see below).

## Champion Three-Year-Old Colt or Gelding

| | |
|---|---|
| 1936 | Granville |
| 1937 | War Admiral |
| 1938 | Stagehand |
| 1939 | Challedon |
| 1940 | Bimelech |
| 1941 | Whirlaway |
| 1942 | Alsab |
| 1943 | Count Fleet |
| 1944 | By Jimminy |
| 1945 | Fighting Step |
| 1946 | Assault |
| 1947 | Phalanx |
| 1948 | Citation |
| 1949 | Capot |
| 1950 | Hill Prince |
| 1951 | Counterpoint |
| 1952 | One Count |
| 1953 | Native Dancer |
| 1954 | High Gun |
| 1955 | Nashua |
| 1956 | Needles |
| 1957 | Bold Ruler |
| 1958 | Tim Tam |
| 1959 | Sword Dancer |
| 1960 | Kelso |
| 1961 | Carry Back |
| 1962 | Jaipur |
| 1963 | Chateaugay ✓ |
| 1964 | Northern Dancer |
| 1965 | Tom Rolfe |
| 1966 | Buckpasser |
| 1967 | Damascus |
| 1968 | Stage Door Johnny |
| 1969 | Arts and Letters |
| 1970 | Personality |
| 1971 | Canonero II |
| 1972 | Key to the Mint |
| 1973 | Secretariat |
| 1974 | Little Current |
| 1975 | Wajima |
| 1976 | Bold Forbes |
| 1977 | Seattle Slew |
| 1978 | Affirmed |
| 1979 | Spectacular Bid |
| 1980 | Temperence Hill |

## THREE-YEAR-OLD FILLIES

| STAKES | TRACK | ADDED MONEY | FUR-LONGS |
|---|---|---|---|
| **Grade I** | | | |
| Acorn S. | Bel | $ 75,000 | 8 |
| Alabama S. | Sar | 100,000 | 10 |
| Coaching Club Am. Oaks | Bel | 125,000 | 12 |
| Delaware Oaks | Del | 75,000 | 9 |
| Fantasy S. | OP | 150,000 | 8.5 |
| Hollywood Oaks | Hol | 100,000 | 9 |
| Kentucky Oaks | CD | 100,000 | 8.5 |
| Mother Goose S. | Bel | 100,000 | 9 |
| Santa Susana S. | SA | 100,000 | 8.5 |
| **Grade II** | | | |
| Ashland S. | Kee | $ 50,000 | 7 |
| Black-eyed Susan S. | Pim | 100,000 | 8.5 |
| Cotillion S. | Key | 50,000 | 8.5 |
| Del Mar Oaks | Dmr | 75,000 | 9T |
| Gazelle H. | Bel | 50,000 | 9 |
| Monmouth Oaks | Mth | 50,000 | 9 |
| Test S. | Sar | 50,000 | 7 |
| **Grade III** | | | |
| Athenia H. | Bel | $ 75,000 | 10T |
| Boiling Springs H. | Med | 40,000 | 8.5 |
| Comely S. | Aqu | 40,000 | 7 |
| Honeymoon H. | Hol | 50,000 | 8.5T |
| Linda Vista H. | SA | 50,000 | 8.5 |
| Little Silver H. | Mth | 50,000 | 8.5T |
| Poinsettia S. | Hia | 50,000 | 9 |
| Post-Deb S. | Mth | 40,000 | 8, plus 70 yds. |
| Princess S. | Hol | 40,000 | 8.5 |
| Pucker Up S. | AP | 50,000 | 9.5 |
| Railbird S. | Hol | 40,000 | 7 |
| Ruthless S. | Aqu | 50,000 | 9 |
| Santa Ynez S. | SA | 60,000 | 7 |

The major emphasis in three-year-old racing is on colts. Although fillies are eligible for all the graded three-year-old stakes, very few have competed successfully against top-class males at this age. In fact, between Silver Spoon's fifth-place finish in the 1959 Kentucky Derby and Genuine Risk's stunning triumph in the 1980 Derby, not a single filly even competed in a Triple Crown event.

The long-standing prejudice against fillies, only recently eroded, has slowed the development of a filly Triple Crown that would match in prestige the races dominated by colts. The generally accepted filly Triple Crown today is the New York Racing Association's Acorn Stakes, the Mother Goose Stakes and the Coaching Club American Oaks, all run at Belmont Park. This triple was created in 1957, when the Mother Goose was elevated to stakes status. Five fillies have swept the three events: Dark Mirage (1968), Shuvee (1969), Chris Evert (1974), Ruffian (1975) and Davona Dale (1979).

Some sentiment has existed over the years that the major races for fillies at Churchill Downs, Pimlico and Belmont should be certified as the Triple Crown for fillies. That triple consists of the Kentucky Oaks (held the day before the Derby), the Black-eyed Susan (held the day before the Preakness) and the Coaching Club American Oaks (three weeks after the Belmont). The first two races, however, are diminished by their proximity to the Derby and Preakness, and changes would have to be made to give them the exposure needed for truly championship events. Until 1979, two fillies had swept these three races—Wistful (1949) and Real Delight (1952). In 1979, Davona Dale became the only filly in history to record a "double" Triple Crown, sweeping all five races.

The three-year-old filly championship is influenced strongly by the five races above, but not as strongly as the Triple Crown influences the championship for colts. The Test Stakes and the historic Alabama Stakes at Saratoga are very important, as are a three-year-old's performance against older fillies and mares in such fall races as the Beldame and the Ruffian Handicap.

**Champion Three-Year-Old Filly**

| 1939 | Unerring |
| 1941 | Painted Veil |
| 1942 | Vagrancy |
| 1943 | Stefanita |
| 1944 | Twilight Tear |
| 1945 | Busher |
| 1946 | Bridal Flower |
| 1947 | But Why Not |
| 1948 | Miss Request |
| 1949 | Two Lea & Wistful |
| 1950 | Next Move |
| 1951 | Kiss Me Kate |
| 1952 | Real Delight |
| 1953 | Grecian Queen |
| 1954 | Parlo |
| 1955 | Misty Morn |
| 1956 | Doubledogdare |
| 1957 | Bayou |
| 1958 | Idun |
| 1959 | Royal Native |
| 1960 | Berlo |
| 1961 | Bowl of Flowers |
| 1962 | Cicada |
| 1963 | Lamb Chop |
| 1964 | Tosmah |
| 1965 | What a Treat |
| 1966 | Lady Pitt |
| 1967 | Furl Sail |
| 1968 | Dark Mirage |
| 1969 | Gallant Bloom |
| 1970 | Office Queen |
| 1971 | Turkish Trousers |
| 1972 | Susan's Girl |
| 1973 | Desert Vixen |
| 1974 | Chris Evert |
| 1975 | Ruffian |
| 1976 | Revidere |
| 1977 | Our Mims |
| 1978 | Tempest Queen |
| 1979 | Davona Dale |
| 1980 | Genuine Risk |

## TWO-YEAR-OLDS

| STAKES | TRACK | ADDED MONEY | FUR- LONGS |
|---|---|---|---|
| **Grade I** | | | |
| Arlington-Washington Fut. | AP | $ 75,000 | 7 |
| Champagne S. | Bel | 125,000 | 8 |
| Futurity S. | Bel | 100,000 | 7 |
| Hopeful S. | Sar | 75,000 | 6.5 |
| Laurel Futurity | Lrl | 100,000 | 8.5 |
| Norfolk S. | SA | 150,000 | 8.5 |
| Sapling S. | Mth | 100,000 | 6 |
| Young America S. | Med | 200,000 | 9 |
| **Grade II** | | | |
| Breeders' Futurity | Kee | $ 50,000 | 7 |
| Cowdin S. | Bel | 50,000 | 7 |
| Del Mar Futurity | Dmr | 100,000 | 8 |
| El Camino Real S. | BM | 100,000 | 8.5 |
| Heritage S. | Key | 100,000 | 8.5 |

| | | | |
|---|---|---|---|
| Hollywood Juven. | | | |
| Champ. | Hol | $100,000 | 6 |
| Remsen S. | Aqu | 100,000 | 9 |
| Sanford S. | Sar | 40,000 | 6 |
| Saratoga Special S. | Sar | 40,000 | 6 |
| **Grade III** | | | |
| Hawthorne Juvenile S. | Haw | $ 75,000 | 8.5 |
| Kentucky Jockey | | | |
| Club S. | CD | 50,000 | 8.5 |
| Sunny Slope S. | SA | 40,000 | 7 |
| World's Playground S. | Atl | 75,000 | 7 |

Two-year-olds are the babies of the Thoroughbred world, and most trainers with promising two-year-olds are reluctant to rush them to the races too quickly. The first significant races for two-year-olds aren't carded until late summer, when racing's elite display the pride and joy of their current crop in such tests as the Sanford Stakes and the Hopeful Stakes. Other top colts may not make their first appearance until fall. The reputation of a two-year-old may rest on his performance in just one or two major stakes. Unlike in the older divisions, it's common for the top contenders for the two-year-old crown not to face each other.

As a result of the above, the voting for championship two-year-old is often very close. In recent years, however, electors have favored colts with a strong showing in such late-fall Eastern tests as Belmont's Champagne Stakes and the Laurel Futurity over the West Coast colts who distinguish themselves in the races like the Norfolk Stakes, the El Camino Real Stakes and the Hollywood Juvenile Championship.

## GREAT HORSES: NATIVE DANCER

The old saw that "good things are worth waiting for" was never more true than when Alfred G. Vanderbilt's mare Geisha finally dropped her month-overdue foal on March 27, 1950. The new arrival, a gray colt by 1945 Preakness winner Polynesian, was the great Native Dancer, who captured twenty-one of twenty-two starts in a brilliant career. Racegoers loved the horse they called "Dancer" or the "Gray Ghost." Crowds surrounding the paddock were awed by the majestic bearing and icy calmness the horse displayed before races; then they rushed to the rail to watch Native Dancer charge down the stretch to victory from way behind, eating up incredible ground with his twenty-nine-foot stride, the longest ever measured.

Native Dancer's reputation preceded him to his very first outing in April of his two-year-old season. He went to the post a seven-to-five favorite and sprinted to a four-and-a-half-length victory in his maiden race. The outing took so little out of him that he came back just four days later to roar to victory in the Youthful Stakes as the four-to-five public choice. Never in the rest of his career did Native Dancer go off at higher odds.

The gray colt bucked his shins after the Youthful, but he came back to the races in tremendous form at Saratoga in August. He swept his next seven starts, with the highlight of equaling the world record for six and a half furlongs in the Belmont Futurity. His performance was so impressive that he became the first juvenile to be named Horse of the Year by the Thoroughbred Racing Association and *Turf & Sport Digest* (the *Daily Racing Form* gave the nod to the Belmont Stakes winner, One Count).

Ankle problems delayed Dancer's first three-year-old start until the Gotham Stakes, two weeks prior to the Kentucky Derby. A two-length victory there, followed by a four-and-a-half-length romp in the Wood Memorial the next Saturday, established the Vanderbilt colt as the overwhelming favorite for the Run for the Roses. What followed instead was the colt's only defeat. The chart of the 1953 Derby tells the story: "Native Dancer, roughed at the first turn by Money Broker, was eased back to secure racing room, raced wide during the run to the upper turn, then saved ground entering the stretch and finished strongly, but could not overtake the winner, although probably best." Jockey Eric Guerin blamed the roughing on the first turn for the loss, while other observers pointed at suspiciously large ankles. All observers agreed that another stride would have turned Dark Star's head victory into a Native Dancer triumph.

After three hard races in three weeks, trainer Bill Winfrey was expected to give his gray colt a rest. Instead he shipped him to New York, where he triumphed in the Withers Stakes. On the next weekend, Dancer added a victory in the Preakness, his fifth race in five weeks. After a three-week breather, Native Dancer won the Belmont Stakes, which he followed with four victories, making his record for the year nine out of ten. Unfortunately, soreness in his left foot prevented the colt from meeting four-year-old sensation Tom Fool in the prestigious fall races. As a result, Tom Fool was named Horse of the Year.

Physical problems continued to plague Dancer at age four, and he only got to the track three times. However, his victories in the Metropolitan Handicap and the Oneonta Handicap (carrying 137 pounds) were so impressive that Native Dancer was finally accorded unanimous Horse of the Year honors before he retired to the breeding shed.

At stud, Native Dancer has been surpassed only by Bold Ruler in the last quarter-century. Dancer compiled a 3.15 average earnings index and sired forty-five stakes winners, including the 1966 Derby and Preakness winner, Kauai King. Yet his major influence has been as a sire of sires. His son, Raise a Native, sired the 1969 Derby and Preakness winner, Majestic Prince, who in turn got 1979 Belmont winner, Coastal. Another son of Raise a Native is Exclusive Native, sire of Triple Crown winner Affirmed and Kentucky Derby-winning filly Genuine Risk. Native Dancer has been an equally brilliant broodmare sire. His daughters have produced the superb filly Ruffian and the great Northern Dancer, one of the world's most influential sires.

*Race Record:*

STS. 1ST 2ND 3RD EARNINGS
22   21   1   0   $785,240

NATIVE DANCER, by Polynesian out of Geisha by Discovery

| 1941 | Alsab |
| 1942 | Count Fleet |
| 1943 | Platter |
| 1944 | Pavot |
| 1945 | Star Pilot |
| 1946 | Double Jay |
| 1947 | Citation |
| 1948 | Blue Peter |
| 1949 | Hill Prince |
| 1950 | Battlefield |
| 1951 | Tom Fool |
| 1952 | Native Dancer |
| 1953 | Porterhouse |
| 1954 | Nashua |
| 1955 | Needles |
| 1956 | Barbizon |
| 1957 | Nadir |
| 1958 | First Landing |
| 1959 | Warfare |
| 1960 | Hail to Reason |
| 1961 | Crimson Satan |
| 1962 | Never Bend |
| 1963 | Hurry to Market |
| 1964 | Bold Lad |
| 1965 | Buckpasser |
| 1966 | Successor |
| 1967 | Vitriolic |
| 1968 | Top Knight |
| 1969 | Silent Screen |
| 1970 | Hoist the Flag |
| 1971 | Riva Ridge |
| 1972 | Secretariat |
| 1973 | Protagonist |
| 1974 | Foolish Pleasure |
| 1975 | Honest Pleasure |
| 1976 | Seattle Slew |
| 1977 | Affirmed |
| 1978 | Spectacular Bid |
| 1979 | Rockhill Native |
| 1980 | Lord Avie |

**Champion Two-Year-Old Colt or Gelding**

| 1936 | Pompoon |
| 1937 | Menow |
| 1938 | El Chico |
| 1939 | Bimelech |
| 1940 | Our Boots |

## TWO-YEAR-OLD FILLIES

| STAKES | TRACK | ADDED MONEY | FURLONGS |
|---|---|---|---|
| **Grade I** | | | |
| Frizette S. | Bel | $100,000 | 8 |
| Matron S. | Bel | 75,000 | 7 |
| Oak Leaf S. | SA | 100,000 | 8.5 |
| Selima S. | Lrl | 100,000 | 8.5 |
| Sorority S. | Mth | 100,000 | 6 |
| Spinaway S. | Sar | 75,000 | 6 |

**Grade II**

| | | | |
|---|---|---|---|
| Alcibiades S. | Kee | $ 50,000 | 7 |
| Arlington-Wash. | | | |
| Lassie | AP | 50,000 | 6 |
| Del Mar | | | |
| Debutante S. | Dmr | 100,000 | 8 |
| Demoiselle S. | Aqu | 75,000 | 9 |
| Hollywood | | | |
| Lassie S. | Hol | 75,000 | 6 |

**Grade III**

| | | | |
|---|---|---|---|
| Adirondack S. | Sar | $ 40,000 | 6 |
| Anoakia S. | SA | 40,000 | 7 |
| Astarita S. | Bel | 40,000 | 6.5 |
| Golden Rod S. | CD | 50,000 | 7 |
| Schuylerville S. | Sar | 40,000 | 6 |
| Tempted S. | Aqu | 50,000 | 8 |

Like two-year-old colts, two-year-old fillies seldom compete until late summer and often the top prospects don't meet each other. The most prestigious early test for young fillies is the Spinaway Stakes at Saratoga. Key fall tests are the Selima Stakes at Laurel, the Frizette Stakes at Belmont and the Oak Leaf Stakes at Santa Anita.

Voting for champion two-year-old fillies is usually extremely close, with particularly vociferous arguments between supporters of East Coast and West Coast candidates.

**Champion Two-Year-Old Filly**

| | |
|---|---|
| 1938 | Inscoelda |
| 1939 | Now What |
| 1940 | Level Best |
| 1941 | Petrify |
| 1942 | Askmenow |
| 1943 | Durazna |
| 1944 | Busher |
| 1945 | Beaugay |
| 1946 | First Flight |
| 1947 | Bewitch |
| 1948 | Myrtle Charm |
| 1949 | Bed o' Roses |
| 1950 | Aunt Jinny |
| 1951 | Rose Jet |
| 1952 | Sweet Patootie |
| 1953 | Evening Out |
| 1954 | High Voltage |
| 1955 | Doubledogdare |
| 1956 | Leallah |
| 1957 | Idun |
| 1958 | Quill |
| 1959 | My Dear Girl |
| 1960 | Bowl of Flowers |
| 1961 | Cicada |
| 1962 | Smart Deb |
| 1963 | Tosmah |
| 1964 | Queen Empress |
| 1965 | Moccasin |
| 1966 | Regal Bleam |
| 1967 | Queen of the Stage |
| 1968 | Gallant Bloom |
| 1969 | Fast Attack |
| 1970 | Forward Gal |
| 1971 | Numbered Account |
| 1972 | La Prevoyante |
| 1973 | Talking Picture |
| 1974 | Ruffian |
| 1975 | Dearly Precious |
| 1976 | Sensational |
| 1977 | Lakeville Miss |
| 1978 | Candy Eclair & It's In the Air |
| 1979 | Smart Angle |
| 1980 | Heavenly Cause |

## OLDER HORSES

### Three-Year-Olds and Up

| STAKES | TRACK | ADDED MONEY | FURLONGS |
|---|---|---|---|
| **Grade I** | | | |
| Amory L. Haskell H. | Mth | $125,000 | 9 |
| Brooklyn H. | Bel | 200,000 | 12 |
| Californian S. | Hol | 250,000 | 8.5 |
| Canadian International | | | |
| Championship S. | Wdb | 200,000 | 13T |
| Century H. | Hol | 100,000 | 11T |
| Gulfstream Park H. | GP | 150,000g | 10 |
| Hollywood Gold Cup H. | Hol | 500,000g | 10 |
| Hollywood Invitational H. | Hol | 250,000g | 12T |

|                          |       | ADDED    |          |
| STAKES                   | TRACK | MONEY    | FURLONGS |
| ------------------------ | ----- | -------- | -------- |
| Jockey Club Gold Cup S.  | Bel   | $350,000 | 12       |
| Man o' War S.            | Bel   | 125,000  | 11T      |
| Marlboro Cup H.          | Bel   | 300,000g | 9        |
| Metropolitan H.          | Bel   | 125,000  | 8        |
| Oak Tree Invitational H. | SA    | 150,000g | 12T      |
| Suburban H.              | Bel   | 150,000  | 10       |
| Sunset H.                | Hol   | 150,000  | 12T      |
| Turf Classic             | Aqu   | 300,000  | 12T      |
| United Nations H.        | Atl   | 125,000g | 9.5T     |
| Vosburgh S.              | Aqu   | 100,000  | 7        |
| Washington, D.C.,        |       |          |          |
|   International S. | Lrl | 200,000g | 12T      |
| Widener H.               | Hia   | 125,000  | 10       |
| Woodward S.              | Bel   | 200,000  | 10       |

**Grade II**

| Ak-Sar-Ben               |       |          |      |
| ------------------------ | ----- | -------- | ---- |
|   Cornhusker H. | Aks  | $150,000 | 9    |
| American H.              | Hol   | 100,000  | 9T   |
| Arlington Park H.        | AP    | 100,000  | 12T  |
| Bel Air H.               | Hol   | 50,000   | 9    |
| Bowling Green H.         | Bel   | 125,000  | 11T  |
| Carleton F. Burke H.     | SA    | 75,000   | 10T  |
| Carter H.                | Aqu   | 75,000   | 7    |
| Del Mar H.               | Dmr   | 125,000g | 10   |
| Dixie H.                 | Pim   | 100,000  | 12T  |
| Donald P. Ross H.        | Del   | 50,000   | 9T   |
| Donn H.                  | GP    | 75,000   | 9    |
| Excelsior H.             | Aqu   | 100,000  | 10   |
| Fall Highweight H.       | Bel   | 75,000   | 6    |
| Gallant Fox H.           | Aqu   | 50,000   | 13   |
| Hawthorne Gold Cup H.    | Haw   | 100,000  | 10   |
| Hialeah Turf Cup H.      | Hia   | 125,000  | 12T  |
| John B. Campbell H.      | Bow   | 100,000  | 10   |
| Lakeside H.              | Hol   | 50,000   | 9T   |
| Manhattan H.             | Bel   | 75,000   | 10T  |
| Meadowlands Cup S.       | Med   | 350,000  | 10   |
| Michigan Mile and        |       |          |      |
|   One-Eighth H. | Det  | 100,000  | 9    |
| Pan American H.          | GP    | 150,000g | 12T  |
| Paterson H.              | Med   | 150,000  | 9    |
| Seminole H.              | Hia   | 50,000   | 9    |
| Stars and Stripes H.     | AP    | 50,000   | 8.5T |
| Tidal H.                 | Bel   | 50,000   | 11T  |
| Whitney S.               | Sar   | 100,000  | 9    |

**Grade III**

| Ak-Sar-Ben Board of      |       |          |      |
| ------------------------ | ----- | -------- | ---- |
|   Governors' H. | Aks  | $ 50,000 | 8.5  |
| Ben Ali H.               | Kee   | 40,000   | 9    |
| Bernard Baruch H.        | Sar   | 50,000   | 11T  |
| Bougainvillea H.         | Hia   | 50,000   | 9.5T |
| Brighton Beach H.        | Bel   | 50,000   | 10T  |
| Canadian Turf H.         | GP    | 50,000   | 8.5  |
| Citation H.              | Hol   | 100,000  | 8.5  |
| Clark H.                 | CD    | 50,000   | 9    |

| STAKES | TRACK | ADDED MONEY | FURLONGS |
|---|---|---|---|
| Display H. | Aqu | $ 75,000 | 18 |
| Dominion Day H. | Wdb | 50,000 | 9 |
| Eddie Read H. | Dmr | 60,000 | 9T |
| Edgemere H. | Bel | 75,000 | 10T |
| Fayette H. | Kee | 50,000 | 9 |
| Fort Marcy H. | Aqu | 50,000 | 8.5T |
| Golden Gate H. | GG | 100,000 | 8.5T |
| Grey Lag H. | Aqu | 75,000 | 9 |
| Knickerbocker H. | Aqu | 50,000 | 11T |
| Longacres Mile H. | Lga | 100,000 | 8 |
| Longfellow H. | Mth | 50,000 | 9T |
| Los Angeles H. | Hol | 50,000 | 6 |
| Massachusetts H. | Suf | 100,000 | 9 |
| Nassau County H. | Bel | 50,000 | 9 |
| Native Diver H. | Hol | 50,000 | 8 |
| Niagara S. | FE | 50,000 | 12T |
| Queens County H. | Aqu | 50,000 | 9.5 |
| Riggs H. | Pim | 50,000 | 8.5T |
| Rolling Green H. | GG | 75,000 | 11T |
| Salvator Mile H. | Mth | 40,000 | 8 |
| Saul Silberman H. | Crc | 50,000 | 9 |
| Seneca H. | Sar | 50,000 | 13T |
| Stuyvesant H. | Aqu | 100,000 | 9 |
| Stymie H. | Aqu | 50,000 | 9 |
| Tanforan H. | BM | 75,000 | 9T |
| Washington Park H. | AP | 75,000 | 9T |
| Westchester H. | Aqu | 50,000 | 8 |
| W. L. McKnight H. | Crc | 75,000 | 9T |

## Four-Year-Olds

| STAKES | TRACK | ADDED MONEY | FUR-LONGS |
|---|---|---|---|
| **Grade I** | | | |
| Charles H. Strub S. | SA | $200,000 | 10 |
| | | | |
| **Grade II** | | | |
| Malibu S. | SA | $ 75,000 | 7 |
| San Fernando S. | SA | 100,000 | 9 |

## Four-Year-Olds and Up

| | | | |
|---|---|---|---|
| **Grade I** | | | |
| San Antonio S. | SA | $125,000 | 9 |
| San Juan Capistrano Invitational H. | SA | 200,000g | 14T (abt) |
| San Luis Rey S. | SA | 150,000 | 12T |
| Santa Anita H. | SA | 300,000 | 10 |
| | | | |
| **Grade II** | | | |
| Oaklawn H. | OP | $150,000 | 8.5 |
| San Bernardino H. | SA | 100,000 | 9 |
| San Carlos H. | SA | 75,000 | 7 |
| San Luis Obispo H. | SA | 100,000 | 12T |
| San Pasqual H. | SA | 75,000 | 8.5 |

| | | | |
|---|---|---|---|
| **Grade III** | | | |
| Arcadia H. | SA | $ 60,000 | 10T |
| New Orleans H. | FG | 125,000 | 10 |
| Razorback H. | OP | 75,000 | 8.5 |
| San Gabriel H. | SA | 60,000 | 9T |
| San Marcos H. | SA | 60,000 | 10T |

Three champions are determined by the above races: Older Colt, Horse or Gelding (formerly titled "Handicap Horse"); Grass Horse or Gelding; and Champion Sprinter.

Of these, the most prestigious is the Older Horse title, which fifteen times in the last twenty years has gone to the Thoroughbred named "Horse of the Year." This championship is primarily determined by horses that distinguish themselves in three sets of three races: The Charles Strub Series at Santa Anita; the Handicap Triple Crown at Belmont; and Belmont's Fall Championship Series.

The first on the yearly agenda is the Charles Strub Series, named for the founder of Santa Anita. While three-year-olds are beginning their preparations for the Kentucky Derby, the previous year's top three-year-olds go west to compete in the Malibu Stakes, the San Fernando Stakes and the Charles H. Strub Stakes. This triple was swept by Ancient Title in 1974 and by Spectacular Bid in 1980. The four-year-olds that distinguish themselves in the Strub Series next go on to meet older horses in the $400,000 Hollywood Gold Cup.

Many horsemen consider sweeping Belmont's Handicap Triple Crown the most difficult task in all of racing. It consists of the Metropolitan Handicap, the Suburban Handicap and the Brooklyn Handicap. The only horses ever to sweep the three contests are Whisk Broom II (1913), Tom Fool (1953) and Kelso (1961). The task is so difficult that a three-time Horse of the Year, Forego, who won eight runnings of these contests, was never able to win all three in one year.

In the fall, the very top three-year-olds get a chance to compete for Horse of the Year honors by taking on older horses in Belmont's famous Fall Championship Series—the Marlboro Cup, the Woodward Stakes and the $500,000 Jockey Club Gold Cup. The latter may be, after the Kentucky Derby, the most important horse race of the year. It was in this race in 1979, for example, that the argument that had raged all year about the relative merits of Affirmed and Spectacular Bid was settled by the older horse's convincing victory over the challenging one-and-a-half-mile course.

**Champion Older Colt, Horse or Gelding**
(Handicap Horse prior to 1971)

| | |
|---|---|
| 1936 | Discovery |
| 1937 | Seabiscuit |
| 1938 | Seabiscuit |
| 1939 | Kayak II |
| 1940 | Challedon |
| 1941 | Mioland |
| 1942 | Whirlaway |
| 1943 | Market Wise & Devil Diver |
| 1944 | Devil Diver |
| 1945 | Stymie |
| 1946 | Armed |
| 1947 | Armed |
| 1948 | Citation |
| 1949 | Coaltown |
| 1950 | Noor |
| 1951 | Hill Prince |
| 1952 | Crafty Admiral |
| 1953 | Tom Fool |
| 1954 | Native Dancer |
| 1955 | High Gun |
| 1956 | Swaps |
| 1957 | Dedicate |
| 1958 | Round Table |
| 1959 | Sword Dancer |
| 1960 | Bald Eagle |
| 1961 | Kelso |
| 1962 | Kelso |
| 1963 | Kelso |
| 1964 | Kelso |
| 1965 | Roman Brother |
| 1966 | Buckpasser |
| 1967 | Damascus |
| 1968 | Dr. Fager |
| 1969 | Arts and Letters |
| 1970 | Fort Marcy |
| 1971 | Ack Ack |
| 1972 | Autobiography |
| 1973 | Riva Ridge |
| 1974 | Forego |
| 1975 | Forego |
| 1976 | Forego |
| 1977 | Forego |
| 1978 | Seattle Slew |
| 1979 | Affirmed |
| 1980 | Spectacular Bid |

## OLDER FILLIES AND MARES
### Three-Year-Olds and Up

| STAKES | TRACK | ADDED MONEY | FURLONGS |
|---|---|---|---|
| **Grade I** | | | |
| Beldame S. | Bel | $150,000 | 10 |
| Delaware H. | Del | 100,000 | 10 |
| Ladies H. | Aqu | 100,000 | 10 |
| Ruffian H. | Bel | 125,000 | 9 |

| STAKES | TRACK | ADDED MONEY | FURLONGS |
|---|---|---|---|
| Spinster S. | Kee | $100,000 | 9 |
| Top Flight H. | Aqu | 100,000 | 9 |
| Vanity H. | Hol | 125,000 | 9 |
| Yellow Ribbon S. | SA | 150,000g | 10T |

**Grade II**

| | | | |
|---|---|---|---|
| Arlington Matron H. | AP | $ 75,000 | 9T |
| Black Helen H. | Hia | 50,000 | 9 |
| Diana H. | Sar | 50,000 | 9T |
| Firenze H. | Aqu | 50,000 | 9 |
| Flower Bowl H. | Bel | 100,000 | 10T |
| Gamely H. | Hol | 75,000 | 9T |
| Hempstead H. | Bel | 50,000 | 9 |
| Maskette H. | Bel | 75,000 | 8 |
| Matchmaker S. | Atl | 55,000 | 9.5T |
| Milady H. | Hol | 50,000 | 8.5 |
| Molly Pitcher H. | Mth | 50,000 | 8.5 |
| Ramona H. | Dmr | 100,000 | 9T |
| Sheepshead Bay H. | Bel | 100,000 | 11T |
| Sheridan H. | AP | 100,000 | 10 |
| Shuvee H. | Bel | 50,000 | 8.5 |

**Grade III**

| | | | |
|---|---|---|---|
| Affectionately H. | Aqu | $ 50,000 | 8.5 |
| Barbara Fritchie H. | Bow | 75,000 | 7 |
| Bed o' Roses H. | Aqu | 50,000 | 8 |
| Beverly Hills H. | Hol | 75,000 | 9T |
| Chrysanthemum H. | Lrl | 50,000 | 9 |
| Correction H. | Aqu | 50,000 | 6 |
| Distaff H. | Aqu | 50,000 | 7 |
| Falls City H. | CD | 50,000 | 8.5 |
| Gallorette H. | Pim | 75,000 | 8.5 |
| Las Palmas H. | SA | 60,000 | 9 |
| Long Island H. | Aqu | 100,000 | 12T |
| Long Look H. | Med | 100,000 | 9 |
| Nettie S. | Wdb | 60,000 | 10T |
| New York H. | Bel | 50,000 | 10T |
| Next Move H. | Aqu | 75,000 | 9 |
| Orchid H. | GP | 100,000 | 8.5T |
| Queen Charlotte S. | Med | 100,000 | 10 |
| Vagrancy H. | Aqu | 50,000 | 7 |
| Wilshire H. | Hol | 50,000 | 8.5 |
| Yerba Buena H. | BM | 100,000 | 11T |

**Four-Year-Old Fillies**

**Grade I**

| | | | |
|---|---|---|---|
| La Canada S. | SA | $125,000 | 9 |

**Grade III**

| | | | |
|---|---|---|---|
| El Encino S. | SA | $ 60,000 | 8.5 |

**Four-Year-Olds and Up (Fillies and Mares)**

**Grade I**

| | | | |
|---|---|---|---|
| Santa Barbara H. | SA | $100,000 | 10T |
| Santa Margarita Invitational H. | SA | 150,000 | 9 |

**Grade II**

| | | | |
|---|---|---|---|
| Apple Blossom H. | OP | $150,000 | 8/70 |
| Santa Maria H. | SA | 75,000 | 8.5 |
| Santa Monica H. | SA | 60,000 | 7 |

Older fillies and mares seldom compete with the top older males over a distance on dirt, and they rarely appear in the top handicap contests listed above. Females do compete successfully in the top grass races and sprint contests, however, so we'll move on to discuss the top handicap female races before moving to the grass and sprint championships.

Just as three-year-old fillies lack races with the supreme prestige of the male Triple Crown, older females have no series of championship races to match the Handicap Triple or the Fall Championship season. Rich races for older fillies and mares are contested all year long, all over the country. Although the most important are probably Belmont's fall races, the Beldame Stakes and the Ruffian Handicap, horses do distinguish themselves in earlier campaigning, making for very close balloting for the Eclipse Award.

**Champion Older Filly or Mare**
(Formerly Handicap Mare)

| 1938 | Marica |
| 1939 | Lady Maryland |
| 1940 | War Plumage |
| 1941 | Fairy Chant |
| 1942 | Vagrancy |
| 1943 | Mar-Kell |
| 1944 | Twilight Tear |
| 1945 | Busher |
| 1946 | Gallorette |
| 1947 | But Why Not |
| 1948 | Conniver |
| 1949 | Bewitch |
| 1950 | Two Lea |
| 1951 | Bed o' Roses |
| 1952 | Real Delight |
| 1953 | Sickle's Image |
| 1954 | Parlo |
| 1955 | Misty Morn |
| 1956 | Blue Sparkler |
| 1957 | Pucker Up |
| 1958 | Bornastar |
| 1959 | Tempted |
| 1960 | Royal Native |
| 1961 | Airman's Guide |
| 1962 | Primonetta |
| 1963 | Cicada |
| 1964 | Tosmah |
| 1965 | Old Hat |
| 1966 | Open Fire |
| 1967 | Straight Deal |
| 1968 | Gamely |
| 1969 | Gallant Bloom |
| 1970 | Shuvee |
| 1971 | Shuvee |
| 1972 | Typecast |
| 1973 | Susan's Girl |
| 1974 | Desert Vixen |
| 1975 | Susan's Girl |
| 1976 | Proud Delta |
| 1977 | Cascapedia |
| 1978 | Late Bloomer |
| 1979 | Waya |
| 1980 | Glorious Song |

## GRASS CHAMPION

In recent years, turf racing has skyrocketed in popularity, as attested by the fact that fifty-six graded races for three-year-olds and older are now contested on the grass. The most prestigious of these races, however, are those held in late fall, when champions from France and England journey across the Atlantic to meet the top grass horses of the United States and Canada. These exciting contests are the Man o' War Stakes at Belmont; the Canadian International Championship Stakes at Woodbine; Aqueduct's Turf Classic; and finally, the most splendid of them all, the Washington, D.C., International at Laurel.

Since females do compete successfully with males on the turf, the grass championship was a single title until 1979, when the category was broken into separate awards for male and female grass horses. Performance in the above four events, however, continues to be given prime consideration in the competition for both awards.

**Champion Grass Horse**

| 1953 | Iceberg II |
| 1954 | Stan |
| 1955 | St. Vincent |
| 1956 | Career Boy |
| 1957 | Round Table |
| 1958 | Round Table |
| 1959 | Round Table |
| 1960 | ——— |
| 1961 | T. V. Lark |

| | | | |
|---|---|---|---|
| 1962 | —— | 1951 | Shellas Reward |
| 1963 | Mongo | 1952 | Tea-maker |
| 1964 | —— | 1953 | Tom Fool |
| 1965 | Parka | 1954 | White Skies |
| 1966 | Assagai | 1955 | Berseem |
| 1967 | Fort Marcy | 1956 | Decathlon |
| 1968 | Dr. Fager | 1957 | Decathlon |
| 1969 | Hawaii | 1958 | Bold Ruler |
| 1970 | Fort Marcy | 1959 | Intentionally |
| 1971 | Run the Gauntlet | 1960–65 | None |
| 1972 | Cougar II | 1966 | Affectionately |
| 1973 | Secretariat | 1967 | Dr. Fager |
| 1974 | Dahlia | 1968 | Dr. Fager |
| 1975 | Snow Knight | 1969 | Ta Wee |
| 1976 | Youth | 1970 | Ta Wee |
| 1977 | Johnny D. | 1971 | Ack Ack |
| 1978 | Mac Diarmida | 1972 | Chou Croute |
| 1979 | Bowl Game (Male) | 1973 | Shecky Greene |
| | Trillion (Female) | 1974 | Forego |
| 1980 | John Henry (Male) | 1975 | Gallant Bob |
| | Just a Game (Female) | 1976 | My Juliet |
| | | 1977 | What a Summer |
| | | 1978 | Dr. Patches & J. O. Tobin |
| | | 1979 | Star de Naskra |
| | | 1980 | Plugged Nickle |

## SPRINT CHAMPION

In horse racing, true championship ability means carrying speed over distance of ground. That's why very few major races for older horses are contested at what would be considered "sprint" distances of less than a mile. However, racing does honor those horses that display brilliant speed by awarding an annual Eclipse Award to the best sprinter.

Because gender has little to do with speed over short distances, this championship has gone to both male and female horses. These Thoroughbreds have followed so many different routes to their titles that no clear pattern exists. Recently, however, the elevation of Aqueduct's Vosburgh Stakes to a Grade I contest has singled that event out as the key sprint of the year.

**Champion Sprinter**

| | |
|---|---|
| 1936 | Myrtlewood |
| 1937–46 | None |
| 1947 | Polynesian |
| 1948 | Coaltown |
| 1949 | Delegate & Royal Governor |
| 1950 | **Shellas Reward** |

## HORSE OF THE YEAR

| | |
|---|---|
| 1936 | Granville |
| 1937 | War Admiral |
| 1938 | Seabiscuit |
| 1939 | Challedon |
| 1940 | Challedon |
| 1941 | Whirlaway |
| 1942 | Whirlaway |
| 1943 | Count Fleet |
| 1944 | Twilight Tear* |
| 1945 | Busher* |
| 1946 | Assault |
| 1947 | Armed |
| 1948 | Citation |
| 1949 | Capot |
| 1950 | Hill Prince |
| 1951 | Counterpoint |
| 1952 | One Count |
| 1953 | Tom Fool |
| 1954 | Native Dancer |
| 1955 | Nashua |
| 1956 | Swaps |

* Denotes Filly

| 1957 | Bold Ruler | 1969 | Arts and Letters |
|------|------------|------|------------------|
| 1958 | Round Table | 1970 | Fort Marcy |
| 1959 | Sword Dancer | 1971 | Ack Ack |
| 1960 | Kelso | 1972 | Secretariat |
| 1961 | Kelso | 1973 | Secretariat |
| 1962 | Kelso | 1974 | Forego |
| 1963 | Kelso | 1975 | Forego |
| 1964 | Kelso | 1976 | Forego |
| 1965 | Roman Brother | 1977 | Seattle Slew |
| 1966 | Buckpasser | 1978 | Affirmed |
| 1967 | Damascus | 1979 | Affirmed |
| 1968 | Dr. Fager | 1980 | Spectacular Bid |

# *Handicaps*

The word "handicap" comes from a very old English game of chance in which two parties put up articles of different value as wagers. Before the game began, each party put a forfeit fee into a hat or cap. A third party who served as umpire then announced the "odds" that would compensate for the different values of the two wagers. Each participant would then stick his hand in the cap. If he pulled out the forfeit, it indicated he didn't accept the odds; an empty "hand in the cap" indicated acceptance.

Today, a handicap race is one in which an impartial umpire—the racing secretary or "handicapper"—examines the past performances of horses entered in a race and makes a judgment as to their relative abilities based on those performances. Instead of assigning different odds or prizes for each one, he apportions different weights based on his appraisal; the highest weight is assigned to his selection as the "best" horse and the lowest weight to the horse whose past performance reflects the least ability.

Assigning weights for handicaps is probably the most difficult and certainly the most controversial part of a racing secretary's job. Central to an understanding of how handicaps are assigned and, beyond that, to how conditions of all other races are written, is an understanding of the question of weight on the Thoroughbred.

## WEIGHT ON THE THOROUGHBRED

From the time men began to ride horses competitively, they noticed the far greater effect of weight carried on a horse's back as opposed to weight pulled in a cart or char-

iot. The difference exists for the same reason that it's far easier to pull a small child in a wagon than to carry the child on one's shoulders. For horses as well as people, the effect is more pronounced as distance increases.

In the earliest Thoroughbred racing in England, horses were fully mature animals (age six and over) which were ridden by the owners in races of three or four miles. The main concern with weight was that it be even for all parties, which meant that the weight for the race was that of the heaviest rider. When King Charles II rode his horses in the King's Plates, the other owners were not about to ask him to go on a diet to meet a lower weight. As a result, for more than a hundred years, all horses in King's Plates carried 168 pounds. The average in other races was about 140 pounds.

Even weights didn't always make for good races, however, because horses inevitably varied considerably in ability. Horsemen gradually became interested in finding a way to compensate for those differences. Around 1700, at a time when importation of foreign stallions and intense selective matings were having a profound effect on the English racehorse, the most obvious difference noted in racehorses was in their size. To compensate for differences in size, a type of race called a "give and take" was instituted. Before such a race, the height at the withers of every contestant was measured, and weight differences were assigned based on about seven pounds to the inch.

This sounded like an easy system, but the weight-for-size races were open to considerable fraud. At first, trainers taught their horses to stand with their feet widely apart to lower their height. To prevent this, horses were made to place their front feet on marks painted on a stone. Trainers responded by beating their horses repeatedly on the withers in the stables, so that they would learn to shrink when touched by the measuring rod. This fraud was one reason that give-and-take races ceased in the late eighteenth century.

A second and more important reason for the death of give-and-take races was the racing of horses of different ages. As we've seen, first five-year-olds, then four-year-olds were competing in the first half of the eighteenth century; by 1780, three- and two-year-olds also went to the post. Differences in the weight-carrying ability of horses of the same age were found to be far less important than the differences between the weight-carrying capacity of horses of different ages. Weight that a mature horse could carry crippled two- and three-year-olds. Thus, beginning at the time when five-year-olds began competing with six- and seven-year-olds, races were carded under "weight-for-age" conditions.

Determining this weight-for-age ratio, however, was a highly subjective task over which arguments have raged for two and a half centuries. The unavoidably arbitrary nature of such assignments was recognized from the beginning, when weight-for-age contests were known as "Whimsical" Plates. Whimsical though it may be, the concept has survived until the present day.

The first weight-for-age scale was included in the controversial 1740 Act of Parliament, an attempt by the British gov-ernment to bring some order to the sport of racing. The Act assigned 140 pounds to five-year-olds, 154 pounds to six-year-olds and 168 pounds to older horses. Like the rest of the provisions of the Act, this particular scale met with strong protest, and was repealed in 1745. Scales varied from race to race, and from race meet to race meet.

One identifiable trend among racetracks was, however, the reluctance to assign heavy weights to two- and three-year-olds. When the classic Epsom Derby was instituted, the three-year-old participants carried 112 pounds. The first two-year-old to race at Newmarket was assigned 84 pounds. When the Ascot Gold Cup, the first great weight-for-age race, was initiated in 1807, three-year-olds were given a significant weight concession, based on the grueling two-and-a-half-mile distance of the race:

*Ascot Gold Cup* (1807)

| | |
|---|---|
| Three-year-olds | 96 lbs. |
| Four-year-olds | 114 lbs. |
| Five-year-olds | 124 lbs. |
| Six-year-olds | 130 lbs. |

As racing became a truly professional sport in the nineteenth century, the lack of a strong central authority seriously threatened the sport. That problem was solved when a retired admiral, Henry Rous, became so influential that he was referred to as the "dictator of the turf." Among Rous's many contributions to the sport was the formulation and implementation of the first weight-for-age scale to be followed by tracks all over Britain. Below is a part of the scale:

*Distance: One Mile*

| AGE | APRIL | MAY | JUNE | JULY | AUG | SEPT. | OCT. | NOV. |
|---|---|---|---|---|---|---|---|---|
| 2 | 58 | 63 | 68 | 70 | 72 | 73 | 74 | 75 |
| 3 | 96 | 97 | 99 | 102 | 104 | 105 | 106 | 107 |
| 4 | 119 | 119 | 119 | 119 | 119 | 119 | 119 | 119 |
| 5 | 126 | 125½ | 125 | 124½ | 124 | 123¼ | 123 | 122 |
| 6 & up | 127 | 126 | 125¼ | 125 | 124 | 123¼ | 123 | 122 |

The main features of the scale were a diminishing of *weight differentials* to *recognize the maturing that took place as the year progressed,* and the *substantial weight reductions given to two- and three-year-olds.* While the first principle has continued in subsequent revisions of the scale, the second has been largely cast aside. Beginning in the 1880s, two- and three-year-olds were asked to carry greatly increasing weights. By 1884, three-year-old colts were asked to carry 126 pounds in the Epsom Derby, fourteen pounds higher than the original weight. The twelve-pound advantage three-year-olds had over older horses at a distance of a mile in November was cut in half, and the actual weight to be carried jumped from 107 to 120 pounds.

In America, in the 1700s, weights were assigned along the lines of the weight-for-age scales in use at major English tracks. Around the time of the Civil War, though, when dash racing replaced heat racing, the weights carried were substantially reduced. The reason was the American obsession with speed. To produce the fastest possible times, Americans skinned the grass off their racecourses and raced on the harder dirt. Realizing that harder surfaces produced more stress on the horses' legs, however, they reduced significantly the weight carried by the horse. For example, Lexington, perhaps the best racehorse of the nineteenth century, a horse that led the sire list for an incredible fourteen consecutive years, never carried more than 103 pounds. The three-year-olds competing in the first Kentucky Derby carried 100 pounds.

Gradually, however, the weights in America, just as in England, began to greatly increase. One reason was the increasing size of the average American, which made finding capable jockeys who could ride at under 100 pounds next to impossible. The main reason, however, was the horse owners' desire to prove the championship quality of their young horses by having them carry higher weights. As a result, the weight for the Kentucky Derby jumped from the original 100 to the present 126 pounds. Some horsemen today feel that's too much weight, and the huge number of horses suffering serious injury at ages two and three proves the stress dirt racing places on young legs. It's significant to note in this regard that the seven highest-priced yearlings purchased in 1979 were all sent to France, where horses are brought along more slowly and race exclusively on the turf. Their owners refused to risk their million-dollar purchases under the stress of American dirt racing.

Today, perhaps more frequently argued than the amount of weight carried by young horses is the difference in weights mandated by the scale published by the Jockey Club. The first scales adopted by the Jockey Club after its formation in 1894 were closely modeled on the English scales. Gradually, the differences between weights assigned to three-year-olds and older horses were reduced. In 1953, at a time when three-year-olds appeared to have a clear advantage in the fall weight-for-age classics, the scale was revised for the last time. Below is the current Scale of Weights for Age:

### Scale of Weights for Age

| DISTANCE | AGE | JAN. | FEB. | MAR. | APRIL | MAY | JUNE | JULY | AUG. | SEPT. | OCT. | NOV. | DEC. |
|---|---|---|---|---|---|---|---|---|---|---|---|---|---|
| One-half Mile | Two years | x | x | x | x | x | x | x | 105 | 108 | 111 | 114 | 114 |
| | Three years | 117 | 117 | 119 | 119 | 121 | 123 | 125 | 126 | 127 | 128 | 129 | 129 |
| | Four years | 130 | 130 | 130 | 130 | 130 | 130 | 130 | 130 | 130 | 130 | 130 | 130 |
| | Five years and up | 130 | 130 | 130 | 130 | 130 | 130 | 130 | 130 | 130 | 130 | 130 | 130 |
| Six Furlongs | Two years | x | x | x | x | x | x | x | 102 | 105 | 108 | 111 | 111 |
| | Three years | 114 | 114 | 117 | 117 | 119 | 121 | 123 | 125 | 126 | 127 | 128 | 128 |
| | Four years | 129 | 129 | 130 | 130 | 130 | 130 | 130 | 130 | 130 | 130 | 130 | 130 |
| | Five years and up | 130 | 130 | 130 | 130 | 130 | 130 | 130 | 130 | 130 | 130 | 130 | 130 |
| One Mile | Two years | x | x | x | x | x | x | x | x | 96 | 99 | 102 | 102 |
| | Three years | 107 | 107 | 111 | 111 | 113 | 115 | 117 | 119 | 121 | 122 | 123 | 123 |
| | Four years | 127 | 127 | 128 | 128 | 127 | 126 | 126 | 126 | 126 | 126 | 126 | 126 |
| | Five years and up | 128 | 128 | 128 | 128 | 127 | 126 | 126 | 126 | 126 | 126 | 126 | 126 |

| DISTANCE | AGE | JAN. | FEB. | MAR. | APRIL | MAY | JUNE | JULY | AUG. | SEPT. | OCT. | NOV. | DEC. |
|---|---|---|---|---|---|---|---|---|---|---|---|---|---|
| One and a Quarter Miles | Two years | x | x | x | x | x | x | x | x | x | x | x | x |
| | Three years | 101 | 101 | 107 | 107 | 111 | 113 | 116 | 118 | 120 | 121 | 122 | 122 |
| | Four years | 125 | 125 | 127 | 127 | 127 | 126 | 126 | 126 | 126 | 126 | 126 | 126 |
| | Five years and up | 127 | 127 | 127 | 127 | 127 | 126 | 126 | 126 | 126 | 126 | 126 | 126 |
| One and a Half Miles | Two years | x | x | x | x | x | x | x | x | x | x | x | x |
| | Three years | 98 | 98 | 104 | 104 | 108 | 111 | 114 | 117 | 119 | 121 | 122 | 122 |
| | Four years | 124 | 124 | 126 | 126 | 126 | 126 | 126 | 126 | 126 | 126 | 126 | 126 |
| | Five years and up | 126 | 126 | 126 | 126 | 126 | 126 | 126 | 126 | 126 | 126 | 126 | 126 |
| Two Miles | Three years | 96 | 96 | 102 | 102 | 106 | 109 | 112 | 114 | 117 | 119 | 120 | 120 |
| | Four years | 124 | 124 | 126 | 126 | 126 | 126 | 126 | 125 | 125 | 124 | 124 | 124 |
| | Five years and up | 126 | 126 | 126 | 126 | 126 | 126 | 126 | 125 | 125 | 124 | 124 | 124 |

To the above scale are added *weight allowances for sex.* Two-year-old fillies get three pounds' advantage; female three-year-olds and upward get five pounds' before September 1, three pounds' after September 1.

## THE EXPERIMENTAL FREE HANDICAP

In any sport that places the emphasis on winning, arguments continually rage about which competitors are the "best." One interesting offshoot of the handicap race, in which horses' relative abilities are translated into relative weights, is the concept of rating all the horses in a certain age group by weight. In the later nineteenth century, in England, it became customary for the official handicapper of the Jockey Club to review at the end of the year the records of the nation's best two-year-olds. The purpose of this review was to assign weights in a manner that reflected the relative ability shown by these animals. Gradually, this assessment, called the Experimental Free Handicap, gained importance among owners, breeders and racing officials as a measure of merit. Considerable prestige was attached to the annual top-weighted youngster.

In 1933, U. S. Jockey Club handicapper Walter Vosburgh began an Experimental Free Handicap of American two-year-olds. This practice has continued to the present day. Recently, the two-year-olds have been weighted by the same three racing officials who participate in the annual grading of American stakes races. While the criterion for the weighting is performance at age two, not prediction of performance at age three, it's interesting that in the last decade all three Triple Crown winners have topped the list, as did Riva Ridge and Spectacular Bid, winners of two jewels in the Triple Crown.

While the Jockey Club restricts its rankings to two-year-olds, both the *Daily Racing Form* and *The Blood-Horse* magazine publish free handicap weights for older horses. Even though they carry no official standing, such rankings have a great influence on racing secretaries in their assignment of weights for handicap races held early in the year.

## THE HISTORY OF THE HANDICAP RACE

The origin of the handicap race lies in the early match races, which were as much betting affairs as sporting contests. Because shipping horses any great distance was difficult, the most talented animals in any region met each other frequently and their relative raw abilities were well established. To make rematches a more interesting wagering opportunity, two horse owners would obtain the services of an impartial third party, who would examine the past records of the two competitors and assign a handicap to the one he considered the superior animal. If both owners accepted the handicap as fair, the match was on.

Through most of the 1700s, almost all races between groups of horses were conducted under weight-for-age conditions. While such races generally proved which was the best horse, they were often lopsided affairs with little betting interest. To increase the betting appeal of certain races, the present-day type of handicap was initiated. In the words of turf dictator Admiral Rous, "A handicap is intended to encourage bad horses and to put them on a par with the best. It is a racing lottery—a vehicle for gambling on an extensive scale, producing the largest field of horses at the smallest expense."

The first handicap, called the Subscription Handicap Plate, was run at Newmarket in 1785, and it attracted fourteen horses, a huge field for the time. The winner was the high-weight, a mare that carried 136 pounds. Six years later, another handicap, the Oatland Stakes, was run at Ascot. Both of the above were considered daring "experiments," and were frowned on by more traditional doyens of the turf. By 1839, though, with the inauguration of the famous Cesarewitch and Cambridgeshire races, handicaps became an integral part of the racing calendar.

The first "handicaps" run in the United States, around the time of the Civil War, were essentially weight-for-age events in which the certain horses were given "reductions" from scale weights to help fill fields. The first present-day-style handicap of any importance was the Suburban Handicap at Sheepshead Bay in 1884. The event immediately became the most talked-about race in the country. Entries closed in January of the year. Weights were assigned, then enormous pre-race wagering was taken during the months before the race. The 1886 race produced the heaviest betting on record, which stimulated the inauguration of the Brooklyn Handicap the next year at Gravesend. In 1891, the Metropolitan Handicap had its first running at Morris Park. These three famous races formed the Handicap Triple Crown. Because the weights of the winner are increased for the season's subsequent events, sweeping this triple crown is racing's most difficult task.

The handicap has today become the most popular type of stakes race for older horses, making up 75 percent of such races run in 1980. Additionally, handicaps make up a majority of the non-stakes features run at many tracks. These features attract the best horses on the grounds and get the largest purses. Nationally, the average non-stakes handicap purse was $11,785, twice the overall average purse and 11 percent more than the average purse for allowance races.

## HOW HANDICAPS ARE DETERMINED

One of the most frequently bandied-about clichés in racing is that "weight can stop a freight train." While it's true that weight is an undeniable factor in racing, arguments about how much weight produces how much advantage have raged unabated for centuries. Each racing secretary and each horseman have personal ideas about the relationship between added pounds and the number of lengths' advantage those pounds provide at each distance.

Despite the confusion, two general statements can be made. The first is that weight is far more important at distances over a mile than it is at sprint distances. The great sprinter Dr. Fager, for example, set a world record for the mile (1:32⅕) carrying 134 pounds, and he set an Aqueduct track record for seven furlongs (1:20⅕, two-fifths of a second off the world mark) carrying an awesome 139 pounds. No world or American record at distances over a mile has ever been set by a horse carrying over 130 pounds.

The second generalization involves weight carried in certain ranges. Weight is assumed to have the least effect on relative ability under 120 pounds. The ability to win carrying over 130 pounds, however, is the mark of a superior, championship horse. The short list of horses who've captured at least one of the three Handicap Triple Crown races carrying 130 pounds or more in the last twenty years forms one of racing's most elite circles. These horses are: Kelso, Forego, Damascus, Buckpasser, Dr. Fager, Gun Bow, Bold Lad, and Cox's Ridge.

The racing secretary begins with the weight-for-age scale when he sits down to examine the record of horses nominated for a handicap. For the rich Marlboro, run in September at a distance of a mile and an eighth, the scale calls for three-year-olds to carry 121 pounds, four-year-olds and up, 126 pounds. Scale weight is only assigned, however, to horses of the very top caliber. Although older horses are the high-weights in almost all handicaps, even in the very best handicaps run in 1978—those with gross purses in excess of $100,000—in only eleven of fifty-seven was the high-weight assigned scale weight or higher. The high weight carried was *under 120 pounds* in eleven of the fifty-seven, *under 125 pounds* in another twenty-nine.

How much under or over scale the weight assigned to a horse is depends upon the particular formula the racing secretary uses to equate weight with lengths at each distance. A rough consensus is that four to six pounds equals a length at distances under a mile; two to three pounds at a mile to a mile and a quarter; one pound to a length at distances over a mile and a quarter. These allowances fit into the first generalization, that weight is a more significant factor the longer the distance run is.

In determining the relative weights carried by horses in a race, the racing secretary's purpose is to prevent a preponderance of races from being won by overwhelming favorites, yet not to pile on so much weight that the favorite has no chance to win. That they do this job well is

reflected by the following results: On the average, favorites win 33 percent of all races run; among the richest handicaps run in 1978 in which the high-weight carried 126 pounds or less, the high-weight won 33 percent of the time. That these races were more interesting *betting* races is vividly demonstrated by the fact that only three of the forty races were won by odds-on favorites.

While weight differences below scale help to even out the competition, one of the truisms of racing is that the great horses that carry over-scale weight are less frequently stopped by it. Of the rich handicaps run in 1978 in which the high weight carried was 126 pounds or over, 53 percent were won by that high-weighted horse. The highest weight of the year was the 134 pounds assigned to Seattle Slew in the mile-and-an-eighth Stuyvesant Handicap at Aqueduct. Despite giving nineteen pounds to the second-weighted horse, the Triple Crown winner roared to a three-and-a-quarter-length triumph.

Every horse, however, has an upper limit to the weight it can carry successfully. Forego, for example, achieved one of the great victories in the last decade when, despite carrying 137 pounds, he beat Honest Pleasure (who carried 119 pounds) in the 1976 mile-and-an-eighth Marlboro Cup. However, the gallant gelding reached his limit the next year when he lost by a neck, carrying 138 pounds, in the mile-and-a-quarter Suburban Handicap, then trailed the winner by eleven lengths, carrying 137 pounds, in the mile-and-a-half Brooklyn Handicap.

Thus, the final step taken by a handicapper when weighting horses is adjusting the assignments based on recent performances. A horse that wins at a certain distance will carry more weight next time against similar company at the same distance. The amount of extra weight is determined by the margin of victory. The more a horse competes in handicap races, the clearer picture both the racing secretary and the horseplayer get of the weight limit above which the horse is unable to win.

Trainers, looking for an edge, often vociferously disagree with the racing secretary's assessment about that upper limit. In racing, however, for non-stakes races, the higher the purse, the stiffer the competition. Handicap races have the richest purses of all non-stakes events, so horsemen have to accept the penalties assigned by the racing secretary in order to compete.

While the weight assigned by the racing secretary is what keeps higher-class animals from having an overwhelming edge, one might wonder what keeps owners of lower-class horses from cluttering up the fields of these rich races in order to take advantage of huge weight edges. One reason is that huge weight advantages seldom compensate for large differences in class. In not a single one of those fifty-seven handicaps referred to above did a low-weighted horse receiving more than a scale-weight advantage win the race. The second factor preventing frivolous entries is track rules that usually give *preference* to high-weights if more horses enter than can be accommodated by the starting gate. That is, if only twelve horses can start but twenty are entered, the twelve high-weights, as determined by the racing secretary, are the starters.

## GREAT HORSES: THE GREAT GELDINGS—EXTERMINATOR, KELSO, FOREGO

Perhaps the saddest effect of the current economic structure of racing is that so many great champions spend so little time on the track before being retired to the breeding shed. Mitigating this in America, however, are the rich handicaps that provide showcases for talented geldings. In most foreign countries, geldings are barred from classic races and find little opportunity to race. In America, racing fans have been able to watch champion geldings compete season after season. Few horses have competed so gallantly or commanded such public attention as the three great handicap champions of this century: Exterminator, Kelso and Forego.

### Exterminator

One of the great Horatio Alger stories in racing began in 1918 when Willis Sharp Kilmer purchased a three-year-old gelding named Exterminator, who had won a grand total of $1,350 as a two-year-old. Kilmer bought the gelding to serve as a trial horse to tune up his two-year-old champion, Sun Briar, for the Kentucky Derby. Exterminator showed well in workouts, but Kilmer, who thought so much of Sun Briar that he named his lavish estate after him, scoffed at the "trial" horse's ability, saying, "I don't consider Exterminator in the same class as Sun Briar."

Suddenly, however, Sun Briar went lame, and Kilmer found himself with Exterminator as his Derby horse. The gelding went postward on May 11, 1918, as the thirty-to-one long shot in his very first race of the year. To everyone's surprise, he roared through the mud to win the coveted crown by a length.

That victory launched one of the most remarkable careers in racing. A big, ungainly horse who was affectionately known as "Old Bones," Exterminator started one hundred times through the age of nine. He won fifty races, was out of the money only sixteen times, and earned over a quarter of a million dollars. Exterminator triumphed at sixteen different tracks at distances from five and a half furlongs to two and a quarter miles, carrying as much as 138 pounds. Often referred to as the "supreme weight carrier," Exterminator got better as he got older. As a seven-year-old in 1922, he won ten out of sixteen races, and only twice carried less than 130 pounds. His performance was so distinguished that he has remained one of the only fourteen horses allotted a slot in the *Daily Racing Form*'s Hall of Fame.

*Racing Record:*

| STS. | 1ST | 2ND | 3RD | EARNINGS |
|------|-----|-----|-----|----------|
| 100 | 50 | 17 | 17 | $252,996 |

EXTERMINATOR, by *McGee out of Fair Empress by Jim Gore

## Kelso

Just as Willis Kilmer's purchase of Exterminator is a story of luck, the breeding of Kelso is a story of love and intuition. Mrs. Richard DuPont was determined to breed her mare, Maid of Flight, to the stallion, Your Host, who had suffered a shoulder injury so severe he was almost destroyed. Mrs. DuPont wanted a foal to name after her friend, Kelso Everett, who was a good "hostess." Kelso turned out to be an ugly, under-sized foal, but from the moment of his birth he won the heart of his owner.

He took longer to prove himself on the racetrack. As a yearling, he was gelded in the hope that it would help him grow. He won his first outing at age two in September 1959, and followed with two seconds, but as a three-year-old he entirely missed the Triple Crown races, and didn't go to the post the first time until June 22. That race, however, was a smashing ten-length victory, followed by a twelve-length triumph in an allowance race at Aqueduct. Kelso stumbled in his first stakes outing of the year at Arlington Park, but followed with six straight smashing stakes triumphs, including a victory over older horses in the Jockey Club Gold Cup. At the end of the year, Kelso became the first horse since voting began in 1936 to be named champion three-year-old without a Triple Crown victory, and he capped that by being voted Horse of the Year.

His next campaign produced an even more important achievement. Kelso joined his great-great-great-grandfather, Whisk Broom II, and Tom Fool as the only winners of the coveted Handicap Triple Crown, sweeping the Metropolitan, Suburban and Brooklyn Handicaps. He added an eight-length triumph in the Woodward Stakes and a second straight Jockey Club Gold Cup before faltering in the Washington, D.C., International. His reward was a second straight Horse of the Year award.

For most horses, Kelso's achievements would have constituted a career, but the gelding affectionately known as "Kelly" went on to win twenty of thirty-five races as a five-, six- and seven-year-old. He was named Horse of the Year each season, for an unprecedented total of five straight nominations as the best racehorse in America. By the time he was retired at age nine, he had won a record $1,977,896, a total that stood until 1979.

*Racing Record:*

| STS. | 1ST | 2ND | 3RD | EARNINGS |
|------|-----|-----|-----|----------|
| 63 | 39 | 12 | 2 | $1,977,896 |

KELSO, by Your Host out of Maid of Flight by Count Fleet

## Forego

Forego was foaled in 1970, the same year as Secretariat. While the young Secretariat showed championship potential as soon as he started to grow, Forego was achieving an awesome reputation as an unmanageable rogue. The huge colt displayed an ungentlemanly interest in fillies, and he had the painful and dangerous habit of savaging with his teeth any human who came near. In desperation, his owner, Lazy F Ranch, had him gelded.

The gelding eventually made him trainable, but Forego didn't get to the races until age three. He "broke his maiden" on the second try and added credible second-place finishes in the Hutcheson Stakes and the Florida Derby, but was a distant fourth as a twenty-eight-to-one shot in Secretariat's record-smashing Kentucky Derby triumph. Not until fall, with convincing victories in Aqueduct's Roamer and Discovery handicaps, did Forego begin to show signs of greatness.

That supreme talent was apparent right from the beginning of Forego's four-year-old campaign, as he opened with four straight stakes victories. The handsome bay, at seventeen hands impossible to miss even in a crowd of horses, began to win widespread affection from the crowd that loved his thrilling late charges. Horsemen were in awe of Forego's incredible versatility. At the end of 1974, he won the one-and-a-half-mile Woodward Stakes by a neck, then came back three weeks later to beat the best sprinters in the nation by three and a half lengths in the seven-furlong Vosburgh Handicap. Three weeks later, he rolled to a smashing victory over a fine field of distance horses in the grueling two-mile Jockey Club Gold Cup. At the end of this campaign, Forego won three Eclipse Awards: Best Older Horse or Gelding; Best Sprinter; and, of course, Horse of the Year.

He followed with two more Horse of the Year campaigns in 1975 and 1976. In both years, he won two legs of the Handicap Triple Crown, the second year losing the coveted honor in the Suburban Handicap by a heart-breaking nose to Foolish Pleasure. That 1976 campaign was capped, however, by one of the most remarkable victories in racing history in the Marlboro Cup. Honest Pleasure, carrying eighteen pounds less than Forego's hefty 137 impost, moved out to a huge lead in the one-and-a-quarter-mile contest. At the top of the stretch, Forego looked totally out of the race, but jockey Bill Shoemaker moved the huge gelding out into the middle of the sloppy track. Forego started to gobble up lengths in an astounding stretch run that ended with him sticking a head in front in the last stride.

Two years later, Forego was finally forced into retirement by a bad left ankle that had plagued him throughout his entire career. He finished just $40,000 short of passing Kelso to head the all-time money-winning list.

*Racing Record:*

| STS. | 1ST | 2ND | 3RD | EARNINGS |
|------|-----|-----|-----|----------|
| 57 | 34 | 9 | 7 | $1,938,957 |

FOREGO, by *Forli out of Lady Golconda by Hasty Road

# The Allowance Race

The amount of time needed to analyze past performances and assign appropriate weights makes it impossible for a racing secretary to card more than two or three handicaps per week. For the majority of races, the racing secretary sets standard weights based on the weight-for-age scale. Then, to provide for more even competition, he establishes conditions based on *number of races won* and/or *amount of purse money won* under which certain horses are *allowed* to carry less than the standard weight.

Many stakes races are run under such *allowance conditions*. So are most claiming races, such as the example below from Atlantic City:

**SEVENTH RACE**       **CLAIMING 7 PURSE $7,500. FOR FILLIES AND MARES, THREE YEARS OLD AND UPWARD.**

| | |
|---|---|
| Three-Year-Olds | 116 lbs. |
| Older | 122 lbs. |
| Non-winners of two races | |
|   since April 6, allowed | 2 lbs. |
|     a race since then | 4 lbs. |
|     a race since March 30 | 6 lbs. |

**CLAIMING PRICE $22,500**
**for each $1,000 to $18,500**     1 lb.
(Races where entered for $17,500 or less not considered.)

                       **SIX FURLONGS**

While the running of races under allowance conditions goes back to the early days of racing, *allowance races* are a more recent development. They stem from the need to provide racing opportunities for horses too good or too valuable to be risked in claiming races, but who are not ready or able to compete with the highest-quality horses in stakes or handicaps.

Since the kind of weight spread possible under allowance conditions couldn't compensate for the wide range of ability within racing's "middle class," racing secretaries began to card races with certain *conditions of entry* based on the number and kind of races run and/or purse earnings. Because these were the same criteria used in allowance conditions, these races were called *allowance races*. Allowance races now make up about 15 percent of the races run annually at U.S. tracks.

Because the purpose of such races is to bridge the rather considerable gap between the large numbers of *claiming horses* and the relatively small group of *stakes performers,* the caliber of competition in an allowance contest varies considerably. In looking at a horse's past performances in *The Daily Racing Form,* the designation "Allowance" for its last race tells much less about the company it met than either the designation "Clm. $20,000" or "Stakes." Evaluating the caliber of competition depends instead on looking back to see the conditions for entry of the race and the purse for which it was run.

Since at any track there are far more lower-quality claiming horses than stakes performers, more of the allowance races carded are for horses at the lower end of the scale. The single most common allowance race is for horses that have just broken their maiden and for horses that have been campaigning successfully at the upper end of the track's claiming scale. The entry condition for this most basic allowance race usually reads, *"For non-winners of a race other than maiden, claiming, or starter."* The purse value of such a race is the lowest of any allowance race; comparing that purse to those of claiming races shows at what dollar figure the claiming and allowance classes at that track overlap. At Fairmount Park, for example, the lowest allowance purse is $4,000, the same as races for $7,000 claimers. At Atlantic City, the purse is $6,500, the same as for $14,000 claimers. At the Meadowlands, the $12,000 purse is the same as for $25,000 claimers; at Santa Anita, the $17,000 purse equals that for $30,000 claimers. Thus, a horse at the Meadowlands, for example, that goes from a $25,000 claiming race to a race for "non-winners of a race other than maiden, claiming or starter" is not making a significant class jump. That same $25,000 claimer from the Meadowlands who is shipped to compete in the lowest-level allowance race at Atlantic City, however, has an enormous class advantage.

After winning at the lowest allowance class, horses move up to compete in races with conditions for "non-winners of two races other than maiden, claiming or starter." Many horses are unable to make this jump and go back to the claiming ranks. The number of horses that fall by the wayside increases greatly by the time conditions read "non-winners of four races other than maiden, claiming or starter." The significance of the class jump in this progression is shown by the increase in purses offered for such races at the Meadowlands:

| CONDITIONS | PURSE |
|---|---|
| Non-winners of one race | $12,000 |
| Non-winners of two races | 14,000 |
| Non-winners of three races | 17,000 |
| Non-winners of four races | 20,000 |

The $8,000 increase in purse offered from the bottom to the top is equivalent to a $20,000 increase in claiming price at the same track.

The horses that reach the top of this ladder are close to stakes caliber. The racing secretary, in arranging races for these animals, groups them with stakes horses coming off a lay-off who need prep races before big stakes and with horses that move back and forth between stakes and allowance races. The conditions for entry in a race for such horses varies with the exact past performances of those horses at the track who need racing opportunities. The only general statement about such conditions is that they usually involve having won a *certain number of races* at a *stated purse value to the winner* within a *stated period of time* and, in some cases, at a *stated distance or over*. An example is the following race from Santa Anita.

EIGHTH RACE       ALLOWANCE PURSE $40,000. FOR FOUR-YEAR-OLDS AND UPWARD WHICH ARE NON-WINNERS OF $19,000 TWICE AT ONE MILE AND ONE-EIGHTH OR OVER SINCE JULY 23.

| | |
|---|---|
| Four-year-olds | 121 lbs. |
| Older | 122 lbs. |
| Non-winners of two such races at one mile or over since then allowed | 3 lbs. |
| of such a race at one mile and one-eighth or over since October 4 | 5 lbs. |
| of such a race since July 23 or two such races of $16,000 at one mile or over since June 1 | 8 lbs. |

(Claiming races not considered)
**\*ONE MILE AND ONE-EIGHTH (ON THE TURF)**

The dollar value given (e.g., non-winners of $19,000) refers only to the *amount of money received for winning a race*. Since at Santa Anita the winner of a race gets 55 percent of the total purse, a horse would win $19,000 by capturing a race with a total purse of over $35,000.

Since the average racing fan doesn't have at his fingertips the past performances of all horses at the track, he has a very difficult time comparing the quality of two such allowance races by comparing conditions. The best indication of the quality of such a race is the purse offered. For example, the above race at Santa Anita, with a purse of $40,000, is obviously for stakes-class horses. At the Meadowlands, entry conditions such as "for three-year-olds and upward which have not won $6,605 three times since October 8, 1978" are undecipherable in themselves. However, the purse offered is $25,000, $5,000 higher than that offered for "non-winners of four races other than maiden, claiming or starter." The racing secretary obviously intends this race to attract horses who've moved up from that level.

Horses who are unable to compete successfully at the next highest allowance level are said to have "run out of conditions." These horses have to be either dropped back into the claiming ranks or shipped to another track.

# The Claiming Race

The allowance race was developed to serve as a stepping-stone for horses with the potential to move up to join the small percentage of animals able to compete successfully in stakes and handicap company. The vast majority of horses needed to fill the majority of races at most tracks have no such potential. The easiest way for a racing secretary to produce competitive contests between such animals is to pass the responsibility for appraising a horse's class to the owner and trainer. The way this is accomplished is the claiming race, in which the horseman has to *balance the chances of capturing a stated purse with the risk of losing the horse for a stated claiming price.* Such claiming races make up over 70 percent of all races run in the United States.

## THE HISTORY OF THE CLAIMING RACE

The idea of keeping owners honest by making them risk the loss of their horse at a stated price in order to enter a race dates back to the very beginnings of Thoroughbred racing. The first on record took place in England in 1689, where the conditions of a race stipulated that the winner could be purchased for 40 guineas by "him that throws most at three throws with two dice." Such stipulations were unpopular with owners, however, and few such races were run until the mid-1800s. By that time, in both Great Britain and the United States, the purpose of carding races was to create betting opportunities. The most effective method of creating large, well-matched fields that encouraged heavy betting was this old-fashioned concept that was called the "selling" race.

The name "selling race" was applied because the conditions of the race stated that the winner would be sold at auction immediately after the race, with a stated price serving as the opening bid. The winning owner could bid on his horse, but rival owners were free to run the price up, forcing the owner who had entered his horse too low either to lose the animal or pay a higher sum to buy the horse back. The difference between the stated price and the final bid went, in some cases, to the owner of the second-place horse (to compensate for getting beat by an undervalued animal). In some cases it went to the track, to be added to the purse pool; in other cases, it was divided between the track and the losing owners.

Numerous variations on the above concept sprang up. In some races, only owners with horses in the race were allowed to bid. In others, the winner could be claimed, for the stated price, by other owners in the race, with the order of finish determining the preference. There were also races in which any runner could be claimed, with the order of preference again determined by finish position.

All of these races admirably accomplished the purpose of discouraging owners from entering their horses for too low a price. Entering a horse at too high a price, on the other hand, was futile, for the horse had little chance of earning a share of the purse. As a result, these races tended to be competitive and popular with the betting public.

As more such races were carded, however, post-race selling became increasingly unpopular with horsemen. For one thing, the turnover of horses was tremendous. More importantly, since buyers could wait until after a horse proved its condition before making a bid or submitting a claim, the trainer who had worked hard to improve a horse was punished as severely as an owner who dropped his horse in value to try to get a purse. The best horsemen ended up losing the most horses.

In response to pressure from horsemen, post-race selling gave way to a system under which the buyer had to make an irrevocable commitment to purchase a horse at a stated price, *before the race was run*. Thus the modern claiming race was born.

## GREAT HORSES: STYMIE

In golf, a stymie is an attempt to block or impede one's opponent. No better name could have been chosen for the gallant chestnut who was to become the "people's horse," the object of the unbridled affection of racing fans all over the country. Stymie was the epitome of the "come from behind" horse, not only in his racing style, but in his career. This symbol of hope for all trainers everywhere rose from the ranks of $1,500 claimers to top the all-time leading money-winners list.

For his time, Stymie's breeding was unusually all-American—he had no foreign horse in his first three generations. He was closely inbred: Man o' War had sired the dam of both his sire and his dam. His breeding indicated a horse of incredible stamina.

Such stamina, however, often means a slow development of speed. Stymie showed so little

promise that in his third race, as a two-year-old in 1943, he was dropped into a $1,500 claimer, in which he was picked up by trainer Hirsch Jacobs. Jacobs had led the nation's trainers in races won for eleven years, but his success had come primarily with cheap claimers. It was the fortuitous claim of Stymie that was to change his career, boosting him into the ranks of top trainers of stakes horses.

It took a long time after Jacobs' haltering of Stymie for the value of his investment to become apparent. Ten times after his claim, Jacobs entered Stymie in claiming races; there were no takers. Stymie finally worked his way out of claiming ranks, but in his first two years he failed to capture a stakes race. He paid for himself with $52,260 in earnings, but that was accomplished through very hard work: fifty-seven starts, seven victories.

As a reward for that work, Jacobs turned Stymie out for a very long rest at the end of 1944. When he came back to the races he was a different horse. At age four, Stymie reeled off six stakes wins and was only out of the money in two of nineteen races. His $225,000 in winnings led to his being named Handicap Horse of the Year. Rested again before 1946, he responded with eight victories, nineteen of twenty finishes in the money and $238,650 in winnings. After spirited back-and-forth jousting with the great horses Armed and Assault, Stymie finally moved into the all-time money-winning lead in 1947. Only an unfortunate cracking of a sesmoid at mid-season in his age-seven campaign prevented him from becoming the first equine millionaire, and this $1,500 claimer finished his career as the greatest claim of all time.

*Race Record:*

| STS. | 1ST | 2ND | 3RD | EARNINGS |
|------|-----|-----|-----|----------|
| 131  | 35  | 33  | 28  | $918,485 |

## THE CLAIMING PROCEDURE

Claiming is conducted at every track under rules established by state racing commissions. In most states, the privilege of claiming is restricted to owners who have started at least one horse at that current race meeting. This means that a new owner has to first purchase a horse privately before being able to play the claiming game. Big stables with a large number of starters also have a big advantage early in a meeting. As a result, restricted claiming has come under attack from people who believe racing should be less of an "insider's game." In recent years, California, Louisiana and Illinois, among a handful of states, have passed rules that "open" claiming to any individual who meets the requirements for the granting of an owner's license.

States with both open and restricted claiming have similar rules to discourage frivolous claiming. In every state, for thirty days after being claimed, a horse cannot run for a claiming price less than *25 percent higher than the price for which it was obtained*. That is, a horse claimed for $10,000 must be entered for at least $12,500 for the first thirty days. Horsemen refer to a horse being "in jail" during this thirty-day period.

In addition to the above restrictions, most states prohibit an owner from either selling a claimed horse privately or from shipping the claimed horse to another track during the duration of the meeting at which the horse was claimed. The purpose of this rule is to prohibit horsemen at one track from "raiding" another track and depleting the reservoir of horses available for racing there.

An owner wishing to claim a horse in any given race puts his claim in a sealed envelope and drops it into a locked box in the racing secretary's office by the mandated "closing time" (usually ten to fifteen minutes before post time). The amount of the claim plus the sales tax due on the purchase must be on deposit with the horseman's bookkeeper. At the closing time, the box is opened by the stewards. If the claim is in order, the person making it becomes the owner of the horse "when the start of the race is effected, whether it [the horse] be alive or dead, sound or unsound or injured before or during the race or after it." If more than one claim is made for a horse, lots are drawn to determine which claimant gets the animal. The owner from whom the

claim was made doesn't find out that the horse has been lost until after the race, when an official comes up and places a tag on the horse's halter (that's why a horse in a claiming race is commonly referred to as "racing for a tag"). Although the ownership officially changes hands when the race is started, the original owner is entitled to all purse money won in the race.

## THE CLAIMING PRICE

Below is a table of the distribution of races and purses by claiming price in 1980:

| CLAIMING PRICE | NO. OF RACES | % OF RACES | % OF PURSES | AVE. PURSE |
|---|---|---|---|---|
| $0 to $1,999 | 3,914 | 5.7% | 1.4% | $ 1,607 |
| $2,000–$2,999 | 9,650 | 14.1% | 4.9% | 2,301 |
| $3,000–$3,999 | 5,106 | 7.5% | 3.5% | 3,121 |
| $4,000–$4,999 | 2,632 | 3.9% | 2.0% | 3,426 |
| $5,000–$5,999 | 4,324 | 6.3% | 3.8% | 3,968 |
| $6,000–$6,999 | 2,652 | 3.9% | 2.7% | 4,512 |
| $7,000–$7,999 | 1,173 | 1.7% | 1.4% | 5,224 |
| $8,000–$8,999 | 1,810 | 2.7% | 2.1% | 5,187 |
| $9,000–$9,999 | 37 | .1% | .1% | 6,270 |
| $10,000–$14,999 | 4,330 | 6.4% | 6.3% | 6,621 |
| $15,000–$19,999 | 1,917 | 2.8% | 3.5% | 8,082 |
| $20,000 & up | 2,922 | 4.3% | 7.5% | 11,554 |
| | 40,467 | 59.3% | 39.2% | $ 4,355 |

At the upper end of the claiming scale, as we've seen, ability is equal to or better than that of allowance class horses. The average purse for an allowance race was $10,602; the average for a claimer involving horses worth $20,000 or more was $11,554.

These higher-value claiming races make up a little more than than 4 percent of the races run every year. At most tracks around the country, the staple is the cheap claiming race. More races are run each year for $1,000 to $3,000 claimers than for all allowance horses combined. Nearly a third of all races run in the United States are for horses racing for a claiming price of under $5,000. Races for claimers under $10,000 make up almost half the races run annually. These horses race for substantially lower purses; to make money for their owners and trainers they have to race more frequently and they suffer far more than their share of physical problems. By any measure, theirs is the lowest class of horse racing.

While claiming price is a rough indication of class, it is an unreliable measure of exact class when comparing two horses racing at different tracks, at different times of the year at the same track, or of different ages at the same track.

First, the difference between tracks. On the same day, in the fall of 1979, the purse for a $3,500 claimer for four-year-olds and up was *$2,800* at the Finger Lakes; *$3,700* at Penn National; and *$4,500* at Keystone. Placed in the same race, the winner of the race at Keystone would in all likelihood trounce the winner of the race at the Finger Lakes. Why, then, are they running for the same claiming price? The major single factor is the age-old influence of supply and demand. The Finger Lakes is located in upstate New York, far from other racing circuits. The horses produced by the still-relatively-small local breeding industry race, not in these "open" claimers, but in richer races restricted to "New York-breds." As a result, the owner who has a horse claimed finds it much more difficult and expensive to replace that horse than does the owner at Keystone, which is within a hundred-mile radius of a dozen other tracks and several major breeding areas.

For precisely the same reason, the claiming price of the same horse fluctuates considerably from season to season on some circuits. In the fall, for example, many major stables ship their horses from the New York tracks to Florida and California. As a result of this exodus and the resulting shortage of racing-fit horses, the value of a $7,500 claimer jumps to $10,000 to $15,000. In late spring, when the major stables return, the value of the horse drops back again.

Finally, the claiming price of horses racing at the same track at the same time often depends on the age and experience of the animal. Two- and three-year-olds tend to be healthier than older horses. Also, because they are still maturing, the limit of their ability has not been conclusively proven. Thus, their claiming prices reflect potential, and are higher for the same level of demonstrated ability than are the claiming prices of older horses. This inflation in claiming prices is reflected in the purse values for the following races at Rockingham Park:

*Claiming Price: $10,000*
Distance: 5½ or 6 furlongs

| AGE | PURSE |
|---|---|
| two-year-old maidens | $4,000 |
| two-year-olds | 5,000 |
| three-year-olds | 5,500 |
| three-year-olds and up | 6,000 |

## WRITING THE CLAIMING RACE

At tracks with a well-rounded mix of horses of different abilities, the racing secretary can assure competitive contests by writing conditions of entry based solely on *age, sex, distance* and *claiming* price. Differences of ability for horses that meet the entry requirements are adjusted by writing *allowance conditions.* In addition, horses of slightly lower value are given weight allowances if entered for a lower claiming price within a stated range. An example of this typical claiming race is the one below from the Atlantic City Race Course condition book for June 13:

**SIXTH RACE          CLAIMING**
**6  PURSE $6,500. FOR THREE-YEAR-**
**OLDS**                          122 lbs.
Non-winners of two races since April 13,
allowed                           2 lbs.
                 a race since then      4 lbs.
                 a race since April 6   6 lbs.
**CLAIMING PRICE $14,000 for each**
**$1,000 to $12,000**             2 lbs.
(Races where entered for $11,000 or less not considered.)

**SIX FURLONGS**

Under the above conditions, a horse that hadn't entered a race for horses of more than $11,000 value in the last two months would carry 116 pounds, an allowance of 6 pounds off the 122-pound stated impost. If the horse's owner wished to enter it for $13,000, instead of $14,000, the weight carried would be 114 pounds; if entered for $12,000, the weight would drop another 2 pounds to 112.

For the tracks at the low end of the purse scale, however, the vast majority of the horses are in a very narrow range of claiming price. At these tracks, the racing secretaries are forced to separate the horses at each claiming price into a number of classes, *using the same kind of entry conditions written for allowance races.* At the Finger Lakes, for example, a condition book may contain as many as 9 different classes of races for $2,500 claimers.

At the bottom of the scale for any claiming price is the race for "non-winners of two races lifetime"—in other words, a race for animals whose only victory came in a maiden race. At some tracks, the lowest race may read "non-winners of a race in 1980–81." Steps upward would be "non-winners of a race in 1981," "non-winners of two races in 1981," etc. At the top of the heap at any level is the "open" claimer, the conditions of which simply read, "For three-year-olds and upward. Claiming price $2,500."

These classes within a claiming price are extremely important to the horseman and horseplayer alike. The jump in ability from one step to the next can be as influential in determining the winner of a race as a $5,000 jump in claiming price at a major track. Since the purse offered for classes within one claiming price may be the same, a judgment of class has to come from reading the conditions.

## STARTER ALLOWANCES, STARTER HANDICAPS AND OPTIONAL CLAIMERS

Owners of claiming horses have to live with the risk that a tag may be placed on the halter of their horses after any race. Many tracks occasionally give owners a breather by scheduling races for classes of claiming horses in which the entrants *are not subject to claim.*

One common such race is the *starter allowance.* An example is the one described below, run at Golden Gate Fields:

### NINTH RACE
**STARTER ALLOWANCE PURSE $8,500. For four-year-olds and upward, which have started for a claiming price of $12,500 or less in 1979–80 and since that start have not won a race other than maiden or claiming or a claiming or starter race exceeding $12,500.**

|  |  |
|---|---|
|  | 122 lbs. |
| Non-winners of two starter races since December 10 | 3 lbs. |
| two such races since November 1 | 5 lbs. |
| one such race since December 10 | 8 lbs. |

(Maiden, starter and claiming races for $10,000 or less not considered.)

**ONE MILE AND ONE-EIGHTH**

Eligibility for a starter allowance is determined by placing an *upper limit* to the claiming price at which a horse has won during the eligibility period. To enter the race, a horse cannot have won a race when entered for more than $12,500 since starting for $12,200. Weights are assigned under allowance conditions.

A second kind of race for claiming horses is the *starter handicap,* such as the one below, run at Pimlico:

### THIRD RACE    STARTER/HANDICAP "THE BELVEDERE HANDICAP"
**Closing Wednesday, March 12**
**Purse $8,000. A Handicap for Three-Year-Olds and Upward, which have started for a Claiming Price of $5,000 or less since September 30, 1979.** Weights and Declarations by 9:30 A.M., Thursday, March 13. **ONE MILE AND ONE-SIXTEENTH**

Eligibility for the starter handicap is determined by the *lowest claiming price* a horse has started at during the eligibility period. Unlike the starter allowance, there are no upper limits to the kind of race the horse may have won during the same period. Because many tracks prohibit claiming on the first day of any race meeting, some stables enter horses far below their normal value on those days simply to make them eligible for these starter races. Since these races do attract horses of more widely varying classes than starter allowances, racing secretaries handicap the races, assigning weights based on their appraisal of individual past performances.

A third kind of race, which is similar to the starter allowance, is the *optional claimer,* such as the race below from Oaklawn Park:

**SIXTH RACE — (Optional Claiming)**
**Purse $6,500. For Four-year-olds and Upward entered to be claimed for $7,500**

and those which have started for $7,500 or less and have not won for a claiming price over $7,500 or a race other than claiming since last starting for $7,500 or less. Four-year-olds, 121 lbs. Older, 122 lbs. Non-winners of three races since October 30 allowed 3 lbs.; two races, 6 lbs.; a race, 9 lbs. If entered to be claimed for $7,500 allowed 3 lbs. (Horses not to be claimed preferred.)
**SIX FURLONGS**
1st Call_____ 2nd Call_____

For these races, any owner can enter any horse to be claimed at the stated price. Horses that are not entered to be claimed, however, are subject to an *upper limit* to the claiming price at which they have won, just like in starter allowances. If a horse entered not to be claimed wins such a race, it has to compete in a race where it is subject to be claimed at that price, before competing in another optional claimer.

# The Maiden Race

Class in racing is primarily determined by the caliber of races won. For that reason, races for *maidens,* horses which have never won a race, are the lowest class of race at any track.

This doesn't mean, of course, that maiden horses don't have any class, just that the class is yet to be defined. Three months after competing in the same maiden race, one animal may be running successfully in rich stakes events, while another may be repeatedly trounced in cheap maiden claimers. Predicting performance from potential is the most difficult judgment in racing.

Most horses make their first starts in non-claiming maiden races, which at Eastern tracks are called "maiden special-weight" races (special weight simply meaning the races are run at other than scale weights). The conditions for such races are the simplest of any races run. An example below is from Santa Anita.

**FOURTH RACE                MAIDEN**
**PURSE $14,000. FOR MAIDEN COLTS**
**AND GELDINGS THREE YEARS**
**OLD.**                        118 lbs.
**ONE MILE AND ONE-SIXTEENTH**

Other than meeting age and gender requirements, the only conditions a horse has to meet to start for the first time in such a race are a specified number of timed workouts (usually three) and a certificate from the track's starter certifying that it has been properly schooled from the starting gate. Exactly how ready the horse is to race, however, depends on the abilities and intention of its trainer and owner. Some trainers win a very high percentage of races with their first-time starters. Others consider the first race or two part of the training program, and instruct the riders not to push the horse until later starts.

About a third of every crop of Thoroughbreds get to the racetrack at age two, and about 40 percent of those break their maiden. The great majority of the rest of the horses that survive training well enough to get to the track make their first appearance at age three. Only the rare horse hasn't revealed its potential by the time it reaches age four. The abilities of maidens age five and up are so limited that most tracks bar them from racing.

Between 20 percent and 25 percent of all horses break their maidens the first time out. Another quarter win the second time out. From then on, the chances of a horse winning decreases as the number of losses increases. Many non-winners are dropped out of non-claiming maiden races into maiden claimers, where they meet animals of generally more limited ability. Because maidens still haven't conclusively demonstrated their potential, however, maiden claiming prices are significantly inflated. The winner of a $20,000 maiden claimer is, in general, unlikely to be competitive in a $20,000 claiming race for winners.

Just as for other kinds of races, purse values for maiden races vary considerably from track to track. The purse for a non-claiming race for three-year-olds may be $15,000 at Aqueduct, $10,000 at Gulfstream Park and $7,000 at Suffolk Downs. While the average level of winners of such races increases with purse value, drops in class are not nearly as significant as drops in class for horses that have won races. The reason is that class isn't demonstrated *until a horse has won*. Some horses simply refuse to win; for these reluctant athletes, respectable finishes in "higher class" races doesn't necessarily mean that they're likely to change their habits when the level of company is changed.

# Groupings Within Kinds of Races

Conditions of entry and weight assignment largely define the kinds of races that make up the class ladder at racetracks. To make competition within classes even closer, racing secretaries additionally group horses by age and gender, as well as preferred distance and racing surface.

## AGE

When racing first began to flourish in England, horses weren't raced until they reached full maturity at about six years of age. The increasing cost of racing animals and the expense of maintaining them led to the pressure to race younger Thoroughbreds. By 1727, racing five-year-olds was common, and the first stakes for four-year-olds began a rise in popularity that culminated nineteen years later in the organization of the Epsom Derby, which redefined "classic" racing to mean the racing of these younger horses over dash distances.

Preparing horses for classic race at age three necessitated giving them racing experience at the tender age of two. The first two-year-old appeared in a match race at Newmarket in 1769. The first race carded specifically for these equine youngsters was run in November 1773. By 1775, two-year-old racing was firmly established.

Today, races are run in one of five age groupings: *two-year-olds, three-year-olds, four-year-olds, three-year-olds and up* and *four-year-olds and up*. Below is a table of the distribution of races by age groupings and purse:

*Summary of Runners by Age in 1980*

| AGE | NO. OF RUNNERS | % OF RUNNERS | % OF RACES | % OF EARNINGS | AVER. EARNINGS PER RUNNER |
|---|---|---|---|---|---|
| 2 | 11,561 | 17.9% | 8.8% | 11.9% | $4,610 |
| 3 | 18,151 | 28.1% | 15.7% | 33.4% | 8,270 |
| 3 and up | | | 49.4% | | |
| 4 | 13,647 | 21.2% | .8% | 24.4% | 8,058 |
| 4 and up | | | 25.3% | | |
| 5 | 8,505 | 13.2% | | 16.0% | 8,458 |
| 6 and up | 12,634 | 19.6% | | 14.3% | 5,091 |

## Two-Year-Olds

Two-year-old racing begins in early spring, as the most precocious youngsters compete in four- and five-furlong sprints. Many of the more highly regarded colts and fillies don't make their first appearances until late summer (many fashionable Eastern stables schedule the debuts of their promising two-year-olds for the Saratoga meeting in August). The first important stakes for juveniles are run at a distance of six furlongs in late summer; by November, distances have stretched to a mile and an eighth.

In 1980, 38 percent of the two-year-olds registered with the Jockey Club went to the racetrack. Of these 11,547 starters, 4,272 (37 percent) won a race. Since only 6,110 races for two-year-olds were run, the vast majority of these victories obviously came in maiden races. These maiden races have the fullest fields in all of racing—two-year-olds made up 17.9 percent of all starters, but two-year-old races were only 8.8 percent of races run. Two-year-olds never compete against older horses.

## Three-Year-Olds

Although every horse's official birthday is January 1, most don't reach the chronological age of three until sometime between March and May. That's the reason why, except for maiden races, three-year-olds seldom compete against older horses until late spring. Except for the important races leading to the Triple Crown and the major filly races, most races for three-year-olds before June are carded at a mile or less.

In 1980, 18,151 three-year-olds raced, the largest number for any age group. The 15.7 percent of all races run that are restricted to three-year-olds only are primarily grouped in the first half of the year. A whopping 49.4 percent of all races were open to three-year-olds and up; most of these are carded from May onward.

## Four-Year-Olds

Although horses don't reach physical maturity until age six, in racing they're consid-

ered fully mature by March of their fourth year. The 566 races restricted to "four-year-olds only" were run in January and February. The 25.3 percent of all races open to "four-year-olds and up" are generally carded before June, when three-year-olds begin to compete with their elders.

Most four-year-olds healthy enough to race continue to compete. By age five, most animals with breeding potential are retired to the farm; a far larger number have their careers or lives cut short by the accumulated wear and tear of racing too often, too young. In 1980, 13,647 four-year-olds raced, but only 8,505 five-year-olds. The quality of the five-year-olds racing, however, matched that of three- and four-year-olds. The average earnings per runner for five-year-olds is virtually identical to that of the younger horses.

The decline in ability, which is generally caused by the accumulation of physical problems, sets in increasingly by age six. In 1980, 12,634 horses age six and over raced; 83 percent of these were male (mostly geldings). Their average earnings, however, were nearly 40 percent lower than for five-year-olds, which reflects the fact that most older horses race at minor tracks.

# GENDER

Just as in every other area of life, racing people have their share of preconceptions about the relative abilities of the two genders. Genuine Risk's smashing triumph in the 1980 Kentucky Derby was a much-needed blow for "women's lib." It exposed many prejudices that just don't hold water under close examination.

Because of inherent differences in size and physical strength, it is true that the very top colts have an advantage over the very top fillies at distances over a mile. This, though, is not the reason that so few females have competed successfully against males in the last few decades. Rather, the reason is that so many rich stakes restricted to fillies and mares have been inaugurated, making it unnecessary for females to challenge males to win substantial prizes.

## GREAT HORSES: KINCSEM

According to a perhaps apocryphal story, on a dark night in 1876 gypsies broke into the barn of a noted Hungarian horseman. Although the barn contained forty expensive, handsome horses, the gypsies stole only one horse, a ewe-necked, mule-eared, sleepy-eyed, scrawny two-year-old filly. When the authorities captured the gypsy chief, they asked him why in heaven's name he had taken such an unlikely-looking animal. The gypsy replied that the filly had qualities far more important than beauty, and that she would be a far greater racehorse than any other in the barn.

The gypsy prophecy turned out to be one of the shrewdest in racing history. In the next four years Kincsem won *all 54 races in which she was entered*, establishing the most incredible racing record in the long history of the sport. Forty-one of her fifty-four triumphs came in European classic races. She won at distances from a half-mile to two and five-eighths miles; she won in Austria, Germany, France, England, Italy, Romania and Poland; she won over any kind of ground in any weather; she carried high weights as she beat male and female horses alike.

As amazing as her record was her disposition and racing style. Kincsem was an extremely lazy horse who hated training. This laziness even afflicted her at the start of races. Commonly, she dwelled badly at the start, chewing at grass and looking around at the scenery. Uncannily, though, she seemed to sense exactly how many lengths she could give away. By the end of the race she had stormed from behind to bury her opponents.

Only once in her long career did she come close to making a miscalculation. At the Grand Prix of Baden, Germany, in 1878, she had to make a ferocious rush in the stretch for a dead heat with a horse named Prince Giles. At that time, racing regulations in Germany called for a run-off before the results were made official. Kincsem promptly went back out and buried Prince Giles by five lengths to leave her record unblemished.

Kincsem's achievement is made even more remarkable by the tiring traveling conditions of the day. She had to be shuttled back and forth across Europe by railroad car, but she seemed to thrive on the travel and the attention. When her car passed, people lined the railbed to cheer. Kincsem began to demand the prerequisites of royalty. She would eat no food and drink no water other than that brought from her home farm in Hungary—at Baden, she once refused to touch a drop for two days until resupplied. She refused to enter the railroad car unless accompanied by her two best friends—her trainer and a disheveled formerly stray cat, which one writer described as "resembling a drunken charwoman."

After her fifty-fourth victory at age five, Kincsem was retired to breed. Among her five foals were no less than three stakes winners. Kincsem remained a champion in everything she did.

---

The dangers in judging ability by sex are most apparent in the rich turf races. Since tracks have to date carded few rich turf races for females, top female turf performers have regularly and successfully competed against males in such races as the Man o' War Stakes, the Turf Classic and the Washington International. The great Dahlia won the Washington, D.C., International in 1973, and was voted Grass Horse of the Year in 1974. Waya triumphed in both the Man o' War and the Turf Classic. In 1979, Trillion beat every contestant except the gelding Bowl Game in the richest turf events.

While it isn't true that colts will always beat fillies, it is true that at the major tracks a female that moves from an allowance or higher value claiming race restricted to her own sex to similar open races against males is *moving up in class*. The reason is that many more females have breeding value. The owner of a potential broodmare will be reluctant to enter her for a claiming price that doesn't reflect a certain breeding value on top of the racing value. For that reason, the claiming price of a female averages 20 percent to 25 percent higher than for males of the same ability.

Because most horsemen feel that a mare's prime breeding years are from age six to age thirteen, most females are retired from the racetrack by age four or five. Those racing older than age six tend to be those who are infertile or those with conformational traits that make breeding them undesirable.

*Summary of Runners by Sex in 1980*

|  | NO. OF RUNNERS | % OF RUNNERS | % OF EARNINGS |
|---|---|---|---|
| Females | 24,692 | 38.3% | 35.3% |
| Males | 39,806 | 61.7% | 64.7% |

## DISTANCE

Horses that can win at longer distances are considered to have more "class" than pure sprinters. Racegoers also find longer races more interesting to watch and to wager on. For these reasons, racetracks offer larger purses to horses that compete at longer distances.

For example, in the same condition book at Aqueduct, $16,000 claimers "four-year-olds and upwards" who entered a six-furlong race competed for a purse of $10,000; those that entered a nine-furlong race were offered $11,000. The purse differential at the Meadowlands between six-furlong races and races over a mile for "non-winners of a race other than maiden, claiming or starter" was $2,000.

The table below shows the preponderance of sprint races and the increase of purse with distance:

*Summary of Races by Distance in 1980*

| DISTANCE | NO. OF RACES | % OF RACES | CUM. % LESS THAN | AVER. PURSE PER RACE |
|---|---|---|---|---|
| Less than 6 furlongs | 9,599 | 15.4% | 15.4% | $ 2,826 |
| 6 furlongs | 26,108 | 42.0 | 57.4 | 5,838 |
| Between 6 and 7 furlongs | 4,921 | 7.9 | 65.3 | 4,963 |
| 7 furlongs | 2,935 | 4.7 | 70.0 | 7,518 |
| Betw. 7 and 8 furlongs | 202 | .3 | 70.3 | 7,672 |
| 1 mile | 6,053 | 9.7 | 80.0 | 6,237 |
| Mile, 70 yds. | 3,762 | 6.1 | 86.1 | 5,896 |
| 1$\frac{1}{16}$ miles | 6,442 | 10.4 | 96.5 | 9,733 |
| 1$\frac{1}{8}$ miles | 1,182 | 1.9 | 98.4 | 20,860 |
| 1$\frac{3}{16}$ miles | 144 | .2 | 98.6 | 15,274 |
| 1$\frac{1}{4}$ miles | 343 | .6 | 99.2 | 26,164 |
| 1$\frac{3}{8}$ miles | 114 | .2 | 99.4 | 25,143 |
| 1$\frac{1}{2}$ miles | 100 | .2 | 99.6 | 48,518 |
| Over 1$\frac{1}{2}$ miles | 220 | .4 | 100.0 | 9,922 |

Omitted from above are all two-year-old races, which are conducted primarily at sprint distances.

## RACING SURFACE

In England and France, where race meetings consist of a few dozen races, all racing is done on grass, the best natural racing surface. However, in the United States during the last century, the vast majority of races have been conducted on dirt. The reasons are that no turf courses could withstand the wear and tear of nine or ten races a day, six days a week. Dirt tracks are far easier and less expensive to maintain under this kind of heavy use.

Recently, however, turf racing has enjoyed a revival in this country. Racing fans have come to increasingly appreciate the spectacle of grass racing, while horsemen appreciate the reduced strain turf racing places on their horses' legs. A number of tracks have added turf courses, and racing secretaries are carding more and more turf races. A large number of new, rich turf stakes races have been established.

The only bar to further increases in turf racing is the still unsolved problem of maintenance. Drainage in rainy weather is a particular problem, for soggy turf gets torn up badly by just a single race. A great deal of research and experimentation is being devoted to the building of more durable grass courses.

Given the limited number of races that can be carded on a turf course, racing secretaries tend to reserve the turf course for higher-class horses. A much higher percentage of stakes, handicaps and allowance races are run on the turf than claiming races. Purses tend to be higher and distances longer than for the average race.

One problem faced by horsemen interested in trying their animals on the turf is that most tracks severely limit training on the turf to reduce wear. This limited training is the reason why a large preponderance of grass races are won by horses that have been racing successfully on the turf, as opposed to horses racing successfully on dirt who move to the turf for the first time.

# The Trainer

While another profession has snared the title of "the world's oldest," horse training is certainly the world's oldest honorable profession. For the millennia from the dawn of civilization to the invention of the internal combustion engine, the horse was mankind's most valuable servant—but the horse was also an animal with a deeply inbred spirit that made bending the animal to man's will a demanding task. That's why the horse trainer had achieved a lofty ranking by the beginning of recorded time, and why treatises on equitation have been found among the earliest known written records.

The job of the modern Thoroughbred trainer is, on the surface, much like that of the manager of a professional boxer. The trainer finds "prospects" to handle, arranges "matches" for them, then brings his charges to the best possible peak of fitness to meet their opponents. While the basic responsibilities of a trainer can be summarized in a sentence, though, the infinite variety of races, racing conditions and racehorses makes the details of the job difficult to summarize in a few paragraphs or pages.

In effect, the entire second part of this book is an explanation of the trainer's job. While the racetrack and racing secretary develop the racing program and create races, the trainer must choose the program with which to be associated. With an understanding equal to that of the racing secretary, the trainer must interpret the conditions of the races that have been created, to determine the best possible races in which to place his charges.

The second and third parts of a trainer's job are equally difficult. One part is the actual process of conditioning the horse. This involves the ability to read minute changes in attitude and health that can translate into poor performance. The second of these jobs is the relationship with the owner. The trainer must balance the needs of the horse with the needs and interests of the owner. Trainers who are the best conditioners in the world will not make money if they can't get along with the people who make the investment in Thoroughbred racing stock.

Because of the variety of experience and knowledge that is required for success as a trainer, we aren't going to try to summarize the job in the same manner as we have the role of the owner-breeder. Instead of telling, we're going to show the trainer in action. The final two chapters in our *Life of the Horse* series could just as well be called *The Life of the Trainer*.

At every American track, there are a small number of very skilled trainers and a larger number of far less competent trainers. Because of the general lack of coverage of racing by the daily newspapers, trainers are little known to the racing fan. Below, we've listed the annual leading money-winning trainers and the top money-winning conditioners of 1980, to alert fans to those at the very pinnacle of the profession. The best way to find out about trainers at one's local track is to pay attention to the trainers' names during visits to the track. Those who consistently enter fit horses that finish at or near the lead will be identified quickly.

*Annual Leading Trainer*
*—Money Won*

| YEAR | TRAINER | NUMBER OF WINS | AMOUNT WON |
|------|---------|----------------|------------|
| 1908 | J. Rowe | 50 | $ 284,335 |
| 1909 | S. C. Hildreth | 73 | 123,942 |
| 1910 | S. C. Hildreth | 84 | 148,010 |
| 1911 | S. C. Hildreth | 67 | 49,418 |
| 1912 | J. F. Schorr | 63 | 58,110 |
| 1913 | J. Rowe | 18 | 45,936 |
| 1914 | R. C. Benson | 45 | 59,315 |
| 1915 | J. Rowe | 19 | 75,596 |
| 1916 | S. C. Hildreth | 39 | 70,950 |
| 1917 | S. C. Hildreth | 23 | 61,698 |
| 1918 | H. G. Bedwell | 53 | 80,296 |
| 1919 | H. G. Bedwell | 63 | 208,728 |
| 1920 | L. Feustal | 22 | 186,087 |
| 1921 | S. C. Hildreth | 85 | 262,768 |
| 1922 | S. C. Hildreth | 74 | 247,014 |
| 1923 | S. C. Hildreth | 75 | 392,124 |
| 1924 | S. C. Hildreth | 77 | 255,608 |
| 1925 | G. R. Tompkins | 30 | 199,245 |
| 1926 | S. P. Harlan | 21 | 205,681 |
| 1927 | W. H. Bringloe | 63 | 216,563 |
| 1928 | J. F. Schorr | 65 | 258,425 |
| 1929 | J. Rowe, Jr. | 25 | 314,881 |
| 1930 | J. Fitzsimmons | 47 | 397,355 |
| 1931 | J. W. Healy | 33 | 297,300 |
| 1932 | J. Fitzsimmons | 68 | 266,650 |
| 1933 | R. A. Smith | 53 | 135,720 |
| 1934 | R. A. Smith | 43 | 249,938 |
| 1935 | J. H. Stotler | 87 | 303,005 |
| 1936 | J. Fitzsimmons | 42 | 193,415 |
| 1937 | R. McGarvey | 46 | 209,925 |
| 1938 | E. H. Sande | 15 | 226,495 |
| 1939 | J. Fitzsimmons | 45 | 266,205 |
| 1940 | T. Smith | 14 | 269,200 |
| 1941 | B. A. Jones | 70 | 475,318 |
| 1942 | J. M. Gaver | 48 | 406,547 |
| 1943 | B. A. Jones | 73 | 267,915 |
| 1944 | B. A. Jones | 60 | 601,660 |
| 1945 | T. Smith | 52 | 510,655 |
| 1946 | H. Jacobs | 99 | 560,077 |
| 1947 | H. A. Jones | 85 | 1,334,805 |
| 1948 | H. A. Jones | 81 | 1,118,670 |
| 1949 | H. A. Jones | 76 | 978,587 |
| 1950 | P. M. Burch | 96 | 637,754 |
| 1951 | J. M. Gaver | 42 | 616,392 |
| 1952 | B. A. Jones | 29 | 662,137 |
| 1953 | H. Trotsek | 54 | 1,028,873 |
| 1954 | W. Molter | 136 | 1,107,860 |
| 1955 | J. Fitzsimmons | 66 | 1,270,055 |
| 1956 | W. Molter | 142 | 1,227,402 |
| 1957 | H. A. Jones | 70 | 1,150,910 |

| YEAR | TRAINER | NUMBER OF WINS | AMOUNT WON |
|------|---------|----------------|------------|
| 1958 | W. Molter | 69 | $1,116,544 |
| 1959 | W. Molter | 71 | 847,290 |
| 1960 | H. Jacobs | 97 | 748,349 |
| 1961 | H. A. Jones | 62 | 759,856 |
| 1962 | M. A. Tenney | 58 | 1,099,474 |
| 1963 | M. A. Tenney | 40 | 860,703 |
| 1964 | W. C. Winfrey | 61 | 1,350,534 |
| 1965 | H. Jacobs | 91 | 1,331,628 |
| 1966 | E. A. Neloy | 93 | 2,456,250 |
| 1967 | E. A. Neloy | 72 | 1,776,089 |
| 1968 | E. A. Neloy | 52 | 1,233,101 |
| 1969 | Elliott Burch | 26 | 1,067,936 |
| 1970 | C. Whittingham | 82 | 1,302,354 |
| 1971 | C. Whittingham | 77 | 1,737,115 |
| 1972 | C. Whittingham | 79 | 1,734,020 |
| 1973 | C. Whittingham | 85 | 1,865,385 |
| 1974 | F. Martin | 166 | 2,408,419 |
| 1975 | C. Whittingham | 93 | 2,437,244 |
| 1976 | J. Van Berg | 496 | 2,976,196 |
| 1977 | L. S. Barrera | 127 | 2,715,848 |
| 1978 | L. S. Barrera | 100 | 3,314,564 |
| 1979 | L. S. Barrera | 97 | 3,563,147 |
| 1980 | L. S. Barrera | 99 | 2,969,151 |

*Leading Trainers*
*Money Won*

January 1–December 31, 1980

| TRAINER | STS. | 1ST | 2ND | 3RD | PCT. | PURSES |
|---------|------|-----|-----|-----|------|--------|
| Barrera, Lazaro S. | 559 | 99 | 83 | 94 | .177 | $2,969,151 |
| Whittingham, Charles | 388 | 57 | 62 | 50 | .147 | 2,571,257 |
| Martin, Frank | 670 | 120 | 88 | 90 | .179 | 2,225,476 |
| McAnally, Ronald | 477 | 75 | 68 | 50 | .157 | 2,066,180 |
| Lukas, D. Wayne | 461 | 63 | 50 | 61 | .137 | 1,982,241 |
| Cantey, Joseph B. | 310 | 54 | 61 | 30 | .174 | 1,981,063 |
| Johnson, Philip G. | 367 | 70 | 71 | 49 | .191 | 1,941,186 |
| Kelly, Thomas J. | 364 | 77 | 42 | 47 | .212 | 1,923,390 |
| Jones, Gary | 489 | 86 | 75 | 53 | .176 | 1,832,435 |
| Carroll, Del W. | 460 | 102 | 64 | 66 | .222 | 1,795,069 |
| Stephens, Woodford C. | 238 | 57 | 50 | 34 | .239 | 1,538,649 |
| Campo, John P. | 620 | 67 | 87 | 97 | .108 | 1,500,991 |
| Penna, Angel | 145 | 46 | 23 | 26 | .317 | 1,468,282 |
| Frankel, Robert | 471 | 77 | 108 | 68 | .163 | 1,453,845 |
| Nerud, Jan H. | 225 | 48 | 43 | 20 | .213 | 1,420,665 |
| Jolley, LeRoy | 186 | 30 | 40 | 20 | .161 | 1,383,612 |
| DiMauro, Stephen | 345 | 63 | 43 | 32 | .183 | 1,348,643 |
| Leatherbury, King T. | 1,147 | 222 | 161 | 143 | .194 | 1,315,891 |
| Adams, William E. | 355 | 49 | 40 | 41 | .138 | 1,231,063 |
| Jerkens, H. Allen | 322 | 51 | 57 | 57 | .158 | 1,226,649 |
| Tesher, Howard M. | 398 | 67 | 57 | 45 | .168 | 1,208,648 |
| Forbes, John H. | 914 | 91 | 96 | 109 | .100 | 1,191,184 |
| DeBonis, Robert | 520 | 61 | 63 | 71 | .177 | 1,181,830 |
| Fanning, Jerry | 440 | 55 | 55 | 56 | .125 | 1,158,517 |
| Alfano, Ronald A. | 727 | 158 | 133 | 97 | .217 | 1,153,532 |

# *Filling Races*

Early mornings are times of feverish activity at racetracks, as over one thousand horses are fed and galloped and cooled down and washed. As the morning wears on, though, horsemen tend to stop whatever they're doing to harken to the loudspeaker that penetrates to every corner of the backstretch. At most tracks, 9:30 or 10 A.M. is closing time for entries. By means of announcements made thereafter, owners find out if their horse is going to get a chance to race two days hence, and what kind of competition it is going to face.

## FINDING THE IDEAL RACE

The trainers of the best horses in the country have the most freedom to choose exactly when and where their charges will compete. The owners of these animals have the resources to ship anywhere in the country and keep paying training bills until the right race comes along. These trainers pay nomination fees to scores of stakes races, then wait to see which race will offer the most advantageous combination of condition, competition and purse value.

For the vast majority of horses, however, "ideal" races seldom come along. For one thing, the selection is limited to those offered in the condition book at the track at which they're stabled. Trainers are pressured to run horses by racing secretaries anxious to fill fields. The best these trainers can do is try to find a race in which their horses have a reasonable chance to win purse money.

The first element trainers consider in evaluating races is the sum of the conditions that we have discussed in great detail above. The "all-American" equine athlete, like the human "all-American," is extremely versatile—Secretariat, for example, captured stakes races at distances from six furlongs to a mile and five-eighths at eight different racetracks; on dirt and grass; under wet as well as dry conditions. The less talented the horse, however, the more narrow the range of conditions under which it performs up to its limited ability. A horse that has never won a race for a claiming price higher than $10,000, never won a race at over six furlongs and never won at a weight higher than 118 pounds is not a very good bet when carrying 124 pounds in a $20,000 claimer at a distance of a mile and a sixteenth. The best race for a horse is one that has conditions close to those of the past races in which the horse has performed well.

Added to the consideration of conditions is the critical matter of evaluation of form. Horses, like humans, undergo slumps in which they're incapable of performing at their best. The onset or the alleviation of injuries and ailments can bring sharp and sudden deterioration or improvement. Recent past performances and recent workouts generally determine whether a horse moves up or down in class.

The evaluation of form is particularly crucial for the trainer of a horse that races in claiming races. Signs of improving form catch the eyes of every sharp competitor. The trainer of an improving horse has to gauge how high to raise his horse to minimize the risk of losing the horse while still maintaining a good chance to win. Conversely, the trainer of a horse that's been having trouble winning wants to drop a horse in class enough to win a purse but not so much as to let the horse go for less than its value.

Finally, when evaluating the condition book, the trainer has to evaluate the competition his horse is likely to face. The best sources of this information are the jockeys' agents, the combination "traveling salesmen" and "town criers" of the racetrack. The job of the jockey's agent is to go from barn to barn every morning to find out which horses trainers plan to enter in which races. From this information and their observations of each horse's recent performances and conditions, they select the horses they want their clients to ride. The best agents are the best handicappers at the track.

Agents get mounts for their riders by offering information and advice. Shrewd trainers learn to evaluate the advice and information offered by different agents, using the best of it as a "second opinion" when gauging the chances of their own horses in upcoming races.

## THE ENTRY PROCEDURE

Until recently, the entry deadline for all races except stakes was traditionally the day before the race. That is why these races are referred to in racing as *"overnight"* races. By now, however, almost every track has adopted the "forty-eight-hour rule," with entries due at 9:30 or 10 A.M. two days before the race. The moving back of the entry time more easily accommodates the assembling of past performances by the *Daily Racing Form,* eases the time deadlines faced by newspaper handicappers and other public selectors, and allows owners and horseplayers alike more time to review and plan for the day's activity.

Trainers enter horses by filling out entry forms. In addition to "vital statistics" such as horse's name, color, sex, age, breeding, owner, trainer and owner's racing colors, the entry form requires the trainer to list the weight allowances his horse can claim for that race; the claiming price at which the horse will run; and, in most cases, the jockey that will ride the horse.

These forms are submitted to an entry clerk, who double-checks the horse's eligibility for the race and eligibility for the weight allowances claimed. The form is then given to the racing secretary, who places it with the other entries for that race.

Beginning a couple hours before the entry deadline, the racing secretary's office is the scene of hectic activity. Every ten or fifteen minutes, the racing secretary announces progress made, over the loudspeakers that reach every area of the backstretch. These announcements include pitches to horsemen to enter races that are filling too slowly. "Attention horsemen," the loudspeaker trumpets, "the third and fifth races are good. The fourth race is close with five. We need your help for the second, seventh and ninth."

To help fill certain races the racing secretary may "open" them. For example, if they don't fill before a certain time, track policy may be to open races written for "fillies and mares" to horses of all sexes; races written "for three-year-olds" may be opened to "three-year-olds and up"; races written for state-breds may be opened to any horse on the grounds.

Of particular concern to the racing secretary is obtaining large fields for races with exotic wagering. Most state laws require at least seven horses for exacta wagering and at least nine horses for trifectas. To allow for inevitable last-minute scratches, racing secretaries prefer ten to twelve entries for such contests. As the entry deadline approaches, the racing secretary often phones the trainers to ask for help. Such favors are repaid in favorable consideration for stall space and by writing race conditions that fit a horse that's been having trouble finding a spot to race.

As the entry deadline arrives, the office fills with jockey's agents and trainers. At

**THE NEW YORK RACING ASSOCIATION INC.**
•
**ENTRY BLANK**

PREFERRED

IF OFF, SWITCH OVER TO:

RACE _____ DISTANCE _____

WEIGHT _____ CL. PRICE _____

PENALTY _____ ALW. _____

JOCKEY _____

RACE _____

DISTANCE _____

OWNER

TRAINER

COLORS

JOCKEY

| NUMBER | HORSE | WEIGHT |
|---|---|---|

| COLOR | SEX | AGE | SIRE | DAM | ALLOWANCE |
|---|---|---|---|---|---|

GRAND SIRE — CLAIMING PRICE

CHANGED EQUIPMENT—BLINKERS ☐ ON ☐ OFF

NOTE: If this entry is signed by other than the owner, the person signing represents that he is authorized to sign on behalf of the owner.

PENALTY

"Rule 25.1 — Every person subscribing to a sweepstakes or entering a horse in a race to be run under these Rules accepts the decision of the Stewards or the decision of the Commission, as the case may be, on any question relating to a race or to racing."

"Rule 25.2 — The nominations or entries of any person or the transfer of any nomination or entry may be cancelled or revoked without notice by the Association, or in the discretion of the Commission or of the Stewards."

BY WHOM ENTERED _____

most tracks, races, with the exception of stakes, that lack at least six entries are tossed out in favor of substitute races listed in the condition book that have drawn enough entries. Since every racetrack has far more cheap horses than good horses, allowance races are usually the hardest to fill.

Maiden races, especially maiden claimers, usually overfill.

If more entries are filed than can be accommodated, the racing secretary turns to the *preference* list. Every time a horse is eliminated from a race because the race overfilled, the horse is awarded a *prefer-*

*ence star*. These stars are good for races written under approximately the same conditions—usually within $500 in price and in one of two distance categories—*short* (under a mile) or *long* (a mile or over). For maiden races at some tracks, two or three stars are needed to get into a race.

In certain races, other preferences may be stated in the condition book. In almost all handicaps, *high-weights* are preferred. In non-maiden races, *winners* are commonly given preference over maidens. In some maiden races, preference is given to horses that have never been entered in *maiden claiming races*.

If spaces in a race are available after all preference stars have been accounted for, the other entries are determined by lot. The other horses are placed on an "also-eligible list"; entrants will be drawn from this list by lot if any horses in the field are scratched.

After reviewing the number of entrants in each race, the racing secretary arranges the races in the order that they will be run two days later. The feature race is normally the next-to-last race on the card. The largest fields become the trifecta races, then the daily double races, then the exacta and quinella races.

## DETERMINING POST POSITION

Post positions for every race are drawn by lot. One volunteer from the crowd in the racing secretary's office draws an entry form from the face-down stack. Another volunteer draws numbered pills from a pillbox or bottle. The name of the horse and the post position are announced and recorded.

The post position drawn becomes the number of the horse on the program, except in the case of *multiple entries*. In some states, such as New York, two horses trained by the same person but owned by separate parties are allowed to run as separate betting interests in non-stake races; in

other states such horses are coupled: e.g., a single bet covers both horses. In all states, horses owned by the same stable must run coupled. The number of entries by one "interest" is normally limited to two in non-stakes races, but is unlimited in stakes events.

In the event of a two-horse entry, the horses are always listed as Nos. 1 and 1A, *regardless of the post position* in which they will start. Three-horse entries are listed as 1, 1A and 1X. If the race draws two coupled entries, the second becomes Nos. 2 and 2A, etc.

After the entries are accounted for, the rest of the numbers are assigned by post position. The horse that has drawn the most inside position apart from the entry becomes No. 2, the next post position, No. 3, etc.

After post positions are completed, the list of entries for every race is typed up and mimeographed. This list is known as the "overnights" or the "overnight sheet."

## SCRATCHES

Because in stakes races horsemen are partly "running for their own money," the nomination fees they've put up, they're given the privilege of scratching their horses as late as forty-five minutes before post time. They don't have to give a reason for scratching—it may be that they don't like the competition they'll face, the post position drawn, the jockey they've been able to get or a slight change in the condition of their horse. Often, a horse may be entered in two stakes at different tracks on the same day, with the trainer and owner waiting until after post positions are drawn and competition determined before making their choice.

For all overnight races, however, scratch time is early on the day of the race. All scratches in overnight races must be approved by the track's stewards. Permission to scratch is always given if the track veterinarian certifies that the horse is lame, has a fever or is otherwise unfit to race. In races with also-eligibles waiting to enter, or with very large fields, permission to scratch is automatic. When the number of entries is near the minimum for exotic wagering, though, the stewards seldom let a trainer "off the hook" without a very convincing reason.

## NAMING JOCKEYS

In California, jockeys must be named by the trainer by the entry deadline. In other states, trainers are requested to make the declaration by entry time, but don't have to name a rider until the afternoon before a race. Changes are permitted until scratch time; after that, permission of the stewards is needed to make a substitution. Most late jockey changes are the result of injury, illness or a jockey's failure to "make the weight" assigned to the horse.

Understanding the important process of selecting a rider for a horse is vital to understanding how a race is run. That, in turn, requires an explanation of the role of the jockey—the most visible of all racing personalities.

# Jockeys

## THE EVOLUTION OF RACE RIDING

The word "jockey" was originally a diminutive or familiar form of "jock," a term applied, often contemptuously, to the common people. Later, the word came to mean "a vagabond." Since among those wandering from town to town were those who were involved in the horse trade, a "jockey" became a horse dealer or horse trainer. That's why the wealthy men who gathered at Tattersall's horse auctions called the organization they formed to administer their sport the *Jockey Club*.

In the early days of racing, owners rode their own horses, but as racing became a professional sport, horsemen increasingly turned to professional riders. One reason was that the trend toward the racing of two- and three-year-olds required riders far lighter than the wealthy horse owners, who heartily indulged in the pleasures of the table. The second reason was the introduction of dash racing, which required a higher degree of riding skill than did heat racing. A four-mile heat conducted over open country, while requiring a certain amount of judgment of pace, left a lot of room for error. In a mile dash featuring ten or twelve horses negotiating tight turns, losing even a few yards in a traffic jam could mean losing the race.

Gradually, the term "jockey" came to be applied only to these professional riders. The word had always had certain connotations of "rogue" and "cheat" attached to it, and these terms appropriately described many of the early professional race riders in England. Bribery was rampant on the turf. Once, having discovered that his jockey had been bribed by bookmakers, the Marquess of Queensberry dramatically threw off his cape and rode his horse in the race himself. Many other owners found their best insurance was a standing offer to more than match the sum of the bribes offered to their riders. Riders who weren't "on the take" often rode miserably because they were drunk or too weak from starvation diets.

The style of riding reflected the greed that was too often reflective of horse racing in this period. Horse trainers, desperate to win, equipped their riders with spurs as well as whips, and instructed them to use both liberally. The following is a description of a horse that had just run at Epsom, site of the Epsom Derby: "He was lacerated and cut up alive, from shoulder to flank, his sheath torn to ribbons, and his testes sorely and dangerously wounded."

In America, heat racing remained popular until the time of the Civil War. During this period, jockeys were primarily black men owned or employed by horse owners. Their role was considered so secondary to the success of the horse that their names were often unrecorded in reports of races.

When heat racing was replaced by dash racing, the importance of the riders grew, just as it had in England more than a century earlier. Until about 1900, many of the best riders were still black—fifteen of the first twenty Kentucky Derbys were won by black jockeys. As in so many other professions, though, when race riding became more lucrative and well publicized, whites

*Annual Leading Jockey
—Money Won*

| YEAR | JOCKEY | MTS. | 1ST | PCT. | AMT. WON |
|------|--------|------|-----|------|----------|
| 1908 | Notter, J. | 872 | 249 | .29 | $ 464,322 |
| 1909 | Dugan, E. | 631 | 143 | .23 | 166,355 |
| 1910 | Shilling, C. H. | 506 | 172 | .34 | 176,030 |
| 1911 | Koerner, T. | 813 | 162 | .20 | 88,308 |
| 1912 | Butwell, J. | 684 | 144 | .21 | 79,843 |
| 1913 | Buxton, M. | 887 | 146 | .16 | 82,552 |
| 1914 | McCahey, J. | 824 | 155 | .19 | 121,845 |
| 1915 | Garner, M. | 775 | 151 | .19 | 96,628 |
| 1916 | McTaggart, J. | 832 | 150 | .18 | 155,055 |
| 1917 | Robinson, F. | 731 | 147 | .20 | 148,057 |
| 1918 | Luke, L. | 756 | 178 | .24 | 201,864 |
| 1919 | Loftus, J. | 177 | 65 | .37 | 252,707 |
| 1920 | Kummer, C. | 353 | 87 | .25 | 292,376 |
| 1921 | Sande, E. | 340 | 112 | .33 | 263,043 |
| 1922 | Johnson, A. | 297 | 43 | .14 | 345,054 |
| 1923 | Sande, E. | 430 | 122 | .28 | 569,394 |
| 1924 | Parke, I. | 844 | 205 | .24 | 290,395 |
| 1925 | Fator, L. | 315 | 81 | .26 | 305,775 |
| 1926 | Fator, L. | 511 | 143 | .28 | 361,435 |
| 1927 | Sande, E. | 179 | 49 | .27 | 277,877 |
| 1928 | McAtee, L. | 235 | 55 | .23 | 301,295 |
| 1929 | Garner, M. | 274 | 57 | .21 | 314,975 |
| 1930 | Workman, R. | 571 | 152 | .27 | 420,438 |
| 1931 | Kurtsinger, C. | 519 | 93 | .18 | 392,095 |
| 1932 | Workman, R. | 378 | 87 | .23 | 385,070 |
| 1933 | Jones, R. | 471 | 63 | .13 | 226,285 |
| 1934 | Wright, W. D. | 919 | 174 | .19 | 287,185 |
| 1935 | Coucci, S. | 749 | 141 | .19 | 319,760 |
| 1936 | Wright, W. D. | 670 | 100 | .15 | 264,000 |
| 1937 | Kurtsinger, C. | 765 | 120 | .16 | 384,202 |
| 1938 | Wall, N. | 658 | 97 | .15 | 385,161 |
| 1939 | James, B. | 904 | 191 | .21 | 353,333 |
| 1940 | Arcaro, E. | 783 | 132 | .17 | 343,661 |
| 1941 | Meade, D. | 1,164 | 210 | .18 | 398,627 |
| 1942 | Arcaro, E. | 687 | 123 | .18 | 481,949 |
| 1943 | Longden, J. | 871 | 173 | .20 | 573,276 |
| 1944 | Atkinson, T. | 1,539 | 287 | .19 | 899,101 |
| 1945 | Longden, J. | 778 | 180 | .23 | 981,977 |
| 1946 | Atkinson, T. | 1,377 | 233 | .17 | 1,036,825 |
| 1947 | Dodson, D. | 646 | 141 | .22 | 1,429,949 |
| 1948 | Arcaro, E. | 726 | 188 | .26 | 1,686,230 |
| 1949 | Brooks, S. | 906 | 209 | .23 | 1,316,817 |
| 1950 | Arcaro, E. | 888 | 195 | .22 | 1,410,160 |
| 1951 | Shoemaker, W. | 1,161 | 257 | .22 | 1,329,890 |
| 1952 | Arcaro, E. | 807 | 188 | .23 | 1,859,591 |
| 1953 | Shoemaker, W. | 1,683 | 485 | .29 | 1,784,187 |
| 1954 | Shoemaker, W. | 1,251 | 380 | .30 | 1,876,760 |
| 1955 | Arcaro, E. | 820 | 158 | .19 | 1,864,796 |
| 1956 | Hartack, W. | 1,387 | 347 | .25 | 2,343,955 |
| 1957 | Hartack, W. | 1,238 | 341 | .28 | 3,060,501 |

| YEAR | JOCKEY | MTS. | 1ST | PCT. | AMT. WON |
|------|--------|------|-----|------|----------|
| 1958 | Shoemaker, W. | 1,133 | 300 | .26 | $2,961,693 |
| 1959 | Shoemaker, W. | 1,285 | 347 | .27 | 2,843,133 |
| 1960 | Shoemaker, W. | 1,227 | 274 | .22 | 2,123,961 |
| 1961 | Shoemaker, W. | 1,256 | 304 | .24 | 2,690,819 |
| 1962 | Shoemaker, W. | 1,126 | 311 | .28 | 2,916,844 |
| 1963 | Shoemaker, W. | 1,203 | 271 | .22 | 2,526,925 |
| 1964 | Shoemaker, W. | 1,056 | 246 | .23 | 2,649,553 |
| 1965 | Baeza, B. | 1,245 | 270 | .22 | 2,582,702 |
| 1966 | Baeza, B. | 1,341 | 298 | .22 | 2,951,022 |
| 1967 | Baeza, B. | 1,064 | 256 | .24 | 3,088,888 |
| 1968 | Baeza, B. | 1,089 | 201 | .18 | 2,835,108 |
| 1969 | Velasquez, J. | 1,442 | 258 | .18 | 2,542,315 |
| 1970 | Pincay, L., Jr. | 1,328 | 269 | .20 | 2,626,526 |
| 1971 | Pincay, L., Jr. | 1,627 | 380 | .23 | 3,784,377 |
| 1972 | Pincay, L., Jr. | 1,388 | 289 | .21 | 3,225,827 |
| 1973 | Pincay, L., Jr. | 1,444 | 350 | .24 | 4,093,492 |
| 1974 | Pincay, L., Jr. | 1,278 | 341 | .27 | 4,251,060 |
| 1975 | Baeza, B. | 1,190 | 196 | .16 | 3,674,398 |
| 1976 | Cordero, A., Jr. | 1,534 | 274 | .18 | 4,709,500 |
| 1977 | Cauthen, S. | 2,075 | 487 | .23 | 6,151,750 |
| 1978 | McHargue, D. G. | 1,762 | 375 | .21 | 6,188,353 |
| 1979 | Pincay, L., Jr. | 1,708 | 420 | .25 | 8,183,535 |
| 1980 | McCarron, C. J. | 1,964 | 405 | .21 | 7,666,100 |

gradually replaced blacks, who were relegated to backstretch work as hot-walkers and grooms.

The styles of the famous riders of this period reflect differences that exist to this very day. The greatest of the black jockeys, and one of the greatest in history, was Isaac Murphy, who piloted 628 of 1,412 mounts to victory, for an incredible 44 percent wins. Murphy disdained use of the whip and spurs, relying instead on the almost mystical communication known as "feel" to coax the maximum performance from his mounts.

In vivid contrast to Murphy were riders like Edward "Snapper" Garrison, one of the first of the prominent white jockeys. Garrison's trademark was liberal use of spurs and whip in headlong charges to the wire that became known as "Garrison finishes."

As racing in both England and the United States progressed into the twentieth century, severe punishment of horses, especially through spurring, became generally recognized as both cruel and ineffective. One practice that died harder was riders' mistreatment of each other. Common practices included whipping other horses and riders, grabbing at saddlecloths and halters, and hooking another rider's leg irons. Far too often, riders who found themselves the victims of such practices retaliated by attempting to put the other rider over the infield fence. For example, early in his career, hot-tempered Eddie Arcaro was banged by another rider while leaving the gate. Furious, he slammed his horse into the other rider's farther along in the race. When asked by the stewards what had happened, Arcaro replied, "I was trying to kill him."

For his conduct, Arcaro was suspended for a year. He returned to the track a changed rider. Such stiff suspensions discouraged the most flagrant fouls, but displays like the 1933 Kentucky Derby, in which jockeys Herb Fisher and Don Meade grabbed and slashed at each other throughout the stretch, continued to mar the sport.

The solution to this problem came with the institution of the *film patrol*. Before World War II, Santa Anita had begun experimenting with filming all of the races. After the war, tracks began to build towers around the course, from which films were made from different angles. These films could be reviewed by the stewards at their leisure when suspected violations were reported by patrol judges stationed around the course. The film patrol resulted in the elimination of most of the obvious rough-riding.

This post-war period probably marked the high point for the riding profession in America. Prospective jockeys honed their knowledge of horses and racing through years of work as hot-walkers and exercise boys before they were allowed on the track. Even licensed apprentices were brought along slowly. Because of this extensive training, the transition from apprentice to journeyman was not abrupt, and the arrival at journeyman level meant full maturity as a rider. With the elimination of the worst of the rough-riding, jockeys could exercise their skills and horsemanship.

At about this time, however, two trends began that were to result in a severe decline in the general ability of race riders. One trend was the overall increase in the *size* of the average American. With fewer small people, trainers were forced to take on potential riders not because of their athletic skills but simply because of their size.

The second trend was the huge expansion of racing. In 1945, 14,000 horses participated in 19,000 races. In 1980, 64,000 horses participated in 69,000 races. At a time when the pool of potential riders was shrinking, the number of new riders needed was skyrocketing. The result was that almost anyone of the proper size could get a job with a trainer, and anyone who learned how to get around a track without falling off ended up as an apprentice, riding in races.

The problem of the shrinking pool of potential riders was partially helped by the increasing number of Latin American jockeys coming to this country and by the gradual acceptance of female jockeys. The training of young potential riders is still generally inadequate, however. The result is the domination of the sport by a small group of talented riders. At the top are the forty or fifty riders whose mounts earn over $1 million a year. While the major California and New York tracks may have a pool of ten to twenty such outstanding riders, owners at small tracks have to compete vigorously for the two or three truly talented riders there. Since these jockeys end up with most of the good horses, the majority of riders struggle to earn $5,000 a year. The turnover is tremendous; the quality of riding, mediocre.

## THE COMPLETE JOCKEY

To a trainer, a competent jockey is one who obtains the maximum level of performance the horse has to give, while avoiding strategical mistakes that prevent the horse from finishing as high as that level of performance would allow. To the casual observer, riding looks "easy" and such competence would seem a matter of course, but the exact opposite is true. Top jockeys are superb athletes whose sport is dangerous as well as physically and mentally demanding.

First, let's consider the physical qualifications. In addition to weighing under 110 or 112 pounds, jockeys must possess the strength and stamina to control a headstrong thousand-pound animal.

Simply maintaining the crouch required for two minutes of racing requires such extraordinary leg strength that inexperienced riders find themselves unable to walk after dismounting. Sophisticated testing by physicians and psychologists has consistently found jockeys to be in the top 10 percent of all athletes.

To this strength and fitness must be added superior reflexes. We all know driving a car on a crowded freeway requires alertness and good reactions. Jockeys pilot horses traveling forty miles per hour inches apart from other animals that may drastically alter course at any instant. Quick reactions and split-second judgments are mandatory to keep a horse out of trouble and on the path to victory.

The need for superior strength, stamina and reflexes is the reason why weight control is one of the big problems in racing.

Every jockeys' room at every track has a steam room in which some jockeys spend hours sweating off extra ounces to "make weight." In desperation, some riders follow dangerous, bizarre diets, even forcing themselves to throw up after every meal. As a result, they're often too weak to ride their best race, and sometimes are so weak that they're a danger to their horse and to other participants in the race.

*Top Five Money-winning Jockeys of All Time* (*Through 1980*)

| JOCKEY | STARTS | WINS | SECOND | THIRD | WIN % | EARNINGS |
|---|---|---|---|---|---|---|
| Bill Shoemaker | 34,220 | 7,925 | 5,336 | 4,257 | .232 | $79,693,453 |
| Laffit Pincay, Jr. | 19,563 | 4,327 | 3,281 | 2,786 | .221 | 55,555,390 |
| Angel Cordero, Jr. | 23,730 | 4,178 | 3,651 | 3,297 | .176 | 55,182,847 |
| Jorge Velasquez | 22,800 | 3,991 | 3,504 | 3,311 | .175 | 50,219,415 |
| Jacinto Vasquez | 25,631 | 3,556 | 3,299 | 3,109 | .139 | 37,554,307 |

A part of the physical side of riding racehorses is the need for physical courage. One rider has described the far-too-common occurrence of a horse breaking a leg as "losing the front wheel of a motorcycle at forty miles per hour." A rider going down is in danger not only of having his horse land on him, but of being trampled by the horses behind. Each year nearly two hundred and fifty riders suffer serious injuries; at this writing, nearly fifty paraplegic riders, including Secretariat's former rider, Ron Turcotte, are receiving disability payments from the Jockey's Guild. In the past two decades more than twenty riders have been killed in racing accidents.

Because of the unavoidable dangers of race riding, officials severely punish reckless riding, but no rider is able to consistently win races by staying safely on the outside. Many races are won by slipping through small holes on the rail or between horses. A rider who grows too cautious, especially after a serious injury, will find it very difficult to get top mounts.

Deciding what constitutes a reasonable risk is part of the all-important area of *judgment,* a skill that comes through experience and exhaustive study of racing films. Inexperienced and incompetent riders are forever getting trapped by a wall of horses, a situation known as a "switch." The best riders are the ones who keep their horses out of trouble by anticipating the moves and strategies of other riders. The top riders study the past performances of other horses in the race and add that to their knowledge of other riders' habits as they make decisions about their strategy, both before and during a race.

Part of the judgment necessary requires a sense of *pace.* Many top jockeys are said to have "a clock in their head." Developing this "clock" takes untold hours of hard work: the jockey first counts mentally while someone else holds a stopwatch, then spends countless hours on the track translating that sense to the racetrack. The lack of a sense of pace is why the only strategy many jockeys are capable of is pushing a horse as hard as they can until it stops. While this "strategy" wins many sprints, it seldom wins in races over a mile.

Implementing proper strategy requires mastering proper *technique*. This means what horsemen call a good *seat* on a horse, sitting low, to cut wind resistance, and as still as possible, to avoid disrupting the horse's running rhythm and balance. Technique also means learning to control a horse in the starting gate and the ability to get the horse out of the gate in good order. It means handling the reins properly to get the horse to relax, to accelerate or to change leads around a turn. Finally, it means handling a whip properly and being able to change over instantly from whipping with one hand to using the other when the need arises. Many jockeys are able to whip only with one hand, a severe disadvantage.

Finally, to all of the above, great jockeys add a final quality known as "great hands" or "feel." This is the essentially indefinable communication between horse and rider that coaxes the maximum performance from an animal. A rider with "feel" can more easily get a horse to relax, can call upon a horse's remaining energy at will and can hold together far longer a horse tiring in the stretch. More than any other quality, "great hands" or "feel" is what distinguishes great riders. While some part of it may be "inborn," as some racing people believe, to a great extent it involves a level of horsemanship that long exposure to horses used to give riders, but that many riders today sorely lack.

## PLACING A JOCKEY ON A HORSE

To obtain the services of most riders, trainers negotiate with jockeys' agents. Who ends up on a horse is primarily a function of the trainer's estimation of the horse's chances and the agent's estimation of the horse's chances. The trainer with the favorite for a race wants to get the best jockey on the grounds; the agent for the best jockey wants to get his rider on the best horse.

At major tracks like Belmont Park and Hollywood Park, trainers have the choice of a dozen or more top riders. The individual choice among them depends to a great extent on the trainer's or owner's personal preference. At smaller tracks, however, one or two jockeys may be clearly superior. At Fairmount Park in 1979, for example, Danny Gall, the nation's leader in races won, rode 224 winners. The runner-up rode 87 during the meeting. Trainers of "live" horses at Fairmount obviously prefer to have Gall ride their stock, and Gall's agent obviously is a shrewd handicapper.

In many races, particularly in the sprints that make up the majority of contests carded, trainers look to hire *apprentices*. A rider is eligible for an apprentice jockey's license at age sixteen. Until they win five races, apprentices get a ten-pound weight advantage in all non-stakes and non-handicap races. This ten-pound advantage is indicated on programs by three asterisks, called "bugs," so a rider who was listed as John Smith*** is called a "triple-bug boy." From the time of the fifth victory until he wins an additional thirty races, he is a double-bug boy, receiving a seven-pound allowance. In every race after the thirtieth win that occurs within a year from the date of the fifth win, the apprentice gets a five-pound allowance. If an apprentice has signed a contract with a stable, the apprentice gets a three-pound allowance for an additional year when riding that stable's horses.

Weight isn't the only reason trainers hire apprentices for the sprints that make up the majority of races. Apprentices tend to take cheaper races more seriously than do more experienced riders; they tend to pay attention to instructions more carefully; and they tend to take more chances than do older riders.

Because one year's apprenticeship is seldom enough time for a rider to really learn

## Top Twenty-five Money-winning Jockeys of 1979

| JOCKEY | MTS. | 1ST | 2ND | 3RD | PCT. | PURSES |
|--------|------|-----|-----|-----|------|--------|
| McCarron, C. J. | 1,964 | 405 | 318 | 282 | .206 | $7,666,100 |
| Cordero, A. Jr. | 1,888 | 377 | 296 | 271 | .200 | 7,174,259 |
| Pincay, L. Jr. | 1,426 | 291 | 225 | 223 | .204 | 6,512,611 |
| Velasquez, J. | 1,373 | 224 | 201 | 201 | .164 | 5,499,614 |
| Asmussen, C. B. | 1,768 | 279 | 257 | 217 | .158 | 5,323,228 |
| Shoemaker, W. | 1,052 | 159 | 140 | 132 | .149 | 5,188,883 |
| Fell, J. | 1,274 | 216 | 186 | 185 | .170 | 5,077,740 |
| Delahoussaye, E. | 1,547 | 237 | 239 | 236 | .153 | 5,036,112 |
| Maple, E. | 1,290 | 164 | 186 | 155 | .127 | 4,714,639 |
| Valenzuela, P. A. | 1,596 | 234 | 229 | 205 | .147 | 4,579,744 |
| Hernandez, R. | 964 | 155 | 127 | 123 | .161 | 3,851,576 |
| Lovato, F. Jr. | 1,774 | 249 | 215 | 238 | .140 | 3,700,041 |
| Hawley, S. | 1,278 | 219 | 184 | 150 | .171 | 3,580,710 |
| McHargue, D. G. | 957 | 140 | 137 | 124 | .146 | 3,430,346 |
| Vasquez, J. | 1,025 | 150 | 149 | 127 | .146 | 3,421,185 |
| Toro, F. | 1,128 | 143 | 136 | 136 | .127 | 3,041,115 |
| Beitia, E. | 1,178 | 166 | 152 | 165 | .141 | 2,973,279 |
| Bracciale, V. Jr. | 1,078 | 215 | 170 | 141 | .199 | 2,896,694 |
| Day, P. | 1,370 | 217 | 218 | 189 | .158 | 2,875,510 |
| Sibille, R. | 1,492 | 269 | 217 | 193 | .180 | 2,844,586 |
| MacBeth, D. | 1,433 | 200 | 179 | 203 | .140 | 2,755,247 |
| Brumfield, D. | 1,205 | 189 | 121 | 113 | .157 | 2,676,422 |
| Romero, R. P. | 1,496 | 282 | 267 | 191 | .189 | 2,661,703 |
| Martens, G. | 1,033 | 128 | 120 | 136 | .124 | 2,504,119 |
| Samyn, J. L. | 720 | 92 | 118 | 111 | .128 | 2,481,473 |

the trade, most jockeys disappear from the track after they "lose their bug"—their apprentice weight allowance. Among the saddest sights at any racetrack are these young men and women hanging around the track in the mornings, begging for chances to work horses in the hopes of getting a ride in the afternoon. The few mounts they get this way seldom win. The contenders in the race go to the few leading journeymen (riders who've completed their apprenticeship) and to the new apprentices who've taken their places.

Competition for top journeymen and apprentices at a track is so keen that jockeys' agents are allowed to commit their riders to two horses at the time of entry. One of the trainers is given "first call" on the jockey's services, the other "second call." If the horse with the "first call" doesn't draw into the race or is scratched, the jockey rides the other.

## JOCKEY FEES

A jockey is a "free agent." Theoretically, the jockey or his agent negotiates his fee for every ride. In practice, such race-by-race negotiation is largely limited to the engaging of top riders to handle top horses in rich races. Some riders do sign contracts with large stables giving the stable "first call" for all races in which it has a horse entered. Sometimes these contracts call for payments above "scale." Top jockeys who give up riding an entire race card at their regular track to ride a horse in a stakes race at another track also receive above-normal compensation.

For most races, however, jockeys receive fees indicated on a fee schedule determined by negotiation between the track, the Horsemen's Benevolent and Protective Association, and the Jockey's Guild. Below is the schedule in effect at most tracks in 1980:

| PURSE VALUE | WINNING MOUNT | SECOND PLACE | THIRD PLACE | LOSING MOUNT |
|---|---|---|---|---|
| $1,000–$1,400 | 10% of win purse | $30 | $25 | $20 |
| $1,500–$1,900 | 10% of win purse | $35 | $30 | $25 |
| $2,000–$3,400 | 10% of win purse | $45 | $35 | $30 |
| $3,500–$4,900 | 10% of win purse | $50 | $40 | $30 |
| $5,000 up | 10% of win purse | $55 | $45 | $35 |

Before a horse goes to the post, its owner must have deposited at least the sum of the losing jockey's fee with the horsemen's bookkeeper. From that fee, which is $30 for the average race, the track deducts $3.50, which goes to the Jockey's Guild for dues and insurance, and another $3, which goes to the valets who clean the jockeys' boots, prepare racing sticks and look after racing equipment. If the jockey has an agent, the agent normally gets 25 percent of all the jockey's earnings. Out of the money that's left, the jockey must pay taxes and buy racing equipment—riding pants, boots, whips and helmets.

The above demonstrates vividly why making a living as a jockey depends on winning races. The top riders, who get the best mounts in rich stakes, make large six-figure incomes. Jacinto Vasquez, who rode Genuine Risk to victory in the 1980 Kentucky Derby, received for his two minutes of work 10 percent of the $250,000 first prize—a nifty $25,000. That figure, however, represents three to five times the yearly earnings of most jockeys at small tracks.

Struggling for money makes a small minority of jockeys susceptible to gamblers. Jockeys are forbidden to bet on any horse except the one they're riding. Those who try to boost income by having others illegally bet on other horses for them may cooperate by holding back their mounts.

## EVALUATING JOCKEYS

The best jockeys at each track are those who appear near the top of the "races won" standings, and those who have ridden at least 15 percent of their mounts to victory. Nationally, winning purses of $1 million or more places a jockey in the elite of his or her profession.

The best way to evaluate jockeys, however, is through observation. Concentrate on watching riders during a few visits to the track. Note which riders get their mounts out of the gate quickly and in an orderly fashion, and those that always seem to get started slowly. Some jockeys consistently use so much of their horse's early speed that the animal fades in the stretch; others strangle off their mount's will to compete; many consistently get trapped in switches or find themselves parked way outside.

Good riders, on the other hand, manage to settle their mounts into a rhythm noticeable to even the casual observer. They keep their mounts on what experience has told them is the fastest part of the racetrack, and they anticipate trouble so well that their horses never seem to be seriously shut off. By the time they reach the top of the stretch, they're positioned to use whatever energy their horses are able to give.

# Life of the Horse: 5. In Training

## The Professional Horse

One of the greatest tragedies of American racing is the national obsession with pure speed.

The horse is a natural endurance animal, built to maintain speeds of about twenty to twenty-five miles per hour comfortably. The modern racehorse, selectively bred and trained to accelerate up to forty mph, is capable of producing greater velocity than mere sinew, bone and cartilage can tolerate. It is the impact of intense speed, rather than repeated mild concussion, that splits bone and rips tendons. Six furlongs at a racing gallop are more erosive than twenty miles at a trot.

In Europe, many Thoroughbreds never set foot on a racetrack until they are three years old. Then they run on the firm but yielding turf surface, not so different from the grassy plains across which *Eohippus* stampeded on his way to evolving into *Equus*. Races are long and relatively slow, emphasizing gameness and endurance over a distance. The mark of a good jockey is that his mount wins by a narrow margin, exerting just enough effort to cross the finish line first.

Although their legs will not be fully ossified until they are over three years old, American two-year-olds are asked to sprint over tracks that are hard and fast. They plunge sharply from the starting gate, reaching out to catch the impact of racing speed on knees and cannon bones that pound themselves into jagged chips just as they are approaching their mature growth. Soreness, injury, lay-ups and ultimately self-destruction are the occupational hazards of being an equine athlete.

Manny Dober is no exception. Everything in her breeding indicates that she will not hit her form until she is three years old, and then only in relatively long races. Her dam, Tanta Prisa, won three races at ages three and four, one at a mile and seventy yards and the other two at a mile and a sixteenth. * Pronto, her maternal grandsire, was strictly a distance horse. Manny has little influence with the racing secretary, though, and her owner, Phil Sagarin, is anxious to begin to recoup the three-and-a-half-year investment that began when Tanta was bred to Native Heritage, so Manny, like 90 percent of all racehorses, has to run before she matures.

Where she is to run is at Suffolk Downs

in East Boston, Massachusetts. Manny was bred in New York to be eligible for the purses enriched by large supplements from the New York State Breeders' Fund. The maiden races for two-year-olds are all short-distance runs, though, and in her training Manny hasn't demonstrated sufficient early speed to sprint with New York-bred maidens. Instead she is exiled to cold Suffolk Downs, where training costs are half those in New York and where the class of horses is very much lower.

Even at Suffolk, Manny is considered too slow to compete in non-claiming maidens. Her first outing is a six-furlong race for $10,000 maiden claimers. Manny breaks in seventh place, drops back to last and finishes eighth in a field of eight. After another equally dismal effort at $10,000, Manny is dropped to $7,500 on December 26. Again, she finishes eighth, ten lengths behind the winner.

These defeats, however, have not quenched the competitive spirit of the daughter of Tanta Prisa. Manny is learning and growing, and in each race she performs as well as her late-maturing body allows. Dropped an additional notch to $5,500 after a three-week rest and equipped with blinkers to encourage early speed, Manny breaks second, manages to stay in second until the quarter-mile pole, then tires and finishes fifth. This performance is encouraging enough to make her move up again to $7,500 claimer, where the public sends her off at 142–1. After settling at the back of the twelve-horse field, underdog Manny puts on an impressive rally, finishing third and covering the distance three seconds faster than she ever has before.

Although her record is far from spectacular, Manny has shown steady improvement. More important, she has demonstrated an unusual tenacity that keeps motivating her to try to win in spite of repeated defeats. At the end of January, the Sagarins make the decision to ship Manny from Suffolk Downs to Belmont. As she steps into the big van, the diminutive chestnut filly is unaware that she has beaten the odds in winning her promotion to racing's big leagues. However, the five low-class races in which she's been forced to prove herself have taken their toll on her still-maturing body. As she shifts her weight to adjust for the bouncing of the horse van, fluid caused by calcium build-up undulates along the bones of her puffy left knee.

"Beautiful Belmont Park"—home of the gracious, oak-lined paddock, and the only one-and-a-half-mile track in the United States—barely blinks an eye at the arrival of a maiden claimer from Boston. Over this hallowed ground the brilliant filly Genuine Risk broke her maiden; Secretariat broke the American record for a mile and a half to complete his Triple Crown; Forego, lugging 137 pounds, broke past Honest Pleasure in the last 100 yards of the 1976 Marlboro Cup to clinch his third consecutive Horse of the Year title; and undefeated Ruffian broke her sesamoid bone in the fatal Great Match with Foolish Pleasure. Champions such as these never knew that tracks like Suffolk Downs, with its one graded (Gr. III) stakes a year, existed. They never paid the dues of running religiously twice a month on the leaky-roof circuit. Champions start at the top.

Manny Dober, in the big van rolling down honky-tonk Hempstead Avenue, flashing bar-lit pink and yellow in the midwinter rain, has no special sense of expectation, of having made it. The muscles of her haunches feel tense from the long trip down from Massachusetts. When the van pumps to a stop and the door opens in front of Barn 34, the stable of top New York trainer Robert DeBonis, she staggers out into the darkness and down the strange aisle willingly enough. A pigeon coos softly from its nest up in the rafters. From farther down the dark row of stalls comes the muffled clatter of a "stall-walker" who spends all night pacing restlessly back and forth. There is a familiar smell in the air, the smell that emanates from all racetrack barns, blotting out even the permeating scents of sweet hay, salty urine and humid horsehide. Manny Dober locks her knees and stifle joints and drowses to sleep inhaling the comforting, tingly scent of Absorbine liniment.

At 4 A.M., she is awakened, both by the squeak of wagon wheels coming down the dirt aisle and the sounds of thirty-nine other hungry Thoroughbreds, pawing, nickering, pushing against their stall screens, waiting to be fed. In the dawn light filtering through the small, high windows of the concrete barn, these animals look gigantic compared to the less classy Thoroughbreds Manny is used to. There is the proud bay head and neck of the turf horse T.V. Series, a winner of the Kent Stakes and more than $125,000, swooping impatiently from side to side in the morning shadows. The slick yellow teeth of Misty Native, winner of the Correction Handicap and $200,000 in stakes races, yawn toward the feed wagon heaped with oats. Intercontinent, a stormy chestnut, pins his fine ears and lashes out, threatening to savage a small bay filly as she pokes her face hopefully toward the night watchman who tenders her breakfast in a plastic feed tub. When the tub is hung safely before her, her eyelashes blink demurely as Intercontinent's teeth grind against the large patch of bare wood and cracked paint he has etched onto the wall between their stalls.

If horses had a conscious sense of recognition, Manny might nicker out to the bay filly, Wandaful Candy J, who has not let Intercontinent's daily threat interfere with her appetite. Wanda, who is even smaller than Manny, has been with DeBonis since she left Elloree. In spite of her small stature, she can sprint and is well suited to the short distances and early speed of the two-year-old and New York-bred races. Nevertheless, it is solely through having been foaled and bred in New York that both Wanda and Manny found their way to the prestigious barn of Robert DeBonis at Belmont. In 1973, before a special series of rich races for horses bred and foaled in New York was instituted to encourage the state's breeding industry, fillies of their class would not have been thought worthy of the $40 per day it costs to keep a Thoroughbred in training on Belmont's back-

stretch. Even though Manny Dober shares the same paternal grandsire as Triple Crown winner Affirmed (Raise a Native), a little name-dropping on her pedigree chart would not have gotten her into Belmont. Because of the highly selective standards and carefully enforced regulations characteristic of the past 240 years of Thoroughbred breeding, all horses trace back to great ancestors, if the genealogist digs back far enough. Three of Manny Dober's great-grandsires—Timor, Tim Tam and Native Dancer—proved in performance that they had the speed and stamina, heart and class to win on any track, at any distance, in any company. A Thoroughbred's pedigree gives it the right to go to the track, but once there, it must fight in order to stay.

"New York horses are head and shoulders above all the others," says Bob DeBonis, standing in the center of his barn and watching the forty horses in his care parade for their morning soundness check. "If they can make it here, they can go up against the best in the world."

A tall, robust man with a comfortable manner which masks his discerning blue-gray eyes, DeBonis was an inveterate gambler before he decided that if he couldn't beat the races, he might as well join them. He started out working with trotters in his extra time. In 1959, when most married men his age with children to support were trying to figure out the fastest way to make it to the top, DeBonis went back to the bottom. He took a meagerly paid job as assistant trainer in a Thoroughbred racing barn. Working as an apprentice trainer in the mornings to gain experience and holding down an administrative job at *Life* magazine in the afternoon and night to keep his family afloat, he managed, by 1967, to get his own trainer's license. Today, with a staff of thirty, a payroll of $1.5 million and a statistical average of winning 20 percent of his races, DeBonis runs one of the most successful barns on the New York circuit.

"I run a high-priced claiming operation with some allowance and stakes horses," he says, sipping coffee and watching horses' legs move as he speaks. "I buy most of the horses for my clients and I learned a lot about picking horses from my gambling days. Gambling was a painful experience because I lost so much money, but being a bettor turns you into a pretty good handicapper. I used to study trainer patterns. Every trainer has his special way of doing things, places he sends a horse when it's sore, places he sends it when it's ready to win. As far as being a trainer, though, there are no special qualifications. You don't need athletic ability like a football player or a brain like a scientist. The only things you really have to have are dedication, a love for the animal and a willingness to get out of bed in the morning."

It is just 6:10 A.M. as the horses parade down one long aisle, around the end of one row of stalls and up along a row of stalls on the other side. The aisle, a dirt rectangle around the central stall area, seems to revolve like a merry-go-round as the horses march.

"Check that ankle. Better rub it with some more witch hazel," says DeBonis to one of the grooms as he and his horse swirl past. "Stop a minute," he says to another, bending down to feel Intercontinent's left front leg. "Okay, he still has some heat there. Ice water and then poultice." The horses continue, walking round and round, black, bay, brown and chestnut, up one aisle, turn, down the other aisle, turn, always, as on the racetrack, to the left. "Oh, here she is, the new one, Manny Dober. Looks like she's a little tight behind. They said she had some problems up in Boston tying up. A little fluid in the left knee." He presses the soft spot gently between two fingers. "Okay, we'll see how she works and decide what to do next."

A.M. radios and P.A. system announcements from the NYRA blast down from the ceiling. Whole families of pigeons swoop past the horses' ears. Quick but silent cats wend between the cutting hooves in search of a cat's breakfast. Spanish-speaking grooms, singing American pop tunes, bustle around flanks and haunches with plastic tubs full of ice or soiled bedding. In one stall, a dreamy-eyed girl groom kneels in a pile of sawdust, tenderly winding a thick sheaf of cotton bandaging around a sore and bulging tendon sheath. By the stable clock, on the face of which galloping horses replace the numerals for 12, 3, 6 and 9, it is exactly six-thirty. Though today is Wednesday, it could be any day of the week.

"Okay, let's go, first set," says DeBonis to his crew of exercise riders. "See you out at the training track in about five minutes. Mark, I want a slow gallop and then a sharp four furlongs from Cat Song if she'll do it."

"Yeah, I haven't been on her for a while. I want to see what the hell she's all about."

The exercise riders, all weighing 130 pounds or less, are hoisted up onto their first mounts of the morning. It is their job, with strong arms and an internal sense of the pace, to work the horses according to the trainer's specifications and to report back how the horse "felt," both physically and emotionally. All of DeBonis' riders fill out daily sheets on the horses they ride. A perceptive exerciser is one of the trainer's most accurate gauges of when a horse is hurting, when a horse is peaking, and what sort of an attitude the horse has both toward running and toward itself.

The horse's back is extremely sensitive. Just as humans project a certain emotional attitude by the way they carry their backs, horses convey their feelings through their spines. The exercise rider, who is perched directly on top of the horse's central nervous system, should be able to tell from the way the horse moves and responds whether it is feeling tense, hesitant, cocky, depressed, angry, relaxed, lazy, worried or any of the numerous other ways a horse may feel. In many ways, he is the horse's mouthpiece, reporting symptoms. It is then up to the trainer to make a diagnosis and decide on the appropriate psychological or physical treatment.

Horses, like people, need self-confidence in order to perform well. Young horses or horses that have been on losing streaks sometimes need to be bolstered with a few easy wins in order to bring out their best form and attitude. Horses whose "hearts have been broken" by repeated defeats due either to insurmountable weight or class differentials, stop trying to win, even against much slower and less talented horses. An astute exerciser can help a trainer identify and solve such problems before they become serious.

Feet dangling out of the stirrups, reins loose, knuckles pressed into the horses' necks, the exercise riders sit so still, apparently guiding their temperamental hulks of horse down the barn aisles by telepathic communication. Out in daylight, they wander, mostly without lead ponies, through the gravel drives and clotheslines fluttering with horse laundry, to the one-mile training track. There, some of the two thousand other horses stabled at Belmont are already at work.

"Slow down, pretty girl. Slow down, pretty girl. Slow down, pretty girl," chants an exerciser from Tartan Farms, rocking back over the red plaid saddle pad and rowing back and forth with the reins in an attempt to ease an overly keen chestnut filly.

"Oh, give me a home, where the buffalo roam," sings another at the top of her lungs, to divert the attention of the nervous black colt she is jogging from the construction going on at one of the nearby barns.

To the inside of the training track, horses gallop past, three abreast. Lone horses, doing speed drills, charge in paths of irresistible force like Kamikaze pilots along the rail. Just as at Elloree Training Center, most horses go out to the track in sets of two to four in which they all do the same thing.

"Horses, being natural herd animals, love company," says DeBonis, waiting up by the clockers' stand to watch Manny Dober's first slow gallop on the beige loam of New York. "But each one is different. As a trainer, you're essentially dealing with a six-month-old baby that doesn't talk or cry. Sometimes he doesn't eat. He runs badly and you wonder why.

"Look at this horse," he says, pointing to Bolting Sam, a consistent winner, who is jogging in sidesteps along the edge of the training track and bucking under his rider. "I only galloped him a half-mile this morning because he's in a race today. He's saying, 'Come on. Come on. Why did it stop?'

"Usually, you train a horse the way it likes to run. If it likes to finish fast, you gallop it easily and ask it to pick up speed at the end. If it likes to sprint, you give it shorter, faster works. A speed work puts an edge on a horse and helps bring it to its peak for a race. That's the whole idea of training, taking that edge off, putting it back on, always having your horse at its peak on the day it's going to run.

"Most horses will run right back to their breeding. Ninety percent of all good horses are well bred. I don't believe a horse can't run, though. I just believe that they refuse to. There are lazy horses as there are lazy people."

A big blood-bay colt by Raise a Native refuses even to jog forward on the training track. Rearing and twisting sideways, penis erect, he slaps one foreleg over the rump of his gelded Appaloosa lead pony in a desperate attempt to mount. While the exercise rider leaps deftly to the ground and the pony, chosen for its patience, shifts from under the colt's weight, two assistants with lead chains rush between galloping Thoroughbreds to clear him from the track. Although he has shown some speed on the few occasions on which he agreed to run, his lustful behavior leaves little hope that he will race successfully. Either he will be castrated to steady his temperament or, if his breeding warrants, retired unraced to stand at stud.

Manny Dober, a settled racehorse now, is numb to such shenanigans. She follows Mrs. Wiggans, another filly who is being exercised for the first time, out onto the seventy-foot-wide track. All of Belmont looms around her, the 30,000 seat grandstand, the three concentric ovals of dirt and turf, the infield with its clusters of vegetation, giant mutuel boards and two lakes. What interests Manny Dober more, though, is sizing up her social status on the training track.

Like a girl sent off to boarding school or someone at a new job, Manny is apprehensive. Horses in a herd have a well-defined dominance structure of superiority and submission. Although they may not overtly threaten each other on the track, they have a fine sense of their own worth and class in relation to the horses they are with. Until they have established their position in the group, they tend to be anxious and hyperactive.

Compared to these sleek, massive, well-bred beasts, Manny is a poor relative, progeny of a stallion whose stud fee was only $1,000 and an unknown mare of Argentine descent. Only fifteen hands high and never yet having broken her maiden, she seems hardly fit for the company of Sophisticate, a strapping bay filly by top stallion Vaguely Noble, whose average earnings index, 5.83, is the highest in the United States. Mrs. Wiggans turns her head away in deference as Sophisticate struts regally past, but Manny, raised by Tanta, the survivor, arches to the limits of her small stature and glints her black eyes imperiously. Six Crowns, by Secretariat and out of filly Triple Crown winner Chris Evert, leers toward them, frowning with flattened ears and pinched nostrils, the traditional equine threat. Mrs. Wiggans bends tactfully toward the outside rail. Manny bites at her bit and jogs forward, trying to yank the reins loose from the rider's hands. Although she has never won a race, her innate pride is still intact.

"Feisty little thing, aren't you?" asks Phil, her exercise rider, as he guides her to the inside rail and sets her off into a slow gallop. At the half-mile pole, he kneels on her shoulders, flattens his chest to her neck and asks her to breeze.

Generally, a horse in full training gallops at least one and a half to two miles a day. After a brief warm-up jog of about a quarter-mile to loosen its muscles, it is asked to run at a rate of 18 to 19 seconds per furlong to build up wind, strength and stamina. Normally, seven days before a race it will get a speed work—three, four or five furlongs in 12 to 13 seconds per furlong. Each horse's individual training

schedule is different and today DeBonis is breezing Manny and Mrs. Wiggans lightly to see how they like to run. When Phil urges her gently forward, Manny easily opens up her stride.

"He's just letting her run off a little now, not trying to kill her," says DeBonis, stopwatch in hand. Manny reels off the next half-mile in a consistent 13 seconds per furlong. "Fifty-two seconds," says DeBonis, shaking his head. "Well, she's not fast, but she's even. If she's anything, she's probably a stayer. Hey," he yells up to the clocker who times early-morning workouts for the *Daily Racing Form*, "what did you get for Mrs. Wiggans? Fifty-four? I got fifty-three. Wo-oh, she's slow," he mutters to himself.

Mrs. Wiggans' exercise rider has no problem easing her at the mile marker. Manny, who is just hitting her stride and feeling tuned up to run after four furlongs, doesn't want to stop. "Oh, now you want to run a little?" Phil asks her. "Now that it's all over?" He braces his toes in the stirrups, stands straight up on her galloping shoulders, and leans back, pulling the reins up to his chest like a water-skier. The leverage of his weight and strength rocking backward compresses Manny's body and shortens her strides until she eases to a stop.

"She's a gutsy little thing," Phil tells DeBonis. "She's not hard to rate, but she'll fight you all the way if she gets it in her head."

DeBonis is more impressed with Manny's spirit than her time. Ideally, a trainer likes to see a horse that can do "twelves"—run each furlong in twelve seconds.

"If they can't do twelves, they're not a racehorse," comments DeBonis, driving back to the barn to get the next set ready to work on Belmont's main track. "If they do twelves, it means they can win."

Manny Dober has been able to do twelves when pushed, even on the training-track surface, which is usually a little slower than the main track, but her preferred style of running is steady, enduring thirteens. Wanda, who likes to do her first furlong in eleven, the second in twelve, the third in thirteen, and the fourth in fourteen.

has the classic pattern of a sprinter, early speed winding down as the distance increases. Mrs. Wiggans, who has shown neither speed nor consistency, is still a bafflement.

## GREAT HORSES: ROUND TABLE

On April 6, 1954, in the same barn at Claiborne Farm, two great horses were foaled. One was Bold Ruler, the most influential son of the great Nasrullah. The other was Round Table, the greatest son of Princequillo. While Bold Ruler's incredible performance at stud has perhaps a slightly higher niche in racing history, Round Table was the unquestioned champion on the track. During four grueling campaigns, Round Table won forty-three of sixty-six races, including thirty stakes. In the process, he set one world record, three American records and twelve track records. By the end of his four-year-old campaign, he had become the all-time leading money winner. His career total of $1,749,869 still places him fourth on the all-time list, behind Spectacular Bid, Affirmed and Kelso. The above achievements made Round Table one of the toughest, most versatile and most durable Thoroughbreds of all time. Winning thirteen of fifteen races on the grass made him perhaps the greatest American grass horse of the century.

As a two-year-old, Round Table raced in the colors of his breeder, Arthur B. Hancock, Jr., of Claiborne Farm. While his five wins as a juvenile indicated promise, it wasn't performance alone that boosted the price Hancock was asking for the colt from $40,000 to $175,000. Rather, it was the incredible thrust the son of Princequillo generated from his hindquarters. When Round Table walked, he overstepped his front hoofprints by about a foot when he put his hind feet down. That meant that when Round Table was running on a surface on which he could get a sufficient hold, he could generate great speed and great stride length.

In February of his three-year-old campaign, after Round Table finished sixth in an allowance race at Hialeah (won by the future Kentucky Derby winner, Iron Liege), Hancock finally sold the colt to Travis M. Kerr for $175,000. The shrewd head of Claiborne Farm did retain 20 percent of the breeding rights to Round Table, however. That retention proved to be extraordinarily profitable.

After his purchase, Round Table won an allowance race at Hialeah, went west to nab one stakes race in three tries, then came east to set a track record in the Blue Grass Stakes. He couldn't translate that promise into a Kentucky Derby (as he finished third to Iron Liege and Gallant Man), but on his return to the West Coast, he really hit his stride. After a second-place finish, Round Table reeled off eleven consecutive stakes triumphs. Twice it was so difficult to find opposition for Round Table that special races were carded, in which all starters received the same money regardless of the order of finish. Round Table finished the year with $600,383, tops of any horse, and he was voted the first of his three consecutive grass-horse championships.

His four-year-old campaign was even more impressive. Round Table won fourteen of twenty races against the best horses in the land. Traveling from coast to coast to find competition, he at one point reeled off eight straight victories, during which he set five consecutive track records. His $662,780 in earnings led all horses for the second straight year; his total of $1,336,489 propelled him past Nashua as the leading money earner of all time; he was named Horse of the Year.

Although most horses would have been retired to stud by this time, Kerr gave his tough campaigner another year. At age five, Round Table won nine of fourteen races. In his first eleven races he carried 130 pounds or more, and despite these burdens set three American turf records. During the year, he won seven races carrying over 132 pounds, including a track-record victory in the Manhattan Handicap at a grueling mile and five-eighths.

In 1960, Round Table was finally sent to the breeding shed, where he continued his outstanding success. Through 1979, Round Table had an average earnings index of 4.20, which placed him eleventh on the all-time list. He has sired 78 stakes winners—20 percent of his named foals. Like so many other sons of Princequillo, Round Table has become an outstanding sire of turf horses.

| | | Prince Rose |
|---|---|---|
| | Princequillo | |
| | | Cosquilla |
| Round Table | | |
| | | Sir Cosmo |
| | Knight's Daughter | |
| | | Feola |

*Racing Record:*

| STS. | 1ST | 2ND | 3RD | EARNINGS |
|---|---|---|---|---|
| 66 | 43 | 8 | 5 | $1,749,869 |

Back at the barn, DeBonis marks down what each horse in the set did that morning, "W" for worked, "G" for galloped, "B" for breezed and "P" for ponied. Extensive records must be kept on every horse in the barn so that the trainer can know what program works most effectively for each individual and so he has a clear idea of what upcoming races each one will be eligible and suited for. The trainer tries to find the races in which each of his horses will have the most advantages in terms of factors like weight, distance, experience and class, with the least possible competition and the greatest possible purse. The ability to strategically read a "condition book"—the fourteen-day listing of specifications of races to be offered—is one of a successful trainer's greatest assets.

The racing secretary makes up the races based on the classes and types of horses stabled at the track for the meeting. If the barns are full of cheap fillies that have never won a race, he cards a lot of maiden claimers for fillies and cuts down on the number of allowance races and races for geldings and colts. The responsibility of the racing secretary is to devise enough different types of races so that each horse on the premises has a fair chance to run and win at least once every fourteen days. It is the job of the trainer to sort out the various races in which he thinks his horse will have an edge. This means not only careful reading of the condition book, but studied awareness of what the competition may be like in each race.

It is not the trainer's job to try to teach

$10,000 claimers how to run like Secretariat. A trainer cannot improve upon a horse's basic running ability. What he must be able to do is analyze how each horse in his care runs best, condition it to its optimum potential, assess its class and find races for it in which it is able to win. Winning races is how owners and public trainers like Bob DeBonis earn money. The idea is not to take a mediocre horse and push it to run in prestigious races in which it has only a slim chance of winning against good horses, but rather to find the richest possible races that it can win against the worst possible horses. As old-time trainer Phil Chinn once said, "I always put my horses in the worst company I can find for them and keep myself in the best company I can find."

"Hey, you!" calls DeBonis entering his barn and snapping his fingers jovially at an arrogant bay colt who charges to the door of his stall and thrusts his muzzle back and forth toward DeBonis' moving hands in mock threat. "What was that all about, that racing business?" The colt, World Pennant, who had the first race of his life the day before, curls his fat, gray upper lip back toward his nostrils, exposing gums the color of watermelon studded with thick incisors. "Don't worry," laughs DeBonis. "I predict good things for you. If you had run a little faster, he wouldn't have had to hit you." World Pennant, who finished fifth, twelve lengths behind the winner, snaps his front teeth together, unconvinced.

If a horse breaks his maiden his first time out, it is often a sign that he will be an exceptionally good racehorse, but many horses take longer to develop. Although the horse is a natural runner, it has to learn for itself how to run in races, how to concentrate on what its rider is telling it while surging in the crowd of other horses and screaming jockeys with sand and dirt pelting it in the face and chest. Running and racing are two related but entirely different tasks. A horse may run perfect twelves in his workouts, but become "chicken" when confronted with other horses and never show the speed he possesses during the race. Other lazy types don't bother to give their all unless they are forced to by the pressure of competition. The only certainty in dealing with racehorses is that no amount of human prodding forces a horse to run faster than it wants to go.

"Once a horse has shown his form," DeBonis comments, "he belongs to the betting public. It is unfair to run him unless you think he has a chance to win. With a horse like World Pennant that hasn't done anything yet, it's different. Why is somebody going to bet on him? Because they like his name?"

After giving World Pennant his pep talk, DeBonis rushes to the racing secretary's office to see if a horse he requested to have scratched has been allowed out of today's race.

By 8 A.M., trainers, jockeys and jockeys' agents have congregated in the racing secretary's office to hear the day's declarations. It is here that a jockey may pick up a mount if his horse has been scratched and where agents vie to get rides for their clients on the best possible horses in each race. Great jockeys are expert riders, but the horse is the primary athlete in any race. Although a good jockey can get the most out of whatever horse he happens to be on, he has to have good mounts in order to win consistently. Jockeys' agents are the supreme handicappers. Their business is to appraise the performance of every single horse at the meet, pick the probable winner for each race, and see that the jockey they represent is on it.

For almost all races except stakes, entries are taken 48 hours before the race is to be run. If there are enough entries, the race "goes." Because big fields attract bettor interest, NYRA tracks do not like to have less than six horses run in a race. For this reason, DeBonis' entry is a "stuck horse," not allowed out of the race by the secretary. The horse, which developed a temperature during the night, is finally scratched when DeBonis explains that it has been treated with drugs by the track vet. In New York State, horses are not permitted to run after having been given Butazolidin, Lasix or any other drug that might alter their performance during a race.

"Horses are like strawberries. They spoil overnight," says DeBonis, striding under the leafless February oaks of Belmont's paddock and into the grandstand to watch his next set work on the main racetrack. "They go lame, bow tendons, get cast against the wall of the stall, hang themselves up in the webbing. They're like quicksilver. They run right through your hands."

Leaning on the rail, DeBonis watches the passing Thoroughbreds extend their slim, supple limbs into the ethereal steam rising off the track, committing flesh and bone irrevocably to the vibrant shocks of racing speed. To help the horse bear this stress, "protective" bandages are wrapped on all four legs to keep them from injuring a tendon or bone by striking it with one of their hooves when they run. Around their ankles are wrapped bandages, called "run downs," to keep the sand surface from abrading the tender skin around the heels. Despite the bandaging, however, one false step can cause the pulling of a suspensory ligament. One soft spot in the footing can crack a sesamoid bone in half.

Back at the barn, Manny Dober has been sponged and hot-walked for forty-five minutes. At 10 A.M., after all the sets have worked and been cooled out, she receives her second meal of the day. Racehorses eat grain three times a day, at 4 A.M., 10 A.M. and 3 P.M., but it is only at ten that Manny receives special supplements and vitamins in her oats: orange "stress tex" to prevent dehydration, yellow gelatin to put a good texture on her foot, liquid blood-builder to keep her from becoming anemic, calcium to improve the quality of her bone and to help keep her from "tying up," and extra $B_1$ to keep her calm and encourage her to relax the tense muscles of her hindquarters. Although each horse has a slightly different diet uniquely suited to its needs, Manny's is representative.

"Tying-up," technically "azoturia," is a cramping of the muscles of the loins and the hind limbs. Sometimes called "Monday morning sickness" because it traditionally occurs after a horse on a rich diet is put back into hard work after a period of rest, azoturia can cause paralysis so severe that the horse must be put to death. Mild "tying-up" is common at the track, especially among fillies. Once a horse has "tied up" it is more prone to do it again. Manny "tied up" so badly at Suffolk that she could barely lift one of her hind feet from the floor, but DeBonis' preventive diet and exercise program is designed to keep her from having the problem again.

After lunch she dawdles over her hay and naps in her stall while grooms rake the aisle into immaculate furrows. DeBonis talks with owners to plan strategies. The track vet does pre-race checks on horses entered in the afternoon's races.

By noon, the barn belongs to the cats and the sparrows. Most of the staff has broken for lunch. Horses stretch out in their stalls or stand in the corners, drowsing. DeBonis has already headed over to Aqueduct to make the 1 P.M. post time. Only Dutch, the barn dog, and one slow, arthritic groom watch over the dark stalls breathing quietly with precious horseflesh. Even if a marauder or thief could break through the NYRA's intricate security system, he would never be able to quickly distinguish maiden Manny Dober from her allowance-winning stablemate, Artist Stick, or to distinguish the stakes horse, T.V. Series, from as-yet-unplaced World Pennant. There are no names on the stall doors.

When her groom returns cheerily at two, Manny gets the special, recuperative treatments DeBonis has ordered for her: icing and poulticing.

"In this business, we must constantly fight inflammation and soreness. We must do everything we can to keep the leg cold and tight." Ice from the track icehouse is lugged into the barn every afternoon so that Manny and most of the other horses can stand with their front legs, up to the knees, immersed and chilled in huge tubs. Swelling, which interferes with the flow of blood to the area, may also permanently distend the tendon sheaths so that the legs and joints become puffy with excess fluid. Routine icing averts the effect of inflammation before it has a chance to affect performance.

After Manny has stood in ice, her knees are poulticed with antiphlogistine and wrapped in cotton and "spider bandages" to keep the left knee tight so that excess fluid cannot build up. The spider bandage, which attaches in many ties behind the knee, allows her full range of movement in the joint. Both legs are poulticed because, if only one were treated, she would tend to put extra weight on the other, eventually over-stressing it as well.

Finally, the bottoms of Manny's feet, which have been "picked," or scraped free of damp, rotting manure, are painted with a black dressing to toughen them to a hard callus which will help her withstand the punishment of running. All four legs are wrapped in "standing bandages" to keep her from accidentally injuring them in the stall. Some horses, annoyed or bored, rip off their bandages with their teeth, but Manny is docile and does not have to have her bandage flannels smeared with red pepper to keep her from biting them.

In a small room across from Manny's stall, blue, brown and silver jars and giant bottles of horse medicines line the walls. There are mineral oil and colic medicine for digestive upsets; Absorbine, Irish Reducine, and various strengths of blisters, all used to tighten horses' legs; Bigeloil body brace, Weladol fungus shampoo and antiphlogistine medicated poultice; Dr. Reed's Koffeze for coughs; Vapol decongestant rub; Dr. Reed's Kidnisept diuretic and urinary tract antiseptic; Kaopectate, witch hazel and hydrogen peroxide; elbow-length rubber boots for horses, with attachable hoses at hoof level for heating or cooling treatments; restorative electrolytes and soothing Bowie mud, imported from Maryland.

In the stalls all around Manny, other horses are taking their cures. T.V. Series, like the noble stakes winner he is, dabbles at his hay and tolerates the knowing fingers massaging his fetlocks with alcohol. Likeable, still sore from his last race, sighs and nods to sleep as warm antiphlogistine, containing glycerine, boric acid, kaolin and oil of peppermint, is smoothed onto his legs with a flattened spoon. A bay mare stands patiently soaking her infected foot in hot Epsom salts for twenty minutes, but the instant the groom turns his back to mix up a hot bran poultice to pack the hoof with, she playfully knocks the bucket over onto the floor. Another mare, with sinus problems, wears a special mask through which warm eucalyptus vapor is steamed into her nasal passages. Farther down the aisle, Intercontinent stamps angrily, objecting to the cooling witch hazel being rubbed into his inflamed right tendon. Some horses, like some people, hate to be nursed.

Even with the constant attention a racehorse in a Belmont barn receives, according to DeBonis, "If you're lucky, you get to keep a horse at the track six months." The trainer can only stave off and relieve the effects of injury so far. Eventually the horse must be "laid up" on a farm for a while so that natural healing processes can take place. Lay-ups, which sometimes include swimming and other forms of mild conditioning at equine health spas, "freshen" a horse's body and mind so that it can return with renewed zest to the rigors of the track.

The average horse races every two to three weeks with an occasional thirty-day rest period. Better horses with more earning potential run less. Cheaper horses have to run more frequently to pay their way and to justify keeping them in training. Manny, an average New York-bred, is expected by her owner to run at least twice a month.

It is up to the trainer to keep the horse sound and fit enough to run and to advise the owner which races it should enter. The owner discusses strategy with the trainer and approves the trainer's decisions about when, where and how often the horse will race. A little over a week after her arrival at Belmont, and eleven days after her last race at Suffolk, Manny is entered in a six-furlong maiden special weights race for fillies and mares foaled in New York.

Before running in a race at any NYRA track, a horse must be officially approved to start. Although she may have lost all memory of South Carolina and Elloree Training Center, Manny remembers her quiet lessons at the monstrous starting gate well. The gate at Belmont is longer than Elloree's, with chutes for fourteen horses, but she walks in easily and stands quiet in the 40"-wide stall, surrounded by bright blue rubberized pads which keep her from "goosing," bumping or tickling her sensitive stifles, and by black rubber mats at her side and above her head in case she rears or balks against the seven-ton metal superstructure.

A fractious liver-chestnut filly who is supposed to break with Manny dances sideways, plunging and rearing as she is led to the gate. Horses improperly schooled during their youth—pushed too fast and punished rather than persuaded to be obedient—can learn to associate the gate with fear and pain. If a horse is afraid of something, it does little good to punish it. It will associate the object of its fear with the pain of the punishment and continue to think that the fear was justified. A horse that is whipped for not entering the gate will expect to be whipped every time it is led to the gate again. Eventually, in order to load the liver-chestnut filly, the assistant starter has to put a black hood over her head so she cannot see where she is going. The blindfold makes her totally docile and she is led into the stall next to Manny's with no incident. When the blindfold is removed, she relaxes. It is entering the gate that she fears, not actually being enclosed. When the doors flip open, Manny and the liver-chestnut break aggressively and breeze a slow four furlongs in fifty seconds. The liver-chestnut is required to come back for further schooling, but Manny Dober is "approved to start" at Aqueduct on February 7.

In her first race in New York, Manny breaks sixth, drops back to seventh, and finishes fifth, fourteen lengths behind the winner, American Liberty. Each fraction for this race is a full second slower than the fractions for the race at Suffolk in which she had come in third. The consensus, however, is not that she refused to run, but that she is still recovering from tying-up and is unused to the New York track surface. Thirteen days later, she runs another six-furlong race at Aqueduct. Following the same pattern of dropping back and then rallying, she finishes fourth, only three-quarters of a length behind the winning horse. The effects of her new diet and of the consistent exercise program of slow gallops, along with the attention given to her delicate legs, are beginning to show. On March 6, she finishes second in a six-furlong race for which the fractional times are almost identical to the last race she had run at Suffolk. Although she has managed to adjust her style somewhat to the short distances at which she is forced to run, DeBonis knows that she would do better in longer races. Like Tanta, who won over a distance at ages three and four, Manny is just beginning to mature and find her form.

"Manny likes to run from behind and is usually last in the early part of the race. She doesn't possess natural early speed, which is an inherited characteristic. I would say that she takes after her mother's side. Pronto was always last to the quarter pole and then he came on strong to win. In training, I don't make her use herself early. I let her start slow and then close fast in her workouts. You should always train a horse the way it likes to run.

"Manny has a wonderful disposition," continues DeBonis, sifting through the most recent pile of X rays on his desk in the barn office. "She wants to be a racehorse, but her size and her infirmities limit her a bit."

Racehorses' legs are continually X-rayed for signs of injury. In DeBonis' barn, photographs of two-year-olds' knees are graded in much the same way as tests handed in by schoolchildren. The best receive "A's" while the average get only "C-pluses" and the poorly developed knees, which still have lots of soft cartilage space between the unformed bones, get "D's." Some flunk entirely and are sent back to the farm to grow up.

Knee injuries are very common among racehorses, as they are among other competitive athletes. Although Manny is close to being an actual three-year-old and her knees have nearly "closed" or ossified to full maturity, the left knee has already begun to deteriorate.

When the horse's leg is held straight and pressed vertically into the ground, the eight small bones of the knee joint fit together perfectly, like pieces of a jigsaw puzzle, interlocking to absorb the shock of racing speed. However, if the horse's muscles become too fatigued to hold the leg straight and to set it down vertically, thousands of pounds of accelerating force drive into the small bones at an angle, crushing their edges together unevenly. Repeated intense concussion causes erosion, splitting and chipping of the bones. Although Manny's X ray reveals a slight erosion of bone, which irritates the ligaments, therapeutic treatments and light exercise have kept her "racing sound." The repeated attempts to sprint have aggravated her puffy left knee, but the program of racing every two weeks has improved both her muscle and her style of running. Horses, being predisposed to self-destruction, will continue forcing weight onto an injured leg until it is no longer capable of supporting them and they fall over. Trainers must constantly balance a horse's soreness against its fitness; its ability to win against its probability of breaking down.

Knowing that Manny's knee cannot take a lot of punishment, DeBonis trains her with long, slow easy gallops, rather than the more taxing speed drills. Her infirmity is no different from that of hundreds of other horses running at Belmont or from thousands of other athletes. She is sore, but not lame. The owner is insistent that she race in order to justify her training bill. On March 14, she is entered in a maiden race for fillies at one mile and seventy yards. It is another state-bred race, offering a rich purse for horses of her class, and it is the first race of Manny's eight-race career in which she has had a reasonable chance of coming in first.

# Section 7

# The Racetrack

## THE EVOLUTION OF RACETRACKS

Originally, in England, races were run over any piece of open ground that suited the owners of the competing horses. When "sweepstakes" became popular and the number of participants grew, it made sense to find a central location where horse owners could "meet" to conduct several races over a period of several days. In turn, the running of several races during these "meetings" justified the measuring and marking off of an official course on which the races could be run. The most popular of these courses soon came to be devoted solely to racing, and thus were the first racetracks.

Most of these racing locations were meadows or heath, and the actual course run varied with the shape of the property and the contours of the local terrain. These courses were irregularly shaped, and they included both uphill and downhill stretches. When racecourses began to build facilities to accommodate the increasing numbers of spectators, these structures were built around the existing courses. That's why, to this day, no two racetracks in England are alike. The course at Ascot is shaped like a large triangle; most races at Newmarket are conducted over one straightaway a mile and a quarter long; the track at York is shaped

like a fishhook. Below is a diagram of the course at Epsom, home of the famous Derby:

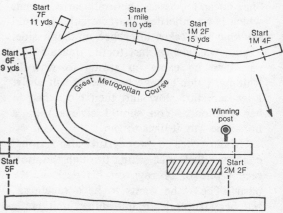

EPSOM (Surrey)

This substantial difference in shape and grading, along with the considerable variances in condition of the grass that provides the footing, makes time comparisons between tracks virtually meaningless. These differences also place a premium on the shrewd jockey who knows from experience how to use the shape and terrain of each course to his horse's best advantage.

The early settlements in heavily forested America often lacked the surrounding open meadows on which the settlers had been accustomed to race. As a result, most racing in the 1600s took place on the streets of the town—in Philadelphia, for example, horses raced through Central Square, dodging trees and, on hanging days, the gallows erected for that purpose. The first English-style course was laid out by Sir Robert Nicholls, first British governor of New York, on a plain near what is now Jamaica, Long Island. With the clearing of land for planting tobacco in the Middle American states, similar courses sprang up in the early 1700s in Maryland, Virginia, Kentucky and South Carolina.

Unlike in England, however, these early racing locations didn't evolve into modern racecourses. One major reason was the American preoccupation with speed. Racing on roads and streets demonstrated that horses ran faster on hard dirt surfaces than on softer grass courses. Dirt also resisted wear and tear far better than turf, which made it possible to extend race meetings for weeks or months. Racing on dirt, in turn, meant that racetracks weren't just laid out over any available grassy meadow, but were built. For maximum spectator visibility, tracks were designed as ovals; in the process of removing the sod and hauling in dirt, contours were eliminated and the courses were made perfectly flat.

Since the change from long heat races to the speedy dashes for which the dirt ovals were built came about the time of the Civil War, the oldest currently operating track is Saratoga, opened in 1864. Although the number of tracks soared to more than three hundred by the 1890s, the wave of anti-gambling sentiment and legislation that swept the country bankrupted the vast majority of them. Besides Saratoga, only seven other tracks date back to before 1900. The construction of the vast majority of the rest of the tracks currently operating started only after states began legalizing pari-mutuel wagering. For example, Maryland became one of the first states to make pari-mutuel wagering legal in 1911; Laurel opened in that year, followed by Bowie in 1914. In the 1930s, Depression-plagued

California jumped on the bandwagon; as a result, Santa Anita opened in 1934, Del Mar in 1937 and Hollywood Park in 1938.

The expansion of racing and the building of new tracks continued into the 1970s. Then, as with many sports, a saturation point seemed to be reached; attendance and wagering figures leveled off. Since 1975, only one major new track, the Meadowlands, has been built. Meanwhile, the number of racing days and of races run annually has remained roughly the same. In 1980, one hundred tracks conducted 7,443 days of racing in North America.

## THE MODERN RACETRACK

Racing associations not only organize racing, but must provide facilities for the racing and training of horses, as well as accommodating fans who come to watch and bet. How well these facilities are designed and maintained plays an important part in the quality of the racing and the enjoyment of racegoers.

Unfortunately, in the midst of racing's postwar expansion, many racing associations concentrated more on increasing short-term profits than on ensuring the long-term health of the industry. That meant seeking to increase income by increasing racing days and pari-mutuel takeout, while minimizing expenses by providing the minimum in facilities and maintenance. The result, inevitably, was a rather sharp drop in attendance, as former racegoers turned to other entertainments that courted them more assiduously.

Today, the racing industry has largely awakened to its dependence on the racing fan. Among other things (such as seeking a reduction in pari-mutuel takeout and vigorous marketing programs), tracks have begun upgrading racing facilities to increase the quality of their "show," and upgrading spectator facilities for better comfort and convenience.

*Table of Comparative Track Records*

(THROUGH JUNE 5, 1980, INCLUSIVE)

Below are track records for distances most frequently raced at courses on the continent.

| TRACK | 5 FUR. | 5½ FUR. | 6 FUR. | 6½ FUR. | 7 FUR. | 1 MILE | 1 MILE, 70 YDS. | 1 1/16 MILES | 1⅛ MILES | 1¼ MILES |
|---|---|---|---|---|---|---|---|---|---|---|
| AGUA CALIENTE | :56⅗ | 1:02 | 1:07⅘ | — | 1:23⅗ | 1:34⅗ | 1:39⅖ | 1:41 | 1:48⅕ | 2:01⅕ |
| AK-SAR-BEN | :57 | 1:02 | 1:07⅖ | — | — | — | 1:39⅖ | 1:40⅗ | 1:47⅖ | — |
| ALBUQUERQUE | :57 | 1:02⅗ | 1:08⅗ | 1:15⅗ | 1:21 | 1:36 | 1:41⅗ | 1:42⅕ | 1:51⅖ | 2:03⅘ |
| ARLINGTON PARK | :57⅕ | 1:03 | 1:08⅖ | 1:15 | 1:20⅖ | 1:32⅕ | 1:42⅘ | 1:41⅖ | 1:46⅘ | 1:59⅖ |
| AQUEDUCT | :57 | 1:02⅗ | 1:08⅗ | 1:15 | 1:20⅕ | 1:33⅕ | — | — | 1:47 | 1:59⅕ |
| AQUEDUCT (Inner) | — | — | 1:08⅘ | — | — | 1:40⅖ | 1:40⅖ | 1:42⅘ | 1:49⅕ | 2:03⅗ |
| †ASSINIBOIA DOWNS | :56⅗ | 1:03⅕ | 1:09⅗ | — | 1:23⅕ | 1:35⅘ | — | 1:42⅘ | 1:47⅗ | 2:05⅖ |
| ATLANTIC CITY | :57⅖ | 1:03⅘ | 1:08⅖ | — | 1:20⅖ | — | — | 1:41 | 1:47⅗ | 2:01⅘ |
| †ATOKAD PARK | — | 1:05⅕ | 1:11⅖ | 1:16⅖ | — | 1:38 | 1:42⅕ | 1:43⅗ | 1:50⅖ | — |
| †BERKSHIRE DOWNS | :59⅕ | — | — | *1:24⅕ | — | — | — | *1:48⅕ | 1:55⅖ | — |
| BELMONT PARK | — | 1:03 | 1:08⅖ | 1:15⅕ | 1:20⅖ | 1:33⅗ | — | 1:40⅖ | 1:45⅖ | 2:00 |
| BEULAH PARK | :58 | 1:04 | 1:09⅕ | — | — | 1:36⅕ | 1:40⅗ | 1:41⅖ | 1:49 | 2:03⅗ |
| †BROCKTON FAIR | *:59⅕ | — | — | *1:22 | — | — | — | *1:48⅘ | *1:53⅕ | — |
| †BILLINGS | :57⅘ | — | 1:14⅘ | 1:19⅖ | — | 1:42⅕ | 1:43⅗ | 1:46⅕ | 1:53⅕ | — |
| BAY MEADOWS | :57⅗ | 1:02⅖ | 1:08 | — | — | 1:33⅘ | 1:41⅗ | 1:39⅘ | 1:46⅖ | 2:00⅖ |
| BAY MEADOWS FAIR | :57⅗ | 1:02⅖ | 1:08 | — | — | 1:33⅘ | 1:41⅗ | 1:39⅘ | 1:46⅖ | 2:00⅖ |
| BALMORAL | — | 1:06⅗ | 1:12⅖ | — | — | 1:40⅖ | 1:43⅗ | 1:45⅘ | — | — |
| †BOISE | :57⅖ | — | 1:12⅕ | 1:17⅗ | 1:23⅗ | 1:37 | — | — | 1:52⅖ | 2:04⅗ |
| BOWIE | :58 | 1:03⅘ | 1:08 | 1:18 | 1:21 | 1:39 | 1:43 | 1:41⅕ | 1:49 | 2:04 |
| CHURCHILL DOWNS | :57⅘ | 1:04⅗ | 1:09⅕ | 1:16 | 1:21⅖ | 1:33⅘ | 1:41⅗ | 1:41⅗ | 1:48⅖ | 1:59⅖ |
| †COEUR D'ALENE | — | 1:07⅕ | 1:13 | 1:19 | 1:25⅖ | 1:40 | — | 1:46⅖ | — | 2:08⅖ |
| †CALGARY | :58⅗ | — | — | 1:19⅕ | 1:24⅖ | — | — | 1:45⅗ | 1:50 | — |
| CENTENNIAL RACE TRACK | :56⅖ | 1:02⅖ | 1:08 | — | — | 1:35⅘ | 1:39⅘ | 1:41⅖ | 1:49 | 2:02⅗ |
| †CAHOKIA DOWNS | :57 | 1:08⅖ | — | 1:17⅕ | 1:23⅖ | 1:37 | 1:40 | *1:42⅕ | — | 2:06⅖ |
| †COLUMBUS | — | 1:05⅕ | 1:11⅕ | 1:17⅕ | — | 1:46⅘ | 1:42⅘ | 1:44⅖ | — | — |
| †COMMODORE DOWNS | :57⅗ | — | 1:14⅗ | 1:17 | 1:24⅖ | 1:38⅕ | 1:42⅗ | 1:44⅕ | 1:53⅖ | 2:08⅗ |

| TRACK | | | | | | | | | | |
|---|---|---|---|---|---|---|---|---|---|---|
| †CALDER RACE COURSE | :59 | 1:05 | 1:10²/₅ | 1:17 | 1:23¹/₅ | 1:37³/₅ | 1:42 | 1:43⁴/₅ | 1:50 | 2:07 |
| †CHARLES TOWN | 1:00 | — | 1:11⁴/₅ | 1:17 | 1:24 | — | — | 1:44 | 1:50¹/₅ | 2:05³/₅ |
| †DELTA DOWNS | :58²/₅ | — | — | 1:19³/₅ | 1:24³/₅ | 1:38 | 1:42²/₅ | 1:43¹/₅ | 1:58⁴/₅ | 2:10¹/₅ |
| DELAWARE PARK | :57¹/₅ | 1:03³/₅ | 1:09 | — | — | 1:35¹/₅ | 1:39²/₅ | 1:41³/₅ | 1:47²/₅ | 2:00²/₅ |
| DETROIT | :57²/₅ | 1:01³/₅ | 1:08 | — | — | 1:35⁴/₅ | 1:39²/₅ | 1:40³/₅ | 1:47²/₅ | 2:02³/₅ |
| DEL MAR | :56²/₅ | 1:02¹/₅ | 1:07³/₅ | — | — | 1:33¹/₅ | — | 1:40 | 1:46 | 2:03²/₅ |
| ELLIS PARK | :58¹/₅ | 1:04 | 1:10 | 1:17 | 1:23³/₅ | 1:36²/₅ | — | 1:45 | 1:50¹/₅ | 2:04¹/₅ |
| †EXHIBITION PARK | — | — | 1:10²/₅ | 1:15³/₅ | — | — | 1:40²/₅ | 1:42¹/₅ | 1:48²/₅ | — |
| †EVANGELINE DOWNS | :58¹/₅ | 1:04¹/₅ | 1:09³/₅ | — | — | 1:36⁴/₅ | 1:42³/₅ | 1:43³/₅ | 1:53⁴/₅ | — |
| FLORIDA DOWNS | :57³/₅ | 1:04¹/₅ | 1:09 | — | — | 1:42³/₅ | 1:41⁴/₅ | 1:43⁴/₅ | 1:52 | 2:07²/₅ |
| FORT ERIE | :57³/₅ | 1:04³/₅ | 1:09²/₅ | 1:15⁴/₅ | — | — | 1:40³/₅ | 1:42¹/₅ | 1:48 | 2:03²/₅ |
| †FERNDALE | :58 | — | 1:15 | 1:19³/₅ | 1:25⁴/₅ | — | — | 1:43²/₅ | 1:54⁴/₅ | — |
| FAIR GROUNDS | :59²/₅ | 1:03³/₅ | 1:09 | 1:19¹/₅ | 1:24²/₅ | 1:37⁴/₅ | 1:41 | 1:42²/₅ | 1:48⁴/₅ | 2:02¹/₅ |
| FINGER LAKES | :58¹/₅ | 1:04²/₅ | 1:10⁴/₅ | — | *1:26⁴/₅ | 1:37 | 1:43 | 1:44¹/₅ | 1:52³/₅ | 2:06 |
| FRESNO | :55²/₅ | 1:03 | 1:08 | — | — | 1:34¹/₅ | — | 1:39⁴/₅ | 1:50¹/₅ | 2:01²/₅ |
| †FONNER PARK | — | 1:04²/₅ | 1:10²/₅ | 1:17³/₅ | — | 1:37²/₅ | 1:41 | 1:46 | 1:54 | — |
| FAIRMONT PARK | :57²/₅ | 1:03²/₅ | 1:08³/₅ | — | — | 1:38²/₅ | 1:40³/₅ | 1:42¹/₅ | 1:49²/₅ | 2:03²/₅ |
| †GREAT BARRINGTON FAIR | 1:00¹/₅ | *1:05³/₅ | 1:20⁴/₅ | *1:21 | — | — | 1:51¹/₅ | *1:52²/₅ | 1:57³/₅ | — |
| †GREAT FALLS | :57⁴/₅ | — | 1:14²/₅ | 1:26²/₅ | — | 1:41³/₅ | 1:45⁴/₅ | 1:46³/₅ | 1:53³/₅ | — |
| GOLDEN GATE FIELDS | :56⁴/₅ | 1:02¹/₅ | 1:07⁴/₅ | 1:15 | — | 1:33³/₅ | — | 1:40³/₅ | 1:46³/₅ | 1:58¹/₅ |
| GULFSTREAM PARK | :57¹/₅ | 1:03²/₅ | 1:07⁴/₅ | 1:20⁴/₅ | — | 1:39³/₅ | 1:40⁴/₅ | 1:46²/₅ | 1:59¹/₅ | |
| †GREENWOOD | — | — | — | 1:17¹/₅ | 1:23 | 1:36 | — | 1:42 | — | 2:03 |
| GRANTS PASS | — | 1:07⁴/₅ | 1:12¹/₅ | *1:23³/₅ | — | — | — | 1:50³/₅ | — | — |
| HAWTHORNE | :58²/₅ | 1:02²/₅ | 1:08¹/₅ | 1:14³/₅ | 1:24⁴/₅ | 1:37¹/₅ | 1:41¹/₅ | 1:39⁴/₅ | 1:46⁴/₅ | 1:58⁴/₅ |
| HIALEAH PARK | :57¹/₅ | 1:05²/₅ | 1:08³/₅ | 1:15⁴/₅ | 1:20³/₅ | 1:36³/₅ | — | 1:40³/₅ | 1:46²/₅ | 1:59³/₅ |
| HOLLYWOOD PARK | :56 | 1:02¹/₅ | 1:07²/₅ | 1:14 | 1:19²/₅ | 1:33¹/₅ | — | 1:39 | 1:46³/₅ | 1:58¹/₅ |
| HAZEL PARK | — | 1:06¹/₅ | 1:10²/₅ | 1:16 | — | 1:36³/₅ | 1:44 | 1:42⁴/₅ | 1:50 | — |
| IMPERIAL | :59⁴/₅ | — | — | 1:20⁴/₅ | — | — | — | 1:45⁴/₅ | — | — |
| †JEFFERSON DOWNS | :58 | — | *1:11 | 1:17 | 1:24 | *1:42¹/₅ | 1:41³/₅ | — | 1:53 | 2:05⁴/₅ |
| JUAREZ | :57⁴/₅ | 1:03⁴/₅ | 1:09²/₅ | — | — | 1:38¹/₅ | 1:42²/₅ | 1:44²/₅ | 1:51¹/₅ | 2:03³/₅ |
| KEENELAND | — | 1:05⁴/₅ | 1:08²/₅ | 1:15²/₅ | 1:21¹/₅ | — | — | 1:41¹/₅ | 1:47²/₅ | 2:03³/₅ |

| TRACK | 5 FUR. | 5½ FUR. | 6 FUR. | 6½ FUR. | 7 FUR. | 1 MILE | 1 MILE, 70 YDS. | 1¹⁄₁₆ MILES | 1⅛ MILES | 1¼ MILES |
|---|---|---|---|---|---|---|---|---|---|---|
| KEYSTONE RACETRACK | :57⅗ | 1:04 | 1:08⅖ | 1:14⅗ | 1:21⅖ | — | 1:40 | 1:40⅘ | 1:47 | 2:02 |
| LOS ALAMITOS | — | — | 1:09⅖ | 1:15⅖ | 1:21⅘ | — | — | 1:42 | 1:47⅕ | — |
| LOUISIANA DOWNS | :59 | — | 1:09⅘ | 1:16⅖ | 1:24⅕ | — | 1:40 | 1:44⅕ | 1:50 | 2:05 |
| LA MESA | :56⅕ | 1:02⅗ | 1:09⅘ | — | 1:23⅖ | 1:36⅖ | — | 1:43⅘ | 1:49⅘ | — |
| LATONIA | :57⅗ | 1:03⅖ | 1:09⅗ | 1:16⅕ | — | 1:35⅘ | 1:40⅗ | 1:42 | 1:49 | 2:04⅕ |
| †LETHBRIDGE | *:57 | — | — | — | 1:27 | — | — | — | *1:51⅖ | — |
| LONGACRES | :56 | 1:02⅖ | 1:07⅕ | 1:13⅘ | — | 1:33⅘ | 1:42 | 1:40⅖ | 1:46⅗ | 2:00⅗ |
| †LINCOLN STATE FAIR | — | — | 1:10⅗ | — | — | 1:37⅗ | 1:42⅖ | 1:42⅗ | 1:51⅖ | — |
| LAUREL RACE COURSE | :57⅕ | — | 1:09⅕ | — | 1:22⅕ | 1:34⅗ | — | 1:41⅗ | 1:49⅕ | 2:03 |
| †MADISON | :59⅕ | — | — | 1:18 | 1:24⅖ | — | 1:44⅗ | — | 1:53⅖ | — |
| †MARLBORO | — | — | 1:13 | 1:19⅗ | — | 1:41 | 1:44⅖ | 1:47⅘ | — | — |
| †MARQUIS DOWNS | — | 1:05 | 1:11 | — | — | 1:37⅘ | — | 1:43⅖ | 1:52 | — |
| MEADOWLANDS | — | — | 1:08⅗ | — | — | — | 1:40⅕ | 1:41⅘ | 1:46⅗ | 2:01⅕ |
| †MARSHFIELD FAIR | *1:02⅘ | — | — | *1:25⅖ | — | — | — | *1:52⅘ | — | — |
| MONMOUTH PARK | :57⅕ | 1:03 | 1:08 | — | — | 1:34⅗ | 1:39⅕ | 1:41 | 1:47 | 2:00⅖ |
| †NORTHAMPTON | *:54⅘ | — | — | *1:21⅘ | — | — | — | *1:49⅕ | — | — |
| †NORTHLANDS PARK | — | 1:04⅖ | 1:10 | — | — | 1:36⅗ | — | 1:43 | — | — |
| OAKLAWN PARK | :57⅗ | 1:03⅗ | 1:09 | — | — | — | 1:39⅕ | 1:41⅗ | 1:48⅗ | 2:04 |
| PENN NATIONAL | :57⅕ | 1:03⅕ | 1:08⅘ | — | — | 1:36⅕ | 1:40 | 1:41⅕ | 1:50⅖ | 2:03⅗ |
| PIMLICO | :57 | 1:04⅕ | 1:09⅕ | — | 1:26 | 1:37⅗ | 1:41⅖ | 1:41 | 1:48⅖ | 2:04⅕ |
| †PARK JEFFERSON | :59⅖ | 1:06⅗ | 1:11⅕ | 1:19⅗ | 1:25⅖ | — | 1:44 | 1:46⅖ | 1:54⅘ | 2:08⅕ |
| †PLAYFAIR | :59⅕ | 1:05 | 1:10 | 1:17 | — | 1:36⅖ | 1:40⅘ | 1:43⅘ | 1:49 | 2:07⅗ |
| PLEASANTON | :57⅕ | 1:02⅖ | 1:08⅘ | — | — | 1:40⅕ | 1:40 | 1:41⅕ | 1:47⅕ | 2:01⅖ |
| PORTLAND MEADOWS | :58 | 1:02⅘ | 1:09⅖ | — | — | 1:36⅕ | 1:41⅕ | 1:43⅕ | 1:48⅘ | 2:05⅕ |
| †POCONO DOWNS | — | 1:04⅘ | 1:11 | *1:14⅗ | — | 1:38⅘ | 1:40⅗ | — | — | — |
| †POMONA | :58⅕ | 1:03⅗ | 1:08⅘ | — | — | — | — | 1:42⅖ | 1:48⅘ | 2:03⅗ |
| PUERTO RICO | :57⅕ | 1:03⅗ | 1:09⅗ | 1:15⅘ | 1:23⅗ | — | — | 1:42⅗ | 1:50 | — |
| †PRESCOTT DOWNS | :59⅘ | 1:04⅘ | — | — | 1:26 | — | — | 1:47⅕ | 1:54⅘ | — |
| RIVER DOWNS | :58 | 1:03 | 1:08⅗ | — | — | 1:36⅘ | 1:40 | 1:41⅘ | 1:49 | 2:02 |

| | | | | | | | | | | |
|---|---|---|---|---|---|---|---|---|---|---|
| †REGINA | :59 | — | — | 1:21⅕ | 1:25⅕ | — | — | 1:46⅗ | 1:52 | — |
| †RILLITO | — | 1:05 | 1:11⅕ | 1:17⅕ | 1:24 | 1:39 | — | 1:45⅘ | 1:54⅘ | 2:10⅖ |
| ROCKINGHAM PARK | :56⅘ | 1:04 | 1:08⅘ | — | 1:26 | 1:35⅖ | 1:39⅕ | 1:42 | 1:48⅕ | 1:59⅘ |
| †RUIDOSO | — | 1:05⅕ | 1:11⅗ | 1:17⅗ | 1:24⅗ | 1:39 | 1:43⅗ | 1:45⅖ | 1:51⅖ | — |
| SANTA ANITA PARK | :58⅗ | 1:02⅘ | 1:07⅘ | 1:14 | 1:20 | 1:33⅘ | — | 1:40⅕ | 1:45⅘ | 1:57⅘ |
| SACRAMENTO | :57⅗ | 1:02 | 1:09 | — | — | 1:35⅕ | — | 1:41 | 1:46⅘ | 2:02 |
| †SALEM | — | 1:05⅕ | 1:11⅕ | — | — | 1:37⅘ | — | 1:44⅘ | — | — |
| †SANDOWN PARK | — | — | 1:11⅖ | 1:18⅗ | — | 1:38 | 1:41⅖ | 1:45⅗ | — | — |
| SARATOGA | :57⅘ | 1:03⅖ | 1:08 | 1:14⅖ | 1:20⅖ | 1:34⅘ | — | — | 1:47 | 2:00 |
| SANTA FE | :57 | 1:03 | 1:09 | 1:16 | 1:22 | 1:36⅗ | — | 1:42⅖ | 1:52⅖ | 2:05 |
| †SHENANDOAH DOWNS | — | 1:05⅕ | 1:10⅘ | — | — | 1:38⅖ | 1:43⅖ | 1:44⅗ | — | — |
| †SOLANO | :57⅖ | 1:02⅗ | 1:08⅘ | 1:17⅗ | 1:24⅘ | 1:35⅖ | — | 1:41⅘ | 1:48⅘ | 2:03⅖ |
| †SPORTSMAN'S PARK | — | — | 1:10⅕ | 1:15⅖ | — | 1:36 | — | 1:42⅘ | 1:49⅕ | — |
| †SANTA ROSA | :57⅖ | 1:02⅘ | 1:08⅘ | — | — | 1:35⅕ | — | 1:41⅖ | 1:49⅕ | *1:58 |
| STOCKTON | :59 | 1:03⅗ | 1:10 | — | — | 1:35⅗ | — | 1:41⅕ | 1:49⅘ | 2:02⅕ |
| †STAMPEDE PARK | — | 1:03⅘ | 1:09⅘ | 1:19⅖ | 1:24 | 1:36 | — | 1:43⅕ | 1:49 | — |
| SUFFOLK DOWNS | :57⅖ | 1:04⅗ | 1:08⅕ | — | — | 1:35⅖ | 1:40 | 1:41⅘ | 1.48⅕ | 2:01 |
| SUNLAND PARK | :56⅖ | 1:02⅗ | 1:08⅖ | 1:15 | — | 1:35⅘ | — | 1:42 | 1:48⅕ | 2:04⅕ |
| THISTLEDOWN | :57⅖ | 1:03⅘ | 1:08⅘ | — | — | 1:35⅘ | 1:41⅖ | 1:42 | 1.47⅖ | 2:03 |
| THISTLEDOWN (Inner) | *:58⅗ | — | — | — | — | 1:39 | 1:43⅗ | — | — | — |
| †TIMONIUM | — | — | — | *1:16⅖ | — | 1:38⅕ | 1:42⅗ | 1:44⅕ | 1:51⅗ | — |
| TURF PARADISE | :55⅖ | 1:01⅗ | 1:07⅖ | 1:14⅕ | — | 1:33⅘ | — | 1:39⅗ | 1:48⅕ | 2:02 |
| VICTORVILLE | 1:01 | 1:06⅖ | 1:13 | — | 1:28⅕ | — | — | 1:28⅕ | 1:59⅘ | — |
| WASHINGTON PARK | :59⅘ | 1:06 | *1:11 | — | — | 1:39⅕ | 1:42⅖ | 1:49⅕ | — | — |
| WATERFORD PARK | :57⅖ | 1:03⅖ | 1:09⅕ | — | — | 1:35 | 1:41⅘ | 1:42 | 1:47⅖ | 2:04⅖ |
| WOODBINE | :57⅖ | 1:03⅖ | 1:08⅗ | 1:12⅘ | 1:21⅘ | — | 1:40⅗ | 1:41⅘ | 1:48⅖ | 2:01⅕ |
| YAKIMA MEADOWS | :56 | 1:03 | 1:09 | — | — | 1:35⅕ | 1:42⅖ | 1:43⅖ | 1:48⅗ | 2:03⅕ |
| LAST UPDATE DATE | :56⅗ | 1:02⅗ | 1:08⅖ | 1:16 | 1:20⅖ | 1:33⅗ | — | 1:40⅗ | 1:47 | 2:00 |

† Track is less than one mile in length
* Races were run at approximately the indicated distance

# Racing Facilities

## THE TRACK

Because North American racetracks are neat ovals, rather than English-type courses that meander over hill and dale, many people believe that one track is pretty much like another. However, substantial differences from track to track, and substantial changes in the racing surface of the same track from day to day, make time comparisons for the same horses running the same distance very misleading. Also, just as in Britain, shrewd, experienced jockeys who can exploit the peculiarities of each track have a big advantage.

The most obvious difference between racetracks is their *length*. Most major tracks are one mile in length. The longest is Belmont Park, at one and a half miles. Several tracks that run short race meetings during fairs are half-mile ovals; the shortest tracks with regular race meetings are five furlongs (five-eighths of a mile).

To avoid starting races on turns (which would give a big advantage to horses with inside post positions), almost all racetracks have at least one *chute,* a spur that leads onto the main track. Most one-mile tracks have chutes off the backstretch that allow a straight start for six-furlong races (called a six-furlong chute), and a chute off the homestretch that allows a straight start for one-and-a-quarter-mile races.

The major effect of the length of the racetrack on the time of the race is the *number of turns* around which the horses have to travel. Horses, like automobiles, have to slow down to negotiate turns. A six-furlong race at a one-mile track goes around one turn; at a five-furlong oval, the same distance wraps around two turns. A good example of the effect on time is the comparison between the track records at two Chicago tracks with the same level of racing—Hawthorne Park, a one-mile track, and Sportsman's Park, a five-furlong track. The six-furlong record at Hawthorne is 1:08⅕; at Sportsman's Park, it is 1:10⅕.

Because the horses at five- or six-furlong tracks are always going around turns, these tracks are commonly known as *bullrings.* Since horses have to travel farther on the outside of turns, bullrings tend to favor horses with *early speed* and *inside post positions.*

A second difference between tracks, even those of the same length, is their *shape*. Five-furlong Hazel Park, for example, has a total homestretch length of 714'; five-furlong Sportsman's Park has a total homestretch length of 1016'. Obviously, the turns at Sportsman's Park are much sharper; horses thus have to decelerate and accelerate more abruptly and must exert more stress on their inner legs to avoid drifting out on the turns. Given these physical demands, many horses have trouble adapting to racetracks with sharper turns.

A third difference between tracks is the *placement of the finish line*. This placement, together with the shape of the track, determines the *length of the stretch*. The stretch length, or the distance between the last turn and the finish line, varies at one-mile tracks from 1,346 feet at the Fair Grounds to 832 feet at Del Mar. Long stretches generally favor come-from-behind horses; short stretches favor speed horses. One problem traditionally faced by Kentucky Derby entrants from the West Coast has been the change from the short stretches of Santa Anita (990 feet) and Hollywood Park (970 feet) to the long stretch at Churchill Downs (1,234 feet).

## THE RACING SURFACE

We explained in the section of this book dealing with conformation the tremendous force placed on the horse's slender legs during each stride. How well a horse stands up under the strain depends to a great extent on the condition of the surface over which it races. The ideal racing surface gives enough to absorb some of the shock of impact, and is elastic enough to return most of the energy to help the horse spring forward.

Hard surfaces are the fastest surfaces, because they offer the least resistance. However, because they absorb little or none of the force of impact, they place a great deal more stress on the horse's tendons, bones and joints. The effect is quite similar to the knee and ankle problems commonly suffered by people who jog on asphalt roads.

Racecourses that are too loose or too soft, on the other hand, absorb a lot of energy but don't give any back. This means the horse has to supply much more muscle power and tires more easily. The effect is much like that which people face trying to run on the beach or in mud.

Turf is the closest nature comes to providing the best racing surface. The grass helps absorb the shock of impact and the root structure holds the soil together to provide a "springiness" that returns much of the energy to the horse. The problem with the turf course is that the grass is quickly worn away and becomes slippery and easily torn in wet weather.

Dirt courses have been designed to provide safe racing in all kinds of weather

while emulating as closely as possible the advantages of natural grass. The courses are built in three layers. The bottom layer is crushed stone or gravel, which provides drainage. Next comes a six- to eight-inch mixture, primarily clay, that provides firmness. On the top is an approximately three-inch layer of sand and loam that serves as the cushion.

The exact composition and depth of each layer results in wide variations in surface from track to track. Hollywood and Santa Anita, for example, have relatively hard surfaces that produce very fast times. Tracks in the East, such as Belmont Park and Churchill Downs, tend to be deeper, more tiring and slower.

Another element of track construction that affects both speed and the wear and tear on horses is the degree of *banking of turns*. Banking helps relieve the strain on the horse's inside legs; makes it easier to avoid drifting; and allows the turns to be negotiated at a higher speed. Unfortunately, the more pronounced the banking of turns, the more difficult the course is to maintain. Rain and gravity cause the top cushion to move toward the rail; "tracks" form on the course and interfere with the running of races. Because the expense of maintaining the racetrack comes out of their pockets, track managements have tended to subordinate the welfare of the horses to the maintenance savings that come from flatter tracks.

Inadequate maintenance is another reason that many tracks develop pronounced "track biases," which have a profound effect on the running of races. At some tracks the rail gets pounded hard as asphalt, giving horses with inside post positions a big advantage. At other tracks, natural contours result in the rail becoming heavier and deeper. Horses with inside post positions tire more quickly, which gives the advantage to outside posts. The best jockeys are quick to notice track biases that occur from meeting to meeting or from day to day, and they concentrate on putting their mounts on the ideal track.

# TRACK CONDITIONS

Even well-maintained racing strips differ substantially from day to day due to the weather. Differences in draining and drying can make one part of the track faster than another. The following general track conditions are posted for the racing public:

*Fast:* The cushion is dry and the base is firm. "Dry," however, can vary from dusty to moist enough to press into clods, and the range caused by these differences can mean as much as a two- or three-second variation in time over six furlongs. Many horses dislike the footing that results when clods form under their hooves. This condition is referred to as a "cuppy" track.

*Sloppy:* The track surface is covered with puddles, but the base is firm. Sloppy tracks are generally about as speedy as "fast" tracks, but because some come-from-behind horses dislike having slop splashed back in their faces, such tracks tend to favor speed horses.

*Muddy:* Tracks are labeled muddy when water has had a chance to seep into the track's base, making it soft. The softer or "heavier" the track, the greater the effect on horses that tend to tire more easily.

*Good:* This term is most commonly used to describe a drying track that's progressing from muddy to fast; it is sometimes used to describe a track moving from fast to sloppy. Conditions within the label "good" vary widely, depending on exactly how much moisture has been absorbed by the cushion and the base.

*Slow:* Seldom used today, this description applies to a track between muddy and good.

*Heavy:* Rarely used today, this word describes a track worse than muddy, in which the base has become gooey rather than soft as a result of a long stretch of wet weather.

### Dangerous Racing Surfaces

*Too deep*—When a racetrack is too deep it takes longer to dry following rain. Deep tracks are very tiring to horses and tired horses are also prone to injury. If a horse has knee or shoulder trouble, deep tracks aggravate the trouble because a horse uses these parts of his body to climb out of deep going. Deep tracks also cause a horse to "run down."

*Too sandy*—If too much sand is added to a track, horses will run down and cut the fetlocks, making it impossible for the horse to run his race and extending the recovery period.

*Too much clay* takes too long to dry out following rain. It becomes slippery and slimy. When drying it clumps, causing a dangerous, uneven surface.

*Uneven*—Causes many breakdowns because a horse will run from a deep to a shallow area unexpectedly.

*Ridges on base*—If the base is disturbed or cut up to any extreme it will make the footing uneven and rolling and will tend to cause stumbling.

*Cupping out*—This condition, which results from lack of moisture in the track and a hard base, causes a horse to slip in his stride.

*Stones* in the track cushion can cause bruises to the foot and can fracture the pedal bone. Stones can also be thrown up and injure horses' eyes. When the track is muddy and the cushion is sloppy a horse runs in the base. If stones are not removed, this is an optimum time for such injuries to occur.

*Too fast*—A track becomes too fast when there is a minimum cushion covering the base and the base is too hard. This type of track causes breakdowns because the horse travels too fast during works and races: the faster the horse runs, the greater the chance of injury. When a track is too fast horses become sore more easily and it takes them longer to recover.

# TURF COURSE CONDITIONS

Because track officials are anxious to avoid expensive damage to fragile turf courses, most races carded to be run on the turf are moved to the main dirt track when rain comes. As a rule, only major stakes races are run on the grass under less than ideal conditions. The following are terms used by tracks to describe turf conditions:

*Firm:* The turf course's equivalent to "fast." A thick cushion of grass absorbs impact above slightly springy soil held together by grass roots.

*Hard:* Heavy use combined with blazing sun thins out grass on racetracks just as it does on front lawns. The lack of a cushion of thick grass makes the course hard and fast.

*Yielding:* Moisture has softened the soil to the extent that some of the springiness has been removed, but not so much that the horse's hooves sink through the surface.

*Soft:* Course is so wet that horses sink into the soil as they do into mud. Racing on such turf courses is very tiring and causes a great deal of damage to the course.

*Good:* The condition between firm and yielding. This label is infrequently used and difficult to decipher.

## THE TRAINING TRACK

To reduce congestion and wear and tear on the main track, many tracks build and maintain training tracks. Such tracks tend to be shorter and deeper than main tracks. Thus workout times on training tracks tend to be slower than those recorded on the main track.

## PADDOCK AND WALKING RING

The word "paddock" was a British dialectical version of the word "parrock," which comes from the same root as the words "part" and "partition." A paddock was originally a fenced-in area adjacent to stables or barns, where horses were let out to run; the word retains this meaning at modern breeding farms.

At a racetrack, though, the paddock is the area to which horses are brought to be saddled. The practice of saddling in public began when bettors demanded a chance to take a good, close look at horses before placing their bets. Because horses are often excited by crowds, trainers would prefer to cut down on time spent in the paddock, but they face fines if their horse is not in the enclosure twenty or thirty minutes prior to post time, in accordance with the applicable racing rules.

Admission to the paddock itself is limited to jockeys, trainers, owners, grooms and racing officials. The viewing areas surrounding the paddock and the walking ring are accessible from both the grandstand and the clubhouse at most tracks.

## THE STABLES

All tracks provide stables for horses racing at each meeting. We've described the allotment of these previously. These stables are normally located either in barns or in shed rows; they're normally covered and enclosed, but unheated. Along with stables, trainers are assigned tack rooms, which serve as offices as well as storage for racing and training equipment. Rooms for storage of hay, straw and feed are also provided.

For reasons of security, access to the stable areas is restricted to horsemen, their employees, racetrack employees and the press. Others seeking admittance must be screened by track security before being issued a stable pass. For reasons of safety, tracks strictly enforce restrictions on smoking, driving and parking, drinking and other harmful behavior. Violations result in either fines, suspensions or revocation of licenses.

The stable areas of tracks, which are referred to as the "backstretch," become communities during race meetings. Many grooms and other employees sleep either in track-provided dormitories or tack rooms. The track provides recreation rooms for leisure activities; the track kitchen serves up three meals a day at reasonable prices; shops sell racing gear, feed and various sundries for human beings. One of the serious problems facing racing today is finding the money to improve living conditions for these "racetrackers," without whom the racing industry couldn't survive.

## SPECTATOR FACILITIES

*The Grandstand:* In the early days of racing, spectators watched races standing up. How good a view one got depended on how close one got to the horses. As a result, fans jostling for position often spilled onto the course, barely leaving a narrow path for the racehorses. Such conditions were both dangerous and uncomfortable.

When racetracks began to depend on spectator admissions as a source of revenue for purses and operating expenses, spectator comfort became a prime concern. Tracks built large grandstands, just like those at baseball parks, where fans could sit and watch the action. Admission fees made up a much more significant part of a track's income in the days before pari-mutuel wagering and, by today's standards, they were high. Grandstand admission at the opening of Belmont Park in 1905 was $2—the same price charged seventy-five years later, when the dollar had declined to a small fraction of its 1905 value. To attract and keep customers at those prices, grandstand areas had to be comfortable and well maintained.

Today, the track's basic admission charge provides entrance to the grandstand, where spectators find a certain number of unreserved seats. The best grandstand seats, those toward the finish line, are normally reserved for those who pay an extra charge. At some tracks, grandstands are comfortable and well maintained. However, because tracks now get most of their income from wagering rather than from admissions, many more grandstands are shabby and uncomfortable, with long waiting lines at pari-mutuel windows and concession stands on weekends.

*The Clubhouse:* While the average spectator watched early races on foot, the "gentry" who organized the races and owned the horses watched from horseback or carriages. The most prestigious spot to watch from was the porch of the judges' stand, a structure built right on the finish line so judges could determine the winners. These stands were small, and they quickly became packed and uncomfortable.

When racing became more professional, jockey clubs and racing associations built

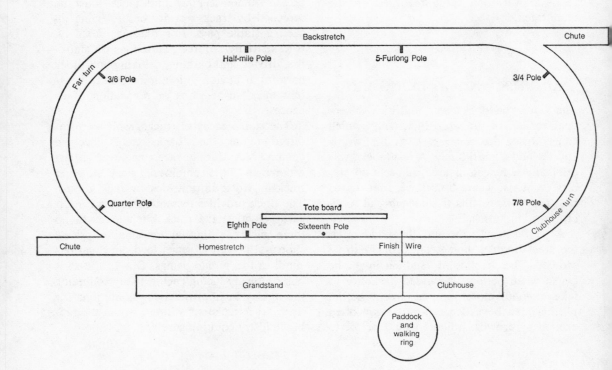

clubhouses for their members, which replaced the old judges' stands. These clubhouses were often lavish, containing dining rooms, ballrooms and even sleeping facilities.

Today, only at Keeneland is the clubhouse restricted to members only. At other tracks, an extra $1.75 or $2 over grandstand admission gets one into this less crowded, more comfortable and more pleasant part of the racetrack. Seats in the clubhouse stands are of three types: boxes, most of which are rented by the season by horse owners and wealthy bettors; reserved seats, available by the day for an extra charge; and unreserved seats.

*Dining Facilities:* Almost all tracks have clubhouse dining rooms that overlook the racetrack. Reservations must normally be made in advance for such rooms, and most have dress restrictions. Grandstand eating facilities are usually limited to stand-up food stands, a cafeteria and, in some places, picnic areas. At most tracks, special dining rooms are available for group outings.

*Parking:* The firt day of racing at Belmont Park in 1905 was delayed by the unexpected arrival of so many patrons in the newfangled "horseless carriages." Today, tracks are more prepared to deal with the large percentage of fans arriving in automobiles. At the larger tracks, three kinds of parking services are available: *valet* parking, available to fans who want to pay extra for the privilege of driving up to the door; *special* parking, self-parking near the gate; and general parking, the least expensive and the farthest from the track.

---

## STATE RACING COMMISSIONS AND RACETRACKS

*Arizona*
**Arizona Racing Commission**
1645 W. Jefferson
Phoenix, AZ 85007
PRESCOTT DOWNS (½ mile)
P. O. Box 952
Prescott, AZ 86301

RILLITO DOWNS (⅝ mile)
4502 N. First Avenue
Tucson, AZ 85718
TURF PARADISE (1 mile)
P. O. Box 9186
Phoenix, AZ 85068

*Arkansas*
**Arkansas State Racing Commission**
P. O. Box 3076
Little Rock, AR 72203
OAKLAWN PARK (1 mile)
P. O. Box 699
Hot Springs, AR 71901

*California*
**California Horse Racing Board**
455 Capitol Mall
Sacramento, CA 95814
BAY MEADOWS (1 mile)
P. O. Box 5050
San Mateo, CA 94402
DEL MAR (1 mile)
P. O. Box 700
Del Mar, CA 92014
FERNDALE (½ mile)*
P. O. Box 637
Ferndale, CA 95536
FRESNO (1 mile)*
1121 Chance Avenue
Fresno, CA 93702
GOLDEN GATE FIELDS (1 mile)
P. O. Box 6027
Albany, CA 94706
HOLLYWOOD PARK (1 mile)
P. O. Box 369
Inglewood, CA 90306
LOS ALAMITOS (⅝ mile)*
4961 E. Katella Avenue
Los Alamitos, CA 90720
PLEASANTON (1 mile)*
P. O. Box 579
Pleasanton, CA 94566
POMONA (½ mile)*
Pomona, CA 91766
SACRAMENTO (1 mile)*
P. O. Box 15649
Sacramento, CA 95813
SANTA ANITA PARK (1 mile)
Arcadia, CA 91006
SANTA ROSA (abt. 1 mile)*
P. O. Box 1536
Santa Rosa, CA 95402

* Indicates Fair Meeting

SOLANO (⅞ mile)*
P. O. Box 9
Vallejo, CA 94590
STOCKTON (1 mile)*
P. O. Box 6310
Stockton, CA 95206

*Colorado*
**Colorado Racing Commission**
Room 220, State Office Bldg.
201 E. Colfax Avenue
Denver, CO 80203
CENTENNIAL RACETRACK (1 mile)
5300 S. Federal Blvd.
Littleton, CO 80123

*Delaware*
**Delaware Racing Commission**
P. O. Box 2103
Wilmington, DE 19899
DELAWARE PARK (1 mile)
P. O. Box 6008
Wilmington, DE 19804

*Florida*
**Florida Division of Pari-mutuel Wagering**
1350 N.W. 12th Avenue
Miami, FL 33136
CALDER RACECOURSE (1 mile)
210th Street and N.W. 27th Avenue
Miami, FL 33056
FLORIDA DOWNS (1 mile)
P. O. Box E
Oldsmar, FL 33557
GULFSTREAM PARK (1 mile)
Hallandale, FL 33009
HIALEAH PARK (1⅛ miles)
Hialeah, FL 33011

*Idaho*
**Idaho State Horse Racing Commission**
4747 Glenwood
Boise, ID 83704
COEUR D'ALENE (⅝ mile)
Route 5, Box 203A
Coeur d'Alene, ID 83814

*Illinois*
**Illinois Racing Board**
160 N. LaSalle Street
Chicago, IL 60601

ARLINGTON PARK (1⅛ miles)
P. O. Box 7
Arlington Hgts., IL 60006
BALMORAL (⅝ mile)
P. O. Box 158
Crete, IL 60417
CAHOKIA DOWNS (¾ mile)
East St. Louis, IL 62205
FAIRMOUNT PARK (1 mile)
U. S. Route 40
Collinsville, IL 62234
HAWTHORNE RACECOURSE (1 mile)
3501 S. Fifty-second Avenue
Cicero, IL 60650
SPORTSMAN'S PARK (⅝ mile)
3301 S. Laramie Avenue
Cicero, IL 60650

*Kentucky*
**Kentucky State Racing Commission**
P. O. Box 1080
Lexington, KY 40588
CHURCHILL DOWNS (1 mile)
P. O. Box 8427
Louisville, KY 40208
JAMES C. ELLIS PARK (1⅛ miles)
322 W. Third Street
Owensboro, KY 42301
KEENELAND (1¹⁄₁₆ miles)
P. O. Box 1690
Lexington, KY 40592
LATONIA (1 mile)
Price Pike
Florence, KY 41042

*Louisiana*
**Louisiana State Racing Commission**
Suite 1020, 1 Shell Square
701 Poydras Street
New Orleans, LA 70139
DELTA DOWNS (¾ mile)
P. O. Box 188
Vinton, LA 70668
EVANGELINE DOWNS (⅞ mile)
P. O. Box 3508
Lafayette, LA 70501
FAIR GROUNDS (1 mile)
1751 Gentilly Blvd.
New Orleans, LA 70119
JEFFERSON DOWNS (¾ mile)
P. O. Box 550
Kenner, LA 70063

LOUISIANA DOWNS (1 mile)
8000 Highway 80 East
Bossier City, LA 71111

*Maryland*
**Maryland Racing Commission**
701 St. Paul Street
Baltimore, MD 21202
BOWIE RACECOURSE (1 mile)
Bowie, MD 20715
LAUREL RACECOURSE (1⅛ miles)
P. O. Box 130
Laurel, MD 20810
PIMLICO RACECOURSE
Baltimore, MD 21215
TIMONIUM (⅝ mile)
Timonium, MD 21093

*Massachusetts*
**Massachusetts State Racing Commission**
1 Ashburton Place
Boston, MA 02108
GREAT BARRINGTON (½ mile)*
South Main Street
Great Barrington, MA 10230
MARSHFIELD FAIR (½ mile)*
Main Street
Marshfield, MA 02050
NORTHAMPTON (½ mile)*
78 Main Street
Northampton, MA 01060
SUFFOLK DOWNS (1 mile)
P. O. Box B
East Boston, MA 02128

*Michigan*
**Michigan Racing Commission**
485 S. Main
Plymouth, MI 48170
DETROIT RACECOURSE (1 mile)
28001 Schoolcraft
Livonia, MI 48150
HAZEL PARK (⅝ mile)
1650 E. Ten Mile Road
Hazel Park, MI 48030

*Montana*
**Montana Board of Horse Racing**
LaLonde Building
Helena, MT 59601
BILLINGS (½ mile)
P. O. Box 1302
Billings, MT 59103

GREAT FALLS (½ mile)*
P. O. Box 1524
Great Falls, MT 59401

*Nebraska*
**Nebraska State Racing Commission**
P. O. Box 652
Nebraska City, NE 68410
AK-SAR-BEN (1 mile)
63rd & Shirley Streets
Omaha, NE 68106
ATOKAD PARK (⅝ mile)
P. O. Box 518
South Sioux City, NE 68776
COLUMBUS (⅝ mile)
P. O. Box 455
Columbus, NE 68601
FONNER PARK (⅝ mile)
P. O. Box 490
Grand Island, NE 68801
LINCOLN (⅝ mile)
Main Post Office Box 81223
Lincoln, NE 68501

*New Hampshire*
**New Hampshire Racing Commission**
105 Loudon Road
Concord, NH 03301
ROCKINGHAM PARK (1 mile)
Salem Depot, NH 03079

*New Jersey*
**New Jersey Racing Commission**
404 Abbington Drive
Twin Rivers Center
East Windsor, NJ 80520
ATLANTIC CITY (1⅛ miles)
P. O. Box 719
Atlantic City, NJ 08404
THE MEADOWLANDS (1 mile)
P. O. Box C-200
East Rutherford, NJ 07073
MONMOUTH PARK (1 mile)
Box MP
Oceanport, NJ 07757

*New Mexico*
**New Mexico State Racing Commission**
P. O. Box 8576, Station C
Albuquerque, NM 87108
ALBUQUERQUE (1 mile)*
P. O. Box 8546
Albuquerque, NM 87108

LA MESA PARK (⅞ mile)
P. O. Box 1147
Raton, NM 87740

RUIDOSO DOWNS (⅝ mile)
P. O. Box 449
Ruidoso Downs, NM 88346

SANTA FE (1 mile)
Rte. 2, Box 199 R.T.
Santa Fe, NM 87501

SUNLAND PARK (1 mile)
P. O. Box 1
Sunland Park, NM 88063

*New York*
**New York State Racing & Wagering Board**
2 World Trade Center
New York, NY 10047

AQUEDUCT (1⅛ miles)
P. O. Box 90
Jamaica, NY 11417

BELMONT PARK (1½ miles)
P. O. Box 90
Jamaica, NY 11417

FINGER LAKES (1 mile)
P. O. Box 364
Canandaigua, NY 14424

SARATOGA (1⅛ miles)
P. O. Box 564
Saratoga Springs, NY 12866

*Ohio*
**Ohio Racing Commission**
30 E. Broad Street
Columbus, OH 43215

BEULAH RACETRACK (1 mile)
P. O. Box 6
Grove City, OH 43123

RIVER DOWNS (1 mile)
6301 Kellogg Avenue
Cincinnati, OH 45230

THISTLEDOWN (1 mile)
P. O. Box 7050
Cleveland, OH 44128

*Oregon*
**Oregon Racing Commission**
520 State Office Building
1400 S.W. Fifth
Portland, OR 97201

PORTLAND MEADOWS (1 mile)
1001 N. Schmeer Road
Portland, OR 97217

SALEM FAIRGROUNDS (⅝ mile)
2330 Seventeenth Street, N.E.
Salem, OR 97310

*Pennsylvania*
**Penn. State Horse Racing Commission**
#2 Riverside Office Center
2101 N. Front Street
Harrisburg, PA 17110

KEYSTONE RACETRACK (1 mile)
P. O. Box 1000
Bensalem, PA 19020

PENN NATIONAL (1 mile)
P. O. Box 100
Grantville, PA 17028

POCONO DOWNS (⅝ mile)
Route 315
Wilkes-Barre, PA 18702

*South Dakota*
**South Dakota Racing Commission**
State Capitol
Pierre, SD 57501

PARK JEFFERSON (½ mile)
P. O. Box 278
Jefferson, SD 57038

*Washington*
**Washington Horse Racing Commission**
210 E. Union Avenue
Olympia, WA 98501

LONGACRES (1 mile)
P. O. Box 60
Renton, WA 98055

PLAYFAIR (⅝ mile)
Terminal P. O. Box 2888
Spokane, WA 99220

YAKIMA MEADOWS (1 mile)
P. O. Box 213
Yakima, WA 98907

*West Virginia*
**West Virginia Racing Commission**
1018 Kanawha Blvd. East
Charleston, WV 25301

CHARLES TOWN (¾ mile)
P. O. Box 551
Charles Town, WV 25414

WATERFORD PARK (1 mile)
P. O. Box 254
Chester, WV 26034

*Canada*

ASSINIBOIA DOWNS (1¾₁₆ mile)
3975 Portage Avenue
Winnipeg, Manitoba
Canada R3K1W5

EXHIBITION PARK (⅝ mile plus 208′)
Exhibition Park
Vancouver, British Columbia
Canada V5K3N8

FORT ERIE (1 mile)
P. O. Box 156
Rexdale, Ontario
Canada M9W5L2

GREENWOOD (¾ mile)
P. O. Box 156
Rexdale, Ontario
Canada M9W5L2

LETHBRIDGE (½ mile)
3401 6th Avenue South
Lethbridge, Alberta
Canada T1J1G6

MARQUIS DOWNS (⅝ mile)
P. O. Box 407
Saskatoon, Saskatchewan
Canada S7K3L3

NORTHLANDS PARK (⅝ mile)
Box 6360, Station C
Edmonton, Alberta
Canada T5B4K7

REGINA (½ mile)
P. O. Box 1363
Regina, Saskatchewan
Canada S4P3B8

SANDOWN PARK (⅝ mile)
837 Burdette Avenue
Victoria, British Columbia
Canada

STAMPEDE PARK (⅝ mile)
Box 1060
Calgary, Alberta
Canada T2P2K8

WOODBINE (1 mile)
P. O. Box 156
Rexdale, Ontario
Canada M9W5L2

*Puerto Rico*

EL NUEVO COMANDANTE (1 mile)
P. O. Box 29500
65th Infantry Station
Río Piedras, Puerto Rico 00929

*Mexico*

CALIENTE (1 mile)
Tijuana, Baja California
Mexico

HIPODROMO DE LAS AMERICAS
 (15⁄16 mile)
Lomas de Sótelo
Mexico 10, Distrito Federal
Mexico

JUAREZ RACETRACK (1 mile)
P. O. Box 1349
Ciudad Juarez, Chihuahua
Mexico

*Abbreviations for*
*North American Tracks*

AC — (Agua) Caliente, Mexico
Aks — Ak-Sar-Ben, Omaha, Neb.
Alb — Albuquerque, N. Mexico
AP — Arlington Park, Illinois
Aqu — Aqueduct, New York
AsD —*Assiniboia D'ns, Win'g. Can.
Atl — Atlantic City, N. Jersey
Ato —*Atokad Pk., S. Sioux C., Neb.
BB —*Blue Bonnets, Canada
BD —*Berkshire Downs, Mass.
Bel — Belmont Park, New York
Beu — Beulah Park, Ohio
BF —*Brockton Fair, Mass.
Bil —*Billings, Montana
BM — Bay Meadows, California
BmF— Bay Meadows Fair, Cal.
Bml — Balmoral, Illinois
Boi —*Boise, Idaho
Bow — Bowie, Maryland
CD — Churchill Downs, Ky.
Cda —*Coeur d'Alene, Idaho
Ceg —*Calgary, Alberta, Can.
Cen — Centennial Race Tr'k, Colo.
Cka —*Cahokia Downs, Illinois
Cls —*Columbus, Nebraska
Com —*Commodore Downs, Pa.
Crc — Calder Race Course, Fla.
CT —*Charles Town, W. Va.
Cwl —*Commonwealth, Ky.
 Formerly Miles Park
DeD —*Delta Downs, La.
Del — Delaware Park, Delaware
Det — Detroit, Michigan
Dmr — Del Mar, California
ElP — Ellis Park, Kentucky
EP —*Exhibit'n Pk., B.C., Can.

* Track is less than one mile in circumference.

EvD —*Evangeline Downs, La.
FD — Florida Downs, Fla.
FE — Fort Erie, Canada
Fer —*Ferndale, California
FG — Fair Grounds, N. Orleans, La.
FL — Finger Lakes, Can'gua, N.Y.
Fno — Fresno, California
Fon —*Fonner Park, Nebraska
FP — Fairmount Park, Illinois
GBF —*Great Barrington, Mass.
GF —*Great Falls, Montana
GG — Golden Gate Fields, Cal.
GM —*Green Mountain, Vermont
GP — Gulfstream Park, Florida
Grd —*Greenwood, Can.
GrP —*Grants Pass, Ore.
GS — Garden State Park, N.J.
Haw — Hawthorne, Illinois
Hia — Hialeah Park, Fla.
Hol — Hollywood Park, Cal.
HP —*Hazel Park, Michigan
JnD —*Jefferson Downs, La.
Jua — Juarez, Mexico
Kee — Keeneland, Kentucky
Key — Keystone Race Track, Pa.
LA —*Los Alamitos, California
LaD — Louisiana Downs, La.
LaM —*La Mesa P'k, Rat'n, N. Mex.
Lat — Latonia, Kentucky
Lbg —*Lethbridge, Alberta, Can.
LD —*Lincoln Downs, R.I.
Lga — Longacres, Washington
LnN —*Lincoln State Fair, Neb.
Lrl — Laurel Race Course, Md.
MD —*Marquis Downs, Can.
Med — Meadowlands, N.J.
Mex —*Mexico City, Mexico
MF —*Marshfield Fair, Mass.
Mth — Monmouth Park, N.J.
Nar — Narragansett Park, R.I.
Nmp —*Northampton, Mass.
NP —*Northlands Park, Canada
OP — Oaklawn Park, Arkansas
Pen — Penn National, Pa.
Pim — Pimlico, Maryland
PJ —*Park Jefferson, S.D.
Pla —*Playfair, Washington
Pln — Pleasanton, California
PM — Portland Meadows, Ore.
Pmf — Portland Meadows Fair, Ore.
Poc —*Pocono Downs, Pa.
Pom —*Pomona, California
PR — Puerto Rico (El Com'te)
Pre —*Prescott Downs, Ariz.
RD — River Downs, Ohio

Reg —*Regina, Canada
Ril —*Rillito, Arizona
Rkm — Rockingham Park, N.H.
Rui —*Ruidoso, New Mexico
SA — Santa Anita Park, Cal.
Sac — Sacramento, California
Sal —*Salem, Ore. (Lone Oak)
San —*Sandown P'k., B.C., Can.
Sar — Saratoga Springs, N.Y.
SFe —*Santa Fe, New Mexico
ShD —*Shenand'h Downs, W. Va.
Sol —*Solano, California
Spt —*Sportsman's Park, Ill.
SR —*Santa Rosa, California
Stk — Stockton, California
StP —*Stampede Park, Alberta, Can.
Suf — Suffolk Downs, Mass.
Sun — Sunland Park, New Mex.
Tdn — Thistledown, Ohio
Tim —*Timonium, Maryland
TuP — Turf Paradise, Arizona
Was — Washington Park, Ill.
Wat — Waterford Park, W. Va.
WO — Woodbine, Canada
YM — Yakima Meadows, Wash.

---

### HUNT MEETINGS

Aik — Aiken, S. Carolina
AtH — Atlanta, Roswell, Ga.
Cam — Camden, S. Carolina
Clm — Clemmons, N. Carolina
Fai — Fair Hill, Maryland
Fax — Fairfax, Reston, Virginia
FH — Far Hills, New Jersey
Fx — Foxfield, Virginia
Gln — Glyndon, Maryland
GN —*Grand Nat'l, Butler, Md.
Lex — Lexington, Kentucky
Lig — Ligonier, Pennsylvania
Mal — Malvern, Pennsylvania
Mid — Middleburg, Virginia
Mon — Monkton, Maryland
Mtp — Montpelier, Virginia
Oxm — Oxmoor, Kentucky
Pro — Prospect, Kentucky
PW — Percy Warner, Tennessee
SH — Red Bank, New Jersey
RB — Strawberry Hill, Virginia
SoP — Southern Pines, N.C.
Try — Tryon, North Carolina
Uni — Unionville, Pennsylvania
War — Warrenton, Virginia
Wel — Wellsville, Pennsylvania

# Section 8

# The Race

The race is the culmination of all the enormous activity described in this book. The race provides the ultimate test of the skill and judgment of the breeder, owner, trainer and jockey, as well as supplying the entertainment for the racing fan on whom the industry depends for its support. The time between the snapping open of the starting gate and the crossing of the finish line may be only a scant minute or two, but in that period are condensed more excitement and thrills than occur during hours in some other sports.

Descriptions of the race, however, can't focus solely on the minute or two in which the horses are actually competing. Each race involves a twenty-five- or thirty-minute cycle of activity that begins with the horses entering the paddock and ends with the lighting of the "Official" sign on the tote board. In this section, we'll explain this race cycle.

GREAT HORSES: SPECTACULAR BID

Spectacular Bid, the last of the great racehorses of the 1970s, retired from racing as the all-time leading money winner, banking an incredible $2,781,608 in his thirty career races. The sleek gray colt triumphed in twenty-six of these contests, including an astonishing twenty graded stakes. Unfortunately, more controversy swirled around Spectacular Bid than around any champion of the century. Such factors as the inexperience of his first rider, the conservative judgment of his owners and his trainer, a safety pin and a sprained right ankle combined to prevent this marvelous racehorse from receiving the unrestrained adulation accorded Secretariat and Affirmed.

The story of Spectacular Bid began when trainer Grover C. "Bud" Delp, on behalf of his client Hawksworth Farm, purchased the colt at the 1977 Keeneland fall yearling sale for $37,000. Delp, a Maryland-based trainer who perennially placed among the top ten trainers in races won, but who had never trained a champion, recalled, "He didn't stand out over the other individuals we bought."

Bid was so lightly regarded that in his first start he went off at a generous 6 to 1. He led wire to wire, then equaled the Pimlico track record for 5½ furlongs in his second start. Bid then went on to capture five of his next seven races, including the prestigious Champagne Stakes, the Young America Stakes and the Laurel Futurity. The colt was a landslide winner of the Eclipse Award as champion two-year-old.

Sent to Florida to prep for the Triple Crown, Spectacular Bid easily captured the

Hutcheson and the Fountain of Youth Stakes. In the Florida Derby, though, jockey Ronnie Franklin, a young apprentice who was Delp's protégé, repeatedly got the colt in serious trouble. Only a courageous final run on the far outside brought Bid to the wire in front. After the race, Delp loudly berated his rider in the paddock. The next day, Delp and Hawksworth Farm owners Harry, Teresa and Tom Meyerhoff met to consider a change to a veteran rider, a move counseled by the vast majority of the racing community. Several days later, Bid's owners announced their controversial decision to stay with Franklin.

After Spectacular Bid rushed to convincing victories in the Flamingo, the Blue Grass, the Kentucky Derby and the Preakness, the critics appeared to have been silenced. In the week before the Belmont Stakes, speculation centered not on whether the colt would capture the Triple Crown, but on whether he would break Secretariat's Belmont record.

The talk evidently went to the head of Ronnie Franklin, for when the gate opened he set the gray colt down to a blistering pace. At the top of the stretch, Bid began to tire, and he finished a well-beaten third to Coastal and Golden Act. The controversy brought about by Franklin's ride greatly intensified when Delp told reporters that Bid had stepped on a safety pin the morning of the race. Bid was judged sound enough to run before the race, but the press asked, "Was the pin just an excuse?" and "Did the injury prevent Bid from winning?" In the *Thoroughbred Record,* Delp gave his view: "Ronnie didn't ride him too well. I think a great jockey could have won on him under the circumstances. And without the pin Ronnie would have won on him by as much as he wanted."

Bid took the summer off to recover from an infection caused by the pin. When he came back to the track, Delp gave the reins to the great veteran Bill Shoemaker. In the Marlboro Cup, Spectacular Bid avenged his Belmont defeat by trouncing Coastal by five lengths. Then Bid met Affirmed, the 1979 Triple Crown winner, in the Jockey Club Gold Cup. Bid was 100 percent healthy, but Affirmed got off to an early lead, controlled the pace and fought off two challenges by the younger gray colt to win by three-quarters of a length. Despite his great year, Bid failed to win Horse of the Year honors.

Spectacular Bid went to California to begin his four-year-old campaign with three goals: to become the all-time leading money-winner; to become Horse of the Year; and to demonstrate his true greatness by becoming the first horse ever to capture the Marlboro Cup, the Woodward and the Jockey Club Gold Cup. By fall, the undefeated Bid had won seven stakes races, ensuring fulfillment of the first two goals. Then the Belmont racing secretary assigned him a weight of 136 pounds for the Marlboro Cup. Unwilling to concede 13 pounds to Winter's Tale, winner of the Suburban and of the Brooklyn Handicap, Delp and the Meyerhoffs declined to run their horse.

Racing fans were further disappointed when an injury to Winter's Tale prevented his scheduled meeting with Bid in the weight-for-age Woodward. All other contenders refused to challenge the great gray colt, and Bid captured the first walkover since Citation won in a walkover in 1949. All that remained for Spectacular Bid to prove was that he could win at one and a half miles by besting Belmont winner Temperence Hill and champion turf horse John Henry in the Jockey Club Gold Cup. However, less than an hour before post time, Delp scratched Bid, citing a slight sprained ankle. Again rumors swirled, fueled by Delp's refusal to allow the track veterinarian to examine Bid. Amid the controversy, Delp contended that the horse's record $22 million syndication justified not risking running him in the Jockey Club Gold Cup. So Spectacular Bid was retired, a great champion whose career was tarnished by personalities and incidents beyond his control.

| Spectacular Bid | Bold Bidder | Bold Ruler |
| | | High Bid |
| | Spectacular | Promised Land |
| | | Stop on Red |

*Racing Record:*

| STS. | 1ST | 2ND | 3RD | EARNINGS |
|------|-----|-----|-----|----------|
| 30 | 26 | 2 | 1 | $2,781,608 |

## THE PADDOCK

Approximately twenty minutes before post time, each horse is led by its groom from the stable to the paddock. The groom takes his charge for a turn or two around the walking ring to settle it down, while fans crane for a first look at the contenders. At most tracks, horses entering the paddock have a tag with their race number clipped to their halter so they can be recognized by the public.

Then the horses are led into the stalls labeled with the number they'll wear in the race. Waiting in the stall are the trainer and the jockey's valet, who carries the saddle, the numbered saddle cloth, the saddle pad and the girths that hold the saddle on the horse. The trainer then proceeds to saddle his charge, working from the horse's left side.

While the horse is being saddled, three officials are moving from stall to stall. The first is the *paddock judge,* whose job is to verify that each animal is fitted with the authorized bit and other equipment. Changes of equipment from race to race, with the exception of the addition or removal of blinkers, must be approved prior to the race by the paddock judge.

The second official is the *horse identifier,* who lifts the upper lip of each entrant to compare the number tattooed there with the identification number on that horse's Jockey Club Foal Certificate. This final check is additional protection against substitution of ringers for legitimate entrants.

Finally, all horses in the paddock are inspected by the *track veterinarian.* The vet has the authority to scratch any horse up until post time if he detects physical problems that would prevent the horse from running a true race. In particular, in the paddock he looks for certain tell-tale signs normally displayed by an animal that's been drugged.

The horses, once saddled and inspected, are led around the walking ring while the trainer gives last-minute instructions to the jockey. Most trainers with experienced riders limit these instructions to a reminder of the horse's racing characteristics and habits—the horse has a tendency to loaf on the lead; the horse won't move into a narrow hole between two horses; the horse bears out if whipped left-handed, etc. These trainers generally leave exact race strategy up to the judgment of the rider, since the exact manner in which a race will unfold is difficult to predict ahead of time. Eddie Arcaro, in his autobiography, told the story of receiving instructions from a trainer to "lay back fourth at the half, move up to third at the head of the stretch, then at the eighth pole come on to win." When the starting gate opened, however, the horse immediately dropped far back and stayed there. After the race, the irate trainer screamed furiously at the rider for not following instructions. Arcaro replied, "What did you want me to do, leave the horse behind?"

About ten minutes before post time, the paddock judge cries out, "Riders up." Traditionally, the trainer boosts the jockey into the saddle. The horses make one circle of the walking ring in numerical order before going onto the track.

## JOCKEY PREPARATION

Supervising the jockeys during a race program is the responsibility of the *clerk of scales.* All jockeys must report to the clerk of scales at least an hour and a half before the first race. From that time until they've completed their last assignment for the day, they may not leave the jockey's quarters except to race, and they may not receive visitors or make phone calls except under the supervision of security personnel.

When they first check into the jockeys' room, the riders are weighed in by the clerk of scales, who then compares their weights with those assigned to each rider's mount for the day. Overweights are posted and announced to the public before the racing program begins and before each race—for example, "In the fourth race, number 3, Wooden Leg, 2 pounds over." Racing rules generally require a change if the rider is five or more pounds overweight.

Included in the weight of the rider are:

Racing Silks
Riding Pants
Boots
Saddle
Saddle Pads

Together, these generally come to about four pounds over the rider's body weight.

Not weighed with the rider, but carried on the horse, are the following:

| | |
|---|---|
| Safety Helmet and Cap | 1¼ lbs. |
| Number Cloth | 1¾ lbs. |
| Blinkers, if worn | ½ lb. |
| Whip | negligible |
| Bridle | 1¼ lbs. |

In some states, such as New York, the overgirth (the strap that holds the saddle in place, which weighs about half a pound) is weighed with the rider; in other states, such as California, it is not weighed with the rider.

As the horses are entering the paddock for the race, the clerk of scales weighs the riders once again. Additional overweights or corrections are announced. If the rider is *under* the assigned weight, enough lead weights are inserted into a saddle pad to bring the total up to the program weight.

After the final weigh-in, the clerk of scales makes one more check of equipment before the jockeys proceed to the paddock. In the early part of this century, when the safety helmet was first introduced, many jockeys disdained wearing such "sissy" protection. Some clerks of scale took to randomly rapping jockeys over the head with a wooden stick as they exited the jockeys' quarters. After a few lumps, even the most recalcitrant riders got the message. Today, clerks of scale seldom have to worry about ill-equipped riders.

## THE POST PARADE

Arrival of the horses on the track is heralded by the bugler's "First Call," the old U. S. Cavalry signal for moving horses from the picket line to the parade ground. As the contestants enter the track, the great majority are met by riders on *lead ponies*. European trainers scoff at the American practice of relying on lead ponies during pre-race warm-ups, attributing it to a lack of proper training. But the presence of the ponies calms most horses, provides additional insurance against runaways, and helps conserve the jockeys' strength.

The riders of the lead ponies are generally independent contractors who are paid per race. At some tracks, the fee charged the owner of the racehorse goes directly to the rider of the lead pony. At other tracks, the lead ponies are paid for by management, and the fee charged the racehorse owner goes to a special welfare fund for backstretch employees.

After entering the track and meeting their lead ponies, the racehorses are paraded in front of the stands and back while the track announcer reads off their names and connections. Then the jockeys move their mounts out for the vital *pre-race warm-up*. The heavily muscled Thoroughbred must be allowed to thoroughly loosen up, just as basketball players run lay-up drills and baseball players take batting and infield practice. Warm-ups are also a time for the horse to get the feel of the racing surface and work off nervous energy built up in the paddock.

While every horse warms up slightly differently, certain patterns of warm-ups indicate how a jockey plans to ride the race. A rider who wants his mount to get out of the gate in a hurry warms the horse up hard, possibly even using the whip. A jockey who wants his horse to relax and rate back off the pace, on the other hand, may follow a brief gallop with a long, calming walk. In general, the thickly muscled sprinters tend to need more vigorous warm-ups than do distance horses, who have longer, less bunchy muscles.

During the warm-ups, the horses are closely supervised by the red-jacketed *outriders,* who respond to any jockey's call for help and chase down runaway horses. The track veterinarian also closely watches the warm-ups, looking again for any physical problems that might result in a scratch.

# THE TRACK ANNOUNCER

As the horses warm up, the track announcer is in a booth high above the racetrack, preparing for his call of the race. His job is a relatively new one in racing; the first public address system was installed at Bowie in 1927. Calls that accurately sorted out the blur of horses on the backstretch proved to be so appreciated by spectators that the idea rapidly spread. Today, Keeneland is the only American track without a public address system.

Calling races is a demanding job requiring an extremely agile and retentive mind. Because saddle-cloth numbers are often hidden in a crowd of horses, announcers identify horses by the colors of jockeys' racing silks and caps. In an amazingly short period of time, these announcers commit firmly to memory as many as twelve or more names and the exact colors worn. The most serious problem is entries; two or more horses wearing the same silks. In these cases, the announcer distinguishes the horses by their coat color or markings.

The announcer follows the action through powerful binoculars, which are sometimes mounted on a swiveling turret like the coin-operated viewing devices commonly placed on top of tall buildings and at scenic overlooks. The microphone is hung from the announcer's neck. This leaves the race caller's hands free to use the binoculars and operate the equipment on which race calls are recorded. Most tracks make

tapes of race calls available to one or more local radio stations for rebroadcast.

# THE START

The start is the most crucial and most dangerous part of a horse race. More races have been lost by bad starts than from any other cause. Jockeys have been seriously wounded, even killed, when horses went wild in the gate. Horses coming out of the gate sometimes veer and slam into other animals, throwing them off stride or causing serious injury.

## The Starting Gate

As dangerous as the start is, the problems of getting a field off safely and in good order were enormously reduced by the development of the modern starting gate. The concept of starting horses from enclosed stalls is a very old one. In Rome's Circus Maximus, horses started from "carceres" or "prison stalls." When the officials dropped a napkin and blew a trumpet, men pulled open hinged doors that released the chariots.

Starts weren't much of a problem when races were run in four-mile heats, but dash racing required an even start. Horses had to be schooled to stand in close company at a starting line, waiting for the sound of a pistol or the drop of a flag. Unfortunately, in almost every field were one or more bad actors who wouldn't learn their lessons and were determined to cause trouble. Such animals snapped and kicked out at starters and other horses, sometimes injuring them badly. False starts were numerous as horses went out of control or jockeys tried to anticipate the start. To maintain control, assistant starters used bull whips, nose chains that rubbed the skin raw and lip twitches. When these didn't work, the only remedy was to start the horse four or five lengths behind the rest of the field, an unfortunate handicap bettors couldn't anticipate.

For large fields, the process of starting a race commonly took ten to fifteen minutes, with half-hour delays not unusual. In the infamous American Derby of 1893, the start took an hour and forty minutes. No less than forty false starts occurred. Worse, in lashing out with a bull whip to try to establish some order, the starter inadvertently put out the eye of one of the racehorses. The race was won by Boundless, Snapper Garrison's mount, but Garrison forfeited his $1,000 riding fee when the starter penalized him for causing half the false starts.

Such nightmares led to experiments with starting gates. In 1894, at Maspeth, New York, horses were lined up behind a single long gate. As a gong sounded, the gate was swung out of the way. The gong disturbed the horses; the gate couldn't be swung out quickly enough to enable a fair start; and, finally, horses still slammed into each other behind the barrier.

In the 1920s, several tracks experimented with gates that had separate stalls for each horse. Some of these gates simply had an old-fashioned starter's tape across the opening, which was dropped at the start. Others had doors that had to be opened manually, but the majority had doors that opened electrically.

These electric gates were by far the fairest and the fastest, but frequent circuit failures resulted in uneven starts, or no starts at all for one or more horses. Finally, this problem was solved by the perfection of the modern starting gate. In this model, stall doors are held closed by electromagnets working against a strong spring. When the starter presses two tongs together, the electric current is shut *off*, and the gates immediately spring open. Thus a power failure would cause the gates to fly open—not at the right instant, but all at the same instant.

## The Starter

The starter has the most influence on the running of the race of any racing official.

With the assistance of seven or more assistant starters, he has the responsibility of seeing that all contestants get off evenly and in good order.

While the starting gate has eliminated the huge delays at starts, it has produced the necessity of schooling young Thoroughbreds to the rather frightening experience of being shut up in the tiny enclosure and to respond to the opening of the gates with a rapid, straight burst of speed. Every morning, the starter and his assistants work with trainers and exercise riders to school young horses, as well as older horses that either have misbehaved or have broken slowly from the gate. Before a young horse can appear in its first race, the starter must certify that it has been properly schooled in the gate. Trainers apply to the starter if they wish to add or remove blinkers; the starter usually requires that the horse break successfully from the gate in the morning before such approval is given.

Despite intensive schooling, some horses still have problems that demand special handling. Some have to be backed into the gate; some are granted permission to be the last horse entered, regardless of post position; in rare cases, some are blindfolded. Just prior to each race, the starter meets with his assistants in front of the gate. Referring to a book he meticulously keeps, the starter reminds his assistants of each horse's peculiarities. The starter assigns assistants to stand in the stall with horses that must be held by the bridle or tail to keep them still. Other assistants are stationed behind horses to slap them on the rump when the gate opens.

A small number of horses fail to behave despite the best of handling. Some chronically rear up, lash out at assistants or break through the gate for false starts. Others simply refuse to leave the stall when the gate opens. Chronic misbehavers are placed on the *"starter's list,"* which prohibits them from being entered in a race until the starter is satisfied that their problems have been solved.

Just before the horses are to be brought into the gate, the starter mounts a tall stand positioned just inside the rail, about ten feet ahead of the gate. He watches carefully, waiting until every horse is standing straight in its stall, head still and feet close together. Jockeys and assistant starters call out if they have problems. At the instant when his judgment tells him that it is the optimum time for the start, he presses the tongs together, the bell rings, the current is cut off, the gates fly open and the horses surge forward.

No matter how good the starter is, however, some horses and jockeys are caught unprepared. A horse may be bobbing from side to side or up and down, causing it to "dwell" for an instant when the gates open. Others may suddenly rear up, causing them to "break in the air." Some jockeys may be inattentive causing their mounts to get off slowly.

Some jockeys, on the other hand, have a reputation as good "gate boys." They have the ability to relax the horse in the gate while maintaining the keen alertness necessary to urge the horse forward the instant the gates open. At the same time, they have to anticipate any sudden veering that may cause the horse to slam into the animal on one side or another.

## TIMING RACES

When races were timed only by hand-held stopwatches, vociferous arguments sometimes raged over the exact time of a race. No matter how alert the timer, no matter how keen the hand-eye coordination, mistakes were inevitable.

Today, photo-electric eyes are imbedded in the distance poles all around the track. The instant the first horse breaks the beam sent out by the electric eye, the time is recorded. Certain split times are flashed onto the tote board in the middle of the infield and superimposed on closed-circuit television screens.

In Europe, races are run from a standing start. In America, however, the starting gate is set up a few yards behind the starting line, so horses get a *running start*.

The track's *timer* is responsible for the accurate recording of race times. To ensure against malfunction of the photo-electric timers, the timer and one or more assistants clock the race with stopwatches. In order that the timers know when the horses reach the starting line, an employee stationed at the starting line raises a flag just before the horses are released from the gate. When the first horse reaches the line, the employee drops the flag and the timers start their watches.

The inaccuracy still possible when the photo-electric system malfunctions was demonstrated in Secretariat's 1973 Preakness victory. In the absence of an accurate electrically recorded time, Pimlico announced the time as 1:54⅖. The *Daily Racing Form* caught the race in 1:53⅖, a new Preakness record. Reporters who repeatedly timed the videotape of the race confirmed the faster time, but Pimlico officials refused to change. Thus the Preakness time record is universally considered "tainted."

## THE PHOTO FINISH

Arguments about the proper time for a race before the advent of photo-electric timing were far outdistanced in number and intensity by arguments about who won a close race in the days before the photo finish was perfected. No matter how trained and acute, human eyes are inadequate for registering the exact order in which the bobbing noses of two or more Thoroughbreds reach an imaginary finish line.

When the motion picture camera was developed, it seemed the natural solution to the problem. However, the movie camera operates by opening and closing the shutter to produce a series of sequential images that, when projected at a certain speed, give the impression of movement. The problem for timing races was that the finish often came during one of those brief instants when the shutter was closed. Faster cameras were developed, but they were very unreliable.

In the early 1930s, an optical engineer at Paramount Studios named Lorenzo del Riccio invented a new camera. A report prepared by the Thoroughbred Racing Protective Bureau described the invention:

In this camera there is a precisely machined vertical slit at the front of the camera box and just behind the lens. The slit averages $\frac{5}{1000}$ to $\frac{1}{100}$ of an inch in width and if recorded in a still picture, would show a strip of from 3″ to 6″ wide across the track at the finish line. There's *no shutter* between the lens and the film. Light passes through the lens and through the narrow slit and is recorded on the film. *The action is stopped by reason of the fact that the film, when recording a picture, is moved from right to left across the slit at a speed proportionate to the speed of the horses.*

As the nose of the first horse reaches the finish, it is recorded on the film as it enters the leading edge of the 6″ wide strip seen through the slit. Then the head is recorded, etc. The moving film in this manner makes a picture of the whole horse and those that follow as they cross in front of the slit. The important thing to remember is that the picture on every part of the film is the picture of the narrow strip of track at the finish point and everything that passes through it.

In other words, the camera continuously records the images crossing the finish line just as a tape recorder continuously registers sound. The result is a long strip of film that shows horses in the exact order and exact distance apart that they crossed the finish line.

Fans viewing the race from the stands or on closed circuit TV often differ with the official placement. The reason is that the angle of vision from any vantage point other than right on the finish line produces an optical illusion. Any viewing angle to the *left* of the finish line makes the *outside* horse look farther ahead. Any angle from the *right* side (clubhouse side) makes the inside horse seem to be ahead.

The photo-finish camera is bolted down, and periodically a surveyor is called in to ensure that the left side of the narrow slit is exactly on the finish line. Before each racing day begins, the camera operators take a test photo to confirm that the camera is working. In particular, they want to check that the narrow mirror placed on the inside of the finish line, which provides a valuable "mirror image" to double-check placements, is in the proper position.

The responsibility for determining the exact order of finish lies with the two or more *placing judges,* who sit in a booth right on the finish line. Immediately after each race, the placing judges determine a preliminary order of finish that is displayed on the infield tote board. If any of the first three finishers were determined by a narrow margin, the word "photo" is flashed on the board. The judges then call down to the camera operator, who prepares an 8″ × 10″ print of the part of the film strip that contains the horses in question. This print is sent up to the placing judges, who then turn off the "photo" sign and post the order of finish. Meanwhile, the camera operator makes one or more additional prints to be posted on the track's photo display board and shown over the track's closed-circuit TV system.

One interesting element of the photo-finish camera is that it doesn't record stationary objects. That's why the finish line on the photos displayed to the public is not the wire stretched over the track at the finish line. The wire, no matter how tightly stretched, sways in the breeze. The finish line on the pictures is *drawn in* after development, using a sophisticated technique that ensures accuracy.

## POLICING THE RACE

While the placing judges determine the order in which the horses crossed the finish line, they aren't the ones that make the race "official." That responsibility rests with the track's three *stewards,* the track's most senior racing officials. The "Official" sign is lit only when the stewards have determined that no violations of racing rules have taken place during the course of the race.

In the early days of racing, the most common racing rule was "every man for himself." Rough-riding was the rule rather than the exception; cutting off or slamming into other horses was an everyday occurrence. Racing officials were appointed to their positions not because of their racing knowledge, but because of their prominence in the community. Their rulings tended to be restricted to placing horses at the finish line.

When the Jockey Club was formed to provide central administration for the then-chaotic sport of racing, the members formulated racing rules that included prohibitions of rough-riding and other dangerous race tactics. Enforcing them, however, still depended on how keenly developed were the powers of perception of the racing officials, and on how skillful they were in interpreting racing law. With only their eyes and memories to guide them, many violations were missed and many violators went unpunished.

The solution came with the institution of the film patrol. While, to this day, professional football, baseball and basketball resist using slow-motion cameras as a backup for the judgment of their officials, racing has used this sophisticated technique since after World War II. Today, at least four different cameras, placed on towers around the racetrack, record each race.

As good as tapes and films are, however, they have to be interpreted. Racing still depends on the skill of its racing officials. In the 1930s, the Jockey Club formed its School for Racing Officials. This rigorous training program is today a prerequisite for obtaining a job as an official at most tracks.

Every race is reviewed by at least seven officials. Four or more patrol judges are stationed at critical points around the track —the start, the turns and the finish line.

These patrol judges are in constant communication with the three *stewards,* who sit in the stewards' booth high above the track. In front of the stewards are at least four television sets, which show the race as seen by each of the four or more cameras. In addition, the stewards watch the race through binoculars.

What the patrol judges and stewards are watching for are violations considered in light of the following Rules of Racing:

153. (a) When clear, a horse may be taken to any part of the course provided that crossing or weaving in front of contenders may constitute interference or intimidation for which the offender may be disciplined.

   (b) A horse crossing another so as actually to impede him is disqualified, unless the impeded horse was partly in fault or the crossing was wholly caused by the fault of some other horse or jockey.

   (c) If a horse or jockey jostles another horse, the aggressor may be disqualified, unless the impeded horse or his jockey was partly in fault or the jostle was wholly caused by the fault of some other horse or jockey.

   (d) If a jockey willfully strikes another horse or jockey, or rides willfully or carelessly so as to cause other horses to do so, his horse is disqualified.

Note that in the above rules no mention is made of *winning.* Whether or not the foul was flagrant enough to keep a horse from winning is *not* part of the decision to disqualify. Actual contact is also not necessary for a foul—only that the horse be "impeded" or caused to alter course.

If the placing judges or the stewards notice any suspicious incidents in the course of the race, the stewards may hold up the posting of the official results for a *steward's inquiry*. Even if no inquiry is posted by the stewards, any trainer or jockey may lodge an *objection,* which causes the stewards to conduct an inquiry.

The stewards follow a two-step procedure during an inquiry or objection. First they talk by telephone to the riders involved— first to the rider of the horse allegedly interfered with, then to the rider of the alleged offender. Then they carefully replay tapes of the incident from all available cameras, going over them as many times as needed before making a decision.

Until the last three decades, horses that were disqualified were placed last. Under the present rules of racing, however, if the stewards decide to disqualify, the offending horse is placed back only as far as needed to place it behind the injured party. Thus, a winner who's disqualified for interfering with the third-place horse is placed third; the second finisher becomes the winner and the third finisher becomes the place horse.

To discourage time-consuming *frivolous* claims, the stewards have the authority to fine the jockey or trainer making such a claim.

The morning after a horse is disqualified, the stewards meet again with the offending jockey to determine if the incident took place because of the rider's careless or dangerous riding. If they decide the jockey is at fault, a suspension is ordered. The most common suspension is three or seven days.

Even if no inquiry or objection is lodged for a race, the stewards need one more signal before the race is pronounced "official." After a race, each rider dismounts and then is weighed out under the supervision of the clerk of scales or his assistant. After allowance is made for mud picked up on wet days, the weight is checked off against the pre-race weight. If all is in order, the clerk of scales picks up a telephone and notifies the stewards. At this point, the race is pronounced "official," prices are posted and the public moves to the windows to collect their winnings and place their bets for the next race.

## DRUG TESTING

While the public gets paid when the "official" sign is posted, the owners have to wait for their purses. After every race, the winner, the second-place finisher, the beaten favorite, and any other horses designated by the stewards proceed directly to the drug-testing barn (known around the track as the "spit barn"). Here blood and urine samples are taken and labeled, then shipped to a drug-testing laboratory. If a horse, as sometimes happens, refuses to cooperate immediately with a urine sample, the animal has to stay in the barn under guard until the sample is obtained or for a specified number of hours.

The incredible variety of pharmaceutical substances and the constant appearance of new products makes drug testing incredibly complicated. Presently, laboratories routinely conduct tests for nearly a hundred different substances. If any drugs have been found by racing security at the track involved, additional tests for those substances may be run. This drug testing, depending on the state, can take from five to fifteen days.

If the drug reports are negative, the stewards order the release of the purse money to the owner. If they test positive, the horse is disqualified to last place and the purses are ordered distributed in the new order of finish. The most famous such redistribution is the disqualification of Dancer's Image in the 1968 Kentucky Derby. The horse, owned by Peter Fuller, was found to have traces of Butazolidin, an anti-inflammatory drug which, ironically, was later legalized for use on horses in Kentucky, though it is now banned.

As of 1980, pre-race drug testing was introduced at New York tracks in a further effort to protect the betting public.

# Life of the Horse: 6. Racing

# The Race

Banknote, the yearling, flapping her lower lip up and down at the strangeness of the bit in her mouth and reeling and squatting, slippery as an eel under the weight of her first rider, has no inkling, but Tanta, witchy and sultry in the stall with her newborn foal, remembers. Sir Wimborne, posing in solitary majesty on his private knoll at Akindale Farm; Take Your Place, galloping frantically to the limits of his paddock; Amber Dancer, beatific as a madonna in the stable light and heavy with foal; even Toga Nut, sighing weakly as he watches the mares saunter down the road to their forbidden fields, knows. They have felt the edgy frustration of the morning workout that ends too abruptly and the tension when the hay and the water are removed from their stalls at 11 A.M. Everything in their breeding, instinct, metabolism, upbringing, training and physique was geared to this day. The race is the most exacting, brutal and enervating moment of a Thoroughbred's life. It is a consummate experience that no horse ever forgets.

Manny Dober, standing patiently in the "receiving barn," where all horses not sta-bled at Aqueduct are brought before the race, knows something is different. The large vein running around her eye and down along the edge of her nose throbs, fat with blood. One of the NYRA horse identifiers has twisted her upper lip inside out so he can read the serial number tattooed there and compare it to the number on her certificate. Another kneels in the sawdust, comparing the shapes of her "night-eyes" to those in the life-size photographs in her registration credentials and checks to see that her cowlicks and markings match those entered on the sheet.

"Okay, I guess you're who you say you are, Manny Dober," says one of the identifiers.

"Hey," yells a groom, "ask her if she's going to win."

Next the vet visits her to conduct the pre-race veterinary check. In order to run, a horse must be approved "racing sound," which means not that it is in perfect physical condition, but rather that it is sound enough not to break down in the race it is about to run.

Manny executes the obligatory blinks

when the vet cups his hand past her long eyelashes. A horse must have normal vision in at least one eye in order to race. When he holds his hands under each of her twitching nostrils, she exhales equally through both of them. Favorites have been known to lose because a piece of sponge was shoved up one of their nasal passages. This trick, last discovered at a New York track in 1946, does not interfere with a horse's speed, but it severely hinders its endurance. Any horse with impaired breathing or a nose bleed is automatically scratched.

At the vet's request, Manny is jogged away from him and then back toward him. She sets her feet down evenly, but his gaze fixes on her puffy left knee. He pops a thermometer into her rectum and, while waiting to read it, palpitates the puffy spot, picks up her leg and flexes it tightly at the knee. Then he presses against it to see if she will flinch in pain. There is no heat in the joint and she ignores his insistent fingers. When he flexes the other knee, for good measure, she cranes her head around and nibbles on his neck.

"Guess she's not hurting that bad," he comments, probing down each of her legs to find any swelling or heat in the tendons and ligaments, any unhealed injury in the ankles or cannon bones which is painful enough to cause her to be lame. He feels to see that the nerve trunks on the back of her legs have not been severed to deprive a painful foot of sensation. The only form of "nerving" allowed in New York is the slicing of the digital posterior nerve below the ankle and just above the hoof.

Finally, he examines her hooves to see that they have not been pared down so low that the sensitive part of her foot will become sore during the race. This strategy ensures that even a good horse will be hurting so badly that it cannot run its best. If the horse is a favorite, a corrupt trainer may pare down its hooves to make sure that it loses. By the time it runs again, the odds on it will have changed, new hoof will have grown in, and the horse will once again have a good chance to win—at higher odds.

Manny's neat, wide hooves are smooth-textured and perfect. Just shod two weeks earlier and painted daily with hoof tar, they are tough and resilient. Hooves which are dry and "shelly" often crack under the pressure of racing speeds. Quarter cracks and sand cracks, like split fingernails, are painful and must be given a chance to grow out so that the pressure applied during work does not split them further. Sometimes they can be patched with silicone successfully enough so that the horse can continue to race while the foot repairs itself.

"One hundred degrees," says the vet, pulling the thermometer from under her swishing tail. "Normal." He makes a note of the puffy knee and points it out to the Hispanic groom who speaks only racetrack English. "Hielo. You know, ice. Ice," advises the vet.

## COMMON RACING AILMENTS AND INJURIES

*Bleeding:* Some horses have a predisposition to hemorrhaging from the nostrils during or after a race or workout. The blood comes from veins ruptured in the nostrils, the pharynx or the lungs.

*Bone spavin:* The formation of bony deposits on the small flat bones at the lower part of the hock. Causes lameness.

*Bowed tendon:* A severe strain of one or both of the flexor tendons that run along the back of the cannon bone. Because of swelling and fluid accumulation, the tendons have a bowed appearance. This condition causes lameness and requires long rest.

*Bucked shins:* An inflammation of the membrane covering the front of the cannon bones of young horses, caused by excessively hard training on immature legs.

*Heat exhaustion:* Caused by over-exertion in hot weather. The horse stops sweating and its body temperature soars. This is often the cause of a horse collapsing after a race.

*Osselets:* Arthritis of the fetlock joint, which causes a hot, painful swelling.

*Popped knee:* A swollen knee that contains an excess of fluid; caused by an inflammation within the knee joint, often because of a bone chip.

*Quarter crack:* A crack found in the wall of the hoof in the area of the quarter.

*Ring bone:* A bony enlargement in the front and sides of the pastern.

*Sand crack:* A crack in the toe of the hoof.

*Sesamoiditis:* An inflammation of the tendon sheath covering the sesamoids, two bones at the rear of the fetlock joint.

*Sinusitis:* An infection of one or both sinuses, causing breathing problems.

*Splints:* Young horses overworked too early often develop bone enlargements between the splint and cannon bones that cause considerable pain.

*Stifle out:* This term refers to dislocation of the stifle joint.

*Suspensory ligament strain:* The suspensory ligament, which runs behind the cannon bone, becomes thickened and inflamed.

*Whistling:* The wheezing sound made by a horse suffering from an inflammation of the respiratory tract.

---

Horses with chronic conditions that are acting up, unhealed surgery or soreness so marked that even numbing ice will not prevent them from limping on the track are given the dreaded pink slips, which mean they are on the vet's list and may not race until he has seen them work out soundly. Some states permit the use of Butazolidin (an analgesic, anti-inflammatory drug) and Lasix, a drug which keeps horses from bleeding from the lungs. In New York, however, horses must run "cold turkey." The theory is that when a horse feels better than it actually is, it is more likely to push itself past the limit of its capabilities and break down. It is also a fact that both "bute" and Lasix are capable of masking the presence of other forbidden substances, such as tranquilizers and stimulants, so that they are undetectable in post-race drug tests.

Breaking down is serious. When a horse falls or even falters on the track, it is not like a basketball player breaking his ankle during a game or a tennis player dislocating her shoulder. The thirty-mile-per-hour or so momentum of the race has already been established and the life of every horse and rider on the track is at stake. Bute is not technically a pain-killer. It reduces fever and inflammation in bones, joints and soft tissues, thus relieving pain. Bute cannot make a horse perform any better than it would if its limbs were not inflamed, but it can make it impossible for a vet to determine whether a horse has deteriorated past the point of being a safe ride.

In 1978, the bute controversy came to a head when a cheap claimer named Easy Edith, running on bute to reduce inflammation in her left knee, shattered her cannon bone banking around the final turn of a six-furlong sprint at Pimlico. She went down, causing three other horses that were unable to stop or turn in time to go down with her. A twenty-five-year-old jockey, Robert Pineda, was killed in the spill and two others were seriously injured. Although no hard evidence has ever linked bute directly to breakdowns, it is widely believed that rest, which would allow inflamed joints to heal, would be preferable to bute, which simply reduces the soreness enough so that they can continue to be stressed.

Sand and dirt cake up and stick to the fronts of Manny's hooves as her groom walks her out of the receiving barn and toward the track. The hoof, which is 60 percent water and very fibrous, absorbs like a sponge. Horses which are so sound that they don't require icing walk into the paddock with dry, clean hooves, but no matter how thoroughly a groom tries to dry a horse's hooves so that it will look like a sound, attractive claiming prospect, a hoof that has been iced will always cake.

Other horses fall into file as Manny

crosses the backstretch and wends her way along the sand path lining the parking lot. Like many of the others, she wears elasticized "run down" bandages on her hind legs to protect her ankles from being rubbed raw and sore by the sand track. One filly, however, wears front-leg bandages, a sign that she may have serious tendon problems which require extra support. Another, whose hind feet do not step far enough forward to land in or ahead of the prints left by her front hooves, looks as though she may be stiff and sore. Ideally, to produce a long, sweeping stride, a Thoroughbred's hind foot should overstep the print left by the front foot by six inches. Manny walks soundly enough, tail arched to reveal an anxious patch of foamy sweat rubbed up between her black-skinned buttocks. Her groom holds her bridle. "Tranquilamente, tranquilamente," he advises, as she crunches the metal D-bit between her teeth. This bit, the same as the full-cheek snaffle except that the cheeks are shaped like the letter "D," is the preferred bit at most racetracks. Manny's is equipped with round rubber pads at the corners to keep the metal from pinching her sensitive lips.

Coming toward her, horses, their chests and faces smeared cocoa brown with sand and mud from the sloppy track, return after the fourth race. Some, still keyed up to run, trot semicircles beside their grooms. The fatigued pant through aching nostrils and walk with their heads bowed to their knees. Others limp. But the winner parades behind them with the vibrant, relaxed steps and cool eye of one who knows he is the best.

The silver hoods in the parking lot glint like a lake in the sunshine. From an enclosure above the paddock, DeBonis watches the other horses led down for the fifth race, looking to see if there is one he might want to try to buy or claim.

"Sloppy today," he remarks with some concern as Manny picks her way down into the gravel paddock. "It's hard for a come-from-behind horse. There is a tremendous amount of sand thrown back at them anyway, and it hurts. It feels like buckshot going into their skin and their eyes. They are more afraid of the rider's whip than they are of getting sand in the face, but a horse at the back of the field can pick up three or four extra pounds on a day like today."

"Some days are great for closers," sighs Phil, Manny's exercise boy, who has come to watch her race. "The guy who rakes the track could make a fortune if he knew what he was doing. The footing can change so much. If he makes it a little wetter, it's fast. If it's dry, it's a dull track. Remember that day when every twelve position came in? You could have ripped up the program." Although the track conditions may be against Manny, the wind direction, pointed out by an orange Day-Glo weather vane on the backstretch, will be with her. "Horses take shelter behind each other like race-car drivers," says Phil. "When the wind is blowing hard down into the starting gate, your closer is in luck. You just hide behind the other horses, let them take the wind in their face. By the head of the lane, the leaders are dead. Then you slip through and the wind is with you now, coming down the homestretch."

The breeze blowing tufts of her chestnut forelock back around her ears is the least of Manny's worries as she enters the paddock. She is listening and watching all around her, trying to size up her status in this strange, pre-selected herd. The skin running along the crest of her neck tingles and she looks warily out from the corners of her eyes for the threat. Outdorable, a dark-brown filly racing for the third time today, was last in her first two starts. She rears and kicks the side of her saddling stall nervously under Manny's appraising gaze. This filly doesn't worry Manny. Unconsciously, she is alert for some sign of dominance reminiscent of American Liberty, Mesina Judge or Miss Andrea F., the horses that beat her in her last three races.

On one level, a race is a stampeding herd of horses. Competition relies not just on speed, but on intimidation and the will to dominate. Trainers and jockeys can influence a horse's attitude about itself only so far. The trainer can put his horse in the optimal race, at the optimal weight and perfect distance. The jockey can give it the ideal ride. But, in the final analysis, the way a horse runs is probably as much influenced by the rules of the herd as by the rules of racing. It is the fault of the trainer if he works a horse so hard in the morning that it "leaves its race on the track," but it is the fault of temperament and nerves if a Thoroughbred becomes so lathered with fright that it "leaves its race in the paddock."

Manny sucks her belly up into her flanks nervously as she passes Belwood Lady, a filly who did beat her by two necks for second place three weeks ago. Tail swishing in threat and hocks flexing with excitement, Manny jogs into her stall, number seven, with elevated, fitful animation. No one can say if she recognizes Belwood Lady, but it is certain that she is reacting to some warning vibration.

"Easy, easy," hums assistant trainer Eligio Betancourt, Jr., placing the three-pound racing saddle on her back and securing it with the elasticized girth. This light perch covered with vinyl so mud can be wiped from the seat, and equipped with light aluminum stirrups, is a feat of technology and streamlining compared to the first saddles used by the Chinese in 200 B.C. Built with a bone framework, they resembled miniature thrones, heavily bejeweled and cushioned with plush fabrics. All the equipment used by a racehorse is designed, not for repose or opulence, but rather for lightness and efficiency.

Strange as it may seem, the first aluminum horseshoes of the type nailed to Manny's hooves were fashioned by Tiffany's. Although the ancient Celts invented the nailed-on metal horseshoe (an invention as revolutionary at the time, about 450 B.C., as the pneumatic tire was for the automobile) it was Pierre Lorillard, owner of the renowned Rancocas Stud of the late nineteenth century, who had the brilliant idea that if he could have his horses shod in a light metal, they would be able to run faster. He ordered Tiffany's to make shoes for him out of the new wonder metal, aluminum, which was still very expensive. The use of aluminum lightened each shoe by an ounce and a half. The new method was so effective that, when the price of aluminum decreased, it became the standard material used to make "racing plates."

## TYPES OF RACING PLATES

*Front*—The front or plain horseshoe is a standard plate fashioned with a "toe" and used on a fast or dry track.

*Outer rim front*—A variety of the front shoe. It has a "grab" around the outer rim to keep a horse standing level and to reduce hoof shock. It can be used on either the turf or the dirt.

*Jar calk*—A shoe used on the front hooves for muddy and sloppy tracks.

*Mud calk*—A plate with a "toe" and a sharp "sticker" on the heel, which gives a horse a better grip or tread on a muddy track.

*Block heel*—A shoe constructed with raised blocks behind and used to prevent horses from running down on their heels and to prevent slipping.

*Inner rim front* and *Inner rim block heel*—These are used to keep a horse standing level at all times, and are excellent plates on the grass.

*Block heel sticker*—A plate that prevents a horse from running down and at the same time incorporates the features of the mud calk.

---

Manny wears four standard racing plates, each one weighing about two ounces. A groove running along the center line of each shoe helps to give her foot traction. Her front shoes are fitted close against her foot and a bit short of the edges of her heels to keep the shoes from being wrenched off. The hind shoes are set slightly back from her toe to prevent injury caused by striking the back of a foreleg with a hind foot while running. Although the track is muddy, she is not wearing calks. By law, mud calks, attached to shoes to dig in and give the foot extra grip on slippery surfaces, may be only a quarter-inch long. Many trainers never use mud calks, because they judge that their potential to do damage to a joint or tendon outweighs the good they may do by providing traction. It is of interest to note that the 1980 Belmont Stakes winner, 53-to-1 long-shot Temperence Hill, was the only horse which ran the race in calks.

## WHY IS THE HORSESHOE LUCKY?

The horseshoe's reputation as a lucky charm originated with an apocryphal story about Saint Dunstan, the tenth-century Archbishop of Canterbury who, it seems, moonlighted as a horseshoer. Late one night, while Dunstan was at the forge catching up on some work, cloven-footed Satan suddenly appeared at the door and demanded that Dunstan repair one of his shoes. Confronted with the possibility of facing the wrath of the Prince of Darkness, Dunstan agreed.

Once Dunstan had one of the legs of Satan lashed to his anvil, though, he made a demand of his own: that Satan never menace a house that had a horseshoe nailed over the entrance-way. The Prince of Darkness finally agreed, and supposedly he's stuck to the deal to this day. Those wanting to take advantage of the charm have to be careful, however—the protection is only good if the horseshoe is nailed on with the open end up. Otherwise, the luck runs out.

As Junior hikes up the overgirth, a second girth which goes on top of the saddle to make sure it will not slip during the race, Manny kicks out anxiously. Her pink blinker hood with French cups—semicircles of plastic rimming the eyeholes—prevents her from seeing behind her, but not to the side, where Belwood Lady waits calmly. Blinkers help to keep the horse's attention focused toward the finish line. The earliest known set of blinkers dates from the fourteenth century B.C. Egyptians overlaid bark with gold leaf to construct facial armor for the horse in war, both to guard the horse's eyes and to keep it from shying. The Assyrians were reputed to use ivory blinkers. The horses of the Crusaders wore metal hoods. Because the horse was the supreme instrument of warfare, capable of being used both as a weapon to trample infantry and as a shield to protect its rider from slashing swords, most equipment racehorses wear was originally designed for use on the battlefield.

Manny Dober looks like a fighter as she is led back up to the paddock circle to be mounted. She is small, but proud and stocky. The energy her hind legs generate by pushing down against the gravel path whips the muscles of her haunch into a burnished tensile coil emanating throughout the length of her back and up into the crest of her neck. Her gaze is determined, but not yet commanding. She squeezes her eyes shut with fearless disdain as she walks past Romanallah, whom she beat by three-quarters of a length in her last race. As she struts past, Romanallah ducks her gray head down and up, down and up, fretfully. From across the paddock, Belwood Lady spies Manny Dober. It is hard to tell from its eyes where a horse is looking, but the furry lining of her ear angled ever so slightly in Manny's direction gives her away. A horse can tell when another horse is checking it out. Manny makes a point of turning her head to stare at Belwood Lady. A head-on stare is challenging to a horse. The horse, in fear, turns its body away to run from danger, but a brave horse stands its ground and fights. Belwood Lady, keeping her eye and ear pointed in Manny's direction, elegantly arches her long, black tail and drops a few golden balls of manure onto the circular path.

Horses are nomadic and communal by nature, rather than territorial. A horse turned out in a pasture does not mark it off with spore like a dog. A horse made nervous by a social situation will pass manure. When Manny has circled the paddock, she smells Belwood Lady's droppings on the path below her. She glances over at the other mare briefly, then sighs with boredom and walks on, pulverizing the droppings with a hind foot. Small white bubbles of lather begin to scrub up under the reins on Belwood Lady's neck.

Standing in the grassy center of the paddock ring, Robert DeBonis is not concerned with Manny's subtle climb up the social ladder. He is more interested in giving the final pre-race instructions to her jockey, Eric Beitia, whose five-pound apprentice allowance has lightened Manny's load from 114 pounds to 109 pounds for this race. Apprentice jockeys receive an allowance of ten pounds until they win five races. They receive a seven-pound weight allowance until they have ridden thirty more winners. Following their thirty-fifth win, they receive a five-pound weight allowance for one year (dated from the day of the fifth race they won). After this, they lose their "bug boy" status and may become licensed journeymen, riding with no weight advantage. (The one exception being a three-pound weight allowance for one more year in races ridden for their original contract owner.) The disadvantage of apprentices is their inexperience, which makes it hard for them to see patterns develop in the field, follow the trainer's instructions and make quick judgments when problems develop. Beitia, however, is currently the second winningest jockey at this meet.

"With this horse, as you know, Eric, you can't rush her," mutters DeBonis intensely, but not loud enough for any other jockey or trainer, who might be standing behind his shoulder, to hear. "She'll go all day. Just lay back and try to make your one run." Beitia nods knowingly as the groom stops Manny in front of him and Junior hoists him up into the tiny stirrups. He rode Manny in her two previous races and has some idea of what to expect. Although some jockeys consistently ride certain horses, they must be willing to accept new, unknown mounts at least several times a day. Generally, the five minutes or so between the time when the jockey is catapulted into the saddle in the paddock and then loaded into the starting gate at the other side of the track is his only opportunity to test out an unfamiliar horse.

Manny, in her pink blinker hood and green "shadow roll"—a fleece noseband which encourages her to lower her head to see the ground and thus lengthen her stride —relaxes completely under Beitia's steady seat. Knees folded to a kneeling position on her withers, hands lightly gripping the texturized rubber reins, Beitia is led around the paddock once. Then Manny is delivered to the outrider on a calm lead pony who will guide Manny through the post parade and up to the starting gate. Manny, last in the parade because she has drawn the number-seven post position, steps along so coolly beside her Appaloosa lead pony that the outrider seems unnecessary. Up ahead, Outdorable, who has drawn the number-one spot, lashes her neck toward the paddock and canters sideways, trying to go back. Number two, the muscular gray Romanallah, and number three, You're All Heart, jog with their heads bobbing and hiding against their ponies' necks. Belwood Lady, number four, appears more composed, but her left ear still twists back toward Manny and her shoulderblades are articulated with satin sweat. Legs Long and Ever Swift, both in the second start of their careers, gape at the clerk of scales, the babbling crowd along the rail, the finish posts and the fluttering Racing Forms; only peripherally aware of the threats of dominance and anxious postures of submission surrounding them.

"I see you, man," screams a Jamaican railbird at one of the jockeys as the post parade begins to jog and warm up past the fans. "I look at you. You hold him back, man. How my family gonna eat, man?"

The jockey sucks his cheeks together, stares directly at the harasser, and shoots a big glob of white spit onto the track between them. The Jamaican waves his torn-up win tickets in a voodoo hex.

Jockeys rank among the world's most courageous athletes. Every racing afternoon from 1 P.M. to 5 P.M., they routinely mount unpredictable and extremely excited horses, most of which they have never ridden before, and attempt to push them to the limits of their capabilities. At its best, racing is dangerous. A hard bump at high speed can knock a horse and jockey into the rail with about the same force as an automobile traveling at 40 mph. A soft spot in the track can cause a horse to go down so fast that the horses behind it have no time to turn away or even slow up before they are trampling it. Accidents have more to do with luck than a rider's skill. Ron Turcotte, who piloted the great Secretariat to his Triple Crown victory, was later the victim of a spill—in a normal race on a normal racing day—that paralyzed him for life. In order to win, a jockey cannot be intimidated by the fact that in the two minutes between the time his horse breaks from the gate until it crosses the finish line, his life is at stake.

A good jockey is totally fearless and so is able to concentrate all of his attention on winning the race. He must be able to relax a flighty horse, excite an unenthusiastic one, give confidence to a green horse and rate a strong one. He must have an exceptional sense of timing and the pace of a race, as well as a sixth sense about "how much horse he has left" to run at any given moment. He is also a strategist and must analyze how the other horses in the field like to run and how their riders will probably ride them. A jockey cannot make a horse run faster than it is physically capable of going and mentally willing to go, but he can make sure that it has an opportunity to run its best race under the circumstances.

Certain jockeys have specialties. William Shoemaker, known as "the Shoe," is re-nowned for the finesse of his delicate hands and his ability to "communicate with" or coax the best performance out of difficult horses. Laffit Pincay, the first jockey to win $7,000,000 in one year, is known for his strength, which makes him successful with strong, brutish types. Although the verb "to jockey" means "to trick, cheat or deceive," most of the jockeying on the racetrack today is the result of pure riding skill rather than chicanery. A sprinter, for instance, can "steal" a longer race full of "come-from-behind horses" if the rider seizes the lead and fools the other jockeys by setting a slower than normal early pace. By the time the other jockeys have figured out that the pace is too slow, the finish line will be approaching and the sprinter will be able to make his one dash before the come-from-behind horses have time to catch up. The one modern device commonly used to inspire horses to run at their maximum speed is a transistorized buzzer, about the size of a matchbook, which is pressed against the horse's skin to give it an electric shock. However, the efforts of the Thoroughbred Racing Protective Agency and the threat of a lifetime suspension from race riding have prevented even most unscrupulous jockeys from resorting to this device.

Beitia glances up at the pari-mutuel pool board and sees that Manny Dober is the favorite, at seven to five, as he gallops her slowly toward the starting gate on Aqueduct's inner dirt track. The kelly-green-and-white racing silks of owner Phil Sagarin billow in the favorable winds while Manny quietly awaits her turn to be loaded. The distance for the race is one mile and seventy yards. Because the oval inner dirt track is only one mile in length, the starting gate is rolled into place seventy yards before the finish line. Races may begin at various locations on the oval, but all of them end between the same two red-yellow-and-blue striped poles across from the paddock. As racetrackers are quick to remark, "That's where the money is."

The seven horses scheduled to start mill anxiously as the assistant starter refers to the notes he has made on his program and instructs his crew.

"Okay," he says, pointing to a bay mare, "that's an OG." An "OG," according to his notation, is a horse which will not enter the gate unless the front door is left open. Others of the fillies may have been marked "H," indicating that someone must hold their heads straight inside the gate; "O," meaning that someone has to stay in the adjoining ("off-side") chute to restrain them to keep them from breaking out too early; "B," meaning that they will not enter the chute without a blindfold; "S," indicating that they must be slapped with a leather strap when the bell goes off in order to break properly; or "T," reminding the starters that if the horses' tails are not held and lifted once they have been shut in their chutes, they will either sit down or rear up. Manny, because she has sensitive stifles, is listed as "HG," meaning that she is "goosey" and must have extra padding placed beside her flanks to keep her from tickling herself and jumping around once in the gate.

The starter ascends the steep wooden steps to his tiny perch to watch the horses being loaded. In order of their post position, Outdorable, Romanallah, You're All Heart, Belwood Lady, Legs Long, Ever Swift and at last, Manny Dober, are closed inside the gate. One instantly breaks through the front; another rears in sympathy.

"You see," says the starter, watching as patiently as God from his crow's nest of a perch twenty feet above the gate, "if I had pushed the button just before she reared, everyone would say I was a bad starter because she didn't have a fair chance to break, but she wouldn't have been rearing when I pushed it."

Down below, from the jockeys, there are screams of, "Not yet!" "No way! No way!"

Manny Dober squats slightly, digging her oval-shaped hind feet into the slop in front of the rubber-coated metal "stumbling bar" at her heels. Beitia perches over her withers, one hand grasping the reins, the other grabbing her mane to keep him from falling backward when she bolts forward out of the gate. Next door, Ever Swift backs up and tries to sit down, but her held tail is lifted over the door and pulled down by the assistant to keep her up on all four feet. The horse that broke early is backed into the chute. The rearer sets her front feet down for an instant. The starter presses his tongs together. The front doors all fly open. The air screams with the jockeys' blood-curdling "Aiiiee. Aiiiee." And, they're off.

Manny Dober is only vaguely aware of the bell ringing behind her and the flag dropping to alert the manual timer that the race has begun. Her head is up and her hocks are bent. Her hind feet push in unison against the stumbling bar and she rears forward, fifth out of the gate. Her hooves slide on the sloppy mud surface and penetrate all the way down to the hard clay base, as she scrabbles to find her footing. Beitia, poised over her shoulders so that she can carry his weight with her skeleton and not her muscles, calmly angles her toward the center of the field, closer to the rail. He flattens his chest to her neck in the "monkey crouch" first popularized by the jockey Tod Sloan, to reduce wind resistance, and places her in a spot just outside the haunch of the fourth-placed horse. The statuesque gray, Romanallah, has seized the lead. By the quarter-mile pole, Romanallah is first, Belwood Lady, who beat Manny in February, a driving second, and Manny Dober, still working into her rhythm, has dropped back to sixth.

Some horses are unable to handle sloppy tracks, which have a watery surface and a firm bottom. Although running well in the slop is thought to be inherited to some extent, certain horses, no matter what their breeding, seem to lack confidence on a slippery track for fear of falling. Belwood Lady has no such trouble. As the half-mile marker approaches, she splashes forcefully along the outside to pass Romanallah. Ten lengths back, Manny, running evenly as ever in the soupy going, has just begun to hit her stride. She is third now, leading the rest of the field. Beitia waits in the irons, letting her work up a rhythm under him. His goggles are thick with sand and mud, so he flips them down on his chest. The three clean pairs underneath will all be dangling around his neck by the time the race is over. Manny, who has a third eyelid which acts as a windshield wiper, involuntarily clears the worst of the sand from her eyes. She is traveling about fifty feet per second and her heart is beating at four times its normal rate.

By the time she sails past the six-furlong pole, the distance at which all of her previous races ended, Manny is six lengths behind Belwood Lady, four lengths behind Romanallah, and ten lengths ahead of the rest of the field. On the far turn, Beitia taps her shoulder and she automatically changes leads in mid-flight. The cables of her tendons, finely tuned as piano strings by De-Bonis' training program, catapult her through the slop toward Romanallah's gray and tiring rump. The sand burning under her eyelids may limit her vision, but Manny's ears are pinned at the gray, and her head, with its demon eyes—the imperious eyes of Tanta, the survivor—angles out in threat. They run head to head for several strides, until the gray defers and drops back half a length. At the top of the stretch, Manny is one length behind Belwood Lady. Beitia, ready to make his big move, takes the reins in one hand and reaches back with the whip. It is less than a thousand feet to the rainbow-colored finish posts. Before the whip can strike her, Manny digs her toes into the mud and surges forward into her one run.

Horses are predisposed to self-destruction. A horse with the heart to want to win is perfectly capable, with no urging from its rider, of running itself to death. Eric Beitia, reaching for his whip, has no knowledge of the swelling and erosion in Manny's left knee. Like most jockeys, he has not been informed of the various flaws in the machine he is dealing with. As far as he is concerned, he must give her her best chance to win the race.

It is a fact of American racing that the horse's left front leg is overstressed. The horse, like a motorcycle, leans into its turns. Because races are run counterclockwise, the left leg, closest to the rail, bears the brunt of the impact. This problem is exacerbated by the design of the racing surface. Tracks are not banked to provide level footing, so the horse, traveling at more than 30 mph, lands repeatedly on the left edge of its left front foot, an area smaller than the average human fist.

## GREAT HORSES: RUFFIAN

Every so often, perhaps once every fifteen or twenty years, there comes to racing a horse so perfectly conformed, so talented and so tragic that it breaks the hearts of even the most hardened horsemen. Such a horse was the filly Ruffian.

By Reviewer and out of Shenanigans, Ruffian was huge for a filly. At age three, she stood sixteen hands, two inches. Her coat was bay, her temperament, difficult. In her eye was the "look of eagles" passed down from her paternal grandsire, Bold Ruler, and her maternal grandsire, Native Dancer. According to the Belmont and Aqueduct veterinarian, Manuel Gilman, "She was the most perfectly put together large filly I've ever seen."

Trained by Frank Whitely, Ruffian won her first ten starts easily. In her first start as a two-year-old in 1974, Ruffian broke late out of the gate, but quickly made up for lost time, blazing across the finish line fifteen lengths ahead of the second-place horse and equaling the track record for the distance (5½ furlongs). She was undefeated in her next four races, thus earning the title of champion two-year-old filly. A hairline fracture of the right hind leg sidelined her until April of her three-year-old year, when she came back sound and full of fight.

As a three-year-old in 1975, Ruffian won five races, including the filly Triple Crown: the Acorn, the Mother Goose and the Coaching Club American Oaks. She had proven that she was a champion, both at sprinting and staying distances, but 1975 was five years before Genuine Risk and the Bertram Firestones pioneered the way for fillies to run in the major classics against colts. The media concocted a championship race for Ruffian—the Great Match.

Horsemen hate match races. Pitting two champions against each other in head-to-head competition almost assures that one will be run into the ground. Whitely tried to protect Ruffian's best interests, but the die was cast. On July 6, 1975, Ruffian paraded to the post at Belmont Park to meet the champion two-year-old colt of 1974, Foolish Pleasure, over a mile and a quarter distance. Foolish Pleasure, which had won eleven of his fourteen starts, had won the Derby, but had come in second in the Preakness and the Belmont Stakes.

The two horses broke from the gate almost together, with Foolish Pleasure just a hair ahead. After a few strides, Ruffian moved up beside him. They ran side by side, clocking their first quarter in 22⅕ seconds. Then, suddenly, Ruffian's jockey, Jacinto Vasquez, heard the horrid sound of bone cracking. Foolish Pleasure zoomed past.

Embattled and confused, Ruffian struggled on. It took Vasquez thirty strides to ease her to a halt. As Foolish Pleasure crossed the finish line to a hollow victory, an air cast was placed on Ruffian's leg and she was moved to Dr. William Reed's Veterinary Hospital across the street. The injury diagnosed was a common one—compound fracture of the sesamoid bone at the back of the fetlock joint.

Ruffian's surgery was successful, but she had such a violent reentry into consciousness that she not only destroyed all the good that had been done, but attacked the vet's assistants in her fear. Due to her mental and physical condition, or the fact, as some horsemen noted, "that she was too much horse," Ruffian was humanely "put down" and buried in the Belmont infield.

Plenty of $2,500 claimers had been destroyed due to cracked sesamoids, but Ruffian was a star. Her tragedy spurred new inquiry into the American obsession with pure speed, and into the viability of racetrack facilities. The American Association of Equine Practitioners set up guidelines for handling badly injured horses. New ambulances were designed. Track veterinary facilities were expanded and improved. Many tracks discontinued the practice of specially preparing track surfaces "for world's records." New York came up with the innovation of hooking a giant magnet to a tractor, which drags the racing strip to clear it of such objects as hoof picks, nails and cigarette lighters, all of which can cause severe damage to horses moving at high speeds. However, projects involving the proper banking of turns and more suitable racing surfaces have mainly been abandoned as impractical or too expensive. Although the treatment facilities have improved, severe injury will persist until the causes of excess concussion due to unnatural speed, irregularities in the strip and overstressing of underdeveloped bone are eliminated. Until that time comes, the enormously talented Ruffian is just another tragic statistic.

| | | Bold Ruler |
| | Reviewer | |
| | | Broadway |
| Ruffian | | |
| | | Native Dancer |
| | Shenanigans | |
| | | Bold Irish |

*Racing Record:*

| STS. | 1ST | 2ND | 3RD | EARNINGS |
|------|-----|-----|-----|----------|
| 11* | 10 | 0 | 0 | $313,429 |

* Broke down in match race vs. Foolish Pleasure for only loss.

---

Every time the horse sets his foot down at a racing gallop, the entire bone column from fetlock to knee is overloaded. At a normal canter, the bone simply expands and contracts to absorb shock, but at racing speed, it begins to microcrush. After three or four thousand strides, the bone fractures. Only sufficient rest for bone repair between races can combat the effects of repeated stress.

Inhaling as her hind legs push off, exhaling as her front legs hit the ground, Manny responds with a sudden burst in response to the popping sound made by Beitia's twenty-one-inch whip and the sting as the fiber glass covered with leather hits her flank. The finish is only a matter of lengths away now. These final strides seem borne from breaths deep under her loins and sudden flexions at the base of her spine. She is the color of cocoa sand, except for the red, glimmering lining of her nostrils. Whatever sight she has left is focused on Belwood Lady. Her tongue, tied down with gauze to keep her from swallowing it, hangs out the side of her mouth.

If there is pain in Manny's knee now, she doesn't feel it. "The wind is up her tail" and her legs swing with the regularity of metronomes. She is an instrument of rhythm, direction and speed. At the seven-eighths pole, she draws up to Belwood Lady and fixes her with a black-and-amber stare. For two fleeting lengths, Manny matches the big bay filly stride for stride. Then, suddenly, the inevitable happens. Horses generally run back to their breeding. Sir Wimborne's class, Tanta's eye, *Pronto's drive, Manny's will prevail. Belwood Lady breaks stride under the pressure of Manny's insistent, challenging rhythm. She tires and drops back.

The brown track pitted with silvery puddles lies clear before her as Manny Dober runs alone. From behind, she can hear the faltering thuds and sucking sounds as Romanallah, now in second place, attempts a comeback. Manny, still prepared to "run all day" if necessary, stretches out even farther into the lead. The tired gray is no match for the enduring *Pronto blood. Belwood Lady straggles in third place as Manny, "much the best" according to the past-performance sheet, finishes first by a good three lengths. Although the time, 1:48⅘, is hardly outstanding, even in the slop, Manny has broken her maiden and proved that, given the proper distance, she is a winner. As horsemen say, "She ran her race and she won it."

There are no Derby roses, no blanket of Preakness black-eyed Susans, no Belmont white carnations or antique silver trophies waiting for her as Manny is eased and then jogged rapidly back to the winner's circle at Aqueduct. Horses of her class only rate a check and a photograph. The Sagarins are there, though, ready to hold her bridle and pat her neck for the camera, along with Junior Betancourt, who watched over her therapy, and Phil, who conditioned her in daily gallops. DeBonis, arms folded over the front of his tweed jacket, grins as proudly as if one of his horses had won a major stakes event. Although Manny's share of the $20,000 purse is $12,000 and his 10 percent of that is only $1,200, DeBonis has taken a filly plagued by problems of size and infirmity and helped her to actualize her potential as a racehorse. Perhaps proudest of all is Manny's groom, who rubbed her legs when they were sore, and stayed with her to keep her company while she stood in the ice, and poulticed her bad knee, and brushed her coat and all the time sang to her in Spanish to keep her relaxed.

When the picture is snapped, Beitia leaps off, unfastens his saddle and heads toward the clerk of scales to weigh out. The Sagarins, along with DeBonis, Phil and Junior, head back up to the Man o' War room to celebrate. The horses for the sixth race are already entering the paddock, lathering, chewing their bits, staring each other down across the asphalt ring. Anyone who bet on Manny to win has already cashed in and received the $4.80 return on his $2.00 ticket.

Ten minutes after making the best effort of her life, Manny is sauntering along the path back to the receiving barn. Her chestnut sides, mottled gray with mud, heave within the net of twitching veins. Mucus drips from her left nostril and white flecks of sweat mixing with sand and dirt line the corners of her eyes.

"Who won the fifth?" calls one of the hot-walkers to another as she passes.

"The number-seven horse," replies the other.

"The gray?"

"No, the little horse, I think it was a chestnut."

"Oh, hell," says the first hot-walker, dropping a wad of tickets into the manure pit.

Limping slightly from the pain in her left knee, Manny fades into the file of "also rans" on their way to the backstretch.

At the Test Barn, she turns away from the others and is led past two Pinkerton guards at the "Casilla de Orina," the Urine Stall. Every first- and second-place finisher, the first four finishers in stakes and added-money events, the horses that pay off in exotic wagering such as trifectas, and any other animals designated by the stewards must submit to drug tests immediately following the race.

In a special chain-link-fenced area, Manny is washed with lukewarm water. As she sighs wearily under the pleasant warmth of the natural sponge, the drug testers wait, hoping that she and Romanallah will pee quickly so they can collect the samples. As soon as the sand has been wiped from her nostrils and her skin is drenched clean and scraped of sweat and dirt, one of the testers jabs her in the neck with a needle and extracts 20 cc's of blood. The blood test, which eclipsed the saliva test five years ago, is the most accurate measure of whether or not a horse has been drugged. Samples are examined by gas chromotography, which can identify a wide spectrum of forbidden substances in the blood, including bute, Lasix, and a variety of stimulants and depressants.

After her blood has been collected and she has been hand-walked to cool out, Manny is taken into one of the NYRA's urine stalls to pee. Most horses naturally urinate within ten minutes after going into a stall. As the drug tester stands by, holding a metal rod attached to a large cup, Manny's groom whistles to her, coaxing. Every time a groom sees a horse about to pee in its stall, he whistles to it to teach it to associate whistling with urination. Manny spreads her legs, lifts her tail and pees straight down into the outstretched cup.

In the old days, heroin, rubbed on a horse's tongue to stimulate it before a race, was so common that it became nicknamed "horse." Testing procedures were much less stringent and sophisticated. Horses that refused to urinate had to remain with the testers until their bladders became so full that they finally gave in. Even then, tests were so spotty that by constantly switching to the latest new drug, unscrupulous horsemen could stay one "hop" ahead. Nowadays the testing methods are more technologically advanced. The blood test can screen for almost any substance, so a horse

which has not urinated within two hours following its race is allowed to leave. In the evening, the samples are flown to the Cornell Veterinary School for analysis. Manny's, as expected, is negative. A positive test prompts a hearing by the stewards and mandates a forty-five-day suspension for the parties involved.

When the testing is done, Manny is taken back to the receiving barn. The soreness in her knee is more evident now that her muscles have cooled out and her adrenaline level is down. Although she walks almost evenly, her lower leg swings out slightly before she steps on her left foot. In the dim, dusty light of the receiving barn, her groom kneels in the straw and smooths the thick, cooling antiphlogistine up her legs with a flattened spoon. The viscous white poultice is applied against the direction in which her hair grows so that it will penetrate right to the skin. Wrapped in brown paper and flannel bandages, it will stay on for forty-eight hours, soothing and drawing heat and inflammation out of the joints and tendons of both her front legs.

"Please, ho, ho. Please," whispers her groom softly, as he stretches her right eye open with two fingers and blows hard into it. Manny tosses her head, trying to pull away. "Please, now, ho," asks the groom again, trying to blow out excess sand and activate her natural windshield wiper. Exhausted, but feisty to the end, Manny half-rears and hops backward into the corner. At last the groom gives up, tosses a cooler over her and loads her into the van back to DeBonis' barn at Belmont.

Manny automatically chews a sheaf of hay in her net, but loses interest suddenly and lets the strands hang from between her teeth. She is too tired to eat. Her feet are sore from pounding. The fluid throbs in her left knee. Granules of sand still cake the corners of her eyes.

"Ladies and gentlemen," booms a voice over the inescapable P.A. system, "it is now post time."

Manny closes her eyelids, locks her legs and, all alone in the dark van, falls asleep.

# Afterward

When a horse in DeBonis' barn wins a race, every employee involved in the care and training of that horse receives a bonus. The horse receives a "loaded jug." In more gracious days gone by, Thoroughbreds were given a warm gruel spiked with brandy or whiskey to relax and rejuvenate them after the race. The morning after her victory, Manny is hand-walked for an hour to encourage circulation and loosen any stiffness. Then she is dosed with the less hospitable but more scientific modern brew: Ambex, a combination of sugar water and vitamins, dripped intravenously into her system to combat the depletion and dehydration of extreme physical effort.

"With a racehorse, you have to put back in what you take out," remarks DeBonis, pleased that she has worked out of her soreness and is "cleaning up her feed." Some horses come out of races hurting so badly that they refuse to eat.

On the second day after her race, Manny is walked again. If she were a colt or a strong filly, she might be jogged lightly. On the third day, when many horses would be in full training again, galloping a mile and a half, Manny is jogged. By day four, her knee seems to have responded well to rest and she is put back on her steady program of slow gallops. On March 26, she breezes four furlongs on the training track in 53 seconds—slow, but consistent. On April 7, she breezes three furlongs in a fast, for her, 37⅗ seconds. This short, quick work is designed to put an edge on her for the state-bred allowance race in which she is entered on April 8.

Unfortunately for Manny Dober, she cannot always run at her ideal distance.

Few racehorses can, particularly if they are stayers, which need long races, and if they are cheap enough so that they must run every two or three weeks. In Manny's case, very few long races are carded for New York-breds the year that she is running. Even the talented jockey, Velasquez, cannot force her to "fire" soon enough in the seven-furlong allowance, but Manny has more heart and will than her stride can satisfy. She moves from last, ten lengths off the pace, at the half-mile pole, to fourth by the early finish, only 2¼ lengths behind the winner. Most horses have only one distance at which they can win. Judged against her own standard, Manny ran even better and faster than she did on the day she won. She pushed herself so hard that the calcium deposit on her knee severely microcrushed.

Although Manny is still able to train and is "racing sound," DeBonis suggests to the owners that she rest. A period of time is needed for the fragmented bone to "remodel" itself and strengthen through the body's regenerative processes. Forcing her to race before the fissures have sealed up is risking greater and possibly irreparable damage.

The trainer, however, is simply an expert adviser and conditioner. The owner has the last word about whether or not the horse will race. Every time an owner enters a horse in a race he takes a calculated risk that all the money he has spent on breeding or purchase and training will best have its chance to be returned during that particular two-minute interval—and that his major property, the horse, will remain intact. Trainers are not omniscient. They are not always the most perfect judges of their horses' needs and capabilities. In the spring of 1980, when asked if he would enter Genuine Risk in the Kentucky Derby, the excellent trainer LeRoy Jolley said, "Absolutely not." Several days later, Mrs. Bertram Firestone, the filly's owner, announced that she would be running. Even Jolley could find no fault with this decision after Genuine Risk became the second filly, and the first since 1915, to win the Kentucky Derby.

The Clinton, a six-furlong race for fillies and mares three years old and upward, foaled in New York, which have never won a race other than maiden, claiming or starter, is hardly of the same caliber as the Derby. Manny's chances are dubious at the short distance. Nevertheless, the Sagarins, like all racehorse owners, have eternal faith in their horse's ability and indomitable gambling spirit. Manny is entered to run on April 23, just fifteen days after her last race.

April 23 does not begin well for Manny. It is a damp, muggy sort of day that causes the irregularity in her knee joint to ache. It is also her regular groom's day off, so the gentle singing and practiced hands to which she is accustomed are missing. No one scratches the crest of her neck to soothe her anxious spirits. No one whispers, "Tranquilamente, tranquilamente," on the long walk to the paddock. Things aren't right.

In the paddock, there are three fillies, all of which won their last races, parading, arched as peacocks, with wicked stares. In Manny's little stall, DeBonis and Junior are nervous. Her jockey, an apprentice with a seven-pound weight allowance, is four pounds "over." Instead of carrying 103 pounds as planned, she will have to lug 107. Manny kicks out as the girth is tightened. No one is there to fondle her upper lip.

"Don't rush her," says DeBonis to the overweight bug boy. "Just lay back and try to make your one run."

When the strange boy gets onto her, she falters under him. He is inexperienced and his weight is not quite balanced over her shoulders. His reins are strong and tight,

causing her to shake her head with anger and nervousness. Manny has drawn the second post position and, as usual, she breaks slowly, letting the early speed go on ahead. As she is fumbling for her footing, just preparing to settle and establish her stride, the bug boy gets nervous about being so far behind the rest of the field and swats her with his stick.

"Don't rush her. Don't rush her," intones DeBonis from his box in the clubhouse.

"Leave her alone, kid," mutters Phil, her exercise rider.

Manny turns on what early speed she has to pass two other horses, but they charge on by her.

"Now she went back to last," says Mrs. Sagarin. The jockey, confused and frustrated, whips Manny's flank every stride.

"Leave her alone," says DeBonis out loud as they go into the turn. Manny, like most stayers, needs time to work up a rapid, synchronized, leg-swinging tempo. Only as her tempo builds will she be able to pick up speed.

As she rounds the turn, Manny begins to quicken her pace a bit and passes two other horses.

"Come on, Manny," cries Mrs. DeBonis, "we know it's only six furlongs!" The winner has already crossed the finish, though, with Manny running evenly in the middle of the field. Her race ended before she had a chance to warm up.

"The thing he did," remarks DeBonis, "he used her too early. That's bad. That's the sort of thing you have to put up with, with a young rider."

"If you use them early, they don't finish," says Phil. "She ran even. She has to have a long race. She was just coming on at the end. Just starting to run."

Back at the receiving barn, Manny is angry. She kicks at the strange groom. Her black-and-amber eyes glitter with confusion. When he tries to blow out the sand, she rears and strikes at him with her left foot. He passes a chain under her lip to restrain her. As she walks her to the van, the wrinkles over her eyes crease black with sweat. Her left toe drags through the dirt each time she tries to swing her leg forward and straighten the knee.

The next day, back at Belmont, things seem worse, not better. Bandaging, ice, antiphlogistine—the miracle cures, are useless. The calcium deposit in her knee has finally fragmented and broken off into a common, but excruciatingly painful, bone chip.

"The knee is like a bunch of rubber bands, tendons and ligaments, stretched over a joint and lubricated with fluid," explains DeBonis, studying the new X rays taken of Manny's leg. "The fracture that caused the original calcium deposit to form makes the smooth bone surface rough, grating the ligaments passing across it. When the chip breaks off, it becomes wedged in the joint and makes it impossible for the horse to bend it fully."

In many cases, large bone chips can be surgically removed. At Dr. William O. Reed's veterinary hospital across the street from Belmont, this is a routine operation which takes about forty minutes. The knee is shaved and scrubbed with antiseptic soaps. The horse is anesthetized and "dropped" onto a metal table which is flush with the floor. All four feet, the tail and the neck are tied down. A wooden block is stuck in the animal's mouth to keep it open and oxygen tubes are inserted into its lungs. Then the metal table is raised to a working level. While attendants monitor pulse rate and breathing, the surgeon slices open the knee, picks out the chips and sews it back up. When the operation is over, the table, with the patient still on it, is tilted almost vertical. The sliding wall panels of the padded recovery stall are opened. The horse is unstrapped and falls, with careful guidance, onto the cushioned stall floor. The most crucial aspect of equine recovery is the re-entry into a conscious state. Following a successful operation, many horses damage themselves so badly, struggling to get up or to run from the pain, that they have to be humanely destroyed.

In Manny's case, however, there is no hope of operating. A sample of liquid drawn from the swelling on her knee consists of blood, not fluid, indicating that the ligaments have been torn and frayed from abrasion. X rays show that the chip in her knee shattered into so many tiny pieces that any attempt to operate would be totally useless. Manny is simply another victim of physical afflictions, unfavorable distances, over-racing at a young age, financial considerations and breeding that produced a fighting spirit too large for her small stature to tolerate.

"Manny won't run again," says DeBonis, striding down the aisle of Barn 34 to take his final look at her. "I won't run her. I won't run a lame horse. I have a reputation to protect and I have spent years building up the trust of the track vet, whom I have to work with day after day."

Manny's head, curious and friendly, reminiscent of Banknote, pops out of her stall at the sound of voices approaching. She looks perfectly healthy and her chestnut coat gleams over muscles so taut and fit that they drove her to her own destruction.

"Every horse will break down," explains DeBonis. "It's just a question of how and when. Some will break down after three races. Others will be okay for ten or twenty. The problem we are constantly dealing with is that Thoroughbreds are bred for ability, not durability.

"This one here," he continues, pointing out Manny to a man in a black jacket.

Bandaged with bright-green shipping wraps on all four legs, Manny willingly follows the man onto a small horse trailer. Although her left leg cannot swing freely, she walks almost evenly up the ramp and sinks her teeth lustily into a flake of clover hay. If Manny had been a gelding, she might have been "put down," but due to her sex, her life is spared. Her usefulness as a race animal is over, but her career as a broodmare is only beginning.

The small van rolls gently down Hempstead Avenue where, on a rainy night only three months ago, Manny inhaled her first scent of "Beautiful Belmont." Although she will never prick her ears to the sound of the bugle calling her to the post again, it will take months for her to "come down," both physically and mentally, from the high of being in training. Her racing career has been shorter and richer than most. She ran for six months and won $19,552.

Today—April 30, 1980—is three years and one week after Manny's actual birthday. In another six months, her shoulders, forearms, hocks, gaskins and femurs will have matured to adult proportions. In a year, her spinal column and hipbone will have finished developing.

The van glides up the Major Deegan Expressway to Route 684. It passes the town of Carmel, where, at Scargo Farm, Tanta bosses her new foal (by Take Your Place) into a shady corner of the pasture and where Banknote, the yearling, opens her nostrils to the afternoon breeze and tests her racing legs on the rolling New York hills. The van moves north. It passes through Patterson and Pawling and near Akindale Farm, where Manny Dober was born. At last, it turns down Route 44 toward Millbrook. Here, at Closeburn Farm, Manny will be bred to a New York stallion, Fratello Ed. Wobbling in the van, knees braced as well as possible, Manny has no inkling of the lazy days that lie before her. She is lithe, fit and virginal—crippled, but still an athlete at the top of her form.

At the farm they will take away her bandages and her shoes. There will be the panic and the strangeness of the breeding shed: the screaming stallion, the mild scent of ivory soap and the twitch. Then there will be nothing to it—just waking up and sleeping and waking up again to see the same lush pastures, the immovable trees,

the static shadows of the fence line in the soundless afternoons.

Manny has had her moment of glory, that fine thirty seconds on the homestretch of Aqueduct Racetrack on March 14, the day she was the best. Her entire life, from the time Tanta went into the breeding shed to meet Native Heritage, was geared toward sending her alone down that last three lengths on a sloppy track. Three years of worry, nurture, training and expense were devoted to preparing her for that one brief, perfect effort. She has performed her mission, provided her owners and the betting public with the excitement for which she was bred.

At first, she will wake at 4 A.M. and pace, wanting to be fed. In the mornings, she will gallop as best she can, working off energy reserves built up during her conditioning. She will wait impatiently and wonder when they are coming with the ice and the poultice. She will sniff with excitement at the least whiff of Absorbine.

Then, quite suddenly, it will settle over her. Her hair will grow long and scruffy. Among the other mares, she will begin to slow down her ritualized exercise program, to sag and grow wide with dreams. Slowly, her eyes will glaze over until the hints of her black fire shine only in the deepest corners and in rare moments of temper. With rest, her knee will heal enough not to bother her except in the dampest weather. By the time her first foal drops in the spring of 1981, Manny Dober will be a full-grown horse.

# Part Three

# PLAYING THE HORSES

# Section 9

# *Handicapping*

---

*"When you go to the track, don't eat, don't go to the bar, and don't bring a girl friend. That's a three-horse parlay and nobody hits three-horse parlays."*

—John Bilous
Winner, NYRA's annual
handicapping contest

Much of the fun of being a sports fan is testing one's knowledge by making predictions about upcoming events. Wherever fans meet, from barrooms to boardrooms, conversation inevitably turns to friendly arguments about who's going to win "the game tonight," "the fight next week," "the pennant," etc. More than occasionally, opinions are backed up by a wager or two.

One of the great pleasures of Thoroughbred racing is that the fan can participate right at the track by matching his knowledge against all the other horseplayers. In the pari-mutuel system, players wager against each other, not against the "house." In contrast to most casino games, in which winning depends upon being lucky enough to beat a fixed house percentage, winning at the track can be achieved by forming educated opinions that are better than average. While the steady rise in pari-mutuel takeout to the 15 percent to 20 percent range has changed the criterion for success from "better than average" to "much better than average," a significant number of horseplayers, relying on keen judgment instead of luck, come out consistently ahead over weeks, months and years.

The way these winners evaluate horse races is exactly the way opinions are formed by other kinds of experts—doctors, stockbrokers, baseball managers, lawyers, etc. The process has three stages:

1. *Gathering information:* Forming an expert opinion on a complex subject requires obtaining as much information as possible. A doctor wouldn't dream of recommending major surgery after just recording a patient's pulse rate and blood pressure. Horseplayers, on the other hand, often wager hundreds of dollars on the basis of systems that concentrate on only one or two bits of information, such as the horse's final time in its last race or its total earnings.

2. *Interpreting information:* To use information properly, a person has to be taught what it means. For example, learning that a horse is wearing blinkers for the first time is meaningless if one doesn't know what blinkers are and why they are used.

3. *Weighing information:* The vital and complex third stage in forming an opinion is using one's experience to weigh the relative importance of the information one has gathered and in-

terpreted. Will a ten-pound-lower weight assignment, for example, allow a horse to carry its speed a furlong farther than it ever has before? The art of weighing all these factors, which together determine the outcome of a race, is called *handicapping*.

Unfortunately, most racegoers never learn how to play the game of handicapping. The problem is twofold: one, they lack a large body of important information —about the characteristics of horses, for example; secondly, they are confronted with an even larger body of information they can't understand, much less evaluate— the past performance charts, results charts, etc. Since few tracks make any attempt to educate their customers, racegoers are left to try to decipher the information on their own. After a few futile and frustrating attempts, most give up the task as "impossible."

Psychologically, failure leaves them open to the large number of "easy" answers to the problem of how to bet their money. One route is to become a "chalk" player, slavishly following the opinion of the crowd by betting on favorites. Some horseplayers hearken to the conspiracy theory, scrounging for "inside" information, even following trainers and grooms to the betting windows to watch them place their wagers. Many racegoers simply buy opinions, following the selections of newspaper handicappers, tip sheets, telephone tip services and touts. Finally, a lot of horseplayers who still hunger to become knowledgeable about the sport succumb to the lavish ads that "guarantee" to teach successful handicapping. In exchange for their $10 to $50, they receive systems into which they're instructed to plug information they still don't fully understand. Buying systems is really the same as buying tip sheets, only a lot more expensive.

Good handicapping doesn't involve reliance on a mechanical system. Rather, handicappers, like physicians or financial analysts, develop a *systematic method* of weighing the information they've gathered and interpreted. Inevitably, just as winning football coaches have different philosophies, different winning handicappers place more weight on certain information. *Speed* handicappers, for example, place special emphasis on the final times a horse has achieved; *class* handicappers judge a horse primarily by the company it's been keeping; *pace* handicappers concentrate on the horse's time and position at various points within its past races.

Although the speed handicappers weigh final times most heavily, they by no means *ignore* class, pace, distance, track condition, weight or any other single factor. Through experience, these handicappers have realized that the most sophisticated rating of a horse's speed won't help it win if it's entered at the wrong distance, against higher-class animals, on a track it can't handle, when its physical condition has deteriorated. Complex judgments cannot be reduced to a few simple rules or mathematical manipulations.

Explaining exactly how different kinds of handicappers weigh all the factors that affect the performance of all different kinds of horses in different kinds of races is a formidable task that would require many volumes. Our purpose in this book has been to provide the information racing fans need to become experts on their own. Accordingly, in this section we're going to concentrate on the first two steps involved in forming an opinion—*gathering* and *interpreting* the information available to handicappers. While we can't go into detail on handicapping procedures, we also will describe and evaluate those who offer, for a fee, to help you get to *stage three*—offers that range from touts and tip sheets that provide dubious opinions to valuable texts by skilled handicappers.

# The Handicapper's Tools

Before we start explaining the information available to handicappers, we'll first talk about the general approach almost all handicappers use in picking winners. The process of picking winners involves making two separate two-part judgments.

The first judgment is determining the ability of each horse entered in a race. Rating each requires first analyzing past performance to determining the level of ability the horse has demonstrated. Depending on the handicapper's preference and experience, the kind of evidence used in making this determination may be final times, pace, earnings, number of wins and/or a combination of other factors. Secondly, once past performance is analyzed, the handicapper must determine how a horse's performance today is likely to compare to that past performance. The kinds of evidence used to judge current form include recent improvement or decline in performance; the ability of the trainer; appraisal of the horse's appearance in the paddock; and other factors.

The second judgment, after each horse is appraised, is comparing the horses to each other. The first part of this judgment is separating the contenders from the non-contenders. While a racing secretary tries to write conditions for each race that bring the entrants as close together as possible, in most races these conditions still produce a field with a wide range of ability. Factors such as distance, class, weight and form can be used to eliminate a number of horses from serious consideration. The second and final step in picking a winner is determining the relative probability of each of the contenders' winning the race. The key word here is probability. No horse is a certainty.

A handicapper makes money only when he is able to identify horses that have a better chance to win than the public thinks they have. In other words, the handicapper is looking for a horse he feels has a 2–1 chance to win a race, but that goes to the post at 5–1 or 6–1 odds.

This last point is the reason most professional handicappers place serious bets on only a handful of races a week; some may place as few as ten wagers in the course of an entire race meeting. A fact of horse racing is that in a lot of races two or more horses may be so close in ability that the chances of successfully choosing between them are less than the odds offered. While the professional, who has to make money, sits out race after race, though, most racegoers who go to the track for recreation enjoy playing every race. If these racegoers become skilled enough handicappers to consistently identify the contenders, they'll do far better than the average horseplayer and will derive a lot of pleasure out of their afternoons at the races.

Knowledge is the basis of sound judgment. To obtain the information necessary for informed opinions, the handicapper has to make the best use of the tools available. Below, we'll discuss the tools, or sources of information, available to the racing fan.

## THE DAILY RACING FORM

The *Daily Racing Form* is not only the richest source of information for the handicapper, it is the official statistician for the entire racing industry. The statistics compiled by the *Daily Racing Form* are considered official by the Thoroughbred Racing

Association, the National Association of State Racing Commissioners and the Jockey Club. The *Daily Racing Form* is also the main supplier of race results, race charts and racing information to the wire services and daily newspapers. The *Form* is indispensable to the racing industry and indispensable to the handicapper.

### History of the Daily Racing Form

The paper was started in 1896 by Frank Brunell, an ex-Chicago *Tribune* sportswriter. In 1922, it was purchased for $400,000 by businessman Moses Annenberg. When Annenberg died in 1942, the business was taken over by his son Walter, who was later to become U. S. Ambassador to Great Britain under the Nixon administration.

When Moses Annenberg purchased the *Form,* the paper had two competitors, the *American Racing Record* and the *Morning Telegraph.* The first of these went out of business in the 1930s, and the *Morning Telegraph* succumbed to a printers' strike in 1972.

Today, the *Daily Racing Form,* which has no competition, is part of Annenberg's Triangle Publications, which also owns *TV Guide* and *Seventeen* magazine.

### Production of the Daily Racing Form

Depending on which tracks are operating, the *Daily Racing Form* is published in as many as thirty editions. The *Form* has fully computerized printing facilities in Hightstown, New Jersey; Chicago, Illinois; and Los Angeles, California. When there is racing in the area, editions are published in Seattle, Washington; Toronto, Canada; and Vancouver, Canada. The paper also has a working arrangement with a publisher in Mexico City, Mexico.

The circulation of the paper averages 150,000 daily, soaring to 400,000 on Kentucky Derby day. Circulation doesn't seem adversely affected by the $1.50 price, which makes the paper the most costly daily in the country. The reason for the current price is that the paper attracts relatively little advertising revenue to offset the very high costs of production and distribution. The publication is a very heavy user of air freight, and very seldom does the *Form* fail to reach tracks by post time.

The huge expansion of the racing industry after World War II made it necessary for the *Daily Racing Form* to introduce sophisticated technology. Today, the *Form* has to record the details of over 69,000 races and the past performances of over 63,000 horses annually. To collect this information, the *Form* employs about eight hundred people across the country. At each track, the publication has an average of three people who clock all workouts, prepare feature articles and prepare detailed charts of every race run.

The information collected by the paper's employees is fed by Teletype into the paper's computer system. This system gives everyone in the three locations complete access to all the information stored. In an instant, the system can recall the complete records of any current or former jockey, trainer or horse. The computer takes approximately eleven seconds to recall and set into type an individual horse's past-performance record.

### Contents of the Daily Racing Form

#### 1. *The Results Chart*

The sources of all racing statistics are the "results charts" prepared by the *Daily Racing Form* for every race run in North America. Fortunately for handicappers, these "charts" include far more than just a record of the order of finish, the time of the race and the payoffs. Rather, they might more properly be labeled "race stories," for in a remarkably concise fashion they tell a handicapper how a race was organized and run.

Below is a results chart from a race at Keystone Racetrack:*

**FOURTH RACE**
**Keystone**
**NOVEMBER 18, 1979**

**6 FURLONGS. (1.08⅘) CLAIMING. Purse $4,000. 3-year-olds and upward, which have not won a race since May 17. Weights; 3-year-olds, 118 lbs. Older, 120 lbs. Non-winners of a race since April 17, 3 lbs. A race since March 17, 6 lbs. Claiming Price $3,500.**

**Value of race $4,000, value to winner $2,400, second $800, third $440, fourth $240, fifth $120. Mutuel pool $51,167. Trifecta Pool $75,293.**

| Last Raced | Horse | Eqt. | A. | Wt | PP | St | ¼ | ½ | Str | Fin | Jockey | Cl'g Pr | Odds $1 |
|---|---|---|---|---|---|---|---|---|---|---|---|---|---|
| 9Nov79 $^{4}$Key$^{12}$ | Nobody Near Us | b | 6 | 109 | 7 | 3 | $4^{1}$ | $1\frac{1}{2}$ | $1^{3}$ | $1\frac{1}{2}$ | Trebino A P$^{5}$ | 3500 | 54.80 |
| 2Nov79 $^{4}$Key$^{2}$ | W. C. Kennedy | b | 4 | 115 | 2 | 5 | $5\frac{1}{2}$ | $4^{1}$ | $2^{3}$ | $2^{1\frac{1}{2}}$ | St Leon G | 3500 | 2.30 |
| 2Nov79 $^{4}$Key$^{7}$ | Please N Reason | b | 8 | 117 | 6 | 8 | $8^{1\frac{1}{2}}$ | $7^{3}$ | $3^{1}$ | $3^{2}$ | Black A S | 3500 | 9.10 |
| 9Nov79 $^{4}$Key$^{7}$ | Tipsy Native | b | 4 | 114 | 10 | 6 | $6^{1\frac{1}{2}}$ | $5^{1}$ | $4^{2}$ | $4^{3}$ | Anaya A | 3500 | 32.70 |
| 4Jly79 $^{1}$Del$^{3}$ | Do It My Way | b | 8 | 115 | 1 | 10 | $11^{5}$ | $8^{2}$ | $6^{1\frac{1}{2}}$ | $5^{2}$ | Le Fore J C | 3500 | 16.20 |
| 15Sep78 $^{9}$Med$^{1}$ | Vanish | b | 4 | 109 | 5 | 4 | $3\frac{1}{2}$ | $3^{1\frac{1}{2}}$ | $5^{2}$ | $6^{1\frac{1}{2}}$ | Rogers K L$^{5}$ | 3500 | 5.10 |
| 6Nov79 $^{4}$Key$^{10}$ | Fraternal | | 6 | 120 | 8 | 7 | $7^{2}$ | $9^{1\frac{1}{2}}$ | $8^{2}$ | $7^{2}$ | Velez H Jr | 3500 | 9.30 |
| 28Oct79 $^{9}$Key$^{7}$ | Super Tune | b | 4 | 113 | 12 | 1 | $2\frac{1}{2}$ | $2^{hd}$ | $7^{2}$ | $8^{3}$ | Galluccio J$^{7}$ | 3500 | 57.80 |
| 5Oct79 $^{9}$Key$^{11}$ | Package Store | | 6 | 114 | 3 | 2 | $1\frac{1}{2}$ | $6^{2}$ | $9^{2}$ | $9^{nk}$ | Klidzia S | 3500 | 5.10 |
| 28Oct79 $^{4}$Key$^{9}$ | Try Good Bye | b | 5 | 120 | 9 | 9 | $10^{1}$ | $10^{1\frac{1}{2}}$ | $10^{1}$ | $10^{nk}$ | Lanci H L | 3500 | 9.00 |
| 9Nov79 $^{4}$Key$^{8}$ | Princely Glow | b | 6 | 114 | 4 | 12 | $9^{hd}$ | $11^{3}$ | $11^{2}$ | $11^{2}$ | Pagano S R | 3500 | 5.30 |
| 26Oct79 $^{9}$Key$^{11}$ | Kristen's Pride | b | 6 | 114 | 11 | 11 | 12 | 12 | 12 | 12 | Baker D S | 3500 | 153.40 |

**OFF AT 2:17, EST. Start good for all but PRINCELY GLOW, Won driving. Time, :23⅕, :48, 1:14⅖ Track fast.**

| $2 Mutuel Prices: | | | |
|---|---|---|---|
| 7–NOBODY NEAR US | 111.60 | 32.20 | 12.60 |
| 2–W. C. KENNEDY | | 4.40 | 4.00 |
| 6–PLEASE N REASON | | | 5.40 |

**$3 TRIFECTA 7–2–6 PAID $3,682.80.**

**B. g, by Flag Raiser—Handi Work, by Fulcrum. Trainer Duffield Frank A. Bred by Fisher Mary V (Ky).**

NOBODY NEAR US dueled for command between rivals to the stretch, drew clear and was hard ridden to hold safe W. C. KENNEDY. The latter lacked room behind the leaders to midturn, came side and finished willingly. PLEASE N REASON rallied widest into the stretch and hung in midstretch. TIPSY NATIVE vied on the outside to the stretch and weakened. DO IT MY WAY was outrun. VANISH had speed for a half and tired. SUPPER TUNE had speed to the stretch and gave way. PACKAGE STORE held a short lead to the turn went sore in the left foreleg. PRINCELY GLOW hesitated and reared up at the start.

**Owners**— 1, Duffield F A; 2, Kady T E; 3, Baddeley C W; 4, Delaney Kathryn & Watters; 5, Menarde J; 6, Keegan W A Jr; 7, Engle C; 8, Pisano M; 9, Fallon M L; 10, Mosca D; 11, Drayer G; 12, Braun & Martino.

**Trainers**— 1, Duffield Frank A; 2, Clemson Ralph H Jr; 3, Baddeley Charles W; 4, Delaney Ralph J Jr; 5, Menarde Frank J; 6, Cogswell Chester; 7, Andris Charles J; 8, Pisano Mario; 9, Fallon Martin L; 10, Jenkens Suzanne H; 11, Sipp Burton K; 12, Martino Clem.

**Overweight:** W. C. Kennedy 1 pound; Do It My Way 1.

**Princely Glow was claimed by Vance D R; trainer, Vance David R.**

**Scratched**—Martin Hagley ( 2Nov79 $^{4}$Key$^{5}$); Bidding Fool (10Nov79 $^{1}$Key$^{10}$); Vitamin C ( 9Nov79 $^{4}$Key$^{3}$).



At the top of the chart are the *conditions* for the race, just as they appeared in the condition book issued by the racing secretary. The kind of race, the way weights were assigned and the dollar value of the purse allow an accurate appraisal of the *class* of the race.

Below the conditions is the purse distribution. After the race, the *Daily Racing Form* computer adds the appropriate amount to the record of each horse, trainer, jockey and owner.

Next comes the "chart" with information about each horse. The chart is prepared by the paper's "trackman" or "chart caller." Before each race, the chart caller memorizes the names and colors of each horse, just like the race announcer. After the horses break from the gate, the chart man, with incredible speed and accuracy, calls out the placing of each horse at each point of call and that horse's margin over the following animal.

For example, in the chart above, Nobody Near Us broke third from the gate, was fourth by one length over the fifth place horse at the quarter-mile pole, moved to a half-length lead at the half-mile pole, had a three-length lead at the top of the stretch, and held on to win by half a length.

After the race, the caller immediately sits down at a typewriter to write a *narrative* of the race action. The winner's race above was described as "Nobody Near Us dueled for command between rivals to the stretch, drew clear and was hard ridden to hold safe." In his narrative, the trackman pays particular attention to any trouble or problems that occurred during the course of the race: "W. C. Kennedy . . . *lacked room behind the leaders";* "Package Store . . . *went sore in the left foreleg";* "Princely Glow *hesitated and reared up at the start."*

After writing the race narrative, the chart caller reviews the video tape of the race to adjust any errors in his original call. When the information on pari-mutuel wagering and payoffs is received from the track management, the entire information contained in the chart is transmitted by Teletype to the *Daily Racing Form* computer.

The charts are published a day or two after the race in the appropriate editions of the *Daily Racing Form.* Condensed charts of every race run each month are published in the *Monthly Chart Books,* which are available singly or by subscription from Triangle Publications.

Virtually all professional handicappers keep files of all results charts for the tracks in their area, because the vital first part of making a judgment about the ability of a horse is evaluating its past performances. Results charts are the most complete available record of those past performances, a valuable source for determining exactly how a horse ran and what competition it faced.

For the racing fan, reading results charts whenever one buys the *Form* is the best

## EASTERN EDITION

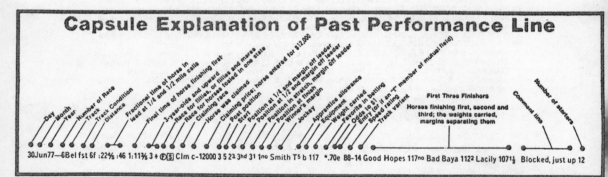

## WESTERN EDITION

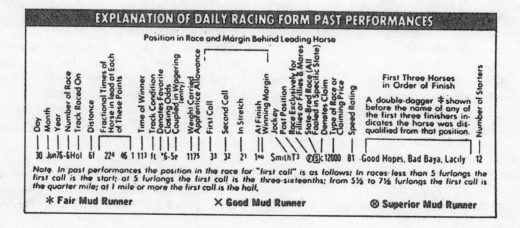

30Jun77—6Bel fst 6f :22⅘ :46 1:11⅗ 3↑Ⓕ[S] Clm c-12000 3 5 2$^3$ 3$^{hd}$ 3$^1$ 1$^{no}$ Smith T$^5$ b 117 *.70e 88-14 Good Hopes 117$^{no}$ Bad Baya 112$^2$ Lacily 107$^{1\frac{1}{2}}$ Blocked, just up 12

**DATE RACE WAS RUN** — The day, month and year. This race was run on June 30, 1977.

30Jun77—6Bel fst 6f :22⅘ :46 1:11⅗ 3↑Ⓕ[S] Clm c-12000 3 5 2$^3$ 3$^{hd}$ 3$^1$ 1$^{no}$ Smith T$^5$ b 117 *.70e 88-14 Good Hopes 117$^{no}$ Bad Baya 112$^2$ Lacily 107$^{1\frac{1}{2}}$ Blocked, just up 12

**NUMBER OF RACE AND TRACK RACED ON** — This was the sixth race at Belmont Park. A complete list of track abbreviations is published in the past performance section of each issue of Daily Racing Form. A ◆ symbol preceding race number denotes track located in foreign country.

30Jun77—6Bel fst 6f :22⅘ :46 1:11⅗ 3↑Ⓕ[S] Clm c-12000 3 5 2$^3$ 3$^{hd}$ 3$^1$ 1$^{no}$ Smith T$^5$ b 117 *.70e 88-14 Good Hopes 117$^{no}$ Bad Baya 112$^2$ Lacily 107$^{1\frac{1}{2}}$ Blocked, just up 12

**TRACK CONDITION** — The track was fast. Track condition abbreviations are, for dirt tracks: fst-fast; fr-frozen; gd-good; sl-slow; sly-sloppy; my-muddy; hy-heavy; for turf, steeplechase and hurdle races: hd-hard; fm-firm; gd-good; yl-yielding; sf-soft.

30Jun77—6Bel fst 6f :22⅘ :46 1:11⅗ 3↑Ⓕ[S] Clm c-12000 3 5 2$^3$ 3$^{hd}$ 3$^1$ 1$^{no}$ Smith T$^5$ b 117 *.70e 88-14 Good Hopes 117$^{no}$ Bad Baya 112$^2$ Lacily 107$^{1\frac{1}{2}}$ Blocked, just up 12

**DISTANCE OF RACE** — The race was at 6 furlongs (or 3/4 of a mile — there are 8 furlongs to a mile). An asterisk * before distance means it was not exact (*6f—"about" 6 furlongs). Turf course symbols (following distance): Ⓣ—main turf course; [T]—inner turf course; [•]—inner dirt track (at racecourses that have two dirt strips).

30Jun77—6Bel fst 6f :22⅘ :46 1:11⅗ 3↑Ⓕ[S] Clm c-12000 3 5 2$^3$ 3$^{hd}$ 3$^1$ 1$^{no}$ Smith T$^5$ b 117 *.70e 88-14 Good Hopes 117$^{no}$ Bad Baya 112$^2$ Lacily 107$^{1\frac{1}{2}}$ Blocked, just up 12

**FRACTIONAL TIMES** — The first fraction (:22 4/5) is the time of the horse in front at the quarter; the second fraction (:46) is the time of the horse in the lead after a half-mile. Fractional times used vary according to the distance of the race. For a listing of the fractions at various distances, see reverse side.

30Jun77—6Bel fst 6f :22⅘ :46 1:11⅗ 3↑Ⓕ[S] Clm c-12000 3 5 2$^3$ 3$^{hd}$ 3$^1$ 1$^{no}$ Smith T$^5$ b 117 *.70e 88-14 Good Hopes 117$^{no}$ Bad Baya 112$^2$ Lacily 107$^{1\frac{1}{2}}$ Blocked, just up 12

**FINAL TIME** — This is the time of the first horse to finish (when the winner is disqualified, this is HIS time, not the time of the horse awarded first money).

30Jun77—6Bel fst 6f :22⅘ :46 1:11⅗ 3↑Ⓕ[S] Clm c-12000 3 5 2$^3$ 3$^{hd}$ 3$^1$ 1$^{no}$ Smith T$^5$ b 117 *.70e 88-14 Good Hopes 117$^{no}$ Bad Baya 112$^2$ Lacily 107$^{1\frac{1}{2}}$ Blocked, just up 12

**RACE FOR 3-YEAR-OLDS AND UPWARD** — This is used ONLY when 3-year-olds and upward were eligible to start in the race.

30Jun77—6Bel fst 6f :22⅘ :46 1:11⅗ 3↑Ⓕ[S] Clm c-12000 3 5 2$^3$ 3$^{hd}$ 3$^1$ 1$^{no}$ Smith T$^5$ b 117 *.70e 88-14 Good Hopes 117$^{no}$ Bad Baya 112$^2$ Lacily 107$^{1\frac{1}{2}}$ Blocked, just up 12

**RACE FOR FILLIES AND MARES** — The symbol Ⓕ means the race was restricted to fillies or fillies and mares.

30Jun77—6Bel fst 6f :22⅘ :46 1:11⅗ 3↑Ⓕ[S] Clm c-12000 3 5 2$^3$ 3$^{hd}$ 3$^1$ 1$^{no}$ Smith T$^5$ b 117 *.70e 88-14 Good Hopes 117$^{no}$ Bad Baya 112$^2$ Lacily 107$^{1\frac{1}{2}}$ Blocked, just up 12

**RACE FOR STATE-BREDS** — The symbol [S] means the race was restricted to horses foaled in a specific state (a closed race). The state where the horse was foaled follows the name of his breeder, directly below the horse's pedigree.

30Jun77—6Bel fst 6f :22⅘ :46 1:11⅗ 3↑Ⓕ[S] Clm c-12000 3 5 2$^3$ 3$^{hd}$ 3$^1$ 1$^{no}$ Smith T$^5$ b 117 *.70e 88-14 Good Hopes 117$^{no}$ Bad Baya 112$^2$ Lacily 107$^{1\frac{1}{2}}$ Blocked, just up 12

**CLAIMING PRICE OR TYPE OF RACE** — The horse was entered to be claimed for $12,000. The letter c preceding the claiming price indicates the horse was claimed. For a complete list of the various race classifications, see reverse side.

30Jun77—6Bel fst 6f :22⅘ :46 1:11⅗ 3↑Ⓕ[S] Clm c-12000 3 5 2$^3$ 3$^{hd}$ 3$^1$ 1$^{no}$ Smith T$^5$ b 117 *.70e 88-14 Good Hopes 117$^{no}$ Bad Baya 112$^2$ Lacily 107$^{1\frac{1}{2}}$ Blocked, just up 12

**POST POSITION** — The horse left the starting gate from post position number 3. This figure can differ from the official program number because of late scratches, horses coupled in the wagering (an "entry") or horses grouped in the mutuel field.

30Jun77—6Bel fst 6f :22⅘ :46 1:11⅗ 3↑Ⓕ[S] Clm c-12000 3 5 2$^3$ 3$^{hd}$ 3$^1$ 1$^{no}$ Smith T$^5$ b 117 *.70e 88-14 Good Hopes 117$^{no}$ Bad Baya 112$^2$ Lacily 107$^{1\frac{1}{2}}$ Blocked, just up 12

**FIRST CALL** — The horse's position immediately after leaving the starting gate. He was fifth at this point. Points of call vary according to the distance of the race. In races of 1 mile and longer, the start call is omitted and the horse's position at the 1/4-mile or 1/2-mile is given instead. A table listing the points of call for races at the most frequently run distances is on the reverse side.

30Jun77—6Bel fst 6f :22⅘ :46 1:11⅗ 3↑Ⓕ[S] Clm c-12000 3 5 2$^3$ 3$^{hd}$ 3$^1$ 1$^{no}$ Smith T$^5$ b 117 *.70e 88-14 Good Hopes 117$^{no}$ Bad Baya 112$^2$ Lacily 107$^{1\frac{1}{2}}$ Blocked, just up 12

**SECOND CALL** — The horse was second, three lengths behind the leader (2$^3$) at the 1/4-mile point. The large figure indicates the horse's running position; the small one his margin behind the leader. If the horse had been in front at this point (1$^3$), the small figure would indicate the margin by which he was leading the second horse.

30Jun77—6Bel fst 6f :22⅘ :46 1:11⅗ 3↑Ⓕ[S] Clm c-12000 3 5 2$^3$ 3$^{hd}$ 3$^1$ 1$^{no}$ Smith T$^5$ b 117 *.70e 88-14 Good Hopes 117$^{no}$ Bad Baya 112$^2$ Lacily 107$^{1\frac{1}{2}}$ Blocked, just up 12

**THIRD CALL** — The horse was third at this call, at the 1/2-mile point, a head behind the leader (3$^{hd}$).

30Jun77—6Bel fst 6f :22⅘ :46 1:11⅗ 3↑Ⓕ[S] Clm c-12000 3 5 2$^3$ 3$^{hd}$ 3$^1$ 1$^{no}$ Smith T$^5$ b 117 *.70e 88-14 Good Hopes 117$^{no}$ Bad Baya 112$^2$ Lacily 107$^{1\frac{1}{2}}$ Blocked, just up 12

**STRETCH CALL** — The horse was third, one length behind the leader (3$^1$), at this point. The stretch call is made 1/8 mile from the finish.

30Jun77—6Bel fst 6f :22⅘ :46 1:11⅗ 3↑Ⓕ[S] Clm c-12000 3 5 2$^3$ 3$^{hd}$ 3$^1$ 1$^{no}$ Smith T$^5$ b 117 *.70e 88-14 Good Hopes 117$^{no}$ Bad Baya 112$^2$ Lacily 107$^{1\frac{1}{2}}$ Blocked, just up 12

**FINISH** — The horse finished first, a nose before the second horse (1$^{no}$). If the horse is second, third or unplaced, the small figure indicates the total distance he finished behind the winner.

30Jun77—6Bel fst 6f :22⅘ :46 1:11⅗ 3↑Ⓕ[S] Clm c-12000 3 5 2$^3$ 3$^{hd}$ 3$^1$ 1$^{no}$ Smith T$^5$ b 117 *.70e 88-14 Good Hopes 117$^{no}$ Bad Baya 112$^2$ Lacily 107$^{1\frac{1}{2}}$ Blocked, just up 12

**JOCKEY** — The horse was ridden by T. Smith. The small figure following the jockey's name (Smith T$^5$) indicates the amount of the apprentice allowance claimed. When an apprentice allowance is claimed the exact number of pounds of the claim is listed.

30Jun77—6Bel fst 6f :22⅘ :46 1:11⅗ 3↑Ⓕ[S] Clm c-12000 3 5 2$^3$ 3$^{hd}$ 3$^1$ 1$^{no}$ Smith T$^5$ b 117 *.70e 88-14 Good Hopes 117$^{no}$ Bad Baya 112$^2$ Lacily 107$^{1\frac{1}{2}}$ Blocked, just up 12

**EQUIPMENT CARRIED** — The letter b indicates the horse was equipped with blinkers. Other abbreviations which may appear here: s-spurs; sb-spurs and blinkers.

30Jun77—6Bel fst 6f :22⅘ :46 1:11⅗ 3↑Ⓕ[S] Clm c-12000 3 5 2$^3$ 3$^{hd}$ 3$^1$ 1$^{no}$ Smith T$^5$ b 117 *.70e 88-14 Good Hopes 117$^{no}$ Bad Baya 112$^2$ Lacily 107$^{1\frac{1}{2}}$ Blocked, just up 12

**WEIGHT CARRIED IN THIS RACE** — The horse carried 117 pounds. This is the weight of the rider and equipment (saddle, lead pads, etc.) and includes the apprentice allowance when an allowance is claimed.

30Jun77—6Bel fst 6f :22⅘ :46 1:11⅗ 3↑Ⓕ[S] Clm c-12000 3 5 2$^3$ 3$^{hd}$ 3$^1$ 1$^{no}$ Smith T$^5$ b 117 *.70e 88-14 Good Hopes 117$^{no}$ Bad Baya 112$^2$ Lacily 107$^{1\frac{1}{2}}$ Blocked, just up 12

**CLOSING ODDS** — The horse was 70 cents to the dollar (he was 7-10 in the wagering). The star * preceding the odds indicates he was the favorite. The symbol ♦ between the weight and the odds would mean he finished in a dead-heat with one or more horses. The letter e following the odds means the horse was coupled in the betting (an entry) with one or more horses. The letter f in this position would indicate he was in the mutuel field; the symbol [D] means that the horse was disqualified.

30Jun77—6Bel fst 6f :22⅘ :46 1:11⅗ 3↑Ⓕ[S] Clm c-12000 3 5 2$^3$ 3$^{hd}$ 3$^1$ 1$^{no}$ Smith T$^5$ b 117 *.70e 88-14 Good Hopes 117$^{no}$ Bad Baya 112$^2$ Lacily 107$^{1\frac{1}{2}}$ Blocked, just up 12

**SPEED RATING AND TRACK VARIANT** — The first figure is the speed rating; the second the track variant. For an explanation of how speed ratings and track variants are compiled see reverse side.

30Jun77—6Bel fst 6f :22⅘ :46 1:11⅗ 3↑Ⓕ[S] Clm c-12000 3 5 2$^3$ 3$^{hd}$ 3$^1$ 1$^{no}$ Smith T$^5$ b 117 *.70e 88-14 Good Hopes 117$^{no}$ Bad Baya 112$^2$ Lacily 107$^{1\frac{1}{2}}$ Blocked, just up 12

**FIRST, SECOND AND THIRD HORSES AT THE FINISH** — The horses who finished 1-2-3 in the race, the weight each carried and the margins separating each one from the next horse. If any of these horses was disqualified or finished in a dead-heat, the symbol [D] for disqualified or [DH] for dead-heat precedes the horse's name.

30Jun77—6Bel fst 6f :22⅘ :46 1:11⅗ 3↑Ⓕ[S] Clm c-12000 3 5 2$^3$ 3$^{hd}$ 3$^1$ 1$^{no}$ Smith T$^5$ b 117 *.70e 88-14 Good Hopes 117$^{no}$ Bad Baya 112$^2$ Lacily 107$^{1\frac{1}{2}}$ Blocked, just up 12

**COMMENT LINE** — A capsule description of the horse's performance, with special emphasis on pointing out any trouble he may have encountered.

30Jun77—6Bel fst 6f :22⅘ :46 1:11⅗ 3↑Ⓕ[S] Clm c-12000 3 5 2$^3$ 3$^{hd}$ 3$^1$ 1$^{no}$ Smith T$^5$ b 117 *.70e 88-14 Good Hopes 117$^{no}$ Bad Baya 112$^2$ Lacily 107$^{1\frac{1}{2}}$ Blocked, just up 12

**NUMBER OF STARTERS** — Twelve horses started in this race.

way to build an understanding of how races are run. One particularly valuable technique is for the fan to make notes after watching a race through binoculars or on closed-circuit television, then checking those notes against the official results chart printed in the *Daily Racing Form.*

2. *Past Performances*

From the results charts, the *Daily Racing Form* extracts important information listed on each line of each horse's past-performance listing. These past performances are marvels of condensation which, properly interpreted, provide a remarkably clear story of the recent history of each horse entered in a race. While professional handicappers prefer to make their final decisions based on the more complete picture of previous races provided by the results charts, the past performances do provide ample information to identify the leading contenders in a race. They are the single most important tool for the recreational handicapper.

The exact format of the past performances varies with the edition of the *Daily Racing Form.* The full-size Eastern editions published in Hightstown, New Jersey, contain more information than those in the tabloid-size Western editions. Because they contain more information important to handicapping, we're going to use the past performances from the Eastern editions in this book.

The first step in using the past performances is learning how to read them. Below are capsule explanations of the past-performance lines in both editions, then the *Daily Racing Form*'s detailed explanation of the data in the Eastern edition. For easy track reference, a handy booklet on how to read the *Form* is also available free of charge at most track newsstands that sell the paper.

### Interpreting Past Performances

After learning to read the past performances, the racing fan next has to learn how to interpret the information. Interpretation is by definition an expression of opinion rather than irrefutable fact. Skilled, winning handicappers differ widely in their interpretation of past-performance data. To do justice to all possible uses and interpretations of the data in the space available here is impossible. Instead, we're going through the past performances to briefly present a range of opinion within which the views of a large number of handicappers fall.

BREEDING

**Sugar And Spice *** B. f. 3, by Key To The Mint—Sweet Tooth, by On-And-On
Own.—Calumet Farm Br.—Calumet Farm (Ky) Tr.—Veitch John M **121**
St. 1st 2nd 3rd Amt.
1980 5 3 0 1 $128,930
1979 1 1 0 0 $9,000
8Jun80- 8Bel sly 1⅛ :46⅕ 1:11⅕ 1:49⅗ ⒻMotherGoose 4 5 53¾ 2½ 1hd 1hd Fell J 121 9.50 79-23 SugrAndSpice121hdBold'NDetrmind1218¾Erin'sWord1213½ Driving 8
24May80- 8Bel fst 1 :44⅘ 1:09⅗ 1:36⅘ ⒻAcorn 4 7 68 56½ 44½ 34 Fell J 121 15.50 80-17 Bold'NDetermined1212¾MiteyLively1211½SugrAndSpic1213½ Wide 8
2May80- 8CD fst 1 1/16 :48⅗ 1:13⅗ 1:44⅘ ⒻKy. Oaks 6 4 64 62¼ 69½ 612 Fell J 121 2.50 72-18 Bold'NDetermined1211½MiteyLively121½HonestAndTru1213 Wide 8
19Apr80- 8Kee fst *7f 1:27⅕ ⒻAshland 9 1 42½ 2½ 1hd 13¼ Fell J 113 *.80 87-16 SugarAndSpice1133¼NiceAndSharp1141¼StinRiber1161¼ Drew off 9
19Apr80-Run in Two Divisions: 7th & 8th races.
1Apr80- 2Aqu my 6f :22⅗ :46 1:10⅗ ⒻAllowance 3 5 21 31½ 2hd 1½ Fell J 116 *1.50 91-19 Sugar And Spice 116½ Shake The Beat 1165½Karand1161¾ Driving 7
5Sep79- 6Bel fst 6½f :22⅘ :46⅗ 1:19 ⒻMd Sp Wt 7 8 2hd 2½ 1½ 11¼ Velasquez J 117 4.10 81-22 Sugar And Spice 1171¼ Harrowing 117no Erin'sWord117nk Driving 11
LATEST WORKOUTS Jun 25 Bel 6f fst 1:15⅘ b ●Jun 19 Bel 1 fst 1:44 b Jun 15 Bel 4f fst :52 b Jun 7 Bel 3f sly :36⅕ b

The past performances include the *sire, dam* and *maternal grandsire,* as well as the *name of the breeder* and *the state in which the horse was bred.* For example, Sugar and Spice is by the outstanding sire Key to the Mint, out of Sweet Tooth (dam of Alydar and champion filly Our Mims) by On-and-On. She was bred in Kentucky by the famed Calumet Farm.

The class that a horse has demonstrated

by racing successfully is a much more reliable indication of likely performance than the potential class demonstrated by the animal's breeding. However, while breeding in itself is not an adequate reason to bet on a horse, it can caution a handicapper not to bet heavily against a first-time starter with a pedigree such as that of Sugar and Spice, who in fact did win her first race. Similarly, a pedigree that includes a stallion known as an outstanding sire of turf horses can alert a horseplayer not to disregard a first-time starter on the grass.

Even the best breeders produce far more untalented than outstanding horses. Some handicappers consider the breeder's retention of ownership of a horse to be a positive sign, if the stable is known to retain only promising prospects.

## TRAINER

**Silver Fir *** — B. g. 16, by Swoon's Son—Snow White, by Counterpoint — $2,000 — Br.—Whitney C V (Ky) — Tr.—Strange Bill — 120
Own.—Strange Mrs B

| | St. | 1st | 2nd | 3rd | Amt. |
|---|---|---|---|---|---|
| 1979 | 5 | 2 | 0 | 1 | $2,935 |
| 1978 | 8 | 5 | 0 | 0 | $6,955 |

| | | | | | | | | | | | | | | | | | | | | | |
|---|---|---|---|---|---|---|---|---|---|---|---|---|---|---|---|---|---|---|---|---|---|
| 26Sep79- 6FL | fst | 6f | :24⅖ | :48⅘ | 1:15 | 3↑ | Clm 2000 | 1 | 1 | $1^{hd}$ | $2^{hd}$ | $2^{hd}$ | $3^{2}$ | Laiz G | 119 | 4.20 | 77–28 | Marked Copy $122^{1}$ Silent Roamer $122^{1}$ Silver Fir $119^{4}$ | Weakened | 12 |
| 3Sep79- 4FL | gd | 6f | :24 | :48⅕ | 1:14⅘ | 3↑ | Clm 2000 | 5 | 6 | $7^{8}$ | $7^{8\frac{1}{2}}$ | $6^{8}$ | $4^{8\frac{3}{4}}$ | Villar H Jr | 120 | *1.60 | 72–21 | Back Hitch $120^{3\frac{1}{2}}$ Roman Ball $108^{4}$ Chuckle Patch $107^{\frac{3}{4}}$ | No rally | 7 |
| 18Aug79- 9FL | fst | 6f | :24 | :48 | 1:14⅘ | 3↑ | Clm 2000 | 9 | 3 | $1^{2}$ | $2^{3}$ | $2^{1\frac{1}{2}}$ | $1^{1\frac{1}{2}}$ | Villar H Jr | 121 | 5.30 | 82–15 | Silver Fir $121^{1\frac{1}{2}}$ British Boy $116^{\frac{3}{4}}$ Happy Jerry $121^{no}$ | Driving | 11 |
| 4Aug79- 2FL | fst | 6f | :24 | :48⅗ | 1:15⅗ | 3↑ | Clm 2000 | 9 | 3 | $4^{4}$ | $4^{8\frac{1}{2}}$ | $5^{8}$ | $6^{7\frac{3}{4}}$ | Villar H Jr | 120 | *2.20 | 69–24 | Simcoe Treasure $120^{nk}$PinPanDan$117^{3\frac{1}{2}}$BritishBoy$118^{2}$ | No excuse | 9 |
| 21Jly79- 9FL | fst | 6f | :24⅖ | :48⅘ | 1:15 | | Clm 2000 | 4 | 8 | $3^{1}$ | $2^{1\frac{1}{2}}$ | $2^{1}$ | $1^{hd}$ | Villar H Jr | 120 | *1.40 | 79–22 | Silver Fir $120^{hd}$ Captain Chubby $120^{1}$ Fast Velocity $120^{3}$ | Driving | 10 |
| 7Nov78- 4FL | fst | 6f | :23⅗ | :47⅘ | 1:14⅕ | 3↑ | Clm 1500 | 5 | 5 | $6^{6\frac{1}{2}}$ | $6^{6}$ | $6^{5\frac{1}{4}}$ | $5^{5\frac{3}{4}}$ | Laiz G | 122 | *.90 | 77–17 | Happy Fortune $120^{1}$ Native Outcast$117^{1}$BlackyKhal$119^{1\frac{1}{4}}$ | Dull try | 6 |
| 28Oct78- 3FL | gd | 1 | :48⅘ | 1:15⅗ | 1:43⅘ | 3↑ | Clm 1500 | 4 | 4 | $3^{4}$ | $2^{1\frac{1}{2}}$ | $1^{2}$ | $1^{6\frac{1}{2}}$ | Laiz G | 120 | *1.00 | 66–22 | Silver Fir $120^{6\frac{1}{2}}$ Stature Snatcher $115^{1\frac{1}{2}}$ Silent Shield $108^{7}$ | Easily | 7 |
| 22Oct78- 4FL | fst | 6f | :24⅕ | :48 | 1:14⅘ | 3↑ | Clm 2000 | 2 | 3 | $3^{1}$ | $1^{\frac{1}{2}}$ | $1^{1\frac{1}{2}}$ | $1^{4}$ | Laiz G | 119 | *1.60 | 81–20 | Silver Fir $119^{4}$NickaJackBreeze$117^{1}$PuffandStuff$122^{\frac{3}{4}}$ | Ridden out | 7 |

The job of the trainer is to keep a horse as fit as possible, then to enter the horse in a race with the class and conditions best suited to the horse's abilities and fitness. At any track, a small number of competent trainers win a large percentage of races. A much larger number of incompetent trainers damage or ruin the careers of their unfortunate charges.

One measure of the competence of a trainer is win percentage. At the Finger Lakes, regular racegoers know that Bill Strange has saddled well over 30 percent winners year after year. Strange's abilities are such that he has been able to even coax seven victories from sixteen-year-old Silver Fir in the last two years. Consequently, Finger Lakes horseplayers have learned to consider almost all horses trained by Strange to be legitimate contenders.

In general, a win percentage of 15 percent or higher is an indication of competence. Unfortunately, track programs include only the records of a few top trainers. Many handicappers take a few minutes a day to keep their own records.

Even more valuable than a record of a trainer's overall percentage are records of *trainer patterns.* Just as in any other complicated profession, in horse training practitioners develop more skill in certain specialties. Some trainers are outstanding handlers of two-year-olds; others work wonders with fillies; some achieve great success training horses for turf races. Also, most trainers develop patterns in their selection of races for their stock. Some win more races by moving animals up in class; some prefer dropping horses slightly; others have a high rate of success entering former sprinters in distance races.

The average racegoer can learn a surprising amount about the trainers at a track by paying attention to the names of trainers when going to the races and reading race results. Also informative are profiles of trainers in the "Turf Topics" section of the *Form.*

## AGE

**Astrid's Pride** — Dk. b. or br. (3), by My Gallant—Aloha Nui, by Thinking Cap or Social Climber — $60,000
Own.—Hirsch M — Br.—Hofmann Mr-Mrs P B (Fla) — Tr.—Gustines Heliodoro
116 — Turf Record: St. 2, 1st 0, 2nd 0, 3rd 0

| | St. | 1st | 2nd | 3rd | Amt. |
|---|---|---|---|---|---|
| 1980 | 14 | 3 | 2 | 1 | $43,840 |
| 1979 | 3 | M | 1 | 0 | $2,860 |

| | | | | | | | | | | | | | | | | | | | | |
|---|---|---|---|---|---|---|---|---|---|---|---|---|---|---|---|---|---|---|---|---|
| 19Sep80- | 9Bel | fst | 7f | :23⅕ | :46⅘ | 1:24⅘ | ⒻClm 50000 | 7 | 2 | 73 | 84½ | 53 | 11¾ | Pincay L Jr | b 117 | 7.20 | 79-18 | Astrid's Pride 1171¾ Oh Dora 1161¾ Dolly By Golly 116no | Driving | 9 |
| 30Aug80- | 1Bel | fst | 1 | :46⅘ | 1:11⅘ | 1:37⅘ | 3↑ ⒻClm 50000 | 4 | 3 | 32 | 41½ | 44 | 35½ | Mora G | b 112 | 11.90 | 75-17 | BlessedPrincss107hdFourA.M.1145½Astrid'sPrid112½ | Fairly evenly | 5 |
| 14Aug80- | 1Sar | fst | 7f | :22⅘ | :46 | 1:24 | 3↑ ⒻClm 50000 | 4 | 7 | 64 | 64 | 53½ | 43½ | Vasquez J | b 114 | 6.90 | 78-12 | Curl 1131½ Dolly By Golly 112½ Lalim 1121½ | Wide | 7 |
| 1Aug80- | 2Sar | fm | 1⅛ | ⓣ:48 | 1:12 | 1:56 | 3↑ ⒻAllowance | 3 | 3 | 43 | 64½ | 1013 | 1015 | Lovato F Jr5 | b 107 | 32.20 | 71-21 | O'Connell Street 1172¼ Hemlock 113½ Utmost Celerity1121½ | Tired | 10 |
| 16Jly80- | 7Bel | fst | 1 1/16 | :47⅘ | 1:12⅘ | 1:42⅘ | 3↑ ⒻAllowance | 1 | 3 | 21 | 65 | 617 | 521 | Gonzalez M A5 | b 111 | 10.60 | 67-17 | Patty Pumpkin 1063¾ Kelley's Day 1131½ Rio Rita 1113¾ | Tired | 6 |
| 29Jun80- | 6Bel | hd | 1¼ | [T]:49 | 1:37⅘ | 2:02⅘ | 3↑ ⒻAllowance | 5 | 1 | 21½ | 815 | 818 | 822 | Mora G | b 114 | 5.30 | 58-06 | Sparklet 1091½ Diffluence 1171 Loving Lady 1092½ | Stopped | 8 |
| 11Jun80- | 5Bel | fst | 1⅜ | :49⅘ | 1:40⅘ | 2:07⅕ | 3↑ ⒻAllowance | 3 | 4 | 3½ | 13 | 14 | 15 | Gonzalez M A5 | b 104 | 7.20 | 64-23 | Astrid'sPride1045MissRebecc1143WinterRomnce112½ | Ridden out | 7 |
| 1Jun80- | 5Bel | fst | 7f | :23 | :46 | 1:25⅘ | 3↑ ⒻAllowance | 2 | 6 | 42½ | 74½ | 89½ | 611 | Mora G | b 111 | 28.60 | 63-25 | Rokeby Rose 1142½ What A Year 109hdUtmostCelerity1132½ | Tired | 8 |
| 5May80- | 2Aqu | fst | 7f | :23 | :46⅘ | 1:24 | ⒻAllowance | 5 | 4 | 45½ | 45 | 48½ | 46½ | Mora G | b 121 | 18.70 | 74-19 | Popular Game 116½ Madura 1161½ Bang The Drums 1214¾ | Evenly | 8 |
| 17Apr80- | 6Aqu | fst | 7f | :23⅕ | :47⅕ | 1:26⅕ | 3↑ ⒻMd Sp Wt | 4 | 3 | 41½ | 4¾ | 11½ | 1½ | Mora G | b 113 | 4.30 | 70-23 | Astrid's Pride 113½ Pink Supreme 108¾LuckyOleAxe1132½ | Driving | 8 |

LATEST WORKOUTS Oct 2 Bel [T] 4f fm :48⅘ h Sep 25 Bel 3f fst :37 b Sep 18 Bel 3f sly :35 h Sep 12 Bel 6f fst 1:14 h

The primary time a handicapper need consider age is when three-year-olds meet older horses. For example, when Astrid's Pride moved from a $50,000 claimer open to older horses to a $50,000 claimer restricted to three-year-olds, she was dropping in class and responded with a victory. The *Daily Racing Form* has added to its Eastern editions a symbol indicating that a race was open to three-year-olds and up. Readers of the Western editions have to look up results charts to obtain the same information.

## SEX

**Genuine Risk** — Ch. f. 3, by Exclusive Native—Virtuous, by Gallant Man
Own.—Firestone Mrs B R — Br.—Humphrey Mrs G W Jr (Ky) — Tr.—Jolley Leroy
121

| | St. | 1st | 2nd | 3rd | Amt. |
|---|---|---|---|---|---|
| 1980 | 5 | 3 | 1 | 1 | $339,210 |
| 1979 | 4 | 4 | 0 | 0 | $100,245 |

| | | | | | | | | | | | | | | | | | | | | |
|---|---|---|---|---|---|---|---|---|---|---|---|---|---|---|---|---|---|---|---|---|
| 17May80- | 9Pim | fst | 1 3/16 | :47⅘ | 1:11⅕ | 1:54⅕ | Preakness | 5 | 6 | 44 | 43½ | 21 | 24¾ | Vasquez J | 121 | *2.00 | 94-12 | Codex 1264¾ Genuine Risk 1213½ColonelMoran1267 | Bothered turn | 8 |
| 3May80- | 8CD | fst | 1¼ | :48 | 1:37⅗ | 2:02 | Ky Derby | 10 | 7 | 74½ | 11½ | 12 | 11 | Vasquez J | 121 | 13.30 | 87-11 | Genuine Risk 1211 Rumbo 1261 Jaklin Klugman 1264 | Driving | 13 |
| 19Apr80- | 8Aqu | fst | 1⅛ | :47⅘ | 1:11⅗ | 1:50⅘ | Wood Mem'l | 3 | 3 | 32 | 31½ | 32 | 31½ | Vasquez J | 121 | 8.20 | 79-17 | PluggedNickle1261½ColonelMorn126hdGenuinRisk1213¾ | Game try | 11 |
| 5Apr80- | 7Aqu | gd | 1 | :46⅘ | 1:12 | 1:38⅘ | ⒻHandicap | 4 | 4 | 32 | 11½ | 11 | 12½ | Vasquez J | 124 | *.20 | 73-20 | Genuine Risk 1242½ TellASecret1153½SprucePine11311 | Ridden out | 4 |
| 19Mar80- | 7GP | fst | 7f | :22 | :44⅘ | 1:22⅘ | ⒻAllowance | 3 | 5 | 44 | 32½ | 1½ | 12½ | Vasquez J | 113 | *.40 | 91-20 | Genuine Risk 1132½ Sober Jig 1123½ Peace Bells1151½ | Ridden out | 6 |
| 17Nov79- | 8Aqu | fst | 1⅛ | :48⅕ | 1:13⅕ | 1:51⅕ | ⒻDemoiselle | 6 | 4 | 3½ | 2hd | 2hd | 1no | Pincay L Jr | 116 | 1.20 | 79-21 | Genuine Risk 116no Smart Angle 1216¾ Spruce Pine 1123¾ | Driving | 7 |
| 5Nov79- | 8Aqu | fst | 1 | :46 | 1:10⅖ | 1:36 | ⒻTempted | 4 | 5 | 51½ | 11½ | 12 | 13 | Vasquez J | 114 | *.90 | 86-18 | Genuine Risk 1143 Street Ballet117½TellASecret1144½ | Ridden out | 9 |
| 18Oct79- | 6Aqu | fst | 1 | :47 | 1:11⅘ | 1:36⅖ | ⒻAllowance | 6 | 2 | 21 | 2hd | 12 | 17½ | Vasquez J | 115 | *.60 | 84-18 | Genuine Risk 1157½ Going East 1175 Cinto Tora 1154½ | Ridden out | 6 |
| 30Sep79- | 4Bel | sly | 6½f | :22⅗ | :45⅖ | 1:18 | ⒻMd Sp Wt | 8 | 11 | 45 | 46½ | 23 | 11¾ | Vasquez J | 118 | *3.10 | 86-24 | Genuine Risk 1181¾ Remote Ruler 11813 Espadrille 1181¾ | Driving | 11 |

LATEST WORKOUTS Jun 4 Bel 5f fst 1:00⅘ h May 28 Bel 6f fst 1:14⅖ b ●May 14 Pim 5f fst :59 h ●Apr 30 CD 5f sl 1:02⅖ b

As Genuine Risk proved so admirably, females can compete successfully with males on the racetrack. Because of their breeding value, the claiming price of fillies and mares is higher than that of male horses with the same racing ability. Therefore, a female moving from a $25,000 claimer restricted to fillies and mares to an open $25,000 claimer is moving up in class. This distinction is far less important, however, for animals entered for less than $10,000.

## WEIGHT

**Winter's Tale** — B. g. 4, by Arts And Letters—Christmas Wind, by Nearctic
Own.—Rokeby Stable — Br.—Mellon P (Va) — Tr.—Miller Mack
123

| | St. | 1st | 2nd | 3rd | Amt. |
|---|---|---|---|---|---|
| 1980 | 6 | 4 | 1 | 0 | $282,800 |
| 1979 | 4 | 3 | 0 | 0 | $25,200 |

| | | | | | | | | | | | | | | | | | | | | |
|---|---|---|---|---|---|---|---|---|---|---|---|---|---|---|---|---|---|---|---|---|
| 2Aug80- | 8Sar | fst | 1⅛ | :46 | 1:09⅗ | 1:48⅕ | 3↑ Whitney | 7 | 7 | 79 | 88 | 711 | 714 | Fell J | 126 | 3.70 | 80-10 | State Dinner 120½ Dr. Patches 114½ Czaravich 1232½ | Outrun | 8 |
| 19Jly80- | 8Bel | fst | 1½ | :51⅗ | 2:05 | 2:28⅗ | 3↑ Brooklyn H | 4 | 3 | 21 | 11½ | 13 | 15 | Fell J | 120 | 3.40 | 77-20 | Winter's Tale 1205 State Dinner1213½RingofLight1142 | Ridden out | 5 |
| 4Jly80- | 8Bel | fst | 1¼ | :47⅘ | 1:36 | 2:00⅗ | 3↑ Suburban H | 1 | 2 | 1½ | 2½ | 11 | 1hd | Fell J | 114 | 2.70 | 97-14 | Winter's Tale 114hd State Dinner 117hd Czaravich 1271½ | Driving | 7 |
| 15Jun80- | 8Bel | fst | 1⅛ | :46⅗ | 1:10⅖ | 1:47⅕ | 3↑ Nassau Cty H | 8 | 1 | 1½ | 11 | 14 | 17¾ | Venezia M | 111 | 3.90e | 91-17 | Winter's Tale 1117¾ Crow's Nest1095DewanKeys114nk | Ridden out | 8 |
| 7Jun80- | 5Bel | sly | 1 | :46⅖ | 1:10⅘ | 1:35⅗ | 3↑ Allowance | 7 | 5 | 62 | 51¾ | 22½ | 25½ | Fell J | 115 | *1.90 | 84-17 | Thin Slice 1155½ Winter's Tale 1152 Son Of A Dodo 112hd | Wide | 7 |
| 26May80- | 9Bel | fst | 7f | :22⅘ | :46 | 1:23⅖ | 3↑ Allowance | 3 | 10 | 74½ | 63½ | 31 | 12½ | Fell J | 119 | 3.60 | 85-20 | Winter's Tale1192½RainPrince112½DynamicMove114hd | Ridden out | 10 |
| 3Dec79- | 7Aqu | fst | 1 | :46⅗ | 1:11⅗ | 1:37⅖ | 3↑ Allowance | 2 | 4 | 54¾ | 75¼ | 57 | 58½ | Fell J | 115 | *.60 | 70-22 | Lark Oscillation1173Pianist1151¾WaveForever1172½ | Lacked room | 8 |
| 19Nov79- | 8Aqu | fst | 7f | :23 | :45⅘ | 1:22⅖ | 3↑ Allowance | 1 | 4 | 35 | 22 | 2hd | 14½ | Fell J | 120 | *.80 | 89-18 | Winter's Tale 1204½RoyalReasoning120hdTermPaper1172¼ | Handily | 5 |
| 8Nov79- | 7Aqu | fst | 7f | :23 | :45⅘ | 1:23⅘ | 3↑ Allowance | 6 | 7 | 54 | 43½ | 1½ | 13¼ | Fell J | 120 | *1.50 | 82-19 | Winter's Tale 1203¼ Contare 1151½ Mon AmiGus115no | Ridden out | 7 |
| 26Oct79- | 4Aqu | fst | 6f | :23 | :47⅕ | 1:12 | 3↑ Md Sp Wt | 8 | 7 | 44 | 31½ | 2hd | 12½ | Fell J | 119 | 2.20 | 83-24 | Winter'sTle1192½LordOfTheSe119½SpeedyMgrdy1194½ | Ridden out | 9 |

LATEST WORKOUTS Sep 2 Bel 7f fst 1:26 h Aug 19 Sar tr.t 4f fst :51⅖ b Aug 16 Sar tr.t 3f my :37 b Jly 30 Sar 5f fst :58 h

How much weight a horse is assigned in a race or how much weight it is giving away is not as important as its past history of carrying weight. For example, stakes-winning Winter's Tale has won handily carrying 120 pounds, but was badly beaten in the Whitney Stakes carrying 126 pounds. Handicappers would be reluctant to wager heavily on Winter's Tale until he proves he can carry weights of 126 pounds and above.

RACING RECORD

**Barbara's Turn** B. f. 3, by Turn To Reason—Sundare, by Prince Dare
$10,000 Br.—Goldsmith Mr-Mrs C O (Md)
Own.—Dillon L G Tr.—Gray Clifford T Jr
119 Turf Record St. 1st 2nd 3rd: 1 0 0 0

| | St. | 1st | 2nd | 3rd | Amt. |
|---|---|---|---|---|---|
| 1979 | 22 | M | 4 | 4 | $5,653 |
| 1978 | 3 | M | 1 | 0 | $1,100 |

| | | | | | | | | | | | | | | | | | | |
|---|---|---|---|---|---|---|---|---|---|---|---|---|---|---|---|---|---|---|
| 14Sep79- 5Tim sly | 4f | | :22⅖ | :47⅕ | 3↑ⒻMd Sp Wt | 1 | 4 | | 35 | 25 | 34¾ | Sierra J A | 117 | 3.60 | 85-09 NiceChoice1174¾MostleyGrey117nkBarbara'sTurn1173¾ | | No excuse | 7 |
| 5Sep79- 9Tim sly | *6½f | :24⅕ | :49⅕ | 1:21⅕ | 3↑ⒻMd Sp Wt | 2 | 2 | 21 | 22½ | 22½ | 26 | Torre M J | 118 | 4.50 | 70-29 Cool Flack 1186 Barbara's Turn 1181 LizzieBeFrank113¾ | | 2nd best | 10 |
| 30Aug79- 5Tim fst | *6½f | :23⅗ | :48⅗ | 1:20⅗ | 3↑ⒻMd Sp Wt | 8 | 5 | 41¾ | 2½ | 21½ | 33½ | Lewis W R Jr | 115 | 6.60 | 77-16 FrolickingMiss1161MissilPrincss1152½Brbr'sTurn1151¾ | | Weakened | 9 |
| 23Aug79- 9Tim fst | *6½f | :24⅕ | :49⅘ | 1:21⅗ | 3↑Md 8000 | 8 | 1 | 2hd | 22 | 22 | 23½ | Lewis W R Jr | 115 | 5.30 | 71-20 Miss D. C. W.1123½Barbara'sTurn1152EarlyGovernor115¾ | | 2nd best | 8 |
| 17Aug79- 6Tim fst | *6½f | :23⅗ | :48⅗ | 1:20⅗ | 3↑ⓈMd Sp Wt | 4 | 5 | 45½ | 24 | 34½ | 52¾ | Lewis W R Jr | 115 | 4.80 | 77-10 PassTheShoe115hdFithfulWill105noLuckyMotive1151½ | | No late bid | 10 |
| 9Aug79- 6Bow fst | 6f | :22⅘ | :46⅘ | 1:11⅘ | 3↑ⒻⓈMd Sp Wt | 7 | 4 | 66 | 54½ | 58 | 610 | Lewis W R Jr | 115 | 2.50 | 71-20 CountyQust122hdWlkingAmbition1158BigPt'sWish1151 | | No factor | 8 |
| 3Aug79- 1Bow gd | 6f | :23 | :47⅗ | 1:14⅘ | 3↑ⒻMd c-5000 | 3 | 6 | 45 | 32½ | 1hd | 2½ | Grenier G | 115 | *.90 | 67-24 A Sassi Spirit115½Barbara'sTurn115nkIrishConcorde115nk | | Gamely | 8 |
| 27Jly79- 2Bow fst | 6f | :23⅕ | :46⅘ | 1:12⅗ | 3↑ⒻⓈMd 5000 | 4 | 2 | 21½ | 11 | 2½ | 21 | Grenier G | 115 | 9.20 | 76-20 Okla Homer 1161 Barbara's Turn 1151 Cry Out 1222½ | | Gamely | 8 |
| 12Jly79- 2Bow fst | 6f | :22⅘ | :47⅕ | 1:13⅗ | 3↑ⒻⓈMd 5000 | 8 | 1 | 76¾ | 56½ | 64¾ | 510 | Cline V L | 115 | 11.00 | 63-26 Salem'sSerende1103HrpyBird115¾HsAChoice1156 | | Unruly pre-post | 9 |
| 4Jly79- 9Bow sly | 6f | :23 | :47⅗ | 1:14 | 3↑Md 5000 | 1 | 5 | 34 | 44½ | 413 | 621 | Cline V L | 110 | 3.60 | 49-21 Reassignment 1157 Scholarship 1154½ Sirens Boy 1155 | | Tired | 11 |

Since the purpose of racing is to win races, one measure of racing class is the number of races won. Fifty years ago, Robert Dowst, whose writings represented perhaps the first substantive handicapping instruction, emphasized the importance of *consistency* in picking winners. Dowst preferred horses that had won at least 20 percent of their races and that had demonstrated recent success at the level at which they were competing on any given day. Dowst's system worked so well that it drove down mutuel payoff on such consistent horses to the point where it became unprofitable to play them.

The statistics reviewed in our section on "Defining Class" demonstrate the relationship between consistency and class. For example, the 14 percent of all horses that won three or more races in 1979 captured 50 percent of all the races run that year. The more frequently a horse wins, the more likely it is to win in the future.

Another important handicapping reminder is that even horses that manage a respectable number of seconds and thirds can be chronic losers. For example, Barbara's Turn may be on the way to becoming a classic "sucker" horse. This three-year-old filly finished in the money in six of her last eight races. In every one of these contests she went off at odds of less than ten to one, and once the public made her an odds-on favorite. However, a record of twenty-six straight losses, together with running line comments such as "no excuse" and "second best" indicate that it isn't talent, but the animal's refusal to win that is the problem. Horses that have a competitive attitude find a way to win frequently; horses without that attitude usually manage to discover a way to lose.

EARNINGS

**Beautiful Contest** Dk. b. or br. c. 3, by Sham—You Picked Abeauty, by Intentionally
$37,500 Br.—Hillbrock Farm Inc (Ky)
Own.—Altan Stable Tr.—Marcus Alan B
115 Turf Record St. 1st 2nd 3rd: 1 0 0 0

| | St. | 1st | 2nd | 3rd | Amt. |
|---|---|---|---|---|---|
| 1979 | 23 | 4 | 7 | 1 | $62,880 |
| 1978 | 10 | M | 1 | 1 | $5,240 |

| | | | | | | | | | | | | | | | | | | |
|---|---|---|---|---|---|---|---|---|---|---|---|---|---|---|---|---|---|---|
| 5Nov79- 2Aqu fst | 1⅛ | :48⅘ | 1:13⅖ | 1:51⅕ | Clm c-30000 | 8 | 7 | 79½ | 79½ | 710 | 79¾ | Pincay L Jr | b 119 | 3.40 | 69-18 General H. D.112nkSal'sDream1194¾FollowThatDream117¾ | | Outrun | 8 |
| 24Oct79- 6Aqu fst | 1⅛ | :48 | 1:13⅗ | 1:54⅗ | Clm 25000 | 5 | 6 | 67 | 52½ | 1½ | 11½ | Pincay L Jr | b 119 | *2.10e | 62-28 Beautiful Contest 1191½ Wimpfybell110¾Royaldate1153½ | | Driving | 8 |
| 15Oct79- 3Bel gd | 1⅛ | :49⅖ | 1:15 | 1:53⅗ | Clm 35000 | 3 | 2 | 2½ | 32½ | 510 | 523 | Pincay L Jr | b 117 | 3.00 | 36-31 Sal's Dream 1141¾ General H. D. 1104 Pull A Cutie 1177 | | Tired | 6 |
| 30Sep79- 2Bel sly | 1⅛ | :47⅕ | 1:12⅗ | 1:52⅗ | Clm 25000 | 1 | 2 | 21½ | 11½ | 12 | 1½ | Pincay L Jr | b 117 | *1.20 | 64-24 Beautiful Contest 117½ Harry J. 1174½ Daring Do 1152½ | | Driving | 6 |
| 17Sep79- 3Bel fst | 1 | :46⅘ | 1:12⅕ | 1:37⅖ | Clm 30000 | 5 | 7 | 64½ | 53½ | 67½ | 614 | Asmussen C B | b 117 | *2.50 | 67-21 Birkhill 1171½ Properly Person 119½ Fun Hour 1177½ | | No factor | 7 |
| 29Aug79- 2Bel sly | 1⅛ | :46⅘ | 1:12⅕ | 1:50 | Clm 35000 | 6 | 2 | 22 | 13 | 1hd | 2¾ | Saumell L | b 117 | *1.20 | 76-15 PullACutie117¾BeautifulContest1172ProperlyPerson11316 | | Gamely | 6 |
| 12Aug79- 3Sar my | 1⅛ | :49⅕ | 1:14⅕ | 1:53 | Clm 35000 | 3 | 5 | 57 | 43½ | 21½ | 22½ | Saumell L | b 117 | *2.40 | 67-25 BroadwayBuck1172½BeautifulContest1175¾PokieJoe1175½ | | Drifted | 8 |
| 29Jly79- 5Bel fst | 7f | :23⅗ | :47⅖ | 1:25 | Clm 35000 | 7 | 1 | 63 | 42 | 65½ | 56½ | Hernandez R | b 117 | *2.20 | 70-21 Dapper Escort 1173½ General H.D.108¾TermPaper1191¾ | | No excuse | 7 |
| 13Jly79- 9Bel fst | 7f | :23 | :46 | 1:24⅘ | Clm 35000 | 4 | 7 | 75½ | 56 | 42 | 2½ | Hernandez R | b 117 | 3.60 | 77-16 TermPper117½BeutifulContest117hdByeByBlus1122½ | | Wide, missed | 10 |
| 4Jly79- 1Bel fst | 6f | :22⅖ | :45⅖ | 1:11⅖ | Clm 50000 | 3 | 8 | 711 | 912 | 97¾ | 83½ | Hernandez R | b 117 | 7.00e | 81-16 Subordinate 112no Third of July 117nk Silver Screen117no | | Outrun | 10 |

LATEST WORKOUTS Nov 17 Bel 4f fst :50 b Oct 31 Bel 4f fst :49⅗ b Oct 22 Bel 4f fst :48⅗ h Oct 9 Bel 4f fst :48⅕ h

Since one of the most reliable indications of the class of a race is the purse offered, the purses that a horse has earned are reflective of its class. Handicappers have developed several methods for comparing the earnings of horses to separate contenders from non-contenders.

The best indication of current class is the purse offered in each of the most recent races in which a horse raced well. However, this information is available only by looking at past results charts.

Handicappers who must use past performances use one of three methods. The first is comparing *total earnings* for the year. Beautiful Contest, for example, earned $62,860 through November 5, 1979. By referring to a table earlier in this book, one can find that these earnings place Beautiful Contest in the top 1.5 percent of all horses that raced that year. These earnings may indicate that Beautiful Contest has demonstrated more class over the year than another horse that has raced about the same number of times, but comparing total earnings against those of more lightly raced horses in the same race can be very misleading.

To solve the problem of dealing with the relationship of races to earnings, many handicappers divide the number of races into total earnings to obtain each horse's average earnings per start. Beautiful Contest, for example, has earned $62,860 in 23 starts, for an average of $2,622 per start. To make the calculation easier, most people using this method drop the last three digits of the total earnings, dividing 62 by 23 to get a "rating" of 2.7. While some computer studies have shown that this is a useful way to identify contenders in certain kinds of races, average earnings per start are misleading for horses that have been racing without winning in tougher company than today's race. For example, a horse that has been finishing third or fourth in stakes races may have a lower average earnings per start than an animal winning lower-class allowance contests.

To correct this problem, one school of handicappers has adopted a third method of comparing earnings. This somewhat more complicated method uses the horse's record plus total earnings to arrive at an approximation of the average total purse offered in races in which the horse earned money.

Computing the average total purse is based on the percentage of each purse that is distributed to each horse. In the easiest, albeit crudest method, one starts with the fact that an average 60 percent of the purse in a race goes to the winner; an average 20 percent to the second-place horse; an average 10 percent to the third-place finisher. Converting to decimals, the handicapper then multiplies the number of wins the horse has achieved by .6, the number of seconds by .2 and the number of thirds by .1. Dividing the sum of these multiplications into the total earnings provides a rough approximation of the average purse. For example, the computation for Beautiful Contest is:

Wins  $4 \times .6 = 2.4$    $\$62,860 \div 3.9 = \$16,118$
$7 \times .2 = 1.4$
$1 \times .1 = \phantom{0}.1$
$\overline{\phantom{0}3.9}$

This method does not, of course, take into consideration the exact percentage applicable at each track, nor does it account for prize money awarded for places below third place. Horseplayers interested in making more accurate ratings using this system might want to investigate the Kel-Co Class Computer, a small hand-held unit which has been cleverly programmed to make these complex calculations. Information about the Kel-Co Class Computer is available from Cannella Corporation, P. O. Box 6213, Syracuse, NY 13217.

## TURF RECORD

**Bowl Game** — B. g. 5, by Tom Rolfe—Around the Roses, by Round Table
Br.—Greentree Stud Inc (Ky)
Own.—Greentree Stable
Tr.—Gaver John M Jr

| Turf Record St. | 1st | 2nd | 3rd | | St. | 1st | 2nd | 3rd | Amt. |
|---|---|---|---|---|---|---|---|---|---|
| 13 | 8 | 2 | 3 | 1979 | 10 | 5 | 2 | 2 | $585,738 |
| | | | | 1978 | 10 | 6 | 3 | 1 | $311,265 |

| | | | | | | | | | | | | | | | | | | | | |
|---|---|---|---|---|---|---|---|---|---|---|---|---|---|---|---|---|---|---|---|---|
| 10Nov79- 8Lrl | sf | 1½ | Ⓣ:57⅗ | 2:23⅖ | 2:51 | 3↑ Wash D C Int | 7 | 3 | $2^{1\frac{1}{2}}$ | $2^{1}$ | $2^{hd}$ | $1^{\frac{3}{4}}$ | Velasquez J | 127 | 3.60 | — — | Bowl Game 127¾ Trillion $124^{no}$ Le Marmot 128 | Driving | 8 |
| 27Oct79- 8Aqu | fm | 1½ | Ⓣ:48⅕ | 2:04⅘ | 2:28⅕ | 3↑ Turf Classic | 2 | 3 | $3^{12}$ | $2^{2}$ | $2^{2\frac{1}{2}}$ | $1^{nk}$ | Velasquez J | 126 | 2.80 | 120 — | Bowl Game $126^{nk}$ Trillion $123^{nk}$ Native Courier $126^{4\frac{3}{4}}$ | Driving | 7 |
| 8Oct79- 8Bel | sf | 1⅜ | Ⓣ:51⅗ | 1:42 | 2:19 | 3↑ Man O' War | 3 | 3 | $3^{6}$ | $3^{2\frac{1}{2}}$ | $2^{4}$ | $1^{hd}$ | Velasquez J | 126 | 2.60 | 67-38 | Bowl Game $126^{hd}$ Native Courier $126^{11}$ Czaravich $121^{2\frac{3}{4}}$ | Driving | 4 |
| 1Sep79- 8AP | fm | 1½ | Ⓣ:48 | 2:06⅕ | 2:32⅕ | 3↑ Arlington H | 2 | 9 | $10^{24}$ | $4^{7}$ | $1^{\frac{1}{2}}$ | $1^{4\frac{1}{2}}$ | Velasquez J | 124 | *.70 | 78-28 | Bowl Game $124^{4\frac{1}{2}}$ YoungBob110 Liveinthesunshine105½ | Drew out | 14 |
| 21Jly79- 8Bel | fst | 1½ | :50⅗ | 2:03⅗ | 2:28⅘ | 3↑ Brooklyn H | 2 | 3 | $4^{2\frac{1}{2}}$ | $3^{4\frac{1}{2}}$ | $3^{1\frac{1}{2}}$ | $2^{\frac{3}{4}}$ | Velasquez J | 119 | 5.10 | 75-24 | The LiberalMember114¾BowlGame$119^{hd}$StateDinner$123^{2\frac{3}{4}}$ | Gamely | 5 |
| 1Jly79- 8Bel | fm | 1⅜ | Ⓣ:48⅗ | 1:37⅘ | 2:13⅕ | 3↑ Tidal H | 2 | 2 | $2^{hd}$ | $3^{nk}$ | $1^{1}$ | $2^{hd}$ | Velasquez J | 125 | *.70 | 103-11 | GoldenReserve$109^{hd}$BowlGm$125^{nk}$ScythinGold$110^{1\frac{3}{4}}$ | Failed to last | 5 |
| 16Jun79- 8Bel | fm | 1⅜ | Ⓣ:48 | 1:35⅗ | 2:11⅗ | 3↑ Bowl Green H | 3 | 4 | $4^{9\frac{1}{2}}$ | $6^{7\frac{1}{4}}$ | $2^{2\frac{1}{2}}$ | $3^{4}$ | Velasquez J | 123 | 5.20 | 108-01 | Overskate $117^{4}$ Waya $125^{hd}$ Bowl Game $123^{1\frac{3}{4}}$ | Gave way | 7 |
| 14Apr79-11Hia | hd | 1½ | Ⓣ | | 2:26⅗ | 3↑ Turf Cup H | 7 | 6 | $6^{4\frac{1}{2}}$ | $3^{\frac{1}{2}}$ | $2^{\frac{1}{2}}$ | $1^{\frac{3}{4}}$ | Cordero A Jr | 122 | 2.90 | 99-10 | Bowl Game 122¾ Noble Dancer II $130^{5}$ Great Sound$111^{hd}$ | Driving | 7 |
| 4Apr79- 9Hia | fm | *1⅛ | Ⓣ | | 1:46⅗ | Allowance | 5 | 5 | $5^{8\frac{1}{2}}$ | $5^{3\frac{1}{2}}$ | $4^{3\frac{1}{2}}$ | $3^{5\frac{1}{2}}$ | Velasquez J | 114 | *1.20 | 97-08 | That's A Nice $114^{4\frac{1}{2}}$ Fed Funds $114^{1}$ Bowl Game 114½ | Bumped | 7 |
| 22Mar79- 9Hia | fst | 6f | :23 | :46⅗ | 1:10⅘ | Allowance | 1 | 8 | $7^{4\frac{3}{4}}$ | $7^{6\frac{1}{2}}$ | $5^{7\frac{1}{2}}$ | $5^{10}$ | Velasquez J | 114 | *.80 | 80-18 | North Course$119^{4}$GetPermission$122^{1\frac{1}{2}}$Robb'sCharm$119^{4\frac{1}{2}}$ | Slow st. | 8 |

A recent and very valuable addition to the past performances is each horse's career record on the turf. Most studies have shown that a horse's record on the dirt is not a reliable indication of its performance on grass. With the exception of animals whose breeding indicates good turf-racing potential, the contenders in most such contests are those horses that, like 1979 Eclipse award-winning grass horse Bowl Game, have demonstrated success on the "weeds."

## DATE LAST RACED

**Dewan Keys** — Ch. h. 5, by Dewan—Eleven Keys, by Royal Union
Br.—Keyes F (Fla)
Own.—Morrissey J O Jr
Tr.—Johnson Philip G
**114**

| Turf Record St. | 1st | 2nd | 3rd | | St. | 1st | 2nd | 3rd | Amt. |
|---|---|---|---|---|---|---|---|---|---|
| 2 | 0 | 0 | 1 | 1980 | 5 | 2 | 0 | 1 | $51,636 |
| | | | | 1979 | 13 | 3 | 6 | 2 | $136,819 |

| | | | | | | | | | | | | | | | | | | | | |
|---|---|---|---|---|---|---|---|---|---|---|---|---|---|---|---|---|---|---|---|---|
| 15Jun80- 8Bel | fst | 1⅛ | :46⅗ | 1:10⅖ | 1:47⅕ | 3↑ Nassau Cty H | 6 | 2 | $4^{2}$ | $4^{3}$ | $3^{9}$ | $3^{13}$ | Skinner K | 114 | *1.70 | 78-17 | Winter's Tale $111^{7\frac{3}{4}}$ Crow's Nest $109^{5}$ Dewan Keys $114^{nk}$ | Hung | 8 |
| 7Jun80- 7Bel | my | 1¼ | :48⅕ | 1:38 | 2:02⅗ | 3↑ Allowance | 2 | 2 | $2^{2}$ | $2^{\frac{1}{2}}$ | $1^{1}$ | $1^{4}$ | Skinner K | 117 | *1.20 | 87-17 | Dewan Keys $117^{4}$ Lucy's Axe 117½ Knight's Tale$117^{nk}$ | Ridden out | 6 |
| 22May80- 8Bel | gd | 1$\frac{1}{16}$ | :46⅗ | 1:11 | 1:42 | 3↑ Allowance | 3 | 4 | $3^{4}$ | $2^{4}$ | $2^{2}$ | $1^{hd}$ | Skinner K | 121 | 1.60 | 92-11 | Dewan Keys $121^{hd}$ Lucy's Axe $119^{5\frac{1}{2}}$DamascusSilver$121^{7\frac{1}{2}}$ | Driving | 7 |
| 3May80- 8Aqu | fst | 7f | :22⅘ | :45⅕ | 1:21 | 3↑ Carter H | 4 | 6 | $6^{5}$ | $6^{6}$ | $6^{8\frac{3}{4}}$ | $6^{8\frac{1}{2}}$ | Castaneda M | 113 | 25.70 | 87-12 | Czaravich $126^{nk}$ Tanthem $122^{hd}$ Nice Catch $120^{nk}$ | Trailed | 6 |
| 20Apr80- 7Aqu | fst | 6f | :21⅘ | :44⅕ | 1:09⅘ | 3↑ Bold Ruler | 5 | 5 | $6^{14}$ | $6^{17}$ | $6^{12}$ | $6^{8\frac{3}{4}}$ | Asmussen C B | 119 | 15.50 | 85-16 | Dave's Friend $123^{2\frac{3}{4}}$ Tilt Up $121^{1\frac{1}{2}}$ Double Zeus 121¾ | Outrun | 6 |
| 22Nov79- 8Aqu | fst | 1$\frac{3}{16}$ | :48⅕ | 1:12⅖ | 1:56⅘ | 3↑ Queens Cty H | 4 | 3 | $3^{2}$ | $3^{\frac{1}{2}}$ | $2^{hd}$ | $1^{\frac{1}{2}}$ | Maple E | 112 | 3.90 | 78-20 | Dewan Keys 112½ Mr. International$108^{no}$GallantBest$116^{no}$ | Driving | 8 |
| 15Nov79- 6Med | fst | 1⅛ | :47 | 1:11⅘ | 1:51⅕ | 3↑ J'ky Holow H | 2 | 5 | $5^{4\frac{1}{2}}$ | $6^{1\frac{3}{4}}$ | $3^{\frac{1}{2}}$ | $2^{no}$ | Maple E | 114 | 13.10 | 77-25 | Silent Cal $118^{no}$ Dewar Keys $114^{1\frac{1}{4}}$ Smarten $122^{8\frac{1}{2}}$ | Jostled | 7 |
| 3Nov79- 8Aqu | sly | 1⅛ | :47⅘ | 1:12⅖ | 1:50⅖ | 3↑ Stuyvesant H | 1 | 4 | $3^{1\frac{1}{2}}$ | $3^{\frac{1}{2}}$ | $1^{hd}$ | $3^{hd}$ | Maple E | 112 | 5.50 | 83-23 | Music of Time $114^{no}$ What A Gent $111^{hd}$DewanKeys$112^{2}$ | In close | 6 |
| 27Oct79- 7Aqu | fst | 1 | :45⅘ | 1:10⅘ | 1:36 | 3↑ Allowance | 3 | 4 | $4^{8}$ | $4^{6}$ | $3^{7}$ | $2^{6\frac{1}{2}}$ | Shoemaker W | 115 | 5.00 | 79-22 | Dr. Patches $115^{6\frac{1}{2}}$ Dewan Keys $115^{hd}$ TimtheTiger$114^{2}$ | Up for 2nd | 6 |
| 13Oct79- 7Bel | sly | 7f | :23⅗ | :47⅕ | 1:24⅗ | 3↑ Allowance | 3 | 4 | $4^{4}$ | $4^{3\frac{1}{2}}$ | $2^{hd}$ | $2^{nk}$ | Maple S | 119 | 3.80 | 79-27 | GallantBest$119^{nk}$DewanKeys$119^{1\frac{1}{2}}$ChopChopTomhwk$117^{7}$ | Gamely | 5 |

LATEST WORKOUTS ●Sep 2 Bel 6f fst 1:12⅘ h Aug 29 Bel tr.t 5f fst 1:01 h Aug 24 Sar tr.t 6f fst 1:14 h ●Aug 21 Sar tr.t 5f fst 1:00 h

A recent race, particularly a recent good race, is generally a sign of fitness. As a result, the authors of many handicapping systems require a horse to have raced within ten or fourteen days of today's race. While this guideline can be useful, it doesn't take into account the difficulties some classes of horses have finding adequate opportunities to race, nor does it take into consideration the pattern the horse has followed successfully in the past.

One particularly useful pattern to note is how the animal returns from a layoff. While some trainers are consistently able to fully prepare certain of their charges for top efforts immediately upon their return to action, most horses are brought back more slowly. For example, trainer P. G. Johnson entered stakes-winning Dewan Keys in two sprint stakes following a five-month freshening. This chestnut horse's record shows that these short races aren't his cup of tea, but they served as valuable prep races. His speed sharpened, Dewan Keys went on to capture two allowance races at distances over a mile.

## TRACK WHERE LAST RACED

**Golden Act** ✻ — Ch. c. 3, by Gummo—Golden Shore, by Windy Sands
Br.—Oldknow & Phipps R W (Cal)
Tr.—Rettele Loren
Own.—Marino Beach Stable

127

| | Turf Record St. | 1st | 2nd | 3rd |
|---|---|---|---|---|
| | 3 | 2 | 0 | 1 |

| | St. | 1st | 2nd | 3rd | Amt. |
|---|---|---|---|---|---|
| 1979 | 11 | 5 | 3 | 2 | $532,453 |
| 1978 | 8 | 2 | 3 | 3 | $127,320 |

| | | | | | | | | | | | | | | | | |
|---|---|---|---|---|---|---|---|---|---|---|---|---|---|---|---|---|
| 16Sep79- 8Bel | fm | 1½ | Ⓣ:47⅘ 2:02⅘ 2:27⅗ | Lawrence R'n | 7 | 4 | $4^{4\frac{1}{2}}$ | $2^{\frac{1}{2}}$ | $1^{\frac{1}{2}}$ | $1^{2}$ | Hawley S | b 126 | *.80 | 86-15 Golden Act $126^{2}$ Smarten $126^{\frac{3}{4}}$ T. V. Series $114^{4}$ | Bore in, clear | 7 |
| 3Sep79- 8AP | fm | 1½ | Ⓣ:51 2:08⅗ 2:32⅘ | Secretariat | 2 | 5 | $3^{2}$ | $2^{hd}$ | $1^{hd}$ | $1^{nk}$ | Hawley S | b 126 | 1.20 | 75-28 Golden Act $126^{nk}$ Smarten $120^{10}$ Flying Dad $120^{2}$ | Driving | 6 |
| 11Aug79- 8AP | gd | 1⅛ | Ⓣ:48⅗ 1:14⅖ 1:53⅘ | Rnd Table H | 7 | 8 | $9^{5\frac{3}{4}}$ | $7^{2\frac{3}{4}}$ | $1^{\frac{1}{2}}$ | $2^{no}$ | Hawley S | 126 | *.60Ⓓ | 68-38 Rossi Gold $108^{no}$ ⒹGolden Act $126^{1\frac{1}{2}}$ LordBawlmer $116^{3\frac{1}{4}}$ | Lugged in | 10 |
| 11Aug79-Disqualified and placed third | | | | | | | | | | | | | | | | |
| 22Jly79- 8Hol | fst | 1¼ | :46⅖ 1:35 1:59⅗ | Swaps | 5 | 5 | $6^{4}$ | $6^{4\frac{1}{2}}$ | $5^{5\frac{1}{2}}$ | $4^{5}$ | Hawley S | 126 | 2.50 | 89-17 Valdez $120^{2\frac{3}{4}}$ Shamgo $114^{\frac{3}{4}}$ Paint King $114^{1\frac{3}{4}}$ | No rally | 6 |
| 9Jun79- 8Bel | fst | 1½ | :47⅗ 2:02⅖ 2:28⅗ | Belmont | 6 | 5 | $5^{5}$ | $3^{3\frac{1}{2}}$ | $3^{2}$ | $2^{3\frac{3}{4}}$ | Hawley S | 126 | 10.10 | 74-17 Coastal $126^{3\frac{1}{4}}$ Golden Act $126^{nk}$ SpectacularBid $126^{3\frac{1}{4}}$ | Good effort | 8 |
| 19May79- 8Pim | gd | 1 3/16 | :46⅘ 1:10⅘ 1:54⅕ | Preakness | 3 | 5 | $5^{7\frac{1}{2}}$ | $5^{4\frac{1}{4}}$ | $2^{6}$ | $2^{5\frac{1}{2}}$ | Hawley S | 126 | 27.20 | 93-09 Spectacular Bid $126^{5\frac{1}{2}}$ GoldenAct $126^{4}$ ScreenKing $126^{1\frac{1}{2}}$ | Went well | 5 |
| 5May79- 8CD | fst | 1¼ | :47⅖ 1:37⅗ 2:02⅖ | Ky Derby | 1 | 8 | $9^{15}$ | $7^{5\frac{3}{4}}$ | $3^{6\frac{1}{2}}$ | $3^{5\frac{3}{4}}$ | Hawley S | 126 | 19.20 | 79-14 SpectculrBid $126^{2\frac{3}{4}}$ GnrlAssmbly $126^{3}$ GoldnAct $126^{1\frac{3}{4}}$ | Brushed Start | 10 |
| 14Apr79- 9OP | fst | 1⅛ | :47⅘ 1:11⅘ 1:50 | Ark Derby | 8 | 8 | $6^{6}$ | $6^{5\frac{1}{2}}$ | $3^{\frac{1}{2}}$ | $1^{nk}$ | Hawley S | 126 | *1.40 | 93-23 Golden Act $126^{nk}$ Smarten $120^{6}$ StrikeTheMain $115^{nk}$ | Hand ridden | 10 |
| 18Mar79- 9FG | fst | 1⅛ | :45⅖ 1:11⅕ 1:51⅕ | La Derby | 5 | 9 | $9^{14}$ | $5^{7}$ | $1^{\frac{1}{2}}$ | $1^{1\frac{3}{4}}$ | Hawley S | 123 | *1.10 | 88-17 Golden Act $123^{1\frac{3}{4}}$ Rivalero $115^{\frac{3}{4}}$ Incredible Ease $120^{1\frac{1}{2}}$ | Drew out | 9 |
| 3Mar79- 8GG | fst | 1 1/16 | :45⅗ 1:09⅖ 1:40⅗ | Calif Derby | 7 | 7 | $7^{13}$ | $6^{9\frac{1}{2}}$ | $2^{8}$ | $2^{5}$ | Pincay L Jr | 122 | *1.50 | 96-09 Beau's Eagle $112^{5}$ Golden Act $122^{3}$ CrestoftheWave $119^{6}$ | 2nd best | 8 |

LATEST WORKOUTS Sep 29 Bel 7f fst 1:28⅕ b   Sep 24 Bel 5f fst 1:00⅕ h   Sep 10 Bel 6f fst 1:13 b

The past performance of half-million-dollar-plus winner Golden Act shows ten excellent races over eight different tracks on both dirt and grass. This colt obviously demonstrated the highest degree of versatility.

Because tracks vary considerably in shape and surface, the vast majority of Thoroughbreds need time to adapt to a new home. For many, the old adage "horses for courses" holds true. These animals only perform to the maximum of their ability on certain tracks. As a result, most handicappers prefer entrants with at least one recent race over a track, especially those who have demonstrated a marked fondness for the oval.

## TRACK CONDITIONS

**Codex** — Ch. c. 3, by Arts and Letters—Roundup Rose, by Minnesota Mac
Br.—Tartan Farms (Fla)
Tr.—Lukas D Wayne
Own.—Tartan Stable

126

| | St. | 1st | 2nd | 3rd | Amt. |
|---|---|---|---|---|---|
| 1980 | 7 | 4 | 0 | 1 | $509,600 |
| 1979 | 7 | 2 | 2 | 0 | $25,576 |

| | | | | | | | | | | | | | | | | |
|---|---|---|---|---|---|---|---|---|---|---|---|---|---|---|---|---|
| 17May80- 9Pim | fst | 1 3/16 | :47⅘ 1:11⅕ 1:54⅕ | Preakness | 3 | 3 | $3^{2}$ | $1^{hd}$ | $1^{1}$ | $1^{4\frac{3}{4}}$ | Cordero A Jr | 126 | 2.70 | 99-12 Codex $126^{4\frac{3}{4}}$ GenuineRisk $121^{3\frac{1}{4}}$ ColonelMoran $126^{7}$ | Wide, ridden out | 8 |
| 13Apr80- 8Hol | fst | 1⅛ | :45⅖ 1:10 1:47⅖ | Hol Derby | 8 | 6 | $7^{6\frac{1}{2}}$ | $6^{3}$ | $2^{hd}$ | $1^{2}$ | Delahoussaye E | 122 | 4.30 | 95-19 Codex $122^{2}$ Rumbo $122^{1\frac{1}{2}}$ Cactus Road $122^{5\frac{1}{2}}$ | Drew clear | 11 |
| 30Mar80- 8SA | fst | 1⅛ | :46⅕ 1:10 1:47⅗ | S A Derby | 9 | 4 | $3^{1}$ | $3^{nk}$ | $1^{2\frac{1}{2}}$ | $1^{nk}$ | Valenzuela P A | 120 | 25.30 | 91-13 Codex $120^{nk}$ Rumbo $120^{7\frac{1}{2}}$ Bic's Gold $120^{3}$ | Lasted | 9 |
| 16Mar80- 5SA | fst | 1 1/16 | :46⅘ 1:11 1:42 | Allowance | 2 | 1 | $1^{1\frac{1}{2}}$ | $1^{\frac{1}{2}}$ | $1^{2\frac{1}{2}}$ | $1^{5\frac{1}{2}}$ | Valenzuela P A$^{5}$ | 111 | 5.70 | 91-12 Codex $111^{5\frac{1}{2}}$ Egg Toss $120^{no}$ Jihad $120^{3\frac{1}{2}}$ | Easily | 9 |
| 2Feb80- 6SA | fst | 1 1/16 | :46⅕ 1:10⅖ 1:41⅗ | Allowance | 2 | 4 | $4^{3}$ | $3^{1\frac{1}{2}}$ | $4^{2}$ | $4^{1\frac{1}{4}}$ | Valenzuela P A$^{5}$ | 113 | 6.30 | 92-09 Rumbo $114^{\frac{3}{4}}$ Score Twenty Four $116^{nk}$ Proven Jewel $120^{\frac{3}{4}}$ | Evenly | 7 |
| 19Jan80- 4SA | sl | 1 | :47⅘ 1:13⅗ 1:39⅖ | Allowance | 1 | 2 | $3^{1\frac{1}{2}}$ | $6^{6}$ | $6^{13}$ | $6^{22}$ | Hawley S | 116 | 2.10 | 50-30 Bold 'N Rulling $109^{7}$ ScoreTwentyFour $118^{5}$ ProvenJewel $116^{8}$ | Tired | 6 |
| 9Jan80- 6SA | sly | 1 | :45⅗ 1:10⅘ 1:37⅕ | Allowance | 4 | 4 | $3^{3}$ | $5^{2\frac{3}{4}}$ | $4^{6}$ | $3^{6\frac{1}{4}}$ | Shoemaker W | 118 | *2.10 | 77-18 Dandy Wit $114^{1}$ Moorish Star $120^{5\frac{1}{2}}$ Codex $118^{no}$ | Even try | 7 |
| 28Oct79- 8SA | fst | 1 1/16 | :46⅕ 1:09⅘ 1:41⅗ | Norfolk | 4 | 7 | $7^{4}$ | $6^{9}$ | $6^{11}$ | $5^{7\frac{3}{4}}$ | Hawley S | 118 | 9.50e | 85-13 The Carpenter $118^{hd}$ Rumbo $118^{2}$ Idyll $118^{2\frac{1}{4}}$ | Wide | 8 |
| 14Oct79- 7SA | fst | 1 1/16 | :46⅖ 1:11⅖ 1:42⅘ | Allowance | 6 | 3 | $3^{nk}$ | $3^{nk}$ | $1^{\frac{1}{2}}$ | $1^{\frac{3}{4}}$ | Hawley S | 115 | ·3.90 | 87-09 Codex $115^{\frac{3}{4}}$ Halpern Bay $115^{\frac{3}{4}}$ Rumbo $118^{2\frac{1}{2}}$ | Driving | 7 |
| 21Sep79-11Pom | fst | 6f | :21⅕ :44⅗ 1:11⅖ | Beau Brummel | 3 | 3 | $4^{4\frac{1}{2}}$ | $5^{8\frac{1}{2}}$ | $6^{9}$ | $4^{\frac{3}{4}}$ | Ramirez R | 114 | *.60 | 88-17 Marimia's Son $114^{hd}$ ⒹLe Caporal $114^{\frac{3}{4}}$ StormyPrince $114^{hd}$ | Rallied | 7 |

LATEST WORKOUTS Jun 2 Bel 5f fst 1:00⅘ b   May 27 Bel 5f fst 1:00⅗ b   ●May 10 Hol 5f fst :58⅗ h   May 2 Hol 5f fst :59⅖ h

The performance of a few horses improves dramatically on "off" tracks; the performances of many more falls off precipitously. For example, the connections of Codex were crestfallen when rain fell the night before the 1980 Belmont Stakes. While Codex had performed brilliantly on dry tracks, he had finished a dismal twenty-two lengths behind the winner under conditions similar to those featured on Belmont day. Although bettors still made Codex the Belmont favorite, he ran true to his past record, finishing eighteen lengths up the track.

Unfortunately, the ten races shown in the past performances often don't include enough races on wet tracks to form a reliable picture of the animal's preferences. In the absence of conclusive evidence, many experts prefer speed horses on sloppy tracks (because they escape having slop kicked into their faces), and come-from-behind horses on tiring, muddy tracks.

## DISTANCE

**Ethnarch** — Dk. b. or br. h. 5, by Buckpasser—Reveille II, by Star Kingdom

Own.—Silver Pals Stable — Br.—Claiborne Farm (Ky) — Tr.—Imperio Dominick A — 116

| Turf Record | | | | | St. | 1st | 2nd | 3rd | Amt. |
|---|---|---|---|---|---|---|---|---|---|
| St. 1st 2nd 3rd | | | | 1980 | 3 | 0 | 0 | 0 | $9,350 |
| 12 | 2 | 2 | 0 | 1979 | 15 | 5 | 3 | 1 | $119,280 |

| | | | | | | | | | | | | | | | | | | | |
|---|---|---|---|---|---|---|---|---|---|---|---|---|---|---|---|---|---|---|---|
| 2Apr80- 8Aqu | fst | 1⅜ | :48⅕ | 1:38⅕ | 2:16⅖ | Handicap | 2 | 5 | $5^{6}$ | $5^{2\frac{3}{4}}$ | $4^{6}$ | $4^{5\frac{3}{4}}$ | Velasquez J | 122 | *1.00 | 93-18 | Roscoe Blake $113^{3\frac{1}{4}}$ Properly Person $111^{2\frac{1}{4}}$ Imitating $113^{nk}$ | Tired | 6 |
| 16Mar80- 9FG | fst | 1¼ | :46⅗ | 1:38 | 2:04⅗ | N Orleans H | 2 | 6 | $5^{13}$ | $3^{\frac{1}{2}}$ | $4^{2}$ | $5^{5\frac{3}{4}}$ | Velasquez J | 118 | 1.70 | 82-15 | Pool Court$111^{hd}$FiveStarGeneral$112^{1\frac{3}{4}}$BookofKings$113^{3\frac{1}{4}}$ | Off slow | 7 |
| 24Feb80- 9FG | fst | 1⅛ | :47⅗ | 1:12 | 1:50⅕ | F G Classic | 4 | 7 | $7^{11}$ | $7^{7\frac{1}{4}}$ | $5^{3\frac{1}{2}}$ | $4^{2}$ | Velasquez J | 120 | 2.60 | 91-17 | BookofKings$115^{no}$ALettrToHrry$125^{1}$PoolCourt$111^{1}$ | Finished well | 7 |
| 30Dec79- 8Aqu | fst | 2¼ | ⊡:49⅖ | | 3:55⅘ | 3↑Display H | 6 | 8 | $8^{19}$ | $3^{2}$ | $1^{4}$ | $1^{5}$ | Velasquez J | 119 | 2.70 | 89-23 | Ethnarch $119^{5}$ Damascus Silver $116^{4}$ Identical $116^{3}$ | Ridden out | 9 |
| 15Dec79- 8Aqu | fst | 1⅝ | ⊡:48⅕ | 2:04⅗ | 2:43⅗ | 3↑Gallant Fx H | 6 | 7 | $6^{9\frac{1}{2}}$ | $6^{8}$ | $3^{5\frac{1}{2}}$ | $2^{6}$ | Velasquez J | 118 | 3.70 | 102-15 | Identical $110^{6}$ Ethnarch $118^{2\frac{1}{4}}$ Land of Eire $114^{\frac{3}{4}}$ | 2nd best | 12 |
| 5Dec79- 6Aqu | fst | 1½ | ⊡:49⅕ | 2:05⅕ | 2:31 | 3↑Handicap | 2 | 5 | $5^{6\frac{1}{2}}$ | $4^{2}$ | $1^{2}$ | $1^{5}$ | Velasquez J | 116 | 4.20 | 96-13 | Ethnarch $116^{5}$ Land of Eire $118^{\frac{3}{4}}$ Properly Person $117^{4\frac{3}{4}}$ | Driving | 7 |
| 22Nov79- 8Aqu | fst | 1 3/16 | :48⅕ | 1:12⅖ | 1:56⅘ | 3↑Queens Cty H | 8 | 8 | $7^{6\frac{1}{4}}$ | $4^{1}$ | $5^{3\frac{1}{4}}$ | $6^{4}$ | Velasquez J | 113 | 18.10 | 74-20 | Dewan Keys $112^{\frac{1}{2}}$ Mr. International $109^{no}$ GallantBest$116^{no}$ | Tired | 8 |
| 15Nov79- 7Aqu | gd | 1 | :45⅗ | 1:09⅗ | 1:34⅕ | 3↑Allowance | 2 | 6 | $6^{6\frac{1}{4}}$ | $6^{5\frac{1}{2}}$ | $4^{5\frac{1}{2}}$ | $3^{4}$ | Pincay L Jr | 119 | 4.80 | 91-15 | Hugable Tom $117^{1\frac{1}{4}}$ Rivalero $115^{2\frac{3}{4}}$ Ethnarch $119^{1}$ | Rallied | 6 |
| 5Nov79- 7Aqu | sf | 1⅛ | Ⓣ:50 | 1:15⅖ | 1:54⅘ | 3↑Allowance | 4 | 9 | $9^{11}$ | $7^{7\frac{1}{2}}$ | $5^{8}$ | $5^{9\frac{3}{4}}$ | Pincay L Jr | 119 | 3.90 | 60-30 | Sten $117^{7}$ Old Crony $117^{2}$ Two Point Poppy $108^{nk}$ | No threat | 10 |
| 21Oct79- 7Aqu | fst | 1⅛ | :49⅕ | 1:13 | 1:50⅖ | 3↑Allowance | 5 | 6 | $5^{9\frac{1}{4}}$ | $5^{8}$ | $4^{4}$ | $4^{2}$ | Vasquez J | 119 | *1.20 | 81-16 | Musical Phantasy $117^{\frac{1}{2}}$ Morning Frolic $117^{1\frac{1}{4}}$ Sten $117^{nk}$ | Wide | 6 |

LATEST WORKOUTS Mar 31 Bel tr.t 5f sly 1:03⅗ b Feb 12 Hia 1⅛m fst 1:53 h

The ideal Thoroughbred combines speed and stamina, and can thus win at distances from six furlongs to two miles. Most horses, however, can win only in a narrow range of distances.

Speed is easier to breed into a horse than stamina, which is the reason over 70 percent of all races are run at distances under one mile. Most handicappers are reluctant to place a large wager on a sprinter going a distance unless the trainer has proven his ability to get speed horses to "stretch out" in the past.

Some horses, like Ethnarch, can only dominate at longer distances—the past performances of this son of Buckpasser show that his two recent triumphs were at one and a half miles and two and a quarter miles. Because raw speed is nearly impossible to train into a horse, distance horses are very seldom successful dropping down into sprints.

## FINAL TIME

**In Patient** — B. g. 4, by Towson—Carlmult, by Carlduro — $9,500

Own.—Payne L P — Br.—Christmas Mr-Mrs W G (Md) — Tr.—Dearstyn Alan T — 115

| | St. | 1st | 2nd | 3rd | Amt. |
|---|---|---|---|---|---|
| 1980 | 6 | 5 | 0 | 0 | $13,916 |
| 1979 | 3 | M | 0 | 0 | |

| | | | | | | | | | | | | | | | | | | | |
|---|---|---|---|---|---|---|---|---|---|---|---|---|---|---|---|---|---|---|---|
| 29Sep80- 5Bow | fst | 6f | :23⅖ | :47⅖ | 1:13⅕ | 3↑Clm c-6500 | 7 | 4 | $2^{hd}$ | $1^{2\frac{1}{2}}$ | $1^{2}$ | $1^{1}$ | Kupfer T | 117 | *1.30 | 74-29 | In Patient $117^{1}$ Dark Hope $117^{4\frac{3}{4}}$ Emperor Ralph $119^{nk}$ | Driving | 7 |
| 22Sep80- 9Bow | fst | 6f | :23⅕ | :46⅖ | 1:12 | 3↑Clm c-5000 | 12 | 3 | $2^{1}$ | $2^{2}$ | $1^{1\frac{1}{2}}$ | $1^{2}$ | Whitacre $G^{7}$ | 112 | 5.00 | 80-20 | In Patient $112^{2}$ Land Lightly $117^{nk}$ Fats' Chic $112^{\frac{3}{4}}$ | Drew clear | 12 |
| 1Sep80- 6Tim | fst | *6½f | :24 | :47⅖ | 1:17⅘ | 3↑Clm 5000 | 4 | 1 | $2^{hd}$ | $1^{\frac{1}{2}}$ | $1^{3\frac{1}{2}}$ | $1^{2\frac{3}{4}}$ | Whitacre $G^{7}$ | 112 | *1.10 | 93-08 | In Patient $112^{2\frac{3}{4}}$ Land Lightly $113^{1\frac{3}{4}}$ Last Activate $116^{3}$ | Driving | 5 |
| 17Aug80- 3Pen | fst | 6f | :22⅕ | :46 | 1:11⅘ | 3↑Clm 5000 | 5 | 3 | $2^{hd}$ | $1^{hd}$ | $1^{hd}$ | $1^{2}$ | Rice C L | 116 | 3.20 | 85-15 | In Patient $116^{2}$ New Patriot $116^{3}$ Sar's Quest $116^{1}$ | Driving | 7 |
| 13Jun80- 5Pen | fst | 6f | :21⅗ | :44⅘ | 1:12 | Clm 5000 | 10 | 2 | $2^{4}$ | $3^{7}$ | $2^{4}$ | $4^{4}$ | Sasser B | 119 | 3.40 | 80-19 | Marshmellow $116^{2}$ Big Kas $116^{1}$ Morty's Boy $122^{1}$ | Weakened | 12 |
| 13May80- 1Pim | gd | 6f | :23⅗ | :47⅘ | 1:14⅖ | 3↑Md 5000 | 5 | 5 | $1^{hd}$ | $1^{hd}$ | $1^{3}$ | $1^{12}$ | Pilar H | 122 | 8.10 | 74-21 | In Patient $122^{12}$ Lenso's Boy $113^{\frac{3}{4}}$ Hi Jane $117^{2}$ | Ridden out | 12 |
| 15May79- 1Pim | fst | 6f | :23⅘ | :48 | 1:15 | 3↑Md 5000 | 2 | 10 | $10^{8\frac{3}{4}}$ | $11^{11}$ | $9^{6\frac{1}{4}}$ | $7^{3\frac{1}{2}}$ | Sasser B | 112 | 5.60 | 67-21 | Caber Toss $122^{hd}$ PerfectReturn$112^{\frac{3}{4}}$NeverintheRed$107^{hd}$ | In close | 12 |
| 27Apr79- 1Pim | sly | 6f | :23⅘ | :48 | 1:15 | 3↑Ⓢ Md 5000 | 4 | 9 | $7^{12}$ | $9^{19}$ | $9^{17}$ | $9^{9\frac{1}{4}}$ | Sasser B | 113 | 21.60 | 62-24 | Eee Bee $117^{2\frac{3}{4}}$ Rejuvavate $109^{nk}$ Jets Turn To $122^{nk}$ | No factor | 12 |
| 3Apr79- 1Pim | sly | 6f | :23⅘ | :48⅖ | 1:15⅕ | 3↑Md 5000 | 8 | 12 | $12^{12}$ | $11^{12}$ | $8^{15}$ | $7^{12}$ | Sasser B | 114 | 34.00 | 58-28 | Big King K. $115^{\frac{1}{2}}$ Russell Road $112^{\frac{1}{2}}$ Hilda's Folly $112^{1}$ | Outrun | 12 |

LATEST WORKOUTS Sep 11 Bow 3f fst :36⅕ h

Since in any kind of racing the winner is the competitor who covers the distance the fastest, most people draw two conclusions about horse racing. The first, that relative speed is a measure of class, is true. The second, that comparing the final times listed in the *Daily Racing Form*'s past performances will point out the fastest horse, is false. Most racegoers who handicap strictly from the past performances would be far better off totally ignoring final time than trying to make a judgment based on raw figures or figures adjusted using "easy" time charts or systems.

In our section on "The Racetrack," we discussed several reasons why final times vary from track to track—length, shape, construction and composition of track surface. At each track, wind and track conditions can produce a wide variance in times for the same class horses from day to day. For example, In Patient won six-furlong races over "fast" tracks at Bowie in times that varied by 1⅖ seconds.

Another factor, other than track and weather conditions, that can affect final time is the manner in which the race was run. A horse that sprints to an early lead and hugs the rail all the way to the wire is obviously going to have a faster final time than the horse that runs into traffic and has to swing wide to win.

Comparing times at different distances is another complicated problem. How, for example, does the time of one horse at a mile and a sixteenth compare with that of another horse at a mile and seventy yards or that of a third at a mile and an eighth? "Parallel Time Charts" that claim to make these comparisons often ignore the rather substantial differences between tracks and between day-to-day track conditions.

Finally, determining the exact time for horses finishing behind the winner depends on the speed of the horses and the distance of the race. The oft-repeated rule of thumb is that one-fifth of a second equals one length, but in fact, a horse that covers six furlongs in 1:12 covers an average of *six* lengths in one second, not five.

To assist handicappers in making some sense out of final times, the *Daily Racing Form* began to compute a "speed rating" for the past performances of each horse. To arrive at this rating, the *Form* uses one hundred points as the numerical rating for the track record at each distance. For every fifth of a second a horse runs slower than the track record, the paper deducts one point. For example, the winner of a six-furlong race at Arlington Park finishes in 1:10. This time is one and three-fifths seconds, or eight-fifths of a second, slower than the track-record time of 1:08⅖. Thus, the winner's speed rating would be 100 − 8, or 92. For horses that finish behind the winner, the traditional one-length-equals-a-fifth of a second (or one point) formula is used.

This system is so crude, however, as to be of little value. Speed ratings are of no use in comparing races at different tracks because the track records vary so widely. Because average horses run closer to track records at shorter distances than at long distances, these simple speed ratings have limited value in comparing the speed of horses at different distances. Furthermore, the speed rating doesn't account for the substantial changes in racing conditions from day to day.

To compensate for this final deficiency, the *Daily Racing Form* lists a *"track variant"* for each racing day in its Eastern editions. This variant is computed by *averaging the difference between the final times and the track records for all races run on one day*. For example, if the average difference was three seconds below the track records, the track variant, at one point for each fifth of a second, would be twelve.

This variant is unfortunately even more misleading than the speed rating. The major problem is that the difference between final and track-record times depends on the quality of races run that day and on the distance of those races. Only very low or very high ratings indicate that the track was particularly fast or slow on a given day.

For all of the reasons above, the average racegoer should concentrate on other factors besides final time when handicapping from past performances. However, the extraordinary success achieved in recent years by speed handicappers has proven that final times can be used to compare horses. These speed handicappers analyze past performances to prepare their own speed ratings and track variants. Their computations are very time-consuming and complicated—far too complicated to go into here—and the ratings arrived at can be used successfully only by those individuals who have a sound knowledge of all factors in handicapping. Those readers interested in speed handicapping will find descriptions of this art in the books recommended at the end of this section.

## FRACTIONAL TIMES

**Temperence Hill** — B. c. 3, by Stop The Music—Sister Shannon, by Etonian
Br.—Polk A F Jr (Ky)
Tr.—Cantey Joseph B
Own.—Loblolly Stable
**119**

| Turf Record | St. | 1st | 2nd | 3rd |
|---|---|---|---|---|
| | 2 | 0 | 0 | 1 |

| | St. | 1st | 2nd | 3rd | Amt. |
|---|---|---|---|---|---|
| 1980 | 13 | 6 | 3 | 1 | $501,052 |
| 1979 | 3 | M | 0 | 0 | $900 |

| | | | | | | | | | | | | | | | | | | | | | | |
|---|---|---|---|---|---|---|---|---|---|---|---|---|---|---|---|---|---|---|---|---|---|---|
| 16Aug80- 8Sar | fst | 1¼ | | :45⅘ | 1:36⅕ | 2:02⅘ | | Travers | 3 | 9 | $9^{15}$ | $5^{5}$ | $3^{nk}$ | $1^{1\frac12}$ | Maple E | | 126 | 3.80 | 86-13 | Temperence Hill $126^{1\frac12}$ First Albert $126^{no}$AmberPass$126^{6\frac34}$ | Driving | 9 |
| 19Jly80- 8Bel | fst | 1½ | | :51⅗ | 2:05 | 2:28⅗ | 3↑ | Brooklyn H | 1 | 2 | $3^{2}$ | $4^{5\frac12}$ | $4^{8}$ | $4^{11}$ | Maple E | b | 114 | 2.10 | 66-20 | Winter's Tale $120^{5}$ State Dinner $121^{3\frac12}$ Ring of Light $114^{2}$ | Tired | 5 |
| 5Jly80- 8Bel | fst | 1⅛ | | :45⅕ | 1:09⅕ | 1:49 | | Dwyer | 7 | 6 | $6^{11}$ | $5^{7\frac12}$ | $4^{6}$ | $2^{1}$ | Maple E | b | 129 | 8.20 | 81-17 | Amber Pass $114^{1}$ Temperence Hill $129^{hd}$ Comptroller$119^{3}$ | Rallied | 8 |
| 22Jun80- 8Bel | hd | 1 | Ⓣ | :45⅖ | 1:09⅗ | 1:33⅘ | | Saranac | 2 | 10 | $12^{10}$ | $12^{11}$ | $9^{11}$ | $7^{7\frac34}$ | Maple E | b | 128 | 4.90 | 88-05 | Key To Content $114^{3}$ Current Legend $114^{\frac12}$BenFab$123^{3}$ | No threat | 13 |
| 7Jun80- 8Bel | my | 1½ | | :50⅕ | 2:04 | 2:29⅘ | | Belmont | 3 | 7 | $8^{5}$ | $3^{\frac12}$ | $2^{hd}$ | $1^{2}$ | Maple E | b | 126 | 53.40 | 71-17 | TemperenceHill$126^{2}$GnuinRisk$121^{1\frac12}$RockhillNtiv$126^{2}$ | Brisk urging | 10 |
| 31May80- 7Bel | fm | 1 1/16 | Ⓣ | :45⅘ | 1:10 | 1:42⅗ | 3↑ | Allowance | 6 | 4 | $5^{12}$ | $4^{12}$ | $3^{3}$ | $3^{1\frac34}$ | Maple E | b | 113 | 8.10 | 81-19 | French Colonial$121^{nk}$Perceran$117^{1\frac12}$TemperenceHill$113^{no}$. | Gaining | 6 |
| 26May80- 8Key | fst | 1⅛ | | :47⅖ | 1:11⅗ | 1:48⅘ | | Pa Derby | 7 | 7 | $7^{13}$ | $6^{10}$ | $6^{12}$ | $5^{11}$ | Haire D | b | 122 | *.70 | 80-15 | Lively King $122^{4}$ Mutineer $122^{nk}$ Stutz Blackhawk $122^{4}$ | No rally | 7 |
| 10May80- 8Aqu | fst | 1 | | :45⅘ | 1:09⅕ | 1:34⅖ | | Withers | 3 | 7 | $7^{8\frac34}$ | $6^{9\frac12}$ | $2^{8}$ | $2^{5\frac12}$ | Haire D | b | 126 | 3.30 | 88-13 | Colonel Moran $126^{5\frac12}$ Temperence Hill $126^{4\frac34}$J.P.Brother$126^{\frac12}$ | Wide | 7 |
| 12Apr80- 9OP | fst | 1⅛ | | :46⅖ | 1:10⅘ | 1:50⅗ | | Ark. Derby | 8 | 9 | $9^{18}$ | $8^{9\frac34}$ | $4^{1\frac12}$ | $1^{1\frac14}$ | Haire D | b | 123 | 4.60e | 90-21 | TemperenceHill$123^{1\frac14}$Bold'NRulling$117^{3\frac34}$SunCatcher$120^{nk}$ | Driving | 10 |
| 29Mar80- 7OP | sly | $1^{70}$ | | :48 | 1:12⅘ | 1:42⅕ | | Allowance | 1 | 3 | $3^{1\frac12}$ | $3^{3}$ | $2^{3}$ | $2^{4\frac34}$ | Maple E | b | 121 | 1.60 | 80-23 | Loto Canada $121^{4\frac34}$ TemperenceHill$121^{1\frac34}$RaiseAKid$112^{2\frac14}$ | 2nd best | 7 |

**LATEST WORKOUTS** ●Sep 5 Bel 3f fst :35⅕ h Sep 1 Bel 6f fst 1:13 h Aug 15 Sar 3f sly :38 b ●Aug 11 Sar 1⅛m fst 1:53⅗ b

The *Daily Racing Form*'s past-performance records include two fractional times achieved by the *leading horse* at that point of call (see the point-of-call chart for the distance for each race).

In England, horses are held in check in the early part of a race, then are let out at the end. In American racing, the first quarter of a race is almost always the fastest quarter; the last quarter, the slowest. Horses that come on in the stretch are not accelerating, they're just tiring less quickly. As a result, American races are won in one of two ways—either a horse sets a pace that no other horse can overcome, or the initial pacesetters tire as a horse with more energy in reserve passes them by.

Predicting the outcome of a race obviously involves trying to determine which horse will be the pacesetter and whether the pace can be sustained throughout the race. In making that prediction, handicappers have learned that a horse that can get a clear early lead can often save enough energy to maintain that lead at the finish. If two or more horses vie for the early lead, however, natural competitiveness may cause them to expend more energy. These "speed duels" can often work to the advantage of a horse that lays off the pace, such as 1980 Belmont Stakes and Jockey Club Gold Cup winner Temperence Hill.

The above observations are the basis of *pace handicapping*. While pace analysis is a sound handicapping fundamental, pace handicapping systems that assign numerical values to fractional times are suspect. The problem is the large variances in time produced by the multitude of factors we discussed under "Final Time."

## POST POSITION

**Likeable** — B. g. 3, by Olden Times—Her Delight, by Herbager
$16,000
Br.—Hexter Stable (Ky)
Tr.—Russo Anthony J
Own.—Donnelly W R
**117**

| | St. | 1st | 2nd | 3rd | Amt. |
|---|---|---|---|---|---|
| 1980 | 7 | 3 | 1 | 0 | $20,460 |
| 1979 | 12 | M | 2 | 4 | $9,970 |

| | | | | | | | | | | | | | | | | | | | | | |
|---|---|---|---|---|---|---|---|---|---|---|---|---|---|---|---|---|---|---|---|---|---|
| 8Apr80- 1Aqu | fst | 6f | | :22⅘ | :46⅕ | 1:11⅗ | Clm 20000 | 4 | 9 | $9^{9}$ | $6^{6}$ | $4^{4}$ | $2^{3}$ | Saumell L | b | 117 | 3.70 | 82-21 | Dover Prince $117^{3}$ Likeable $117^{\frac34}$ Beachhead $112^{3}$ | Broke in air | 9 |
| 5Mar80- 9Aqu | fst | 6f | ⊡ | :22⅗ | :46 | 1:12⅗ | Clm 16000 | 1 | 5 | $2^{1}$ | $3^{2}$ | $2^{1\frac12}$ | $1^{\frac34}$ | Asmussen C B | b | 119 | 5.30 | 81-22 | Likeable $119^{\frac34}$ Catchy Thought $112^{nk}$ Rollicking Jeff$112^{1\frac34}$ | Driving | 11 |
| 22Feb80- 2Aqu | gd | 6f | ⊡ | :22⅗ | :46⅗ | 1:13 | Clm 16000 | 2 | 1 | $4^{2\frac12}$ | $3^{3}$ | $2^{1}$ | $1^{hd}$ | Asmussen C B | b | 117 | 3.30 | 79-19 | Likeable $117^{hd}$ Chrisy's Decision $112^{\frac34}$ Good and Fine$119^{4}$ | Driving | 7 |
| 11Feb80- 3Aqu | fst | 6f | ⊡ | :22⅕ | :46 | 1:12⅗ | Clm 16000 | 7 | 1 | $6^{3\frac12}$ | $7^{7\frac12}$ | $7^{7}$ | $5^{7\frac34}$ | Santiago A | b | 119 | 3.30 | 73-23 | Last Goodie $117^{2}$ Ole Bear $117^{5}$ Whambang $117^{nk}$ | Wide | 7 |
| 1Feb80- 1Aqu | fst | 6f | ⊡ | :22⅘ | :47⅕ | 1:13⅗ | Clm 20000 | 7 | 4 | $5^{4\frac12}$ | $4^{5\frac12}$ | $5^{7}$ | $4^{7}$ | Garramone A | b | 119 | 18.30 | 70-25 | CatchyThought$114^{1\frac12}$BlueEyedIke$108^{2\frac12}$QuietSm$117^{3}$ | Slightly wide | 9 |
| 14Jan80- 4Aqu | gd | 6f | ⊡ | :23 | :48 | 1:13⅗ | Md 18000 | 1 | 7 | $4^{2}$ | $3^{nk}$ | $1^{3}$ | $1^{5\frac34}$ | Asmussen C B | b | 122 | *1.00 | 76-23 | Likeable $122^{5\frac34}$ Bello Boy $115^{1}$ Guess What's Up $112^{3}$ | Ridden out | 12 |
| 4Jan80- 4Aqu | fst | 6f | ⊡ | :23⅕ | :47⅕ | 1:14 | Md 20000 | 10 | 1 | $6^{3\frac12}$ | $3^{1\frac12}$ | $4^{3\frac12}$ | $5^{6\frac34}$ | Maple E | b | 122 | *2.40 | 67-22 | Jim Hilt $122^{1\frac34}$ Droll Troll $122^{hd}$ Scarlet Castle $122^{3}$ | No rally | 12 |
| 19Dec79- 1Aqu | gd | 6f | ⊡ | :23⅘ | :48 | 1:13⅘ | Md 20000 | 3 | 3 | $3^{nk}$ | $3^{1\frac12}$ | $1^{hd}$ | $4^{2\frac14}$ | Velasquez J | b | 118 | *1.30 | 73-19 | HighProfile$108^{1\frac14}$NtiveStnd$114^{nk}$[D]BrookvilleSport$118^{\frac34}$ | Weakened | 9 |
| 19Dec79-Placed third through disqualification | | | | | | | | | | | | | | | | | | | | | |
| 15Nov79- 9Aqu | fst | 6f | | :22⅖ | :46⅖ | 1:12⅕ | Md 20000 | 11 | 1 | $1^{hd}$ | $2^{hd}$ | $2^{hd}$ | $2^{2\frac14}$ | Asmussen C B | b | 116 | *2.50 | 80-15 | Duffys Brother $116^{2\frac14}$ Likeable $116^{2}$ Deedee's Deal$120^{1\frac14}$ | Game try | 11 |
| 26Oct79- 5Aqu | fst | 6f | | :23⅕ | :47⅘ | 1:13⅕ | Md 20000 | 7 | 2 | $1^{2}$ | $1^{hd}$ | $1^{hd}$ | $2^{\frac34}$ | Gonzalez M $A^{5}$ | b | 113 | *1.80 | 76-24 | Quiet Sam $109^{\frac34}$ Likeable $113^{1\frac12}$ Red Weaver $118^{1\frac14}$ | Weakened | 8 |

**LATEST WORKOUTS** Apr 19 Bel tr.t 5f fst 1:03⅕ h Apr 2 Bel 6f fst 1:17⅘ b Mar 27 Bel tr.t 3f fst :36 b Mar 17 Bel tr.t 6f fst 1:17⅗ b

The sharpness of the turns on a track, the location of the starting gate in relation to the turns at each distance, and variations in track surface can all result in pronounced biases of certain post positions at certain distances. For example, the sharp turns of Aqueduct's inner dirt course favor horses starting on the inside, especially horses that like to get out to an early lead. Likeable raced well when he drew an inside post position, but in the races in which he started in post position seven or worse, he expended so much energy that he tired badly in the stretch.

A few enlightened tracks include updated post position surveys in their programs (such as the one below for Aqueduct's inner dirt course).

(SPRINTS)

| P.P. | STS. | WINS | % | P.P. | STS. | WINS | % |
|---|---|---|---|---|---|---|---|
| 1. | 312 | 36 | .12 | 8. | 215 | 15 | .07 |
| 2. | 312 | 49 | .16 | 9. | 192 | 15 | .08 |
| 3. | 312 | 35 | .11 | 10. | 148 | 12 | .08 |
| 4. | 312 | 35 | .11 | 11. | 103 | 11 | .11 |
| 5. | 311 | 34 | .11 | 12. | 65 | 6 | .10 |
| 6. | 310 | 33 | .11 | 13. | 15 | 1 | .07 |
| 7. | 272 | 33 | .12 | 14. | 10 | 0 | .00 |

Handicappers at other tracks will find it wise to make their own.

Normal track biases can change dramatically on off tracks. Noting the results of two or three races before wagering can pay off in these conditions.

POINTS OF CALL

```
Pearl Necklace *          Ch. m. 5, by Ambernash—Another Jane, by Traffic Judge           Turf Record        St. 1st 2nd 3rd      Amt.
                                   Br.—Webster R N (Md)                              124  St. 1st 2nd 3rd  1979 10  6   2   2   $274,250
  Own.—Webster R N                 Tr.—Laurin Roger                                       13   8   3   1   1978 13  4   5   2   $223,637
12Sep79- 8Bel fst 1      :45⅗ 1:09⅗ 1:34⅘ 3+ⒻMaskette      1 4 2½  1hd 1hd 3nk Fell J        125 *1.10 94-20 Blitey 112nk It's In the Air 122no Pearl Necklace 125¾ Weakened 5
 1Sep79- 8Bel gd  1¼ Ⓣ:48   1:37⅗ 2:02⅕ 3+ⒻFl'wr Bwl H  6 1 1½  11  1½  1½  Shoemaker W   125 *1.20 83-17 PerlNecklce125½TheVeryOne112¹½Terpsichorist118nk Handy score 8
19Aug79- 8Sar yl  1⅛ ⓣ:46⅗ 1:11⅗ 1:48⅘ 3+ⒻDiana H       3 5 55  32½ 21  1¾  Fell J        124 *1.30 83-17 Pearl Necklace 124¾ Island Kiss 114¹¾ Terpsichorist119³¾ Handily 9
 2Jun79- 8Bel fst 1⅛     :45⅖ 1:09⅕ 1:48⅗ 3+ⒻHempstead H  2 2 22  14  16  15  Fell J        122  *.30 84-25 Pearl Necklace 122⁵ Miss Baja115¹⁰SweetWoodruff108¹½ In hand 5
23May79- 8Bel sly 1¹⁄₁₆    :45⅕ 1:09⅖ 1:41⅖ 3+ⒻShuvee H      7 1 1½  1hd 12½ 13½ Fell J        121  1.80 95-22 Pearl Necklace 121³½TingleStone120³Kit'sDouble109¹¾ Hand ride 8
15May79- 8Pim fst 1¹⁄₁₆    :47⅕ 1:10⅘ 1:43⅕ 3+ⒻⓈGeisha H    4 2 2hd 1hd 13  14  Hernandez R   121  *.30 89-21 Pearl Necklace 121⁴ Kit's Double 113³ Debby's Turn 115½ Easily 6
 7May79- 8Pim fst 1¹⁄₁₆    :47⅘ 1:11⅘ 1:43⅖ 3+ⒻⓈAllowance   6 1 13  13  17  16  Hernandez R   115  *.10 88-17 Pearl Necklace 115⁶ JamilaKadir119²½TopStorm108⁴½ Easily best 6
28Apr79- 8Aqu sly 1⅛     :48   1:12⅖ 1:50⅘ 3+ⒻTop Flight H  7 2 21½ 2½  12  2nk Hernandez R   120  2.50 81-17 Waya 128nk Pearl Necklace 120⁷ Island Kiss 112¹ Best of others 8
13Apr79- 8Aqu fst 1      :46   1:11⅖ 1:37⅘ 3+ⒻBed Roses H   4 3 31½ 1hd 1hd 3½  Hernandez R   121  *.50 76-24 One Sum 118½ Reflection Pool113noPearlNecklace121½ Weakened 7
     13Apr79-Run in Two Divisions: 7th & 8th races.
31Mar79- 8Bow fst 7f     :22⅗  :45  1:22⅗ 3+ⒻB Fritchie H 4 3 2½  21  23  23½ Amy J         122 *1.70 89-18 Skipat 125³½ Pearl Necklace 122¹½ The Very One 113½ 2nd best 8
  LATEST WORKOUTS     ●Sep 19 Bel 6f fst 1:12 h     Sep 9 Bel 5f fst 1:00⅘ b     Aug 30 Bel 4f sly :48⅕ b     Aug 15 Sar ⓣ 1 fm 1:39⅗ h
```

The listings of the position of each horse and the number of lengths behind the leader at each point of call are a very valuable handicapping tool. These positions can provide hints about a horse's form as well as providing an overall picture of how the race is likely to be run.

A majority of races are won by horses on or near the lead at the end of the first quarter-mile. A horse like the very successful Pearl Necklace is far less subject to traffic problems and bad racing luck than a horse that comes from far back. A jockey on a leader can usually choose the exact time he wants to make a move; a jockey on a horse in heavy traffic often has to wait until an opening presents itself.

Being on or near the lead is no advantage if a horse has the tendency to expend so much energy that it tires badly. Such horses can win only if they get a big early lead. A horse like Pearl Necklace, on the other hand, that can sustain its energy and determination under heavy pressure is a strong contender in any race.

Because horses tend to repeat their previous patterns, handicappers look for *changes in race patterns* as an indication of improving or declining form. Such changes indicating possible *improvement* include:

*A display of early speed:*

| | | | | | |
|---|---|---|---|---|---|
| 29Apr | 8 | $2^{1}$ | $2^{3}$ | $6^{7}$ | $8^{10}$ |
| 20Apr | 9 | $9^{10}$ | $8^{8}$ | $8^{7}$ | $7^{6}$ |

*Carrying speed further in succeeding races:*

| | | | | | |
|---|---|---|---|---|---|
| 29Apr | 3 | $1^{2}$ | $1^{1}$ | $2^{2}$ | $6^{9}$ |
| 20Apr | 3 | $1^{1}$ | $3^{4}$ | $5^{7}$ | $8^{12}$ |

*Significant gain of ground in the stretch:*

29Apr 7 $8^{14}$ $7^{10}$ $5^{8}$ $4^{3}$

*Making two separate runs at the leader:*

29Apr 8 $5^{3}$ $2^{2}$ $3^{3}$ $2^{1/2}$

All past performances should be reviewed in light of available information on how the race was run. The "comment line" in the Eastern editions of the form can be enlightening. Comments such as "block," "steadied," "bumped," "lost whip," or "saddle slipped" can excuse what appears to be a poor performance. Others, such as "gamely," "rallied," or "sharp" can be positive signs. These comments are taken from the narratives printed under results charts. Access to these full narratives contributes substantially to the success of accomplished handicappers.

Even the occasional racegoer can become remarkably proficient at interpreting points of call by trying to predict how a race will be run, then immediately after the race analyzing the actual results in light of the prediction. Practical exercises make the numbers in the *Form* come to life.

## FINAL FINISH

**Coup De Chance ✱**
Own.—Levesque J L
Br.—Angus Glen Farm Ltd (Can)
Tr.—Starr John

**115**

| Turf Record | St. | 1st | 2nd | 3rd | | St. | 1st | 2nd | 3rd | Amt. |
|---|---|---|---|---|---|---|---|---|---|---|
| | 7 | 2 | 1 | 2 | 1979 | 16 | 5 | 6 | 2 | $69,780 |
| | | | | | 1978 | 12 | 3 | 2 | 3 | $55,869 |

| | | | | | | | | | | | | | | | | | | | |
|---|---|---|---|---|---|---|---|---|---|---|---|---|---|---|---|---|---|---|---|
| 21Oct79- 5WO | fst | 6f | :22⅖ | :45⅖ | 1:10⅕ | 3↑ Nearctic | 3 | 4 | $4^{3½}$ | $4^{1}$ | $5^{5½}$ | $6^{8¾}$ | Souter J P | b 116 | 2.40 | 83-16 | Ocean Emperor $118^{2}$ Stutz Bearcat $128^{½}$ Viceera $114^{2¾}$ | Tired | 7 |
| 4Oct79- 7WO | sly | 6f | :23⅕ | :46⅗ | 1:13⅖ | 3↑ Allowance | 4 | 5 | $1^{½}$ | $1^{2}$ | $1^{4}$ | $1^{5}$ | Souter J P | b 112 | *1.10 | 76-34 | Coup DeChance$112^{5}$BillyRedcoat$117^{nk}$CourtlyDancer$114^{2}$ | Handily | 8 |
| 27Sep79- 7WO | fst | 6f | :23⅕ | :45⅘ | 1:10⅗ | 3↑ Allowance | 3 | 5 | $2^{½}$ | $2^{hd}$ | $2^{hd}$ | $2^{hd}$ | Souter J P | 117 | 2.20 | 90-18 | Ocean Emperor $120^{hd}$ Coup De Chance$117^{4}$Viceera$117^{3}$ | Game try | 6 |
| 5Sep79- 7WO | fm | *7f | (T):23 | :46 | 1:24⅘ | 3↑ Allowance | 3 | 7 | $7^{7¼}$ | $5^{3¾}$ | $2^{1½}$ | $1^{¾}$ | Souter J P | 117 | *.60 | 96-03 | Coup De Chance $117^{¾}$ Risk Shot $114^{3}$ Portage Bay $120^{2}$ | Driving | 9 |
| 25Aug79- 8FE | hy | 6f | :22⅖ | :46⅗ | 1:12⅘ | 3↑ Allowance | 5 | 5 | $5^{5¼}$ | $5^{3½}$ | $3^{1}$ | $2^{1½}$ | Souter J P | 117 | *2.25 | 81-27 | Nice Bippy $114^{1½}$ Coup De Chance$117^{no}$GoldenBaffle$117^{½}$ | Gamely | 7 |
| 7Jly79- 8WO | fm | 1 | (T):46⅘ | 1:11 | 1:36⅕ | Heresy | 6 | 7 | $6^{3½}$ | $5^{2}$ | $4^{3}$ | $3^{3}$ | Souter J P | 123 | 3.60 | 89-09 | Admiral Twit $115^{2¾}$ The Loaf $117^{nk}$ Coup De Chance$123^{1½}$ | Rallied | 9 |
| 30Jun79- 7WO | sly | 1¼ | :45⅖ | 1:38⅗ | 2:06⅗ | [S]Queens Plate | 6 | 3 | $3^{3½}$ | $6^{11}$ | $8^{27}$ | $8^{30}$ | Souter J P | 126 | 15.45 | 43-21 | Steady Growth $126^{2½}$ Bold Agent $126^{2}$ Ram Good $126^{½}$ | Tired | 9 |
| 16Jun79- 8WO | fst | 1 1/16 | :47⅘ | 1:11⅖ | 1:42⅘ | [S]Plate Trial | 3 | 4 | $5^{2¼}$ | $5^{3}$ | $5^{6½}$ | $6^{10}$ | Souter J P | 126 | 3.80 | 85-09 | Bold Agent $126^{5}$ Lover's Answer $126^{3½}$ Villa Dancer $126^{½}$ | Tired | 9 |
| 16Jun79-Run in two divisions 6th and 8th races. | | | | | | | | | | | | | | | | | | | |
| 26May79- 8WO | sf | 1 1/16 | (T):48⅖ | 1:13⅘ | 1:48⅘ | Toronto Cup | 9 | 3 | $3^{2½}$ | $2^{1}$ | $2^{1½}$ | $1^{hd}$ | Souter J P | 119 | 4.60 | 62-38 | Coup De Chance $119^{hd}$ Bridle Path $116^{1½}$ TheLoaf$115^{2½}$ | Prevailed | 13 |
| 12May79- 8WO | fst | 1 1/16 | :46 | 1:10 | 1:42⅗ | Marine | 3 | 2 | $2^{½}$ | $1^{½}$ | $1^{hd}$ | $2^{2½}$ | Souter J P | 117 | *1.30 | 92-14 | FlashingEgle$114^{2½}$CoupDeChnce$117^{hd}$Lover'sAnswer$120^{½}$ | Gamely | 13 |

Most handicappers consider as contenders only those horses that have demonstrated the ability to compete at a certain class, distance and weight by running a recent "good" race under those conditions. By "good," they generally mean in the money or within two or three lengths of the winner.

Some place special emphasis on horses that have finished second in their last race. The reason is that winning horses often have to move up in class or are penalized for their victory under allowance conditions. Either situation benefits the second-place finisher.

## KIND OF RACE

**Hawaiian Regent**
Own.—Frantz Dorothy
B. g. 6, by Hawaii—Autumn Serenade, by Royal Serenade
**$10,000**
Br.—Schmidt C E (Ky)
Tr.—Sigler Ward

**$112^{7}$**

| Turf Record | St. | 1st | 2nd | 3rd | | St. | 1st | 2nd | 3rd | Amt. |
|---|---|---|---|---|---|---|---|---|---|---|
| | 4 | 1 | 0 | 0 | 1981 | 5 | 4 | 1 | 0 | $13,000 |
| | | | | | 1980 | 15 | 4 | 1 | 2 | $12,385 |

| | | | | | | | | | | | | | | | | | | | |
|---|---|---|---|---|---|---|---|---|---|---|---|---|---|---|---|---|---|---|---|
| 8Mar81-10Pen | fst | 5f | :22⅕ | :46 | :58⅘ | Clm 10000 | 4 | 6 | $5^{1¾}$ | $3^{3}$ | $3^{2}$ | $1^{no}$ | Egan R $R^{7}$ | b 106 | 7.20 | 92-21 | HawiinRegent$106^{no}$BrillintCounty$113^{nk}$ChristmsPrty$119^{4½}$ | Driving | 8 |
| 1Mar81- 1Pen | fst | 5f | :22⅗ | :47 | :59⅘ | Clm 8000 | 8 | 5 | $2^{½}$ | $2^{½}$ | $1^{1}$ | $1^{1½}$ | Egan R $R^{7}$ | b 108 | 5.90 | 87-21 | Hawaiian Regent $108^{1½}$ Missy's Chance$115^{no}$FourBits$115^{1}$ | Driving | 8 |
| 14Feb81- 7Pen | gd | 6f | :22⅘ | :46⅖ | 1:12⅘ | Clm 6250 | 4 | 6 | $1^{1}$ | $1^{½}$ | $1^{½}$ | $1^{2}$ | Egan R $R^{7}$ | b 112 | *2.10 | 80-30 | Hawaiian Regent $112^{2}$ Power Master $111^{nk}$ TimeTix$112^{4½}$ | Driving | 8 |
| 31Jan81- 7Pen | fst | 6f | :22⅗ | :45⅖ | 1:11 | Clm 6250 | 2 | 7 | $3^{1½}$ | $3^{2½}$ | $1^{hd}$ | $2^{½}$ | Egan R $R^{7}$ | b 108 | 5.30 | 88-19 | [D]Up Is O. K. $112^{½}$HawaiianRegent$108^{5}$[D]BettheLimit$114^{5}$ | Gamely | 8 |
| 31Jan81-Placed first through disqualification | | | | | | | | | | | | | | | | | | | |
| 26Jan81- 6Pen | fst | 5f | :22⅗ | :46⅗ | :59⅗ | Clm 5000 | 1 | 5 | $2^{1½}$ | $5^{3½}$ | $4^{3½}$ | $2^{3}$ | Egan R $R^{7}$ | b 106 | *2.00 | 86-18 | Hickory Cap $113^{3}$ Hawaiian Regent $106^{1}$ LuckyRuler$110^{nk}$ | Rallied | 7 |
| 28Dec80- 9Key | fst | 6f | :22⅗ | :46⅕ | 1:12⅗ 3↑ | Clm c-3500 | 1 | 5 | $9^{6¼}$ | $9^{7¾}$ | $4^{6}$ | $3^{1½}$ | Nied J Jr | b 119 | 5.40 | 77-22 | Wind Gauge $108^{hd}$ Jaime Jen $113^{1½}$ HawaiianRegent$119^{1½}$ | Rallied | 10 |
| 13Dec80- 4Key | fst | 7f | :22⅗ | :45⅘ | 1:25⅘ 3↑ | Clm 5000 | 11 | 1 | $2^{hd}$ | $4^{2}$ | $9^{7¾}$ | $9^{10}$ | Nied J Jr | b 119 | 10.70 | 68-21 | Tinsel Town $113^{1½}$ Quill Prince $113^{1½}$ Cosmopolitan $113^{hd}$ | Tired | 12 |
| 22Nov80- 2Key | fst | 6f | :22⅘ | :46⅗ | 1:13⅕ 3↑ | Clm 5000 | 1 | 11 | $1^{hd}$ | $2^{½}$ | $2^{1½}$ | $5^{3¼}$ | Merlino $J^{7}$ | b 115 | 3.70 | 73-19 | Take theStand$114^{¾}$NationsHonor$114^{1}$NearlyAMan$114^{1}$ | Weakened | 12 |

The steady rise in class from $5,000 claimer to $10,000 claimer of Hawaiian Regent is readily apparent from the *Daily Racing Form*. As we demonstrated in our descriptions of the different kinds of races, though, accurate appraisals of class require investigation of conditions and purses offered. Those facts, unfortunately, can only be obtained from results charts.

One clue available to the *Form* readers is the "company line," the names of the horses that finished first, second and third in each race. Recognition of the ability of horses stabled at a track gradually comes to those who make a habit of reading race results.

## JOCKEY

**Spectacular Bid** *    Gr. c. 3, by Bold Bidder—Spectacular, by Promised Land    Br.—Gilmore & Jason Nimes (Ky)    Tr.—Delp Grover G

Own.—Hawksworth Farm

| | | | | | | | | | | | |
|---|---|---|---|---|---|---|---|---|---|---|---|
| 8Sep73- 8Bel fst 1½ | :47½ 1:11 1:46½ | 3 ↑ Marlboro H | 5 3 1hd 1½ 13 15 | Shoemaker W | 124 | *.50 | 94–17 SpectacularBid124⁵GeneralAssembly120½Coastal122½ | Ridden out 6 |
| 15Aug73- 7Del gd 1½ | :46½ 1:11½ 1:41½ | Allowance | 3 3 2½ 1⁶ 112 117 | Shoemaker W | 122 | *.05 | 101–14 Spectacular Bid 122¹⁷ Armada Strike1127NotSoProud112⁶ Easily 5 |
| 9Jun73- 8Bel fst 1½ | :47½ 2:02½ 2:28¾ | Belmont | 3 2 2½ 13 2½ 33½ | Franklin R J | 126 | *.30 | 73–17 Coastal 126³¼ Golden Act 126⁴ᵏ Spectacular Bid 126³¼ Tired 5 |
| 19May73- 8Pim gd 1¼ | :46½ 1:10½ 1:54½ | Preakness | 2 4 45 1hd 16 15¼ | Franklin R J | 126 | *.10 | 99–09 Spectacular Bid 126⁵¼GoldenAct126⁴ScreenKing126½ Ridden out 5 |
| 5May73- 8CD fst 1¼ | :47½ 1:37½ 2:02¼ | Ky Derby | 3 7 6¹⁰ 2hd 11½ 12¾ | Franklin R J | 126 | *.60 | 85–14 SpectacularBid126²½GenerlAssembly126³GoldenAct126½ Driving 10 |
| 28Apr73- 7Kee fst 1½ | :46½ 1:10½ 1:50 | Blue Grass | 4 4 1hd 12 15½ 17 | Franklin R J | 121 | *.05 | 87–20 SpectaculrBid121⁷LotO'Gold121⁸Bishop'sChoice121¹⁰ Easily best 4 |
| 21Mar73-10Hia fst 1½ | :46 1:09½ 1:48½ | Flamingo | 8 3 1½ 1⁰ 1¹⁰ 112 | Franklin R J | 122 | *.05 | 90–16 SpectculrBid122¹²StrikeTheMin118³SirIvorAgin122ⁿᵈ Ridden out 8 |
| 3Mar73-11GP fst 1½ | :47½ 1:11½ 1:48½ | Fla Derby | 5 5 47½ 3½ 11½ 14¼ | Franklin R J | 122 | *.05 | 90–14 SpctculrBid122⁴¼LotO'Gold122¾Fntsy'NRlity122³ Four wide, clear 7 |
| 19Feb73- 9GP fst 1½ | :47¾ 1:10½ 4:41½ | Ftn Of Youth | 2 3 1hd 13 14 18½ | Franklin R J | 122 | *.10 | 95–12 SpectaculrBid122⁸¼LotO'Gold117³Bishop'sChoice122¹ Ridden out 6 |
| 7Feb73- 9GP fst 7f | :22½ :44½ 1:21½ | Hutcheson | 1 2 2hd 12 13 13½ | Franklin R J | 122 | *.05 | 97–22 SpectculrBid122³½LotO'Gold114⁷NorthernProspect114½¼ In hand 4 |

121 | St. 1st 2nd 3rd | Amt.
1979 10 9 0 1 $862,183
1978 9 7 1 0 $384,484

**LATEST WORKOUTS**    ● Oct 4 Pim   4f fst :47¾ h     ● Sep 30 Pim   5f fst :58½ h     Sep 26 Pim   1½m fst 1:50½ h     ● Sep 21 Del   6f fst 1:11½ h

Aside from the jockeys active at the major New York and California circuits, the ranks of competent riders at American racetracks are thin. Because trainers with live horses want the best possible riders, and because jockeys' agents want to see their clients on the best mounts, a handful of jockeys end up with most of the victories at any track. Most handicappers prefer to see one of these top riders or the current

"hot" apprentice on contenders. They consider it a sign of improving form when a trainer replaces a less talented rider with a top jockey. After his controversial trip in the Belmont Stakes, for example, young Ron Franklin was replaced as rider of Spectacular Bid by the great Bill Shoemaker, a move applauded by racing experts who wanted to see the gray colt perform up to his awesome potential.

## BLINKERS

**\*Caraquet**    Ch. g. 4, by Gulf Pearl—Dreamy Idea, by Double Jump    Br.—Ballykisteen Stud (Ire)    Tr.—Kuhn Marvin H

Own.—Hartenstein H W

| | | | | | | | | |
|---|---|---|---|---|---|---|---|---|
| 31Mar80- 5Pim fst 1½ | :48½ 1:14½ 1:49½ | Clm c-6500 | 6 4 46 11½ 12 13¾ | Imparato J | 114 | 3.50 | 57–31 Caraquet 114³¾ Sir Dignity 109¹ Monty G. 114⁸ Driving 7 |
| 22Mar80- 3Pim fst 1½ | :48½ 1:14¾ 1:46½ | Clm 5000 | 6 3 3³ 3½ 1hd 1¾ | Imparato J | 113 | 17.10 | 71–21 Caraquet 113¾ Count Jud 113⁴¼ Right Pot 113¼ Driving 9 |
| 17Mar80- 1Pim sly 1½ | :47½ 1:13¾ 1:48½ | Clm 3000 | 9 6 2¹½ 1½ 4¹½ 3¹½ | Adams J K | b 113 | 7.50 | 60–24 Big Chain 113¾ Flying Pass 119¹ Caraquet 113²½ Bore in 9 |
| 1Mar80- 1Bow fst 7f | :23 :46½ 1:25½ | Clm 3000 | 9 7 75¼ 7¹⁰ 6¹² 67¾ | Adams J K | b 113 | 18.40 | 72–18 Ronny Robot 106⁵ Double Quill 113¹ Foxbriar 113¹ No threat 12 |
| 15Feb80- 2Bow fst 1½ | :48½ 1:14¾ 1:54½ | Clm 5000 | 6 6 56½ 67½ 8¹¹ 8¹⁸ | Faine C⁷ | b 106 | 73.90 | 53–34 IvanSkvinsky113²½CountJud108²½PutThatGunAwy108¹ No threat 8 |
| 5Feb80- 2Bow fst 1½ | :49½ 1:14½ 1:49½ | Clm 5000 | 7 9 9¹³ 9¹² 5¹² 6¹⁴ | Adams J K | b 113 | 93.60 | 45–30 Lion Lamb 109⁷ Wincoma's Fiddle 113¾ Right Pot 114³¾ Outrun 12 |
| 28Jan80- 9Bow fst 6f | :23 :46½ 1:13 | Clm 6500 | 9 2 12⁹½12¹⁰12¹⁴12¹² | Adams J K | b 114 | 45.10 | 63–32 Easy Sweazy 113ⁿᵒ Nod For Love 119¹½ Sir Mort 114¼ Outrun 12 |
| 14Jan80- 5Bow fst 7f | :23 :46 1:25½ | Clm 11500 | 8 7 74¾ 7⁸ 10¹⁹11¹⁸ | Fazio J J | b 114 | 37.90e | 60–29 Pocketino 114¹ Oglesnops 114¹ Leeward Tilt 115²½ No factor 11 |
| 5Dec79- 9Grd fst 7f | :23¾ :49¾ 1:28¾ | 3 ↑ Clm 8000 | 10 10 10⁹¼10⁷¾ 64¾ 66½ | Latorre R | b 121 | 16.00 | 66–28 PoliticalPractice114½¼IrishReward117¾BidAndTell124²¾ No factor 9 |
| 27Nov79- 3Grd sl 7f | :24¾ :49¾ 1:30⅘ | 3 ↑ Clm 6250 | 3 3 4³ 3² 2² 1½ | Latorre R | b 121 | 6.15 | 61–35 Caraquet 121¾ Redeye Ray 117² Fiddling Leo 118⁶ Driving 6 |

110 | Turf Record    St. 1st 2nd 3rd | Amt.
St. 1st 2nd 3rd    1980 8 2 0 1 $8,340
6 1 1 1    1979 5 1 0 0 $3,120

**LATEST WORKOUTS**    Apr 10 Lrl   5f my 1:05⅘ b

Generally, the addition of blinkers is thought to promote early speed. The removal of blinkers, conversely, sometimes helps a horse relax early in a race and save

its energy for the finish. The removal of blinkers from Caraquet, for example, seems to have contributed to a substantial change in running style and in results.

## ODDS

**Affirmed** * — Ch. c. 4, by Exclusive Native—Won't Tell You, by Crafty Admiral
Own.—Harbor View Farm
Br.—Harbor View Farm (Fla)
Tr.—Barrera Lazaro S
**126**

| | St. | 1st | 2nd | 3rd | Amt. |
|---|---|---|---|---|---|
| 1979 | 7 | 5 | 1 | 1 | $800,200 |
| 1978 | 11 | 8 | 2 | 0 | $901,541 |

| | | | | | | | | | | | | | | | | | | | |
|---|---|---|---|---|---|---|---|---|---|---|---|---|---|---|---|---|---|---|---|
| 29Aug79- 0Bel | sly | 1 | :45 | 1:09⅗ | 1:34 | 3↑ Allowance | 3 | 1 | $1^{1/2}$ | $1^{1}$ | $1^{2}$ | $1^{6}$ | Pincay L Jr | 122 | | 98-15 | Affirmed $122^{6}$ Island Sultan $115^{14}$ Prefontaine 117 | Ridden out | 3 |
| 29Aug79-No wagering. Exhibition Race Run between 7th & 8th Races. | | | | | | | | | | | | | | | | | | | |
| 24Jun79- 8Hol | fst | 1¼ | :45⅗ | 1:34⅕ | 1:58⅗ | 3↑ Gold Cup H | 1 | 2 | $1^{hd}$ | $1^{hd}$ | $1^{hd}$ | $1^{3/4}$ | Pincay L Jr | 132 | *.30 | 99-13 | Affirmed $132^{3/4}$ Sirlad $120^{4}$ Text $119^{6}$ | Driving | 10 |
| 20May79- 8Hol | fst | 1⅛ | :44⅘ | 1:09⅕ | 1:41⅕ | 3↑ Californian | 2 | 1 | $1^{1}$ | $1^{1}$ | $1^{2}$ | $1^{5}$ | Pincay L Jr | 130 | *.30 | 89-16 | Affirmed $130^{5}$ Syncopate $114^{4}$ Harry's Love $117^{3/4}$ | Driving | 8 |
| 4Mar79- 8SA | fst | 1¼ | :46⅗ | 1:34⅕ | 1:58⅗ | S Anita H | 3 | 2 | $2^{1}$ | $1^{1/2}$ | $1^{4}$ | $1^{4 1/2}$ | Pincay L Jr | 128 | *1.30 | 103-09 | Affirmed $128^{4 1/2}$ Tiller $127^{3}$ [DH]Painted Wagon 115 | Speed to spare | 8 |
| 4Feb79- 8SA | gd | 1¼ | :47 | 1:35⅘ | 2:01 | C. H. Strub | 8 | 2 | $3^{1}$ | $1^{1}$ | $1^{2}$ | $1^{10}$ | Pincay L Jr | 126 | *.90 | 91-17 | Affirmed $126^{10}$ Johnny's Image $115^{4}$ Quip $115^{7}$ | Handily | 9 |
| 20Jan79- 8SA | gd | 1⅛ | :45⅗ | 1:09⅗ | 1:48 | San Fernando | 4 | 3 | $4^{9 1/2}$ | $5^{7 1/2}$ | $3^{3 1/2}$ | $2^{2 3/4}$ | Cauthen S | 126 | *.50 | 89-14 | Radar Ahead $123^{2 3/4}$ Affirmed $126^{nk}$ Little Reb $120^{4}$ | Drifted out | 8 |
| 7Jan79- 8SA | fst | 7f | :22⅘ | :45 | 1:21 | Malibu | 2 | 1 | $3^{2}$ | $3^{2 1/2}$ | $3^{2 1/2}$ | $3^{2 1/2}$ | Cauthen S | 126 | *.30 | 96-13 | Little Reb$120^{2 1/2}$RadarAhead$123^{hd}$Affirmed$126^{3}$ | Hemmed in to str. | 5 |
| 14Oct78- 8Bel | sly | 1½ | :45⅕ | 2:01⅘ | 2:27⅕ | 3↑ J C Gold Cup | 2 | 2 | $2^{hd}$ | $3^{7}$ | $4^{15}$ | $5^{10}$ | Cauthen S | 121 | 2.20e | 65-13 | Exceller$126^{no}$SeattleSlew$126^{14}$GretContrctor$126^{4 3/4}$ | Saddle slipped | 6 |
| 16Sep78- 8Bel | fst | 1⅛ | :47 | 1:10⅕ | 1:45⅘ | 3↑ Marlboro H | 1 | 2 | $2^{2 1/2}$ | $2^{2 1/2}$ | $2^{3}$ | $2^{3}$ | Cauthen S | 124 | *.50 | 95-12 | Seattle Slew $128^{3}$ Affirmed $124^{5}$ Nasty And Bold $118^{4}$ | No excuse | 6 |
| 19Aug78- 8Sar | fst | 1¼ | :48 | 1:36⅘ | 2:02 | Travers | 3 | 2 | $2^{hd}$ | $1^{1/2}$ | $1^{2}$ | $1^{1 3/4}$ | Pincay L Jr | 126 | *.70[D] | 91-14 | [D]Affirmed $126^{1 3/4}$ Alydar $126^{3 1/2}$ Nasty And Bold $126^{15}$ | Came over | 4 |
| 19Aug78-Disqualified and placed second | | | | | | | | | | | | | | | | | | | |

LATEST WORKOUTS Sep 20 Bel 4f fst :47 b Sep 15 Bel 7f fst 1:25⅕ b Sep 9 Bel 1⅛m fst 1:49⅕ h ●Sep 5 Bel 5f fst :58⅘ h

Surveys have shown that the public is a pretty shrewd handicapper. That is, horses win about as frequently as their odds indicate they should. The only exceptions are on the ends of the range. Perhaps because some horseplayers are looking for the "big payoff," longshots tend to be overbet; perhaps because of their low payoffs, odds-on favorites such as Affirmed tend to be underbet.

## WORKOUTS

**Flighty Passer** * — Dk. b. or br. g. 3, by Fast Passer—Honeys Flight, by Misty Flight
Own.—Dewitt Virginia
$20,000
Br.—Ritzenberg M (Va)
Tr.—DeWitt Virginia
**117**

| | St. | 1st | 2nd | 3rd | Amt. |
|---|---|---|---|---|---|
| 1979 | 10 | 2 | 0 | 1 | $12,195 |
| 1978 | 0 | M | 0 | 0 | |

| | | | | | | | | | | | | | | | | | | | |
|---|---|---|---|---|---|---|---|---|---|---|---|---|---|---|---|---|---|---|---|
| 17Sep79- 2Bel | fst | 6f | :22⅘ | :46⅕ | 1:11 | Clm 25000 | 9 | 4 | $4^{2}$ | $4^{5 1/2}$ | $6^{9 1/2}$ | $5^{12}$ | Maple S | b 117 | 19.30 | 75-21 | Ex Governor $117^{4}$ Pokie Joe $110^{1 3/4}$MidnightRacer$117^{3 1/2}$ | Weakened | 10 |
| 19Aug79- 9Sar | sly | 7f | :23⅕ | :46⅗ | 1:24⅘ | 3↑ Clm 16000 | 6 | 3 | $1^{1/2}$ | $1^{1}$ | $1^{3}$ | $1^{3}$ | Maple S | b 115 | 28.30 | 80-21 | Flighty Passer $115^{3}$ Pompini $113^{2 1/2}$ Plethora $117^{hd}$ | Ridden out | 9 |
| 15Jun79- 2Bel | fst | 7f | :23 | :46⅗ | 1:26 | Clm c-14000 | 9 | 5 | $2^{1}$ | $3^{2}$ | $9^{11}$ | $11^{21}$ | Velez R I | b 117 | 8.90 | 51-22 | NowAndLater$113^{3 3/4}$Bravo'sFlame$113^{3 3/4}$Topian$106^{1 1/2}$ | Roughed start | 11 |
| 15Jun79-Placed tenth through disqualification | | | | | | | | | | | | | | | | | | | |
| 29May79- 5Mth | fst | 6f | :22⅕ | :45⅗ | 1:11⅗ | Clm 16000 | 6 | 1 | $1^{hd}$ | $1^{1}$ | $2^{hd}$ | $3^{1}$ | Velez R I | b 119 | 5.90 | 82-20 | CelticTresure$116^{3/4}$RiseThRhythm$114^{nk}$FlightyPssr$119^{2}$ | Weakened | 6 |
| 21May79- 4Aqu | gd | 7f | :22⅗ | :45⅕ | 1:24⅘ | Clm 14000 | 9 | 1 | $8^{10}$ | $8^{12}$ | $8^{7 1/2}$ | $5^{3 3/4}$ | Martinez P $Jr^{10}$ | b 109 | 9.70 | 75-17 | Illegal Motion $115^{2 1/2}$ Bravo'sFlame$112^{3/4}$SkySpeeder$119^{1/2}$ | No factor | 9 |
| 27Apr79- 4Aqu | sly | 7f | :22 | :45⅗ | 1:25 | 3↑ Md 12000 | 11 | — | — | — | $2^{4}$ | $1^{3/4}$ | Martinez P $Jr^{5}$ | b 104 | 35.00 | 76-21 | Flighty Passer $104^{3/4}$ Italian John $117^{6 1/2}$ El Intrigante$122^{nk}$ | Driving | 12 |
| 11Apr79- 9Aqu | fst | 6f | :22⅗ | :46⅕ | 1:12 | 3↑ Md 12000 | 2 | 11 | $6^{6}$ | $5^{10}$ | $6^{12}$ | $5^{12}$ | Rolfe D $L^{5}$ | b 109 | 8.60 | 71-23 | Sky Speeder $113^{6 1/2}$ Gee Best $117^{1 1/2}$ Flamer $113^{2 3/4}$ | No rally | 11 |
| 15Mar79- 6Hia | fst | 6f | :22⅘ | :45⅘ | 1:10 | Clm 16000 | 4 | 8 | $5^{5}$ | $4^{6 1/2}$ | $6^{12}$ | $6^{19}$ | Guerra W $A^{7}$ | b 109 | 37.60 | 74-17 | CremeDeLFete$116^{12}$ForeignBrnch$111^{nk}$NewsChif$116^{1 1/2}$ | No factor | 8 |
| 1Mar79- 4GP | fst | 7f | :22⅗ | :45⅘ | 1:24 | Md 20000 | 11 | 10 | $7^{6}$ | $7^{7 1/2}$ | $8^{14}$ | $9^{20}$ | Venezia M | b 118 | 5.80 | 64-22 | Salute Royale $120^{6}$ The Assyrian $120^{6}$ Arctic Voyage $115^{3}$ | Outrun | 12 |
| 31Jan79- 4GP | fst | 6f | :21⅗ | :44⅘ | 1:09⅗ | Md Sp Wt | 10 | 10 | $8^{14}$ | $9^{17}$ | $9^{15}$ | $9^{16}$ | Cruguet J | 120 | 51.00 | 75-16 | Gallant Serenade $120^{3/4}$ Bolger $120^{2}$ Captain Clay $120^{2 1/2}$ | Outrun | 12 |

LATEST WORKOUTS Aug 14 Bel tr.t 6f fst 1:17⅘ h ●Aug 9 Bel tr.t 6f fst 1:15 h Aug 5 Bel tr.t 6f sly 1:19⅘ b Jly 31 Bel tr.t 6f fst 1:18 b

The *Daily Racing Form* clocks and publishes workouts conducted at North American tracks. Stories about the workouts that the clockers missed or mistimed are like stories of the fish that got away—such rumors are usually exaggerated. The clockers, with the cooperation of trainers, catch the vast majority of morning trials.

Like final times of races, workout times vary substantially depending on track conditions, weight of the exercise rider, type of saddle and equipment used, how far from the rail the horse raced, and what the pace of the workout was. Betting on one horse over another because its workout was a second or two faster is foolish. Only occasionally, for example, does an outstanding workout like that turned in by Flighty Passer on August 9 indicate a sharp form reversal. Much more important is the frequency and pattern of workouts. Frequent workouts are a positive sign of fitness, and many handicappers like to see a race or workout per week.

One valuable indication of the way a horse is training is the comment line underneath the daily reports of workouts. A sample appears on p. 326:

## BELMONT PARK — Track Fast

| Three Furlongs | | | | Four Furlongs | | | | Five Furlongs | |
|---|---|---|---|---|---|---|---|---|---|
| Bing | :36⅗ b | Speed City | :36 h | Folge | :50⅗ b | Admiral Rix | 1:02 h | | |
| Celia Bonita | :35½ h | Stand Firm | :37⅗ b | Free Again | :46⅗ h | Bang the Drums | 1:00 h | | |
| ChampgneMooa | :36⅗ b | Sue Babe | :37⅗ b | Friendly Frolic | :50 b | Flying South | 1:05 b | | |
| Clint Maroon | :37⅗ b | Sweet Cyane | :39⅗ b | Fun Worthy | :49⅗ b | Forever Sparkle | 1:01 b | | |
| Con Celia | :34⅘ b | Topical | :37⅗ b | Harrowing | :49 b | Invigorating | 1:01 b | | |
| Culcita | :37⅗ b | Torsion Messàge | :38 b | Heavenly Cause | :48⅗ b | KingofMardiGras | 1:00⅕ h | | |
| Dandy Current | :36½ h | Trieze | :37⅗ b | Jay Bird | :49 hg | Silent Dignity | 1:00 h | | |
| DeterminedMary | :36½ h | Turnstone | :36 hg | Jet Lag Jane | :48⅗ hg | Singularity | 1:03 b | | |
| Distinctive King | :35⅗ h | Two Cents Extra | :35⅗ b | Joe Montage | :47⅗ h | Sir Ivor Again | 1:02 b | | |
| Dont Tell Mama | :36½ b | Veiled Prophet | :36⅗ b | Judge Henderon | :49⅗ b | Suite of Dreams | 1:03⅗ b | | |
| Eleutheros | :37⅗ b | Will of Iron | :35⅗ h | Key to Content | :49⅗ b | Switcheroo | 1:03⅗ b | | |
| Ellen Terry | :37⅗ b | Wycoff | :35⅗ h | Lionize | :49⅗ b | Tanthem | 1:02 b | | |
| French Colonial | :38⅗ b | **Four Furlongs** | | Little Linny | :49⅗ hg | Tweak | 1:03½ b | | |
| Gleaming Jewels | :39 b | AnonymousPrinc | :49⅗ b | Lord Darnly | :49⅗ bg | WanderingCloud | 1:02½ b | | |
| Gleaming Smile | :39 b | Belongingness | :53⅗ b | Majestic Robert | :50 hg | What A Year | 1:02 b | | |
| Hammerhead | :38 b | Blitey | :49⅗ b | Onalaska | :47⅗ h | **Six Furlongs—1:08¾** | | | |
| High Jinxs | :37 b | Bowl Game | :47⅗ b | Premier Ministre | :49⅗ b | Groton High | 1:18 b | | |
| James Boxwell | :35⅗ b | Bowstring | :53 b | Present | :48 b | Honest Moment | 1:12⅗ h | | |
| Laurial | :38⅗ b | Buck O Halperin | :49⅗ b | Prince Robair | :51⅗ b | Indeed Gallant | 1:13⅗ h | | |
| Lets Have Fun | :37⅗ b | Cannibal | :48⅗ hg | Proud Reason | :53 b | Relaxing | 1:12 h | | |
| Like A Tiger | :38 b | Chieffo | :49 b | Rightful Ruler | :48⅗ h | Rose of Morn | 1:15 b | | |
| Mark's Mill | :37⅗ b | Crazy Chief | :48 b | Savage Mac | :51 b | **Seven Furlongs—1:20½** | | | |
| Napur | :35⅗ h | Dancinginthedrk | :49⅗ h | Startop Ace | :49 hg | Worth A Bet | 1:30½ b | | |
| Promising Star | :35⅗ h | Debussy | :48⅗ hg | Thin Slice | :48 b | **1 Mile—1:33⅘** | | | |
| Sea Holme | :35⅗ h | Early Settler | :52 b | Tudor Tarheel | :50⅗ hg | Damask Fan | 1:46 b | | |
| SilverProspector | :35⅗ h | Easter Thunder | :49⅗ h | Valiant Order | :49 b | | | | |
| SomethingUniqu | :37⅗ b | Farewell Letter | :50⅗ b | Whyte Angle | :50⅗ b | | | | |
| | | Flitalong | :48 b | Winter's Tale | :47⅗ h | | | | |

**CON CELIA** (3f) was full of run. **BOWL GAME** (4f) is doing well. **CRAZY CHIEF** (4f) holds his form. **HONEST MOMENT** (6f) acts good. **RELAXING** (6f) went evenly.

Horses mentioned in the above comments are worth watching. Also, because past performances only list the horse's last four workouts, handicappers looking for patterns keep files of daily reports of workouts, or index cards listing a horse's yearly workouts.

## THE TRACK PROGRAM

The track program is the only source for final program numbers, weights, scratches and jockey assignments. The listing for each horse also includes the colors of the racing silks to be worn by the jockey—helpful information for fans who want to identify the horses they're watching through the binoculars.

Perhaps because fans have to buy a program to get the information above, track managements haven't seen fit to include other kinds of information that would be of great assistance in handicapping races and making a day at the races more enjoyable. Alone among major sports managements, the administrators of Thoroughbred racetracks seem to feel that it's the fan's responsibility to keep vital statistics on the participants. While harness tracks print complete, up-to-date records of all trainers and drivers, no Thoroughbred track provides the records for more than a handful of top trainers and jockeys. Less than a third of the programs compute the win percentages of those listed. While all harness programs include up-to-date post-position surveys, only two of twenty programs we recently reviewed contained that information. Few programs even provide a complete diagram of seating and other spectator facilities; thus, the first-time racegoer is forced to wander around to find out what the track has to offer.

## THE MORNING LINE

In the days before pari-mutuel wagering, bookmakers survived through the keenness of their handicapping. Before a single bet was taken on a race, bookmakers had to post an opening "line" on each horse, this line being the odds at which he would accept bets. While the odds were later adjusted to reflect actual betting, the bookie was committed to paying off bets taken at his original figures. Those that couldn't accurately predict how the public would bet ended up bankrupt.

Today, the pari-mutuel system has replaced bookmaking, and the public, through its actual wagering, sets the odds on each horse. In each track program, though, the listing for each horse contains "probable odds," otherwise known as the "morning line." This morning line is a throwback to the opening line of the bookmaker, in that it is an attempt to predict the final odds the public will set for each horse. It is not an attempt to handicap the race itself.

The accuracy of the morning line varies considerably from track to track, depending on the ability of the person who prepares it. Even the best practitioners of this art are beset by the same problems as public selectors—they don't have the benefit of late scratches, late weather conditions, observing the horses in the paddock, etc. For these reasons, the morning line is an extremely unreliable handicapping tool, and systems that purport to pick winners by relating actual odds to the morning line are total wastes of time.

---

Track managements counter the above argument by saying that most racegoers haven't asked for this kind of information, and adding more material would increase the program cost. They do not seem to believe that the more educated fans are, the more interested they become. In any case, an additional 35¢ for a track program is not a lot to pay for information that helps a horseplayer select more wisely the horses on which he or she wagers an average of $120 per day.

### How to Read the Program

A typical page of the daily program at The Meadowlands is shown on page 328. The information on the left explains what appears on the racing program in each race and can be utilized for identifying the horses and for wagering purposes. The page is of the 1978 Young America.

## PERSONAL NOTEBOOK

One's personal observations are among the best handicapping tools. Recording these observations is an excellent learning experience, for amid the noise and excitement of the track, details soon slip from even the best of memories.

Particularly important are notes on the way horses look and behave in the paddock and during warm-ups. Comparing these notes with actual performances of the horses will soon help a racegoer discern obviously unfit or unruly animals that have little chance to win.

Notebooks can also help handicap subsequent races. No matter how good chart callers may be, oversights or space limitations lead to the omission of important details about problems certain horses faced. If a horse's actual performance was better than the past performances and the results chart indicated, the horse may go off at odds higher than they should be.

## DAILY NEWSPAPERS

The coverage of Thoroughbred racing in daily newspapers is scanty at best. Many print only race results and a list of entries taken from the "overnight sheet" provided by the track. While some print condensed charts purchased from the *Daily Racing Form,* these seldom contain the information needed to compile trainer profiles.

While daily newspapers can't be expected to provide the wealth of statistical information compiled by the *Daily Racing Form,* they should provide the kind of hard reporting on racing that they give to fans of other major sports. However, many trackmen assigned by newspapers are handicappers instead of reporters. They concentrate on making daily selections instead of seeking stories beyond information contained in the track's press releases. Racing and racegoers would benefit from much more of the entertaining, skilled reporting provided by excellent journalist-handicappers such as Ray Kerrison of the New York

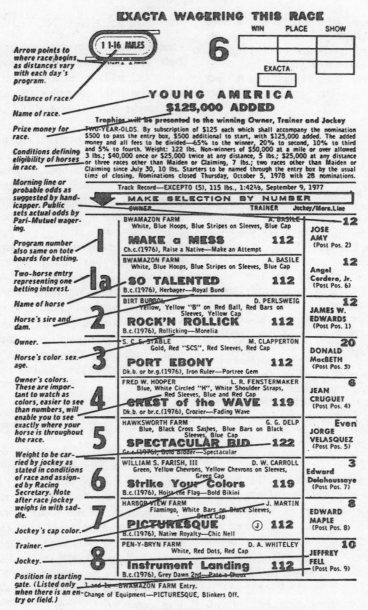

**EXACTA WAGERING THIS RACE**

| | WIN | PLACE | SHOW |
|---|---|---|---|

**6**

EXACTA

Arrow points to where race begins, as distances vary with each day's program.

Distance of race.

Name of race.

Prize money for race.

Conditions defining eligibility of horses in race.

Morning line or probable odds as suggested by handicapper. Public sets actual odds by Pari-Mutuel wagering.

Program number also same on tote boards for betting.

Two-horse entry representing one betting interest.

Name of horse.

Horse's sire and dam.

Owner.

Horse's color, sex, age.

Owner's colors. These are important to watch as colors, easier to see than numbers, will enable you to see exactly where your horse is throughout the race.

Weight to be carried by jockey as stated in conditions of race and assigned by Racing Secretary. Note after race jockey weighs in with saddle.

Jockey's cap color.

Trainer.

Jockey.

Position in starting gate. (Listed only when there is an entry or field.)

1 1-16 MILES   START ▲ ▲ FINISH

**YOUNG AMERICA**
**$125,000 ADDED**

Trophies will be presented to the winning Owner, Trainer and Jockey

TWO-YEAR-OLDS. By subscription of $125 each which shall accompany the nomination $500 to pass the entry box, $500 additional to start, with $125,000 added. The added money and all fees to be divided—65% to the winner, 20% to second, 10% to third and 5% to fourth. Weight: 122 lbs. Non-winners of $50,000 at a mile or over allowed 3 lbs.; $40,000 once or $25,000 twice at any distance, 5 lbs.; $25,000 at any distance or three races other than Maiden or Claiming, 7 lbs.; two races other than Maiden or Claiming since July 30, 10 lbs. Starters to be named through the entry box by the usual time of closing. Nominations closed Thursday, October 5, 1978 with 28 nominations.

Track Record—EXCEPTO (5), 115 lbs., 1:42⅖, September 9, 1977

**MAKE SELECTION BY NUMBER**

OWNER     TRAINER     Jockey/Morn.Line

**1** — BWAMAZON FARM    A. BASILE
White, Blue Hoops, Blue Stripes on Sleeves, Blue Cap
**MAKE a MESS** 112
Ch.c.(1976), Raise a Native—Make an Attempt
JOSE AMY 12 (Post Pos. 2)

**1a** — BWAMAZON FARM    A. BASILE
White, Blue Hoops, Blue Stripes on Sleeves, Blue Cap
**SO TALENTED** 112
B.c.(1976), Herbager—Royal Bund
Angel Cordero, Jr. 12 (Post Pos. 6)

**2** — BIRT BURBOL    D. PERLSWEIG
Yellow, Yellow "B" on Red Ball, Red Bars on Sleeves, Yellow Cap
**ROCK'N ROLLICK** 112
B.c.(1976), Rollicking—Monelia
JAMES W. EDWARDS 12 (Post Pos. 1)

**3** — S. C. S. STABLE    M. CLAPPERTON
Gold, Red "SCS", Red Sleeves, Red Cap
**PORT EBONY** 112
Dk.b. or br.g.(1976), Iron Ruler—Portree Gem
DONALD MacBETH 20 (Post Pos. 3)

**4** — FRED W. HOOPER    L. R. FENSTERMAKER
Blue, White Circled "H", White Shoulder Straps, Red Sleeves, Blue and Red Cap
**CREST of the WAVE** 119
Dk.b. or br.c.(1976), Crozier—Fading Wave
JEAN CRUGUET 6 (Post Pos. 4)

**5** — HAWKSWORTH FARM    G. G. DELP
Blue, Black Cross Sashes, Blue Bars on Black Sleeves, Blue Cap
**SPECTACULAR BID** 122
Gr.c.(1976), Bold Bidder—Spectacular
JORGE VELASQUEZ Even (Post Pos. 5)

**6** — WILLIAM S. FARISH, III    D. W. CARROLL
Green, Yellow Chevrons, Yellow Chevrons on Sleeves, Green Cap
**Strike Your Colors** 119
B.c.(1976), Hoist the Flag—Bold Bikini
Edward Delahoussaye 3 (Post Pos. 7)

**7** — HARBOR VIEW FARM    J. MARTIN
Flamingo, White Bars on Black Sleeves, Black Cap
**PICTURESQUE** Ⓙ 112
B.c.(1976), Native Royalty—Chic Nell
EDWARD MAPLE 8 (Post Pos. 8)

**8** — PEN-Y-BRYN FARM    D. A. WHITELEY
White, Red Dots, Red Cap
**Instrument Landing** 112
B.c.(1976), Grey Dawn 2nd—Pate a Choux
JEFFREY FELL 10 (Post Pos. 9)

1 and 1a—BWAMAZON FARM Entry.
Change of Equipment—PICTURESQUE, Blinkers Off.

**Selections 5—6—4—7**

---

*Post*, Russ Harris of the New York *Daily News* and Dave Feldman of the Chicago *Sun-Times*.

## PUBLIC SELECTORS

Relying solely on the selections of newspaper handicappers, *Daily Racing Form* selectors or tip sheets to make one's bets is like going out to the golf course, paying the greens fee and caddy fee, and then watching someone else play. Doing one's own handicapping is the best way to maximize one's enjoyment of racing.

It's also the only way to profit from betting on horses. Professional selectors work under severe handicaps, being forced to make their selections before final scratches,

racecourse where spectators met to wager, became known as the Tattersalls.

Shortly after 1800, a new kind of bettor began to appear in the Tattersalls. These "legs," as they were called, invented the principle of laying bets at different prices on every horse in the field. This practice was first called "making the rounds"; then, because the "legs" had to keep careful records of their wagers, the phrase "making a book" was used.

These "bookmakers" could make a decent profit if they were able to obtain the right balance of bets on all contenders. They soon realized, however, that the surest way to make big money was to ensure that the favorite, on which most of the money was bet, didn't win the race. Bribery of jockeys and drugging of horses became rampant, as did the substitution of ringers. Settling disputes concerning allegations of misdeeds became a full-time job for the members of the Jockey Club. Finally, the Jockey Club washed its hands of such affairs in 1842. Under the stern, morally upright leadership of Admiral Rous, the organization concentrated, successfully, on cleaning up racing. As racing became more honest, the honest bookmaker began to appear in the Tattersalls.

While plenty of person-to-person wagering took place in early American racing, another form of betting called the auction pool was very popular prior to the Civil War. To form the pool, a "betting interest" in each horse would be auctioned to the highest bidder. Generally, the horses with the best chances to win attracted the largest bids. The auctioneer took a portion of the total pool as his commission, then the rest went to the "owner" of the winning horse.

The problem with auctions was that bettors didn't know the odds they would end up with until after all the horses were auctioned off. The desire to get a pre-determined price led to the increasing popularity of bookmakers after the Civil War. At the major tracks, these bookmakers tended to be honest. At the numerous smaller tracks that sprang up all over the country, the kind of chicanery that had plagued racing in Britain was common. Bookmakers' abusive practices in large part led to the wave of anti-gambling sentiment that shut down so many tracks in the early 1900s.

## HOW BOOKMAKING WORKS

In person-to-person wagering, the odds agreed upon determine the percentage of money each party puts up. If two people agree that a horse's chances of winning are 3–1, the person betting on the horse puts up 25 percent of the total "pool" while the person betting against the horse puts up 75 percent. The winner of the bet gets his stake returned, plus the total of the money bet by the loser or losers.

Obviously, someone who sets up in the business of taking bets can't afford to pay out all the money he takes in, because that would leave no profit. Instead, bookmakers set their odds to obtain a total percentage of money bet that would be over 100 percent, with the amount over that figure being their profit. The example below is a five-horse race:

| ODDS OFFERED | PERCENTAGE | MONEY COLLECTED |
|---|---|---|
| 1–1 | 50% | $100 |
| 3–1 | 25 | 50 |
| 4–1 | 20 | 40 |
| 9–1 | 10 | 20 |
| 19–1 | 5 | 10 |
| | 115% | $230 |

If the bookmaker offered true odds, he would return $130 to the person who wagered $100, making the payoff $1.30 for every $1.00 wagered. However, he offers only 1–1 odds, paying off $100 for the $100 wagered if that horse finishes first. The additional $30 left in the pool is the bookmaker's profit, or "commission."

The sharper bookmakers used their keen knowledge of handicapping to secure high percentages and high profits. They would offer higher-than-normal odds to elicit wagers on horses that had no chance to win, while dropping the odds on clear favorites to a minimum. As wagers were placed before a race, bookmakers sent runners to keep abreast of the progress of betting around the ring, changing their odds to protect themselves.

The major disadvantage faced by bookmakers was that laying fixed odds left them vulnerable to shrewder handicappers with big money to wager. The most famous bettor of the nineteenth century, "Pittsburg Phil," won an estimated $3 million by taking advantage of bookmakers. "Phil" would send anonymous confederates to place small wagers on other horses to boost the odds on the horse he thought would win. Then these confederates would simultaneously place large wagers at the high odds. The bookmakers had no time to adjust their odds, which then sank to nothing for small bettors, who found themselves caught between the bookmakers and the big gamblers.

Although some bookmakers who took unnecessary risks went bankrupt, most made huge profits. The big gamblers benefited from the system also. However, a significant part of the betting public distrusted bookmakers and disliked the constant feeling of being taken advantage of.

## OFF-TRACK BETTING

All the way around the world, from the granite rotunda of Grand Central Station in midtown Manhattan to England, France, Japan, Australia and back to Puerto Rico, government agencies offer horse racing's primary patron, the bettor, the convenience of wagering his money around the corner from home, rather than at the track. Off-track betting not only attempts to curtail illegal bookmaking, in which bettors take the risk of being cheated out of their bets, it also generates extra revenues for local governments. In the United States, all legal off-track betting organizations are Public Benefit Corporations, the revenues of which are plowed directly back into city and state budgets and the state racing and breeding industries.

New York City was the first location in the United States to institute off-track betting. In its first ten years of operation, it became the largest retail business in New York City, outselling even Bloomingdale's and Macy's. In the 1980 fiscal year, New York City's 156 OTB parlors accepted a record of $893.9 million worth of bets on flat and harness racing, earning $60.2 million for the city, $19.2 million for the state, $8.9 million for local governments and $49.5 million for the racing industry and state breeding fund.

Due mainly to the success of New York City OTB, five other OTB corporations were approved by the state legislature and licensed by the state for operation in Nassau County (25 offices), Suffolk County (26 offices), Catskill Region (24 offices), Western Region (65 offices), and the Capital Region (41 offices). All six New York State OTB Corporations are separate entities, both financially and administratively. Nevertheless, they are connected by telephone wires and computers, take the same bets, and give the same odds and paybacks.

The bettor who walks into a New York branch office of OTB to place a bet has the option of wagering on the day's card of races from various harness and Thoroughbred tracks in New York and New Jersey. On Tuesdays, when New York tracks are dark, he or she may bet on selected cards from tracks such as Keystone in Pennsylvania and Calder in Florida, with which OTB has agreements. Races with special appeal, such as the Kentucky Derby, are also offered by OTB. In out-of-state wagering, New York City and New York State receive their normal cut of the take.

The only state other than New York to have legalized OTB is Connecticut, which has an entirely different organization and offers teletrack coverage of New York races. With teletrack, bettors pay an admission fee, just as at the track, to enter a theater in which the day's races from Belmont, Aqueduct or whatever card is being offered are projected on a large screen. Bettors place wagers at ticket windows and may buy food and drink in booths in the theater. Although New York does not yet offer teletrack, many proponents of racing believe that it is the key to the growth of the Thoroughbred industry.

In New York, bettors who do not wish to go to the trouble of going to their OTB office can open OTB telephone accounts and bet over the phone until the cash in their account runs out. No matter how a person wishes to bet at OTB, he or she must place a wager of at least $2.00. There is no upper limit. Bets must be placed on the day of the race, before post time. All the varieties of exotic wagering offered at the track are also available at OTB. However, if the bettor cashes a really big winning ticket, OTB will ask for his social security number and report his winnings to the IRS.

In the eighties, OTB hopes to branch out into other sports, offering wagering on football, basketball and other non-horse-related competitions. Whether this will be sanctioned by the state and what effect casino gambling, if it is legalized, will have on racing and on OTB still remain to be seen. Certainly, however, the trend in racing's next decade is television-oriented and OTB is prepared to get in on the ground floor. Simulcasting—broadcasting the call of the race and simultaneously airing the video in OTB parlors—is expected to become a new and pleasant feature for OTB patrons. If network television begins to broadcast racing, as many in the industry hope it does, the day may soon arrive when a bettor can call in a bet, watch the race and collect the winnings (which will be credited to a telephone account), all from the comfort of a favorite armchair.

## THE DEVELOPMENT OF THE PARI-MUTUEL SYSTEM

Among those who resented the high percentage taken out by bookmakers was a Paris perfume merchant named Pierre Oller. Oller believed that the fairest wagering system was one in which the actual odds would be determined by the ratio of the money bet on one horse to the money bet on all the other horses. He proceeded to set himself up in the business of collecting what he called "mutual wagers" or, in French, "pari-mutuels." For his services, Oller deducted 5 percent of the total money bet.

The system proved popular with small bettors, who were comforted by the knowledge that 95 percent of the money would be returned to the winners. The system was also logical, mathematical and easily understood. Oller built "pari-mutuel" machines, which issued tickets and recorded the number of bets made on each horse. Payoffs were computed after each race.

In 1877, the pari-mutuel system was given tryouts in the United States, first at Morris and Jerome Parks in New York, and then at several other tracks, but the fierce opposition of bookmakers resulted in the experiments being dropped by track managements. However, in 1908, as we explained in our history of the Kentucky Derby, promotional genius Col. Matt Winn dusted off old pari-mutuel machines to get around a Louisville City Council ban on bookmaking. The experiment was successful, and it spread to other states, where abuses by bookmakers had led to the banning of gambling. By 1941, when New York State banned bookmaking, pari-mutuel wagering was the only form of horse-race betting permitted at American tracks.

## THE PARI-MUTUEL SYSTEM TODAY

In 1980, 55 million horseplayers poured $7.2 billion through the windows at North American tracks, an average of $129 per day per bettor. The percentage of this total "handle" taken off the top of the mutuel pool has climbed from Pierre Oller's 5 percent to an average of 17 percent on straight bets and up to 25 percent on "exotic" wagering.

The development of wagering other than the traditional win, place and show betting has been controversial. While track managements argue that such forms of betting are vital to sustain the current level of handle, other racing experts decry the "lottery" atmosphere they've given to racing and blame exotic betting for the recent spate of race-fixing accusations involving some of the nation's best-known riders.

## HOW PAYOFFS ARE CALCULATED

The advantage of playing the horses as opposed to most forms of casino gambling is that at the track one is playing against other bettors instead of against a fixed house percentage that assures losing in the long run. The disadvantage is that the high percentage of pari-mutuel takeout, combined with an unfair method of rounding off payoffs, means that only a small percentage of bettors end up winning in the long run.

For our example of how payoffs are calculated, we're going to use a win pool of $100,000 at a track where the takeout percentage is 17 percent. We'll assume that the winner of the race attracted a total of $40,000 in bets. If *no percentage* were taken off the top, the people who put up that $40,000 would win the $60,000 put up by the losers. For each $1.00 they bet, they would get back $1.50. Thus, the "true" odds would be 1.5–1, or, in track terms, 3–2. The payoff on a $2.00 win ticket would be $3.00 plus the $2.00 original wager, which makes a total payoff of $5.00.

To compute the actual payoff, however, we must first *deduct the 17 percent* that goes to the track, to the state and to horsemen's purses from the total mutuel pool:

$100,000×.17=$17,000

```
   $100,000 total pool
 −   17,000 to track, etc.
   ─────────
   $ 83,000 to be distrib-
            uted
```

Next, the $40,000 wagered by the public must be set aside to be returned to them:

```
   $83,000
 −  40,000
   ────────
   $43,000 net profit to be distributed
```

This $43,000 is then *divided by* the $40,000 wagered to determine the return for every one dollar wagered:

$$\$43,000 \div \$40,000 = \$1.07$$

Thus, the 17 percent takeout reduced the payoff from $1.50 on $1.00 to $1.07 on $1.00—a 43-cent or 29 percent reduction in profit.

That's burdensome enough, but tracks use another procedure that reduces the payout further. Arguing that handling pennies is too difficult for mutuel clerks and patrons, tracks *round off the payment,* a technique called "breakage." At first, tracks "broke" payoffs to the next lowest *nickel* (nickel breakage). Using nickel breakage, the $1.07 would be "broken" to $1.05. The profit on two dollars would be $2.10 instead of $2.14, another 1 percent profit for the track on top of the 17 percent already deducted.

Not satisfied with nickel breakage, however, tracks came up with the much more onerous *dime breakage.* Under this hard-to-justify system, all payoffs for $1.00 wagered were broken to the nearest dime. Thus, the $1.07 payoff would be broken to $1.00. Instead of winning $2.14, the bettor now wins just $2.00. Dime breakage in this case has given the track an additional 3 percent on top of the 17 percent. The odds paid by the winner are now 1–1, or even money; the return, $2.00 profit plus the original $2.00 wager, is $4.00. The track has kept $20,000 of the original $100,000 pool.

The cumulative effects over a nine- or ten-race program of this high takeout plus breakage are startling. On a race day when the public brings $300,000 in cash to the track, the handle will be about $1,000,000. Through the course of the day, this $300,000 is recirculated through the windows, shrinking, of course, with the takeout on every race. Assuming breakage averages 1.5 percent on top of the 17 percent takeout, the total dollar takeout on a handle of $1,000,000 is $185,000. When this is subtracted from the $300,000, bettors go home with $115,000. The public lost 62 percent of its money; the guy who brought a $20 bill went home with $7.66.

The figures above vividly demonstrate why the racing industry has vigorously argued for a reduction in takeout percentage. For every 1 percent the takeout is reduced, the public would go home with about 3.5 percent more money. The New York Racing Association's experiment with a reduction in takeout from 17 percent to 14 percent gave the average bettor more than a 10 percent break.

## THE PHILOSOPHY OF BETTING

Given the high percentage of betting capital eroded by the pari-mutuel takeout, making money requires a lot more than just picking winners. Rather, it means seeking out situations in which the handicapper believes that the odds established by the general public are substantially higher than the horse's actual chances of winning the race. In other words, the handicapper looks for a horse going off at 5–1 that really has a 2–1 chance to win the race. In racing, this situation is known as an *overlay*.

An *underlay,* on the other hand, is a situation in which a horse has been overbet. For example, a horse that really has a 2–1 chance to win goes off at 1–1. Many horseplayers seek to take advantage of underlays by betting against short-priced favorites.

The chances of finding overlays and the difficulties involved in the search vary with the different types of bets.

### Win Betting

Most experts consider win wagering the "best bet" in horse racing. The primary reason is that the updating of actual odds every thirty seconds allows a handicapper to make the most accurate assessment of *risk* versus *return* before placing a bet.

Surveys of race results demonstrate that the public does an excellent job of hand-

icapping. Nationally, favorites chosen by bettors win about 33 percent of all races, a percentage higher than that attained by 99 percent of all public selectors. Betting on all favorites produces about a 10 percent loss—not desirable, but much better than the statistical average of more than 17 percent produced by the takeout percentage.

Most surveys have also found that, by and large, horses win about as often as the public believes they should. That is, a horse on which 25 percent of the money is wagered wins about 25 percent of the time. Of course, because of the pari-mutuel takeout, a horse that receives 25 percent of the wagering goes off not at the "true" odds of 3–1, but at 2.32–1. That's why the average bet produces a 17 percent loss.

### Place and Show Betting

Handicapper Robert Dowst believed that any handicapper good enough to make money on place and show wagering could get a much higher return betting only to win. While place and show wagering produces more winning tickets, payoffs are considerably lower than on win bets. Also, because actual payoffs depend on which horses actually finish in the money, measuring risk versus return, the vital step in making money at the track, is extremely difficult.

Before explaining why place and show bets are statistically less attractive, we'll show how place bets are computed. We'll assume that the horse that paid $4.00 to win (the example we used above) had an equal percentage of money wagered on him in the place pool. Assuming a place pool of $50,000, that would mean that $20,000 was bet on the winner. And we'll assume that the horse that finished second was a longer-priced horse that attracted only $5,000 in bets.

The first step is taking the 17 percent off the top:

$50,000×.17=$8,500   $50,000 total pool
                     —   8,500 to track, etc.
                     ————————————————
                     $41,500 gross distribution

Next, the track subtracts the money wagered on each horse, a total of $25,000:

$41,500
− 25,000
_____
$16,500 winnings to be distributed

This $16,500 is *divided equally* between the people who wagered on each horse. This resulting $8,250 is then divided by the dollar amounts wagered on each horse, to determine the gross profit:

Winner:      $8,250÷$20,000=$.41 profit for each $1.00
Place Horse: $8,250÷$5,000=$1.65 profit for each $1.00

Then, the dime breakage is applied to each gross profit to determine net profit:

$.41 rounds to $.40 on $1.00
$1.65 rounds to $1.60 on $1.00

While the breakage in this example is not high, suppose the gross profit for the winner were $.39. That would be broken to $.30, taking away almost 25 percent of the bettor's return.

Finally, the payoffs for a $2.00 bet are double the profit per dollar, plus the original wager. The winner pays $2.80 to place; the second-place finisher pays $5.20.

Show payoffs are computed in the same manner, except that the profit is divided into *thirds*.

The first major problem with place and show wagering is that the odds are impossible to determine ahead of time. In the above example, the horse that paid 1–1 to win paid 2–5 to place. If a horse that had attracted $10,000 in place wagering had finished second, however, the payoff would have been 1–5. While a handicapper looking at the odds board can weigh a 1–1 payoff against his estimation of the horse's chances to win, he can't accurately estimate the payoff he'll get by betting to place. With a 1–5 profit, he'd have to believe the horse had an 85 percent or better chance to finish first or second, a rather strong vote of confidence.

Compounding the problem is the effect of double breakage on place bets, and triple breakage on show wagering. Because breakage is separately applied, the track's percentage is higher on place and show wagering than on win betting.

Smart bettors can take advantage of place and show wagering in two special situations, however. Because most horseplayers bet to win, sometimes horses going off at 1–2 or less to win will pay about the same to place. The bettor takes less risk for the same reward in such a situation by making a place wager.

Secondly, a few bettors with a lot of capital take advantage of laws requiring tracks to pay at least $2.10 on a $2.00 bet. If the actual amount of money wagered on a horse is so high that the payoff computes to less than $2.10, the track must come up with the money to lift the payoff to that level. This situation is referred to as a "minus pool." At some tracks, bettors seeking a quick 5 percent return have bet as much as $100,000 on an overwhelming favorite to show. The problem is that no horse is a sure thing. These overwhelming favorites sometimes finish out of the money, and the $100,000 takes a long time to recoup.

**The Daily Double**

The daily double was the first multiple wagering to be introduced at American tracks. Traditionally, the daily double involves picking the winners of the first two races on the program. Some tracks offer "late doubles" on the last two races on the card.

Serious horseplayers seldom place a large wager on a daily double. For one thing, picking the winners of two successive races is much more difficult than picking the winners of any two races on the card. Secondly, seldom do two "bettable" races appear as the first and second races on the program.

The relatively recent and much welcome practice of showing approximate daily double payoffs on closed circuit television monitors has led some mathematically minded bettors to specialize in the daily double and other multiple wagers. These horseplayers first handicap a race to predict what each horse in a race should pay to win. Then they compute what a *parlay* on each combination would pay. Parlaying wagers means reinvesting the total proceeds of one wager on the next race (and subsequent races, if one should choose). After determining the approximate payoffs on a parlay, they chart the daily double payoffs that appear on the screen to determine if any combinations will pay significantly higher odds than a parlay.

For example, a parlay on a 3–1 horse in the first race and a 4–1 shot in the second would be computed thusly:

First race payoff: $2.00 wager returns $8.00.

Second race payoff: $8.00 wager returns $40.00.

If the pattern of daily double betting indicates that the combination of these two horses will pay less than $40, the double is an underlay. If the double pays more than $40, it's an overlay.

Of course, making money as a chartist further requires mathematically determining the exact proportion of the bets to be placed on each combination to ensure a profit. An easier course of action followed by other bettors is to compare the profit from *wheeling,* that is, coupling one clearly superior horse in one race with the possible contenders in the second race, to the profit from betting the same amount of money on the superior horse alone.

In some states, the track takes a higher percentage from daily double wagers than from win wagers, a significant consideration for the horseplayer. The exact percentages taken from each type of wager are listed in the *Daily Racing Form*'s headings for the results charts. An example is below:

---

— Official Racing Charts ————————

# Pimlico

### Friday, May 16, 1980

---

## Exactas

Exactas or perfectas require picking the first two finishers in a race in the exact order of finish. These wagers are so popular that the exacta pool for a race is normally higher than the combined win, place and show pools.

Picking the first two finishers in one race is generally more difficult than picking the winners in two successive races. Because most tracks take a higher percentage from exacta pools than win pools, most professionals avoid exactas in most races. The only regular exacta bettors among professionals are the chartists, whose mathematical search for overlays in exacta betting is even more complicated than in the daily double.

Exactas can be attractive bets, however, in races where the favorite is going off at low odds, especially even money or less. Because the public tends to overbet longshot combinations in multiple wagering, just as it does in the win pool, wheeling the favorite with likely second-place finishers can produce a bigger profit than betting the total amount one wagers on the favorite, to win.

Less frequently profitable is the very common practice of boxing two or more horses; that is, placing wagers on all possible combinations. The chances of two horses finishing one-two are considerably less than the chances of one of the two horses winning the race. Therefore, the return for boxing the exacta has to be considerably higher than betting an equal amount of money on both horses to win to justify the investment.

## Quinellas

Quinella betting requires picking the first two finishers in a race, regardless of order. Although one quinella bet equals two exacta bets (a two-horse box), quinella payoffs are normally less than half what an exacta payoff would be. While more bettors cash tickets on quinella races, quinella betting seldom produces overlays that justify taking the risk of picking the first two horses.

## Trifectas

The most controversial form of exotic wagering is the trifecta, or the "big triple," in which the bettor has to pick the exact order of the first three finishers in a race. Trifectas occasionally produce five-figure payoffs that excite bettor interest, but these payoffs also provide the incentive for the fraud that has cast a shadow over the entire sport of racing.

The trifecta, compared with other forms of wagering, is a bad bet, for two reasons.

First, the track takeout on trifecta betting at most courses is 25 percent. If that percentage were applied to all wagering, the average bettor would find 85 percent of his original capital eaten up on every trip to the track. Secondly, probable trifecta payoffs are not flashed to the public, making no intelligent comparison of risk and reward possible. Betting on trifectas is much more like buying lottery tickets than applying sound handicapping techniques to picking winners.

Because of the extraordinarily high takeout percentage, a bettor can only be assured of a reasonably high payoff if the favorite or top two favorites finish fourth or worse. In these cases, placing bets on all possible combinations of the other horses pays off. The next logical step for the criminal-minded is to pay the jockey riding the favorite to make sure his horse does finish out of the money. That practice is the basis of the recent scandals in Thoroughbred racing.

No racing fan can justify trifecta betting as an intelligent wager. Boycotting such betting would be an effective signal to track managements to abolish trifectas.

## Pick Six

The highest pari-mutuel payoff in North American racing history was the $350,204.40 paid to Nacho Gomez at Caliente Racetrack in Tijuana, Mexico, on November 12, 1977. To win the money, Gomez picked the winners of the fifth through tenth races on the card.

GREAT HORSES: SEATTLE SLEW

On the eve of the 1977 Kentucky Derby, Washington *Star* columnist and expert handicapper Andy Beyer wrote that Seattle Slew was "an overrated, improperly trained mediocrity who is not going to win." On the afternoon of May 7, a cheering crowd of 124,000 refused to listen, making Slew a 1–2 favorite in the fifteen-horse field. After a perilous start, the "people's horse" proved the experts wrong as he charged like a fullback through the crowded racetrack to a convincing 1¾-length triumph.

No great horse in the 1970s had to overcome more skepticism than Seattle Slew. A yearling of unprepossessing stature and breeding, Slew was purchased at the 1975 Fasig-Tipton summer sale for a modest $17,500 by Washington State lumberman Mickey Taylor and his wife, Karen, along with Florida veterinarian Dr. Jim Hill and his wife, Sally. Placed in the hands of former steeplechase rider and trainer Billy Turner, the colt demonstrated some ability in impressive victories in a maiden special race and an allowance contest at Belmont in the fall of his two-year-old campaign. When Slew trounced a ten-horse field by 9½ lengths in record time in the prestigious Champagne Stakes, he was voted two-year-old champion.

Experts still doubted the dark bay or brown colt's ability to carry his speed over classic distances. Others deprecated the quality of the horses Slew had beaten. The public, however, who had become "Slewmaniacs," made the colt a 1–10 favorite in his three-year-old debut in a seven-furlong allowance at Hialeah. Slew once again demonstrated his incredible speed by passing the six-furlong pole in 1:08, under the track record, en route to a nine-length win. After additional smashing victories in the Flamingo Stakes (at 1–5) and the Wood Memorial (at 1–10), he headed to Churchill Downs undefeated.

Newspapers were full of features criticizing Billy Turner's novel approach to preparing Slew for the Run of the Roses. Because a number of the best three-year-olds were sidelined for the Derby (J. O. Tobin, Cormorant, Silver Series), Turner decided to train his horse less arduously hoping to save energy for the Preakness and the grueling Belmont to come. Six days before the Derby, when Slew drilled a mile in a leisurely 1:41⅘, the cry went up that Slew would come up "short" in the big race. The cry was wrong.

Coming out of the Derby strong and fit, Slew became the first undefeated Triple Crown winner by winning the Preakness (by 1½

lengths) and the Belmont (by 4 lengths). Only then did his connections make an error, underestimating the physical toll the classics had taken on their colt. Sent to California for the Swaps Stakes, Slew finished a badly beaten fourth to J. O. Tobin and was retired for the year.

The Taylors and Hills made a popular decision, however, when they announced that Seattle Slew, who had been syndicated for $12 million, would race as a four-year-old. However, in January, while preparing for his debut at Hialeah, the courageous Slew found himself facing the greatest of challenges. He was stricken with the deadly virus Colitis X, and his life hung in the balance for several days before his fever finally dropped. When the debilitated horse did make it back to the track in May, a hock injury delayed his comeback for another two months.

By the time Seattle Slew approached the post for the fall 1978 Marlboro Cup, the spotlight in the Thoroughbred world was on the brilliant chestnut colt Affirmed. For the first time in his career, Slew was not the favorite, but in this epic battle of Triple Crown winners Slew sprinted to a commanding lead and easily held Affirmed safe, winning by a stunning three lengths. After two years of gallant triumphs, the greatness of Seattle Slew was universally acknowledged. The encomiums continued as Slew scored a four-length victory in the Woodward Stakes, then lost by a short nose to Exceller in one of the great races of all time, the 1978 Jockey Club Gold Cup. Voted Handicap Horse of the Year, Slew retired to stud, and mare owners from all over the world competed for chances to breed to the "people's horse."

| | | Boldnesian |
|---|---|---|
| | Bold Reasoning | |
| | | Reason to Earn |
| Seattle Slew | | |
| | | Poker |
| | My Charmer | |
| | | Fair Charmer |

*Racing Record:*

| STS. | 1ST | 2ND | 3RD | EARNINGS |
|---|---|---|---|---|
| 17 | 14 | 2 | 0 | $1,208,726 |

In 1980, this form of wagering, called Pick Six, was introduced at California tracks. In the first weeks, payoffs ranged as high as $135,000. Of course, picking six winners in a row is very difficult. Like the trifecta, the Pick Six is essentially a lottery rather than an intelligent investment of betting capital. The only advantage is that Pick Six is virtually impossible to fix. While it's easy for a jockey to hold a horse, it's impossible to bribe a jockey to ensure that his horse will win. Even if one race could be "fixed," thousands of combinations of horses would have to be played in the other races in order to guarantee picking the six winners.

## HOW HONEST IS RACING?

Recent race-fixing trials and accusations of misdoing have unfortunately resulted in very misleading impressions of the integrity of the sport of Thoroughbred racing. Part of this impression results from the dishonesty that marred the early days of racing in both Britain and the United States. The truth is that, in this century, the combined efforts of state governments, the Jockey Club and local racing associations have made Thoroughbred racing the best supervised and best policed of all professional sports. Every racetrack employee, no matter how lowly, is thoroughly investigated in a licensing procedure. Racetracks conduct elaborate pre- and post-race drug testing; they also employ increasingly sophisticated horse identification procedures. The Thoroughbred Racing Protective Bureau, whose investigators are primarily well-trained ex-FBI agents, provides exhaustive surveillance of track activities. State as well as track auditors scrutinize computer printouts of wagering data to detect unusual patterns. Because of such scrutiny, the racing industry has a better record of deterring fraud than most corporations.

This does not mean, however, that certain individuals don't attempt to increase their income by misleading the public.

Given the low purses at many tracks, trainers and jockeys sometimes have to rely on betting to make ends meet. Trainers try to push up odds on a horse by entering it in unsuitable races with unfit conditions, or by instructing the jockey to "hold" the horse. A few trainers even try to ensure success by injecting the horse with some new miracle drug. Fortunately, those trainers who aren't caught seldom succeed in the long run. Horsemen involved in shady practices are rarely competent enough at their profession to train their animals to the peak of fitness necessary to win after the odds have been built up. Although drugs can alleviate painful physical ailments, there's no evidence that they can overcome the limitations of a horse's natural ability. That true ability is usually reflected somewhere in the horse's past performances.

More serious than the isolated maneuvering of trainers and jockeys are betting coups or fixed races. However, the legalization of off-track betting and the increasing volume of betting on football, basketball and baseball has reduced dramatically the amount of illegal betting on horse races. Bookies will take small wagers on races, but they won't accept large bets, because they don't get enough action to justify the risk involved.

To fix a race to ensure that one horse will win, or that certain horses will finish first and second, a prospective fixer would have to pay off several jockeys—a risky proposition. More importantly, to make up the cost of the bribes, the fixer would then have to bet a large amount to win. That large amount, in the pari-mutuel system, would depress odds to the unprofitable level.

Thus, attempts to fix races are almost exclusively limited to trifecta races. As we've said before, eliminating trifecta wagering would eliminate that incentive. On other than trifecta races, the racegoer can bet with the level of confidence with which he bets in casinos or on other professional sports.

## BETTING SYSTEMS

How to bet is determined by the results of one's handicapping. How much to bet, however, requires a separate set of judgments. One of the most common laments of the horseplayer is, "I'm a good handicapper but a lousy bettor."

While handicapping ability is largely a matter of knowledge, successful betting depends on maintaining discipline in what can be emotional and pressure-laden situations. After carefully making his selections, a horseplayer notices a sudden, dramatic drop in the odds on another horse. In such cases, the urge to drop one's own selection and go with the "smart money" is overwhelming. Horseplayers find themselves ignoring horses going off at 3–1 to play longshots, or abandoning win betting to take a flyer on exactas and trifectas.

Even professional horseplayers find themselves succumbing to such pressures. A professional may go to the track to bet on only two races, in which he has spotted sufficiently attractive overlays, but sitting out races is dull. For action, he may find himself placing a small wager or two. In the excitement, small bets grow larger. By the time the races he's been waiting for come up, the profit he anticipated may still leave him a loser for the day.

Even more than the professional, the average racegoer enjoys having some money riding on every race. One solution is to bet the same amount on every race, be it $2 or $10; but, as we've explained in detail, some races are more playable than others. Logic suggests betting more money on some races than on others.

To solve this problem, some professionals divide their wagers into two kinds— "prime" bets and "action" bets. Prime bets are reserved for those overlays on which large profits depend. A professional may set a prime bet at 5 percent of his total betting capital. A typical racegoer who brings $50 to the track may decide to make three $10 prime bets during a day.

Action bets are the smaller wagers that provide entertainment between prime races. A professional may set an upper limit of $20 for action bets; the racing fan may divide the $20 left over after prime bets equally between the rest of the races on the card.

The distinction between prime bets and action bets is also useful in winning and losing streaks. Most experts advise increasing betting during winning streaks, but the money should be added to *prime* bets; increasing action bets, because these bets are primarily for fun, will erode winnings in a hurry. Just as in other activities, in horseplaying one encounters mystifying slumps when winners don't come no matter how hard one tries. The best advice is not to force the situation. Just as an investor cuts back when the stock market is in a slump, a horseplayer on a losing streak should reduce wagers until things start picking up again.

The worst way to react to a losing streak is to fall for one of the progressive betting patterns recommended in "get rich quick" systems. Most of these systems suggest doubling every wager until a winner comes along. This would mean that a bettor who started with a $2 bet would find himself placing a $1,024 wager for the tenth race during a modest losing streak. Progression systems are a sure path to the poorhouse.

### A FINAL WORD

"Eat Your Betting
Money, But Don't
Bet Your Eating Money."
—Sign in the Belmont
Backstretch Cafeteria

# Index

Icecapade, 42, 81
Icy Reply, 53
Idaho State Horse Racing Commission, 270
Identification: blood type, 75; chestnuts, 75; distinctive characteristics, 75; markings, 74–75
Idun, 194, 197
Ildrim, 186
Illinois Derby, 192
Illinois Racing Board, 270
Imp, 166
Impecunious, 160
Imperial, 261
Inbreeding, degree of, 30
Incredible John, 45
Indian Broom, 183
Indian Hemp, 46
Indolence, 48
Influenza, 70
In Patient, 319
In Reality, 40, 41, 45, 80, 185
Insco, 183
Inscoelda, 197
Inside post positions, 264
Inside Tract, 185, 187
Inspector, 186
Instant Sin, 54
Intentionally, 41, 45, 50, 203
Intercontinent, 247, 248
Intermission, 184
Inventor, 182
Invercauld, 186
Inverness, 186
Invigorator, 183
Irish Birdcatcher, 14
Irish Castle, 45, 58, 183, 187
Irish Playboy, 45
Iron Constitution, 185
Iron Liege, 115, 183, 185, 252
Iron Ruler, 45
Iroquois, 37
Isabey, 182
Isinglass, 46, 178
It's In the Air, 197
It's Only Money, 119

Jacinto, 79
Jack Hare, Jr., 184
Jack High, 187
Jacobin, 182
Jacobs, Hirsch, 21, 166, 218, 231, 232
Jacobs, John W., 185, 187
Jacobus, 184
Jaipur, 187, 193
Jaklin Klugman, 183
Jamaica Handicap, 161, 192
James, B., 185, 239
James, E., 183, 185
James Reddick, 182
Jamestown, 183, 187
Jamie K., 185, 187
Jampol, 185
Janney, Stuart S., Jr., 146
Janus, 15
Japhet, 184
Jay Ray, 185
Jay Trump, 166
Jean Bart, 185
Jean Egreaud, 186
Jeep, 187
Jefferson Downs, 261, 270, 274
Jeffords, Walter M., Jr., 146
Jeg, 184
Jericho, 184, 186
Jerkens, H. Allen, 166, 232
Jerome, Leonard W., 142, 189
Jerome Handicap, 169, 192
Jerome Park, 142, 180, 189, 335
Jester, 43, 45
Jet Action, 50
Jet Jewel, 40
Jet Pilot, 183
Jim Dandy Stakes, 192
Jim French, 183, 185, 187
Jim Gaffney, 184
Jim Gore, 182, 211
Jock, 183

Jockey Club (Great Britain), 12, 17, 18, 110, 114, 141, 143, 145, 177, 208, 332, 333
Jockey Club (U.S.), 18, 60, 65, 69, 74–75, 76, 143, 144, 145, 170, 179, 188, 189, 207, 208, 283, 308, 342; membership, 146–47; and naming of horses, 118–19; responsibilities of, 146
Jockey Club Foal Certificate, 277
Jockey Club Gold Cup Stakes, 48, 132, 149, 172, 175, 179, 198, 200, 212, 276, 321, 341
Jockeys, 238–45, 292; annual leading jockey and money won (1908–80), 239–40; apprentices, 243–44; earnings, 241, 245; evaluating, 245; evolution of race riding and, 238–41; fees, 244–45; in Hall of Fame, 166–67; handicapping, 324; judgment and pace, 242–43; naming by entry time, 236; placing on a horse, 243–44; preparation, 277–78; qualifications, 241–43; technique, 243; top five (through 1980), 242; top twenty-five (1979), 244
Jockey's agent, 234–36
Jockey's Guild, 242, 245
Joe Cotton, 182
Joe Daniels, 186
Joc Madden, 164, 186
Joe Morris, 182
John B. Campbell Handicap, 198
John Boulger, 184
John C., 184
John Finn, 182
John Henry, 161, 162, 163, 203, 276
Johnny D., 203
John P. Grier, 39
Johns Joy, 46
Johnson, Albert, 167, 182, 183, 187, 239
Johnson, Philip G., 232
John's Roll, 44
Johnstown, 180, 183, 187
Johren, 186
Jolley, LeRoy, 183, 232, 294
Jolly Johu, 187
Jolly Roger,, 166
Jones, Benjamin A., 115, 166, 183, 185, 187, 188, 231
Jones, Gary, 232
Jones, H. A., 166, 183, 185, 187, 231, 232
Jones, R., 185, 239
Jones, Richard I. G., 146
Jones, Warner L., Jr., 146
Jose Binn, 35
J. O. Tobin, 32, 203, 341
Joyner, Andrew J., 166, 184
Juarez Racetrack, 261, 273, 274
Judge Himes, 182
Judge Murray, 184
June Grass, 184
Just a Game, 203
Just Nosed Out, 119
Juvenile Stakes, 169

Kalitan, 184
Kate Bright, 184
Kathryn's Doll, 160
Kauai King, 180, 183, 185, 196
Kayak II, 200
Keck, Howard B., 146
Keene, James R., 111, 143
Keeneland, 152, 153, 161, 169, 191, 192, 261, 269, 270, 274; Fall Sale of Breeding Stock, 47, 79, 82, 83, 275; July Select Sale, 79; Summer Select Sale, 82
Kel-Co Class Computer, 316
Kelly, Thomas J., 232
Kelso, 161, 163, 166, 193, 200, 204, 209, 210, 252; career of, 212
Kenilworth Park, 169
Kent Stakes, 248
Kentucky Boy, 184
Kentucky Colonel, 54, 60
Kentucky Derby, 4, 33, 36, 58, 94, 104, 109, 149, 169, 170, 172, 173, 176, 178, 189, 192, 193, 195, 200, 207, 211, 212, 226, 238, 240–41, 245, 252, 265, 276, 284, 299, 340; colors of the winners, 60; facts, 188; history of, 180–88
Kentucky Jockey Club Stakes, 195
Kentucky Oaks, 169, 193
Kentucky State Racing Commission, 270